Privilegia Londini:

OR, THE

RIGHTS,
Liberties, Privileges,
LAWS, and CUSTOMS,
OF THE
City of *LONDON*.

Wherein are contained,

I. The feveral Charters granted to the faid City, from K. WILLIAM I. to the Prefent Times.

II. The Magiftrates and Officers thereof, with their refpective Creations, Elections, Rights, Duties, and Authorities.

III. The Laws and Cuftoms of the City, as the fame relate either to the Perfons or Eftates of the Citizens; *viz.* of Freemens Wills, *Feme-Sole* Merchants, Orphans, Apprentices, &c.

IV. The Nature, Jurifdiction, Practice, and Proceedings of the feveral Courts thereof, with Tables of Fees relating thereto.

V. The feveral Statutes concerning the faid City, and Citizens, Alphabetically digefted.

The **Third Edition**, with large ADDITIONS.

By W. BOHUN, *of the* Middle-Temple, *Efq;*

THE LAWBOOK EXCHANGE, LTD.
Clark, New Jersey

ISBN-13: 978-1-58477-994-0
ISBN-10: 1-58477-994-2

Lawbook Exchange edition 2009

The quality and irregular pagination of this reprint is equivalent to that found in the original work.

THE LAWBOOK EXCHANGE, LTD.
33 Terminal Avenue
Clark, New Jersey 07066-1321

Please see our website for a selection of our other publications and fine facsimile reprints of classic works of legal history:
www.lawbookexchange.com

Library of Congress Cataloging-in-Publication Data
Bohun, William.
  Privilegia Londini, or, The rights, liberties, privileges, laws, and customs, of the city of London. Wherein are contained, I. The several charters granted to the said city, from K. William I to the present times. II. The magistrates and officers thereof, with their respective creations, elections, rights, duties, and authorities. III. The laws and customs of the city, as the same relate either to the persons or estates of the citizens ... IV. The nature, jurisdiction, practice, and proceedings of the several courts thereof, with tables of fees relating thereto. V. The several statutes concerning the said city, and citizens, alphabetically digested.
    p. cm.
  Originally published: London : Printed for D. Browne [etc.], 1723. 3rd ed., with large additions.
  Includes bibliographical references and index.
  ISBN-13: 978-1-58477-994-0 (hardcover : alk. paper)
  ISBN-10: 1-58477-994-2 (hardcover : alk. paper)
  1. London (England)--Charters, grants, privileges. 2. London (England)--Politics and government--Early works to 1800. 3. Customary law--England. 4. Courts--England--London. I. Title. II. Title: Privilegia Londini. III. Title: The rights, liberties, privileges, laws, and customs, of the city of London.
  KD8882.B64 2009
  349.421--dc22   2009033975

Printed in the United States of America on acid-free paper

Privilegia Londini:

OR, THE

R I G H T S,
Liberties, Privileges,
LAWS, and CUSTOMS,
OF THE
City of *LONDON.*

Wherein are contained,

I. The feveral Charters granted to the faid City, from K. WILLIAM I. to the Prefent Times.

II. The Magiftrates and Officers thereof, with their refpective Creations, Elections, Rights, Duties, and Authorities.

III. The Laws and Cuftoms of the City, as the fame relate either to the Perfons or Eftates of the Citizens; *viz.* of Freemens Wills, *Feme-Sole* Merchants, Orphans, Apprentices, &c.

IV. The Nature, Jurifdiction, Practice, and Proceedings of the feveral Courts thereof, with Tables of Fees relating thereto.

V. The feveral Statutes concerning the faid City, and Citizens, Alphabetically digefted.

The 𝕿𝖍𝖎𝖗𝖉 𝕰𝖉𝖎𝖙𝖎𝖔𝖓, with large ADDITIONS.

By W. BOHUN, *of the* Middle-Temple, *Efq;*

LONDON,
Printed for D. BROWNE, W. MEARS, R. GOSLING, T. WOODWARD, J. HOOKE, F. CLAY, and J. STEPHENS. M.DCC.XXIII.

To the Right HONOURABLE,

Right Worshipful, &c.

THE

Lord-Mayor and Sheriffs,

Recorder and *Aldermen,*

Common-Council and *Free-Citizens,*

OF

The Antient, Renowned, and Opulent
City of *L O N D O N :*

The Enfuing

TREATISE,

CONTAINING

The *Rights, Liberties, Privileges, Laws*
and *Cuftoms* of the faid *C I T Y* and
C I T I Z E N S,

Is moft Humbly

Dedicated, &c.

A 2

THE

PREFACE.

AVING observed in the Course of our English *History many* Attempts *made (by the* Ministers *of some artful and designing* Princes) *to weaken and undermine the* ancient, *legal, and fundamental* Rights, Liberties, *and* Privileges *of the City and Citizens of* London : *I thought myself obliged to endeavour to collect and ascertain such* Laws, Customs, *and* Usages *of the said City, wherein the original Constitution and Foundation of its* Government *seem to have been laid; and whereby its* Happiness, Opulency, *and* Glory *do (under* God *and his present* Majesty) *evidently subsist.*

Nor can the Collector *hereof be justly censured by any* Briton *who has any regard for his Country;* when he considers, That *within the* Bosom *of this* City *are involved almost all the* Rights, Privileges, *and* Liberties *of* Great Britain *in general: and should these* Bounds *of* Property *contain'd in this* City's Liberties *be once overturn'd, not only* London, *but the whole* Nation *would soon be overspread with a (worse than* Egyptian) Plague *of* Prerogative *and* Arbitrary Power, *and* delug'd

A 3 *with*

with an Inundation *of* Tyranny, Rapine, Injuftice *and* Oppreffion.

For as in Nature, *when ever the* Head *is fubjeʗed to any exterior* Force *or* Injury, *or internal* Malady *or* Diforder, *all the* Members *of the* Body *do confequently fuffer with it, and participate of all its* Pains *and* Agonies : *So in* Civil Polity, *the* Subverfion *of the* Liberties *and* Privileges *of the* Head *or* Chief City, *does infallibly draw after it the* Subverfion *of thofe of the whole* State *or* Kingdom. Examples *hereof have happen'd too near us to have been unobferv'd, and ought to be* Memento's *for our own* Caution, *and the following* Obfervation, *viz.*

That as no Nation, Kingdom, State, *or* City *can fupport itfelf, or be fupported as fuch, without equal and proper* Laws, Cuftoms, *and* Conftitutions *for the due* Government *and Proteʗion of the* People *in the Enjoyment of their* Rights *and* Properties : *So whenever thofe* Laws, Cuftoms, *and* Conftitutions *are* invaded, undermined, fubverted, *or* deftroy'd, *fuch* Nation, Kingdom, State *or* City *muft foon become a* Bedlam *of Diforder, a* Babel *of Confufion, or an* Aceldama *of Blood, Ruin, and Devaftation.*

Inftances *to evidence this* Truth *might be produced from the* Hiftories *of all* Ages, *and all* Nations *in the* World. *Thus the* Luxuries, Extortions, *and* Oppreffions *praʗifed under* Sardanapalus, Pharaoh, Rehoboam, Zedekiah, Belfhazzar, Cleopatra, *&c. fubverted (by fubverting the* People's Rights) *the refpeʗive* Kingdoms *of* Affyria, Egypt, Ifrael, Judæa, Babylon, *&c.*

And whoever will, may obferve from the Hiftories of Marcellinus *and* Procopius (*and efpecially from what the incomparable* Grotius *has remark'd in his* Books de Bello Gothico, *&c.) that the Deftruction of* Rome *and the* Weftern *Empire was occafioned by the* Avarice, Extortion, *and* Oppreffion

of

of the Exarchs *of* Italy, *and others the* Emperor's Miniſters *there ; ſo that the* People *choſe rather to be govern'd by the barbarous* Goths *and* Vandals, *than the tyrannick* Dominion *of their own* unnatural, *tho'* native Governours.

Nor was the miſerable Fate *of* Conſtantinople *and the* Ruin *of the* Eaſtern *Empire, and its Subjection to the* Dominion *of the* Turks, *effected from any other mediate* Cauſe, *than the* Extortions, Exactions, *and* Oppreſſions *of the* Emperor *and his* Miniſters ; *who, by* miſapplying *the* Moneys *given for* publick Services, *and extorting vaſt* Sums *from the* Subjects *without* cauſe, *created ſuch a* Jealouſy *and* Odium *in the* People, *as that they refuſed even* neceſſary Supplies *when their* City *was actually* beſieg'd, *and in* imminent Danger *of being* taken *; the* Invaſion *of their* Rights *and* Properties *rendering them indifferent in their* Choice *of being* Slaves, *either to a* Chriſtian *or a* Turkiſh Tyrant.

See *Knolles's Turkiſh* Hiſtory, 348. That 2 of the Emperor's Miniſters appointed to repair the Walls and Fortifications of that City, miſapply'd 70000 Florens collected to that end; and yet (it ſeems by the Emperor's Connivance) the Walls were not repair'd, whereby the *Turks* eaſily won the City, &c.

And were it not for the Odiouſneſs *of* homebred Examples, *and an* Averſion *to expoſe the* Wounds *of my* Country's Liberties, *I might here ſhew the like* Cauſes *have always had the like* Effects *in this* Iſland : *and that the ſeveral* Conqueſts *thereof, by the* Romans, Saxons, Danes *and* Normans, *were owing to the* Tyranny *and* Injuſtice *of* Caſſibellan, Vortigern, Ethelbald, Edred, Harold, &c.

And indeed what a famous Judge *long ſince obſerv'd, is founded on a* Divine *and* Eternal Truth, *viz.* Si Principes ſine Fræno, *i. e.* ſine Lege regunt, clamabunt ſubditi ad Dominum, &c. Et Dominus vocabit ſuper eos Gentem robuſtam, longinquam & ignotam, cujus Linguam ignorabunt;

Vid. *Bracton.* pag. 34, 107.

A 4   quæ

quæ deftruet eos, & evellet radices eorum de Terra, quia fubditos noluerunt jufte judicare, &c.

How happy *then* (*yea*, thrice happy *compared with others*) *ought the* City *and* Citizens *of* London *to efteem themfelves, and be efteem'd, who have hitherto preferved fuch evident and* noble Remains *of that* Liberty *and* Freedom, *and of thofe* Rights *and* Privileges *whereof the* whole Nation *were poffefs'd in the Times of our* Britifh *and* Saxon Anceftors! *when the* Free-People *of this* Ifland *enjoy'd the* Right *of electing all their* Civil *and* Military, *as well as* Spiritual Magiftrates, Officers, *and* Superintendants; *as may be fully evidenced from the* Hiftories *and* Monuments *of thofe ancient Times; efpecially from the* Laws *of* Edward the Confeffor, *which* Laws *the* Kings *of the* Norman Race *were for many Succeffions* fworn *to obferve.*

And that W. 1. *and his* Succeffors *fwore to the Obfervation of thofe* Laws, *and alfo executed* Grants *or* Charters *to that purpofe, is fully proved by all the* Hiftorians *of thofe Times; as* Ingulphus, Eadmerus, Mat. Paris, Willielmus Newbrigenfis, *&c. Indeed fome of thofe* Kings *are* ftain'd *with this unlucky Character, viz.* Quod nimis impudenter fregit Sacramentum fuum: *But* this *it feems was then a* Royal Cuftom.

And it may be here obferved, That altho' the Charters *to the* City *of* London (*as they are here recited by* 15 Car. II.) *do begin with thofe of* W. 1. *yet it muft not be underftood as if any of the* City Rights, Liberties, *or* Privileges, *were originally owing to the* Grants *of that* Prince. *For 'tis evident, the faid* City *and* Citizens *had and enjoy'd moft of the* Liberties *and* Privileges *mention'd in the following* Charters (*befides divers others not* therein *enumerated*) *by* immemorial Ufage *and* Cuftom *long before the* Arrival *of* W. I.

Thus

Thus 'tis apparent the Citizens *of* London *enjoyed a certain* Privilege *antecedent to the suppposed Conquest,* That if any Person of a servile Condition Vid. 7 H. 6. abode in the said City for a Year and a Day 32. 37 H. 6. peaceably, he from thence became a free Citizen 27. of *London,* and was for ever after freed from his Lord and Master. *This is indeed said to have been granted to the said City by a Charter of* Edward *the* Confessor ; *but 'tis evident the same* Custom *or* Privilege *was in being in the* Time *of the* Britons, *particularly in the Reign of* Dunwallo Molmutius, *who began* circ. A. D. 480.

And from the very Words of the following Charters *'twill appear,* That many of the particular Privileges *therein mentioned as* new Grants, *were not only originally* Saxon, *if not* British *Customs, but* Vid. 5 Stow. *had been from* Time *immemorial enjoyed by the* Citi- 346. zens *of* London, *and their Ancestors. And the* Charters *of* H. 1, &c. *shew,* That their Courts *of* Hustings, Folkmotes *and* Wardmotes ; *their* Magistrates, *viz.* Portreves, Ballivi *or* Sheriffs, Domesmen, *or* Justices *and* Aldermen ; *the* Privileges *of their* Sokes *and* Portsoken, Hustings, &c. Fitz Coron. *their* Suits *of* Foreign Attachments, Withernams, &c. *and their* Exemptions *from* Foreign Pleas, Wager *of* Battle, Miskennings, Scot *and* Lot, Tolls *of* Passage, Lastage, &c. *were all of* Saxon, *if not* British *Original.*

Besides, 'tis observable the Charter *of* W. 1. *was not penn'd in the* Norman *Dialect, nor in the Stile of a* Conqueror : *But he, as a King of* Englishmen, *grants, or rather* confirms *to the Citizens of* London, *their antient* English *Rights and Privileges, in the following* Saxon, *or Old English Words; viz.*

William

Ƿilliam Kyng gret Ƿilliam Bisceop; and Gosfregth Porterefa, and ealle tha Burh-warn binnen London Frencisce & Englisce freondlice ; And ic kithe eow thaet ic wille thaet get ben eallra theera laga weorthe the git weeran on Eadwerdes Daege Kynges. And ic wille that aelc child beo his Faeder Yrf nume aefter his Faeder daege. And ic nelle gewolian thaet aenig Man eow eanig wrang beode. God eow geheald.

Now as those general Words in this Charter, I will that all there, (i. e. *all the* Burhwarn *or* Citizens *within* London) be Law worthy as they were in King *Edward's* Days, *do plainly imply the said Citizens were possess'd of divers* Rights, Privileges *and* Customs *in the Confessor's Days ; so 'tis apparent, not only* London, *but the whole Nation, was then possess'd of the like* Rights, Customs *and* Privileges, *as the* Free Election *of their* Sheriffs, Aldermen, Domesmen, Justices, Coroners, *and particularly of all their* Heretochs *or Commanders of Military Forces,* &c. *as appears by the* 33 *and* 35 *Laws of the Confessor, and other Laws of the* Saxon *and* Danish *Kings.*

But of the Citizens Right *of electing their Magistrates, sufficient has been already said in the ensuing* *Vid. pag. 39, 41, 42. 45, 49, 51, 52, 55, &c. *Treatise : I shall therefore only add a Collection of some of the many Sums of Money, which in* H. 3 d's *Time were* exacted, *and I may say* extorted *from the* City *and* Citizens *of* London, *under the Pretence of granting their* Charters, *or* confirming *or* restoring *their* Rights *and* Liberties. *For as* R. 1. *exacted from them* 1500 *Marks for one of their* Charters *of* Liberties, *and* K. John 3000 *Marks for another ; so it appears from the Authority of* H. 3 d's

H. 3d's † *Hiſtoriographer, that in that Prince's Reign* † Mat. Paris. *there were exaƈted from them, on the like Pretences,* Edit. Lond. *the following Sums,* viz. 1571.

Anno 1217. (1 *H. 3.*) *The* Citizens *paid for ſecu*- Pag. 449. *ring their* Liberties, *&c.* 5000 l.

—— 1218. (2 *H. 3.*) *A Fifteenth was given of all their* movable Goods.

—— 1225. (9 *H.3.*) *Another Fifteenth was given on*   432. Hubert de Burgo's *Propoſal and the* King's Pro- miſe of *granting the* Charter of Liberties.

—— 1227. (11, 12 *H. 3.*) *Cives Londinenſes* (Ca- ib. 449. vilatorum conſilio) compulſi ſunt ſolvere Re- gi 5000 Marcas argenti. *And yet by* Hubert de Burgo's *Counſel, the* King *cancelled all his Charters :* Et cepit præterea quintam decimam partem omnium Mobilium *Londinenſium,* &c.

—— 1230. (14 *H. 3.*) *Cives Londinenſes* ad gra- ib. 488. viſſimam Redemptionem compulſi ſunt.

—— 1231. (15 *H. 3.*) *The King exaƈts* Scutage, ib. 491. i. e. 3 *Marks of every Scute or Eſquire's Fee.*

—— 1232. (16 *H. 3.*) *An Aid demanded, and a* Pag. 498, 505. Quadrageſm *granted. See its Colleƈtion,* pa. 508.

—— 1235. (19 *H.3.*) *The King takes* Carvage, ib. 558. i. e. 2 *Marks for every Carve of Land on the Mar- riage of his Siſter.*

—— 1236. (20 *H. 3.*) *The* Londoners *bore the* ib. 562, 563. *Charge on the young Queen's Coronation.*

—— 1237. (21 *H. 3.*) Rex exegit triceſimam ib. 582, 583. partem omnium mobilium. *But this ſeems to be* & vid. 596. *afterwards confirm'd in Parliament, on Condition the King confirm'd the Charters,* &c.

—— 1240. (24 *H.3.*) Rex abraſit impudenter pe- ib. 701. cuniam. *And the itinerant Juſtices were employ'd* Vid. 713. & *to get the King Money on pretence of diſtributing* 780. *Juſtice.*

Anno

ib. 737.

Anno 1241. (25 H. 3.) *The King exacts* 20000 *Marks from the* Jews. Et abstulit violenter

ib. 740.

a *Majori Londinenfi, the* 40 l. (*or rather* 400 l.) *yearly Revenue given by the City for Support of his Dignity.* — Nec multum poft *Cives Londinenfes* contra Confuetudinem & Libertatem Civitatis, quafi Servi ultimæ cònditiònis, non fub Nomine aut Titulo *liberi Adjutorii,* fed *Tallagii,* &c. numerare funt coacti——*Quære the Sum.*

ib. 777.

——1242. *(26 H. 3.) A Parliament held at* London, *a Recital of the King's Exactions and Debates thereon.*

ib. 806.

——1243. *(27 H. 3.) Cives Londinenfes* compulfi funt ad graviffimam Redemptionem, quæ *Tallagium* dicitur. *And fee* pag. 814. *a great Exaction from the* Jews, *&c.*

ib. 862, 868.

——1244. (28 H. 3.) *An Aid demanded, and* Scutage *granted,* i. e. 20 s. *a* Scute *of all that held* in Capite. *See there a Recital of the King's Extortions,* &c. *Alfo a Contribution by the* Londoners, *on Condition of obferving the Charters,*

ib. 879.

granted. But, fays the Hiftorian, qualiter Promiffa & Pacta adimplebit Rex, noverit ille qui nihil ignorat. *And the fame Year he importunately (not to fay moft impudently) demanded another Aid in Parliament. But failing therein,* Et avide & fitienter inhians Pecuniæ inconfulta à Regni univerfitate, &c. à *Civibus*

Nota.

Londinenfibus 1500 Marcas, *violenter & impudenter extorfit,* &c. Et compulfi funt *Cives* Memoratam Pecuniam *alienigenis* difpergendam numerare.

ib. 920.

——1246. (30 H. 3.) *Cives Londinenfium* ad Redemptionem Solutionis, fub nomine *Talla-*

quinque, *omitted as fuppos'd.*

gii, ad — millium Marcarum, non fine multo gravamine & diminutione Catallorum fuorum & cordium amaritudine funt compulfi.

Anno

Anno 1248. (32 *H.* 3.) *The Courtiers to get Mo-* ib. 994.
ney advised the King to sell his Plate and Jewels
to the Londoners, *and thereby cheat 'em of their*
Money: And note the King's Words, Abundant
illi *Rustici Londinenses,* qui se *Barones* appel-
lant usque ad Nauseam, Urbs illa est puteus
inexhaustus; Et statim concepit in animo ip-
sos *Cives* bonis suis spoliare. *Whereupon about*
Michaelmas *the King proclaims throughout* Lon- ib. 997.
don, &c. *That a Fair should be held for* 15
(some say 40 *) Days at* Westminster, *and that*
no Goods, Wares or Merchandizes, should be
bought or sold in London *during that Time.*

—— 1249. (33 *H.* 3.) Rex regalis magnificen- ib. 1005.
tiæ Terminos impudenter transgrediens à *Ci-*
vibus Londinensibus exegit *Primitiva,* i. e. *New-*
Years-Gifts. And soon after taking Counsel how ib. 1006.
further to oppress the Citizens, got from 'em 2000l.
on a Pretence of suppressing the Fair at Westminster. *And yet in the following Year,*

—— 1250. (34 *H.* 3.) *He again invades the* ib. 1040.
City's Liberties in favour to the Abbot of Westminster; *and two Years after,*

—— 1252. (36 *H.* 3.) *He extorted,* precibus ib. 1135.
imperiosis, *from the said* Citizens 200 *Marks of*
Gold, and yet compell'd 'em to attend the said Fair
at Westminster *as before. And, as the Lord*
Chief Justice Treby *observed in his Argument*
on the Quo Warranto, pag. 132. *The Redemp-*
tion of this Fair cost the City 8000 l. *which*
amounts to above 160,000 l. *of our Money.*

—— 1253. (37 *H.* 3.) *The next Year he swears* ib. 1148,
to the great Charter, but soon breaks his Oath; 1151, 1169.
and his Malice continuing against the City, magnam summam à *Civibus* extorsit, *besides* 100
Marks Contribution, under Colour of which the
King's Collectors, à *Civibus* magnam quantita-
tem pecuniæ exegerunt.

Anno

ib. 1203, &c.
1204.

Anno 1254. (38 H. 3.) *And the following Year,
tho' the* Londoners *had given the King* 100 l. *as
a New-Year's Gift, (now by Cuſtom exacted as a
Duty) and alſo a Veſſel of Plate and Jewels that
coſt them* 200 l. *yet he extorts from 'em as a*
Tallage, &c. 3000 *Marks more, calls the Magiſtrates* Slaves, &c. *and impriſons divers of
'em.*

ib. 1237,
1240.

—— 1256. (40 H. 3.) *And ſee in the next Year
the King's Proclamation for* Knighthood, *and
his Project to get Money thereby; alſo the ſame
Year he taxes the* Londoners *at* 500 *Marks,*
ad arbitrium ſuum, non obſtante aliqua Libertate, &c. *ſo that the Citizens,* quaſi Servi
ultimæ Conditionis Jugum ſubibant ſervi-
tutis.

It ſeems
5000.

1263.
1266.
1270.

—— 1257. (41 H. 3.) *In this Year,* 52000
*Marks were granted to the King by Parliament,
on Condition to obſerve the great Charter, which
Sum he contemns; and note, 'tis there obſerv'd,
That the King had ſpent of the Peoples Money*
800000 *Marks, and* 150000 *Marks, and that*
42000*Marks were granted by the Prelates the ſame
Year. And in the next,*

ib. 1282.

—— 1258. (42 H. 3.) *A Tax having been laid on
the Citizens of* London, *on Pretence of employ-
ing it in rebuilding their Walls, &c. the Collectors
thereof embezled the better part thereof (as the
Practice then was in moſt other Caſes;) and tho'
the Criminals were arraign'd and convicted
thereof, yet they were delivered, (and I ſuppoſe
pardoned) at the Interceſſion of* John Manſel, *who
had been the King's Chancellor and chief Coun-
ſel-*

1287.

lor. And the ſame Year the Citizens of London
being accuſed of divers pretended Crimes, redempti
& multiformiter puniti erant; *ſo that* Ralph
Hurdel *the Mayor* præ dolore obiit.

But

But as thefe Exorbitances of the King drew on him the Odium *not only of the* Londoners, *but of the* Nation *in general, fo this very Year the* Barons de-1301. clared *War againft him, and the* Citizens *in a* Common-Council *refolved to affift them therein, and fortify'd the* City *in their favour, as is obferved hereafter, pag.* 43. *and foon after feiz'd and im-*ibid. *p.*1329, prifon'd *divers of the* King's Officers *and* Minifters,1330, &c. *particularly the* Judges *and* Barons *of his* Exchequer. See Mat. Paris, *pag.* 1327.

The faid War continuing till 1264, i. e. 48 H. III. *both the* King *and* Prince Edward *his Son were that Year taken* Prifoners *by the* Barons *at the* Battle of Lewes : *And thereupon, in the following Year, the* King *renews and regrants the* Great Charter *of the* Liberties *of* England, *wherein efpecial Provifion is made,* That *the faid* City *fhall have all their* ancient Liberties *and* Cuftoms. *Which Charter*Vid. poft. *in effect, was at firft granted by* H. I. *and after*p. 473. *him by* H. II. *and King* John, *as* Mat. Paris *pag.* 74, 134,319,320, &c. *has fhewn ; and contain'd but a part of thofe* Rights *and* Liberties *to which the whole* Nation, *as well as* London, *were juftly entitled.*

Thefe Particulars I have here added by way of Preface, *which, together with what is hereafter ob-*ferved *from pag.* 40, *to* 48, *may be* Memento's *of the* Attempts *of former* Times, *and* Cautions *for the future. But for the prefent (Thanks to the Divine Providence) we are now under the juft and* mild Government *of a* Prince, *who makes the* Laws *of the* Land *the* Rule *and* Meafure *of all his* Actions; *and by whom the* Rights, Liberties, *and* Privileges *not only of this* City, *but of the whole* Nation, *will undoubtedly be held* facred *and* inviolable.

I

I shall add no more, but desire the Reader to insert in their proper Places the following Paragraphs, viz.

At the foot of pag. 188.—*Yet in the case of* Soan & Mace, Hill. 2 & 3 Jac. 2. *in* B. R. Holt *moved for a* Procedendo *in an Action against a* Feme-

Feme-Sole Merchant. Sole Merchant *in* London, *removed into* B. R. *For that, both by the* Custom *and* Charters *of the said City, it ought to be tried there; and the Court*

Vid. Cumber- *granted a* Procedendo *accordingly. And so in* Tre-**bach. 42.** by*'s Argument, in the* Quo Warranto Case, *Fol.* 8, &c. *the same is affirm'd: And altho' the* Hus*band is to be named for Conformity, yet the Action is properly against her, and the Judgment is severally (solely) against her, and the Debt must be levy'd of her Estate.*

Statutes, *And at* pag. 473. *before the* Stat. *of* Gavelett, **Pleas of** *add—See also the* Statute *of* Gloucester, 6 Ed. I. **Land, &c.** cap. 11, 12, 13, 14. *touching Pleas of Land, and other Proceedings in the Courts of* London.

AN
ABSTRACT,
Of the Great Charter
OF
CONFIRMATION,

Granted 15° Car. Secundi.

WILLIAM *the Conqueror* grants the City of *London* two Charters; in the firſt of which he confirms to them the Laws they enjoy'd in the Reign of King *Edward the Confeſſor*, appoints every Child to be his Father's Heir after his Death; and promiſes to ſuffer no Man to do them wrong: And the ſecond to the ſame Effeÿt.

Will. Conq.
Charter 1. 2.
Vide Stow,
lib. 5. *p.* 347.

Edw. Confeſſ.
Laws con-firmed.

Henry the Firſt grants them likewiſe a Charter, wherein he grants the Citizens of *London* to hold *Middleſex* to Farm for Three Hundred Pounds, upon Account, to them and their Heirs, and that the ſaid Citizens ſhall place whom they will among themſelves as Sheriffs,

Hen. I. Charter.
Vide Bohun's *Right of Elec-tions,* 193, &c. *And* Stow, *ib.* 347.
Midd. Farm'd

B

Sheriffs chosen. Sheriffs, and also as Justices, to keep the Pleas of the Crown, and none other to be Justice over them; and that the Citizens shall not plead without the Walls of the City concerning any Plea; also to be free from *Scot and Lot*, and from *Dane-guilt*, and from all *Murther*; excuses them from waging of Battel; and that if any Citizen be impleaded concerning the Pleas of the Crown, the Man of *London* shall discharge himself by his Oath, which shall be adjudg'd within the City.

Nemo faciat Bellum.

And further, that none of the King's Houshold, or any other, shall be lodged in the City of *London* by force, and that the Citizens and their Goods should be free, and that all their things throughout *England*, and the Sea-Ports, be free from all Toll, Passage and Lastage, and from all other Customs: And that the Churches, and *Barons*, and Citizens should peaceably hold their Sokes, so that the Strangers that should be lodg'd in the Sokes, should pay Custom to him only to whom the Soke doth belong, or to his Officer.

Toll, &c.

Barons.

Fleta, Lib. 1. c. 47. Amercements.

Also that no Citizen should be amerc'd, *nisi a fa* were, *i. e.* not above 100 *s.* for any pecuniary Punishment; that there should be no Miskenning in the *Hustings*, nor in the Folk-Mote, nor in any other Plea within the City. That the Hustings sit once a Week, *viz.* on *Mondays*, and that the Citizens enjoy their Lands, Bond Promises, Debts, &c. according to the Laws of the City. And if any shall take Toll or Custom of any Citizen, the Citizen shall within the City take of the Burrough or Town where the Toll or Custom was so taken, so much as the Citizen gave for Toll, and as he receiv'd Damage thereby,

Hustings.

thereby. And all Debtors who owe the Citizens any Debts, fhall pay them in *London*, or difcharge them themfelves there, that they *Attachments.* owe none ; but if they will not pay the fame, nor come thither to clear themfelves, the Citizens to whom fuch Debts are due, may take *Namia fua, i. e.* Goods within the City of that Burrough-Town, or County where he remains who owes the Debts. And alfo to have their Chafes and Hunt in *Chiltre, Middle-* *Chafe and* *fex,* and *Surry,* in as full and ample manner *Hunt.* as any of their Anceftors ever had.

> ☞ Note, *That King Stephen granted a Charter to the whole Kingdom, confirming all the Liberties granted by* Hen. I. *and alfo all the good Laws and Cuftoms of* Edward the Confeffor. See 5 *Stow* 348.

Henry the Second grants them another Char- *Hen.* II. *Mo-* ter, by which he confirms to them all their *nyers.* former Privileges; and further grants, That no Citizen excepting only his Monyers and Officers, fhould be impleaded without the Walls of the City, but only in foreign Tenures. He *Foreign Te-* alfo acquits them of *Murder (i. e.* of Payments *nures.* made for it*)* within the City and the Portfoken thereof, and that no Citizen fhall wage Battel ; and that of Pleas of the Crown, they may difcharge themfelves according to the old Ufage of the City. No Man to take Lodgings there by Force, or by Delivery of the Marfhal ; alfo, that all the Citizens fhall be quit of Toll and Leftage throughout *Eng-* *Toll, &c.* *land,* and the Ports of the Sea; and that none fhall be adjudged for Amerciaments of Money, but according to the Law of the City which they had *Temp. Hen.* I. and that there fhall be no Miskenning in any Plea within the City, and that the Huftings fhall be kept once *Huftings.*

a Week, and they juftly have their Lands, Tenures and Premiffes, and all their Debts, who-
foever do owe them ; and that Right be done
them according to the Cuftom of the City, of
all their Lands and Tenures which be in
the City, and of all their Debts which were
lent at *London*, and of Promifes or Contracts
there made Pleas to be holden at *London*. He

Huntings. alfo grants their Huntings wherefoever they
had them *Temp. Hen.* I. and if any in all *England* fhall take any Cuftom or Toll of or from
the Men of *London*, after he fhall fail of Right,
the Sheriffs of *London* may take Goods thereof at *London* ; and further grants them to be

Scotale. free from all Bridtoll, Childwite, Jerefgive
and Scotale, fo as the Sheriff of *London*, or
any other Bailiff may take no Scotale, *&c.*
all which Privileges are granted to them and
their Heirs, to hold the fame by Inheritance
of the faid King and his Heirs.

Rich. I.   *Richard* the Firft, *Ann.* 5°, grants them not to
Ch. 1. plead or be impleaded without the Walls of the
City, excepting Foreign Tenures, and his own
Monyers and Minifters. He grants them like-
wife an Acquittal of Murther within the City,

Wager of Bat- and in *Portfoken.* That none wage Battel :
tel. That they difcharge themfelves of the Pleas
of the Crown, according to the Cuftom of
the City. That none take Lodgings in the
City by force, or delivery of the Marfhal ; that
they be free from Toll and Leftage through-

Hen. II. out *England*, and the Sea Ports, *&c.* and con-
Grants con- firms, *verbatim*, all their former Grants made
firmed. by King *Henry* his Predeceffor.

Rich. I.   *Richard* the Firft, *Ann.* 8°, grants them a fe-
Ch. 1. cond Charter, by which all the Wears in the
Wears in the River of *Thames* are to be remov'd ; and the
Thames re- Keepers of the *Tower* for the future not de-
moved. mand

City of London.   5

mand or exact any thing of any Person by
reason of the said Wears for ever.

King *John* grants the City of *London* five *John, Ch.* 1.
several Charters: In the firſt, *Ann.* 1°, he confirms to them all the Grants made to them
by his Anceſtors, and is almoſt *verbatim* as
thoſe of *Hen.* II. and *Rich.* I.

In the Second, *Ann.* 1°, he confirms to them *John, Ch.* 2.
the Sheriffwick of *London* and *Middleſex*, with *Sheriffwick of*
all the Cuſtoms belonging to it, both by *Middleſex.*
Land and Water, as well within the City as
without, to hold the ſame at the Annual Rent
of 300 *l.* payable in equal Proportions at the
Eaſter and *Michaelmas* Exchequer.

He further grants them Power to chooſe and
remove their Sheriffs, and makes the ſaid Sheriffs preſentable and accountable to the Juſti-
ces of his *Exchequer*; and in caſe the ſaid She- *Sheriffs inſol-*
riffs themſelves ſhould prove Inſolvent, and not *vent.*
able to ſatisfy the Amerciaments and Farm, *Amercia-*
then the Citizens to be accountable, ſaving to *ments.*
the ſaid Citizens their Liberties aforeſaid.
The ſaid Sheriffs likewiſe to enjoy the Liberty
of other Citizens, and not to be amerc'd a- *Citizens to*
bove 20 *l.* and that not to endamage any of *make it good,*
the other Citizens, tho' the Sheriffs are not *ſaving, &c.*
ſufficient.

And that if the Sheriffs commit any Of- *Sheriffs trya-*
fence, by which they incur the loſs of their *ble by Citizens.*
Lives or Members, they ſhall be adjudg'd ac-
cording to the Laws of the City; that is, be
tried by Citizens before the Juſtices of the
Exchequer. He likewiſe confirms to them the
Sheriffwick of *London* and *Middleſex*, at 300 *l.*
per Ann. and forbids all Perſons to do any
Damage to the Citizens of *London*, in thoſe
things that belong to the Sheriffwick; and
withal he grants, that if any thing ſhould be

B 3   given

given away by him or his Heirs, which of Right belongs to the Sheriffs of *London*, the same to be allow'd on Account in the *Exchequer*.

John, *Char.* 3.   In the Third, *Ann.* 1°, he again commands all Wears in the *Thames* and *Medway* to be re-

Wears in the mov'd, and that no Wears for the future be
Medway re- put up any where in the *Thames* and *Medway*,
moved. upon the forfeiture of Ten Pounds Sterling. He likewife clearly remits all that the Keepers of the *Tower* of *London* were wont to exact yearly upon the Account of the faid Wears, and forbids the faid Keepers to exact any Money, or to give any Perfon any Trouble by reafon of the fame.

John, *Char.* 4.   In the Fourth, *Ann.* 10, or 16. he likewife commands the removal of all Wears, *&c.* and grants to the *Barons* of the City of *London*

Mayor to be yearly to chufe a Mayor ; the faid Mayor to
chofen. be prefented to him, or in his abfence to his Juftices : At the end of the Year to proceed to choofe another, or to retain the fame, prefenting him again to him, or in his abfence

Chamberlain- to his Juftices. He likewife confirms to them
ſhip reſerved. all their former Immunities, faving only the *Chamberlainſhip* to himfelf.

John, *Char.* 5.   In the Fifth Charter, faid to be *Ann.* 3", he
Weavers Guild. grants that the Guild of the Weavers fhall not be in the City; and that whereas the faid Guild were wont to pay him 18 Marks yearly, he agrees with the Citizens to pay him 20 Marks into the *Exchequer* for a Gift, *&c.*

Henry III.   *Henry* the Third, *Ann.* 11", grants the City
Char. 1.   of *London* a new Charter, confirming the Sheriffwick of *London* and *Middlefex* at the yearly Rent of 300 *l. per Ann.* as aforefaid ; as alfo,

Liberty

Liberty to chufe and remove their Sheriffs ; *Shereffwick*
orders the faid Sheriffs to be prefented at the *confirmed.*
Exchequer ; and the Citizens (if the Sheriffs do
not anfwer the Amerciaments, and the Farm,)
to do it themfelves, faving their Liberties as
aforefaid, and the faid Sheriff their other Liberties.

He orders the Amercements of the Sheriffs *Amercements*
not to exceed 20 *l.* and that if they do any *20 l.*
Offence whereby they ought to incur the lofs
of their Lives or Members, that according to
the Law of the City they be judg'd before
the Juftices of the *Exchequer.* He repeats a-
gain their former Grant of holding the Sheriffwick of *London* and *Middlefex* quietly, ho-
nourably, and wholly by the Farm of 300 *l.*
per Ann. and provides, that if himfelf or any
of his Juftices fhall grant to any Perfon any
Thing belonging to the Sheriffwick of *London, &c.* that it fhall be accounted for to the
Citizens of *London,* in the Acquittal of the faid
Farm in the *Exchequer.*

In his Second Charter, *Ann.* 11°, he grants Henry III.
to the *Barons* of *London* the Liberty to chufe a *Char.* 2.
Mayor; orders that he be Prefented, after his *Mayor con-*
Election, to him, or in his abfence to his Ju- *firmed.*
ftices. That at the end of the Year they pro- *Barons.*
ceed to a new Choice : That the faid *Barons*
enjoy all their former Liberties, faving only *Chamberlain-*
the *Chamberlainfhip* to himfelf. *fhip referved.*

In his Third Charter, *Ann.* 11°, he commands Henry III.
the removal of all the Wears in the River of *Char.* 3.
Thames and *Medway.* He forbids the Keepers
of the *Tower* of *London* to demand any thing as
they were wont formerly upon the account of
the Wears, and declares the faid Wears to be *Wears re-*
injurious not only to the City of *London,* but *mov'd.*
to the whole Realm.

B 4　　　　　Note,

☞ Note, *It is said by* Calthorp, *in his Tract of the Cities Liberties, p. 15. That the King's Hand, as well as Seal, was set to this Charter ; the like whereof (says he) I never did hear or read of before.*

Hen. III. Char. 4.

In his Fourth Charter, *Ann.* 11°, he grants that no Citizen plead without the Walls of the City, excepting his Monyers and Ministers, and in Foreign Tenures. He likewise grants them an Acquittal of all *Murther* within the Walls of the City. That no Citizen be oblig'd to wage Battel, and that they have liberty to discharge themselves of the Pleas of the Crown according to the Custom of the City. That none be lodg'd upon them by force. That they be free from all *Toll, Lestage, &c.* throughout *England.* That they be amerc'd according to the Law of the City. That there be no Miskenning in any Pleading in the City. That *the Hustings* sit once a Week. That they enjoy their Debts, *&c.* according to the Custom of the City. That Pleas for Debts lent in *London,* be holden in the City. That they enjoy their former Liberty of Hunting. That they be quit of all *Bridtoll, Childwite, Jeresgive,* and of all *Scotale,* as aforesaid ; and that they and their Heirs hold their Liberties of him and his Heirs hereditarily.

pleadings within the City.

Amercements. Hustings.

Hunting.

Liberties held.

Hen. III. Ch. 5. Warren of Stanes granted.

In his Fifth Charter, *Ann.* 11°, he grants the Warren of *Stanes, &c.* to the Inhabitants of the County of *Middlesex,* and gives leave that the same should be diswarren'd and disforrested, *&c.*

Hen. III. Char. 4.

In his Sixth Charter, *Ann.* 31°, the Covenant between the King's Brother *Richard,* Earl of *Cornwal,* and the Mayor and Commonalty

of

of *London,* concerning *Queen-Hith,* is repeated, Queen-Hith and *Queen-Hith* granted to the City at the *granted.* Yearly Rent of 50 *l.* to be paid at two equal Proportions every Year in *Clerkenwell;* which Grant not long after was solemnly confirm'd by the King for him and his Heirs, *&c.*

In his Seventh Charter, *Ann.* 37°, he grants Hen. III. to the Citizens of *London, &c.* all their Li- *Ch.* 7. berties and Free Customs, which they had in the Reign of *Henry* his Grandfather. He ap- *Mayor to be* points that the Mayor be yearly presented to *presented.* him, or in his absence, to the Barons of the *Exchequer* at *Westminster;* and allows to the Sheriffs of *London* yearly 7 *l.* upon account for the Liberty of St. *Paul's,* and that the Citi- St. Paul's *Li-* zens throughout all his Dominions, both here *berty.* and beyond Sea, be quit of all Toll and Custom, *&c.*

In his Eighth Charter, *Ann.* 50°, he grants Hen. III. to the Citizens of *London* to traffick with their *Ch.* 8. Merchandizes where they pleas'd, as well by *Traffick by* Sea as Land, and grants them a general Im- *Sea and Land.* munity from all Toll, *&c.*

In his Ninth Charter, *Ann.* 52°, (the Citi- Hen. III. zens having forfeited their former Charters) *Ch.* 9. he is reconcil'd to them, and grants as follows; *Former Char-* That none of them be compelled to plead with- *New Grant.* out the Walls of the City, except Foreign Tenures, and his Monyers and Officers, and such other Matters which are contrary to the Peace of the Realm, *&c.* He grants them likewise Acquittal of Murther, in the City and *Portsoken,* and that none of them may wage Battel, and that they may discharge themselves of the Pleas of the Crown according to their antient Custom; except only that they shall not swear upon the Graves of the *Note.*

Dead,

Dead, but that others be chosen to do that which the Deceased should have done in his Life : And he also grants, that none shall lodge within the Walls of the City, and in *Portsoken*, by force, or by delivery of the Marshal.

Free Trade any where. He further grants them Liberty to dwell with their Merchandizes, and to trade free in any part of his Dominions, and as well on this, as beyond the Seas, to be free in all his Sea-Ports from all Toll, Lestage, &c. except- *Prizage.* ing only his Custom and Prizes of Wine, which was for one Tun before, and another behind the Mast 20 s. and withal grants, that if any Person take any Toll of them contrary to his Grant, that the Sheriff of *London* shall take *Withernam,* their Goods by Withernam at *London*.

Hustings, Also that the *Hustings* be holden once a *Ante 2, 8.* Week, and that the Citizens have right done them within the City for their Lands and Te- nures, according to the antient Custom of the City ; that they have liberty to appoint their *Attorneys.* Attorney, as well in Pleading as Defending there, as elsewhere in our Courts. That there be no Miskenning in their Pleas, *i. e.* where they have not declared altogether well. And that of all Debts, Promises, &c. made in *Pleadings in* *London*, Pleas be there holden, according to *London.* their antient Custom, and that all be quit of *Childwite* and *Jerisgive*, and from *Scotale*. That the Citizens have and hold their Lands, Debts, and Tenures as formerly. That there be no *No Forestalling.* Forestalling, &c. upon the forfeiture of the Goods bought after that manner, and Impri- sonment.

Also that no Goods be put to sale before *Customs levied.* the Custom be levied, without great Punish- ment, and the forfeiture of the said Goods.
That

That no Stranger buy any Goods before they *Goods weighed*, be weighed at the King's Beam, upon forfeiture of the faid Goods. Further he grants, that the Citizens, for the better fecurity of *Citizens Debts* their Debts, might have liberty to enrol them *enrolled in the* in the *Exchequer;* but no Debt to be enrolled *Exchequer,* unlefs teftified by fix or four Witneffes, and that they pay for every Pound fo enrolled one Penny for his ufe; and likewife grants, that they enjoy all their former Cuftoms, provided they are not contrary to right Law and Ju- *Jews and* ftice, making a referve to himfelf touching *Merchant* *Jews*, and Merchant Strangers. *Strangers.*

Edward the Firft by his Charter, *Ann.* 26°, *Edw. I,* appoints, That the Mayor and Sheriffs of the faid City be prefented in his Abfence to the Barons of the *Exchequer* at *Weftminfter*, till his next coming to *Weftminfter* or *London,* and then to be prefented to himfelf, *&c.* Or in *Mayor pre-* cafe that he, nor the faid Barons fhall be at *fented.* *London* or *Weftminfter*, then that he fhall be prefented to the Conftable of the *Tower.* He alfo grants to the Citizens aforefaid, that they be for ever free from Pannage, Pontage, and *Or Paviage.* Murage. That the Sheriffs of *London* be a- merced as the Sheriffs of other Counties; and that the Citizens enjoy all their former Liberties, Freedoms, Quittals and Free Cuftoms.

Edward the Second, *Ann.* 15°, in return for *Edw. II,* feveral Kindneffes mentioned at large in his Charter, (granted to the Citizens of *London, viz.* That whereas they had affifted him with armed Footmen at the Caftle of *Leeds* in *Kent, &c.*) Grants that the fame *Aids, &c.* fhall not be prejudicial to the Mayor, *&c.* nor be drawn into Example,

Edward

Edw. III. *Edward* the Third, *Ann.* 1°, grants the Citi-
Ch. 1. zens of *London* a very large and beneficial
Charter; wherein according to the Great
Charter or the Liberties of *England*, i. e. *Mag-*
na Charta, all their Antient Liberties and Customs are restored, and all Usurpations of
their former Liberties revoked and annulled.

The Mayor a He grants that the Mayor and his Successors
Justice for the be one of the Justices of the Goal Delivery
Goal Delivery of *Newgate*, to be named in every Commis-
of Newgate. sion ; and that they have In-fangtheft, and
Out-fangtheft, and Chattels of Felons, &c.

> ☞ See Hollinshead, 343. *That by this Chárter the*
> *King granted, that the Franchises of the City*
> *should not thenceforth be seized into the King's*
> *Hands for any Cause, but only for Treason*
> *and Rebellion, shewed by the whole City.* Sed
> vide post the Stat. 28 E. 3. c. 10.

Also that, according to former Charters,
Sheriffwicks. they only pay 300*l. per Ann.* for the Sheriffwick
of *London* and *Middlesex.* He also grants to the
Citizens, liberty to devise their Lands in *Lon-*
Mortmain. *don* in Mortmain, or otherwise as they were
wont in former times. He likewise grants
that the Sheriffs of *London* should not be a-
Amercements merced any otherways for the Escape of
of Sheriffs. Thieves, &c. than other Sheriffs on this side
Trent ; and that the Citizens of *London* should
not be charged with the Custody of those that
fly to the Churches within their Liberty for
Sanctuary, otherwise than of old accustomed, and that they may remove all Weares in
Thames and *Medway*, and have the Punish-
ments thereof.

Sale of Mer- That all Merchant Strangers that come to
chant Stran- *England* to sell their Merchandizes, &c. should
gers Goods, be obliged to dispose of them in 40 Days :
That

That they should not keep Houses, but sojourn with the Citizens, &c. He also grants
that neither the Marshal, Steward, nor Clerk *Clerk of*
of the Market of his Houshold should sit or *Market.*
exercise any Power within the Liberty of the
City. That the Citizens should not be forced to plead out of the City. That no Es- *Escheator.*
cheator exercise any Power within the City,
but that the Lord Mayor for the time being,
execute the Office of Escheator, and take an
Oath for the due performance thereof, and
account with the King and his Heirs.

That the Citizens from henceforth, should *War out of*
not be obliged to go or send to War out of the *the City.*
City. That the Constable of the *Tower,* &c.
should not make any Prizes in any respect, or
arrest any Boats bringing Victual to the said
City. That the Citizens, as they were wont
formerly, should have their Keepers among
themselves to hold their Pleas touching their
Covenants or *Contracts* in the good Fairs of
England. That the Sheriffs of *London* take no
Oaths at the *Exchequer,* but upon the giving
up their Accounts. He likewise restores to
them all their former Liberties and Customs, *Former Liber-*
which the Justices of the *Tower* in their Cir- *berties and*
cuit had compelled them to claim, &c. He *Customs re-*
grants, that one Writ of Allowance of their *stored.*
Charters should be sufficient for one King's
time; and that no Summons, Attachments or
Executions be made by any the King's Officers within the Liberties of the City, but
only by the Officers of the City; and that
the Sheriffs of the said City may lawfully take
the Forfeitures of Victuals and other Things
and Merchandizes. He likewise grants, that
if in the last Circuit of the *Tower,* any Thing
was done or attempted contrary to their Liberties,

berties, that the fame fhould not be prejudicial to them, &c.

That the Citizens of *London* fhould be taxed
in Subfidies as other Commons of the Kingdom, and not as Citizens. That they be quit
of Tallage, and that the Liberty of the City
be not taken into the King's Hands for any
Perfonal Trefpafs or Judgment of any Minifter of the City; neither fhall a Keeper of the
City for that reafon be deputed, but the fame
Minifter fhall be punifhed only according to
his Offence.

Purveyors.

Prizage.

That no Purveyor, or any other Officer
belonging to him, or his Heirs, fhould make
any Prize of the Goods belonging to Citizens
without their confent, nor make any Prize of
their Wines againft their Wills, &c. He likewife forbids his Purveyors or other Officers
to Merchandize in any Commodity that rela-
ted to their Office. That all Lands without the City, belonging to the Officers of
the fame, be kept harmlefs, as their Tenements are within the faid City. He alfo grants

*No Market
within feven
Miles.
Inquifitions
taken in
St.* Martin's
le Grand.

that no Market be within feven Miles of *London.* That all Inquifitions be taken by the
Juftices of *London,* in St. *Martin's le Grand,*
and not elfewhere, except the Inquifitions to
be taken for the *Tower* of *London,* and Goal
Delivery of *Newgate:* And that none of the
Freemen of the faid City fhould be impleaded
or troubled at the *Exchequer,* or elfewhere, by
Bill, except it be by thofe things that concern Us and our Heirs, &c.

Edw. III.
Ch. 2.
Southwark
granted.

In his Second Charter, granted in Parliament, *Ann.* 1°, he grants to the City of *London* the Village of *Southwark,* with the Appurtenances, paying yearly at the *Exchequer*
the Farms thereof due and accuftomed.

In

In his Third Charter, *Ann.* 11°, granted in
Parliament to the City of *London*, the *York*
Statute is recited, wherein is enacted, That
all Merchant Strangers, as *English*, should sell
their Commodities, of what sort soever, at
any Cities, Towns, or Boroughs, notwithstanding their Charters, Liberties, *&c.* granted
to the contrary. Nevertheless, the Citizens
of *London* are to enjoy their Customs accor-
ding to *Magna Charta, &c.* *Ed. III. C. 34 Customs ac- cording to Magna Charta,*

In his Fourth Charter, *Ann.* 28°, he grants,
That the Serjeants of *London* may bear Maces
of Gold or Silver within the Liberties of the
City of *London*, or without, in their Attendance
upon the King or Royal Family. *Edw. III. Ch. 4. Maces of Gold and Sil- ver.*

In his Fifth Charter, granted, *Ann.* 50°, in
Parliament, he grants to the City of *London*,
that the Merchant Strangers coming into *England* should board with a free Host of the
City, and not keep Houses; and that there
should be no *Brokers* from henceforth, but
what were chosen by the Merchants which
belong to the Mystery in which the said Bro-
kers exercise their Office. *Edw. III. Char. 5. Merchant Strangers to board, and not to keep Houses. Brokers.*

In the same Charter, upon the humble Petition of the Mayor, Aldermen, *&c.* The King
in Parliament grants to the City of *London,*
That no Stranger should sell any Goods by
retail, or keep any House, or be a Broker
in the said City or Suburbs. *Strangers not to sell by retail.*

Note, *A Charter was granted in Parliament
to the City of* London, Ann. 7. R. II. (*which
is omitted in this* Confirmation.) *See* Cotton's *Records,* 294. 466, &c. *By which
Charter all their antient Liberties and Customs are restored and confirm'd; all which
you may find collected, and Alphabetically digested.*

gefted in a Tract faid to be compiled by
Sir Henry Calthorp, *Kt. and printed in the*
Year 1642. Vide ib. pag. 1 & 14.

Henry IV.

Cuftody of
Gates.

Gathering
Tolls.

Tronage.

Edw. IV.
Char. 1.

Liberties and
Cuftoms con-
firmed.

Mayor, Re-
corder and
Aldermen
made Juftices.

Mayor of the
Quorum.

Sheriffs Atten-
dant.

Henry the Fourth in his Charter, *Ann.* 1°, granted to the City of *London* for himfelf and his Heirs, to the Citizens and their Heirs, to have the Cuftody as well of the Gates of *New-gate* and *Ludgate* as of all other Gates and Po-fterns belonging to the faid City ; with the Office of gathering all Toll and Cuftoms in *Cheap, Billinfgate,* and *Smithfield,* and alfo the Tronage, *i. e.* the weighing Lead, Wax, Pep-per, Allom, Madder, and the like.

Edward the Fourth in his Firft Charter, *Ann.* 2°, grants to the City of *London,* for the more firm and entire eftablifhment of the good Government of the fame, That they hold and enjoy all their Liberties and Free Cuftoms, as whole and found as they had, and held them in the time of any of his Proge-nitors. He likewife grants, That the Mayor, Recorder, and fuch Aldermen as have been Mayors, fhall be difcharg'd of the faid Of-fice, and fhall be Juftices of the Peace for the putting all Ordinances which are for the prefervation of the Peace and Good Govern-ment of the City, and of the Suburbs and Li-berty thereof, as well by Land as Water in Execution ; and that the faid Mayor, Recor-der, and Aldermen be Juftices of *Oyer* and *Terminer*; and that the Mayor for the time being, and his Succeffors be of the *Quorum.* And that the Sheriffs of the City of *London* be Attendant upon the faid Juftices, and aiding and affifting to them in preferving the Peace of the City, as aforefaid, faving always to the faid Mayor, Recorder, Aldermen

dermen and Citizens their Cuſtoms, Liber- *Saving the Ci-*
ties, *&c.* *ties Cuſtoms.*

He alſo grants to the City of *London,* That *Cuſtoms cer-*
the Cuſtoms of the ſaid City be certified and *tified by word*
recorded by Word of Mouth; and that the *if Mouth.*
Maior and Aldermen of the City, and their
Succeſſors, do declare by the Recorder, whether the Things under diſpute be a Cuſtom or
not; and alſo grants to the Maior, Aldermen,
and Commonalty of the ſaid City, that there
be no forfeiture of the Premiſes upon the account of any Non-Uſer or Abuſer, *&c.*

Alſo, That all Perſons inhabiting within *Inhabitants*
the ſame, or the Suburbs, or Liberties thereof, *contributary to*
ſhould be contributary in proportion to their *all Taxes, &c.*
reſpective Faculties, *&c.* to all Taxes, Grants
and Talliages, *&c.* excepting only the Mer-
chants of *Almain,* which had a Houſe in *Lon-* *Except Mer-*
don, commonly called, The *Guild-Hall* of the *chants of Al-*
Almains. *main.*

That the Aldermen of the ſaid City ſhould *Maior and*
not be put upon Aſſizes, Attaints, or Juries, *Aldermen ex-*
ſo long as they continue Aldermen; and that *empted from*
thoſe that have bore the Office of Maior, *Juries, &c.*
ſhould be utterly exempted for ever.

Alſo, That the Aldermen of *London* ſhould *And being Col-*
not be Collectors or Taxers out of the City; *lectors of Taxes*
and if they ſhould be choſen to any of the ſaid *out of the City.*
Offices, they ſhould not incur any Penalty or
Impriſonment, upon the account of their refuſal.

And whereas there were certain Doubts
concerning the uſe of ſome Liberties belonging to the Town of *Southwark,* formerly granted
to the Citizens of *London* by King *Edward* the
Third, this King grants to the ſaid City in a
very large and extenſive manner, the ſaid
Town of *Southwark,* with all the Appurte- *Southwark*
C nances *granted.*

nances ; and alfo all Waifs, Eftrayes, &c. and
Felons Goods. all Treafure-trove in the Town aforefaid, of
all Handy-works, Goods, and Chattels of all
Traytors. Traitors, Felons, Fugitives, and Out-Laws.

Alfo all Goods difclaimed, or found in the
Efcheats and faid Town, with all Efcheats and Forfeitures,
other Forfei- as fully and wholly as he fhould have, if the
tures. faid Town were in his own Hands ; and that
Maior, &c. to it fhall be lawful for the Maior, &c. to put
take poffeffion of themfelves into poffeffion thereof.
them.

He alfo grants to the Maior and Commo-
Affize of nalty of *London* the Affize of Bread, Wine, &c.
Bread, &c. Victuals, and things faleable in the faid Town ;
Clerk of the as alfo the Clerkfhip of the Market belong-
Market. ing to the faid Town, with all Forfeitures and
Fines and For- Fines.
feitures.
Execution of And that the Execution and Return of
Writs, &c. Writs, &c. be by the Officers of the City of
London—— and that neither the King's Clerk
of the Market, nor the Sheriff of *Surry*, do in
any refpect intermeddle therein.

A Fair with Alfo to hold a Fair three days in the Year,
a Pypowder *viz.* the 7th, 8th, and 9th days of *September*,
Court. and that they may from time to time have a
Court of *Pypowders*, with all Summons, At-
tachments, &c. belonging to the fame, and alfo
View of that they may have a View of Frankpledge,
F,ank-pledge. with all that thereunto appertaineth, &c.

He alfo grants that the Maior, Commonalty,
or their Deputies may take and arreft all Fe-
Felons, &c. in lons, Thieves, &c. and commit them to *New-*
Southwark, *to gate*, which are apprehended in *Southwark* ; and
be fent to further grants to the Maior and his Succeffors,
Newgate. &c. That they may for ever have the Town a-
forefaid, with all the Liberties, &c. in as
The Town large a manner as if the fame were in his own
granted at 10*l.* Hands, paying for the fame only Ten Pounds.
Rent.
for

for the Antient Farm; the Rights of the Arch- *Archbishops Right excepted.*
bifhop of *Canterbury* only excepted.

In his Second Charter, *Ann.* 3°, he grants to *Edw. IV.*
the Maior, Commonalty, *&c.* the Tronage and *Ch. 2.*
Weighing of Wool, by whom, or from what- *Tronage.*
foever Parts brought to the faid City of *London,*
and that all Wool that formerly was brought
to the Staple of *Weftminfter,* be henceforth
brought to *Leaden-Hall,* within the faid City; *At Leaden-*
and, That there be no other Staple within *Hall.*
three Miles of the fame, *&c.*

In his 3d Char. *Ann.* 18°, he grants to the Citi- *Edw. IV.*
zens of *London, &c.* upon their releafing of 1923*l.* *Ch. 3.*
9 *s.* 8 *d.* out of a certain Sum of 12923*l.* 9*s.* 8*d.*
then owing to the City from the King, Licenfe
to purchafe 200 Marks *per Ann.* in Mortmain; *Purchafe in*
and alfo grants to any perfon, liberty to grant *Mortmain.*
to the City of *London* 200 Marks *per Ann.* in
Mortmain, as aforefaid, to enjoy and hold the
fame, without any Letters Patents, or any
Inquifition upon any Writ of *ad quod damnum,* *Without Li-*
or any other the King's Commandments, *&c.* *cenfe.*
with privilege to have as many Writs of *ad*
quod damnum, as fhall be fufficient for their
utmoft fatisfaction for the faid Sum of
1923 *l. 9 s. 8 d.*

☞ Note, *This Charter was confirmed in* Parl. 3
Hen. 8.

In his Fourth Charter, *Ann.* 18°, he grants *Edw. IV.*
to the faid Citizens of *London* in Parliament, *Ch. 4.*
in confideration of the faid Sum of 70000 *l.*
the refpective Offices of Packing, Portage,
Garbling, Gauging, and Wine-drawing, the *Packing and*
fame to be executed by them, or their fuffi- *Garbling, &c.*
cient Deputies——— (*See the Charter at*
large.) And alfo grants them, in confide-
C 2   ration

Coroner's Office, &c.   ration of the faid Sum of 7000 *l.* the Office of Coroner, with Power to the Maior and Commonalty to grant the faid Office of Coroner to whom they pleafed ; and alfo that the Maior and Aldermen, *&c.* as aforefaid, might have full Power and Authority to exercife the faid Office of Coroner :

Butler and Coroner feparate.   He caufes the Offices of chief Butler and Coroner to be divided, and made two feparate and diftinct Offices—— And that no other Coroner, but the Coroner belonging to the City of *London,* do intermeddle in any refpect in the faid City.

Henry VII.

Merchandize foreign bought, &c. forfeited.

Gauger.

Henry VII. *Ann.* 1ˢ, grants to the City by his Charter, That if any Strangers to the City of *London* buy any Wares or Merchandize of any Perfon, being likewife a Stranger to the faid City, That all Merchandizes fo bought, fhould be forfeited, *&c.* That any Stranger, *&c.* may buy any quantities of Commodities in Grofs, but not to fell again. He likewife confirms to them the Office of Gauger within the faid City, to hold the fame with all Fees, Profits, *&c.*

Hen. VIII. *Ch.* 1. *No Inquifitions to be at St. Martins.*

Henry VIII. in his firft Charter, *Ann.* 10°, grants, That the Inquifitions, *&c.* formerly taken in St. *Martin's le Grand,* fhould be from henceforth taken in *London,* except only Inquifitions taken in Eyre in the *Tower* of *London,* and for the Goal Delivery of *Newgate.*

Hen. VIII. *Ch.* 2. *Keepers of the Great Beam and Common Balance.*

By his Second Charter, *Ann.* 22°, he cancels Sir *William Sidney's* Patent relating to the great Beam and Common Balance belonging to the City of *London,* and declares, That the keeping the faid Beam and Weights pertaining to the City by Prefcription ; and orders, That the

Weights

Weights and Beams for weighing Merchants Commodities, be, and ought to be in the Hands of Persons chosen by the Maior and Commonalty ; and that they shall have the Tronage ; that is, the weighing of Wax, *Tronage.* Lead, Pepper, Allom, &c. and be Keepers of the Great Beam, and Common Balance, as granted by *Hen.* IV.

In the same Charter, the Maior, Commonalty, and Citizens are ordained Keepers of the Beams, Weights, &c. with Power and Authority to make and assign Clerks, Porters, &c. of the said Great Beam and Balance, and of the Iron Beam, and of the Beam of the *Still-Yard* aud Weights aforesaid ——— with all the Fees and Profits thereto belonging, without Account, &c.

Edward VI. *Anno* 4°, in his Charter grants *Edw.* VI. to the Maior of *London,* &c. several Messuages *Southwark* in *Southwark,* with their Appurtenances, except- *Park,* &c. ing the Capital Messuage, called *Southwark Place, The Park* and *Antelope,* with all the Garden-Ground, Buildings, &c. thereto belonging ———

He further grants the Manor of *Southwark, Manor of* belonging to the late Monastry of *Bermondsey, Southwark,* with all the Appurtenances, and also the Manor *and Monastry* and Borough of *Southwark,* late Parcel of the *sey, &c.* Possessions of the Archbishop of *Canterbury,* with several other Lands, Tenements, &c. in as full and large a manner as the Duke of *Suffolk,* or any Abbot of *Bermondsey,* or Archbishop of *Canterbury,* did enjoy the same ; and in as full and large a manner as the same came, or ought to have come to his Father *Henry* VIII. &c.

C 3   He

He likewife grants in confideration of 500
Marks paid into the Treafury, &c. feveral o-
Waifs, Eftrays, ther things to the Maior, &c. viz. Waifs,
Plea 27, 29. Eftrays, Treafure found, Goods of Traitors,
Deodands, &c. Felons, Fugitives, Out-Laws, and Deodands,
and alfo all Efcheats and Forfeitures formerly
belonging to the King and his Heirs, &c.

Affize of Alfo, That the Maior and Commonalty,
Bread, &c. fhould have the Affize of Bread, Wine, Beer,
and Ale, &c. and whatfoever did belong to
the Clerk of the Market; as likewife the
Execution and Return of Writs, Warrants, &c.

Southwark He further grants them a Fair for three
Fair. Days every Year in *Southwark*, with a Court of
Pypowder, with all Liberties and Free Cuftom
to fuch a Court appertaining.

Frank-Pledge. He likewife grants them a View of Frank-
Summons, At- pledge, together with all Summons, Attach-
tachments,Ar- ments, Arrefts, Iffues, Profits, &c. which
refts, &c. therefore may, or ought to belong to the King,
his Heirs, and Succeffors, &c.

He alfo grants them Liberty to apprehend
Felons, Thieves, and other Malefactors with-
Felons fent to in the faid Town, Borough, &c. and to carry
Newgate. them to *Newgate*, there to be kept till they
fhall be delivered by due courfe of Law:
And alfo grants, That the Maior, Commo-
nalty, &c. have the fame Liberties in the Bo-
rough and Town aforefaid, as the King
fhould have, if the fame were in his
Hands.

Jury of South- He likewife grants, That they fhould hold
wark *appear-* Pleas in *London* for Matters in *Southwark*; and
*ing in*London. that the Jurors in *Southwark* making default before the Maior and Sheriffs of *London*, fhould
forfeit their Iffues, and fuffer fuch Amercements as the Men impannelled and fummoned
in the faid City of *London* are liable to.

He

He further grants, That the Maior and *Plaints and* Commonalty, *&c.* have cognizance of all man- *Pleas arising* ner of Pleas, Actions, Plaints, and Suits Per- *in Southwark.* sonal arising in *Southwark*; and also grants, That the Maior, *&c.* may chuse two Coroners *Coroners.* for *Southwark*, and that no Coroner belonging to the King, have any power to intermeddle there.

He likewise grants, that the Maior of *London* be Escheator in *Southwark*, and that no other *Escheators.* Escheator intermeddle: And that the said Maior be Clerk of the Market in *Southwark*, *Clerk of the* and that the King's Clerk of the Market do *Market.* not intermeddle, *&c.*

He further grants them all Franchises, Stal- *Franchises,* lages, Pickages, *&c.* which any Archbishop of *Stallage, Pick-* *Canterbury,*. or the said Duke of *Suffolk*, *&c.* *age,* &c. did enjoy; and that none of the King's Officers or Ministers do intermeddle in any respect in the said Town and Borough of *Southwark*.

He likewise grants, That all and singular *Inhabitants* the Inhabitants of *Southwark* be under the *subject to the* Magistracy and Government of the Maior and *Maior's Go-* Officers of *London*, as the Citizens and Inha- *vernment.* bitants of the said City be; and that the said Maior, *&c.* have the same Jurisdiction in *Southwark* as in *London*, &c.

He grants also, That the Maior, Recor- *Maior and* der and Aldermen, that are Justices of the *Aldermen* Peace in *London*, shall be Justices of the Peace *Justices for* in *Southwark*; and that there be Markets in *Southwark.* *Southwark* four Days a Week. Provided nevertheless, that this Grant doth not prejudice the Steward of the King's House, *&c.*

He moreover grants, to save the City harm- *Corodies,* less against all Corodies, Rates, Fees and An- *&c.* nuities, given out, or to be paid out of the

C 4 the

Premises, referving to himfelf the Services in the faid Charter referv'd, and the Fee-Farm of 10 *l. per Ann.*

James I.
Ch. 1.

*Bailiff of the
River of
Thames.*

King *James* I. in his Charter, grants the Maior, *&c.* to be Chief Bailiff, and have the confervation of the River of *Thames,* and the Extent of his Jurifdiction to be Weftward to *Stanes* Bridge, in the County of *Middlefex,* and Eaftward as far as *Kendal,* alias, *Yendal,* or *Yeenleet,* with all the Fees and Profits thereunto belonging.

*Meafurers of
Coals and
Grain,* &c.

He likewife grants to the Maior, *&c.* to have the Office of meafuring all Coals and Grain, and of all Salt, Apples, *&c.* and to take the Fees and Profits belonging to the faid Office, to the fole Ufe of him the faid Maior, *&c.* without any lett or hindrance of the King, or any other Perfon, and to hold the faid Office without account, and that no other Water-Bailiff, Confervator, or Meafurer intermeddle: And the Grants of the faid Offices to remain firm to the Maior, *&c* notwithftanding any Non-Ufer, or Abufer of the fame.

King James I.
Ch. 2.

King *James* I. in the Preamble of his Second Charter, makes a full and general confirmation of all former Charters granted to the City of *London,* and repeats the feveral Names of the Corporations of *London* ; and likewife grants

*All Liberties
reftored.*

them a Reftitution of all Liberties to all Intents and Purpofes, as fully and largely as their Anceftors enjoy'd them; and although they have not ufed, or have abufed their neverthelefs he grants, that they may ufe them for the time to come.

*Precincts de-
termined.*

He grants likewife, That they hold their Premifes as they were formerly accuftomed, and determines the Liberties of the City of

London.

London to extend and ſtretch forth likewiſe to
Duke's-place, St. *Bartholomew's* Great and Leſs, Duke's-place.
Black-Friers, *White-Friers*, and *Cold-Harbourgh*, Black-Friers.
and the reſpective Inhabitants thereof, to be White-Friers.
within the Precinct of *London*, with a Proviſo
that the Inhabitants of *Black* and *White-Friers*
be exempt from certain Taxes, Fifteens, *&c.*
and that the Inhabitants aforeſaid be quit
from the Office of Conſtable, Scavenger,
&c.

Neverthelefs he grants, That the Maior, *&c.*
by their own Officers may levy all ſuch Aids,
Tallages, Grants, and Contributions, which are
not excepted in the ſaid Charter; and that
the Juſtices of *London* ſhould hold Juriſdiction
in *Black-Friers*, *White-Friers*, *Duke's-place*, *Great* Great *and*
and *Little* St. *Bartholomew's*, and *Cold Har-* Little St. Bar-
bourgh, with power to take Security for the tholomew's.
preſervation of the peace, and to commit the Cold Har-
Refuſers to Priſon——— bourgh.

He further grants, That the Maior and Re- *Juſtices of*
corder, and ſuch other Juſtices that are cuſto- Oyer *and*
marily Juſtices in the City, be Juſtices of Terminer.
Oyer and *Terminer*, and that the Maior for the
Time being, and the Recorder be always of
the *Quorum*, and that no other Juſtices do intermeddle in the City and Liberties aforeſaid,
and that the Sheriffs of *London* be aiding and
aſſiſting to the ſaid Juſtices.

He likewiſe grants, That all Treaſures *Treaſure-*
found within the ſaid City, all Waifs, Eſtrays, *Trove,* Waifs,
and all Goods and Chattels of Felons, Fugi- *Eſtrays,* &c.
tives, *&c.* belong to the ſaid City, and that
they have theſe Letters Patents under the
Great Seal, without any Fee or Fine in the
Hamper, *&c.*

In

James I.
Ch. 3.
Coals meafu-
red.

In his Third Charter, *London* is ftyled his *Royal Chamber*, and therein is granted, That the City have the meafuring of all Coals brought to the City of *London*, as likewife the weighing of Coals, with all the Fees and Profits belonging to the fame; and that the faid Office be executed by the Maior, or his Deputies.

8 d. per Tun.

No unlading
till Notice.

In the fame Charter the Fees for weighing of Coals are fettled at 8 *d. per* Tun, the fame to be to the Ufe of the Maior and Commonalty of the City of *London*; and withal it is provided, that no Merchant unlade his Coals till the Maior have Notice, to the intent, that having a true Eftimate of the Quantity of Coals brought to the City of *London*, he may be able to fatisfy the King in that Particular, when demanded.

Foreftalling of
Coals, and re-
tailing in
Lighters.

In the fame Charter all forftalling and regrating of Coals is prohibited, all felling of Coals by retail in Lighters forbidden, and no Markets for the future to be in Lighters. And further he grants, that if after the fealing of thefe Letters Patents any Defects fhould appear, others fhould be granted more advantageous and effectual.

Car. I.
Ch. 1.

King *Charles* I. begins his 1ft Charter with an Acknowledgment of the good Services of the City of *London*, and confirms all their former Letters Patents, except thofe in the fame Charter excepted. He likewife repeats the feveral Names of the Corporations of *London*, and makes a Reftitution of all their Liberties, except fome few that are therein excepted.

Liberties re-
ftored.

In the fame Charter a Recital is made of the Charter of the 26th of *October*, in the 23d
Year

Year of *Hen.* VI. and likewise the Soil, *&c.* of the Streets, and of the *Thames,* granted to the City; and then all other Charters of the said King *Henry* VI. are made void, and some Doubts mentioned concerning the Validity of the Charter granted to the City of *London* the 10th of *Henry* VII. after which the said King *Charles* grants as follows——

Soil of the Streets and Thames. Charters of Hen. VI. *made void.*

That the Maior, Recorder and Aldermen belonging to the City of *London* be Justices of the Peace; and to commit those to the Prison of *Newgate, &c.* who shall refuse to find Securities for the Preservation of the Peace, as aforesaid; and to do and execute all such things which Justices and Keepers of the Peace in any County of *England* do, or are wont to do.

Maior, Recorder, and Aldermen made Justices.

He likewise grants, that Four of the said Justices, the Maior, or Recorder to be always one, may hold a Sessions, to enquire into several Offences, *viz.* into Weights and Measures, and selling Victuals contrary to the Statutes, *&c.* to receive and inspect into Indictments taken before them, to make and continue Procefs, and punish Offenders according to the Laws of the Kingdom, and the Custom of the City: And also grants them Power to execute the Laws as fully and largely as any other Justices of the Peace in any other County; and that the Sheriffs, *&c.* attend, aid and assist the said Justices when desired.

Sessions to inquire of Weights and Measures, &c. Indictments, Procefs, &c.

He also grants them the Forfeiture of Recognizances, particularly those relating to Bastard-Children, Inmates and Alehouses; with Recognizances for Appearances at the Sessions of Goal-Delivery, Fines and Issues of

Forfeitures of Recognizances, &c. granted.

Jurors

Jurors within the City of *London*, excepting only *Royal Iffues*, &c.

He likewife grants them all Recognizances taken, or to be taken, for the Security of the Peace or good Behaviour, with all Recognizances taken in the Court for the River of *Thames*, and all things thereunto appertaining ; as likewife all Fines, Amerciaments and Penalties adjudg'd by the Maior, *&c.* relating, or any ways belonging to his faid Courts, as Confervator of the River of *Thames* ; and alfo all Fines, *&c.* impofed by Commiffioners of Sewers, the fame to be holden to the faid Maior, *&c.* without Account.

Fines, Amerciaments, and penalties.

He likewife grants to the Maior, Commonalty, and Citizens of *London*, and their Succeffors, the Fields commonly known by the Name of *Moor-Fields*, both Outward and Inward, and likewife the Field commonly call'd *Weft-Smithfield*, with liberty to hold Fairs and Markets in the faid Fields, with all Tolls, Profits, *&c.* thereunto belonging : Referving the Streets, wafte Ground, common Soil, *&c.* within the City and Liberties ; to hold the fame in free Burgage, and not in Capite, with Pardon and Remittance of all Iffues relating to the faid Premifes, without any Writ of *Ad quod Damnum* ; and alfo Pardon of all Intrufions, except fuch which relate to Churches and Church-Walls.

Moor-Fields granted.

Weft-Smith-Field.

Streets, Wafte. Common Soil.

He alfo grants the Office of Garbling Spices, *&c.* to the Maior and Citizens of *London*. The faid Maior, *&c.* to hold and enjoy the faid Office, with all the Fees, Profits, *&c.* without rendring any Account to the King, his Heirs, or Succeffors, the Garbling of **Tobacco** only excepted.

Spices Garbled.

Except Tobacco.

He

He likewiſe grants to the Maior, Commo-　*Office of Gaug-* nalty and Citizens the Office of Gauging,　*ing.* with all the Fees, Profits, and Emoluments lawfully belonging to the ſaid Office, the ſame to be executed by them or their Deputy, without Account, and the Fees, &c. to be appointed and allowed by the Lords, Chan-cellor, Treaſurer, and Preſident of the Coun-cil, and the two Chief-Juſtices of the *King's Bench,* and *Common-Pleas.*

He alſo grants to the Maior, Commonalty,　*Keeper of the* and Citizens, the Office of Keeper of the　*Great Balance.* great Balance or Weight within the City of *London,* for weighing all Merchandizes of *A-ver-du-pois,* and alſo all other Weights for weighing any ſort of Wares or Merchandizes within the ſaid City, with all the Fees and Profits, &c. thereto belonging, &c.

He alſo grants to the Maior, Commonal-　*Outroper's Of-* ty, &c. the Office of Outroper, or Common-　*fice.* Cryer, with liberty to exerciſe the ſame by themſelves, or Deputy. The ſaid Deputy to be choſen by the Maior, Commonalty, and Citizens in Common Council, with Power to take the Fees expreſſed in a Schedule annexed to his ſaid Charter; and that no other pre-ſume to ſell any Goods by Outcries within the City and Liberties of *London,* under the Pain of the Royal Diſpleaſure.

He likewiſe grants, That Freemens Wi-　*Freemens Wi-* dows ſhould uſe their Husbands Arts and Ma-　*dows to uſe* nual Occupations, ſo long as they continued　*Arts,* &c. Widows, notwithſtanding the Statute made the 5th Year of the Reign of Queen *Elizabeth,* or any other Statute to the contrary. He like-wiſe, for the Benefit of the City of *London,*　*No Market* grants, That there be no Market within ſe-　*within Seven* ven Miles of the ſaid City; and further grants,　*Miles.*

3　　　　　　　　　　　　　　　　　　**that**

that according to the ancient Cuſtom of the
ſaid City, the Maior and Aldermen, *&c.*

Cuſtoms re-
corded vivâ
voce.
ſhould record their Cuſtoms by the Mouth of
their Recorder, touching any Plea, Deed,
Cauſe, or Buſineſs relating to the City of
London.

Treaſure-
Trove, Waifs,
Eſtrays, &c.
He further grants to the ſaid Maior, *&c.*
all Treaſure found in the City of *London,* and
Liberty thereof, with all *waived or ſtrayed*
Goods and Chattels *of all Felons, Fugitives,*
&c. He likewiſe grants, that the Maior of

Two Alder-
men, one a Ju-
ſtice for Mid-
dleſex, the o-
ther for Surry.
London, for the Time being, ſhould nominate
Two Aldermen for Juſtices of the Peace, the
one to act, and be inſerted in all Commiſ-
ſions in *Middleſex,* the other in *Surry.*

Freedoms to be
taken up.
He likewiſe grants, touching Freemen, that
the Sons of Freemen and others ſhould be
obliged to take up their Freedom, *&c.* and
that no Perſon ſhould tranſport any Goods
from the Port of *London,* or uſe any Merchandize within ten Miles diſtance of any Port
thereof, without becoming a Freeman, and
producing a Teſtimonial under the Hands of
the Chamberlain, to prove the ſame; and

Merchants
Apprentices.
that no Merchant, free of *London,* from henceforth, take any Perſon to ſerve him after the
manner of an Apprentice, for any leſs Term
than Seven Years.

Court of Con-
ſcience.
He likewiſe grants the City a Court of
Conſcience or Requeſt, for the trying all
ſmall Debts under 40 *s.* the ſaid Court to be
kept in the *Guild-Hall,* and the Proceedings to
be by way of Plaint and Summons, and the
Officers of the ſaid Court to be in the
Choice of the Maior, Commonalty, *&c.* and
to take ſuch Fees which are expreſſed in the
Schedule annexed to his Letters Patents.

He

He alfo grants to the Maior, Commonalty, and Citizens, the Office of Brokers of Pawns, *Brokers of* &c. and that the Fees be the fame that are *Pawns.* exprefled in the Schedule annexed : And that the Citizens for the better finding out their refpective Dwellings, might hang out Signs. *Signs to be* And likewife grants to the faid Maior, Com- *hung out.* monalty, &c. the keeping of the Hofpital called *Bethlehem,* with Manors, Lands, &c. be- *Keepers of* longing to the fame ; and the better to enable *Bethlehem* them to fupport the Burthen of the Poor in *Hofpital.* the Houfe called, The Houfe of the Poor in *Weft-Smithfield,* he grants that the Maior, &c. fhould be Governor of the faid Hofpital of *Bethlehem,* and that the Revenues, &c. be ap- plied to the Ufes before-mentioned.

He alfo declares, that no Leafe of any Ho- *Leafes of Ho-* fpital-Lands fhould be let for any Term of *fpital Lands.* Years, exceeding One and Twenty. He fur- thermore grants to the Maior and Commo- nalty, &c. Liberty to purchafe five Acres of *Five Acres of* Land in St. *Gile*'s in the Fields, notwith- *Land in St.* ftanding the Statute of Mortmain, &c. with *Gile's in the* Liberty to build on the faid five Acres with- *Fields.* out any Royal Licenfe ; and withal grants, that thefe Letters Patents, and the Inrolment fhould be good and firm, and effectual in Law againft him and his Succeffors, without any other Toleration, or Confirmation, &c. and that the faid Letters Patents fhould be fealed by the Great Seal of *England,* without paying or making any Fine or Fee in the Hamper.

Fees to be taken by the **Common Outroper.**

For felling of all Goods $\frac{1}{4}$ in every Shilling.
For writing and keeping the Books 1 *penny* per *l.*
To the Cryer for crying the Goods 1 *s.* ·

Fees taken by the Regifter for Brokers.

	d.	q.
For the Bond to be enter'd into by every Broker, Brogger, or Huckfter in the Chamber,	08	00
For every Bargain, Contract, Pawn, for, or upon which there fhall be lent, or given 1 *s.* or above, and under 5 *s.*	00	0$\frac{1}{4}$
For every the like for which fhall be lent 5 *s.* or under 20 *s.*	00	0$\frac{1}{2}$
For every the like for which fhall be lent 20 *s.* or more, and under 40 *s.*	01	00
For every the like upon which fhall be lent 40 *s.* or more	02	00

Court of Confcience in London, *Clerks Fees.*

	d.	q.
For every Plaint	02	00
For every Appearance	02	00
For every Order	04	00
For every Remittance to the Common-Law	04	00
For every Receipt or Warrant to commit to Prifon	06	00
For every Search	02	00
For every Satisfaction Acknowledged on an Order	06	00

	d.	*q.*
For warning every perfon within the Liberties	04	00
For warning every perfon without the Liberties	06	00
For ferving every Precept or Warrant	04	00

King *Charles* I. in another Charter, in confideration of 4200 *l.* creates the feveral Offices of Package, Portage, or Balliage, and after grants the fame to the Maior, Commonalty, *&c.* of *London*, with all the Fees and Profits expreffed in a Schedule annexed to the faid Charter; and alfo the Office or Employment of Scavage, with all the Fees and Profits exprefs'd in the Table, *&c.* paying yearly to the King and his Succeffors three *Pound* fix *Shillings* and eight *Pence:* He likewife empowers the Maior, *&c.* to adminifter the Oath in the cafe of concealed Goods, *&c.*

All which Charters were confirmed by King *Charles* the Second, at *Weftminfter,* the 24th Day of *June,* in the 15th Year of his Reign.

Car. I.
Char. 24
Package,
Portage.
Scavage.
Charters con-
firmed.

Now for the better underftanding of the foregoing Charters, I fhall here prefent the Reader with an Expofition of fuch old Saxon *and other obfolete Words as are contained therein, viz.*

B Arones, Mat. Paris, *fub Anno* 1253, fays, That the Citizens, or Men of *London,* in refpect of the Dignity of the City and antient Liberties of the Citizens, were wont to be called *Barons.* And the fame Author, *fub Anno* 1258, fays, *Nobiles* Angliæ *convocaverunt totius Civitates Cives quos* Barones *vocant.* And yet Dr. *Brady* thinks, that only the better Sort of the

D   Citi-

Citizens, as the Aldermen, &c. are to be intended by the Word *Barones* in the *London*
Charters, becaufe the Words in 2d Chart.
Hen. I. are & Barones, & Cives : which feem
to put a Difference between *Barons* and Citizens. But this feems a Miftake, for the 4th
Charter of King *John*, and the 2d Charter of
Hen. III. fays, *Scietis Nos concefſiffe & confir-
maffe* Baronibus *noftris de Civitate* London,
quod eligant fibi Maior, &c. which compared
with the other Charters, fhews it to be a
Grant to all the Freemen of the City ; and
confequently that the word *Baro* there, figni-
fies only a *Freeman* of the City. See *Stow, lib.*
5. *pag.* 173, and 332. And Note, thofe *Barons*
feem to be the fame which in the Charter of
W.I. are call'd *Burhwarn*, or Burro-Men. *Ib.* 347.

Bridtoll, i. e. *Bridge-toll*, or Money paid for
paffing a Bridge. *Vide* the Charter of *Hen.* II.
the 4th Charter of King *John*, and the 4th
Charter of *Hen.* III.

Ciltre, or *Chiltre*, part of the County of
Hartford, about St. *Albans* fo called. *Vide Ch.*
Hen. I. *and* Mat. Paris.

Childwite, the fame with *Leirwite*, or *Lecher-
wite*, i. e. Money paid, or a Punifhment for
corrupting or getting a Bondmaid with Child.
Vide ibid.

Corrody, An Allowance of Meat and Drink
out of a Religious or other Houfe, towards
Maintenance of any Perfon whom the King
fhould appoint, or Money paid in lieu thereof.
Vide Charter *Edw.* VI.

Dane guelt, or *Dane-geld*, Money originally
paid to the *Danes* to keep them from Rapines,
and afterwards, a Tax impofed to defend the
Nation againft their Invafions. *Vide* Charter
Hen. I. and the Argument on the *Quo War-*
ranto.   *Deodand*

Deodand, Any thing that caufes a Man's
Death, is faid to be a *Deodand,* and forfeited
to the King. *Vide* Charter *Edw.* VI.

Efcheats, Any Lands, or other Profits that
fall to the King or other Lord, by reafon of
the Death or Forfeiture of any Tenant, or
other Poffeffor. *Vide ibid.*

Folkmote, According to *Stow* and others, fig-
nifies the General Affembly of all the Citizens.
Vide Spelman, and *Somner in Verbo,* and Dr.
Brady's Gloffary, pag. 48. and Chart. *Hen.* I.

Frank-pledge, Signifies a Pledge or Surety
for Freemen of fourteen Years and upwards,
except Clerks and Knights: For all fuch Freemen were to find Security towards the King
and his Subjects ; or elfe, were to be fent to
Prifon. *Vide Cowel in Verbo,* and Chart. 1.
Edw. IV. *vers Finem.*

Guild, A Company or Fraternity, combined
by Laws and Payments for their mutual Support, and confirmed by the King's Grant.
Vide 5th Char. *Johis.*

Hallmote, or *Hallimote Court. Vide* p. 408.

Huftings, derived from *Hus,* a Houfe, and
Thing. Caufa. i. e. a Houfe where Caufes are
tried ; or according to Mr. *Somner,* from the
Saxon Word *Hyhft,* or higheft and *Thing Judi-
cium quafi.* The higheft Court of the City of
London. *Vide* 9th Chart. *Hen.* III.

Jerefgive, Is a Toll or Fine, taken by the
King's Officers, on a Perfon's entring into an
Office ; or rather, a Sum of Money, or Bribe,
given to them to connive at Extortion, or other
Offence in him that gives it. See Chart.
Hen. II. 4th Chart. *Hen.* III. and 9th Chart.
Hen. III.

Infang-

Infanghtheft, A Liberty granted to Lords of Manors, to try and judge any Thief taken in their Fee : *Outfangtheft* is a like Liberty for any Thief taken out of their Fee. See Chart. *Hen.* I. and 1 Chart. *Edw.* III.

Leſtage, A Toll paid for Liberty, for Perſons to carry their Goods up and down in Fairs and Markets. *Vide* Chart. *Hen.* I.

Miskenning, A changing, or varying from a Plea or Count, *i. e.* when one leaves his firſt Declaration or Plea, and gives another. *Vide* Chart. *Hen.* I. Chart. 4 *Hen.* III. and Chart. 9 *Hen.* III.

Murage, A Contribution towards repairing the Walls and Edifices of the City. *Vide* Chart. *Edw.* I.

Murder, or *Murdrum*, Signifies not only the Crime, but the Pecuniary Mulct or Puniſhment due for that Crime ; ſo that to be quit of Murder, was, that the Place where it was committed, ſhould not be fined or amerced, tho' the Murderer eſcaped. *Vide* Chart. *Hen.* I. 4 Chart. *Hen.* III.

Outfangtheft, vide *Infangtheft*.

Namium, Is the taking, attaching, or diſtreining of moveable Goods. *Vide* Withername.

Piccage, vide *Stallage*.

Pannage, or *Pawnage*, a Duty paid to the King for Paſturage of Cattle, &c. *Vide* Chart. *Edw.* I. but it there ſeems to be miſprinted for *Paviage*.

Paſſage, A like Duty paid for paſſing thro Gates, Bridges, &c. *Vide* ibid.

Pontage, A like Duty paid for paſſing over Bridges with Horſes, Carts, Carriages ; or under them with Boats, Ships, or towards repairing ſuch Bridges, &c. ibid.

Portſoken, An Extent of Juriſdiction or Liberty from without the Gates of the City, or as ſome take it, the Liberties within the Port or City of *London.* *Vide* 9th Chart. of *Hen.* III. and 1 Chart. *John.*

Pypowder Court, A Court held in Fairs, &c. for enrolling Contracts and redreſſing Diſorders there committed. *Vide* 1 Chart. *Edw.* IV. & *Pag.* 303.

Scott and *Lott,* Publick Contributions or Impoſitions. *Vide* Chart. *Hen.* I

Scotale, A Practice of the King's Officers who kept Alehouſes or brew'd Liquors, and forced Men to come to their Houſes and pay Contributions (call'd Scotales) for fear of their Diſpleaſure. *Vide* Chart. *Hen.* II. and 4th Chart. *Hen.* III.

Stallage, A Payment for erecting or having a Stall in a Fair or Market ; as *Piccage* is a Payment for breaking the Ground in order to erect ſuch Stall, &c. *Vide* Chart. *Edw.* VI.

Soke, A Liberty or Privilege of Juriſdiction, within a certain Place or Precinct ; alſo the Court there held. *Vide* Chart. *Hen.* I.

Tallage, or *Tailage,* Signifies the paying a part or ſhare of a Man's Subſtance, by way of Tribute, Toll or Tax. 1 Chart. *Edw.* III.

Toll, An Impoſition, or Payment for any Thing bought or ſold in Fairs or Markets. *Vide* Chart. *Hen.* IV. &c.

Tronage, Is a Duty paid at the City Beam for weighing Lead, Wax, Pepper, Allom, &c. *Vide* Chart. *Hen.* IV. 2 Chart. *Edw.* IV. and 2 Chart. *Hen.* VIII.

Withernam, By ſome is defin'd to be *Vetitum Namium,* i. e. an illegal taking of Goods, &c. But others more rightly deriving it

D 3 from

from the *Saxon Wider* (*rurſus*) & *nam* (*Captio*)
have ſhewn, that it ſignifies a Recaption, or
taking again, *i. e.* a taking of ſomething in
lieu of another thing unjuſtly taken or detained. *Vide 9 Chart. H.* III.

Alſo for the further Explanation of the ſaid Char-
ters, I ſhall here add ſome few Obſervations up-
on the ſame, as they relate either to the Officers
or the Liberties of the ſaid City of London —
And firſt of the Officers or Magiſtrates there-
of ; viz. *the Lord Maior,* &c.

Portreve. By the Charter of *W.* I. the chief Magi-
ſtrate of the City is named *Portereſa,* or *Por-*
treve, which in old *Saxon* ſignifies the Ruler
or Governor of the Port or City (*vide Verbo*
Portſoken *ante ;*) yet ſome think him originally
named *Portgrave,* from the *Saxon* Word *Grave,*
ſignifying an Earl or Count, as if he were the
Earl or Count of the City; and that therefore he has the Honour due to a Count, as
well in the King's Preſence, as elſewhere in
London, by having a Sword born before him,
&c. Compare 5 *Stow,* pag. 72. with pag. 100.
However, certain it is, that about the Year
Portgrave. 1184. 32 *H.* II. he was called *Portgrave :* For
in that Year a Patent was granted to the
Weavers of *London,* wherein the *Portgrave* is
mentioned as the principal Officer of the City, and as ſuch ordered to burn ſuch Cloaths
as were weaved with a Mixture of *Engliſh* and
Spaniſh Wooll.

Juſtices.   Some think the ſame Officer is called *Ju-*
ſticiarius in the Charter of *H.* I. whereby he
grants the Citizens Liberty to chooſe *Juſtici-*
arium de ſeipſis ad cuſtodiendum plita Coronæ ;
and he is accordingly ſtyled *Juſticiarius* in the
Book

Book of the *London* Cuſtoms: But as that Book was written *circa Temp.* Ed. IV. ſo in the Charter of *Ed.* IV. *&c.* the Recorder of *London* is nominated *Juſtice,* and poſſibly may *Re·order.* be the Officer intended by the ſaid Charter of *H.* I.

And it may be here noted, that as in the Time of the *Saxons* no Perſon could exerciſe any Office or Authority either Civil or Military over the People of *England,* but ſuch as were freely choſen thereto by the Conſent of the *Elective.* Freeholders or Freemen over whom he was to exerciſe his Office ; ſo no Man could exerciſe any Office or Authority within the City of *London,* but ſuch as were choſen thereto by the Freemen of the ſaid City ; which ancient Right was doubtleſs confirm'd to the Citizens of *London,* by thoſe general Words in *W.* Iſt's Charter, whereby he grants them the Benefit of the Laws of *Edward* the Confeſſor.

Note alſo, that originally all Sheriffs and *Sheriffs, &c.* *Heretokes,* or Lords Lieutenants of Counties, as alſo all Conſervators of the Peace, Eſcheators, Coroners, *&c.* throughout the Kingdom, were eligible by the Freeholders at their reſpective Folkmotes, or County Courts ; which Privilege ſeems to have been chiefly intended when the Kings of the *Norman* Race either granted or confirmed the good Laws and Cuſtoms of *Edward* the Confeſſor. See the Confeſſor's Laws, and *Coke*'s Expoſition on the *Stat Articuli ſuper Chartas.*

'Tis alſo obſervable, that the *Portreves* or *Portgraves* of *London* are often in Records, *circa Temp.* H. II. called Vice-Comites, or Sheriffs, and ſome Authors call them Domeſmen, El- *Domeſmen.* dermen, and Judges of the King's Courts in

London, and mention their Election, *&c.* And *Fitz-Steven* writing about the ſame Time, ſays, the City of *London,* like that of *Rome,* is divided into Wards (now 26.) and has yearly Sheriffs inſtead of Conſuls and Aldermen, that bear the Dignity of Senators ; where his not mentioning any other, ſhews that theſe Sheriffs were then the *Portgreves,* or ſuperior Officers of the City.

Provoſt.

Yet in the Reign of King *Steven,* I find that one *Gilbert Becket* was *Portgrave* of *London,* and *Andrew Buckeret* Provoſt of the ſame ; which Office of the Provoſt ſeems to be the ſame we now call Sheriff, and inferior to that which was then ſo named ; the *Ballivi* or Sheriffs, being then *Cuſtodes Civitatis. Vide poſt.*

Ballivi.

And 'tis evident 1° & 2° *R.* I. *Annis* 1190, 1191, the ſaid City was governed by two Officers, called *Ballivi,* which in old Deeds are called Sheriffs or Portgerifs ; and Note, that in all original and other Writs, the Sheriff's Office is ſtill called *Balliva.*

Maior.

The firſt Maior of *London* is generally agreed to be *Henry Fitz-Alwin,* Draper ; the Grandſon of one *Leoffſtane,* Goldſmith, a *Saxon,* who ſeems to have been Provoſt or Sheriff, *i. e.* Judge of the ſaid City, *Temp. W.* I. & *W.* II. and the ſame who by *Mat. Paris* and others is called *Domeſman.*

This *Henry Fitz-Alwin* was made Maior of *London* 2° *R.* I. *Anno* 1190, and continued in that Office till 14° *Johannis, Anno* 1212, when he dy'd, and *Roger Fitz-Alwin* ſucceeded as Maior for the following Year 1213. But whether theſe were Maiors by Election, or created ſo by the ſole Authority of the King, is not certain.

But

But in the next Year, *i. e.* 1214, King *Elective.*
John, by his Charter 10 *Maij* 16° *Ric.* granted, or rather confirmed (no doubt for a valuable Confideration) to the Barons, *i. e.*
Freemen of *London*, their Right of electing
their Maior yearly. Some fay this Charter *5 Stow 101.*
was 10 *Johannis*, but that feems a Miftake.

But tho' the faid Charter grants them the
Election of their Maior yearly, yet I find afterwards the fame Perfon continued Maior
for divers Years fucceffively ; either by virtue
of a new Election or otherwife till *Anno* 1239.
24 *H.* III. from which time they feldom continued in that Office above one Year.

And in the Year 1241, *Gerrard Batt* having
ferved as Maior the precedent Year, was a-
gain elected to that Office ; but the King
would not admit him, he being charged with
taking Money of the Victuallers. *Quære*, if
the real Caufe.

'Tis faid the Maior and Chamberlain of *Chamberlain,*
the City were formerly the fame, for that *5 Stow 73.*
Sr. *Gregory de Rokeflee*, who was Maior *Anno*
1275. 7° *E.* I. and fo continued till 1282, is
called *Chamberlain* in the City Books, as *lib.*
B. Fol. 3, 9, *&c.* And when *Henry Galleis* or
Walleis, Maior in 1274, was fent beyond Sea,
the King commanded the Sheriffs and Citi- *2 Ed. I.*
zens to appoint two other difcreet Freemen to *i. e. by Elec-*
take the Office in his Abfence, who are call- *tion.*
ed *Chamberlains* alfo in *Lib. B. Fo.* 38. 'tis
faid, That when the faid Maior, *Anno* 1298,
took a Journey towards *Lincoln* about earneft
Bufinefs of his own, he put in his Place *Wil-*
liam de Bethonia, and *Geofry de Norton,* who in
the King's Letter are called *Camerarij Civita- 26 Ed. I.*
tis ; and in the fame Book it appears that the
Maior fupply'd the Office of Coroner, under *Coroner.*

the

the Name of Chamberlain of the City. See
alſo the ſecond Charter of *H.* III. 11 *H.* III.
for electing their Maior yearly, &c. See alſo
5 *Stow* 77. that *E.* II. *Anno* 12. *Rui.* at the
Requeſt of the Citizens granted, that no
Maior ſhould continue in Office above one
Year.

And Note by the ſaid Charters of K. *John*
and *H.* III. He is after ſuch Election to be preſented to the King for his Approbation. But
ſee the Charter of *E.* I. that in the King's
Abſence he is to be preſented to the Barons of
the Exchequer, or in their Abſence to the
Conſtable of the Tower. Alſo by the firſt

Juſtice, Charter of *E.* III. he is to be one of the Ju-
Eſcheator. ſtices of *Newgate,* and *Eſcheator* in *London* ; and
by the firſt Charter of *Ed.* IV. he, with the
Recorder and Aldermen above the Chair, are
Juſtices of to be Juſtices of Peace and of *Oyer* and *Terminer,*
Oyer, &c, within the City and Liberties, and he of the
Quorum; and the ſame Powers are alſo given
him by the ſecond Charter of *Jac.* I. See alſo the Charter of *Ed.* VI. where the like and
other Powers are given him in *Southwark,* &c.
And by the firſt, ſecond, and third Charter
of *Jac.* I. he is to have the Conſervation of
the River *Thames* and *Medway,* and the Office
of meaſuring Coals, Salt, Apples, &c.

Maiors ap- But notwithſtanding the ſaid Charter of
pointed by the King *John* and *H.* III. granting the Citizens
King. the free Election of their Maiors, yet we
find divers ſubſequent Inſtances of Maiors appointed by the King himſelf, without ſuch
Election.

As *Anno* 17 *E.* II. the Office of Maioralty
being in the King's Hands for certain Cauſes
5 Stow 79. (as the Record ſays) he committed it to
Nicholas Farindon, quamdiu Nobis placuerit, and
commanded

commanded the Aldermen, Sheriffs, and Citizens to be obedient to him as Maior; also *Anno* 14 of the said King, the Maioralty being then in the King's Hands, *per Considerationem Curiæ,* i. e. on a Judgment given in the King's Court, he constituted *Robert Kendall* Maior, to do, execute, *&c.* all things that belonged to the said Office. Also *Rich.* II. *Ann.* 20 *Reg.* with assent of his Council, appointed *Richard Whitington* to serve as Maior, in the Room of *Adam Bamme* (who deceased in his Maioralty,) until the Day accustomed for electing a new Maior.

Note, this Officer under the name of Maior, *Custos or Keeper, or Warden of London.* seems to have been without interruption, the chief Magistrate of the City from 1° R. I. 1189, till 1252, i. e. 37 *Hen.* III. In which Year the Liberties of the City were seized, and the Maior displaced, for not looking to the Assize of Bread (as was pretended ;) and the King is supposed to have appointed a *Custos,* i. e. *Lord Warden,* or *Keeper* of the City, but who, I find not. Also in 39 *Hen.* III. the Maior and divers Aldermen, and the Sheriffs of *London* were deprived, and others placed in their Rooms, *Quere* the Cause. And 49 *Hen* III. 1265, the Chains and Posts in *London* were plucked up, the Maior and principal Citizens imprisoned, and *Otho,* Constable of the Tower, made Custos of the City. This seems to have been, for that in the precedent Year, the Citizens fortified the City in favour of the Barons. And in the following Year, *Gilbert* Earl of *Gloucester* entred the City with an Army, and fortified the same, as it seems against the King. For which Reason, as I take it, the King in the same Year, and for divers Years follow-

Observations on the.

following, appointed a yearly *Cuſtos* of the City.

5 Stow, *pag.* 74.
But King *Edw.* I. in the beginning of his Reign, *Ann.* 1273, revived the Office, of Maior; and ſo it continued till 1285, 13 *Ed.* I. when *Gregory Rokeſly* being elected Maior, re-fuſed to appear at the Tower before the King's Juſtices, *&c.* and aſſerted his Privilege

Vide *Char.* Edw. I.
not to be ſummoned out of the City, &c. Where-upon the Office was ſeized, together with the Liberties of the City, by *John de Kirby,* then Lord Treaſurer, and formerly Lord Keeper,*&c.*

2 *Cuſtodes*.
And after the City had been ſome Months, without a Maior, *Ralph Sandwich* and *John Briton,* were appointed *Cuſtodes,* and ſeem to have ſo continued till 1289, when three *Cuſtodes* were appointed, and *Ralph Barnavers,*

3 *Cuſtodes*.
or *Barners,* added to the two former. But in the twenty eight following Years, the ſaid *Briton* and *Sandwich,* ſometimes jointly, and ſometimes ſeverally, ſeem to have been *Cuſtodes* till 1298, 26 *Edw.* I. when *Henry Walleis* was elected and ſerv'd as Maior; and after him, *Elias Ruſſel,* for the two following Years; after whom, Sir *John Blunt* was made *Cuſtos,* and ſo continued till the laſt Year of *Edw.* I. (1306;) when upon *Blunt*'s going to

4 *Cuſtodes.* elected.
the Wars with the King's Son, four *Cuſtodes* were, in obedience to the King's Command, choſen by the City. And 1° *Edw.* II. the ſaid Sir *John Blunt* is again named *Cuſtos;* but from that year down to the preſent Year, ex-cept 15 *Rich.* II. the Office of Maior has con-tinued in a conſtant Succeſſion; only ſome-time, their Election ſeem to have been guided by the King's Nomination.

Note, in 1319, 13 *Edw.* II. Sir *John Giſors* (who had been Maior in 5, 6, and 8 *Edw.* II.)

2   together

together with many other Citizens, fled the City for Matters laid to their Charge, as Confederates with the Lords againſt *Pierce Gaveſton.* In which Year *Walter Stapleton,* Biſhop of *Exeter,* was made Treaſurer, and ſeems to have been a great Incendiary between the King and the Citizens : and that for this Reaſon, the Citizens of *Lond. Ann.* 1326, 20 *Edw.* II. took the ſaid Lord Biſhop, and cut off his Head at the Standard in *Cheap.*

But ſoon after, King *Edw.* III. (he began 25 *Jan.* 1326.) in the firſt Year of his Reign, *viz.* 6 *Martis* 1326. paſſed (as it ſeems in Parliament) that moſt beneficial Charter, whereby (*inter alia*) he grants, That the Liberties and Franchiſes of the ſaid City, ſhould not, after that time, be ſeized into the King's Hands *for any Cauſe,* but *only for Treaſon and Rebellion ſhewed by the whole City.* See *Hollinſhead,* pag. 343. and 5 *Stow,* 109. And in the Recital of that Charter, as it is in that of 15 *Car.* II. it is ſaid, *That the Liberties of the ſaid City ſhall not be taken into the Hands of Us or our Heirs, for any Perſonal Treſpaſs or Judgment againſt any Miniſter of the ſaid City. Neither ſhall any Cuſtos or Keeper be appointed in the ſaid City for that Cauſe, but the ſame Miniſter (only) ſhall be puniſhed according to the Quality of his Offence.* After which, I find few attempts to appoint a *Cuſtos.* Only *John* of *Gaunt,* Duke of *Lancaſter,* on the Deathbed Sickneſs of his Father *Edw.* III. aiming, as was ſuppoſed, at the Crown ; and finding the *Londoners* averſe to his Deſigns, he pretended they had conſpired his Death, *&c.* and under that Colour, by his Power and Intereſt, procured the then Maior, to be depoſed, and another to be elected. He alſo procured the then Aldermen to be diſplaced,

and

He began 25 Jan. 1326.

Note.

Note.

Annis 1376, 1377.

and others to be put in their Places. And not content with this Injuſtice to the City and Citizens; he, in the firſt Parliament of *Rich.* II. being Proteƈtor of the King and Kingdom, procured a Bill to be brought into *Anno* 1378. Parliament in the King's Name, That the City of *London* ſhould no more be governed by a *Maior,* but by a *Cuſtos,* as in *Times* before: And that the Marſhal of *England,* (who was 5 Stow 114. then the Lord *Piercy,* and the Duke's Creature) ſhould have the whole Power of making Arreſts within the City, with other Particulars in Derogation of the Liberties of the City. *Note.* But Sir *John Philpot,* Citizen of *London,* and a bold and worthy Member of that Parliament, on the reading of the Bill in the Houſe of Commons, ſtood up, and ſaid, ſuch a Matter was never heard of before. And that the Maior of *London,* never would ſuffer any ſuch Arreſt within the ſaid City; with more ſuch Words of like Stoutneſs: Whereby he put a ſtop to the Duke's Projeƈt.

But though this Speech procured the ſaid *Philpot* the juſt Eſteem of the Citizens, ſo as in Vide Cotton's the following Year they Eleƈted him Maior; Records, &c, yet the Duke of *Lancaſter* could not forgive him, but ſet on foot that unjuſt Proſecution againſt him; charging him, as I remember, with High Treaſon, for that he had ſome Years before, at his own charge, fitted out certain Ships which had ſcoured the Seas of Pyrates, &c.

Note, *Anno* 1388, and 12 *Rich.* II. A Proclamation was made in *London,* (*Quere* by whoſe Advice) for all the Guilds and Fraternities to bring their Charters into the Chancery before the King, with an Account of their Foundations and Inſtitutions, Goods and Chattels, &c.

And

And *Anno* 1391, 15 *Rich.* II. The Maior of *London* being in the King's Difpleafure (*Quere* the Caufe) was taken into Cuftody, and fent a Prifoner to *Windfor* Caftle. And thereupon the King feized the City's, Liberties, and made a *Cuftos*, or Lord Warden, of the City, &c. *The laft Lord Warden.*

But as thefe, and fome other illegal Acts of that King (procured him the *Odium* of the People, efpecially the *Londoners*) and in Confequence thereof, the lofs of his Crown and Life; fo I do not find that any of his Succeffors ever attempted the like Seizure &c.

But the City of *London* ever afterwards enjoyed a conftant Succeffion of elective Maiors, though fometimes too much influenced in fuch Elections by Court Cabals, &c. till that infamous Judgment on the *Quo Warranto* 35 *Car.* II. Whereby the Liberties and Privileges of the faid City were feized into that King's Hands, on a pretended Forfeiture by the Citizens, in petitioning the faid King for a *Free Parliament*; which, without Doubt, ever was the Birthright of *Englifh* Freemen. Jan. 12, 683.

And in *October* following, Sir *William* Pritchard, Lord Maior, and *Peter Daniel* and *Samuel Dafhwood*, Efqs; Sheriffs of the faid City, were newly appointed by Commiffion from the King, to hold their refpective Offices during his Pleafure. Soon after which, followed that odious and pernicious Practice of furrendring Charters, &c. And thereupon the Magiftrates of the faid City were appointed by Commiffion from the King for fome Years. But this Violence on the City's Privileges continued not many Years: For King *James* II. on the firft Rumour of the Prince of *Orange*'s October 4, 1629. 5 Stow 91, *and* 353.

Pre-

Preparations, fent the Lord Chancellor *Jeffries* (who had been the Principal Inftrument of that King's illegal Actions) to the faid City, and reftored them their former Charter.

And by Stat. 2 *W. M.* Sef. 1. Cap. 8. reciting, That whereas a Judgment was given in the King's Bench in Trinity Term, 35 *Car.*II. in a *Quo Warranto* againft the Maior and Commonalty and Citizens of *London*, that the Franchife of the faid City fhould be feized into the King's Hands as forfeited, which Proceedings were *Illegal* and *Arbitrary :* 'Tis enacted, That the faid Judgment, and every other Judgment given or recorded in the faid Court for feizing the *Franchife* of the faid City into the King's Hands, be reverfed and made void, and Vacats entred upon the Rolls.

And the Maior, Commonalty and Citizens of *London*, do remain a Body Politick, by the Name of Maior and Commonalty, and Citizens of the City of *London*, &c. without any Seizure or Forejudger of the faid Franchife, *&c.* upon pretence of any Forfeiture or Mifdemeanor done, or to be done ; and to have and enjoy all their Rights, Charters, *&c.* which they lawfully had at the time of the recording or giving of the faid Judgment.

That all Charters, Letters Patents, *&c.* for incorporating the Citizens and Commonalty of the faid City, or any of them, and Charters *&c.* concerning any of the Liberties, *&c.* Lands and Tenements, *&c.* Rights, Titles or Eftates made fince the faid Judgment, by the late King *Charles* II. or King *James* II. are thereby declared void.

Alfo all the Officers, Companies and Corporations are reftored, *&c.* and Perfons admitted fince the faid Judgment into Freedoms or Liveries

veries of the faid Companies, according to the Cuftom of the City, fhould enjoy the Rights and Liberties of Freemen and Livery-men ; and this Act is reputed a general and publick Act of Parliament. See the faid Stat. 2 *W. M.*

Note, this Grand Magiftrate is yearly elected on *Midfummer* Day by the Livery Men of the twenty fix Wards. And though the Senior Alderman is moft ufually chofen, yet that is at the Electors Difcretion. And this Officer being thus Elective, his Authority ceafes, not on the King's Death or Abdication (as that of all Commiffion Officers doth.) And therefore it is faid, in fuch a Cafe, the Lord Maior of *London* is the principal Officer in the Kingdom. *Privileges of the Lord Maior.*

Principal Magiftrate.

Note alfo, the Lord Maior for the Time being, is perpetual Coroner and Efcheator within the faid City and Liberties of *Southwark, &c.* And the Coroner's Court is always held before him or his Deputy. *Dyer* 317. *Stamf.* lib. 2. cap. 31. 4 *Inft* 250. *Cro. Jac.* 531. He is alfo Chief Juftice for the Goal Delivery at *Newgate. Vide* 1 Chart. *Edw.* III. And by 1 Chart. *Edw* IV. Juftice of Peace for *London, &c.* And by 2 Chart. *Jac.* I. Juftice of *Oyer* and *Terminer*. *Coroner.*

Efcheator.

Chief Juftice of Goal Delivery.

He has alfo a Right to be the King's Butler at the King's Coronation, as appears by *Rot. Serviciæ* 1° *Hen.* IV. And fee 1 *Roll Rep.* 145. this Claim then allowed. This Right feems to be very antient, for among the Petitions in Parliament, 11° *Edw.* III. is that which follows, *viz.* *King's Butler.*

A Noftre Seignor le Roy. &c. To our Lord the King and his Council, *Rich. de Bettonie,* of *London,* Sheweth, That whereas at the Coronation *The Maior's Petition in Parliament.* 11 *Edw.* III.

tion of our Lord the King that now is, he being then Maior of *London*, performed the Office of *Butler*, with 360 Valets all cloath'd in the ſame Livery, and each bearing in his Hand a white Silver Cup, as other Maiors of *London*, time out of Mind, uſed to do at the Coronation of the Kings your Progenitors; and the Fee appendant to that Service, *viz.* a Gold Cup with a Cover, and with an Ewer of Gold enamelled, were delivered to him by Aſſent of the Earl of *Lancaſter*, and other great Men then of the King's Council, by the Hands of Sir *Robert de Woodhouſe*. Notwithſtanding which, there now comes an Eſtreat out of the Exchequer to the Sheriffs of *London*, for levying of 89 *l.* 12 *s.* 6 *d.* for the ſaid Fee, upon the Goods and Chattels of the ſaid Sir *Richard*, whereof he prays Remedy may be ordained him. Alſo the Maior and Citizens of *Oxford* are bound by their Charter to come to *London* at the Coronation, to aſſiſt the Maior of *London* in ſerving at the ſaid Feaſt, and ſo have always uſed to do. Or if it pleaſe our Lord the King and his Council, we will willingly pay the ſaid Fee, ſo that we may be diſcharged of that Service.

Maior of Oxford to aſſiſt.

See Blunt's *Tenures* 121, *and* quære *the Anſwer*.

Conſervator of the Thames.

Alſo the Lord Maior is Bailiff and Conſervator of the Rivers *Thames* and *Medway*, touching which ſee hereafter under the Title *Court of Conſervacy*, &c.

And Note, if any Apprentice or Citizen of *London* ſhall be carry'd on Shipboard, and there detain'd againſt his Will, the Lord Maior may ſend his Warrant by his Water-Bailiff,

Bailiff, and compel the Captain or Commander of the Veffel to releafe fuch Perfon.

'Tis a Cuftom in *London,* that if one be e- *Maior fined*
lected Maior, and he refufes, to fine him 500*l.* *on Refufal.*
But they ought not to chufe an unfit Man on
purpofe to have the Money.   1 *Roll Rep.* 109.

As to the Manner of his Election, together
with his Prefentation, Oath and Duty, fee
5 *Stow* 74, 75, 76, *&c.*

Now as to the Sheriffs of the faid City, Sheriffs
we may obferve they were anciently called
Ballivi; and feem to have been fuch Officers, *how named.*
who under the firft *Norman* Kings (when
there was no Portreve or Maior elected) had
the Government of the City committed to
them by the King, and were in the Nature
of *Cuftodes,* or Lord Wardens. 'But thofe Officers, thus impofed on the Citizens againft
their Confent, feem to have been rejected by
them as a Grievance, and contrary to the
Confeffor's Laws, *&c.* Wherefore *H.* I. no
doubt on the Citizens Petition, and perhaps a
round Sum paid, granted by Charter, That
the faid Citizens might place whom they *Eligible,* &c.
would among themfelves as Sheriffs ; which
Charter you will find confirmed by King
Stephen in Parliament, and by *H.* II. and King
John's Charters: And by the fecond Charter of
King *John,* and the firft of *H.* III. 'tis exprefly granted, That the Citizens of *London*
may chufe and remove their Sheriffs, *&c.* See
the Charters.

Thefe Magiftrates being thus eligible (as all *Their Power*
other Sheriffs of the Kingdom originally were)
have both a judicial and a minifterial Power
lodg'd in them ; for with refpect to their
own Courts they are the fole Judges, but in
the Court of the Huftings they are not Judges

E 2   alone

alone, but are the Minifters to execute the Judgments and Precepts of the Lord Maior, *&c.*

How elected. They were of old time chofen, as the Charters fpeak, by the Citizens from among themfelves, *i. e.* the Commonalty or Commoners, and oftentimes never came to be Aldermen ; but of later Times they have been made Aldermen before, or prefently after their Election. So 'tis faid, that formerly many Aldermen have been Maiors who never were Sheriffs, as *Nicholas Faringdon,* who was never Sheriff, yet four times Maior, and the like of divers others.

The Charters abovementioned direct the Election of Sheriffs to be by the Citizens in general ; and accordingly 4 *Hen.* V. an Act of Common Council fays, the Sheriffs ought to be freely and indifferently chofen by the more fufficient Citizens fummon'd to thefe Elections : Alfo an Act of Parliament made 7 *R.* II. fays that St. *Matthew's* Day fhall be the Day for electing Sheriffs ; and when the Commons have agreed upon the Perfons, they fhall prefent them to the Maior and Aldermen.

Notwithftanding which, and divers other Precedents, the Lord Maiors of *London* about 32 and 33 *Car* II. being influenced by Court Practices, claim'd a Right of chufing one of the faid Sheriffs, by drinking to him, and nominating him to be Sheriff for the enfuing Year ; which was generally confirm'd by the Commonalty. But as the Commons originally had a difcretionary Power of rejecting the Perfon nominated, fo they feared, by reafon of fome Court Practices then on Foot, that that Cuftom might in Time turn to their

their Prejudice, and utterly deprive them of
fuch difcretionary Power; wherefore they declared againft the faid Practice of the Maior's
nominating one of the faid Sheriffs, and in-
fifted upon their Right granted by the faid
Charters to the Citizens in general.

But this Claim of the Citizens being oppofed by the Court, occafioned great Heats
and Difturbances in the City; and divers e-
minent Patriots (*viz.* Sir *T. Pilkington*, Sir *Pa-
tience Ward*, Sir *S Barnardifton*, *&c*) who appear'd in Defence of the Citizens Rights, were
profecuted at Law for a.pretended Riot in
electing their Sheriffs. And thefe Heats and
Animofities gave Colour for that pretended
Proteftant Plot, whereby Mr. *Cornifh*, and o-
ther worthy Citizens, were unjuftly put to
Death; and within a Year after followed that
quo Warranto Profecution againft the faid City and Citizens before mentioned.

1683.
5 *Stow 91.*

Asto the Authority and Office of Sheriffs, it
belongs to them to ferve the King's Writs both
of Procefs and Executions, be they Summons,
Attachments, orDiftreffes, *&c.* to compel Men
to appeartoanfwerthe Law; as alfo for feizing
on their Goods, Lands, or Bodies: They are
alfo to ferve all Extents, Writs of Poffeffion
or Seizin, *Habeas Corpus's*, Writs of Inquiry,
&c. and for the better Execution of their
Office, they may in certain Cafes raife the
Poffe Comitatus: They are to return all Juries
for Trial of Mens Lives, Liberties, Lands,
and Goods, and ought to fee that fuch Jury-
men be of good Abilities and honeft Repute,
&c. They ought alfo to look after the keeping of the publick Peace, and to fee condemn'd Perfons executed according to their
*Their Authori-
ty and Office.*

Sentence, except pardoned by the King :
and if a Reſcue be made after an Arreſt, they
may ſue the Reſcuer, and compel him to pay
the Debt, to which they themſelves are alſo
liable. Alſo in all Caſes where the King is
Party, they may break open Doors, or untile
the Houſe where Entrance is deny'd ; and ſo
upon Eſcapes and Outlawries after Judgments,
but not upon any Meſne Proceſs.

Under-Sheriff Alſo for better performing their ſaid Office,
they have jointly an Under-Sheriff, who is
always an Attorney, and generally of known A-
bilities, and gives good Security to the Sheriffs
for the juſt Performance of his Office ; but
this Under-Sheriff acts only for the County,
but has nothing to do within the City or Li-
His Deputy. berties, and keeps his Deputy for *Middleſex*
accordingly.

Sheriffs Bai-liffs, &c. Note alſo, As to Sheriffs Bailiffs there is no
need of them in *London* ; for the ſaid Sheriffs
have each their reſpective Compters or Priſons within the ſaid City, and in each Compter their peculiar Officers, as a Secondary, a
Clerk of the Papers, four Clerks Sitters, a
Priſon Keeper, with Serjeants and their Yeomen, for making Arreſts, Attachments, Executions, *&c.*

Sheriffs Courts. They have likewiſe their reſpective Courts,
with a Judge, and Officers belonging to each
Court for Trial of Cauſes on ſuch Arreſts or
Attachments, and of which Courts, *&c.* ſee
hereafter——Note, the Lord Maior and Citi-
zens have the *Shrivalty* of the ſaid City in
Fee ; and the Sheriffs are Guardians of the
City under them. Note alſo, *Anno* 1293, three
Men had their Right Hands cut off at the
Standard in *Cheap*, for reſcuing a Priſoner ar-
reſted by a City Serjeant.

Beſides

Befides the beforenamed Magiftrates, (*i. e.*
the Maior and Sheriffs) 'which are annually e-
lected, and on whom the Government of the
City chiefly relies, there are other Magiftrates, which being once elected, are conti-
nual, as the Aldermen of the feveral Wards, Aldermen,
the Recorder, Chamberlain, Common-Ser-
jeant, Town-Clerk, &c.

In the *Saxon* Times he was called an Alderman, who by Election was vefted with a
judicial Power, (for in thofe Times none Judges. Vide
could exercife any Authority, either civil or poft.
military, but by the free Election of a *Folkmote*, as appears from the Confeflor's, and
other *Saxon* Laws.) And hence it is, that in
thofe Laws the Earls or Aldermen of Counties are mentioned as Judges, and that if
fuch Earl or Aldermen misbehave himfelf in
his Judgments, he fhall forego, or may be de-
pofed from his Office, *i. e.* in a Folkmote, as
was done in the Cafe of *Toftius*, Earl, or Alderman, of *Northumberland. See the* Saxon
Chron. pag. 171.

Now as the Government of the City of
London was an Epitome of that of the whole
Kingdom, fo the Office of Alderman within
his properWard, bore fome Analogy to that of
Earls or Aldermen of the feveral Counties,
and were, in confequence of their Election,
vefted with a judicial Power : And 'tis evident both from Hiftory and Records, that
all the Aldermen of *London* were of old time
annually elected on the Feaft of St. *Gregory*, How elected,
i. e. 2 *Martij*, altho' the fame Perfons when &c.
once elected, were generally continued by an
annual Re-election. And yet in the Year *See* infra,
1249 (25 *Hen.* III.) thofe Aldermen were

E 4   (it

(it ſeems by a Court Trick) all changed; and in 1255 (39 *Hen.* III.) the Maior and divers Aldermen, as alſo the Sheriffs, were deprived, and others placed in their Room by the King: and the like happen'd in 1265, or 50 *Hen.* III. But I find in 1273, 1 *Ed.* I. Sir *Walter Harvey*, who was Maior that Year, was afterward deprived of his Office of Alderman for his Miſdeeds, which ſeems to have been done by the Citizens in a Folkmote or Common Hall.

Deprived.

In 1304 (32 *Ed.* I.) an Alderman was elected to be Recorder of the City, and was appointed, *i. e.* permitted to wear his Apparel as an Alderman.

Made Recorder.
1 oſt 64.

Anno 1354, 28 *Ed* III. 'tis ſaid the Aldermen of *London* were uſed before that time to be changed yearly, but that 'twas then ordain'd they ſhould not be removed without ſome ſpecial Cauſe.

5 Stow 111.

Yet I find that 7 *R.* II. *Anno* 1383, the Citizens petition the King in Parliament, That whereas the Aldermen of *London* are yearly choſen and returned at the Feaſt of St. *Gregory* the Pope, they pray, that a free Choice may be made of the moſt able Men of the City, as well of ſuch as were elected (Aldermen) the Year before as of others, and that yearly. Whereto the King grants, as long as thereby is good Government in the City. So that hitherto the Citizens maintain'd their ancient Right of electing their Aldermen yearly; tho' this Cuſtom was not well reliſh'd by the Court, as appears by the King's Anſwer.

Cotton's *Records* 301.
Vide ſupra

Alſo this Practice of yearly electing Aldermen ſeems to have continued for about
ten.

ten Years afterward, *i. e.* till 17 *R.* II. when an Act was paſſed in Parliament (as 'tis ſaid by the King and Lords only) which enacts, That the Aldermen of *London* ſhould not from thenceforth be yearly choſen, but remain (in Office) till they be put out for ſome reaſonable Cauſe, ſo that their Office is now held *quamdiu ſe bene geſſerunt.* ^{Cotton's *Records* 354.} ^{*Aldermen for Life.*}

And Note, in the ſame Parliament 'twas enacted, that the Men of the Ward of *Faring-don* within *London*, may chuſe an Alderman for the Rule there, and that the Inhabitants of *Faringdon without* may likewiſe chuſe an Alderman for the Rule there ; both of which Aldermen to continue as above ; and thus it continues to this Day. ^{*Faringdon Ward infra and extra,*}

But tho' an Alderman when elected continues in, for Life, *ut ſupra,* yet the Manner of their Election has been frequently controverted between the Lord Maior and Aldermen, or rather the Court on one Side, and the Commonalty of the City on the other, and, *inter alia,* this that follows, *viz. Thurſday, Sept* 11. 1711, Sir *Gilbert Heathcote* Knight, Lord Maior, a Common Council was called on Pretence to paſs the Orphan's Bill ; but there having been a Bill depending for twelve Months paſt, relating to the Election of Alderman, a Queſtion was propoſed, whether that Bill ſhould paſs or not ? Which the Lord Maior oppoſed, and would not put the Queſtion : But after three Hours Debate, a Clauſe of the Bill was left out, which occaſion'd all the twelve Months Conteſt, *viz. That all contro-verted Elections relating to Aldermen ſhould be decided by the Common Council, and not by the Court of Aldermen themſelves ;* which Clauſe, tho' highly juſt, being expunged, the ſaid Bill ^{*Conteſts between the Aldermen and Commons.*} ^{10. Annæ.} ^{5 Stow 82} ^{*About 8 Aldermen preſent.*}

paſs'd

pafs'd, which enacted, That in all future E-
lections for Aldermen, the Ward fhall return
only one Alderman and one Commoner ; that
upon the Demife of the Alderman of *Bridge*
Ward without, the Aldermen above the
Chair may change their Wards for that, and
if they refufe, the Common Council to chufe
one, and that none but Freemen, paying Scot
and Lot, fhall have a Right to poll for Aldermen.　And, 'tis faid, an Order was then
made, That if any Action at Law enfued by
reafon of the faid Act of Common Council,
that it fhould be defended at the City
Charge.　*Heu ! Opprobrium !*

Note alfo, That *December* 6, 1712, another
Act of Common Council paft, for further regulating the Nominations and Elections of
Aldermen and Common Council Men, and
for regulating Elections in Common Halls,
and for obliging Aldermen to nominate and
appoint Common Council Men to be their
Deputies.　See the faid Act, 5 *Stow* 84.

Near 20 Al-
dermen pre-
fent.

But on the 15th of *April*, 1714, another
Act paffed, entituled, An Act for reviving the
ancient Manner of electing Aldermen ; reciting, Whereas by the ancient Ufage and
Cuftom of the City of *London*, when any Ward
became vacant and deftitute of an Alderman,
the Inhabitants thereof, having a Right to
vote in fuch Elections, were wont to chufe
one Perfon only, being a Citizen and Freeman of the faid City, to be Alderman of the
faid Ward.　And whereas feveral Acts and
Ordinances of Common Council have been
heretofore made, to alter the faid ancient
Way and Method of Election, as particularly

21 Ric, II.

on 1 *Aug,* 21 *Ric.* II. it was ordained, That
for the future in the Elections of Aldermen

　　　　　　　　　　　　　　　　　　　two

two at the leaſt, honeſt and diſcreet Men, by
the Men of the Ward ſo deſtitute of an Alderman, ſhould be choſen and preſented to the
Maior and Aldermen ; ſo that either of them
whom they ſhould chuſe, might be admitted
and ſworn. Alſo on 20 *September*, *3 Hen.* IV. it 3 Hen. IV.
was agreed and ordain'd by the Maior and
Aldermen, that in the Elections of Aldermen
thenceforward to be made, there ſhould be
named and choſen four of the moſt honeſt and
ſufficient Citizens of the City, one of which
the Maior and Aldermen ſhould in their Diſcretion, *&c.* admit and ſwear into the ſame
Office; which ſaid Ordinance in a Common
Council held *November* 23 following, was ap-
proved. And whereas by an Act of Common
Council made 11 *September*, 10 *Annæ* (*i. e.* the
Act *ſupra* 1711.) in the Maioralty of Sir *Gilbert Heathcote*, entituled, *An Act to regulate
the Electioms of Aldermen*, the ſaid laſt recited
Ordinance is repeated and made void to all
Intents and Purpoſes whatſoever, and it is
thereby (*inter alia*) enacted, That from thenceforth in all Elections of Aldermen for this City there ſhould be named, elected, and preſented to the Court of Lord Maior and Aldermen for the time being, by the Houſhold-
ers of the Ward deſtitute of an Alderman,
being Freemen of the City, and paying Scot
and bearing Lot, two Perſons and no more, *viz.*
one Alderman, and one able and ſufficient Citizen and Freeman of the City not being an Alderman; which ſaid Alderman ſo to be nominated and preſented, ſhall and may remove
to, and accept and take ſuch Ward, by the Inhabitants whereof (qualified as aforeſaid) he
ſhall be ſo nominated, elected and preſented,
if preſent when the Report of the ſaid Nomination

mination and Election ſhall be made to the
ſaid Court, &c. and ſhall declare his Intention ſo to do; in which Caſe there ſhall be
a Wardmote holden, and the like Nomination and Preſentment made to the ſaid Court
by the Inhabitants of that Court whereof he
was an Alderman, within four Days next enſuing: But in Caſe ſuch Alderman ſhall be
abſent at the time of making the ſaid Report,
or being preſent ſhall declare his Refuſal to
remove, then the other Perſon nominated
and return'd with the ſaid Alderman, ſhall by
the ſaid Court be admitted, accepted, and
ſworn well and truly to execute the ſaid Office of Alderman, as by the ſaid Acts or Ordinances may more fully appear. Which ſaid
ſeveral ways of electing and preſenting more
than one Perſon to the ſaid Court of Lord
Maior and Aldermen on the Vacancy of an
Alderman, have been found to be very incon-
venient, and to create unneceſſary Difficul-
ties in ſettling ſuch Elections in Caſes where
Conteſts do ariſe   'Twas therefore enacted
by the Lord Maior and Aldermen and Commons in the ſaid Common Council of *April*
15, 1714, That the ſaid recited Acts and Ordinances, and all other Acts and Ordinances
of Common Council, ſo far as they require
the Inhabitants of the ſeveral Wards, in E-
Note.   lections of Aldermen, to nominate, elect,
or preſent more than one Perſon to the ſaid
Court, be repealed, and made abſolutely null
and void.

    And for reviving the ancient **Cuſtom** of
the City, and reſtoring to the ſaid Inhabi-
Note.   tants their ancient Rights and Privileges of
chuſing one Perſon only to be their Alderman, 'twas enacted, That thenceforth in all
                    2   Elec-

Elections of Aldermen at a Wardmote to be held for that Purpose, within the time limited by the Laws of the City for holding the same, there fhall be elected, according to the faid ancient Cuftom, by the Houfholders of that Ward, being Freemen of the faid City, and paying Scot and bearing Lot, only one able and fufficient Citizen and Freeman of the faid City, not being an Alderman; which Perfon fo elected fhall be returned by the Lord Maior or other Perfon duly authorized to hold fuch Wardmote, to the faid Court of Maior and Aldermen, within the time for that purpofe by the Laws of the faid City limited and appointed, and fhall be by them admitted and fworn well and truly to execute the faid Office of Alderman: And in cafe of his Re-fufal to take on him the faid Office (unlefs he can difcharge himfelf therefrom by the Laws of the City) he fhall be fubject to all the Pains and Penalties which may be inflict-ed on him by the Laws and Cuftoms of the faid City or otherwife.

Provided, that all former Acts of Common Council relating to the Time of electing, or the method or manner of taking Polls or Scru-tinies, or making Returns of fuch Elections, and all Articles therein not hereby or by any other Act repealed, are to ftand and be in force, *&c.*

And alfo provided, that this Act fhall not extend to alter the manner of conftituting or electing an Alderman of *Bridge* Ward without, but that the method prefcribed by the Act of *September* 20, 1711, be continued and obferved.

Touching the *Wardmote Courts,* fee hereafter in its proper Title.

Note, all Aldermen of *London* above the Chair, and the three eldeft under it, are Juftices *Aldermen's Privileges.*

of

of the Peace within the City by Charter 1. *E.* IV. *Quere* if not fo by the common Law; and by Chart. 2 *Jac.* I. the Maior and Recorder and fuch Aldermen are made Judges of *Oyer* and *Terminer.*

Not to be Ju-rors, &c. They are privileged from ferving on In-quefts, Juries, *&c.*

or Conftables. So they are exempted from ferving of Con-ftables.

Alderman *Abdy* having a Houfe at ———— in *Effex*, where it was pretended that Con-ftables fhould be elected out of the Inhabitants of every Houfe by Prefentment every Year in the Leet, and that he was nominated by the Leet held fuch a Day, to be Conftable there for the following Year; and becaufe he re-fufed, the Steward impofed a Fine upon him; and on moving the Court of B. R. a Writ was granted to difcharge him, for that he ought to be difcharged from that Service by reafon of his being obliged as Alderman to attend the Courts of *London,* and was finable there if abfent; and they alfo held he was not obliged to execute the faid Office of Conftable by De-puty. See *Cro. Car.* 422, 585. 1 *Jon.* 462.

Offences againft them, how pu-nifhed. See 5 *Stow* 156. that one was imprifon'd, and had his Right Hand cut off for affaulting an Alderman, and two others imprifon'd for re-bellious or opprobrious Words fpoken to an Alderman; alfo the Door-Keeper, or Ufher of the Compter, removed from his Office for the like Offence; and in another Cafe, Im-prifonment was for a Year and Day, and Lofs of Freedom for Rebellion to an Alderman, *i. e. beating him.*

And Note 'tis there faid, that none fhall be Aldermen of *London,* unlefs born within the King-dom of *England,* and his Father an *Englifhman.*

There

There are also several other eminent Offi-
cets belongiug to the said City, besides the
Maior, Sheriffs, and Aldermen before-mentioned, *viz.*

First the Recorder, which is usually some **Recorder :**
grave and learned Lawyer, skilful in the Laws
and Customs of the City. He is to be chief **his Office,**
Assistant to the Lord Maior and Aldermen,
for their better Direction in administring Law
and Justice; and taketh place in all their
Councils, and in Courts, before any Man that
hath not been Maior. And being the *Mouth*
of the City, he learnedly delivers the Sentences
and Judgments of their Courts.

His Qualifications are thus set down in the **and Qualifica-**
Book called *Liber albus, viz.* He shall be one of **tions.**
‘ the most skilful and virtuous Apprentices of
‘ the Law of the whole Kingdom. He is to
‘ sit on the right Hand of the Maior in re-
‘ cording Pleas and passing Judgments ; and
‘ by him Records and Processes had before
‘ the Maior and Aldermen, at St. *Martins le*
‘ *Grand,* are to be Recorded by word of
‘ Mouth before the Judges assigned there to
‘ correct Errors. The Maior, and Aldermen
‘ have therefore used commonly to set forth
‘ all the Customs and Business touching the
‘ City before the King and his Council, as
‘ also in the King’s Court by Mr. Recorder,
‘ as a chief Man endued with Wisdom, and
‘ eminent for Eloquence.

His Fees have been sometimes more, some- **His Fees.**
times less, according to his Merit, or the
good Will of the City. It appears by *Liber
albus,* his Fee about that time was settled at
100 Marks, and he was to have of the
Chamber such Vestures, and so lined or faced,
and as often as the Maior and Aldermen had
every

every Year; and his Clerk, such as the Serjeants of the Chamber.

His Oath, &c.   What the Recorder's Oath and Duty was
Temp. Ed. I. *Anno* 1304, appears by *Liber Horne,* which
says, That on *Monday* after the Feast of
St. *Paul*'s Conversion, 32 *Ed.* I. the Maior
and Aldermen (there named) meeting toge-
An Alderman ther, *John de Wengrave,* Alderman and Re-
Recorder. corder, was sworn well and faithfully to render all the Judgments of the *Hustings,* on the
Meeting and Agreement of the Maior and
Aldermen concerning their Pleas, and also all
other Judgments touching the City of *London,* &c. and that he should do Justice as well
to Poor as Rich, and that all the Pleas of the
Hustings, presently after the *Hustings* is fi-
nished, he shall oversee, order and cause to
be enrolled according to the things pleaded,
&c. and that he shall come prepared to dis-
patch the Business of the City, &c. when
he shall be lawfully warned by the Maior and
Bailiffs: For which Labour the said Maior
and Aldermen have yielded to give the said
John 10 *l.* Sterling by the Year out of their
Chamber, and 20 *d.* of each Charter written
and each Testament enrolled in the said *Hustings.*

A Justice of   Note, the Recorder of *London* is appointed
Peace and Oy- to be a Justice of Peace there by the first
er and Ter- Charter of *Ed.* IV. and the first of *Car* I. And
miner. by the second Charter of *Jac.* I. he with the
Maior and principal Aldermen is appointed
a Justice of *Oyer* and *Terminer,* and the Maior
and Recorder to be of the *Quorum*

   Note also, by ancient Custom and by several
Charters, *viz.* 1 Char. *Ed.* IV. and 1 Char.
His Certificate Car. I. the Customs of the City are to be
by Word of certified by word of Mouth, *i. e.* by the
Mouth. Mouth of the Recorder. See *Hob. Rep. Day-
vers*

vers Savage ; as the Cuſtom touching enrolling Apprentices, *pag.* 107. ſo the Cuſtom
touching Freemen, *Deviſes in Mortmain, Free-
bench, Hotchpot, Fem Coverts, Sole Merchants, &c.*

Yet Note, the Cuſtoms of *London* that di- *Note.*
rectly concern the Intereſt of the Corporation,
are not tryable by their Certificate, but by
Jury. *Vide poſt* 80.

The Plaintiff ſurmiſed, that there is a
Cuſtom in *London*, that if any Cuſtom of
London be pleaded, and iſſue thereupon, it
ſhall be try'd by a Writ to the Maior and Aldermen, to certify whether there be ſuch a
Cuſtom ; and they ſhall make their Certificate by the Mouth of the Recorder, *Ore tenus,*
and prayed to have a Writ to certify, &c. and
the Recorder certified, that there was no
ſuch Cuſtom, &c. And after this Certificate
it was moved, that this was a Miſ-tryal ; for
it being a Cuſtom which concerns all the Citizens, ought not to be try'd by ſuch a Certificate, but by Jury : And *Bulſtrode*, who argued for the Defendant, inſiſted much upon
a Caſe in the *Common Bench*, reported by my
Lord *Hobert*, That a Cuſtom of *London*, that
concerns all the Citizens, ſhall be try'd *per
pais :* But after long Deliberation, it was reſolved by all the Court, that the Trial was
good, eſpecially when the Plaintiff hath
ſhewn that there is ſuch a Cuſtom, that it
ſhall be ſo certified, and the Defendant hath
confeſſed it, ſo as the manner of Trial being
as it were by his conſent, he ſhall not after
ſuch Trial except againſt it. And this Cuſtom
doth not concern all the Perſons of *London*,
but only thoſe who uſe manual Trades ; as
if the Cuſtom to deviſe in *Mortmain*, or of

F   foreign

foreign Attachments had been try'd by Certificate. *Vide* 3 *Cro. Appleton* 5. *Stoughton.*

Judgments in *London* on the Outlawries in *London,* are cuſtomarily pronounced by the Recorder, and not by the Coroner, as in County Courts, 1 *Inſt.* 288.

Chamberlain.   Next to the *Recorder* is the *Chamberlain* of the City ; he is an Officer of great Repute and Truſt ; and tho' elected annually on *Mid-*

See 4 *Chart.* *ſummer* Day, yet is ſeldom diſplaced, but
Johannis. continues in for Life, if no juſtCauſe or great Crimes are proved againſt him. He hath the keeping of the Monies, Lands, and Goods of the City Orphans, or takes good Security for Payment thereof when the Parties come to Age ; and to that End he is deemed in

Poſt 324. Law a ſole Corporation to him and his Succeſſors for the ſaid Orphans ; wherefore a Bond made to him and his (Succeſſors) Heirs, &c. is recoverable by his Succeſſors. His Office may be term'd the City's publick Treaſury, he collecting the Cuſtoms, Monies, and yearly Revenues, and all other Duties and Payments belonging to the Corporation of the ſaid City ; and yearly Accounts for the ſame before Auditors aſſigned : He is alſo entruſted with the Counterparts of the City's Leaſes, as alſo Bonds and Securities, and has a Court peculiarly belonging to himſelf ; of which ſee hereafter. Note, there was a Patent 7 *Hen.* III. *Mem.* 5. *Willielmo Jerner de Chamberlaria Londini.*

Common Ser-   The *Common Serjeant*'s Office is to attend
jeant. the Lord Maior and Court of Aldermen on Court Days, and to be of Council with them on all Occaſions both within and without the Precincts or Liberties of the City : He is alſo to take Care of the Orphan's E-
ſtates,

states, both by taking Accounts thereof, and by perusing and signing their Deeds and Indentures, *i. e.* their Securities, before the same passed the Lord Maior and Court of Aldermen. He is likewise to let, set, and manage the Orphans Estates according to his Judgment to their best Advantage.

The *Town-Clerk,* called also the *Common,* or *Town-Clerk.* *Commons* Clerk, keeps the original Charters of the City, as also the Books, Rolls, and other Records, wherein are registred the Acts and Proceedings of the City, so that he may not improperly be termed the City Register, and he is to attend the Lord Maior and Aldermen at their Courts, &c.

Note, the Town-Clerk and Common-Serjeant take place of each other according to their Seniority in Office ; and the ancient yearly Stipend or Fee allowed to the Chamberlain, Common-Serjeant, and Town-Clerk, was only 10 *l.* to each.

As to the Office of Coroner, 'tis observed *Coroner.* before, that the Lord Maior for the time being is Coroner of the City, but he hath his Deputy for the Management thereof. This Office appears by the Mirror to be as ancient as the Time of King *Alfred,* and was formerly of that Esteem, that none could execute it under the Degree of a Knight. *Vide ante* 19 & 22.

And Note, as the Sheriffs are to enquire of all Murders, Homicides, and other Felonies, so the Coroner is to enquire of all sudden Deaths; and to that end he impannels a Jury of Enquiry, and gives them their Charge, and examines Evidence upon Oath, &c.

In 51 *Ed.* III. the Citizens of *London* pray- *Cotton* 147. ed that they might place and displace a Coroner among themselves, answering unto the King what belongeth thereunto; but the King's Answer was, that he would not depart with his ancient Right.

And Note, by a Statute made 3 *Hen.* VII. 'tis provided, that no Coroner demand or take any thing of any Man for doing his Office, yet the Coroner of *London* usually takes extraordinary Fees, more than ought to be taken, and much more than formerly.

The Fees formerly were,

	l.	s.	d.
The Warrant for summoning a Jury,	o	2	6
The Inquisition ——— ———	o	6	8
The Coroner's Fee ——— ———	o	13	4
The Warrant or Certificate to bury the Body ——— ———	o	13	4
	1	5	o

But now instead of 13 *s.* 4 *d.* 'tis said he takes four or five Pounds or more for his Fee, whereas he ought according to the Statute to execute his Office *gratis*, especially where the Relations of the Deceased are poor. This is said to be a great Oppression to the Citizens, and ought to be redress'd either by a Court of Aldermen, or that of a Common Council, who have Power to do it if they think fit.

The City Re-membrancer. The City Remembrancer: This Officer's Business is to attend the Lord Maior on certain Days, and to put his Lordship in mind of the select Days he is to go abroad with the Aldermen, *&c.* He is also to attend daily at the Parliament House during the Sessions, and

to

to report to the Lord Maior their Tranf-
actions, &c.

The Comptroller of the Chamber's Office *Comptroller of*
is to infpect and cheque the Chamberlain's *the Chamber,*
Accompts. Alfo the Cuftom hath been for *the Chamber,*
the Comptroller to draw the Leafes of the
City Lands, and the Clerk of the Chamber
to engrofs them ; the reafon whereof feems
to be becaufe the Clerk of the Chamber is
one of the Chamberlain's Clerks, tho' admitted by the Lord Maior and Court of Aldermen, and the *Chamberlain* or his Clerk are
to examine the Leafes when engroffed before
they are fealed, and when they are examined,
the Chamberlain (and not the Comptroller)
always carries the Leafes into the Court of
Aldermen to be fealed, and takes them back
when fealed.

And Note, the Clerk of the Chamber's *Fees,*
Fee was formerly but 10 *s.* (befides the King's
Duty and Parchment) for engroffing any Leafe
granted to the City, but of late Years he has
taken more, becaufe the Leafes are now made
longer, though not much better than formerly.

Befides the foregoing Officers there are alfo
belonging to the City two Judges of the She- *Judges of She-*
riffs Courts, 4 Common Pleaders, or City *riffs Courts,*
Council, a Regifter of the Orphans Fund, *Council, At-*
8 Attorneys of the Sheriffs Courts, a City *torneys, &c.*
Solicitor, 2 Bridge-Mafters, a Hall-Keeper,
&c.

There are alfo divers Officers peculiarly *Officers of the*
belonging to the Lord Maior's Houfe, where- *Lord Maior's*
of the firft 4 are Efquires by their Places, *Houfhold.*
viz.

The *Sword-Bearer,* who is always to attend *1. Sword-*
the Lord Maior in publick, and is to carry *Bearer,*
F 3 the

the Sword, the Emblem of Juſtice, upright be-
fore him; he hath his Table at my Lord
Maior's, to ſupport which there is 1000 *l. per
Annum* allowed, and has a Houſe or Dwelling
allow'd him by the City at *Juſtice-Hall* in the
Old Baily. See the Charter.

Manner of bearing it.

The Manner of bearing this Sword is ſet
forth in *Leigh*'s Accidence, or Armory, *fol.* 94,
viz. he muſt carry it upright, the Hilts being
held under his Bulk, and the Blade directly
up the middle of his Breaſt to the middle of
his Forehead; this is the Diſtinction from
bearing it in any Town for a Duke, an Earl,
or a Baron. For a Duke, the Blade muſt
lean from the Head between the Neck and
the Right Shoulder; and for an Earl, the
Bearer muſt carry the ſame between the Point
of the Shoulder and the Elbow; and for a Baron there is alſo a different bearing.

2. Common Hunt.

The *Common Hunt.* His Buſineſs is to take
care of the Pack of Hounds belonging to the
Maior and Citizens, and to attend them in
hunting when they pleaſe: His Houſe is in
Finsbury Fields, where the Hounds are alſo
kept; and for keeping thoſe called the Deep-
mouth'd Hounds he hath a good yearly Allowance beſides Perquiſites; and is to attend
the Maior on certein ſet Days weekly. See
the City's Privilege of Huntings, Chart. *H.* I.
and *H.* II. 1 *Johannis,* and 4 Char. *H.* III.

3. Common Cryer.

The *Outroper,* commonly termed the *Common Cryer.* It belongs to him and the Serjeant
at Arms to ſummons all Executors and Adminiſtrators of Freemen to appear and bring
in Inventories of the Perſonal Eſtates of Freemen within two Months after their Deceaſe.
He is alſo to give Notice of Appraiſements,
and to attend the ſame; and is likewiſe to
attend

attend the Lord Maior on fet Days, and at
the Courts held weekly by the Maior and
Aldermen, and has his Dwelling allow'd him
at *Alderfgate.* See Chart. *Car.* I.

The Water Bailiff. This Officer is to look 4. *Water-*
after the Prefervation of the River of *Thames* *Bailiff.*
againft all Encroachments, and to look after
the Fifhermen for Prefervation of the young
Fry, to prevent deftroying them by unlawfull
Nets or Engines; to which End there are
Juries of Enquiry appointed for every County that hath any part of it lying on the Sides
of the faid River; which Juries fummoned by
the faid Water Bailiff, do at certain Times
make Enquiry of all Offences relating to the
faid River and the Fifh therein, and make
their Prefentments accordingly. He is alfo
bound to attend the Lord Maior on fet Days
in the Week. His Houfe is at *Cripplegate.*

Note, Every Fifherman is to appear before
him on St. *Paul's* Day at *Guild-Hall* Chappel,
to regifter their Names in his Book. *Vide
poft,* The *Court of Confervacy,* &c.

Befides which faid Officers there are alfo
divers others belonging to the Lord Maior,
viz.

Three Serjeant Carvers.
Three Serjeants of the Chamber.
A Serjeant of the Channel.
A Yeoman of the Channel.
An Under Water-Bailiff.
Four Yeomen of the Water-Side.
Two Yeomen of the Chamber.
Two Yeomen of the Wood-Wharfs.
Three Meal-Weighers.
The Foreign Taker.

As alfo divers Clerks, and Keepers of
Halls, Prifons, *&c.* Stewards of Manors and
F 4 Lands,

Lands, Gaugers, Packers, Porters, *&c.* too numerous to be here particularized.

And having thus given you an Account of the Royal Charters to the City, and alfo of the Magiftrates and Officers thereof, with their Rights, Privileges, and Duties ; I fhall now proceed to treat of the Cuftoms of the City of *London*, both general and particular ; as the fame do refpectively concern either the Perfons of the Citizens, or their Eftates, *&c.*

Of fuch General Cuftoms of the City, as refpect either the Perfons of the Citizens, or their Houfes, Lands, Goods, &c.

London held in free Burgage.

A N D Note, all the City of *London* and Liberties thereof, are held of the King in free Burgage, without any Mefnalty.

Bargain and Sale of Lands.

It is a Cuftom of *London* to bargain and fell Lands by Parol. 4. *Inft.* 675.

Alfo the Cuftom of *London* is, That Lands pafs by fuch Bargain and Sale, without any Inrollment, according to Stat. 27 *Hen.* VIII. c. 16.

Paffing the Wife's Lands.

Alfo if a Man and his Wife pafs the Wife's Lands in *London*, and fhe be examined (*ut infra*) it fhall bind her by the Cuftom. See 2 *Co.* 57. *Beckwith's* Cafe, *Hob.* 225. *Needler's* Cafe, and 1 *Cro.* 669. *Darman* verfus *Bowyer.*

Lands pleadable in the Hust'ngs.

By the Cuftom of *London* Lands are pleadable in the *Huftings* Court. 4 *Inft.* 147.

And

And no Writ lies of Lands in *London,* but in *London* only. *Dyer* 317.

By the faid Cuftom he who holds Lands or *Joint Tenants may devife.* Tenements in *London* jointly with others, may devife that which belongs to him, without other Severance. See 49 *Ed.* III.

Alfo by the faid Cuftom, and by 1 Chart. *Devife in Mortmain.* *Ed.* III. the Citizens of *London,* being Freemen, may devife their Lands in *Mortmain, &c.* See *Cro. Car.* II. 48, and 57.

But Infants cannot make any Devife of *Infants and Fem Coverts cannot.* Lands or Tenements, nor may Feme Coverts devife their Lands or Tenements, tho' with Licence of their Husbands. *Sed vide* Kitch 151. *contr.*

Nor can the Husband devife his Tenements to his Wife for longer Term than her *Nor the Hufband but* fub *modo.* Life, (but this is faid to be alter'd by Statute) nor the Wife claim any larger Eftate, on Pain to loofe the whole. Neither can the Hufband devife the Tenements of his Wife, nor *Vide Statute* 32 *Hen.* VIII. *of Wills.* thofe which he and his Wife have jointly purchafed; but if the Husband and Wife have *Ancient Cuftoms of* Lond. *pag.* 4. Tenements jointly to them and the Heirs of the Husband, he may devife the Reverfion.

Alfo where a Reverfion or a Rent is de- *ib. pag.* 5. vifed by a Will enrolled in the *Huftings,* the fame Reverfions and Rents pafs prefently after the Death of the *Teftator,* fo as fuch Devifees of Rents may diftrein and avow for the fame, and fuch Devifees of Reverfions may fue a Writ of Waft, *&c.* at their Will, without other Attornement of the Tenants, and they may plead the fame Inrollment if need be, tho' they have not the faid Will to produce.

And

Ibid.

And the ſame Cuſtom holds in caſe of Charters, Indentures, and other Deeds and Writings enrolled in the *Huſtings* of Record, and ſuch Inrollments have always been uſed where ſuch Wills have been publiſhed and proved in full *Huſtings*, and ſuch Charters, Indentures, Deeds, &c. evidenced there, and the Conuſances and Confeſſions of Women have been received to prove the ſame, either before the Maior and one Alderman, or before two Aldermen for Neceſſity, as well out of Court as in, ſo that the ſaid Charters, Indentures, &c. ſo acknowledg'd, be afterwards enter'd and enrolled in ſome of the *Huſtings*, and the Fees thereof paid.

Rents deviſed without Clauſe of Diſtreſs &c. Diſtreinable, ibid 5.

Alſo where a Man has deviſed by his Will ſo enrolled, a certain Rent to ariſe out of his Tenements within the ſaid City, without any Clauſe of Diſtreſs, yet by the Uſage of the City, the Deviſee may Diſtrein and avow the taking, if the Rent be behind. And in the ſame Manner ſhall be done of all antient Rents, called Quit-Rents, within the ſaid City.

Ibid 4. Wills how enrolled.

And Note, all Wills, &c. whereby any Tenements are deviſed, may be enrolled in the *Huſtings* of Record, at the Suit of any that may take benefit thereof. And the Will, &c. ſo to be enrolled, ſhall be brought before the Maior and Aldermen in full *Huſtings*, and be there proclaimed or publiſhed by the Serjeant, and proved by three diſcreet Perſons well known, who ſhall be ſworn and examined as to the Circumſtances of the making thereof, and of the Eſtate and Capacity of the Teſtator, and of his Sealing and Signing, &c. the ſame. And if the Proof be good, then ſhall the Will be enrolled, and the Fees paid for Enrollment. *Ut Supra.* And no Nuncupative, or other Will

Will, can be Enrolled, except the Seal of the Teftator be fet thereto : and yet fuch Wills may be good, tho' not Enrolled or of Record. *Vide poft,* The fpecial Cuftoms touching Freemens Wills, Executors, Devifes, *&c.*

Note, all the City of *London* and Liberties thereof, are held of the King in Freeburgage, as aforefaid. And all the Lands and Tenements, Rents and Services, within the faid City and Suburbs, as well in Rendition as Demeafn, are devifeable by Ufage of the faid City; fo that the Freemen and Women of the faid City, by the faid Ufage, may devife their Tenements, Rents, and Reverfions within the faid City and Suburbs, to whom they will, and of what Eftate they will (except as aforefaid) and may alfo devife a new Rent out of their faid Tenements. *London, Freburgage.* *Calthorp, 103, 104.* *Who may devife, and how.*

It is a Cuftom in *London* to put Ladders, or place Poles (but not to break Ground) upon the Land or Houfes adjoining, for repairing a Man's own, and this for neceffity. *Placing Ladders on other Men's Ground to build.*

And fee the feveral Statutes for rebuilding the faid City, poft, under the Head of General Statutes.

Cuftoms as to Landlords and Tenants.

IF Leffee within the City be a Fugitive, whereby his Goods within the Houfe be arrefted or attached, yer the Landlord fhall be ferved before all others (but the King) being behind by two Years, and for fo much Rent in Arrear, Goods fhall be left in the Houfe to the Ufe of the Landlord. *Leffee Fugitive,*

And tho' the Leffee within the City commit Felony or other Contempt, by which his Goods *Or a Felon.*

Goods and Chattels become subject to Forfeiture, yet the Leſſor ſhall be paid his Rent for two Years, out of the Goods found within the ſame Houſe.

Warning.

By the Cuſtom of *London*, every Tenant before he leaves his Houſe, ſhall give warning to the Leſſor, and ſo the Leſſor to his Leſſee, according to the Laws of the City in that Caſe provided.

Waſte in Houſes.

It is ſaid to be the Cuſtom of the City, That thoſe which have Tenements within the ſaid City, ſhall not be ſuffered to ſtrip or waſte their Tenements in Demeſne, nor to pull them down in deforming or defacing of the City, unleſs it be to amend them, or build them up again; and any that doth it, or beginneth to do it, ſhall be puniſhed by the Maior and Aldermen for the Offence, according to the Cuſtom of the City.

Danger of being Ruinous.

Alſo, if Walls, Penthouſes, or other Houſes whatſoever within the ſaid City ſtretching to the High Street, be ſo weak or feeble, that the People paſſing by, miſtruſt the Peril of ſome ſuddain Ruin, then after it is certified to the Maior and Aldermen by a Maſon, and Carpenter of the City ſworn, or that it be found in the Wardmote that the danger is ſuch, then the ſame Maior and Aldermen ſhall cauſe the Party to be warned to whom the ſame Tenements belong, to amend them and repair them ſo ſoon as conveniently he may; and if after ſuch warning, they be not amended, nor begun to be amended within forty Days then next following, then ſhall the ſaid Tenements be repaired and amended at the Coſt and Charges of the ſaid City, until the Coſts be fully levied of his Goods and Chattels, or other his Tenements, if need be.

Alſo

Also, if any House be found within the said *Cover'd with* City, or the Suburbs of the same, covered with *Thatch,* &c. Straw, Reed, or Thatch, he to whom the House belongeth, shall pay to the Sheriffs for the time being, forty Shillings, and shall be compelled to take away the same Covering.

Also, if any House within the said City *Fire.* be burning, so that the Flame of the Fire be seen out of the House, he which dwelleth in the said House shall pay to the Sheriffs 40 *s.* in a red Purse.

It is a Custom, That Writs of Covenant *Covenant.* are maintainable without Specialty, 27 *H.* VI. *N. B.* 103.

Covenant lies in *London* upon a Bill ; tho' without Specialty, by the Custom, 22 *E.* IV. 2.

It is a Custom of *London,* That Beasts di- *Distresses.* strained, or Goods taken in *London,* shall not be replevisable by Writ out of *Chancery,* but by the Sheriffs of *London. Dyer,* 245. *b.*

And by the Custom of *London,* any Goods *Replevins.* taken in *London,* shall not be replegiable by any Writ out of Chancery, but by the Sheriffs of *London,* only. *Dyer* 345.

It is a Custom of *London,* that an Action of *Pledges.* Debt lies against Pledges without Writing. 43 *Edw.* III. 11. 1 *Edw.* IV. 6.

Action of Debt in *London,* shall be maintain- *Actions of* able in *London* upon a simple Contract, 8 *Rep. Debt main-* 126. and that Debt on single Contract shall *tainable on sin-* be equal to an Obligation. *Snelling's* Case, Ex- *gle Contracts.* ecutors are bound to pay such Debts. *Vide post.* Special Customs.

The Maior and Commonalty of *London* brought an *Indebitatus assumpsi* against *A. B.* for *Where a Free-* 5 *l.* for so much due to them for divers Tuns *man may be a* of Wine brought from beyond the Seas to the *Witness.* Port of *London,* at 4 *d. per* Tun. On *non as-*
sumpsit

sumpsit and Trial at the Bar, divers Freemen of *London* were offered as Witnesses for the Plaintiff, and by *Scrogs, Dolben* and *Raymond* they mere Witnesses. 1 *Ventr.* 351. the Case of the City of *London* concerning the Duty of Water-baylage.

No Lawgager against a Debt for Tabling.
It is a Custom, that in Debt for Tabling, the Defendant shall not have his Law, neither shall Lawgager be allow'd for Tabling against the Testimony of an Alderman.

Nor against a Merchant's Book.
One shall not wage Law against a Merchant's Book. *Perk.* 27.

Of swearing the Truth of a Debt.
It is a Custom in *London*, that if the Plaintiff in a Debt upon a Contract produce two Men afore the Maior, &c. and will swear the Debt is true and real, the Defendant shall be ousted to have his Law. 1 *Edw.* IV. 5.

Action sur concessit solvere.
By the Custom of *London*, a Man may maintain Actions of Debt, *sur concessit solvere.* 1 *Hen.* VII. 22, &c. *N. B.* 161. b.

Debt brought on Obligation, the Defendant pleads, That the Plaintiff was indebted to him, *& concessit solvere*, and pleads a Foreign Attachment in *London.* The Plaintiff *Protestando nul tiel Record, pro placito dicit,* that he *pro diversis denariorum summis per ipsum præfat' R. prius debitis, non concessit solvere,* the said Sum, *modo & forma prout,* &c. The Defendant demurs ; its a good Bar, the Debt being well travers'd. *Coke* and *Brainford,* 1 *Crooke.*

Examination of a Debt by the Lord Maior.
It has been a Custom, Time out of Mind, for the Lord Maior, when a Person is impleaded before the Sheriffs, to send for him and the Record, and to examine him upon his Plea ; and if it appear upon his Examination, that the Plaintiff is satisfied, that he may award that the Plaintiff shall be barred. 8 *Rep.* 126.

It

It is a Cuſtom, that if a Debtor be fugitive, *Debtors ar-*
he may be arreſted before the Day of Pay-*reſted before*
ment, to find better Security : Alſo that the *the Day.*
Creditors may before the Day, arreſt his *Poſt* 306, 308.
Debtor to find better Security. *Hob.* 86. 8 *Co.*
126. 11 *Hen.* VI. 3.

It is a Cuſtom of *London,* for one Obligor *Contribution*
that pays the whole Debt, to have Debt *pro* *pro Rata.*
Rata, againſt his Companion; or one Joint
Obligor ſhall have Contribution againſt his
Companion by the Cuſtom of *London.* *Co.* Li.
Intr. 161.

It is a Cuſtom of *London,* That Attaints *Attaints.*
ſhall not be brought otherwiſe than within the
City, of a Falſe Oath made there. *Kitch.* 567.

It is a Cuſtom of *London,* That they ſhall *Inqueſts.*
not be Impannelled upon Inqueſts out of the
City, and that they ſhall not join with Foreigners on any Inqueſt. *Dyer* 40, 46. 11 *Hen.*
VII. 14.

There is a Cuſtom in the City of *London,* *Granage of*
called *Granage, viz.* That the Lord Maior, *Salt.*
for the Time being, ſhall have of every Alien,
that brings into the Port of *London* any Salt,
the twentieth Part of it. *Dyer, Eliz.* 352.

'Tis a Cuſtom in *London,* That if an Infor- *Adulterers.*
mation be made to a Conſtable there, that
one within their Juriſdiction is with a Woman
in Adultery, that he ſhall take the Beadle, and
others of the ſame Pariſh, and go to the Houſe,
and if they find the Man in Adultery, they
ſhall take and carry him to the Compter, and
leave him there. 3 *Juſt.* 206. 8 *Co.* 126.

Note, by their Cuſtom, the Maior and
Commonalty may limit the Penalties of *By-*
Laws to themſelves : but then, they cannot be
ſued for in the Maior's Court. *Salk.* 307, 308.

                                  And

May prescribe against a Stat. and why.

And it is also said, in *Palmer* 542, That the Citizens of *London* may prescribe against a Statute, because their Liberties and Customs are reinforced and confirmed by Statute. And Note, Sir *Edw. Coke*, in 1 *Roll. Rep.* 105. says, we take Notice of the Customs of *London*, and

Their Customs allowed, in B. R. &c.

allow them in our Courts in *Westminster* Hall. And *Fleetwood*, Recorder of *London*, 1 *Leon.* 284. and 4 *Leon.* 182. says, The King's Courts ought to take Notice, that those in *London* have a Court of Record. And 3 *Leon.* 264. the same Recorder says, That all the Customs of *London* are confirmed by Acts of Parliament; as also by *Magna Charta*, which has been confirmed fifty two times, and also by the Stat. 7. *Rich.* II. See *Treby's* Argument on the *Quo Warranto*, p. 30, 31. That the City of *London* are not bound to plead, or set forth their Liberties, as other Cities and Towns are. And Note, it seems sufficient to certify them by the Mouth of their Recorder. *Vide Tit.* Recorder. *Ante* 64, 65, and Char. *Car.* I.

Where B. R. &c. are bound to take Notice of their Customs.

And see 1 *Roll. Rep.* 106. That if a Judgment be given in *London*, and the same brought into *B. R.* the Judges there ought to take Notice of the Custom of *London*. But if a Custom be in another Place, on an original Action, there, we ought not to take Notice of it without it be alledged. *Per Cur.*

See other general Customs of London, *post*, 306, 308, &c.

Special Customs of *LONDON.*

Concerning Simple Contracts.

IT is a Custom of *London*, That an Action of Debt shall be maintained against Executors upon a Simple Contract. 8 *Co.* 126.

One *Snelling* brought Debt upon an Obliga- 5 *Co.* 82 *b.* tion against an Administrator, who pleads, there is a Custom in *London*, That an Administrator shall pay Debts upon Contract to a Citizen as well as upon Obligation, and that *J. S.* upon a Contract had recovered, and held good.

1. *Resolved, Altho' that Debt is given against an Administrator by the* Stat. *of* 31 *E.* III. *yet because they were charged as Executors before, so that only the Name is changed, the Custom generally alledged is good.*

2. *The Custom bindeth Strangers ; as this same Case is reported by* Cro. Eliz. 409.

. Debt against *Norton* as Administrator of one *Cro.* 1 *part,* *Norton,* upon an Obligation. The Defendant Snelling *v.* shews the Custom of *London* to be, *That if a* Norton, *f.* *Contract be made by a Citizen to pay Money to ano-* 409. *ther Citizen, and he who made the Contract dies, that his Executors or Administrators, shall be chargeable therewith, as if it were upon an Obligation ;* and shews further, how the Intestate was indebted on a Contract to one *A.* who had recovered against him, and that he had *Riens ouster en ses mains, &c.* And it was thereupon demurred.

G   *Glanvil*

Glanvil moved, *That this Cuftom was not good: For firft, It is againft Law, that an Execu-tor, or Adminiftrator, fhould be charged upon a Simple Contract. Secondly, It is againft Law, that a Stranger fhould be barred of his Debt upon a Spe-cialty, by reafon of a Debt upon a Simple Contract. Daniel è contrà.* The Cuftom was always to bind the Executors or Adminiftrators to pay Debts upon Contracts, and Cuftoms in *London* are confirmed by Parliament, and are now as ftrong as a Statute. And therefore in *London,* they prefcribe to give Land in *Mortmain,* which is againft Statute-Law, and there is not any Cuftom but that it deprives, and is againft the Common-Law in fome Point. And this Cuftom is reafonable; for a Debt upon a Contract, is as well due as a Debt upon an Obligation; and therefore there is as great Reafon for the Payment of the one as of the other, although the Law hath given a greater Prerogative, *viz.* a Priority of paying the one, rather than the other. And altho' it might feem hard to have allowed this Cuftom in this Court if it had been originally pleaded here: yet when the Cuftom has been executed againft the Adminiftrator by the Laws of the City whereto he is fubject, it would be mifcheivous unto him to be difallowed it here; for then he fhould be twice charged without Remedy; and this Difference is taken, 1 *Edw.* IV. 8. And *Owen,* Juftice, faid, The Cuftom is rea-fonable, for the Executor is in Confcience bound to pay a Debt upon a Contract, as well as upon a Specialty. And of the fame Opinion, were the other Juftices. See 5 *Co.* 82.

Where

Where particular Cuſtoms in London *are pleadable, or not, in the* B. R. *or* Common Pleas, *or only within* London.

IN Trover and Converſion, the Defendant *Shop a Market* pleaded the Cuſtom of *London*, That the *overt an ill- Plea.* Property ſhall be altered if a Man buy any Goods in an open Shop, by force whereof he converted them, *&c.* This Plea was held not good, for that it amounted only to the General Iſſue. *Vide poſt* Marketovert.

In the Caſe of *Stanton* and *Squire, Moor* 135, it *Feme-Sole* was agreed upon the Book of 1 *Edw.* IV. upon *Merchant where to be* the Cuſtom of a Feme-covert Sole Merchant, *ſued.* and held that this is pleadable, and ſhe is to be ſued in *London*, and not elſewhere.

So the Cuſtom of *London*, that Pledges ſhall *Pledges.* be ſued without Deed; and that Infant ſhall not wage his Law upon Covenant for Tabling, *Infants.* but in the Common Bench, ſuch Infant ſhall wage his Law, and ſuch Woman ſhall not be ſued, and ſuch Pledges ſhall not be ſued without Deed.

But if an Infant binds himſelf as an Ap- *If Infant ſued* prentice in *London*, if he be ſued upon his *in* B. C. *upon* Covenant in *C. B.* as he may, he ſhall not *his Covenant, he ſhall not* plead Nonage in Bar; and *Walmſley* took this *plead Nonage* Diverſity between the ſaid Cuſtoms and this *in Bar.* Covenant; for the ſaid Cuſtoms are things Executory, and theſe are Preſcriptions united *Diverſity.* to the Courts of *London*, for it only appears in Suits and Pleas; but this Covenant by the ſaid Cuſtom is become a ſtrong thing, and allowable by the Law, and ſo pleadable in

G 2 any

any place in *England* ; for the Words of the Plea are, That the Covenant ſhall be of ſuch. Effect and Efficacy, as if he had been of full Age at the Time of the Indenture, and then he ſhall be bound in every Place within the Realm.

The Recorder of *London* moved in another Caſe, that where the Cuſtom was in *London,* that if many are bound in an Obligation as *Sureties contributory.* Sureties, if the Principal fail of Payment, ſo that one of the Sureties be ſued upon the Bond, that he ſhall have a Writ *de Contributione facienda* againſt the other Sureties, and told the Court, ſuch a Writ was brought in *London,* and is now removed *in Banco* ; and pray'd the Juſtices to remand this to *London,* for that the Common-Pleas cannot do right upon that Cuſtom, and his Requeſt was granted.

How the Cuſtoms there are to be certified into other Courts.

Vide ſub Recorder ante.

The Plaintiff upon Iſſue joined upon the Cuſtom, ſurmiſed that there is a Cuſtom in *London,* That if any Cuſtom be pleaded and deny'd, and iſſue thereupon, it ſhall be try'd by a Writ to the Maior and Aldermen, to certify whether there be ſuch a Cuſtom, and they ſhall make their Certificate by the Mouth of their Recorder, *Ore tenus,* and prays to have a Writ to certify, which was awarded accordingly. *Cro. Car.* 516.

Where the Privileges of the Courts of Weſtminſter *have been allowed againſt the Cuſtomary Actions in* London, *viz*.

ACtion *ſur conceſſit ſolvere*, which is a cuſto- Cuſtomary mary Action in *London*, was diſcharged Actions diſ- by the Privilege of the Common-Pleas after a charged by large Debate, 38 *H.* VI. 29 *b.* But the Con- Privilege of trary ſeems to be held by *Cook* in *Croſſe's* Caſe. the Common- 1 *Rol. Rep.* 268. Pleas.

An Action upon the Cuſtom of *London* a- gainſt a Feme-Sole Merchant was diſcharged by Privilege, *eo quod,* the Defendant and her Husband were empleaded in the Common- Pleas, and yet this is a cuſtomary Action that does not lie in the Common-Pleas nor elſe- where out of *London.* 9 *Ed.* IV. 35.

Edward was indebted to one *A.* and deli- vered Goods to *Tetbury,* being a Carrier, to carry them : *A.* attacheth the Goods in the Hands of the ſaid *Tetbury* the Carrier, who being privileged in the Common-Pleas by an Action, was diſcharged of the Attachment. 1 *Leon.* 189.

But Money was attached in the *Hands* of *Turbile,* Clark of *B. R.* and he moved for his Privilege, but it was denied. 1 *Sands* 68. *Vide poſt, Attachments.*

Cuſtoms which take Effect in the Court where the Cuſtom is uſed, and there begins to be in force, theſe are not allowable but in ſuch a Court, City, or Borough where they are uſed ; as in *London* the Cuſtom is, that in Action of Debt on Contract, if the Aldermen of the City will record this, the Defendant in Action againſt him ſhall be ouſted of his

Leygager.

Leygager; and this is a good Custom, and allowable in the Court there; but if the Party bring his Action in *B. R.* the Defendant shall have his *Leygager*, tho' the Alderman comes here and records the Contract. 2 *Bulstr.* 192. in *Burton* and *Palmer's* Case.

Foreign Attachments.

A Debt was recovered in *London* by force of a foreign Attachment, and after the Debtee of him in whose Hands the Money was attached brought an Action, and the foreign

Per Dodridge. Attachment was pleaded in Bar. *Per Dodr.* we ought to allow it; but upon such Custom, by way of original Suit, we cannot do

Procedendo. Right to the party; and a *Procedendo* was awarded by the Court. 1 *Rol. Rep.* 268. *Crosse's* Case.

Prohibition for refusing to accept a Plea to the Jurisdiction.

A Prohibition was awarded to the Court at *Woodstreet* Compter, *London*, in an Action of Debt commenced there, for that the Defendant had pleaded there before any Imparlance taken; that the Cause of Action did arise at a Place out of their Jurisdiction, and offer'd to have sworn his Plea to be true, which they refused to accept. *N. B.* 21.

Note also, That upon such Refusal, a Bill of Exceptions may be made, and Error assigned for that Cause.

Citizens disfranchised, restored.

Note, a Citizen was disfranchised for suing another Citizen in *C. B.* But all the Parties to the Disfranchisement were fined each 100 Marks, and the Party disfranchised restored. 3 *Cro.* 33.

Abusing an Alderman.

A Custom of *London* alledged, to commit to Prison for abusing an Alderman (*i. e.* calling him Fool and Ass) on the *Exchange*, held not good; but they may take Sureties for his good Behaviour. 3 *Cro.* 689.

See

See alfo 2 *Salk.* 425. That the Cuftom of
London to punifh by Information in the Court
of Aldermen, for Affault and contemptuous
Words of an Alderman is good ; *aliter* if to
disfranchife; and in *Clark's* Cafe, 1 *Ventr.* 327.
the Court faid they might fine for fpeaking
opprobrious Words of an Alderman, but the
Cuftom to disfranchife would not hold, notwithftanding the Statutes for confirming their
Cuftoms.

See more of Disfranchifements : Title, the
Chamberlain's Court, *pag.* 345.

The Statute for Payment of Tythes, &c.
in London.

BY an Act of Parliament made in the 22d
and 23d Year of King *Charles* II. it is ordained and enacted, ' That the Annual cer-
' tain Tythes of all and every Parifh and
' Parifhes within the City of *London,* and Li-
' berties thereof, whofe Churches have been
' demolifhed by the dreadful Fire : And
' which faid Parifhes, by Virtue of an Act,
22 *Car.* II. cap. 11. Intituled, *An Additional
Act for Rebuilding of the City of* London, *Uniting
of Parifhes,* &c. ' remain and continue fingle,
' as heretofore they were, or are by the faid
' Act annexed or united into one Parifh re-
' fpectively, fhall be as followeth :

	l.	*s.*
The Parifh of *Alhallows Lombard- ftreet*	110	00
St *Bartholomew Exchange*	100	00
St. *Bridger,* alias *Bridges*	120	00
St. *Bennet Finck*	100	00

G 4

St.

	l.	*s.*
St. *Michael Crooked-lane*	100	00
St. *Chriſtopher*	120	00
St. *Dionys Backchurch*	120	00
St. *Dunſtan's* in the *Eaſt*	200	00
St. *James Garlickhith*	100	00
St. *Michael Cornhill*	140	00
St. *Michael Baſſiſhaw*	132	11
St. *Margaret Lothbury*	100	00
St. *Mary Aldermanbury*	150	00
St. *Martin Ludgate*	160	00
St. *Peter Cornhill*	110	00
St. *Stephen Colman-ſtreet*	110	00
St. *Sepulchre*	200	00
St. *Alhallows Breadſtreet*, and St. *John Evangeliſt*	150	00
Alhallows the Great, and *Alhallows the Leſs*	200	00
St. *Alban Woodſtreet*, and St. *Olaves Silverſtreet*	170	00
St. *Anne* and *Agnes*, and St. *John Zachary*	140	00
St. *Auguſtin*, and St. *Faith*	172	00
St. *Andrew Wardrobe*, and St. *Anne-Black-Friers*	140	00
St. *Antholin*, and St. *John Baptiſt*	120	00
St. *Bennet Gracechurch*, and St. *Leonard Eaſt-cheap*	140	00
St. *Bennet Paul's-wharf*, and St. *Peter's Paul's-wharf*	100	00
Chriſtchurch, and St. *Leonard Forſter-lane*	200	00
St. *Edmond the King*, and St. *Nicholas Acons*	180	00
St. *George Botolph-lane*, and St. *Botolph Blllinſgate*	180	00
St. *Lawrence Jury*, and St. *Magdalen Milk-ſtreet*	120	00

St;

l. s.

	l.	*s.*
St. *Magnus,* and St. *Margaret New-Fiſhſtreet* - -	170	00
St. *Michael Royal,* and St. *Martin Vintry*	140	00
St. *Matthew Friday-ſtreet,* and St. *Peter Cheap* - -	150	00
St. *Margaret Pattons,* and St. *Gabriel Fenchurch* - -	120	00
St. *Mary at Hill,* and St. *Andrew Hubbard* - -	200	00
St. *Mary Woolnoth,* and St. *Mary Woolchurch* -	160	00
St. *Clement Eaſt-cheap,* and St. *Martin Orgars* - -	140	00
St. *Mary Abchurch,* and St. *Lawrence Poultney* - -	120	00
St. *Mary Aldermary,* and St. *Thomas Apoſtles* - -	150	00
St. *Mary le Bow,* and St. *Pancras Soperlane,* and *Alhallows Honeylane*	200	00
St. *Mildred Poultry* and St. *Mary Colechurch* - -	170	00
St. *Michael Woodſtreet,* and St. *Mary Staining* - -	100	00
St. *Mildred Breadſtreet,* and St. *Margaret Moſes* - -	130	00
St. *Michael Queenhith* and *Trinity*	160	00
St. *Magdalen Old-Fiſhſtreet,* and St. *Gregory* - -	120	00
St. *Mary Somerſet,* and St. *Mary Mounthaw* - -	110	00
St. *Nicholas Coleabby,* and St. *Nicholas*	130	00
St. *Olave Jury,* and St. *Martin Ironmongerlane* - -	120	00
St. *Stephen Walbrook,* and St. *Bennet Sheerhogg* - -	100	00
St. *Swithin,* and St. *Mary Bothaw*	140	00
St. *Vedaſt,* alias *Foſters,* and St. *Michael Quern* - -	160	00

'Theſe

' These respective Sums so to be respectively
' assessed, &c. shall be, and continue to be
' esteemed, deemed, and taken to all Intents
' and Purposes, to be the respective certain An-
' nual Maintenance (over and above Glebes
' and Perquisites, Gifts and Bequest to the re-
' spective Parson, Vicar, and Curate of any
' Parish for the time being, or to his or their
' respective Successors, or to other Persons for
' his or their Use) of the said respective Par-
' sons, Vicars, and Curates, who shall be
' legally Instituted, Inducted and Admitted
' into the respective Parishes aforesaid.

In which Act there is a Provision in these
Words :
' That where any of the Parishes within the
' said City, have since the late Fire, by Death,
' or otherwise become Vacant, the surviving
' or remaining Incumbent of the other Parish
' thereto united, or therewith consolidated,
' shall have and enjoy, and have like Remedy
' to recover the Tythes hereby settled to be
' paid, as if he had been actually presented,
' admitted, instituted, and inducted into both
' the said Parishes, since the Union and Con-
' solidation thereof.
' That the Aldermen of such respective
' Ward or Wards within the said City, wherein
' any of the said Parishes lie, and his or their
' Deputy or Deputies, and the Common
' Council-Men of such respective Parish
' wherein the Maintenance aforesaid is re-
' spectively to be assessed, to be nominated by
' such respective Aldermen, Deputy, Common
' Council-Men, and Church-Wardens, or any
' five of them, whereof the Alderman or his
' Deputy to be one, shall at some convenient
' and seasonable time, before the 20th Day of
May,

' *May,* 1671. affemble, *&c.* and they, or the
' major part of them fo affembled, fhall pro-
' portionably affefs upon all Houfes, Shops,
' Warehoufes and Cellars, Wharfs, Keys,
' Cranes, Warehoufes, and Tofts of Ground
' remaining unbuilt, and all other He-
' reditaments whatfoever (except Parfonage
' and Vicarage Houfes) the whole refpective
' Sum by this Act appointed, or fo much of
' it as is more than what each Impropriator
' is by this Act enjoined refpectively to allow,
' in the moft equal way that the faid Affeffors,
' according to the beft of their Judgments, can
' make it; which faid Affeffment fhall be
' made and finifhed' before the 24th of *July*
' then next.

' That if any Variance or Doubt happen
' to arife about any Sum fo affeffed as afore-
' faid, or that any Parifhioner or Parifhioners,
' or Owner or Owners of any Houfe, Shop,
' Warehoufe or Cellar, Wharf, Key, Crane,
' Water-houfe, or other Hereditament within
' any of the faid Parifhes, fhall find himfelf
' or themfelves aggrieved by the affeffing of
' any Sum or Sums of Money in manner and
' form aforefaid, that then upon complaint by
' the Party or Parties aggrieved to the Lord
' Maior and Court of Aldermen of the faid
' City, within fourteen Days after Notice
' given to the Party or Parties affeffed of fuch
' Affeffments made, the faid Lord Maior and
' Court of Aldermen, fummoning as well the
' Party or Parties aggrieved, and the Alder-
' men and fuch others as made the faid Affeff-
' ment, fhall hear and determine the fame in
' a fummary Way, and the Judgment by them
' given fhall be Final, and without Appeal.

' That

' That any Affeffment or Rate to be made
' by Virtue of this Act, fhall, or may in all,
' or any the Parifhes aforefaid, in like manner
' be received or altered, or laid again within
' three Months after the 24th Day of *June*,
' 1674, according to the aforefaid Rules,
' and any fuch Affeffment or Rate fhall or
' may be again received or re-affeffed within
' three Months after the 24th Day of *June*,
' 1681. And that all and every fuch new
' Affeffement and Rate, fhall be liable to the
' like Appeals as aforefaid, and fhall be col-
' lected, levied, and paid as any other Affeff-
' ment or Rate mentioned in this Act, may or
' ought to be.

' That if any the Inhabitants in any refpe-
' ctive Parifh or Parifhes as aforefaid, fhall, or
' do refufe or neglect to pay to the refpective
' Incumbents aforefaid, of any of the faid re-
' fpective Parifhes, any Sum or Sums of Mo-
' ney to him refpectively payable, or appointed
' to be paid by this Act, or any part thereof,
' contrary to the true intent and meaning of
' this Act, being lawfully demanded at the
' Houfe or Houfes, Wharf, Key, Crane, Cel-
' lar, or other Premiffes whereout the fame is
' payable, that then it fhall and may be law-
' ful to and for the Lord Maior of the City of
' *London* for the time being, upon Oath to be
' made before him, of fuch refufal or neglect,
' to give and grant out Warrants for the Offi-
' cer or Perfon appointed to collect the fame,
' with the Affiftance of a Conftable in the Day
' time, to levy the fame Tythes or Sums of
' Money fo due, and in arrear and unpaid,
' by Diftrefs and Sale of the Goods of the
' Party or Parties fo refufing or neglecting to
' pay

' pay ; reftoring to the Owner or Owners,
' the Overplus of fuch Goods over and above
' the faid Arrears of the faid Monies fo due
' and unpaid ; and the reafonable Charges of
' making fuch Diftrefs; which he is to de-
' duct out of the Moneys raifed by fale of
' fuch Goods.

In purfuance of which Act, the Lord
Maior, upon complaint to him made by any
Minifter againft any Parifhioner, for refufing to
pay the Rate affeffed, will caufe fuch Parifhioner to be fummoned to appear before his
Lordfhip ; and if he refufe to appear, or to
pay the Money affeffed on his Houfe or Warehoufe, his Lordfhip will, upon Oath made of
the Demand thereof, grant his Warrant to
diftrain the Goods of fuch Offender : If the
Lord Maior and Aldermen neglect to execute,
the Lord Chancellor or Keeper, or two Barons
of the Exchequer may do it ; and where the
Parifhes became vacant fince the Fire, the fur-
viving Incumbents of Parifhes therewith con-
folidated, fhall have like remedy for Tythes,
as if actually prefented, &c. in both Parifhes
fince the Union.

⚘ Note, That before this Act of Parliament,
the Cafe of *London* for Tythes was argued upon
the Petition of one Mr. *Dun*, Parfon of *Grace-
Church*, exhibited unto the then Lord Maior of
London, againft *Burrell* and *Goff*, and afterwards
upon a fpecial Commiffion granted (Suit
made to the King by Sir *Francis Bacon* then
Lord Chancellor of *England)* to the Archbifhop of *Canterbury*, the faid Lord Chancellor
and divers others Noble and Learned Peers
and Judges. And thereupon (amongft other
things) upon the Point, of what was antiently
paid

paid by the Citizens of *London* for Tythes, and how the Payment grew: It is ſaid, that it appeared by the Records of *London*, That *Niger*, Biſhop of *London*, 13 *Hen*. III. made a Conſtiſtitution in confirmation of an antient Cuſtom

And how theſe Payments grew, Niger *Biſhop of* London*'s* Conſtitution 13 Hen. III.

formerly uſed time out of mind, that Proviſion ſhould be made for the Miniſters of *London* in this manner; that is to ſay, that he which payeth the Rent of twenty Shillings for his Houſe wherein he dwelt, ſhould offer every *Sunday*, and every Apoſtles day, whereof the Evening was faſted, one Half-penny: And he that paid but ten Shillings Rent yearly, ſhould offer but one Farthing; and all this amounted unto but, according to the Proportion of 2 *s*. 6 *d. per* Pound; for there were fifty two Sundays, and but eight Apoſtles days, the Vigils of which were faſted. And if it chanced that one of the Apoſtles days fell upon a *Sunday*, then there was but one Half-penny, or Farthing paid; ſo that ſometime it fell out to be

30 Edw. III.
1.
10 Edw. III.
3.

leſs by ſome little than 2 *s*. 6 *d. per* Pound: and it appeareth by our Book-caſes, in *Edward* the Third his Reign, that the Proviſion made for the Miniſters of *London*, was by Offerings and Obventions, howſoever the Particulars are not deſigned there, but muſt be underſtood according to the former Ordinance made by *Niger*, and the Payment of 2 *s*. 6 *d*. in the

Th Arundel Archbiſhop of Cant. 13 R. II.

Pound, continuing until 13 *Ric.* II. *Thomas Arundel*, Archbiſhop of *Canterbury*, made an Explanation of the Conſtitution made by *Niger*, and thruſt upon the Citizens of *London*, two and twenty other Saints Days than were meant by the Conſtitution made by *Niger*, whereby the Offerings now amounted unto the Sum of 3 *s*. 5 *d. per* Pound; and there being ſome Reluctation by the Citizens of *London*,

London, Pope *Innocent* in 5 *Hen.* IV. granted his *Bull*, whereby the former Explanation was confirmed; which Confirmation (notwithstanding the Difference between the Minifters and Citizens of *London* about thofe two and twenty Saints Days which were added unto their Number) Pope *Nicholas*, alfo by his Bull, in 31 *Hen.* VI. confirmed: Againft which, the Citizens of *London* did contend with fo high a Hand, that they caufed a Record to be made, whereby it might appear in future Ages, that the Order of Explanation made by the Archbifhop of *Canterbury*, was done without calling the Citizens of *London* unto it, or any confent given by them. And it was branded by the Name of an Order furreptitioufly and abruptitioufly gotten, and therefore more fit to have the Name of a Deftructory, than a Declatory Order: The which contending notwithftanding, as it feemeth, the Payment was moft ufually made according unto the Rate of 3s. 5d. in the Pound; for *Linwood*, who writ in the Time of King *Hen.* IV. in his Provincial Conftitutions, debating the Queftion, Whether the Merchants and Artificers of the City of *London* ought to pay any Tythes? Sheweth, that the Citizens of *London*, by an antient Ordinance obferved in the faid City, are bound every Lord's Day, and every principal Feaft Day, either of the Apoftles, or others whofe Vigils are feafted, to pay one Farthing for every ten Shillings Rent, that they paid for their Houfes wherein they dwelt; and in 36 *Hen.* VI. there was a Compofition made between the Citizens of *London* and the Minifters of *London*, that a Payment fhould be made by the Citizens, according unto the Rate of 3 s. 5 d. in the Pound; and if any

Houfe

Houſe were kept in the proper Hand of the Owner, or were demiſed without reſervation of any Rent ; then the Church-Wardens of the Pariſh, where the Houſes were, ſhould ſet down a Rate of the Houſes, and according to that Rate, Payment ſhould be made. After which Compoſition ſo made, there was an Act of Common Council made 14 *Edw.* IV. in *London,* for the Confirmation of the *Bull* granted by Pope *Nicholas*. But the Citizens of *London* finding that by the Common Laws of the Realm, no *Bull* of the Pope, nor Arbitary Compoſition, nor Act of Common Council, could bind them in ſuch things as concerned their Inheritance ; they ſtill wreſtled with the Clergy, and would not condeſcend unto the Payment of the ſaid eleven Pence by the Year, obtruded upon them by the Addition of the two and twenty Saints Days : whereupon there was a Submiſſion unto the Lord Chancellor, and divers others of the Privy Council, and they made an Order for the Payment of Tythes, according unto the Rate of 2 *s.* 9 *d.* in the Pound ; the which Order was firſt promulgated by a Proclamation made, and afterwards eſtabliſhed by an Act of Parliament made 17 *Hen.* VIII. *cap.* 21. In confirmation of which ſaid Order, there was a Decree made 37 *Hen.* VIII. with ſome further Additions ; the which ſaid Decree was confirmed by an Act of Parliament made 37 *Hen.* VIII. *cap.* 12. So as it appeareth by that which hath been ſaid, that the firſt Payment was only according unto the Rate of 2 *s.* 6 *d. per* Pound : afterward, the Payment was increaſed to the Rate of 3 *s.* 5 *d. per* Pound : And laſtly, there was an Abatement and Payment made only according to the Rate of 2 *s.* 9 *d.* in

Submiſſion to the Lord, Chancellor and Privy Council.

Which Decree by the Act, ought to have been enrolled in Chancery in ſix Months ; but ſearch hath been, and 'tis not found.

9 d. in the Pound. The firſt Payment grew
by Cuſtom, the ſecond by Conſtitutions, and
Bulls of the Pope ; the laſt by Decree in the
Chancery.

And as to the laſt Point, which was, Who *Who to be*
ſhall be Judge of the Payment of Tythes for *Judge.*
Houſes in *London*, and the Remedy for the
Recovery of them ? It was ſaid to be apparent out of the Words of the Decree, that the
Maior of the City of *London* is Judge, and
is to give order concerning them ; and Suit is
not to be made in the Eccleſiaſtical Court
for them ; and if it be, a Prohibition is to be
granted, inſomuch that the Party grieved re-
ſorteth unto another Judge than the Statute
hath appointed. But if the Maior do not
give Aid within two Months after Complaint
made, or do not give ſuch Aid as is fitting,
then Reſort is to be made unto the Lord
Chancellor of *England*, who hath three
Months given him for ending of the ſaid
Cauſe.

Note alſo, That one material part of the *What the Par-*
Argument was, Whether by the Common *ſon may by*
Law any thing can be demanded for the *Law demand for Houſes in*
Houſes in *London*? It is to be agreed, and *London ?*
clear, that nothing can be demanded. For *Fitz Herb.*
that which the Parſon ought to demand of *Nat. brev.*
Houſes is Tythes ; and it is improper, and *fol. 53.*
cannot be, that Tythes can be paid of Houſes. Firſt, In regard that Houſes do not increaſe and renew, but rather decreaſe for want
of Reparations, and Tythes are not to be
paid of any thing but ſuch things as do increaſe and renew ; as it appeareth by the Le-
vitical Law, and the Common Law of the
Land. *Secondly,* Houſes are matters of Inheritance, whereof a *Præcipe* lieth at the

H   Common

Common Law. And the Rent reſerved upon a Leaſe made of them, is likewiſe knit
unto the Inheritance and Parcel of it; ſo that
it ſhall go along unto him that hath the Inheritance, and therefore ſhall deſcend unto the
Heir: And it is a Rule in Law, that Tythes
are not to be paid of part of the Inheritance,
but they ought to be paid of ſuch things as
renew; upon which reaſon it is, that
Tythes, by the Common Law of the Land, are
not to be paid of Slate, Stone, and Coal
digged out of the Pit. *Thirdly,* Houſes being
built only for the Receiving, Habitation,
and Dwelling of Men, and for Conveniency
of Protection againſt the ſcorching Heats in
Summer, and tempeſtuous Storms in Winter,
without any Profit at all redounding unto the
Owner; and the Parſon being to have a Benefit otherwiſe, in the Payment of perſonal
Tythes ariſing through his Induſtry in the
Houſe, no Tythes can be demanded for
the Houſes themſelves, or for the Rent reſerved upon them. *Fourthly,* The Decree
made 38 *Hen.* VIII. which exempteth the
Houſes of Noblemen from the Payment of
any Rate-Tythes, ſheweth the Common
Law to be ſo, that Houſes of themſelves are
to be diſcharged of the Payment of Tythes;
and accordingly it hath been adjudged in divers Caſes happening at the Common Law,
that Tythes by the Courſe of the Common
Laws may not be demanded for Houſes, but
they are to be diſcharged. And as to the
Point, which was, Whether Cuſtom can e-
ſtabliſh a Right of Payment of any thing unto the Parſon for Houſes? It ſeem'd clear,
that it well might; for it may well be, that
before ſuch time as any Houſe was built on
the

34 Eliz.
Dawſon's
CaſeK.Bench.

the Ground where the Houfe is, there had
been a Sum of Money paid for the Profits
of the Ground, in the Name of a *Modus deci-
mandi* ; and tho' the Houfe was after built
on the Ground, yet the *Modus* continues.
And there being a Continuance of the *Modus* after the building of the Houfe, Time
has made it to be a Payment for the Houfe;
but this Payment is to be termed a *Modus de-
cimandi*, and cannot well be called a Tythe
paid for Houfes, becaufe, as is formerly faid,
Tythes may not be paid for Houfes : And
all this appears by Dr. *Grant's* Cafe in 11 *Co.
fol.* 16.

Note, That by the Cuftom of the Parifh
of *Alhallows* in *London*, the Parifhioners every
Year ufed to elect Churchwardens one of the
faid Parifh who had born the Office of Scavenger, Sidefman, or Conftable ; and that e-
very Year one that had been elected Churchwarden, is elected to continue a Year longer,
and to be the Upper-Churchwarden, and
another is chofen to him, who is called the
Under-Churchwarden : And fuch a Choice
was made in the faid Parifh, notwithftanding
which Election the Parfon nominated one C.
to be Churchwarden, and procured him to be
fworn in the Ecclefiaftical Court ; and this by
colour of the late Canons ; That the Parfon
fhould have the Election of one of the Church-
wardens; and this being againft the Cuftom,
a Prohibition was prayed, and it was granted : For it being a fpecial Cuftom, the Canons cannot alter it ; efpecially in *London,*
where the Parfon and Churchwardens are a
Corporation to purchafe Lands and demife
their Lands. *Cro. Jac.* 532. *Warner's* Cafe.

The Cuftom of Alhallows touching the Choice of Churchwar-dens.

In London *the Parfon and Church-wardens are a Corporation.*

Cuftom, that the Veftry chufe a Clerk. One was placed as Clerk of St. *Catherine*'s *Colemanftreet* by the Parfon, according to the Canon, That the Parfon of the Church fhould have the placing of the Clerk; but the Parifhioners difturbed him upon Pretence of a Cuftom to place a Clerk there by the Election of their Veftry; and upon that Surmife the Churchwardens and Parifhioners prayed a Prohibition, and it was granted; for it is a good Cuftom, and the Canon cannot take it away. *Cor. Jac.* 670.

Archbifhop never makes any Vifitation in London *Diocefs and City.* The Archbifhop never makes a Vifitation in *London* Diocefs, for there hath been for long time a Compofition between the Bifhop of *London* and the Archbifhop of *Canterbury,* That if any Suit be begun before the Archbifhop, it fhall be always permitted by the Bifhop of *London.* 2 *Cro.* 240.

Note, 'Tis faid to be a Cuftom in *London,* that where one is buried in another Parifh than where he dies, the Burial Duties fhall be paid in both Parifhes. *Hob.* 175. *Stiles* 166.

Yet fee 1 *Salk* 132, 134. No Fees are due for Chriftenings or Buryings, unlefs by Cuftom, and then only to him that does the Office.

Concerning building on old Foundations, and ſtopping of Lights in the City of London.

IT is warrantable by the Cuſtom of *Lon-don,* to rebuild any Houſe upon the old Foundation, where the ancient Houſe ſtood, in Height at pleaſure of the Party, al-though by rebuilding the Lights of his Neighbour be ſtopped up, unleſs there be ſome Writings to the contrary.

The Caſe was thus;

Reginald Hughs being ſeized in his Demeſne as of Fee, of an ancient Houſe in the Pariſh of St. *Olives,* in the Ward of *Queen Hithe,* *London,* in the South Part of which Houſe had been three ancient Lights (time out of Mind.) *Anthony Keem* having taken a Leaſe for 31 Years, from the Rector and Guardians of the Pariſh Church of St. *Michael* at *Queen-Hithe* by Indenture of a ruinous Houſe and Yard next adjoining unto the ſaid Houſe, with a Covenant to beſtow an hundred Marks at the leaſt, upon the repairing or new building thereof; doth within two Years pull down the ſaid Houſe, and build a new one in the Place; and likewiſe upon the Yard; whereby the three ancient Lights of *Hugh's* Houſe were ſtopp'd up. Whereupon *Hughs* brings his Action upon the Caſe againſt *Keem,* for ſtopping up the ſaid Lights; upon which *Keem* pleads a ſpecial Plea in Bar, ſhewing

Trin. Term.
7 Jac. Regis
Rot. 1490.

H 3   the

the Ruinoufnefs of the Houfe, and the Leafe
made by the Rector and Guardians, and the
Covenant comprifed within the Leafe ; and
alfo fhews a Cuftom in *London,* that if one
have an ancient Houfe, wherein there are
ancient Lights, and one other hath a Houfe
adjoining upon that Houfe ; he that hath
the adjoining Houfe may well enough enhance
his Houfe, or build a new Houfe upon his
Ground, and ftop up thofe ancient Lights,
unlefs there be fome Writing to the contrary:
And he doth aver *in facto,* that there was no
Writing to the contrary ; and that he according to the Cuftom, did take down the old
Houfe, and build a new one upon the fame
Foundation, and upon the Yard oppofite unto the faid Lights, whereby they were ftopped up; and hereupon the Plaintiff demurs.

The Queftions of this Cafe are,

Firft, *Whether it be lawful for a Man to build
a Houfe upon his own Ground, whereby the
Lights of an ancient Houfe are ftopped, there
being no Cuftom to enable him ?*

Secondly, *Whether the Cuftom of* London *will
enable a Man to build a new Houfe from the
Ground, where no Houfe formerly was, whereby he may ftop the ancient Lights of his Neighbour's Houfe.*

Thirdly, *Whether upon an ancient Foundation a
Houfe may lawfully be enhanfed, fo as it fhall
ftop up the Light of the Neighbour's Houfe adjoining.*

As

As to the *First*, it is clear by the Opinion *Quest.* 1. of Sir *Thomas Flemming*, Chief Juſtice of the King's Bench, Sir *Chriſtopher Yelverton*, Sir *David Williams*, and Sir *John Crook*, Juſtices of the King's Bench, that there being no Cuſtom, it is not lawful to erect a new Houſe upon a void Piece of Ground, whereby the old Lights of an ancient Houſe may be ſtopped up; for the Rule of Equity and Law ſaith, *Sic utere tuo, ut alienum non lædas*; and the Light which cometh in by the Windows, being an eſſential Part of the Houſe, by which he hath three great Commodities; that is to ſay, Air for his Health, Light for his Profit, Proſpect for his Pleaſure, may not be taken away no more than a Part of his Houſe may be pulled down, whereby to erect the next Houſe adjoining. And with this Reſolution agreeth the Caſe of *Eldred*, reported by Sir *Edward Cook* in his Eldred's *Caſe.* Ninth Report, *fol.* 58. where he ſheweth the ancient Form of the Action upon the Caſe to be *quod meſſuagium horrida tenebritate, obſcuritatum fuit*; but if there be Hindrance Vide Hobart's only of the Proſpect by the new erected *Reports,* 131. Houſe, and not of the Air, nor of the Light, then an Action of the Caſe will not lie, inſomuch that the Proſpect is only a matter of Delight, and not of Neceſſity.

As to the *Second*, It was reſolved by the *Queſt.* 2. Opinion of the aforeſaid Judges, That the Cuſtom of *London* will not enable a Man to erect a new Houſe upon a void Space of Ground, whereby the ancient Lights of an old Houſe are ſtopp'd up: For *Firſt*, The

Owner

Owner of the old Houſe having Poſſeſſion
of a lawful Eaſement and Profit, which hath
been belonging unto the Houſe by Preſcription, Time out of Mind, may not be pre-
ſcribed out of it by another thwarting
Cuſtom, which hath been alſo uſed Time out
of Mind; but the latter Cuſtom ſhall rather
be adjudged to be void ; and Preſcription
againſt a Preſcription will never be allow'd
by the Law. *Secondly,* It may well be that
before time of Memory, the Owner of the
ſaid void Piece of Ground granted unto the
Owner of the Houſe, to have his Windows
that Way without any ſtopping of them ; the
which being ·done, and continued accordingly, hath begotten a Preſcription, which
may not be defeated by the Allegation of
a general Cuſtom : And with this Reſolution
doth agree a Caſe adjudged, *Trin.* 29. *Eliz.*
Rot. 253. in the King's Bench ; whereupon
an Action upon the Caſe brought by *Thomas*
Bloond againſt *Thomas Moſley,* for erecting of a
Houſe in the County of the City of *York,*
whereby the ancient Lights of his Houſe
were ſtopped up: The Defendant did plead
a Cuſtom for the City of *York,* as there is
here for the City of *London,* and adjudged
that the Cuſtom was nought ; whereupon the
Plaintiff had his Judgment : But if the Houſes had been new erected Houſes, or otherwiſe Windows had been newly made Windows in that ancient Houſe, the Erection
of that new Houſe upon that void Space of
Ground would have been lawful, notwithſtanding that the Windows and Lights be
ſtopped up ; for it ſhall not lie in the Power
of the Owner of the ancient Houſe, by ſetting

out

out his new Windows, to prevent him that hath the void piece of Ground, from making the beſt Benefit of it.

As to the *Third Point*, It was conceived, *Queſt.* 3. that if the new Houſe be only erected upon the antient Foundation, without any Enlargement, either in Longitude or Latitude, howſoever, it be made ſo high, that it ſtoppeth up *Quare.* the Lights of the old Houſe, yet it is not ſubject unto any Action, becauſe the Law authorizeth a Man to build as high as he may upon an antient Foundation, and it is no reaſon to forecloſe a Man from making his Houſe convenient unto his Eſtate and Degree, by building up higher, when there is no other Impediment, but only ſome Windows which are built out over his Houſe : And agreeing to this, ſeemeth the old Book of 4 *Edw.* III. 150, to be, where an Aſſize of Nuſans was brought for erecting his Houſe ſo high, that the Light of the Plaintiff, in the next adjoining Houſe, was diſturbed by it ; but if the new builded Houſe exceeded the antient Foundation, whereby that Exceſs is the Cauſe of ſtopping up of Lights, then is he ſubject unto the Action of him whoſe Light is ſtopped up, as it may appear by 22 *Hen.* VI. 25. And in the Caſe at the Bar, Judgment was given for the Plaintiff, becauſe he had brought his Action for building of a new Houſe upon a void piece of Ground, by which his Windows were ſtopped up : And becauſe the Defendant in his Juſtification, did not ſet forth by way of pleading, that he did erect, this his new Building, upon the old Foundation only, as he ought, the Plea was ill ; and the Plaintiff had good cauſe to demur in Law.

Note,

Note, *Alſo the Defendant doth not by way of Allegation, ſet forth the Act of Parliament for confirming of their Cuſtoms ; and that Act is a private Act, of which the Court here is not to take Notice, unleſs the ſame be ſpecially alledged by the Party.*

A Man brings an Action for ſtopping up three antient Lights, *totaliter*.   The Defendant confeſſeth the ſtopping up two of the Lights, and part of the third, and ſhews the Cuſtom of *London* (as aforeſaid) and afterwards takes a Traverſe in this Manner, *abſque hoc*, that he ſtopped up the three Lights, *aliter vel alio modo.* And, *per Cur'* this Plea is not good, for the Traverſe goes only to the two Lights before-mentioned ; but as to the third in part, this is no anſwer at all ; he ſhould have pleaded not Guilty, as to the Reſidue, and not have taken a Traverſe.   1 *Bulſt.* 116. *Newel* and *Barnard.*

See alſo *the Caſe of* Arnot *and* Brown, *poſt Tit. Courts* Tenant *and* Goldwin, *6 Mod.* 314. *and ib.* 116. *and* Palmer *and* Fletcher 1 *Lev.* 122.

And Note, by the Cuſtom of London, *a Man may ſet Ladders, Polls, &c. upon the Lands of another, for building or repairing his Houſe, &c.* Vide ante.

For Preferving and Ordering the Streets of London *againft Annoyances, thefe things were ordered, and ought to be obferved,* viz.

THAT no Man fhall fweep the Dirt, *Dirt.* or Filth of the Street into the Channel of the City, in the time of any Rain, or at any other time, under pain of Six Shillings and Eight Pence.

That no Man fhall caft or lay in the Streets, Dogs, Cats, or other Carrion, or any noifome thing contagious of the Air. Nor no Inholder fhall lay out Dung out of his Houfe, ex- *Dung.* cept the Cart be ready to carry the fame away incontinently, under pain of Forty Shillings.

No Brewer fhall caft willfully Dregs, or *Ale Dregs.* Drofs of Ale or Beer into the Channel, under pain of two Shillings.

No Man fhall incumber the Streets with *Timber, or* Timber, Stones, Carts, or fuch like, under *Stones,* &c. pain of Forfeiture of the fame thing that fo incumbreth the Streets, and alfo twenty Shillings Fine if he remove it not at the warning of the Serjeant of the Market.

Every Builder of Houfes ought to come to *Builders.* the Maior, Aldermen and Chamberlain, for a Special Licenfe for Hourd by him to be made in the High Streets, and no Builder to incumber the Streets with any manner of thing, taken down for the preparing of his New Building, under pain of Forty Shillings, except he make a Hourd of Forty Shillings.

No,

Carts, &c.   No Carts that ſhall be ſhod with Spig-Nails, ſhall come upon the Streets of this City, under pain of Three Shillings and Four Pence.

No Carts uſing daily Carriage within this City, nor Car, ſhall have Wheels ſhod with Iron, but bare, under pain of Six Shillings.

No Man ſhall ſet any Carts in the Streets by Night time, under the pain of Twelve Pence, and recompence to ſuch Perſons as ſhall be hurt thereby.

No Man ſhall ride, or drive his Car, or Cart, a-trot in the Street, but patiently, under pain of Two Shillings.

Budgmen.   No *Budg-man* ſhall lead but two Horſes, and he ſhall not let them go unled, under pain of Two Shillings.

Shooting.   No Man ſhall ſhoot in the Street, for Wager, or otherwiſe, under like pain of Two Shillings.

Galloping.   No Man ſhall gallop his Horſe in the Street, for Wager or otherwiſe, under like pain of Two Shillings.

Bowling, &c.   No Man ſhall bowl, or caſt any Stone in the Street, for Wager, or Gain, or ſuch like, under pain of Two Shillings.

Digging.   No Man ſhall dig any Hole in the Street for any matter, except he ſtop it up again, under pain of Two Shillings, and recompence to any Perſon hurt thereby.

Goung-Fer-mour.   No Man may bury or cover any Dung, or Goung, within the Liberties of the City, under pain of Forty Shillings.

Goung-Fermour ſhall not carry any Ordure till after Nine of the Clock in the Night, under pain of Thirteen Shillings and Four Pence.

No

No Goung-Fermour fhall fpill any Ordure in the Street, under pain of Thirteen Shillings and Four Pence.

No Man fhall bait Bull, Bear, or Horfe in the open Street, under pain of Twenty Shillings. *Bull-baiting.*

No Man fhall have any Kine, Goats, Hogs, Pigs, Hens, Cocks, Capons, or Ducks in the open Street, under pain of Forfeiture of the fame. *Hogs, or Poultry.*

No Man fhall maintain any Biting Curs, or mad Dogs in the Streets, under pain of Two Shillings, and recompence unto every Party hurt therewith. *Dogs.*

No Man fhall burn any Straw, Rufhes, or other things, Linnen or Woollen, in the Streets by Night or by Day, under pain of Three Shillings Four Pence. *Burning Straw, &c.*

No Man fhall blow any Horn in the Night, within this City, or Whiftle, after the Hour of Nine of the Clock in the Night, under pain of Imprifonment. *Blowing Horns, or Whiftling.*

No Man fhall ufe to go with Vizards, or difguifed by Night, under like pain of Imprifonment. And *Vizards.*

That Night-walkers and Evefdroppers, indure like Punifhment. *Evefdroppers.*

No Hammer-man, as a Smith, a Pewterer, a Founder, and all Artificers making great Sound, fhall not work after the Hour of Nine in the Night, nor afore the Hour of Four in the Morning, under pain of Three Shillings and Four Pence. *Hammer-men.*

No Man fhall caft into the Ditches of this City, or the Sewers of this City, without the Walls, or into the Wells, Grates, or Gullers of this City, any manner of Carren, ftinking Flefh, rotten Fifh, or any Rubbifh, Dung, *Sewers.*

2   Sand,

Sand, Gravel, Weeds, Stones, or any other thing to stop the Course of the same, under pain of cleaning them at his own Cost and Charge, under pain of Imprisonment.

Widraughts. No Man shall make any Widraughts in any of the Town-Ditches, or the Town-Gullets, under the pain of Twenty Shillings.

Going Armed. No Man shall go in the Streets, by Night or by Day, with Bow bent, or Arrows under his Girdle, nor with Sword unscabberd; under pain of Imprisonment; or with Hand-Gun, having therewith Powder and Match, except it be in an usual May-game, or Sight.

Sudden Out-cry, &c. No Man shall after the Hour of Nine at the Night, keep any Rule whereby any such sudden Out-cry be made in the still of the Night, as making any Affray, or beating of his Wife, or Servant, or Singing, or Revelling in his House, to the Disturbance of his Neighbours, under pain of Three Shillings Four Pence.

Butchers driving Oxen. No Butcher, or his Servant, shall use to drive any Ox or Oxen a-trot in the Streets, but peaceably; and if an Ox happen to be let go, when he is prepared to slaughter, the Butcher shall forfeit Two Shillings, besides recompence if any Person be hurt thereby.

Scalding Hogs. No Butcher shall scald Hogs, but in the Common Scalding-House, upon pain of Six Shillings and Eight Pence.

Unwholesome Flesh. No Butcher shall sell any Measel Hog, or unwholsome Flesh, under pain of Ten Pounds.

No Butcher shall sell any old stale Victual; that is. to say, above the slaughter of three Days in the Winter, and two in the Summer, under pain of Ten Shillings.

3

No

No Victualler of this City, shall give any *Ill Language.* rude or unfitting Language, or make any Clamour upon any Man or Woman in the open Market, for cheapning of Victual, under pain Three Shillings and Four Pence.

No Butcher shall cast the Inward of Beasts *Beasts En-* into the Streets, Cleaves of Beasts Feet, Bones, *trails.* Horns of Sheep, or other such like, under pain of Two Shillings.

The Pudding Cart of the Shambles shall not *Pudding* go afore the Hour of Nine in the Night, or *Carts.* after the Hour of Five in the Morning, under pain of Six Shillings and Eight Pence.

No Man shall cast any Urine-Boles, or Or- *Urine Boles,* dure-Boles, into the Streets by Day or Night, *&c.* afore the Hour of Nine in the Night: And also he shall not cast it out, but bring it down, and lay it in the Channel, under the pain of Three Shillings and Four Pence. And if he do cast it upon any Person's Head, the Party to have a lawful recompence, if he have hurt thereby.

No Man shall hurt, cut or destroy any Pipes, *Conduit Pipes,* Sesperals, or Windvents pertaining to the Con- *&c.* duits, under pain of Imprisonment, and making Satisfaction, tho' he doth it out of the City, if he may be taken within the City.

No Man within this City may make any Quill, or break any Pipe of the Conduit coming thro' his House, or nigh his Ground, under pain of the Pillory, or take any Water privately unto his House.

That whosoever shall destroy or perish any Cocks of the Conduit, must have Imprisonment, and make Satisfaction.

Note,

Note, *That an Act of Common Council was
made in the Even of St.* Michael, *Anno Regis*
Henrici Octavi 21. *That no Person should lay
any Wares in the Street, or beyond the Edge of
their Stall, upon pain of Forfeiture, the first
Time, Six Shillings and Eight Pence ; the second
Time, Thirteen Shillings and Four Pence ; and
the third Time, the Ware so laid.*

Note, *In what manner the aforementioned Customs,
or Orders concerning the Streets are observed at this
time, I shall not determine : However, by a Statute* 22 & 23 Car. II. cap. 17. *it is Enacted,
That the sole Power of regulating, keeping clear,
Pitching and Paving the Streets of the City
of* London, *with the manner thereof, and of
making and cleansing Drains and Sewers,&c. shall
remain in the Maior, Commonalty and Citizens,
to be executed by such as the Maior, Aldermen,
and Commons in Common Council shall appoint,
or seven of them, being all Members of the said
Court.*

*Also Persons aggrieved by any Charge imposed by
Virtue of this Act, within five Days after demand thereof, may appeal to the Maior and
Court of Aldermen, whose Order therein shall be
final.*

And by Stat. 2 W. *and* M. Seff. 2. cap. 8. [*for
sweeping and cleansing the Streets within the Parishes in the Weekly Bills of Mortality in* Middlefex, Weftminfter, Southwark, *and* Kenfing-
ton, &c.] *It is Enacted, That the cleansing
the Streets, Lanes, and Passages within* London,
*and the Liberties thereof, shall be managed ac-
cording to the antient Usages of the City.*

Of

Of Carts and Carmen in London.

THE Carmen of *London* are an antient Fel- *Carmen, a* lowship, formerly incorporated with the *Fellowship.* Woodmongers, but afterwards Diffolved. They are now fubject to fuch Orders and Regulations, as are from time to time made by the Courts of Aldermen and Common Council.

And for the better ordering and difpofing of *Ordering* Carrs, Carts, &c. there was an Act of Common *them in the* Council, *Anno* 1665, Sir *John Lawrence* Maior, *Woodmongers,* reciting, That the Right of ordering and di f- *&c.* pofing of Carrs, Carts, *Caroons,* Carters, and Carmen, and all Perfons working any Carts or Carrs within the City of *London* and Liberties, is, and hath been in the Maior, Commonalty, and Citizens. And accordingly, the Government of the faid Carrs, Carts, &c. hath been from time to time, by feveral Acts of Common Council, difpofed and committed fometimes to the Prefident and Governors of *Chrift Hofpital ;* and at other times, to the Mafter, Wardens, and Fellowship of Woodmongers, *London ;* and in the Year 1658, to the then Prefident and Governors of the Poor of the faid City ; and lately, again to the Mafter and Wardens of the Fellowship of Woodmongers, by Virtue of an Act of Common Council, made 1661, in the Maioralty of Sir *Richard Brown* (an Woodmonger.) But thereupon divers Complaints were made of many Inconveniences and Grievances brought upon the Citizens and Inhabitants of *London* and the Liberties, as in raifing the Price, and in ufing Deceit in the Weight and Meafure of Coals, by means and pretence of the Pri-

I   vileges

vileges and Powers granted by the ſaid Act. Wherefore that Act is hereby repealed ; and 'tis Enacted,

Now in Chriſt-Hoſpital. That the Preſident and Governors of *Chriſt-Hoſpital*, ſhall for the Time to come, have the Rule, Overſight, and Government of the ſaid Carrs, Carts, &c. during the Pleaſure of the Court, and according to the Rules, Directions, and, Proviſions therein mentioned, *viz.*

Under certain Rules, &c. That no more than 420 Carts be allowed to work within the City and Liberties, and that 7 s. 4 d. *per Ann.* and no more, be received or *i. e. The Licence for a Cart,* &c. paid for a *Caroon*, and 20 s. and no more or greater Fine, upon any Admittance or Alienation of a *Caroon*.

Any Perſon preſuming to work any Carr, Cart, &c. not allowed, to forfeit for every time ſo offending, 40 s.

No Carr, Cart, &c. to be permitted to any Wharf, Wharfinger, or Woodmonger, or kept by them, but by Licenſe of *Chriſt-Hoſpital*, on Penalty of 40 s.

Such as have *Caroones*, not to let them out for hire, without the Approbation and Allowance of the Preſident and Governors of the ſaid *Hoſpital*.

None to be admitted to work any Carr, but ſuch as ſhall be found of civil Carriage, and able and meet for that Imployment, on Pain of 10 s. *per Diem.*

That the Rates and Prices of Carriages, may be moderated as well for the People, as the Carmen ; and hereafter from Year to Year, in the Month of *September*, ſet and appointed by the Court of Aldermen, and ſuch of the Commons and others, as they ſhall think fit

to

to call before them for their Information.
And the faid Prices to be printed and fet upon
the Pofts in publick Places. And if any Carman demand or take more, to forfeit for every
fuch Offence 10 *s.*

That it be lawful for the Marfhals of the
City, and their Men, (who are hereby appointed to affift the Prefident and Governors
of *Chrift-Hofpital*) to take and feize all fuper-
numerary Carrs not allowed, that fhall be
found working in the City. And according
to the *antient Cuftom,* impound them in the
new Store-Yard, at the Poftern belonging to
the City, there to remain till the refpective
Owner fhall conform himfelf to the Government of the faid Prefident and Governors.

That if the yearly Rent of 17 *s.* 4 *d.* a piece *Quere.*
be not paid to the faid Prefident and Governors, the Caroon, or Licenfe of fuch Perfon,
fo neglecting or refufing, fhall be forthwith
fufpended, and his Perfon difabled to work
any longer.

And the Prefident and Governors of the
faid *Hofpital,* are from time to time, to obferve, perform, and execute fuch Acts and Orders as fhall be further made by the Common
Council, or by the Lord Maior and Court of
Aldermen, for and concerning the Regulation
of Carrs, Carts, &c. in *London.* And alfo *Coals and*
touching the Price, Meafure, and Affize of *Fuel.*
Coal-Sacks, Coals, and other Fuel. And in
the fame Act, are contained divers Orders
concerning Sea-Coal, and the Woodmongers.

But for afcertaining the Prices to be taken by *Prices of*
Carmen, for the Carriage of Goods and *Carts,* &c.
Merchandizes from the Wharfs to the feveral *afcertained.*
Places of the City and Liberties, an Act of

Common Council was made *Anno* 1667, Sir *William Bolton* Maior, occaſioned by the daily Complaints of Merchants and Citizens, of the exceſſiveRates demanded and taken byCarmen abovewhat is reaſonable,and had been limited, having been ſo appointed and ſet by the Juſtices of the Peace. And whereas theRule, Government, and Overſight of the Carts and Carmen, and all Perſons working any Carrs and Carts within *London* and the Liberties, was by the aforeſaid Act of CommonCouncil, of 21 *Junij* 1665, ſettled in the Preſident and Gover-

Carts to be nors of *Chriſt Hoſpital.* Now the ſaid Preſident *numbered with* and Governors are *deſired* and directed by this *Figures.* Court, that they cauſe every Carr which ſhall be Licenſed to Work, to be numbered with Figures upon a Piece of Braſs to be fixed upon every Carr and Cart ; and the Carman's Name and ſuch Figures to be fairly regiſtered in a Book, to be kept in *Chriſts-Hoſpital,* there at any time to be ſeen ; to the End, that if any Carman ſhall not conform to the Rates afore-ſaid, or ſhall refuſe to carry Goods at ſuch Rates, the Merchant knowing what Figure is upon the Cart, may more readily find out the Worker thereof. And the ſaid Preſident or Governors, upon the Certificate or Teſtimony of the Party grieved, are hereby anthorized to ſuſpend ſuch Perſon from working ſuch Carr, until he ſhall make Reſtitution.

Preſident, &c. And the ſaid Preſident and Governors, are *to meet every* to meet every *Thurſday* in *Chriſt-Hoſpital,* at *Thurſday.* two in the Afternoon, to hear and determine of Complaints that ſhall be made by any Mer-chant or Citizen, againſt the Carmen.

And the ſaid Preſident and Governors are impowered and authorized to nominate and *Street-Men.* appoint *Street-Men,* ſuch as they ſhall think
ſic

fit, to beOverfeers of the faid Carmen, to fee and take care that Merchants, and other Citizens Goods, be well and faithfully delivered at the following Rates and Prices without any Exactions, Hindrance, or Difturbance, *viz.*

From any Wharf between the Tower and *Rates,* &c. *London* Bridge, to *Tower-ftreet, Gracechurch-ftreet, Fanchurch-ftreet, Billinfgate,* within *Cornhill,* and Places of like Diftance, up the Hill with 1800 Weight, and not exceeding 2000 Weight 2 *s.* 2 *d.* And 2 *d.* for every hundred above 2000 Weight. Provided the Carmen for this Rate, and all other Rates herein contained, help to load and unload their Carts.

From any Wharf aforefaid, to *Broadftreet, Lothbury, Old Jewry, Baffifhaw, Colman-ftreet, Ironmonger-lane, St. Lawrence Jury, Milk-ftreet, Aldermanbury,Cheapfide,Wood-ftreet, Friday-ftreet, Bread-ftreet,* and Places of like Diftance,for the like Weight as aforefaid, 2 *s. 6 d.*

And for Sea-Coal, the Load, 1 *s.* 4 *d.* every Load to be half a Chaldron. And for one hundred of Faggots, the like Rate.

From any theWharfs aforefaid,to *Smithfield-Bars, Holborn-Bars, Temple Bar,* or any of the Bars on the North Side of the City, and places of like Diftance up the Hill with 1800 Weight for every Load, 3 *s.* 4 *d.* And going beyond the faid Places, the Parties to agree with the Carmen.

From any of the Wharfs aforefaid, to *Tower-ftreet,Billinfgate-ftreet,*&c.with 1400Weight, and not exceeding 1800Weight, 1 *s.* 10 *d.* and fo proportionably of the reft.

This Order to be Printed, and Copies thereof faftened, and fet up on Pofts in all publick Places of the City.

I 3 *Of*

Of Hackney-Coaches and Chairs in London.

Hackney-
Coaches and
Chairs.

AND forasmuch as Hackney-Coaches do very much affect the Streets of the City of *London,* and by the Opinion of many ought to be under the Direction and Government of the said City in the same Manner as Carts and Carrs are: I shall insert part of the Act of Parliament of 5, 6. *W. M. cap.* 22. for licensing and regulating Hackney-Coaches, *&c.* which hath respect to the said City, *viz.*

By the sixth Paragraph of that Act 'tis provided, That no Hackney Coachman shall presume to take for his Hire in and about the Cities of *London* and *Westminster,* or within ten Miles thereof, above 10 *s.* for a Day, reckoning twelve Hours to the Day, and by the Hour not above 18 *d.* for the first Hour, and 12 *d.* for every Hour after; and that no Person shall pay from any of the Inns of Court, or thereabouts, to any Part of St. *James's,* or City of *Westminster* (except beyond *Tuttle-street*) above 12 *d.* and the same Prices from the same Places to the Inns of Court, or Places thereabouts; and from any of the said Inns of Court, or thereabouts, to the *Royal Exchange,* 12 *d.* And if to the Tower of *London,* or *Bishopsgate,* or *Aldgate,* or thereabouts, 1 *s.* 6 *d.* And so from the said Places to the said Inns of Court, and the like Rates from and to any Places at the like Distance with the Places beforementioned.

And

'And whereas by the faid Act 'tis alfo provided, That no Perfon fhall be obliged to
pay above 12 *d.* for the Ufe of a Hackney-
Coach for any Diftance (not particularly fet
down in the Act) fo as the fame do not
exceed one Mile and four Furlongs, and 1 *s. 6 d.*
for any Diftance (not therein fet down) a-
bove one Mile and four Furlongs, and not
exceeding two Miles. The Commiffioners
for putting the faid Act in Execution, in
Purfuance thereof, caufed to be admeafured,
and publifhed the feveral Diftances between
the moft noted Places within the Limits of
the weekly Bills, (not fet down in the faid
Act) according to which the faid Rates of
12 *d.* and 1 *s. 6 d.* ought to be paid and re-
gulated aforefaid, *viz.*

One Shilling Rates for Hackney Coaches, viz.

From *Weftminfter-Hall* to *Marlborough-ftreet,*
Albemarl-ftreet, Bolton-ftreet, Soho Square, Bloomf-
bury Square, Little Queen-ftreet Holborn. So
from *St. James's Gate* to *Queen Anne Square*
Weftminfter, or to the neareft Corner of *Red*
Lyon Square, or from *Golden Square* to *Red*
Lyon Square ; fo from *Haymarket Playhoufe* to
Red Lyon Square, Queen Anne Square Weft-
minfter, Thavies Inn, and *Bloomfbury Square.*
So from *Red Lyon Square* to *Guild-Hall ;* or
upper End of *Fetter-Lane Holbourn,* to *Ald-*
gate, or *Royal Exchange,* to *Hoxton Square,* or
Newgate, to the middle of *Greek-ftreet* near
Soho Square ; or the *King's-Head Tavern* in
Southwark, to the Sign of *Sir William Wal-*
worth ; or *Grays-Inn Gate,* to *Sadler's Wells ;* or
Tom's Coffee-Houfe in *Ruffel-Street Covent*
Garden, to *Newcaftle Houfe* by *Clerkenwell*
Church ; or *Temple Bar* to *Billingfgate,* or *Ald-*
gate to *Shadwell Church.*

One Shilling and Six Pence Rates for Hackney-Coaches, viz.

From *Drury Lane Playhouse* to *Queen-Square Westminster.* From *Westminster-Hall* to *St. Paul's Church,* or to *Queens Square* in *Red Lyon Fields;* from *New Exchange* in the *Strand* to the *Royal Exchange; Haymarket Play-house* to *Hatton Garden, Red Lyon Square* to *Westminster-Hall;* St. *James's* to *Marybone-Church; Royal Exchange* to *Bloomsbury Square,* or the *Watch-house* at *Mile-End;* the Outside of *Aldgate* to *Stepney Church; Bedford-street Covent Garden* to *Coleman-street; Bread-street* to *Upper Moore-Fields,* and thence to *Hoxton Square; Austin-Fryars Gate* in *Broad-street* to *Hart-street* by *Bloomsbury Market; St. Martins-Lane* in the *Strand* to *Gold-street* by *Wood-street;* the End of *Lombard street* next *Gracechurch-street* to *Somerset-House;* St. *Lawrence Church* by *Guild-hall* to *Brownlow street* in *Drury-Lane; Royal-Exchange* to *Newington Church* beyond *South-wark; Tom's Coffee-House* by *Covent-Garden* to the *Royal Exchange; Stocks-Market* to *Charing-Cross;* and from *Aldgate* to *Ratcliff Cross.* And so for other Places of like Distance.

Hackney-Chairs.

And whereas by the said Act 'tis also enacted, That no Person shall be obliged to pay to the Chairmen for a Hackney-Chair carried any Distance within the Limits aforesaid, more than two third Parts of the Rates allowed to Hackney-Coaches, viz. not exceeding 1 Mile and 4 Furlongs for 1 s. And if above 1 Mile and 4 Furlongs, and not exceeding 2 Miles, the Fare of 1 s. 6 d. for such Hackney-Coaches; the Fare for a Hackney-Chair is by the said Act directed to be 1 s.

for

for any Diſtance not exceeding 1 Mile and 4 Furlongs.

And the ſaid Commiſſioners, in Purſuance of the ſaid Act, cauſed to be admeaſured and publiſhed the ſeveral Diſtances and Rates allowable by the ſaid Act to Chairmen for their carrying to and from the moſt noted Places where ſuch Chairs are commonly uſed within the City of *London* and Limits aforeſaid *viz.* .

One Shilling Rates for Hackney Chairs, viz.

From *Weſtminſter Hall* to *Covent Garden*, or to *Exeter Exchange*; St. *James's Gate* thro' the *Park* to *Weſtminſter Hall*, or to *Somerſet Houſe*; *Haymarket Playhouſe* to *Eſſex-ſtreet, Bolton-ſtreet, Soho Square*, or to the Entrance of *Lincoln's-Inn-Fields*. So from *Somerſet Houſe* to the upper End of *Hatton Garden*, and from the neareſt Corner of *Golden Square* to *Drury Lane Playhouſe*, or *Bridges-ſtreet*.

One Shilling and Six Pence Rates for the ſaid Chairs, viz.

From *Weſtminſter Hall* to either *Marlborough-ſtreet, Soho Square, Bolton-ſtreet*, or *Temple Bar*. From St. *James's Gate* to *Queen Anne Square, Weſtminſter*; from *Golden Square* to *Red Lyon Square*, and from the *Haymarket Playhouſe* to either *Red Lyon Square, Queen's Square, Bloomſbury Square*, or *Gray's Inn*.

---

*For regulating of the publick Mar-
kets within this famous City, an
Act of Common Council was formerly made, Entituled, An Act
for the Settlement and well-order-
ing of several publick Markets within the City of London : Whereby it
was Enacted,*

'THAT for the better Order and Regu-
' lation to be had of the Market at
' *Leaden-Hall,* and the *Greenyards* there, with
' the other Market-Grounds thereunto be-
' lohging ; and of the Market at *Wool-*
' *Church,* and the Market of *Honey-Lane,* or
' *Milk-street,* as also the Market near *Newgate,*
' and all other common Markets already set-
' tled and appointed, or which hereafter
' shall be settled and appointed within the Ci-
' ty of *London:* Be it Enacted by the Right
' Honourable the Lord Maior, and the Al-
' dermen his Brethren, and the Commons in
' this Common Council assembled, and by
' the Authority of the same, That the
' Rules, Orders, and Directions hereafter
' prescribed, be duly observed by all Per-
' sons that are or may be concerned therein,

' And *First,* Whereas by former Acts of
' Common Council, the Sale of Beef hath
' been restrained and appointed to be only in
' *Leaden-Hall,* and the *Greenyards* there ; which
' if now observed, would be very inconveni-
                                    ent

' ent to the Inhabitants of this City, in re-
' gard the late Butchery of the *Stocks*, and
' St. *Nicholas Shambles*, (which heretofore fur-
' nifhed with Beef and other Flefh Victuals,
' thofe Parts of the City) are now removed
' and otherwife difpofed of : Be it Enacted
' by the Authority aforefaid, That all and e-
' very Butcher and Butchers, Poulterer and
' Poulterers (other than fuch as are hereafter
' excepted) Country Farmer, Victualler, La-
' der, or Kidder, who keepeth no Butch-
' ers or Poulterers Shop or Shops within the
' City of *London*, or Liberties thereof, or
' within two Miles Diftance of the Liberties
' of the fame City, may, from and after the
' Publication of this Act, take to farm, or
' hire Standings, Stalls, or Places in any the
' aforefaid refpective Markets ; and there
' fell, utter, and put to open Shew or Sale
' his or their Beef, Mutton, Veal, Lamb,
' Pork, and other Butchery or Poultry Wares
' or other Provifions upon four Days of
' the Week, in manner as is hereafter ex-
' preffed, *viz.* upon *Mondays*, *Wednefdays*,
' and *Fridays* weekly, between the Feaft of
' the *Annunciation*, and the Feaft of St. *Mi-*
' *chael*, from fix of the Clock in the Forenoon
' until eight of the Clock in the Evening of
' the fame Day; and between the Feaft of
' St. *Michael* and the *Annunciation*, from eight
' of the Clock before Noon, until five of the
' Clock in the Evening of the fame Day, and
' upon every *Saturday* in the Week all the
' Year long, from the aforefaid refpective
' Hours of fix and eight of the Clock before
' Noon, until eight of the Clock in the Even-
' ing of the fame Day, for fo long Time
only

'only as he or they ſhall furniſh the ſaid
'Stalls, Standings and Places with whol-
'ſome Fleſh and other Proviſions in his or
'their own Right, and not as Servant or
'Servants, or otherwiſe in behalf of any o-
'thers ; any thing in any former Act of Com-
'mon Council contained to the contrary
'thereof in any wiſe notwithſtanding.

  'Provided always, That no Butcher or
'Poulterer whatſoever, who keepeth no Shop
'or Shops within the City of *London*, or Li-
'berties thereof, or within two Miles Di-
'ſtance of the ſame City, ſhall in the ſaid
'reſpective Markets, ſell, utter, or put to o-
'pen Shew or Sale, his or their Butchery or
'Poultry Wares upon *Mondays* and *Fridays*
'weekly, upon Pain, that every ſuch Butcher,
'or Poulterer ſhall for every time he or they
'ſhall ſell, utter, or put to open Shew or
'Sale in the ſaid Markets, his or their
'Butchery or Poultry Wares, upon *Monday*,
'or *Friday* in any Week, forfeit the Sum of
'ten Shillings.

  'And to the end the reſpective Hours a-
'foreſaid may the better be obſerved in the
'ſaid Markets, It is further enacted by the
'Authority aforeſaid, That a Market Bell in
'all the ſeveral Markets within the City of
'*London*, ſhall ring twice every Day, (that is
'to ſay) the firſt Ringing from the twenty
'fifth of *March*, yearly, until the twenty
'ninth Day of *September*, at ſeven of the
'Clock before Noon, except upon *Monday*,
'and then the firſt Ringing ſhall not begin till
'eight of the Clock in the Forenoon ; and
'from the twenty-ninth Day of *September*,
'yearly, until the twenty-fifth Day of *March*,
     'at

' at eight of the Clock before Noon, and not
' before, except upon *Monday*, and then the
' firſt Ringing ſhall not begin till nine of the
' Clock before Noon, and that the ſecond
' Ringing of the Market Bell for raiſing of
' the ſaid Markets ſhall begin to ring from
' and after the twenty fifth of *March*, yearly,
' until the twenty ninth Day of *September* (ex-
' cept on *Saturdays*) half an Hour after four
' in the Afternoon, and to continue ringing
' till five of the Clock ; and from and after
' the twenty ninth Day of *September*, until
' the twenty fifth Day of *March* yearly (ex-
' cept on *Saturdays*) to begin to ring half an
' Hour after three of the Clock, and to con-
' tinue ringing until four of the Clock in the
' Afternoon ; and that the ſecond ringing of
' the Market Bell upon *Saturday* weekly
' throughout the Year, ſhall begin half an
' Hour after ſeven of the Clock, and to con-
' tinue ringing until eight of the Clock in the
' Evening of the ſame Day. And if any
' Butcher or Butchers, Poulterer or Poulter-
' ers, Victualler, or Country Farmer, Lader,
' Kidder, or other Perſon whatſoever, ſhall
' ſell, or put to open Sale any manner of
' Butchery or Poultry Wares, or other Provi-
' ſions in the ſaid Markets, before ringing
' of the Market Bell at the ſaid ſeveral
' Hours and Times in the Morning reſpec-
' tively ; ſuch Offender or Offenders ſhall be
' proceeded againſt as Foreſtallers of the
' Market, as by the Law in this Caſe is di-
' rected and appointed. And that no Butch-
' er, Poulterer, Victualler, Country Far-
' mer, Lader, Kidder or other Perſon
' whatſoever, ſhall ſell or put to open Sale
' any Butchery or Poultry Wares, or other

Provi-

' Proviſions after the End of Ringing the Mar-
' ket Bell at the ſaid ſeveral Hours in the Af-
' ternoon reſpectively, but ſhall then depart
' from the ſaid Markets, upon pain that every
' Perſon ſelling Butchery or Poultry Wares,
' or other Proviſions, after the ſaid reſpective
' Hours in the aforeſaid Markets, ſhall forfeit
' the Sum of Ten Shillings for every ſuch Of-
' fence. And .if any Butcher, Poulterer,
' Country Farmer, Lader, Kidder, or other
' Perſon whatſoever, ſell, utter, or put to
' open Sale in the ſaid Markets, any manner
' of Fleſh-Meat upon any other Day or Days,
' then is before hereby limited and expreſſed,
' ſuch Butcher, Poulterer, Country Farmer,
' Lader, Kidder, or other Perſon, ſhall for
' every ſuch Offence, forfeit the Sum of.
' Twenty Shillings.

'	Provided always, That no Butcher,
' Poulterer, Country Farmer, Lader, Kidder,
' or other Perſon whatſoever, ſhall, upon the
' *Saturday* in any Week, bring into any of the
' ſaid Markets, any manner of Fleſh-Meat,
' after Six of the Clock in the Afternoon, be-
' tween the twenty fifth of *March*, and the
' twenty ninth of *September*, yearly ; nor after
' Four of the Clock in the Afternoon, between
' the twenty ninth of *September*, and the twenty
' fifth of *March*, upon pain of forfeiting the
' Sum of ten Shillings for every time any ſuch
' Perſon ſhall bring into any of the ſaid Mar-
' kets, any manner of Fleſh-Meats, after the
' ſaid reſpective Hours.

'	And further be it Enacted, by the Autho-
' rity aforeſaid, That no Stall, Standing, or
' Place within any of the ſaid Markets, ſhall
' from and after the Publication of this Act,
' be letten or alotted to any Butcher or
'	Poul-

' Poulterer, who doth, or shall keep any
' Butchers or Poulterers Shop within the City
' of *London*, or Liberties thereof, or within
' two Miles Distance of the Liberties of the
' said City, for so long time as he or they
' shall keep any Butchers or Poulterers Shop
' within the Limits aforesaid.

' And further, That no Butcher, Poulterer,
' or other Person whatsoever, shall have and
' enjoy more than two Stalls, Standings, or
' Places within any one of the Markets afore-
' mentioned, at one time.

' Provided always, That the Country Peo-
' ple and others resorting to the said Markets,
' being not Butchers, nor Poulterers, nor sel-
' ling any manner of Flesh-meat, or Poultry,
' may stand or sit, and vend their Herbs,
' Fruit, Eggs, Butter, and other such like
' Provisions and Commodities in the Markets,
' upon every working Day in the Week, be-
' tween the Feast of the *Annunciation*, and the
' Feast of St. *Michael* the Arch-Angel, from
' Seven of the Clock in the Morning, until
' Five of the Clock in the Evening of the same
' Day : And upon every working Day be-
' tween the Feast of St. *Michael* and the *An-*
' *nunciation*, from Six of the Clock in the
' Morning, until Four of the Clock in the
' Evening of the same Day, so as the same
' Persons that bring them first to Market, do
' continue the Selling thereof, and do observe
' the Ringing of the Market Bell for keeping
' the said Hours accordingly.

' And it is also further Enacted, (in regard
' that the Market is most principally intended
' for the Benefit of House-Keepers, who buy
' for their own Use and Behoof) that the Re-
' tailers

'tailers and Traders of this City, who buy to
'ſell again, ſhall not enter into any of the a-
'foreſaid Markets to make their Proviſions,
'and buy of any of the Market People there,
'to carry the ſame to their ſeveral Houſes and
'Shops, until the Afternoon of every Day,
'to the End that Houſe-Keepers may provide
'themſelves in the Morning of every Day at
'the firſt Hand, and pay moderate Rates for
'their Proviſions ; upon Pain that every ſuch
'Retailer, or Retailers, or Traders ſhall for
'every time offending herein forfeit Forty
'Shillings.

   'And foraſmuch as all dead Fleſh-Meat,
'and other Victuals, and Proviſions of all
'Sorts of Fruits, Herbs, Fiſh and the like,
'ought to be ſold in open and common
'Markets, allowed and appointed, and not
'under private Stalls, or at Tavern Doors, or
'in any Street or Common Paſſages, or in
'any private Places, or carried up and down,
'and ſold by way of Hawking; by means
'whereof, much unwholſome Proviſions, dan-
'gerous to the Health and Bodies of his Ma-
'jeſty's Subjects may be uttered and ſold :
'Be it Enacted by the Authority aforeſaid,
'That no Butcher, Poulterer, Country Far-
'mer, Lader, Kidder, Victualler, Gardner,
'Fruiterer, Fiſh Seller, or other Perſon or Per-
'ſons whatſoever, ſhall, from and after the
'Publication of this Act, Sell, Utter, or put
'to ſhew or Sale, by way of Hawking, or as
'a Hawker, or in any otherwiſe, any Beef,
'Mutton, Lamb, Veal, Pork, Poultry, Butter,
'Cheeſe, Fiſh, Fruit, Herbs, or other Victuals
'or Proviſion whatſoever, in any Private
'Houſe, Lane, Alley, Inn, Warehouſe, Street-
'ſtall, or Common Paſſage, or other Place or
                                 • Places

'   Places whatfoever, within the City of *London*,
'   or Liberties thereof, but only in his or their
'   own Shop, or Shops, or in the publick Mar-
'   ket-place or Places, and in Market time only,
'   according as is before appointed, upon Pain
'   that every fuch Perfon fo carrying, or offer-
'   ing to put to Sale, by way of Hawking, or
'   in any otherwife, any Flefh-meat, Poultry,
'   or other Victuals whatfoever, as aforefaid,
'   in any Private Houfe, Lane, Alley, Inn,
'   Warehoufe, Street-ftall, or Common Paffage,
'   or other Places whatfoever, being not his
'   or their open Shop, or Shops, or the Com-
'   mon Market-Place, fhall forfeit the fame
'   Goods fo offered to Sale, without any man-
'   ner of Favour, according to the antient
'   Cuftom of the City of *London*, ufed and ap-
'   proved; and the fame fo forfeited, fhall be
'   difpofed of to fuch Prifons within this City
'   of *London*, as the Lord Maior for the time
'   being, fhall direct and appoint.

'   And to the intent that Foreftalling, Re-
'   grating, and Ingroffing of Victuals and other
'   Commodities, may be the better prevented,
'   and the Laws made againft the fame, more
'   effectually obferved. It is Declared and
'   Enacted, by the Authority aforefaid, That
'   no Perfon or Perfons, from and after the
'   Publication of this Act, fhall buy, or caufe
'   to be bought, any Victuals, or other things
'   whatfoever, within the faid City of *London*
'   or Liberties thereof, coming to any the
'   Common Markets of this City, or make
'   any Bargain, Contract, or Promife for the
'   having and buying of the fame, or any part
'   thereof, fo coming as aforefaid, before the
'   fame fhall be brought into one of the faid
'   Markets ready to be there fold : And alfo,

K   ' That

' That no Perſon or Perſons, that ſhall by any
' Means Regrate, Obtain, or Get into his or
' their Hands, or Poſſeſſion, in any the ſaid
' Markets, any Victuals, or other things
' whatſoever, that ſhall be thither brought to
' be ſold, ſhall from henceforth ſell the ſame
' again in their Shop, or Shops, or any of the
' Markets or other Places within this City
' and Liberties thereof, or ſhall ingroſs or get
' into his or their Hands, by buying, con-
' tracting, or otherwiſe, any of the things a-
' foreſaid, in the ſaid Markets, with intent to
' ſell the ſame again, in the ſame, or any other
' Markets or Places within this City, and Li-
' berties thereof, upon Pain that every ſuch
' Foreſtaller, Regrator, and Ingroſſer, ſhall
' for every ſuch Offence, forfeit Forty Shil-
' lings.

' And whereas, for accommodation of
' Market People, with Stalls, Boards, Shelter,
' and all other like things neceſſary for their
' ſtanding in any of the Market Places within
' this City of *London*, and cleanſing and keeping
' clean the ſame ; and otherwiſe for defraying
' the incident Charges of repairing and main-
' taining the ſame Market ; and to gratify
' and reward the Care and Attendance of
' ſuch Perſons as ſhall be imployed therein,
' there hath always been given and paid cer-
' tain reaſonable Rates for the ſaid Accom-
' modations and Charges : And to the intent
' that the ſaid Rates may be aſcertained and
' made publick to all Market People, where-
' by the Perſons that ſhall from henceforth by
' Order of the Committee for letting of the
' City Lands, with Approbation of this
' Court, be imployed therein as Collectors, or
' Receivers of the ſame Rates, may be pre-
' vented

' vented from demanding, or extorting more
' than is allowed, as is herein after expreſſed :
' Be it Enacted by the Authority aforeſaid,
' That all and every Perſon and Perſons, re-
' ſorting to any of the ſaid Markets, to ſell
' and vend their Commodities, ſhall from
' henceforth pay unto ſuch Perſon or Perſons,
' as from time to time ſhall be thereunto ap-
' pointed, as aforeſaid, to take and receive
' the Profits of all, or any of the ſaid Markets,
' to the Uſe of the Maior, Commonalty, and
' Citizens of the City of *London*, of, and from
' all Market People thereunto reſorting, for
' their Stalls, Standings and other Accommo-
' dations, in the ſeveral Market-places afore-
' ſaid, after the Rates following ; (that is to
' ſay) for every Stall or Standing of the
' Length of Eight Foot, and Breadth of Four
' Foot, uſed or employed for Sale of Fleſh-
' meat, or Fiſh, for every Day, Eight Pence,
' or Two Shillings and Six Pence *per* Week ;
' and for every ſuch Stall or Standing, uſed or
' employed for Sale of any other Commodi-
' ties, for every Day, Four Pence, or Eighteen
' Pence *per* Week ; and for every Stall or
' Standing of the Length of Six Foot, and
' Breadth of Four Foot, uſed or employed for
' the Sale of Fleſh-meat, or Fiſh, Six Pence
' for every Day, or Two Shillings *per* Week ;
' and for every ſuch Stall or Standing, uſed
' for other Proviſions or Commodities, for eve-
' ry Day, Three Pence, 'or Sixteen Pence *per*
' Week ; and for every Standing for Tanned
' Leather, Six Pence *per* Day ; and for every
' Raw Hide, an Half Penny ; and for every
' Horſe Load of any Proviſions or Commo-
' dities, not upon Stalls, Three Pence ; and

K 2   ' for

' for every Cart-load of fuch Commodities,
' Six Pence.

' Provided that all Gardners and Country
' People, and others reforting to the faid
' Markets, early in · the Morning to fell
' Herbs, Fruit, and other like Commodities,
' and there continue for no long Space, quit-
' ting the Markets at Eight or Nine of the
' Clock in the Morning, fhall pay for the
' larger Places or Standings, only Three Pence,
' for every time they refort thither; and for
' the leffer Places, or Standings only, Two
' Pence.

' And that the faid Collectors or Receivers
' fhall not demand or require of the Market-
' People more than according to the afore-
' faid Rates, without the free Confent and
' Agreement of the faid Market People, for
' fome extraordinary Conveniency or Accom-
' modation, unlefs in *Leaden-Hall* Market,
' where other and larger Rates have been an-
' tiently paid for Stalls or Standings therein,
' and that no Perfon or Perfons, inhabiting in
' or near to any the faid Market Places, or
' other Perfon or Perfons whatfoever, upon
' pretence of any Right whatfoever, other
' than the Receivers or Collectors of the faid
' Rates and Duties, fhall from henceforth
' provide any Stalls or other Accommoda-
' tions in any of the aforefaid Market Places ;
' or directly, or indirectly, take, require, or
' exact any Sum or Sums of Money, or other
' Reward of the Market People, for any
' Stalls. Standings, or Accommodation of
' their Place and Station in the faid Markets;
' upon pain that every Perfon offending herein,
' fhall forfeit and lofe for every time fo doing
' and offending, Twenty Shillings.

' And

' And for the better order and quiet of the
' Market People, and the reconciling all Dif-
' ferences that may arife therein, betwixt
' them and the Collectors or Receivers in the
' aforefaid Markets ; as alfo that the Rates
' and Duties may be the better collected and
' certainly paid into the Chamber of *London*
' without Fraud, and the faid Markets more
' effectually fupervifed ; for prevention of A-
' bufes and Diforders that may arife therein,
' be it Enacted, That the Committee for let-
' ting the City Lands for the time being, fhall
' and are hereby authorized from time to time,
' by and with the Approbation of this Court,
' to appoint fitting Perfons for Overfeers of
' the faid refpective Markets and Collectors,
' or Receivers of the Profits, or Duties arifing
' or growing out of the fame, and to treat
' and agree with the faid Perfons, and allow
' them for their Care and Pains, fuch Part or
' Portion of the faid Profits, as in their Dif-
' cretions fhall be found requifite : Provided
' the faid Allowance exceed not the Tenth
' Part of the whole clear Profits (all neceffary
' Charges being deducted) upon Condition
' that the faid Overfeers and Collectors or
' Receivers, that fhall from time to time be
' thereunto appointed by Order as aforefaid,
' do give fufficient Security to the Satisfaction
' of the faid Committee, for their Diligence
' and faithful Performance in their Office, and
' overfeeing the Orders and Provifions afore-
' faid obferved, and giving a juft and true
' Account of their Receipts and Payments of
' the Moneys every Week into the Chamber;
' and that the faid Committee do once in
' every Week meet together at the *Guild Hall*,
' and there audite the Accompts and Pay-

' ments

‘ ments of the said Overseers and Collectors
‘ or Receivers, for Prevention of any Abuses
‘ that by neglect thereof might arise or hap-
‘ pen ; and also endeavour upon any Com-
‘ plaints and Grievances of the Market Peo-
‘ ple, against the said Overseers and Col-
‘ lectors, or Receivers, or otherwise to com-
‘ pose and redress the same as soon as possibly
‘ they can ; that so all Disturbances to the
‘ Market People, and unnecessary Suits at
‘ Law may be avoided : And that the said
‘ Overseers and Receivers, or Collectors, shall
‘ frequently attend, and be in the said Mar-
‘ kets, during Market time, and diligently
‘ oversee the same ; to prevent with their
‘ best care, any Abuses or Disorders that may
‘ happen or be committed therein ; and also
‘ to take care that the Provisions and Penal-
‘ ties appointed by this Act against all Offen-
‘ ders, contrary to the same, be duly and con-
‘ stantly put in Execution : And if any of the
‘ said Overseers, and Collectors or Receivers
‘ shall be remiss, or corrupt herein, then they
‘ shall be forthwith displaced and disabled
‘ of any Office or Place touching the said
‘ Markets.

‘ And be it further Enacted, That in case
‘ the aforesaid Committee for letting the Ci-
‘ ty Lands shall at any time hereafter find it
‘ most fitting and advantagious for the benefit
‘ of the Chamber, to let the said Markets
‘ or any of them to Farm; that then the Com-
‘ mittee aforesaid, for the time being, shall
‘ and may treat with any Person, or Persons
‘ for letting the same to Farm, upon the best
‘ terms they can, and report their proceedings
‘ unto this Court for their Approbation
‘ therein.

‘ All

' All which Pains, Forfeitures, and Penal-
' ties, Sum and Sums of Money, to be for-
' feited by Virtue of this Act, shall be recove-
' red by Action of Debt, Bill, or Plaint, to be
' commenced and profecuted in the Name of
' the Chamberlain of the City of *London* for the
' time being, in the Court holden before the
' Maior and Aldermen in the Chamber of the
' *Guild-hall* of the City of *London* ; and that
' the Chamberlain of the faid City for the
' time being, in all Suits to be profecuted by
' Virtue of this Act, againft any Offender or
' Offenders, contrary to the fame, shall reco-
' ver the ordinary Cofts of Suit to be expended
' in and about the Profecution thereof ; and if
' the Suit pafs for the Defendant, then the
' faid Defendant to recover his Cofts ; and the
' Chamberlain for the time being, shall not
' have Power to take lefs of any Offender
' than herein is limited to be forfeited for eve-
' ry Offence.
 ' And further, That one Moiety of all For-
' feitures to be recovered by Virtue hereof
' (the Cofts of the Suit for Recovery of the
' fame being deducted) shall after Recovery,
' and the Receipt thereof, at or before the
' Twenty-fifth Day of *March* yearly, be paid
' and delivered unto the Treafurer of *Chrift's-
' Hofpital*, to be employed towards the Relief
' of the Poor Children, to be brought up and
' maintained in that *Hofpital* ; and the other
' Moiety to him or them which shall firft give
' Information of the Offences, for which the
' Forfeitures shall grow, and profecute Suit
' in the Name of the Chamberlain of the faid
' City, for recovery of the fame, any thing in
' this Act to the contrary notwithftanding.

‘ And whereas the Serjeant and Yeoman of
‘ the Channel, and Yeoman of *Newgate Mar-*
‘ *ket,* and Foreign-taker, while the Common
‘ Markets were kept in *Leadenhall-street, Cheap-*
‘ *side,* and *Newgate-street,* did take care for
‘ sweeping and making clean the said Streets
‘ where the Market People resorted, and paid
‘ for carrying away the Soil thereof ; as also for
‘ furnishing the Market People with Boards
‘ and other Accommodations : In considera-
‘ tion whereof, they received some certain
‘ Allowance by consent of the Market People,
‘ for their care and pains therein.   Now for-
‘ asmuch as the said Markets are removed out
‘ of the Streets, and made Commodious, at
‘ the publick charge of the City, and that the
‘ Revenue thereof ought to be improved for
‘ the benefit of the Chamber : Be it Enacted,
‘ that the several Officers aforementioned,
‘ shall from henceforth be wholly discharged
‘ from the charge of cleansing and carrying
‘ away the Soil of the said Markets, and pro-
‘ viding Boards and other Accommodations
‘ for the Market People ; and likewise from
‘ any ways intermeddling with the Receipt of
‘ any Duties, Fees, or Profits, or taking any
‘ Money of any Persons resorting to, or stand-
‘ ing in any of the Common Markets afore-
‘ said, upon any pretence whatsoever ; but
‘ that instead thereof, the Serjeant and Yeo-
‘ man of the Channel for the time being, shall
‘ during their continuance in the said Places,
‘ each of them have, and receive out of the
‘ Chamber of *London* the Sum of Three Pounds
‘ Weekly ; and *Richard Robinson,* the present
‘ Foreign-taker and Yeoman of *Newgate Mar-*
‘ *ket,* the Sum of Three Pounds every Week,
‘ during the term of his Natural Life: All
              3   ‘ which

' which Sums refpectively, and none other,
' fhall be paid by the Chamberlain out of
' the Profits arifing by the Markets to the
' Perfons aforefaid, in full Satisfaction of all
' their Right, Title, Claim and Demand
' whatfoever, to any Part or Share of the
' Profits to be collected of the Market
' People.

Wagſtaffe.

See more hereafter touching the *Cuſtom* of
Market Overt, and concerning Blackwell
Hall *and* Billingſgate *Markets,*&c. *in the
Acts and Statutes relating to the City of*
London.

Con-

Concerning the Watches to be kept in the City of London. *Note, That an Act of Common Council was made in the Maioralty of Sir* John Robinſon, *Kt.* (*Anno* 1693.) for the better ordering of the Night Watches within the City of *London* and Liberties thereof ; *whichfolloweth in theſe Words.*

' WHereas by the antient, good and
' laudable Cuſtom of the City of *Lon-*
' *don,* all and every Perſon and Perſons which
' do dwell, occupy, or inhabit in any Houſe
' or Houſes within the ſame City or the Li-
' berties thereof, as well ſuch as are not Free
' of the ſaid City, as other the Freemen of
' the ſame, being Perſons able and fit to
' watch, or to find an able and fit Perſon to
' watch for him, her, or them, or in his,
' her, or their ſtead, ought by reaſon of their
' Habitation, Occupation, and Dwelling, to
' keep watch within the Ward wherein he,
' ſhe, or they do occupy and inhabit; for the
' Preſervation of the King's Peace, and for
' the arreſting and apprehending of all Night-
' walkers, Malefactors, and ſuſpected Per-
' ſons which ſhall be found paſſing, wandring,
' and miſ-behaving themſelves : And where-
' as every Conſtable of any Precinct is a Con-
' ſtable to all Intents and Purpoſes, not only
' in the Precinct and Ward where he dwelleth,
' but in all and every other Precinct, Ward,
' and Place within the ſaid City and the Li-
' berties thereof : And whereas there is now
' and of late Years hath been (by reaſon of
         the

' the great Concourfe of People from all Parts
' to the faid City) great Neceffity of a ftrong
' and fufficient Watch to be kept every Night
' within every Ward of the faid City, and
' the Liberties thereof; and it has been thought
' fit and provided by former Orders and Acts
' of Common Council, for the Safety and
' Peace of the faid City, that the Number of
' Men to watch every Night, in every Ward
' throughout the faid City and Liberties
' thereof, fhall be as hereafter particularly fol-
' loweth, *viz.*

Aldgate	34
Dukes-Place	10
Alderfgate	44
St. Martin's le Grand	12
Bifhopfgate	80
Broadftreet	30
Billinfgate	30
Bridge within	25
Baffifhaw	12
Breadftreet	26
Cornhill	16
Candlewick	24
Cordweiner	24
Cheap	25
Cripplegate within	40
Colmanftreet	34
Cripplegate without	90
Caftle Baynard	40
Dowgate	36
Farringdon within	50
Mugwel-ftreet	4
Black-Friers	14
Farringdon without	130
White-Friers	8
Bridewell Precinct	8

Bar-

Bartholomew Great	—	10
Bartholomew Less	— —	4
Lime-street	— — —	11
Langhorn	— —	34
Portsoken	— —	60
Queenhith	— —	49
Tower	— —	40
Vintry	— —	34
Walbrook	— —	29

' Yet neverthelefs the faid Watches are ve-
' ry weak and wanting, by reafon that many
' ill-affected Perfons, not willing to do any
' Duty for the publick Safety, or not Propor-
' tionable to the Number of the Inhabitants
' where they dwell, under Pretence that they
' ought not to watch with any other Con-
' ftable than the Conftable of the Precinct
' wherein they inhabit, whereas feveral Pre-
' cincts within the faid City and Liberties of
' late, by multiplicity of new Buildings, and
' Divifions of Houfes are grown far more
' populous than other Precincts, and many
' Precincts have not Inhabitants to make up
' a third, fourth, fifth, or fixth Part of the
' Number of Watchmen aforefaid, or compe-
' tent Number of Watchmen for fafeguard of
' the faid Ward; fo that without fome Way
' (other than the Inhabitants of every Precinct
' to watch with the Conftable of that Precinct
' or fome new Divifion of every Ward, for
' proportioning and appointing the Number
' therein to keep Watch) a fufficient Watch
' cannot be kept, whereof divers refractory
' Perfons taking Advantage, and pretending
' that they are not byLaw compellable there-
' unto, will not yield Obedience to the Go-
' vernment of the faid City therein, but refufe

' fufe to watch when they are required,
' whereby the Watches are generally much
' neglected, and the Conftables and other Of-
' ficers much troubled and difcouraged, and
' the faid City and Inhabitants therein much
' damaged and indangered thereby, and like-
' wife upon feveral Occafions and Diftur-
' bances of late have been put upon great
' and extraordinary Charge and Trouble, in
' ferving upon Military Guards of the Trained
' Bands and Auxiliary Forces of the faid
' City.

' Now the Right Honourable the Lord
' Maior, the Right Worfhipful the Alder-
' men his Brethren, and the Commons in
' this Common Council affembled, taking
' the Premifes into their confideration, and
' conceiving it very neceffary at all times,
' that their fhould be fufficient Watches kept
' within the faid City of *London* and Liberties
' thereof, for Remedy therein, and for the
' better ordering and eftablifhing of the
' Watches to be hereafter duly kept within
' the faid City and Liberties thereof; do E-
' nact and Ordain, and be it Enacted and
' Ordained by the faid Lord Maior, Alder-
' men, and Commons in this Common Coun-
' cil affembled, and by Authority of the fame,
' that one Conftable with the Beadle in every
' Ward, and the faid Number of Perfons
' refpectively fhall watch every Night in e-
' very of the Wards aforefaid refpectively,
' from nine of the Clock in the Evening, till
' feven of the Clock in the Morning, from
' *Michaelmas-day* till the firft of *April,* and
' from the firft of *April* till *Michaelmas-day*
' from ten of the Clock in the Evening, till
' five of the Clock in the Morning : And
that

‘ that the Alderman, Deputy, and Common
‘ Council-men of every of the said Wards
‘ respectively, or the major Part of them,
‘ shall forthwith take an exact Survey of all
‘ the Inhabitants and House-keepers within
‘ their respective Wards, who are able and
‘ fit to find Watchmen ; and shall nominate
‘ and appoint one Constable in their said
‘ Wards, with the Beadle of their respective
‘ Wards, and the full Number of Inhabitants
‘ within the said respective Wards, according
‘ to the Proportions before mentioned, to
‘ watch every Night within the respective
‘ Wards, beginning at one certain Place within
‘ the said respective Wards, and from thence
‘ to proceed and go forwards in an orderly
‘ Way, and appoint the next Night one o-
‘ ther Constable and the like full Number of
‘ Inhabitants next adjoyning unto those who
‘ watched the Night before, and so to pro-
‘ ceed forward through the Ward, one Con-
‘ stable and the full Number of Inhabitants
‘ to watch every Night, and then to begin
‘ again with those Iuhabitants who first
‘ watched, and proceed forwards every Night
‘ in turn as aforesaid, without respecting any
‘ one Precinct more than another, but that
‘ all the Inhabitants within the said Wards
‘ respectively do watch, or find Watchmen
‘ in their Turns, as aforesaid, who shall
‘ watch with the Constable appointed as
‘ aforesaid, though he be not of the same
‘ Precinct as the Inhabitants be : and that all
‘ the Constables within the respective Wards,
‘ shall in their Turns, one after another,
‘ watch with the said Inhabitants, and when
‘ they have watched all over by Turns as
‘ aforesaid, he that began shall begin again,

and

' and the reft follow in their Turns, and
' fo one after another, as often as it fhall
' come to their or any of their Turns : And
' that the faid Alderman, Deputy, or Com-
' mon Council-men of the refpective Wards
' aforefaid, or the major Part of them fhall
' likewife appoint a certain Place within the
' faid Ward, where the Conftable and all
' the Watchmen fhall every Night firft meet
' for that Night, and agree to what Places
' they fhall afterwards go to watch in the
' faid Ward in fuch manner and order, that the
' Conftables and Watches of every Ward may
' maintain a Correfpondence and Intelligence
' with each other, and be ready upon fome
' Sound or Sign, to be made or given, to
' come in, in an Inftant if there be need, upon
' any Diforder or other Occafion, to the
' Help and Affiftance of one another; and
' fhall alfo appoint the Number of Watch-
' men which fhall be, and continue toge-
' ther in every Place, and caufe the Name
' of the Conftable, and of every Inhabitant
' which is to watch with every feveral Con-
' ftable, and the Times and Places of their
' meeting and watching particularly every
' feveral Night to be printed and delivered
' to every Conftable within their Ward ref-
' pectively, and one or more Papers thereof
' fo printed to be fet upon Pofts or open
' Places, where every Conftable and fuch as
' are to watch with him refpectively dwell,
' that every Conftable and Watchman may
' know the Night, Time, and Places where
' they are to watch : And that the Conftable
' on the Day before his Watch-night, or the
' Beadle of that Ward, do warn every Man
' that is to watch with him accordingly, or
                                        ' leave

' leave Notice thereof in writing at the
' Houfe of every fuch Man: And that the
' Inhabitants of every Ward do take Notice
' hereof, any Pretence of Privilege, Ufage,
' or Cuftom to the contrary hereof in any
' wife notwithftanding.

   ' And be it alfo further Enacted, by the
' Authority aforefaid, That if any Conftable
' fhall make Default in executing his Office,
' or doing his Service in any of the Premiffes
' hereby appointed, or hereafter to be or-
' dered or appointed as aforefaid, without
' juft and reafonable Caufe to be allowed of
' as is hereafter mentioned, that then every
' fuch Conftable fhall forfeit and pay for e-
' very fuch Default five Pounds: And that
' if any perfon appointed and warned to
' watch, or to find an able and fit Perfon to
' watch in his or her ftead as aforefaid, that
' then every fuch Perfon fo refufing or making
' Default as aforefaid, and not having juft
' and reafonable Caufe for fuch his Default,
' as fhall be allowed of by the Lord Mayor
' of the faid City, or the Alderman of
' that Ward for the Time being, fhall for-
' feit and pay for every fuch Default Twenty
' Shillings.

   ' And it is hereby further Enacted, That
' the Aldermen, Deputy, and Common
' Council-men of every Ward, or the major
' Part of them, for the time being, fhall from
' Time to Time nominate and appoint two or
' more honeft able Men of the fame Ward,
' who fhall be called Supervifors, to take
' care and over-fee that the Watches ap-
' pointed in every Ward be from henceforth
' duly kept: And that the Conftables,
' Beadle and Watchmen, execute, do and
                                      ' per-

' perform their Duties and Services therein,
' or otherwife pay the Forfeitures and Pay-
' ments herein before ordained for their De-
' faults refpectively ; and that the fame Su-
' pervifors, or one of them, fhall take No-
' tice of fuch of the faid Inhabitants as ab-
' fent themfelves at any Time from watching
' as aforefaid, and likewife of fuch Con-
' ftables and Beadle as fhall at any Time
' make Default, be remifs or negligent in
' Performance of his or their Duties in the
' Premiffes, and fhall likewife from Time to
' Time prefent the Name of every fuch De-
' faulter to the Lord Maior of the faid City
' for the time being, or to the Alderman of
' the Ward where fuch Default fhall be made,
' that every fuch Defaulter may pay the For-
' feiture and Payment impofed upon him or
' her as aforefaid : And that the Beadle of
' every Ward, or fome trufty Perfon for him,
' fhall in the Prefence of the Conftable and
' one of the faid Overfeers, if they, or either
' of them can be prefent, call over the Names
' of all thofe which fhall be appointed to
' watch each Night refpectively in their
' Courfe as aforefaid, as well at the Hours
' appointed for their meeting in the Evening,
' as alfo at the Time appointed for the break-
' ing up of the Watch in the Morning; and
' that they the Conftable, or Beadle, or one
' of them, or fome other trufty Perfon in
' their or either of their behalf, in cafe the
' Supervifor fhall be abfent at any of the
' faid Times, fhall take a Note in writing
' of the Names and Sirnames of every of the
' Inhabitants then appointed to watch, as
' fhall be abfent from their Watch at any of
' the Hours herein before appointed Evening

L   or

' or Morning, and fhall deliver the faid
' Note the next Day to the Supervifors, or
' one of them: And that the Conftables, Su-
' pervifors, and Beadle of every the faid
' Wards, and every of them, fhall bring be-
' fore the Lord Maior of the faid City for
' the time being, or the Alderman of their
' Ward, every Conftable or other perfon
' making Default in any of the Premifes re-
' fpectively, if fuch Perfon making Default
' will readily and voluntarily go along with
' him ; and every fuch Defaulter fhall then
' prefently pay to the Lord Maior or Alder-
' man aforefaid, fuch Forfeitures and Pay-
' ments as are herein before limited and ap-
' pointed for them refpectively to pay as a-
' forefaid ; and that all Monies fo forfeited
' and paid as aforefaid, fhall be employed
' to and for the Relief of the Poor of the
' faid Ward, as the Lord Maior or Alder-
' man of the Ward where fuch Default fhall
' be made fhall think fit and appoint : But
' if fuch Defaulter fhall refufe to go with the
' faid Conftable, Supervifor, or Beadle, be-
' fore the faid Lord Maior or Alderman as
' aforefaid, or going, fhall refufe or de-
' lay to pay the faid Forfeitures, Penal-
' ties, or Sums of Money, refpectively as
' aforefaid, that then, and in either of the
' faid Cafes, fuch Defaulter fhall forfeit and
' pay treble the aforefaid Penalties or Sums
' of Money: All which Forfeitures hereby
' forfeited fhall refpectively be recovered by
' Action of Debt, Bill, or Information, in
' the Name of the Chamberlain of this City
' for the time being, in the Court holden be-
' fore the Lord Maior and Aldermen of the
' faid City, in the Chamber of the *Guildhall*
of

' of the fame City, to be prosecuted by the
' Beadle of the Ward wherein every of the
' faid Offences aforementioned fhall be com-
' mitted, or any other Perfon or Perfons there-
' unto appointed by the faid Lord Maior or
' the Alderman of fuch Ward : And after re-
' covery thereof, one Moiety of the fame
' after all Charges deducted, fhall be to the
' faid Beadle or other Profecutors, and the
' other Moiety to be imployed to the Relief
' of the Poor of the Ward wherein fuch Of-
' fence fhall be committed, as the Lord
' Maior or Alderman of the fame Ward
' fhall direct and appoint.   In all Suits to be
' brought by Virtue of this Act, the Cham-
' berlain fhall recover his ordinary Cofts and
' Charges to be expended for the Recovery
' of all fuch Forfeitures againft the Of-
' fenders.

' And laftly, be it enacted by the Autho-
' rity aforefaid, That the Beadles of the fe-
' veral Wards of this City, or any of them,
' fhall not hereafter take or have any Allow-
' ance of Watchmen, called Dead-pays, for
' or in Refpect of their Nightly watching, or
' for or in Confideration of any other Ser-
' vice whatfoever, but that the Inhabitants
' of every Ward fhall amongft themfelves
' raife fome convenient Sum of Money for a
' fit and competent Salary and Allowance to
' be made unto the faid Beadles for their faid
' Service : Or if the faid Inhabitants of all
' or any the faid Wards cannot agree upon
' raifing fuch Salary or Sum of Money, then
' the fame to be done by Authority of Com-
' mon Council, by fuch Way and Means, and
' Proportion to the Service and Extent of
' each Ward, as by the faid Common Coun-

' cil ſhall upon further Conſideration he found
' juſt and reaſonable.

The Cuſtom of London *concerning the Priſage of Wine.*

IT is to be obſerved, That King *Edw.* III. in the firſt Year of his Reign, doth by his Letters Patents bearing Date the ſame time, grant unto the Maior and Commonalty of *London,* that no Priſage ſhall be of any of the Wines of the Citizens of *London ;* but they ſhall be free, and diſcharged from the Payment of all manner of Priſage. Now one *George Hanger* being a Citizen and Freeman of *London,* and Reſident within the City, fraught four ſeveral Ships with Merchandize to be tranſported beyond the Seas; the which four Ships being disburthened of the ſaid Merchandize, and laden with Wines, two of the Ships came up the *Thames* of *London,* and before any unbulking of them, *George Hanger* maketh *Frances Hanger,* being his Wife, his Executrix, and dieth. Afterwards the other two Ships came up to *London,* Sir *Thomas Waller* being Chief Butler of the King, by virtue of Letters Patents made unto him, demandeth the Payment of Priſage of the ſaid *Frances Hanger* for the Wines in the ſaid four Ships, *viz.* to have of every of the Ships one Tun before the Maſt, and one other Tun behind the Maſt, that being the Cuſtom; ſhe denieth the Payment of it ; whereupon the ſaid Sir *Thomas Waller*

exhi-

exhibiteth his Information into the King's-Bench againſt the ſaid *Frances Hanger*; who pleadeth a ſpecial Plea in Bar, ſhewing the whole matter as aboveſaid, upon which Sir *Thomas* demurs.

Vide Eaſter-Term 9 Jac. I. Rot. 163. in Banco Regis.

The Queſtions of this Caſe were two.

1. Firſt, *Whether for the Wines which came up the* Thames *in the two Ships before the Death of* George Hanger, *any Priſage ought to be paid unto the King or not ?*

2. Secondly, *Whether any Priſage ought to be paid for the Wines which were upon the Sea in the Ships before the Death of the ſaid* George Hanger, *but came not up the* Thames *until after the Death of* George Hanger?

This Caſe was argued at ſeveral times, by learned Counſel on both ſides; and laſtly by the Judges of the King's Bench.

And Sir *Edward Cook,* Sir *Chriſtopher Yelverton,* Sir *David Williams,* and Sir *John Dodrige* were of Opinion, *That Judgment ought to be given for* Frances Hanger *againſt* Sir Thomas Waller; *and that all the Ships ought to be diſcharged of the Payment of Priſage, by vertue of the ſaid Charter made by* Edward III. *unto the Maior and Commonalty of* London: And that for the Reaſons following.

The Judges for the Defendant.

Firſt, In regard that theſe Wines in each of the four Ships aforeſaid, remained (notwithſtanding the Death of *George Hanger*) to be ſtill the Wines of *George Hanger;* for if *Frances Hanger* the Executrix were to bring an Action for the Recovery of them, ſhe

L 3　　　ſhould

ſhould bring an Action as for the Wines of
George Hanger, and if *Frances Hanger* ſhould be
waived or attainted of Felony or Treaſon,
thoſe Wines ſhould not be forfeited : So if a
Judgment in Debt or other Action ſhould be
had againſt *Frances Hanger* as Executrix of
George Hanger, theſe Wines ſhould be taken
in Execution as the Wines of *George Hanger;*
and therefore they are diſcharged of Priſage
within the Words, Intent and Meaning of
the before recited Charter made by King *Edward* III. which pointed rather at the Wines
than at the Perſon of *George Hanger.*

Privilege to the   *Secondly,* In regard that *Frances Hanger* be-
Repreſentative. ing the Executrix of *George Hanger*, is the repreſentative Perſon of *George Hanger*, as to
theſe Wines ; ſo that ſuch Privileges and Immunities as *George Hanger* was to enjoy if he
had been living, the ſame ſhall *Frances Hanger*
have Benefit of after his Death.   And therefore if *Frances Hanger* had been a Nun, yet
as Executrix and Repreſentative of the ſaid
George Hanger, ſhe ſhall ſue, and be ſued,
as concerning the perſonal Eſtate of the Teſtator, ſo far as *George Hanger* himſelf might
ſue or be ſued.

Thirdly, This Charter made by King *Edward* III. being a Charter only to diſcharge
the Citizens of *London* of the Payment of
Priſage, and not a Charter whereby the Priſage of the Citizens of *London* is granted
unto others, ſhall have a liberal Conſtruc-
tion, and not be ſtrained unto a ſpecial Intent as a Patent of Charge ſhall be : For it
is evident by divers Caſes in our Books, that
Frances Hanger being an Executrix, ſhall be
taken

taken to be within the Remedy of an Act of
Parliament, to difcharge herfelf of a Burthen
impofed upon her in refpect of *George Hanger*
her Teftator, notwithftanding there was never fo much as any mention made of her
as Executrix in the Act of Parliament.
And therefore *Frances Hanger* being an Executrix, fhall have an Attaint upon the Statute of 23 *Hen.* VIII. *chap.* 3. to difcharge
herfelf of a falfe Verdict againft *George* 3 *Eliz.* Dy.
Hanger; whereby his Goods are to be char- 200.
ged; and yet fhe is not named in the Act of
Parliament. So *Frances Hanger* being an Executrix, fhall have a Writ of Error upon the
Statute of 27 *Eliz. chap.* 8. in the Exchequer 26 *Eliz. the*
Chamber, to difcharge herfelf of an errone- *Lord* Mor-
ous Judgment given into the King's Bench dant's *Cafe.*
againft *George Hanger,* whereby his Goods are
fubject to an Execution. Likewife if *George
Hanger* be outlaw'd upon a Writ of *Cap. ad
fatisfaciend.* awarded upon a Judgment given
in Debt, or other perfonal Action againft
him, *Frances Hanger* as *Executrix* of *George
Hanger,* fhall take Advantage of a general
Pardon made by Act of *Parliament* in the
Life of *George Hanger,* and fhall be fuffer'd to
plead it, and to give Satisfaction of the
Judgment given againft *George Hanger,* whereby fhe may be enabled to take Benefit of the
Pardon; the which being fo, that *Frances
Hanger* is a Perfon capable to difcharge her
felf of a falfe Verdict, of an erroneous
Judgment, of an Outlawry pronounced a-
gainft *George Hanger* her Husband, where the
Statute by precife Words doth not relieve
her; *a fortiori* fhall *Frances Hanger* in the Cafe
at the Bar, be enabled to difcharge her felf

of

of the Priſage of theſe Wines, within the Charter of *Edward* III.

Fourthly, There being nothing done in the Caſe at the Bar, to prevent *George Hanger*, whereby his Wines ſhould be made incapable of the Diſcharge of the Payment of Priſage, but only the Death of *George Hanger* before the disburthening and unlading of his Ships; and this being only the Act of God, ſhall not turn to his Prejudice; it being a Maxim and Principle of the Common Laws of the Realm, that the Act of God ſhall never prejudice, in caſe where there is not any Laches in the Party.

Fifthly, It is to be obſerved, that this Charter, to be diſcharged of the Payment of Priſage granted by King *Edward* III. was granted unto the Maior and Commonalty of *London*, which is a Body that never dieth; and ſo however that *George Hanger*, unto whom (as unto a Member of that Body) the Privilege of that Charter is diſtributed, be dead; yet the Maior and Commonalty continuing the Privilege and Immunity of *George Hanger*, to have his Wines diſcharged of the Payment of Priſage will live.

Rot. 9. *Sixthly,* That becauſe this very Caſe had received formerly the Reſolution of three Barons in the Exchequer, upon an Information exhibited there by Sir *Thomas Waller*, that *Frances Hanger* ſhould be diſcharged of Priſage for the Wines in all the four Ships: Whereupon Sir *Thomas* diſcontinued his Information,

formation, and exhibited it *de novo* in the King's Bench, whereby he would take the Opinion of this Court likewise ; and there having been former Opinions conceived for the Difcharge of them, it is more agreeable with Reafon to have this Opinion confirmed than oppofed.

But Sir *Thomas Fleming,* Sir *John Crook,* and Sir *Robert Haughton,* upon the Reafons hereafter enfuing, were for Judgment to be given for Sir *Thomas Waller,* and that Prifage ought to be paid for all the Wines.

Firft, In regard the Charter extendeth only to difcharge fuch a Perfon as is a Citizen of *London* of the Payment of Prifage ; and *George Hanger* being dead, is no longer a Citizen.

Secondly, This Privilege is in refpect of the Perfon who is the Owner of the Wines, and not in refpect of the Wines themfelves; and there being a Remotion of the Perfon, there is a Remotion of the Exemption itfelf : And though a Tenant in ancient Demefne, by the Common Laws of this Realm, be difcharged of the Payment of Toll, yet if he die, his Executors fhall pay a Toll for the Goods of the Teftator : Infomuch, that it was only a perfonal Privilege which dieth together with the Perfon.

Thirdly, Prifage is a Flower of the Crown, and ought to have a ftrict Conftruction ; fo as none may take Benefit of it, but only fuch as are within the precife Words of the Charter ; and though the Wines in the Ship may be faid to be the Wines of *George Hanger* to

a fpe-

a ſpecial Intent; that is to ſay, for the Payment of his Debts, Legacies, &c. yet may
they not be ſaid to be the Goods of *George
Hanger* to every Intent; ſo that *Frances Hanger*
the Executrix may diſpoſe of them according to her Will and Pleaſure.

Fourthly, Priſage being a thing which is
not due until ſuch time as the Bulk be
broken; and the Duty accrued, the Charter
ſhall not extend to diſcharge the Wines in
the Hands of the Executrix of the Payment
of Priſage.

Note, *There were ſeveral Matters conſiderable
in the Caſe :* viz.

The Nature of **1.** The Nature of Priſage: It is a certain
Priſage.   Duty which the King and his Predeceſſors
by themſelves or Officers, by Cuſtom
time out of mind, hath uſed to take for
the Proviſion of his Houſhold, of all *Engliſh* Merchants, of all Wines whatſoever
which they bring from beyond the Seas
into the Coaſt of *England :* It is a Duty
certain, as to the Time when he ſhall take
it; and in reſpect of the Place where to be
taken, and in reſpect of the Quantity. As
to the Time, it is to be taken upon the
breaking of the Bulk of the Ship, and not
before. As to the Place, he ſhall take one
Tun behind the Maſt, and the other
Tun before the Maſt. And as to the certain Quantity, it is manifeſt by divers ancient Records: For if a Ship have ten
Tun in her, and under the Number of
twenty Tuns, then the King is to have
one Tun only; if the Ship containeth
twenty

twenty Tuns and more, then the one to be taken behind the Maſt, and the other before ; the King paying for the Portage 20 *s.*

Now Merchant Strangers by the Charter of *Lex Mercatoria,* 21 *Edw* I. are diſcharged of the Payment of Priſage ; in lieu whereof the Merchant Strangers grant to the King 2 *s.* of every Tun of Wine brought in by them, within 40 Days after it is brought into the Port ; the which 2 *s.* is called by the Name of Butlerage ; becauſe the Chief Butler, by reaſon of his Office, is to receive it ; but they who buy Wines beyond the Seas for their own ſpending, ſhall pay no Priſage.

2. Priſage ſhall not be ſaid to be due till ſuch time as the Bulk be broken ; for the Merchant ought to be ſecured of their ſafe Conduct, till ſuch time as they are come into Port where they unlade ; for they may be driven into Port by Pirates, or Violence of Tempeſt, their Cocket ſhewing their Courſe to be bent unto another Port.

3. The Priſage of Wines is a Flower of the Crown ; yet it is not ſuch an inſeparable Flower of the Crown, but that it may well enough be granted over ; for it is a matter of Profit and Benefit which may redound to the King.

The Merchants bringing Cuſtom to the King, and filling his Coffers, and ſupplying his Subjects with Neceſſaries, do increaſe the Honour of the Nation by Commerce,

Commerce, and the Strength of the Nation by Shipping, and it is reaſon that Charters made in their favour ſhould receive a benign Interpretation; and more eſpecially all Merchant Strangers had at this time a Charter of Diſcharge for the Payment of Priſage, but only that they were to pay 2 *s.* in the Tun; and i the *London* Merchants had not had a Charter of Diſcharge, the Merchant Strangers would have afforded their Wines cheaper.

4. As to what Perſons ſhall be diſcharged of the Payment of Priſage within the Words of this Charter, it will be manifeſted by ſhewing the Diſtinctions and Degrees of Citizens.

Five kinds of Citizens. There is mention made of five manner of Citizens, *viz.*

1. He that is a Citizen of *London* for bearing the Offices of the City, and to ſuch ſpecial Intents, becauſe he is a Freeman of the City; but if he is not a Citizen in Reſidence, but liveth elſewhere; ſuch a Citizen ſhall not be diſcharged of Priſage. *Vide* Trin. 4, 5, 6. *Rot.* 14.

2. Such as are Citizens it reſpect of their Freedom, and likewiſe in regard of Reſidence within the City, but do not keep a Family or Houſhold in the City, but are Inmates or Sojourners, ſuch Citizen is not capable of this Immunity; for ſuch a Citizen is not ſubject to Scot and Lot as he that is an Houſholder. *Vide* Hill 43 *Eliz. Rot.* 22.

3. The

3. The third Sort are fuch as do refide and keep a Family in the City, but are not Free-men of the City, fo as to be chofen into any Office; they are not capable of the Difcharge of Prifage.

4. Some are Citizens and Freemen, and do refide or keep Families in *London*, and are not continuing Citizens at the Time of the Bulk broken, and the Ship unladen; for they were disfranchifed before; thefe fhall not en-joy the Privileges, forafmuch as they were not continuing Citizens at the Time as the Prifage ought to be taken.

5. S   as are Citizens, Freemen, refident with Families, and continuing Citizens at the time as Prifage ought to be taken, thefe are fuch as are intended by this Charter; and fo a Woman is within the Intent of the Charter.

Laftly, He that would have Wines dif-charged of the Payment of Prifage, ought to have a Property in them, *fibi, folum, & femper*; and he ought to have *jus poffeffionis & jus pro-prietatis* : Therefore if a Citizen and a Fo-reigner be joint Merchants of Wines ; now the Wines of thefe joint Merchants fhall not be difcharged of Prifage, for that the Citizen hath not the fole Property in them ; *aliter*, of two Citizens, joint Merchants; becaufe they are the Wines of the Citizens, according to the exprefs Words of the Charter. If a Citi-zen and Freeman have Wines pledged to him by another Citizen and Freeman, thefe Wines upon their coming home, fhall not be dif-charged of the Payment of Prifage, for that
the

the Citizen hath only a ſpecial Property in them. If a Citizen do buy Wines with intent that a Foreigner upon their coming home ſhall have theſe Wines; now theſe Wines ſhall not be diſcharged of Priſage, and this Deceit ſhall avail him no more than if a Citizen buy Cloth in *London* for a Foreigner, he ſhall defeat the Cuſtom of Foreigners to avoid the Forfeiture of them.

Cuſtoms

Cuſtoms of *London* as to Foreigners.

☞ Note, *If a Freeman of* London *ſhall employ a Foreigner to work for him, at any manual Trade, within the ſaid City or Liberties thereof, he forfeits* 5 l. *for every Day he ſo employs him, and an Action of Debt lies againſt him for the ſame, purſuant to an Act of Common Council made in the Mairolty of Sir* William (*or Sir* John) Gerrard, Knt. i. e. An-no - - - - See the ſaid Act in this Treatiſe hereafter. Alſo if any Man that is not a Freeman of London, keep any Shop inward or outward, within the City or Liberty, for the Sale of any Goods or Wares by Retail, he forfeits* 5 l. *for every Day, and an Action of Debt lies againſt him for the ſame, in the Lord Maior's Court, in the Name of the Chamberlain of* London *for the time being, purſuant to an Act of Common Council made in the Mairolty of Sir* Leonard Halliday, Knt. Anno 1605. *which Act is as followeth.*

Note Sir Wil. Gerrard *was Maior in* 1555. *and* Sir John *in* 1601.

' **W**Here by the antient Charters, Cuſtoms, Franchiſes, and Liberties of
' the City of *London,* confirmed by ſundry
Acts

' Acts of Parliament, no Perfon not being free
' of the City of *London*, may or ought to fell
' or put to fale any Wares or Merchandizes
' within the faid City, or the Liberties of
' the fame by Retail, or keep any open or in-
' ward Shop, or other inward Place or Room
' for fhew, fale, or putting to fale, of any
' Wares or Merchandizing, or for ufe of any
' Art, Trade, or Occupation, Myftery, or
' Handicraft, within the fame. And where-
' as alfo *Edward*, fometime King of *England*,
' of famous Memory, the third of that Name,
' by his Charter made and granted to the
' faid City in the Fifteenth Year of his Reign,
' confirmed alfo by Parliament amongft other
' things granted, That if any Cuftoms in the
' faid City, before that Time obtained and
' ufed, where in any Part hard or defective, or
' any thing in the fame City newly arifing,
' where Remedy before that was not ordained,
' fhould need Amendment, The Maior and
' Alderman of the faid City, and their Suc-
' ceffor, with the Affent of the Commonalty
' of the fame City, might put and ordain
' thereunto fit Remedy as often as that fhould
' feem expedient unto them : So that fuch
' Ordinance fhould be profitable to the King,
' for the Profit of the Citizen, and other his
' People repairing to the faid City, and agree-
' able to Reafon : And whereas by Force of
' the faid Cuftoms, Franchifes, and Liberty,
' and of the Charter laft aforementioned, con-
' firmed as is afore fpecified by Parliament,
' The Lord Maior, Aldermen, and Com-
' mons of the faid City, did the twelfth day
' of *October*, in the third Year of the Reign
' of *Edward*, fometime King of *England*, the
' fourth, as a thing thought fit and convenient

for

' for that time, amongſt other things, agree
' and ordain that the *Baſket-makers, Goldwire-*
' *drawers,* and other Foreigners, contrary to
' the Liberty of the ſaid City, holding open
' Shops in divers Places of the City, and
' uſing Myſteries within the ſaid City, ſhould
' not from thenceforth hold Shops within the
' Liberty of the City aforeſaid; But if they
' would hold any Shop, or dwell in the ſame
' City, they ſhould dwell at *Blanchappelton.*
' and there hold Shops, ſo as they might have
' ſufficient dwelling there. And whereas the
' Lord Maior, Aldermen, and Commons of
' the ſame City, did afterwards, the ſixteenth
' Day of *May,* ſeventeenth Year of the Reign
' of our late Sovereign Lord of famous Me-
' mory, King *Henry* the Eighth (as a Courſe
' thought fit and agreeable for that time) Or-
' dain, Eſtabliſh, and Enaɛt, that no manner
' of Perſon or Perſons being eſtrange from the
' Liberties of the ſaid City, from thenceforth
' ſhould hold or keep any open Shop or Shops
' within the ſaid City, or Liberties of the
' ſame, neither with any Lattice before, nor
' yet without Lattice (certain Numbers of
' poor Men occupying the Seat of *Botchers,*
' *Taylors,* and *Coblers* only except) upon Pain
' of Impriſonment, and alſo to forfeit and
' pay forty Shillings to the uſe of the Com-
' monalty of this City, as often-times as he
' or they ſhould do the contrary. And where
' alſo the Lord Major, Aldermen, and Com-
' mons of the ſame City did afterwards, the
' twentieth Day of *January,* in the ſaid Se-
' venteenth Year of King *Henry* the Eighth
' (reciting, that whereas a Common Coun-
' cil holden the ſixteenth Day of *May,* in the
' ſeventeenth of the Reign of King *Henry* the
M   Eighth,

'Eighth, It was Ordained and Enacted,
'That no manner of Perfon or Perfons, be-
'ing eftranged from the Liberty of this City,
'from thenceforth fhould hold or keep any
'Shop or Shops, within this City, or the Li-
'berties of the fame, neither with any Lat-
'tices before, nor yet without any Lattice,
'upon Pain of Imprifonment) further Ordain
'and Eftablifh, that if any Perfon or Perfons
'being Foreign, fhould hold and keep any
'open Shop or Shops, as is aforefaid, he
'fhould forfeit for every time fo doing forty
'Shillings, to be levied by Diftrefs, to the
'Ufe of the Commonalty of the faid City,
'by the Chamberlain for the time being, or,
'other Officer of this City ; and alfo have
'Imprifonment by Direction of the Maior
'and Aldermen for the time being. Now
'forafmuch as divers and fundry Strangers and
'Foreigners from the Liberties of the faid
'City, nothing regarding the faid antient
'Charters, Franchifes, Cuftoms, or Liber-
'ties of the faid City, and Acts and Ordi-
'nances heretofore made according to the
'fame, but wholly intending their private Pro-
'fit, have of late Years devifed and practifed
'by finifter and fubtil Means, how to de-
'fraud and defeat the faid Charters, Liberties,
'Cuftoms, good Orders and Ordinances, and
'to that End do now inwardly in privy and
'fecret Places, ufually and ordinarily fhew,
'fell, and put to fale their Wares and Mer-
'chandizes, and ufe Arts, Trade, Occupa-
'tions, Myfteries, and Handicrafts within
'the faid City and Liberties of the fame, to
'the great Detriment and Hurt of the Free-
'men of the faid City, who pay Lot and
'Scot, bear Offices, and undergo other
Charges

'Charges, which Strangers and others not
'Free are not chargeable withal, nor will
'perform; for Reformation of which Disor-
'ders, and avoiding of such Prejudice and
'Damages as thereby groweth to the Free-
'men of the said City, and is now more of
'late used than was in any time hereto-
'fore suffered, and to provide for the com-
'mon Profit and Good of the Freemen and
'Citizens of this City; It is therefore by
'the Lord Maior and Aldermen and Com-
'mons in this Common Council assembled,
'ordained and established, that no Person
'whatsoever, not being Free of this City of
'*London*, shall at any time after the Feast of St.
'*Michael* now next ensuing, by any Colour,
'Way, or Means whatsoever, either directly
'or indirectly, by himself or by any other,
'shew, sell, or put to sale any Wares or
'Merchandizes whatsoever, by Retail with-
'in the City of *London*, or the Liberties or
'Suburbs of the same, upon Pain to forfeit to
'the Chamberlain of the City of *London* for
'the time being, to the use of the Maior and
'Commonalty of the said City, the Sum of
'five Pounds of lawful Money of *England*,
'for every time wherein such Person shall
'shew, sell or put to sale any Wares or Mer-
'chandizes, by Retail within the said City,
'Liberties, or Suburbs thereof, contrary to
'the true Intent and Meaning thereof. And
'it is further ordained and established, That
'no Person whatsoever, not being free of the
'City of *London*, shall at any time after the
'said Feast of St. *Michael* now next ensuing,
'by any Colour, Way, or Means whatso-
'ever, directly or indirectly, by himself or
'by any other, keep any Shop, or other

' Place whatfoever, inward or outward, for
' fhew, fale, or putting to fale of any Wares
' or Merchandizes whatfoever, by way of
' Retail, or ufe any Art, Trade, Occupa-
' tion, Myftery, or' Handicraft whatfoever,
' within the faid City, or the Liberties or
' Suburbs of the fame, upon Pain to forfeit
' the Sum of five Pounds of lawful Money of
' *England*, for every time wherein fuch Per-
' fons fhall keep any Shop, or other Place
' whatfoever, inward or outward, for fhew,
' fale, or putting to fale of any Wares or
' Merchandizes whatfoever, by way of Re-
' tail, or ufe any Art, Trade, Occupation,
' Myftery, or Handicraft whatfoever, within
' the faid City or Liberty, or Suburbs of the
' fame, contrary to the true Intent and
' Meaning hereof. All which Pains, Penal-
' ties, Forfeitures, and Sums of Money to be
' forfeited by virtue of this Act or Ordi-
' nance, fhall be recovered by Action of
' Debt, Bill or Plaint, to be profecuted in
' the Name of the Chamberlain of the City
' of *London* for the time being, in the King's
' Majefty's Court to be holden in the Chamber
' of *the Guild-hall* of the City of *London*, be-
' fore the Lord Maior and Aldermen of the
' faid City ; wherein no Effoign or Wager
' of Law fhall be admitted or allowed for
' the Defendants. And that the Chamber-
' lain of the City for the time being, fhall
' in all Suits to be profecuted by virtue of
' this Act or Ordinance againft any Offender,
' recover the ordinary Cofts of Suit to be
' expended in and about the Profecution
' thereof ; and farther, that one equal third
' Part of all Forfeitures to be recovered by
' virtue

' virtue hereof, (the Cofts of the Suits for
' Recovery of the fame being deducted
' and allowed) fhall be after the Recovery
' and Receipt thereof, paid and delivered to
' the Treafurer of *Chrift's Hofpital,* to be em-
' ployed towards the Relief of the poor
' Children, to be brought up and maintain-
' ed in the faid Hofpital ; and one other
' fuch equal third Part fhall be paid into
' the Chamber of the faid City ; and one other
' equal third Part to him or them which fhall
' firft give Information of the Offences for
' which fuch Forfeitures fhall grow, and
' profecute Suit in the Name of the Cham-
' berlain of the faid City for Recovery of the
' fame, any thing in this Act to the contrary
' notwithftanding. Provided always, that
' this Act or Ordinance, or any thing herein
' contained, fhall not extend to any Perfon
' or Perfons, for bringing or caufing to be
' brought any Victuals to be fold within this
' City, or the Liberties thereof, but that
' they, and every of them may fell Victuals
' within the faid City, and the Liberties
' thereof, as they might lawfully have done
' at the making hereof, any thing herein con-
' tained to the contrary in any wife notwith-
' ftanding.

As to the Act of Common Council, That no Foreigner shall open Shop, &c.

IN *Waggoner* and *Fisher's* Case : *Waggoner* was arrested upon Plaint in the Lord Maior's Court, in Debt, at the Suit of *Fish*, Chamberlain: The Defendant brought a Writ of Privilege retournable in the *Common-Pleas :* The Retorn was, There is a Custom in the City of *London, That no Foreigner shall keep any Shop, or use any Trade in* London. And there is another Custom, *That the Maior, Aldermen, and Commonalty (if any Customs be defective) may supply Remedy for it ; and if any new thing happen, they may provide Remedies for it, so it be* Congrua & bonæ fidei confuetudo rationi confentanea & pro communiutilitate Regis civium & omnium aliorum ibid. confluentium. That King *Edw.* III. by his Letters Patents, granted, That they might make By-Laws, and the Letters Patents were confirmed by Act of Parliament, and shew several Acts of Common-Council made in the time of *Hen.* IV. and *Hen.* VIII. for inhibiting Foreigners to hold any Shop or Shops, or Lattice, *&c.* and Penalties, imposed, and that after, and shew the Day, an Act of Common-Council was made, That no Foreigner should use any Trade, Mystery, or Occupation within the said City, nor keep any Shop there for Retailing, upon pain of 5 *l.* and gives Power to the Chamberlain to sue for it by Action, *&c.* in the Court of the Maior ; and that such a Day the Defendant held a Shop, and used the Mystery of making Candles, and a Plaint was levied, and the Defendant Arrested.

By-Laws.

It

It was agreed by all that the Cuſtom and *Defect in the Return.*
By-Law was good, but there was a Defect in
the Return ; it does not appear by the Return
that the Defendant had uſed the Trade of
Tallow-Chandler, nor ſold any Candles, but
only he kept a Shop, and uſed the Myſtery
of making Candles ; and it is not the making
them, but the Sale of them is the Wrong ; and
for this Cauſe he was delivered, and not remanded. *Vide* 2 *Brown.* 284.

It was agreed, that a Merchant, or any *What Goods may be ſold in* London, *and by whom*
other Man, may ſell Goods in Grofs as he
may ſell an Hundred Tun of Wines, or Pieces
of Cloth ; and one Tun of Wine to one Man,
and a Piece of Cloth to another, till they
had ſold all ; and this was not a Retailing ;
but they cannot ſell by the Yard, or keep a
Shop.

And in this Cafe it was ſaid by *Coke,* That
they could not inflict Confiſcation of Goods,
or Imprifonment, but may inflict Pecuniary *Pecuniary Puniſhments not Impriſonment,*
Puniſhments.

Alſo if any that is a Freeman of *London,*
ſhall employ a Foreigner to work within the
City or Liberties thereof, he forfeits 5 *l.* a Day,
and an Action lies againſt him for the ſame ;
purſuant to an Act of Common-Council made
in the Maioralty of Sir *William Gerrard,* Knt.
primo Auguſti 3 & 4 *Phil.* & *Mar.* which Act *Vide ante.*
is as followeth.

' WHereas, by the antient laudable
'   Laws, Liberties, and Franchiſes
' of this Noble City of *London,* no Perſon or
' Perſons ſhould be willingly ſuffered to exer-
' ciſe, uſe, or occupy any Manual Occupation or
' Handicraft within the ſaid City or Liberties
' thereof, unleſs he or they were free of the
M 4   ſame

' fame City; or Apprentice, or Apprentices
' with fome that be free of the fame City;
' the which faid antient Laws, Franchi-
' fes, and Liberties, notwithftanding divers
' Artificers and Handicrafts-men being Free-
' men of this City, not regarding or efteem-
' ing the faid Laws, Liberties, Cuftoms,
' and Franchifes, nor the Oath that they have
' taken to the faid City at fuch time as
' they were made Free, for the Maintenance
' and Advancement of the fame City, have now
' of late not only willingly fuffered, hired, and
' fet on work within the faid City and Liber-
' ties thereof, divers Foreigners from the Li-
' berties of the faid City, in divers and fundry
' Handicraft and Manual Occupations, but
' alfo have refufed to take and fet a work in
' the faid Manual Occupations or Handicrafts
' the honeft poor Citizens and Freemen of the
' fame City, to the great Hindrance, Lofs, and
' Prejudice of the faid poor Citizens, and to
' the utter undoing of a great Number of
' the faid poor Handicrafts-men, being Citi-
' zens and Freemen of the faid City, and
' alfo of their poor Wives and Children
' for ever, unlefs fome fpeedy Remedy
' be herein provided. For Reformation
' whereof, be it Enacted, Ordained, and Efta-
' blifhed by the Lord Maior, Aldermen and
' Commons in this prefent Common-Council
' affembled, and by the Authority of the
' fame, That no Perfon or Perfons, now being
' free of this City of *London*, or that hereafter
' fhall be free of the fame, fhall after the Feaft
' of St. *Michael* the Arch-Angel, now next
' coming, by any colour, ways, or means, fet
' at work in any Manual Occupation or
' Handicraft within the faid City, the Liber-
' ties

' ties or Suburbs thereof, any manner of Fo-
' reigner from the Liberties of the said City,
' upon pain of forfeiture of FivePounds of cur-
' rent Money of *Engand*, for every time that
' every such Person or Persons shall offend or
' commit, or do any thing contrary to the pur-
' port, true intent and meaning of this present
' Act.
  ' All and singular which Penalties and For-
' feitures above, and by this present Act li-
' mited and appointed, shall be divided into
' three equal Parts, whereof the one to the *Ante* 165.
' Use of the Maior and Commonalty, and
' Citizens of the said City for the time being;
' and one other part thereof to be to those of
' the first Presenters of the same Offence ; and
' the third Part thereof, to be to those of the
' Company or Fellowship that every such
' Offender shall be free of ; and that all and
' every such Penalty and Penalties and Forfei-
' tures shall be recovered, as well upon the
' proper Confession of the same Offence,
' made by the same Offender or Offenders
' themselves, before the Lord Maior and
' Court of Aldermen for the time being, as
' also upon good and sufficient Proof thereof
' to be made by the Witnesses before the
' said Lord Maior and Court of Aldermen
' for the time being; or by Bill or Plaint
' of Debt to be commenced by any such
' Informer or Presenter in any of the King
' and Queen's Majesties Courts of Record
' within the said City, in the Name of the
' Chamberlain of the said City for the time
' being; wherein no Essoin or Wager of
' Law shall be admitted or allowed for the
' Party Defendant. And be it also Enacted
' by the Authority aforesaid, That it be law-
                                          ful,

' ful for the faid Lord Maior and Aldermen
' of the faid City for the time being, upon
' every confeffion or proof of any fuch Offence
' aforefaid, before them made, or fufficiently
' proved, to commit every fuch Offender or
' Offenders to Ward, there to remain with-
' out Bail or Mainprize, until he or they have
' fully fatisfy'd or paid the faid Forfeiture or
' Forfeitures and Penalties to the Ufes afore-
' faid. Provided always, that this Act of
' Common Council, or any thing therein con-
' tained, fhall not in any wife extend to be
' prejudicial or hurtful to the Mafters or Go-
' vernors of *Chrift's Hofpital* and *Bridewell*, or
' to any other of the Hofpitals belonging to
' the faid City for the time being, or to any
' of them, for the fetting at work either,
' Strangers or Foreigners within the faid
' Houfes, or any of them ; neither to the faid
' Strangers or Foreigners that fhall fo happen,
' to work therein, nor to any of them ; nei-
' ther to any Freeman or Woman of the fame
' City, for having or fetting to work any Ap-
' prentice or Apprentices at any time here-
' after, in any Manual Occupation or Handi-
' craft within the faid City ; nor to any fuch
' Apprentice or Apprentices that fhall fo ferve,
' fo that his or their Indenture of Apprentice-
' hood be inrolled in the Chamberlain's Of-
' fice of the faid City, according to the antient
' Cuftoms of the fame City, in that behalf,
' ufed and obferved. Provided alfo, that this
' prefent Act, or any thing therein contained,
' fhall not extend to be prejudicial or hurtful
' to any Perfon or Perfons now being, or that
' hereafter fhall be free of the faid City, for
' fetting a work at any time or times, any
' Perfon or Perfons being Feltmakers, Cap-

3   ' thickers,

' thickers, Carders, Spinners, Knitters, or
' Brewers, or to any Perſon that now keepeth,
' or hereafter ſhall keep any Brewhouſe with-
' in the ſaid City or the Liberties thereof, for
' working or uſing any of the ſaid Crafts or
' Occupations within the ſame City, or with-
' in the Liberties or Suburbs thereof, this
' preſent Act, or any thing therein contained
' tothe contrary in any wiſe, notwithſt and-
' ing.

But Note, an Action of the Caſe was *Weavers.*
brought by the Weavers of *London,* none being
to intermeddle with their Guild, nor with
their Art within the City or *Southwark,* but
thoſe of the Fraternity. The *Action* ſuppoſed,
That the *Plaintiffs* from time to time, whereof,
&c. were a Corporacion in *London, &c.* paying
for it 20 *s.* and 8*d.* to the Queen *per Annum, &c.*
And that the Cuſtom there, is, *&c.* that none
ought to intermeddle with their Guild, nor
with their Art within *London* or *Southwark,*
but thoſe of the Guild : And that the Defendant being none of their Guild, had bought
forty Pounds worth of Silk of one *R.* to be
woven, and had weaved it, *&c.* The Defendant pleaded, *Not Guilty,* and a ſpecial Verdict found theſe Cuſtoms, *&c.* and that the
Defendant, being a Stranger, had received of
R. forty Pounds worth of Silk to be woven, and
had carried it to *Hackney,* and there had woven
it, and had brought it back to *London,* and received his Salary, *&c. Et ſi, &c.* And hereupon all
the Court reſolved, That it was not any Offence :
for although it were a good Cuſtom, as they
all allowed it was, being uſed time out of
Mind, *&c.* yet this contracting for it in *London,*
and working of it in the Country, is not inter-
                                        ' med-

medling with their Trade in *London*; no more
than if a Taylor fhould buy Cloath, or receive
any other thing in *London*, and make a Gar-
ment thereof in the Country ; and although
it be a contracting in *London*, yet it is not
intermedling with the Trade. Wherefore it
was adjudged for the Defendant. *Vid.* 1 *Cro.*
803. The Weavers *verf. Browne.*

Concerning Buying and Selling betwixt Foreigners.

IT is a Cuftom of *London*, that if one Stranger buy any thing of another Stranger, it
fhall be forfeited to the Maior and Commonalty of the faid City. As to this Cuftom accept this Refolution. 1 *Cro.* 352. *Sams* v.
Fofter.

Action of Trover, and Converfion, of an Ox-
Hide of the Plaintiffs in *Middlefex*; the Defendant pleaded that the City of *London* is an antient City, and that there is a Cuftom there,
that *Si aliquis extraneus forinfecus à Libertate ejuf-
dcm Civitatis* buy any thing *de alio forinfeco à
Libertate prædict'* that it fhould be forfeited to
the Maior and Commonalty of the faid City ;
and faith, That the Plaintiff *Extraneus à Libertate,* did buy the faid Ox-Hide of another
Foreigner ; whereupon he feized it in *London,*
to the Ufe of the Maior, *&c. abfque hoc,* that
he did find it, and convert in *Middlefex.* And
it was thereupon demurred.

Glanvil

Glanvil argued for the Plaintiff, *Firfl*, That it was not a good and lawful Cuftom ; and in Proof thereof, cited the Cafe, 36 *Hen.* VI. of Jewels of the Kings fold, and 21 *Hen.* VII. 40. 3 *Eliz. Dyer,* 186, & 246.   And the Form of the Pleading he faid is not good, *viz. Si aliquis extraneus à Libertate* ; but doth not fhew where the Liberty is, and the Traverfe is not good ; for he ought to traverfe every County befides *London,* and not *Middlefex* only.   *Anderfon* and *Beaumond* conceived the Form of the Pleading to be ill, but for the matter of the Cuftom itfelf, they doubted.   *Owen* faid, The Cuftom was good, and had been allowed before thefe times.

An Act of Common Council, 1ft of June, 18 *King* Hen. VIII. *Concerning making Freemen of the City, againft colouring Foreign Goods.*

AT this Common Council, it is agreed, granted, ordained, and enacted, That if hereafter, any Freeman or Freewoman of this City, take any Apprentice, and within the Term of Seven Years, fuffer the fame Apprentice to go at his large Liberty and Pleafure ; and within, or after the faid Term, agree with the faid Apprentice for a certain Sum of Money, or otherwife for his faid Service; and within or after the End of the faid Term, the Freeman prefent the faid Apprentice to the faid Chamberlain of the City, and by good deliberation, and upon his Oath made to the fame City, the fame Freeman or Freewoman affureth and affirmeth to the faid Chamberlain, that the faid
Appren-

Apprentice hath fully ferved his faid Term as
Apprentice. Or if any Freeman or Freewoman
of this City, take any Apprentice, which at
the time of the faid taking, hath any Wife.
Or if any Freeman or Freewoman of this City, give any Wages to his or her Apprentice,
or fuffer the faid Apprentices to take any part
of their own Getting or Gains. Or if any
Freeman or Freewoman of this City hereafter,
colour any Foreign Goods, or from henceforth buy or fell for any Perfon or Perfons, or
with or to any Perfon or Perfons, being Foreign or Foreigners, Cloaths, Silks, Wines,
Oils, or any other Goods or Merchandize
whatfoever they be ; whether he take any
thing or things, for his or their Wages or
Labour, or not ; or if any Perfon or Perfons,
being free of this City, by any colour or deceitful means from henceforth, do buy, fell, or
receive of any Apprentice within this City,
any Money, Goods, Merchandize or Wares,
without the affent or licence of his Mafter or
Mafters ; and upon Examination, duly proved
before the Chamberlain of the faid City, for
the Time being ; and the fame reported by
the Mouth of the faid Chamberlain, at a
Court to be holden by the Maior and the Aldermen of the fame City, in their Council
Chamber.

That as well the faid Mafter, as the faid
Apprentice, fhall for evermore be disfranchifed.

See hereafter of Disfranchifements, *&c.*

The Cuſtoms of London *as to Appren-*
tices, and ſeveral Caſes adjudged
thereupon.
Vide poſt, *The Chamber-lain's Court.*

THE Cuſtom of *London* as to Inrolling *Inrollment.*
Apprentices, is certified by the Mouth
of the Recorder.

The Apprentice at any time before one
Year (if his Maſter do not Inrol the Indenture)
may exhibit a Petition in *French* to the Lord
Maior and Aldermen, and have a *Scire Facias*
againſt his Maſter, to ſhew why the Indenture
was not Inrolled ; and if he do not ſhew ſufficient cauſe (as that he could not bring the
Apprentice perſonally, as he muſt, or ſome
ſuch Cauſe) then he may ſue out his Indenture, and be diſcharged of his Maſter. *Pal-*
mer 361.

But this Caſe is more fully reported in 2
Roll's Rep. 308. in a Writ of Error between
the Maſter and the Apprentice, they were at
iſſue upon the Cuſtom of *London*, and the *Cer-*
tiorari was awarded to the Maior ; and the
Recorder certified that where any Man within the Age of 21 Years, and not under the
Age of 14, binds himſelf by Indenture, in
which are many Covenants; theſe ſhall bind
the Infant, although the Deed was not inrolled before the Chamberlain within the
Year : but with this Difference, That the
Apprentice may come in before the Maior
and Aldermen, and there ſhew the Matter by
Petition in *French*, that the Deed is not enrolled within the Year ; and upon this, a *Scire*
Facias

Where the Apprentice may be discharged for want of their Inrolment. *Facias* shall issue forth to the Maior, to shew why the Deed was not inrolled. And if upon his default, the Deed was not inrolled, the Defendant (the Apprentice) may sue out his Indentures, and shall be discharged; and if it was not inrolled through the Default of the Apprentice, as if he would not come to be present before the Chamberlain, but absent himself, then he shall not be discharged; for the Deed may not be inrolled, unless the Apprentice be present in Court. 21 *Jac. R. R. Cole* and *Holmes, &c.*

Such Action was brought against an Apprentice, *viz.* that he departed from his Master's Service, *&c.* the Defendant pleads Nonage; the Plaintiff reply'd the Custom of *London,* and that the Indenture was inrolled as it ought to be; and this was certified by the Recorder to be the Custom, and Judgment was given against the Defendant.

Apprentice sued upon his Covenants. Action of Debt on Bond, whereof the Condition was to perform Covenants in Indenture of Apprenticeship in *London :* The Defendant pleads the Custom of *London,* That the Indenture shall be void if it be not inrolled within the Year, and this Custom was traversed.

A Turnover. The Custom of *London* is, to turn over an Apprentice from one to another; and he to whom such Apprentice is turned over, may have Action of Covenant upon special Issues, on the several Breaches assigned; and the Plaintiff in such Case had a Verdict, tho' it was moved in Arrest of Judgment.

1. That *abstraxit se à Servitio,* so many Nights, and during that time did not serve

ferve him ; which *per Cur.* being found
againſt him is good enough.

2. It is ſaid he did not ſerve according to
his Covenants, whereas no Covenant *Covenant.*
was made with the Plaintiff, yet it is
good enough, and the Concluſion, *&*
ſic non tenuit conventionem made with the
Plaintiff, is as good as can be, and
Judgment *pro Quer.* 1 *Keeb.* 250. *Bowcher*
and *Coſter.*

Action of Covenant was brought upon
the Cuſtom of *London,* That an Infant above *The Cuſtom*
14, and under 21, may bind himſelf Appren- *how to be*
tice, and that the Maſter ſhall have *tale re-* *pleaded.*
medium as if he were 21. It is good, and he
need not alledge that the Cuſtom is, That
he ſhall have Action of Covenant againſt him,
for *tale remedium* implies as much. *Mod.*
Rep. 271. *Hord* and *Chandler.*

In Covenant it was laid as a Cuſtom, that *How a Cuſtom*
every Freeman may take an Apprentice, and *is to be al-*
that Infants may bind themſelves to ſerve. *ledg'd in plead-*
ing.

It was objected, That this Cuſtom was
alledg'd *in fieri,* and not *in facto,* for Uſage
is not added to it : As a Cuſtom of a Manor, that every Tenant *potuit & potuiſſet ſur-*
ſum reddere is ill : So *licet & licuit,* for the
Lord to aſſeſs a Pain ; But the *Court contra* ;
as *Old Entries* 141, a Cuſtom that every Citizen and Freeman might demiſe in *Mortmain*
good. 1 *Crok.* 347. and in *Windhurſt* and *Gibb's*
Caſe. *Raym.* 4.

An Infant binds himſelf Apprentice at 16
in *London,* if he be ſued upon his Covenant
in *B. C.* as he may, he ſhall not plead Nonage in Bar ; for this Cuſtom that ſuch Co-
N   venants

venants ſhall bind in *London* is become allowable in Law, and ſo pleadable in any Place in
England, vide ſupra, & vide poſt, Chamberlain's Court, *& pag.* 184, 185.

Where, and in what Caſes, by the
Cuſtom of London, *he who is free*
of one Trade may ſet up another ;
or not.

J T. was Apprentice for ſeven Years in
London to a Wool-packer, and is made
a Freeman; afterwards he leaveth the Trade
of a Wool-packer, and betaketh him to the
Trade of an Upholſterer : *T. A.* exhibits an
Information in the Court of the Lord Maior
of *London, tam pro Dom. Rege quam, &c.* upon
the Stat. of 5 *Eliz.* 4. This Information being removed out of the Maior's Court by
Certiorari into the King's Bench, *J. T.* pleads
the Cuſtom of *London,* That every Citizen
and Freeman of *London,* which hath been an
Apprentice in *London* unto any Trade, by the
Space of ſeven Years, may well and lawfully
relinquiſh that Trade, and exerciſe any other
Trade at his Will and Pleaſure ; and ſheweth
farther, that all the Cuſtoms of *London* were
confirmed by K. *R.* II. in the Parliament
holden in the ſeventh Year of his Reign, and
averreth, that he had ſerved one (   )
in the Trade of a Wool-Packer, as an Apprentice, by the Space of ſeven Years, and
that he was a Citizen and Freeman of *Lon-*
don, and that he did relinquiſh the Trade of
a Wool-Packer, and betook himſelf to the
Trade

Trade of an Upholsterer, *prout ei bene licuit,* and demands the Judgment of the Court, if this Information will lie. *J. T.* demurs to the Plea.

The Queſtion was, Whether this Cuſtom of relinquiſhing one Trade after he hath been Apprentice for ſeven Years , and betaking himſelf to another Trade, wherein he hath not been Apprentice, be good, or not; and it was agreed to be a good Cuſtom, and it might have a reaſonable Commencement; for *London* being a famous City for Traffick and Commerce, cannot but ſometimes have Merchants and Tradeſmen in it, who by Miſadventure of Pirates, or Shipwreck, or by Confiſcation of their Goods in foreign Countries abroad, or by Caſualties of Fire at Home may have their Eſtates ſunk,whereby for want of Means or Stock they are forced to leave that Courſe, and betake themſelves to ſome other Trade, proportionable to the Means which they have ; or through Sickneſs, *&c.* may become infirm in Body, and cannot follow that laborious Trade, *&c.* and this Cuſtom hath had a perpetual Allowance.

It was a Queſtion in this Caſe, Whether the Branch of the Stat. 5 *Eliz.* 4. be a Repeal and Controll of the Cuſtom of *London,* concerning the Exercife of a Trade that he hath not been an Apprentice to by the Space of ſeven Years.

And it was reſolved, that the Cuſtom of *London* was of force, and was not controlled by that Branch.

It was alſo reſolved, That the Trade of an Upholſterer was not within that Stat. of 5 *Eliz.*

Calthr. 9. Allen v. Tolley, Sid. 367. contra, and that it is within the Statute.

This Caſe of *Tolley* was adjudged 12 *Jac.* I. in *B. R.*

Note. But it hath been adjudged ſince, That there is no ſuch Cuſtom in *London* generally, *viz.* That one brought up as Apprentice in a Trade of manual Occupation, as Goldſmith, Cutler, Taylor, *&c.* may exerciſe any other Trade of manual Occupation. But the Cuſtom is, that one of a Trade of buying and ſelling may exerciſe any other Trade of buying and ſelling, as Mercer, Grocer, *&c.* See the Caſe of *Appleton verſ. Stoughton. Cro. Car.* 371, 372. or 516.

See alſo the Caſe of the King againſt *Bagſhaw,* where an Information was againſt *Bagſhaw,* upon Stat. 5 *Eliz.* for occupying the Trade of a Goldſmith, not being an Apprentice to it: The Defendant pleads the Cuſtom of *London,* that one being an Apprentice for ſeven Years, and made a Freeman of *London* of any Trade, may uſe any other Trade in the ſame City, and ſhews he was bound Apprentice to the Art of the Cordweyners, and ſerved ſeven Years, and was made free, and ſo juſtifies: The King's Attorney demurs, and after waved the Demurrer, and took Iſſue upon the Cuſtom, and the Iſſue being joined, whether there were ſuch Cuſtom as is pleaded. *Littleton* Recorder certified, *Ore tenus,* That there was not any ſuch Cuſtom generally, for he ſaid, that the Cuſtom is not, that one brought up as an Apprentice in the Trade of a Goldſmith, Cutler, *&c.* being a Feeeman of *London,* may by colour thereof uſe any other manual Trade; but one of a Trade who uſeth buying and ſelling,

as

as Mercer, Grocer, may exercife another Trade of buying and felling. *Cro. Car.* 347, 361. And it is refolved in *Flerthen* and *Bagfhaw's* Cafe, upon Recorder *Littleton's* Certificate, *Ore tenus,* that there is not any fuch Cuftom generally. 2 *Rolls's Abr.* 573.

K. was indicted at the Seffions in *Suffolk* for ufing the Trade of a Wollendraper at *Framlingham* in the fame County, *&c.* not having ferved as an Apprentice to it, againft Stat. 5 *Eliz. c.* 4. which was removed by *Certiorari* in *B. R.* The Defendant pleads, that he is a Citizen and Freeman of *London,* and that K. *H.* III. by his Letters Patents grants to the Maior and Commonalty of the faid City, and their Succeffors, *Quod omnes* *cives civitat' præd. per totam terram,* &c. *libere* *& fine Impedimento, tam per mare quam per ter-* *ram, de rebus & Mercimoniis fuis extunc impo-* *fterum negotiare poffint prout fibi viderent expe-* *dire ac etiam refiderent & morarentur ubicunque* *voluerint infra hoc regnum Angliæ cum Mercimo-* *niis & Merchandizis fuis emend. & vendend. &* *pro negotiationibus fuis conficiend ;* and pleads the faid Grant, and all the Donations and Cuftoms were confirmed by *R.* II. and that he being a Citizen and Freeman of *London* by all the time mentioned in the Indictment, *apud* *Framlingham præd. refidebat & morabatur cum* *quibufdam Mercimoniis pannariis emend. & ven-* *dend. Mercimonia pannar. præd. pro ut ei bene* *licuit juxta conceffion' & confirmation' præd.* which is the fame ufing the Trade fuppofed in the Indictment. 'Twas held an ill Plea, becaufe the Charter of *Henry* III cannot be a Difpenfation with the Stat. 5 *Eliz.* which

The Charter of K. H. III. *about Citizens of* London *Merchandizing expounded.*

N 3   fays,

That Charter says, *That no Person shall use a Trade*, &c. *to*
no Dispensation which *he has not served as an Apprentice*; it
with the Stat.
5 Eliz. That only gives Liberty to Citizens and Freemen
no Person of *London* to sell their Merchandizes in any
shall use a Places (Boroughs or Corporations) at their
Trade that has Pleasure, it never intended to give Liberty
not been Ap-
prentice, to use a Trade to which he had not been Ap-
yet the Law prentice, for two Reasons. *First,* Because at
seems contrary. Common Law, before the Statute, any one
might use what Trade he would, though he
had not been Apprentice, if he had Skill. *Se-*
condly, It only gave Liberty to reside where
they please, though some Cities and Boroughs claim a Liberty to exclude Foreigners,
Cro. El. 110, 352. *Dyer* 279. *B.* 8. Rep. 128.
Sanderson 311. the King. *v. Kilderby.*

See 3 *Cro.* 803. That by the Custom of
London none shall use the Trade of a Silk-
weaver, but such as are of that Company.

The Custom of *London* pleaded, That Infant may bind himself Apprentice at 16, and
Nonage shall be no Bar, *vide tit. Custom* pleaded. It was moved as an Exception, that it
is alledged that every Citizen and Freeman
may take an Apprentice, and it is not said,
that the Plaintiff is a Citizen, but that he is
a Freeman : But *Fleetwood* Recorder answer'd,
A Freeman That a Freeman may take an Apprentice at
may take an *York* and such Apprentice shall be Freeman
Apprentice at
York. of *London* ; but he said, a Citizen is such a
one as inhabits in the City of *London.*
Moor, 135, 136. and yet see 2 *Bulstr. contra.*
p. 193.

Declaration. And it ought to be laid in the Declaration, that *B.* being a Citizen and Freeman of
London, (*civis & liber homo*) and not a Freeman of *London* only ; and for this Cause a
Judgment

Judgment was revers'd, 2 *Bulstr.* 191. *Burton* and *Palmer*.

See 1 *Salk.* 66. That by the Custom of *London* an Executor shall on the Testator's Death place his Apprentice with another Master.

A Man may be made a Freeman of *London* in three Ways.

One may be made a Freeman of London *three ways.*

   1. *By Service of Apprenticeship.*
   2. *By Redemption, Fine, or Ransom.*
   3. *By Birth, as a Freeman's Son is free.*
2 *Bulstr.* 193.

Yet 'tis said in *Stow, lib.* 5. *pag.* 330. That without serving an Apprenticeship with some Freeman of the City, no Man, tho' he be born in *London*, or of Parents that are *Londoners*, is admitted to be a Freeman or Citizen of *London*, to follow a Trade there; *i. e.* except he be made free in the Court of *Hustings: Quere*, If it may not be done in the Court of Common Council, for that being the City Parliament, and having Power to make By-Laws which shall bind all the Citizens and Freemen, must surely have the Power to make any deserving Person free of the City. See *Calthorp's* Tract, pag 7.

Covenant was brought against an Apprentice on Indentures; Defendant pleads he was within Age: The Plaintiff in his Replication maintained his Action by the Custom of *London*, That he may bind himself at the Age of Fourteen.

Declaration on Covenants in general against an Apprentice.

The Question in 4 *Leon.* 77. and *Cro. Eliz.* 642. *Walker* and *Nicholson's* Case was, Whether this were a Departure in pleading, and it was much doubted there; and 19 *R.* II.

Replies by the Custom of London *it is a Departure.*

was

was cited how that an Infant brought his Action against his Guardian in Socage, who pleaded, that the Plaintiff was within Age. The Plaintiff did maintain his Declaration, That by the Custom of such a Place an Infant at the Age of 18 Years might bring an Account against his Guardian in Socage, and it was held no Departure. In the principal Case it was much argued, in *Mould* and *Wall's* Case, 14 and 15 *Car.* II. *B. R.* because he brought his Action as at Common Law generally, and maintained it by a Custom.

Departure in pleading. Some argued, that it was a Departure, and cited 1 *Inst.* 304, and *Kel.* 76. the Abbot of *Buckface's* Case, which was, Action was brought against *H.* as Bayliff generally. The Defendant pleaded, he was Receiver; Plaintiff reply'd, that the Tenants of the Manor have used to elect a Tenant, which shall be Bayliff, to collect the Lord's Rents, and this was adjudg'd a Departure, 1 *Inst.* 304. *Kel.* 76.

In *Yelv.* 13. Pl. 22. *Wood* and *Hawkshead's* Case, it was argued there, if a Man entitle himself by the Feoffment of one *A.* and the Defendant shews how *A.* was an Infant at the time of the Feoffment, if the Plaintiff in his Declaration will induce a Custom to make the Feoffment good; this is a Departure, the Custom being a Matter of Title, and variant from the Declaration.

Alledges a general Custom, and replies by special Custom ill. And it was agreed by all, that where one alledgeth a general Custom in a Covenant; and replies by a special Custom, that that is not good at Common Law. But here, by *Windham* Justice, this is no Departure in the principal Case, being no Matter varying from the Covenant, that being but supposal, and always general, and this special Matter

3   ter

ter is a good fupport ; and that this is no departure from the Title, but an anfwer to a dif-
bility pleaded in Bar.

Fofter held it to be no departure, the Gift
of the Action being laid in *London*, and the Title is the fame Stile, only the Perfon enabled.
Winch. 63.

But by *Twifden* it is a Departure, and all
the Prefidents are to count on the Cuftom, as
being the ground of the Action. And further *Infant not*
he faid, as in *Gilbert* and *Fletcher's* Cafe, *Hill.* 5 *bound by Col-*
Car. I. the Action is founded on the Covenant, *lateral Cove-*
and not on the Cuftom ; and an Infant is not *nant.*
bound by a Collateral Covenant.

But the Court gave leave to the Plaintiff to
difcontinue his Action; and to declare on the
Cuftom of *London*, That an Infant may bind
himfelf thereby. See *Yelv.* 13, 14.

Covenant was brought upon Indentures of
Apprenticefhip, containing the ufual Covenants
in fuch Indentures, and the Breach was, that
he ran away with his Mafter's Money in *Lon-*
don.

Two Exceptions were taken to this Declaration.

1. In the Indenture the Words are, *That the* Words that
Infant fhall be loyal and faithful, &c. & *fecreta* imply a Cove-
fua celar', without any Words of Covenant nant.
exprefs.

But it was refolved, That the Words imply
a Covenant.

2. It was excepted, That Infants fhall be *That an In-*
bound by Covenant is pleadable no where *fant fhall be*
but in *London* (as the Cuftom is, that In- *bound by his*
fant fhall not wage his Law upon Covenant *Covenants*
for Tabling) *fed non allocatur.* It is pleada- *ble.* *when pleada-*
ble

ble at any Place, this Covenant is allowable
at Law; and the Words are, That the
Covenant shall become of such Effect and
Efficacy, as if he had been at full Age at the
time of his sealing the Indenture; and then
he shall be bound in every Place within
the Realm.

The Court seemed to be of Opinion, that
it was a Good Custom, and that the Action
was well brought, *Moor* 135. *Stanton's* Case.

By-Law can-
not make a
Bond void.   In Action of Covenant on Apprentices In-
dentures, the Defendant pleads a By-Law in
London, by the Common Council there ; That
if a Freeman take to Apprentice the Son of an
Alien, that Bond and Covenant shall be void.
Per Cur. that is no Plea ; for the Common
Council cannot make the Conditions or Cove-
nants void, but may inflict a Fine on such a
Master. *Moor* 411. *Dayzell* and *Peck. See
more of Apprentices,* post, Title *Chamberlains
Court, & ante* 176, 177.

Custom as to Women.

BY the Custom of *London,* the Wife shall
have the Moiety of the Goods whereof
her Husband died possess'd, if he dies without
Children. And by his Will he cannot prejudice her concerning her third Part; yet in his
Life-time, he may give them away, *Cro. Car.*
345.

On Bargain and Sale of Houses in *London,*
by Deed inrolled, if the Feme-Covert be examined, it shall bind her, as a Fine doth at
Common Law.

Women-

Women-Coverts that ufe certain Crafts within the City by themfelves, without their Husbands, may, by the Cuftom of *London,* take Women to be their Apprentices, for to ferve them, and to learn their Crafts, &c.

Of a Feme-Sole Merchant.

THE Words of the Cuftom are, *That where a Woman exercifeth a Trade wherein her Husband doth not intermeddle, fhe fhall have all Advantages, and fhall be fued as a Feme-fole Merchant* by the Cuftom. See 1 *Ed.* IV. 6. 35. *H.* VI. 38.

Feme-Covert, by the Cuftom of *London,* fhall fue without her Husband, as a Feme-Sole Merchant, by *Wray.* But the Action muft be laid within the City, *Chamberlain* and *Sharp's* Cafe. But every Feme which trades in *London* is not a Feme-Sole Merchant.

On *Habeas Corpus* to remove the Body *cum caufa* of the Wife of *B.* it was retorned, that the Action was brought againft her and her Husband, as a Feme-fole Merchant for Wares bought by the Feme, wherein the Husband was named only for Conformity ; and by the Cuftom, the Execution fhall be only againft her, *Cro. Jac.*

Bluet was a Vintner, and preft for a Soldier beyond Sea, and goes over Sea ; the Wife takes a Houfe, and buys Wine of *Langham,* who trufts her, fuppofing her to be a Feme-fole Merchant : After the Husband returns, and the Wife denieth to pay for the Wine, and the doubt was, if the Wife was a Feme fole Merchant by the Cuftom ; and the Words of the Cuftom were read *prout fupra* ; and by *Richard-*
fon

fon and *Yelverton,* fhe is not a Feme-fole Merchant within the Cuftom, for her Husband
exercifed the fame Trade ; and by *Yelverton,*
Feme-fole Merchant ought to be the Widow
of a Tradefman, who takes a fecond Husband,
and fhe after exercifeth the Trade of her firft
Husband : But *Croke, Hutton,* and *Harvey, contra;* if the Husband meddle with the Trade of
the Wife, then fhe is not a Feme-fole Merchant ; but if the Husband be beyond Sea,
or becomes Bankrupt, or leaves his Trade, and
his Wife exercifeth the fame Trade, or they
both exercife the fame Trade diftinctly by
themfelves, and not meddle the one with the
other, the Wife is Sole Merchant,. *Litt. Rep.*
36. 1 *Cro.* 67. *Langham* and *Bluet, Tamen
quære.*

*The Cuftom of
the Feme-fole
Merchant was
alledged in the
Declaration,
and a Proce-
dendo was
awarded.*

Feme was indicted as a Feme-fole Merchant, for felling Ale, and her Husband not
joined. Where fhe ufeth the fame Trade, fhe
doth it as a Servant, and he alone fhall be indicted : Nor will any Action lie in *B. R.* a-
gainft her alone ; and a *Procedendo* was awarded, 2 *Kebl.* 583. *Mereton* and *Packman* ; fo a
Procedendo was afterwards granted in *Royften*
and *Ivery's* Cafe, on Suit of a Feme-Covert,
as a Feme-fole Merchant, the Cuftom being
alledged in the Declaration. 3 *Keb.* 302.

> See the Cafe 9 E. IV. 35. *touching the faid
> Cuftom of Feme-fole Merchant. That the
> faid Privilege fhall not be allowed in* C. B. *if
> fhe be arrefted by Procefs thence ; and Quere how
> fhe may make an Attorney to appear, &c. in*
> C. B. aliter, *if fhe comes in on the Exigent.
> And fee there, touching the Cuftom of arreft-
> ing in* London, *to find better Surety.*

Concerning *Actionable Words spoken of Women.*

IT is a Cuſtom of *London* to maintain an Action on Scandals, and Words of Defamation, that are not Actionable in a Court at *Weſtminſter.* Yet as to this Cuſtom, Note the following Caſes, *viz.* Cro. 3 Part.
Dimmock v
Fawcet. 393
& 394.

One *Margaret Hart* brought an Action in the Sheriffs Court in *London* againſt another Woman for ſaying, *That ſhe was an Arrant Whore, and went from Chamber to Chamber playing the Whore.* This was removed by a *Habeas Corpus* into the King's Bench, and Bail put in. *Stone* moved for the Plaintiff, to have the Cauſe remanded, becauſe for theſe Words, Action lies not here, but they were Actionable there, by the Cuſtom of *London,* becauſe ſhe is puniſhable for ſuch Offence. But the Court denied to grant a *Procedendo,* and ſaid, an Action lies not for theſe Words; but that ſhe ſhould be ſued for Defamation in the Spiritual Court only. *Cro. 3.* Part 350. *Hart's* Caſe.

An Action upon the Caſe was brought in *London,* for Words of the Feme, *Thou art a Whore, and a Twopenny Whore.* Upon an *Habeas Corpus,* this Cauſe being removed, *Croke* ſigned a *Procedendo,* becauſe he was informed, it was a good Cauſe of Action in *London* by the Cuſtom (for they ought to puniſh ſuch Perſons with Carting and Whipping) and that it lies not in this Court. And now *Pheaſant* moved to have a *Superſedeas,* and the Cauſe removed ; for he ſaid it was againſt Law, to ſuffer ſuch Actions to be proſecuted in *London* Cro. 3 Part.
Bower *and*
his Wife, v.
Cooper, f.
486, 487.

upon

upon pretence of a Cuſtom, where they are not maintainable in a Superior Court : But *Stone* prayed, That no *Superſedeas* might be granted, for he ſaid, an Action lies in *London*, for theſe Words by Cuſtom : Becauſe a Whore there is to ſuffer Corporal Puniſhment, *viz.* Carting and Whipping : And it is an Offence preſentable at the *Wardmotes* Inqueſt, and there puniſhable ; ſo being ſubject to a Corporal Puniſhment, it is reaſon ſhe ſhould have her Action there.   And if the Party conceives himſelf grieved, he may have a Writ of Error ; and if againſt Law, may reverſe it : And cited *Trin.* 8. *Car.* ſuch a Cauſe being removed by *Habeas Corpus,* a *Procedendo* was awarded in this Court upon Debate.   And ſo all the Court held here, except *Berkeley* ; who conceived that a *Superſedeas* ought to be granted.   And it was alledged by *Stone,* that by the Statute of 21 *Jac.* after a *Procedendo* is awarded, no *Superſedeas* ought to be granted.   But the whole Court was againſt him in that Point : For when a *Procedendo* unduely *vel improvidè emanavit,* the Uſe is to grant a *Superſedeas.* But here it was conceived by *Jones, Brampſton,* and *Croke,* that the *Procedendo* was well awarded, therefore they denied to grant a *Superſedeas.*

One brought an Action in *London,* for calling the Wife of the Plaintiff Whore ; the Defendant removed this out of *London* by *Habeas Corpus* ; a *Procedendo* was prayed, becauſe the Action was maintainable in *London,* though not at the Common Law ; denied by the Court ; for ſuch Cuſtom to maintain an Action for brabling Words is againſt Law. *Co. Lit.* 4. *f.* 18. *Oxford v. Croſſe.*

Yet all the latter Caſes allow the ſaid Action maintainable in *London* by Cuſtom.

2   *Con-*

Concerning By-Laws, what are Good, or not, and how to be pleaded.

ANY Town may prefcribe to redrefs Nuifances, &c. By Laws: See 21 *Ed.* IV. 54. Pl. 1. *By-Law by the Horners Company.*

The Company of Horners fet forth (in Debt upon a By-Law) that they were incorporated by Letters Patents of King *Charles* I. and were thereby impowered to make By-Laws for the better Government of their Corporation, and that the Mafter, Wardens and Affiftants of the Company, made a Law, that two Men, appointed by them, fhould buy rough Horn for the Company, and bring them to the Hall, there to be diftributed every Month by the faid Mafter for the Ufe of the Company; and that no Member of the Company fhould buy rough Horns within 24 Miles of *London*, but of thofe two Men fo appointed, under a Penalty to be impofed by the faid Maior, &c.

It was argued that this was not a good By-Law.

1. Becaufe it doth reftrain Trade; for the Company are to ufe no Horns but fuch as thofe two Men fhall buy; and if they fhould have Occafion for more than thefe two Men fhould buy, then the Trade is reftrained.

To this it was anfwer'd, That this By-Law is for the Encouragement of Trade, becaufe the Horns are equally to be diftributed, when bought to the Hall, for the Benefit of the whole Company.

2. The Mafter, &c. hath referv'd a Power which they make ufe of to opprefs the Poor, be-

becaufe they make what Agreements they will amongft themfelves, and fet unreafonable Prices upon thofe Commodities, and let the younger Sort of Tradefmen have what Quantity, and at what Rates they pleafe. But the material Objection was, that this being a Company incorporated within the City of *London*, they have not Jurifdiction elfewhere, but are reftrained to the City, and by confequence cannot make a By-law, which fhould bind at the Diftance of 24 Miles ; for if fo, then they may extend it all over *England*, and make it as binding as an Act of Parliament ; and for this Reafon it was adjudged no good By-Law. 2 *Mod. Rep.* 158. The Company of Horners againft *Barlowe.*

Corporations in London are reftrained within the Ju- rifdiction of London.

A Plaint was removed out of the Lord Maior's Court by a *Habeas Corpus,* the Return whereof was, That the City of *London* was an ancient City incorporate, and that time out of mind there was a Cuftom, that the Portage and Unlading of all Coals and Grain coming thither fhould belong to the Maior and Aldermen, &c. that there was a Cuftom for them to regulate any Cuftom within the City, &c. Then they fet forth an Act of Common Council, by which the Porters of *Billingfgate* were made a Fellowfhip; and that the Meeters of Corn fhould from time to time give notice to the Porters to unlade fuch Corn as fhould arrive there ; and that no Bargemen not being free of the faid Fellowfhip fhall unlade any Corn upon the Forfeiture of 20 *d.* to be recovered in an Action to be brought in the Name of the Chamberlain, and that the Party offending fhould have no Effoign or Wager of Law, and fet forth

Porters ; By-laws as to Corn-meeters.

forth the Judgment in the *Quo Warranto*, and the regrant ; and that the Defendant not being of the faid Fellowfhip, did unlade one hundred Quarters of Malt, *&c.*

Exceptions to this By-Law.

1. *It appears upon the Retorn, that the City of* London *hath affumed an Authority to create a Fellowfhip by Act of Common Council, which they cannot do, for it is a Prerogative of the Crown fo to do ; and they have not averred, or fhewed any Special Cuftom to warrant fuch an Authority.* *Authority to create a Fellowfhip.*

2. *They have made this By-Law too general ; for if a Man fhould carry and unlade his own Goods there, he is liable to the Forfeiture ; in which Cafe he ought to be excepted.*

3. *This Act of Common Council prohibits Bargemen not being free of the Fellowfhip of Porters, to unlade any Coals or Grain arriving there ; and they have not averred that the Malt unladen, did arrive,&c. and fo have not purfued the words of the By-Law.*

4. *They fay in this Law, That the Perfons offending, fhall have no Effoign or Wager of Law, which is a Parliamentary Power, and fuch as an inferior Jurifdiction ought not to affume.* 3 *Mod.* Rep. *Anonimus.* *The Offender fhall have no Effoign or Wager of Law.*

28 *Eliz.* An Act of Common Council according to the Cuftom of the City of *London,* was, That none fhould bring any Sand, nor fell, nor ufe any within the City or Suburbs of *London,* but that which was only taken out *An Act of CommonCouncil, not to ufe any but Thames Sand.*

O   of

of the River of *Thames*, &c. and that if any did the contrary, that he fhould forfeit for the firft Fault 5 *l.* and for the fecond Fault 10 *l.* to be recovered in an Action of Debt, wherein no Effoign, Protection, or Wager of Law fhould be allowed; and this Plaint for the forfeiture of 120 *l.* was removed out of *London* into the Common Pleas, by Writ of Privilege; and the Judges did greatly fpeak againft the faid Act of Common Council, as well for the Matter, as for the Form of it: They were informed by Serjeant *Swagg*, That the faid *Thames* Sand was much worfe than the Land Sand, and yet the Price of it was greater, and the Meafure lefs; for of the *Thames* Sand there were but Eleven Bufhels to make a Load, and of the other Sand, there were Eighteen Bufhels; and they faid they were prefumptuous to make fuch Acts fo Parliament like, (*viz.*) that no Effoign, Protection, or Wager of Law, fhould be allowed of, and that they did arrogate to themfelves too high Authority; and they ftirred up the Plaintiff at the next Parliament, to exhibit a Bill againft them for it, and to fue them in the *King's Bench* for their Infolence, and faid it would fhake their Liberties. *Godbolt*, p. 107.

London re-proved for making their Acts of Common Council fo Parliamentary like.

One of the Bricklayers was fued by the Chamberlain of *London*, on Penalty for breaking an Act of Common Council, and had a *Habeas Corpus*, upon which this Matter was retorned, that *Civitas Londini eft antiqua civitas*; and that they, time out of Memory, have made Ordinances for the Government of the City, which binds the Citizens; and that by an Act of their Common Council for ordering the Companies of Bricklayers and Plaifterers, it was ordained that the Bricklayers fhould not

Act of Common Council againft Bricklayers and Plaifterers.

plaifter

plaifter with Lime and Hair, but with Lime and Sand only; and that plaiftering with Lime and Hair, fhould belong only to the Plaifterers; and they which broke, *&c.* fhall forfeit 40 *s.* to be recovered by the Chamberlain of *London*.

The Queftion was, if this be a Good Ordinance?

Object. That it's not good.

I. *It pertains to Bricklayers and Tylers to daub with Hair, and fo this reftrains part of their Trade.*

II. The Retorn was, *That thofe* of London *have* regimen perfonarum in manufactionibus, *which is for the ordering of their Perfons, and prefervation of the Peace : but they have not* regimen manufactionum *to annex that to one Trade, which belongs to another.* But per Cur.

1. This Ordinance is not in deftruction, but for the ordering of Trades; and for any thing that appears by the Retorn, it is indifferent to which of thefe Trades this Matter belongs ; fo the Ordinance is but a determination of a Queftion between the Companies by the Common Council ; but had it appeared upon the Retorn, that daubing with Lime and Hair belongs to the Bricklayers, the Ordinance is not good.

2. That the Retorn, that they have *regimen perfonarum in manufactionibus* goes to their Demeaner in their Myfteries, *Palmer* 395. between

tween the Bricklayers, Tylers, and Company of Plaiſterers.

Orders by the Company of Butchers to dreſs their Kidneys of Veal in the ſame manner as Kidneys of Sheep are dreſſed.

The Corporation of Butchers in *London* was confirmed, by which they had power to them given to make *By-Laws* and *Ordinances* ; they did ordain, That no *Butcher*, or Perſon, being a Stranger, ſhould ſell any Veal within the City of *London*, unleſs they did dreſs the Kidneys of their Veals, in ſuch manner as the Kidneys of Sheep were dreſſed ; and if they did otherwiſe, to forfeit 6 *d.* for every time; and if they refuſe to pay, they are to forfeit the Veal : The Servant of the Plaintiff coming with a Veal to ſell, and not performing the Ordinance, the Defendant in behalf of the Corporation, took the Veal on his Refuſal to pay the 6 *d.* For this the Plaintiff brought Treſpaſs. Defendant pleads in *Bar*, That he took the ſame as forfeited by their Ordinance, but does not ſhew the Ordinance in certain. *Per Cur.*

Ordinances of Companies ought to be ſhewed in certain.

By-Law not good to bind Foreigners.

The Ordinance ought to be ſhewed ſpecial. In pleading of a private Ordinance made by the Butchers in their Corporation, a Stranger is not bound to take notice thereof ; and this By-Law was not good to bind Strangers ; but the ſame had been good, if made to ſuppreſs Fraud, *&c.* uſed by a Foreigner, as Corruption, *&c.* in the Sale of their Meat, and then they ought to take notice of the ſame, but not here, as this Caſe is, and Judgment *pro Quer.* 1 *Bulſt.* 11. *Francklin* and *Green.*

No Statute or By-Law can be made for Matters of Inheritance.

2

The

The Sheriffs of *London* retorned, that for the more indifferent way of Merchandizing, they have a Cuftom, that the Goods, as well *Goods to be* that were fold by Weight, as others of all *weighed at the* Strangers, before Sale, ought to be weighed *Common* at the Common Beam ; and to inforce this, *Beam.* there is a By-Law made, with a pain of paying 40 *s. per* Tun for not weighing. This is a good Cuftom, though it was objected, Men may be forced to weigh, whether they fell or not, becaufe it may have a reafonable commencement. So Goods foreign bought, and foreign fold, fhall be forfeited. It was faid, that notice is not neceffary to a By-Law that is grounded upon the Cuftom of *London, Quære de hoc.* 1 *Keb.* 32, 35, 39. *Player* and *Bernadifton :* It was faid there, That in *London,* By-Laws refemble Acts of Parliament ; but let them have a care that they word them not too much like an Act of Parliament. *Vide fupra.*

The By-Law in *London,* whereby the Num- *By-Law to re-* ber of Carts is reftrained, is a good By-Law, *ftrain the* 1 *Ventr.* 21. *Number if Carts.*

Habeas Corpus to remove *B.* who was taken by Procefs upon a Plaint exhibited in the Sheriffs Court in *London,* and the Return was, That time out of Mind, the Maior, Aldermen, and Common Council of the City, have had the government and regulation of Trade within the faid City, and power to make By-Laws concerning the fame, and that they had made a By-Law, that there fhould be but 420 Carrs allowed to work within the City, all which fhould be licenfed by the Prefident of *Chrift-Church Hofpital* ; and that there fhould be paid for Licenfe of every Carr 20*s.* Fine, and 12 *s. per Ann.* Rent, &c. and that none fhould ufe a Carr without fuch Licenfe, under

O 3   a

a Penalty, *&c.* provided that all Perſons may
ſend their own Carrs to the Wharfs, *&c.* and
carry Goods in their own Carrs from the
Wharfs, except ſuch as ſhall be Traders or
Retailers in Fuel. That *B.* without ſuch Licenſe wrought with a Carr, *pro lucro ſuo proprio,* and for the Penalty a Plaint was levied.

By-Law good when a Cuſtom warrants it.　It was prayed that no *Procedendo* ſhould be.
For tho' the By-Law ſhould be admitted to be
good, having a Cuſtom to warrant it, as
was adjudged in *Player* and *Jenkin's* Caſe,
19 *Car.* II. *B. R.* yet the Plaint is inſufficient,
for that no Cuſtom is alledg'd: And in *Roll.*
364, ſuch a By-Law to limit the Number of
Carrs was held void, becauſe no Cuſtom is
alledg'd. But *per Cur.*

It is not neceſſary to mention the Cuſtom
in the Plaint, for 'tis *Lex Loci,* and they take
notice of their own Cuſtoms in their own
Courts.

But in this *Habeas Corpus* they have returned the Cuſtom, and ſo had good Cauſe
to proceed in the Plaint; for a Cuſtom may
create a Monopoly, as the Caſe in the Regiſter is; a Cuſtom was, that none ſhould
exerciſe the Trade of a Dyer in *Rippon* without
the Archbiſhop of *York's* Licenſe.

But the Court doubted whether this By-
Law was good, becauſe it would reſtrain the
Woodmongers from bringing their Wood, *&c.*
home in their own Carts. *Ventr.* 194. *Brad-
nox's* Caſe.

By-Law of a Company for electing a Livery Man. Sir *Tho. Jones* 149.

By-Law for Reparation of Puddle-Dock.　In *Fiſh* and *Keate's* Caſe they returned the
Uſage, Power, and Cuſtom of the City of
London to make By-Laws by their Common
Council, and that *Puddle-Dock* near *Paul's
Wharf,*

Wharf was an ancient Place for lading and unlading of Ships, Boats, Lighters, &c. and that it was in decay; and that for Reparation of it, it was ordained, *That every Ship that should be loaden and unloaden there, should pay a Penny for every Load; and that every Carman for every Load that he should carry from thence should pay* 1d. The Case was argued in *B. R. Mich. Jacobi* I. but I find it not adjudged.

But see 5 *Rep.*62,&c. the Chamberlain of *Lon.* Case. An Act of Common Council was made, That if any Citizen, Freeman, or Stranger within the said City shall put any Broad-Cloth to sale within the said City of *London,* before it be brought to *Blackwell-Hall* to be view'd and searched, so that it may appear to be vendible, that Stallage shall be paid for it, *viz.* 1 d. for every Cloth : That he shall forfeit for every such Cloth 6 s. 8 d. and that the Chamberlain should have an Action of Debt for it.   This Case was removed, and after a *Procedendo* was granted.   For many Statutes were granted for the true making of Woollen Cloth, which is the principal Commodity of the Realm : And to the intent that the said Statutes might be better executed without Deceit, this Act of Common Council was made, and the assessing the 1 d. was good, it being *pro bono publico.*

Broad-Cloth to be brought to Blackwell-Hall.

King *Charles* I. made the Shoemakers of *London* a Corporation, and gives them Power to make Ordinances ; and they make an Ordinance, *That none shall use that Trade, unless he be free of their Corporation; and if any who was not free use it, he shall forfeit* 40 s. *per Week, and to be committed for it.* After they commit *J. S.* for using the Trade, and not paying

By-Law, that no Shoemaker shall use the Trade, unless he be free of their Corporation, &c.

paying 40 *s.* againſt the ſaid Ordinance. *Per Cur.* It is not lawful to impriſon him. *Hill* 14 *Car.* I. B. K. *Hardcaſtell*'s Caſe, reſolved upon an *Habeas Corpus*, and he was delivered accordingly. 1 *Roll's* Abr. 364.

By-Law by Merchant Taylors. Merchant Taylors of *London* make a By-Law, *That no Merchant put his Cloth to be dreſſed, but to the Clothworkers of their Company.* It is void, as being againſt the Liberty of the Subject. 1 *Roll's* Abr. 364. *Edward's* Caſe.

That none make or uſe an Hot-Preſs. If a By-Law be made in *London, That none ſhall make an Hot-Preſs, nor uſe it within the City, under the Pain of* 10 l. *for the making, and* 5 l *for the uſing;* this is a good By-Law, becauſe uſing of theſe Preſſes is dangerous for Fire, and deceitful alſo, being it makes the Cloth and Stuff better to the Eye than in Truth they are. *Edward's* Caſe, 1 *Roll's* Abr. 365.

Cuſtoms to meaſure Sea-coal. It is a good Cuſtom of *London* that they have uſed at all times, to have the meaſuring of Seacoals *infra portum Lond*², which extends from *Stanes-Bridge* unto *London-Bridge,* and from thence to *Gravefend,* and from thence to *Yealand* ; or *Yendale,* for all this is the Port of *London.* 1 *Roll's* Abr. 557.

The

*The Cuſtom in not removing Body
and Cauſe upon an* Habeas Corpus,
void.

*H*ILL, Citizen and Freeman of *London*, af- *The Cuſtom of*
firms a Petition againſt another Citizen *not removing*
and Freeman of *London* upon a Bond of 100 *l.* *Body and Cauſe upon*
A Summons is awarded againſt the Obligor; Habeas Cor-
and it being returned, that he hath nothing pus.
whereby he may be ſummoned within the
City, upon a Surmiſe made by *Hill* the Obligee, that one *Harrington*, a Citizen and Freeman of *London*, is indebted an 100 *l.* to the
firſt Obligor, a Summons is awarded according to the Cuſtom of *London* of foreign Attachments for the warning of *Harrington*,
who is warned accordingly: Whereupon
Harrington procureth an *Habeas Corpus* for the
removing of his Body, together with the
Cauſe into the King's Bench; upon which
Writ a Return is made in this manner, *viz.*
That London *is an ancient City, and that, time* *The Cuſtom*
out of mind, the Maior, Aldermen, and Citi- *retorned.*
zens of London *have had cognizance of all man-*
ner of Pleas, both real and perſonal, to be holden
before the Maior, Aldermen, and Sheriffs of London, *and that in no Action whatſoever they ought*
to remove the Cauſe out of London *into any other*
Court; and do moreover ſhew a Confirmation made
7. R. II. *of all their Cuſtoms, and therefore they*
had not the Body here, nor the Cauſe.
Exceptions being taken to the Inſufficiency
of this Retorn, it was reſolved *per totam Cur.*
That this Retorn made was ill, for the ſaid
Courſe is, and always hath been, that upon
Habeas

Habeas Corpus, the Body, together with the Cauſe, have been removed out of *London* into the *King's-Bench*; and likewiſe upon *Certiora-ries* awarded out of the *King's-Bench,* Records have been certified out of *London* into that Court; for Juſtice being to be done to the Citizens of *London* as well in that Court as in their own proper Court, the Court of *London* being inferior to the *King's-Bench,* ought to yield Obedience to Writs awarded out of

If it be a ſpe-ſial Cauſe on the Cuſtom, and ſo retorn-ed, it ſhall be remanded.

that Court, as the ſuperior Court: But if the Caſe ſhall be ſuch, that there ſhall be a Fai-lure of Juſtice in *B. R.* upon removing of the Cauſe, becauſe it is an Action merely ground-ed on the Cuſtom of *London,* then a Retorn made of the ſpecial Matter will be warranta-ble ; and if it appear to the Court, that it is ſuch a Cauſe that will not bear an Action at Common-Law, then it may be good, for it is uſual in the *King's-Bench,* that if the Cauſe retorned unto the Court upon the *Ha-*

Cuſtomary Actions to be try'd in the Place only where the Cu-ſtom lieth.

beus Corpus appear to be ſuch a Cauſe as will bear an Action only by the Cuſtom, and not at the Common Law, the Court will grant a *Procedendo,* and ſend it back to *London,* as if the Cauſe retorned appears to be an Action of Debt upon *conceſſit ſe ſolvere,* or Action of Covenant brought upon Covenant by Word without Specialty ; for theſe be mere cuſto-mary Actions, which cannot be maintained but by the Cuſtom of *London,* and therefore ſuch Cauſes ſhall be remov'd, otherwiſe there would be a Failure of Juſtice. *Paſch.* 14 *Jac.*

Cuſtom of London, *to fine one choſen*
to be Sheriff, *if he refuſe to hold.*

CHamberlain, a Citizen and Freeman of
London, being choſen by the Commons according to the Cuſtom of *London,* to be one
of the Sheriffs of the City of *London,* is con-
vened before the Maior and Commonalty to
take the Office upon him, or otherwiſe to
make Oath that he is not worth ten thouſand Pounds: Upon his Appearance he re-
fuſeth to take the Oath, and likewiſe to execute the Office: They fined him 400 Marks
and committed him to Priſon, until ſuch time
as he enter into Bond unto the Maior and
Commonalty to pay it: He becomes bound
accordingly; the Money is not paid at the
Day, whereupon the Maior and Commonalty affirm a Plaint againſt him in *London* for
the ſaid Debt. *Chamberlain* obtains an *Ha-*
beas Corpus to remove the Body and the Cauſe
into the *King's-Bench,* upon Suppoſition he
was to have the Privilege by reaſon of Pri- *Priority of*
ority of Suit in the *King's-Bench,* and upon *Suit.*
Retorn of the *Habeas Corpus* this matter appeared to the Court.

It was moved for a *Procedendo,* it being a *Privilege by*
cuſtomary Suit, merely grounded upon the *reaſon of Pri-*
Cuſtom of *London :* But it was denied by Sir *ority of Suit in*
Edward Coke Chief Juſtice, and the whole *B. R.*
Court, becauſe by the Law, *Chamberlain*
having Cauſe of Privilege by reaſon of the
Priority of Suit againſt him in *B. R.* might
not

not be remanded, and they declared upon the Bond in *B. R.*

It was likewife moved, that the Action upon this Bond might be laid in fome indifferent County, and not in *London*, becaufe the Trial there muft be had by thofe that were Parties to the Action, it being brought by the Maior and Commonalty; but the Court would not, upon this Surmife, take away the Benefit which the Law giveth to every Plaintiff upon a tranfitory Action, *i. e.* to lay it in whatfoever County he will; and if there be any fuch Caufe as is furmifed, then after Plea pleaded, he may make Allegation, that the City of *London* is a County in itfelf, and that all the Citizens there are Parties to the Action which is brought, whereby there may not be an indifferent Trial; and upon this Surmife the Court fhall order the Trial to be in a foreign County, which was done accordingly.

The Cuftom of Market Overt.

WHEN it is faid every Shop is a Marker Overt in *London*, it is to be intended for thofe things only which are ufed to be fold and bought in the Shop, and not for other things; therefore felling of ftolen Plate in a Scrivener's Shop, doth not alter the Property, but the Owner fhall have a Writ of Reftitution.

So Horfes fold in *Cheapfide* alters not the Property: So *Smithfield* is not a Marker Overt for Cloths, but for Horfes and Cattel: So

So Sale in an inner Room in a Shop shall not alter the Property: So behind a Curtain in a Shop: So where the Shop Windows are shut, it is no good Sale to alter the Property of the Owner. *Moor.* 360. the Bishop of *Worcester*'s Case.

Trover for a Silk-Quilt, Silk-Curtains, and a Petticoat and Cloak. The Defendant *quoad* all besides the two last, pleaded, *not guilty,* and *quoad* them he pleaded, the City of *London* is an ancient City, and that within the same is a Market every Day, for all Goods to be sold in every Part of the City in every open Shop, every Day besides *Sundays* and *Holy-days,* betwixt Sun-rising and Sun-setting, so as one of the Contractors be a Freeman, and that he being a Freeman of the Company of Mercers, such a Day, not being *Sunday* or *Holy-day,* bought those things in his open Shop, wherein he had, for a long time used to buy such Wares, *&c.* and justifies the Conversion. *Per totam Cur.* the Plea is not good, for it is laid too general, that every Freeman might buy all manner of Wares in every Shop, for then a Scrivener might buy Plate in his Shop, *&c.* and to buy Petticoats is not agreeable to the Trade of a Mercer; so the Custom is unreasonable, had it been found by special Verdict. *Cr. Jac.* 68. *Taylor* and *Chambers.*

Cuſtom of Innkeepers detaining an Horſe for Meat.

Horſe detain'd. IF one ſets an Horſe at Livery to an Innkeeper, and the Horſe remain there ſo long as the Meat amounts to the Value of the Horſe, then the Innkeeper may call to him four of his Neighbours, and appraiſe the Horſe, and value alſo the Meat ; and if it ſeems that the Meat amount to the Value of the Horſe or more, the Innkeeper may detain the Horſe as his own.

This Cuſtom is only in *London* and *Exeter.* And therefore in *Walbrook* and *Griffith*'s Caſe, the Plaintiff brought an Action on the Caſe for his Horſe, and the Defendant pleads, and laid this to be the general Cuſtom of the Realm, *&c.* and Judgment was given againſt the Defendant, and the Court agreed, that an Innkeeper (Hoſteler) is bound to take Horſes to Livery. If Attorney hires a Chamber in an Inn for the Term, the Innkeeper ſhall not be anſwerable for the Goods ſtolen, but the Innkeeper ſhall anſwer for the Horſe, if the Owner do not come back in 20 Days or more. An Innkeeper may detain an Horſe for the Meat, and yet he may have an Action upon the Caſe for the Meat. *Moor* 876.

Per Serjeant Mountague, Recorder of *London,* the Cuſtom is this: If one bring an Horſe to an Inn, leaves him there, and goes his way, and the Horſe eats up more than his Price, the Innkeeper after Appraiſement

by

by his next Neighbours, may fell the Horfe to pay himfelf, but not if the Debt was for other Horfes; as if one do bring many Horfes into an Inn, and afterwards takes all of them away but one, the Innkeeper cannot fell this Horfe for Payment of that which was due to him for the other Horfes by the Cuftom of *London,* notwithftanding the Debt doth amount to more than the Price of that Horfe; but every Horfe is to be fold by the Cuftom, to fatisfy for the Debt due for his own Meat only. 1 *Bulftrod.* 207. *Mofs. verf. Townfend, vide* 2 *Bulftr.* 186. 1 *Bulftr.* 217. 2 *Bulftrod.* 1.

London

London Cuſtoms, touching Wills, Deviſes, Legacies, Executors, Diſtributions, Orphans, &c.

§ 1. *Of Freemens Wills, and Admini-ſtration of Inteſtates Eſtates.*

EVery Freeman of *London* may make his Will himſelf, and alter it as often as he pleaſes, but he muſt have regard to the Cuſtom of *London*, of giving to his Wife on e third Part of his Perſonal Eſtate, and to his Children another third Part; and the other third Part he may give away to whom he thinks fit. And if he have a Wife and no Child, ſhe ſhall have half his Perſonal Eſtate by the ſaid Cuſtom, and the other Half he may diſpoſe of as he pleaſes. And the like if he have Children only and no Wife, they ſhall have one Half by the Cuſtom, and he may diſpoſe of the other. *Vide infra.*

The Form of a Freeman's Will may be thus.

I W. B. of *London*, Draper, do declare this to be my Will. *Firſt*, I revoke all former Wills. I give my Wife *M. B.* one third of my Perſonal Eſtate, the whole in three equal Parts to be divided: I give to my Children one other third Part thereof, according to the Cuſtom of *London:* And as to the other third, which I have liberty to diſpoſe of as I think fit, I diſpoſe thereof as followeth. I give to my Brother *T. B.* 20 s. to buy him a Ring;

and

and to my Coufin *G.* 20 *s.* to buy him a Ring; and as to the reft and Refidue, I will it fhall be divided into fix equal Parts or Shares, two Parts whereof I give to my Daughter *K.* two other Parts to my Daughter *S.* one Part to my Son *W.* and the other Part thereof I give to my Grandchildren, Share and Share alike ; and I make my faid Wife fole Executrix of this my Will, dated this fecond Day of *November,* 1722.

If a Freeman's Will after this or any other manner be writ with his own Hand, it fhall be a good Will as to all his perfonal Eftate, altho' his Name be not fubfcribed thereto, and although it be without Date or Witneffes, as was adjudged in the Cafe of Sir *William Turner,* Knight and Alderman, who in half a Sheet of Paper writ Inftrudtions for his Will, and what Legacies he would give; and among the reft there was one Legacy of 30000 *l.* to a Nephew's Son : This Paper was brought into *Doctor's Commons* to be proved, which his other Relations oppofed, the fame not being figned by him, and was without Date, or any Witneffes thereto ; in this Caufe there was above 1000 *l.* fpent on both fides ; but it being all of his own Hand-writing, it was adjudged to be a good Will.

But if a Freeman of *London* hath Freehold Lands or Tenements to difpofe of, he muft devife the fame by Will in Writing, purfuant to the Act of 29 *Car.* II. *cap.* 3. *for Prevention of Frauds and Perjuries,* which enacts, *That all Devifes and Bequefts of any Freehold Lands or Tenements fhall be in Writing, and figned by the Party fo devifing the fame, or by fome other Perfon in his Prefence, and by his exprefs Directions, and fhall be attefted and fubfcribed in the Devifor's*

P.　　　　*Prefence*

Preſence by three or four credible Witneſſes, or elſe to be utterly void.

And that no Deviſe in Writing of Lands, Tenements, and Hereditaments, or any Clauſe thereof, ſhall, after the 24th of June, 1677. *be revocable otherwiſe than by ſome other Will or Codicil in Writing, or other Writing declaring the ſame, or by burning, cancelling, tearing, or obliterating the ſame by the Teſtator, or in his Preſence by his Direction and Conſent; but all Deviſes and Bequeſts of Lands and Tenements ſhall remain and continue in force, until ſo burnt, cancelled, torn, or obliterated, or altered by ſome other Will or Codicil, or other Writing as afore-ſaid, any former Law or Uſage to the contrary notwithſtanding.* See the Statute.

Deviſe in Mortmain.   *Note,* By 1 *Bulſtr.* 192, a Foreigner, as well as a Freeman, may deviſe his Fee-ſimple Lands in *London* to another in Fee in *Mortmain,* by the Cuſtom of the City without any Licenſe: But ſee *Dyer* 255, that tho' Foreigners as well as Freemen, may deviſe by the ſaid Cuſtom, yet none but Freemen may deviſe in *Mortmain.* And,

Deviſe of Lands to be inrolled.   By the Cuſtom of *London,* a Deviſe of Lands is invalid, unleſs inrolled within a convenient time. *Cro. Car.* 669. And a Teſtament of Goods muſt be inrolled in the *Huſtings. Hob.* 346.

Reverſions de-viſed by Will inrolled.   It is ſaid, That by the ancient Cuſtom of *London,* where Reverſions of Rents are deviſed by a Will inrolled in the *Huſtings,* ſuch Reverſions are ſo executed, that after the Teſtator's Death the Deviſee may diſtrein and make Avowry, or ſue a Writ of Waſte, without any Attornement of the Tenants, &c. *Vide ante* in general Cuſtoms.

'Tis

'Tis alſo ſaid to be a Cuſtom of *London,* Ex gravi que~ ⌐cela.
that one may have an *ex gravi querela* upon
a Deviſe of Lands there.

I bequeath to my loving Wife Alice *my Live-* Bequeſt of a *lyhood in* London *for the Term of her Life.* By Livelihood. this Will Lands in *London* will paſs by force of the Word *Livelyhood. Owen* 30. And *Brooke* Juſtice there ſaid, it was in ancient Times uſed in divers Places of this Realm, and taken for an Inheritance, to which *Dyer* agreed.

It is ſaid to be the Cuſtom of *London, That* FreemensWills. *if the Father advance any of his Children with any part of his Goods, that ſhall bar them to demand any further part, unleſs the Father under his Hand, or in his laſt Will do expreſs, or declare, that it was but in part of Advancement ; and then that Child ſo partly advanced, ſhall put his Part in* Hotchpot *with the Executrix and* Hotchpot, vide *Widow, and have a full third Part of the Whole,* poſt. *accounting that which was formerly given him as part thereof.* Co. Litt. 176, b. 12 Co. 113.

By the Cuſtom of *London* Probate of Te- *Probate of* ſtaments in *London* is firſt before the Ordina- *Wills in* Lonry, and after before the Maior of *London* in don. his *Huſtings.* See *Regiſter* 246. Perk. §. 577. Cro. Car. 396.

To prove the Will in the *Huſtings* is thus, *The Method.* The Witneſſes thereto muſt be ſworn in open Court, and if their Evidence be full, the Clerk of the Inrollments will enter the Will upon Record, which is the beſt Way of proving Wills touching Eſtates in *London.* See general Cuſtoms *ante.*

As to the Office and Duty of Executors ſee hereafter, *tit. Orphans, &c.* And Note, That by the Cuſtom of *London* an Executor ſhall be charged there to pay a Debt upon a

P 2   ſimple

simple Contract of his Testator. See 5 *Co.* 81. *Cro. Eliz.* 409. 5 *Mod.* 76, 93, &c.

Note also, That in the Case of *King* against *Peck* in *Mich.* 10. *W.* III. *B. R.* 'twas said by *Holt* Chief Justice, that by the Custom of *London*, the Executor shall, on the Master's dying before an Apprentice's Term be expired, put the Apprentice to another Master of the same Trade. And that even in other Places it would be very hard to construe the Death of the Master to be a Discharge of the Covenants. He said it had been held, that the Covenant for Instruction failed, but that he still continued an Apprentice with the Executor, *quoad* Maintenance. 2 *Salk.* 426.

.See 2 *Levinz.* 177. That the Executor is liable in Covenant, if he does not instruct the Apprentice, or find him another Master.

'Tis a Custom in *London* for Executors of Freemen to give Bond as well in the Court of Orphans as in the Spiritual Court. *Hob.* 247.

The third Part of the Goods of a Citizen of London dying Intestate, pertaining by the Custom to his Administrator, is subject to Distribution by the Act of of 22 Car. II. c. 10. for the Settlement of Intestates Estates.

In Attachment on a Prohibition to the Prerogative Court the Plaintiff declares, on the Statute 22 *Car.* II. for settling Intestates Estates, and the Proviso therein, for saving the Customs of *London*, &c. and then shews the Custom of *London*, for Distribution of the Estates of Freemen dying intestate, *viz.* one Part to the Wife, one other to the Child of the Intestate, and the third Part to the Administrator; and further shews, That *D.* the first Husband of the Wife was Citizen and Freeman of *London*, and died Intestate, and Administration was committed to his Widow, who had a Child, and that she had made Distribution according to the Custom, and notwithstanding was sued in Court Christian,

ftian, to make a Diftribution of the Part of
the Adminiftratrix. The Queftion was, *whether the Cuftom were good in Law?* For that e-
very Cuftom muft be time out of Memory,
and an Adminiftrator had Commencement
within time of Memory, for he was confti-
tuted by 31 *Ed.* III. But *per Cur.* the Cuftom
is good, and is the fame with *Coke* 5. *Rep.*
Snelling's Cafe; and the Adminiftrator was
by Common Law, the King as *Parens Patriæ*
being fo. And it was agreed by all the
Juftices, that the Heir by the Cuftom of
London fhall have his Share in the Diftribution. *T. Jones* 204. *& Ux. verf Crifp. Pat.* 32.
Car. II. B. R.

As to the Cuftom concerning the Difpofi-
tion of Freemens Eftates, to what is faid before, we may add thofe Rules in 2 *Salk.* 426. *viz.*

If a Freeman of *London* has no Wife, but
only Children, the half of his perfonal Eftate *Diftribution of*
belongs to his Children, and the other half *Freemens E-*
the Freeman may difpofe of; fo if he has a *ftates.*
Wife and no Children, half of his perfonal
Eftate belongs to his Wife, and the other
half he may difpofe of. But if a Freeman
has a Wife and Children, one third Part
belongs to the Wife, another third Part to his
Child or Children, and the Freeman may
difpofe of the remaining third Part only;
and if fuch Freeman dies Inteftate, the Cuftom can only affect 2 Thirds, and the remaining third is fubject to the Statute of Di-
ftributions, and fo dividing the whole into
Ninths, four Ninths belong to the Wife, and
5 Ninths belong to the Children.

If fuch Freeman has two Sons, and the *Cuftom not ex-*
eldeft Son dies leaving a Son, and then the *tended to*
Freeman dies, the Grandchild, tho' in Law *Grandchildren.*

a Rea Repreſentative of the Son, who never was advanced, has no Part by the Cuſtom of *London*; for the ſaid Cuſtom extends only to the Children and not to the the Grandchildren *per Northey*; and ſo it has been certify'd by the Recorder into Chancery.

Hotchpot only among Children.

If ſuch Freeman has but one Child, and he has received ſome Portion from his ſaid Father, and the Father dies leaving this Child and a Wife; the Child ſhall have his full Orphan's Part, without any Regard to what he has already received; for that Advancement in part is only to be brought into *Hotchpot* with Children, and not with others, *per* Sir *Edward Northey.*

Where 'tis under the Father's Hand, how much a Child has received, &c. yet brought into Hotchpot.

If ſuch Freeman has advanced any of his Children with a Portion, yet if it appears what that Portion was by any Writing under the Father's Hands, or by his Will or Marriage Settlement, and by the ſaid Will or Settlement 'tis ſaid, That the ſaid Portion is or was in full of his Child's Part by the Cuſtom, yet this Child ſhall come in for a Share of the reſt of the Father's perſonal Eſtate, bringing the Portion already receiv'd into *Hotchpot.* Otherwiſe it is, if it does not appear under the Father's Hand what the Advancement was. 2 *Salk.* 427. See *Co. Lit*, 176. *&* 12 *Co.* 13.

If a Freeman gives his Daughter 500 *l.* and ſhe being of full Age gives him a Releaſe of all Claims and Demands ſhe then had or could have in or to the Eſtate which he ſhould have at the time of his Death, and ſhe after marries with or without her Father's Conſent, and her Husband after Marriage gives the Father the like Releaſe; and then the Father dies leaving an Eſtate of
6000 *l.*

6000 *l.* and only two other Daughters, and
by his Will gives thofe two Daughters all his
Eftate, the Releafes in this Cafe, fhall not bar
the married Daughter from claiming an equal
Share of her Father's Eftate, with the other
Daughters, fhe bringing her 500 *l.* into *Hotchpot.*

And the reafon hereof is, becaufe the married Daughter when fole, nor her Husband
after Marriage, had no Right or Claim to any
part of her Father's Eftate, till after his Death.
And therefore the Releafes fealed in her Father's Life-time, were of no Value. So that
there feems no Way to bar a Child from
coming in and claiming the Cuftomary Part of
a Freeman's Eftate, but by caufing fuch Child
to give him Security by Bond, or otherwife
not to claim or demand fuch Part, or elfe a
Covenant to that Purpofe. See more of this
Matter, *poft* 284, 285, *&c.* Tit. *Orphans Court.*

In 26 and 27 *Car.* II. *B. R.* The Cafe was, *Husband vo-*
a Freeman of *London* being poffefs'd of a Term, *luntary Af-*
Affigns it by Deed to his Son for a Provifion, *figns a Term*
and dies; the Mother fues in Chancery for *the Wife to*
her Cuftomary Part, and on iffue try'd before *have her Cu-*
Hales, whether the Feme fhould be bound by *ftomary Part*
this Affignment, fo as to be thereby excluded *thereof.*
from her Cuftomary Part thereof; it was
prov'd, and fo found by the Jury, that fhe was
not bound thereby. And the fame Law, of
Goods, *&c.* 2 *Lev.* 130. City *verfus* City.

So in 1 *Chan. Rep.* p. 84 (10 *Car.* I.) *Nott,* *The Cuftom*
verf. Executors of *Sewfter,* on a *rationabile parte* *allowed on a*
bonorum. The Cuftom of *London* was held *Caufe againft*
good againft a Deed of Truft to the ufe of a *a Deed of*
laft Will. The Suit there, was to have a pro- *ufe of a Will;*
portionable part of a Leafe, and the Profits *and Daugh-*
thereof according to the Cuftom of *London;* *ters to have a*
which Leafe, the Teftator being Father of the *Share with the*
Sons.

Plaintiff, a Daughter, by his Will, directed the Defendants, his Executors, to convey to his two Sons. The Court, on reading the Deed, it appearing to be in Trust to the use of his last Will, declared, that the same was contrary to the Custom of *London*, and that the Plaintiff, according to the Custom, ought to have her Part of the said Lease, and of the Profits thereof.

A Wife relieved against her Husband's Brothers and Sisters. But see 1 *Chan. Rep.* 26. *Havers versus. Burton,* &c. 4 *Car.* I. a Woman that brought a Portion to her Husband, relieved against the Custom, *viz.* The Husband having 1000 *l.* left him by his Father, (who was a Citizen and Freeman) and being an Orphan, and under Age, and his Portion in the Chamber, married the Plaintiff (who brought him a good Portion) and afterwards died before he came of Age; but, by his Will, devised the said 1000 *l.* to the said Plaintiff. The Defendants insisted, that by the Custom of *London*, the said Husband's Portion survived to his Brothers and Sisters, and that 500 *l.* of the said 1000 *l.* in the said Chamber, was a Legacy given to be paid him at Twenty-one; or if he died before, then to go to his Brothers and Sisters. And consequently, that he could not dispose of it.

But the Court conceiving this to be hard against the Wife, who brought a Portion, ordered it to be referred to the Master of the Rolls, and two Serjeants, to settle the Difference; who thereupon ordered the Plaintiff should have 240 *l.* thereof, notwithstanding the said Custom.

Devise of Survivorship of a Customary Part. See also the Case of *Hammond* and *Jones,* *Mic.* 19 *Car.* II. B. R. *viz.* A Freeman of *London* devised, That his third Part should make

make the Cuftomary Part of his Children 500 *l.*
apeice, if their Cuftomary Parts did not
amount to fo much. And if any of them died
before Twenty-one, his Part to be divided a-
mong the others: All the Children die before
Twenty-one, except the Plaintiff's Wife, her
Brother *J.* being the laft that died, and the
Plaintiff had received out of the Father's Part,
fo much as would make his faid Wife's Part
500 *l.* And the Queftion was, if fhe fhould be
intituled by her Father's Will to have the
Cuftomary Part of her Brother *J.* for 'twas
objected, that the Cuftomary Part was not due
by the Will, but by the Cuftom; and to intitle
her thereto, fhe ought to take Letters of Adminiftration to her Brother, and that fhe can't
be intituled by the Father's Will. For he had
no Power to appoint a Survivor of fuch Cuftomary Part. But 'twas held by *Keeling,* Ch.
Juft. &c. That tho' the Father had no Power
to difpofe of fuch Cuftomary Part from the
Children, yet he had Power to appoint a Survivor thereof among the Children themfelves
by his Will. And *Wild,* the Recorder, and
King's Serjeant, faid it was fo lately refolved
in Chancery, in a Caufe wherein he was of
Council; and fo *Keeling* directed the Jury,
who accordingly gave a Verdict for the Plaintiff for the whole.

But notwithftanding the foregoing Cafe, it *That fuch*
has fince been otherwife determined in Chan- *third Part is*
cery, in a Caufe between the Son of Sir *R.* *liable to a*
How, Kt. and Alderman, and his Mother-in- *Diftribution.*
law. For the Cuftom giving one third to the
Wife, and another third to the Child or Children, the remaining third was ufually claim'd
by the Widow, by Virtue of Letters of Adminiftration granted to her of her Husband's
Eftate,

Eſtate, which being thought unreaſonable, was
controverted as aforeſaid; and on hearing the
Cauſe, it was ſettled and decreed to be obſerved as a Rule for ever, That the Deceaſed's third, ſhould be divided into three
equal Parts, and that one third thereof ſhould
go to the Widow, and the other two thirds
to the Child or Children, Share and Share alike,
Note the pursuant to the Stat. 1° *Jac.* II. *For reviving*
Stat. 1 Jac.II. *and continuing of ſeveral Acts therein mentioned.*
Wherein it is (for determining ſome Doubts
ariſen on the Act for better ſettling of Inteſtates
Eſtates) Enacted, &c. ' That the Clauſe in
' the ſaid Act, which provides that the ſaid
' Act, nor any thing therein, ſhall not preju-
' dice the Cuſtoms obſerved within *London*, or
' Province of *York*, was never intended, nor
' ſhall be taken or conſtrued to extend to ſuch
' part of any Inteſtates Eſtate, as any Admi-
' niſtrator, by Virtue only of being Admini-
' niſtrator, by pretence or reaſon, of any
' Cuſtom, may claim to have to exempt the
' ſame from Diſtribution. But that ſuch Part
' in ſuch Adminiſtrators Hands, ſhall be ſub-
' ject to a Diſtribution as in other Caſes
' within the ſaid Act.

And 'tis further provided, &c. ' That if after
' the Father's Death, (*inteſtate*) any of his
' Children ſhall die inteſtate (without Wife or
' Children in the Life-time of the Mother,
' every Brother and Siſter, and the Repreſenta-
' tives of them, ſhall have an equal Share
' with her, any thing in the ſaid Act for
' ſettling Inteſtates Eſtates to the contrary,
' notwithſtanding, &c.

' And Note, The Repreſentatives of every
' Brother and Siſter are their Children.

By

By the Cuftom of *London*, a Freeman's Wi- s *Widow's*dow may require her Widow's Chamber fur- *Chamber.*
nifhed, befides the third Part of his Perfonal
Eftate; and if he fhall make a Will contrary
to the Cuftom, and give away more than a
third Part of his Perfonal Eftate from his
Wife and Children, they may be relieved a-
gainft fuch Will by a Bill, either in the Lord
Maior's Court of Equity, or in the High
Court of Chancery, againft the Executors and
Legatees of fuch Freeman. And fo much
of the Will as fhall be found contrary to the
Cuftom, will be declared void, &c.

If a Freeman fhall in the Time of his laft
Sicknefs, give and deliver any part of his Monies, or Goods, to his Wife, Child, or any
other Perfon, with intent fuch Perfon fhall
keep the fame to their own ufe, fuch Gift is
againft the Cuftom of *London*, and the Goods
or Monies fo given, fhall be accounted part
of the Eftate that belonged to fuch Freeman
at the time of his Death, and may be recovered
in the Lord Maior's Court of Equity, or the
High Court of Chancery as aforefaid. For by
the Cuftom of *London*, a Freeman cannot, in the
time of his Sicknefs whereof he fhall die,
give away any Part of his Eftate, otherwife
than by Will, and then only of his Death's
Part.

Alfo if a Freeman fhall fettle or make over
any part of his Eftate to the ufe of his Child
or Children, with defign to defraud his Wife
of her full third Part, his Widow may fet afide
fuch Settlement, by a Bill againft the Truftees 2 Lev. 130.
and the Children, in either of the Courts aforefaid.

If

If a Freeman ſhall have five **Daughters,** and marries two of them in his **Life-time,** and gives 'em 500 *l.* a piece, and dies poſſeſs'd of an Eſtate of 6000 *l.* Value, and one of the married Daughters afterwards dies, leaving a Child, that Child, as the Repreſentative of his Mother, may claim a further Part of the 600c *l.* Eſtate as the Mother might have done, had ſhe been living.

If a Freeman ſhall have three **Daughters,** and marries one of them in his Life-time, and gives her 1000 *l.* and after dies, leaving an Eſtate but of 500 *l.* Value, in ſuch Caſe the married Daughter cannot be compelled to refund.

See the Caſe of *Hammond* and *Jones,* 1 *Levinz.* 227. A Freeman Deviſes who ſhould be the Survivor of the Cuſtomary Part of his Children, and held good.

Anderſon and *Readſhaw*, verſus *Duck,* *Chandler*, &c.

A Report, or Certificate, by the Lord Maior, *&c.* of *London*, touching the Diſpoſition of Free- mens Eſtates ; and the Lord Chancellor *Cowper*'s Decree there- upon ; *viz.*

To the Right Honourable William *Lord* Cowper, *Baron of* Wingham, *Lord High Chancellor of* Great Britain.

May it pleaſe your Lordſhip.

WHEREAS by an Order of the High Court of Chancery, made the 15th Day of *December* laſt, in a Cauſe there depending between *Joſhua Readſhaw*, Admini- ſtrator of *Juliana* and *Barbara* his late Wives, deceaſed, Plaintiff : *James Duck*, and *Joſeph Chandler*, ſurviving Executors of *Joſeph Ander- ſon*, deceaſed, *William Braſier* and *Hannah* his Wife, Defendants. It was referred to Mr. *Lovibond*, one of the Maſters of the ſaid Court, to ſtate a Caſe touching a Loſs therein menti- oned, and ſend it to the Recorder of the City of *London*, to certify to that Court, the Cuſtom of the City of *London,* upon the Caſe ſo to be ſtated. And whereas the ſaid Maſter hath accord-

The Report of my Lord Ma- ior, &c.

accordingly ſtated the **Caſe** between the ſaid
Parties, in the Words following.

    Jan. 15, 1701. *Joſeph Anderſon,* a Freeman
of *London,* by his Will, directed, that an Inventory ſhould be taken of his Perſonal Eſtate by
his Executors, and that *Barbara,* his Wife,
ſhou'd have her Widow's Chamber; and, after
his Debts and Funeral paid, gave her a third
Part of his Perſonal Eſtate; another third Part,
he gave equally amongſt his Children, *Juliana,*
Hannah, Joſeph and *William,* and *Jane,* who
died in the Eſtator's Life-time. And the remaining third Part, he gave as follows, *viz.*
ſeven hundred and forty Pounds to the ſaid
Hannah, forty Pounds in ſmall Legacies, two
hundred Pounds a piece to the ſaid *Joſeph,*
William and *Jane,* the *overplus* (if any) to be
equally divided amongſt four of his Children,
and to be paid them by his Executors, *viz.* to
his Sons at the Age of twenty-one Years, and
to his Daughters at the Age of twenty-one
Years, or Marriage; and if the third Part of
his Perſonal Eſtate, in his diſpoſe, ſhould by
bad Debts, or other Accidents, fall ſhort, and
not be ſufficient to pay all his ſaid Legacies,
he willed each of the ſaid Legatees ſhould
bear ſuch loſs (whatſoever it amounted to)
in proportion according to their Legacies, and
made *Joſeph Duck, Joſeph Chandler, Samuel*
Greenhile, and *Thomas Greenhile* Executors.

    Mr. *Duck,* Mr. *Chandler,* and *Thomas Green-*
hile, only proved the ſaid Will, and exhibited
an Inventory of their Teſtator's Perſonal
Eſtate into the Chamber of *London,* and entred
into the uſual Recognizance, and paid *Barba-*
ra, the Widow, and Mr. *Readſhaw,* who married *Juliana,* ſeveral Sums on account of their
Cuſtomary Shares.

Thomas

Thomas Greenhill died, and Mr. *Duck* having take out Adminiſtration to him, a Bill was exhibited againſt Mr. *Duck* and Mr. *Chandler,* the two ſurviving acting Executors, for an Account of the Eſtator's perſonal Eſtate, and to have a Diſtribution thereof according to the Cuſtom and the Will.

The Cauſe was heard, and an Account was directed, and the Maſter (to whom the Cauſe was referred) by his Report, charged the Defendant *Duck,* who was become inſolvent, with one hundred ſixty three Pounds one Shilling and ten Pence, as the Balance of his Account; and with two hundred ſeventy nine Pounds and nineteen Shillings, receiv'd by his Inteſtate *Thomas Greenhill,* out of the Teſtator's Eſtate, making together four hundred forty three Pounds and ten Pence. May 30, 1707.

And upon arguing Exceptions taken to the Maſter's Report before the Lord Chancellor, a Queſtion aroſe upon what part of the Teſtator's Eſtate, the Loſs of this Money in caſe it ſhould not be recovered was to fall, whereupon it was order'd, that the ſaid Maſter ſhould ſtate a Caſe touching the ſaid Loſs, and ſend it to the Recorder of the City to certify to the Court the Cuſtom of the City, of *London* upon the Caſe ſo to be ſtated, *viz.* Dec. 15, 1714

Whether by the ſaid Cuſtom the Loſs of the ſaid Freeman's Eſtate by the Inſolvency of his Executors ought to be borne out of the Teſtamentary Part of his Eſtate only, or out of the whole perſonal Eſtate, as well Cuſtomary as Teſtamentary. *Quære.*

We the Lord Maior and Aldermen of the ſaid City of *London,* whoſe Names are ſubſcribed, do in Obedience to the ſaid Order,

by

by *William Thomſon*, Eſq; Recorder of the ſaid City *Ore tenus*, humbly certify unto your Lordſhips.

That if a Freeman of *London* dies, leaving a Widow and Children, his perſonal Eſtate, after his Debts paid (and the Cuſtomary Allowances for his Funeral) and for the Widow's Chamber, being firſt deducted thereout, is by the Cuſtom of the ſaid City to be divided into three equal Parts, and diſpoſed of as followeth, *viz.* one third Part thereof belongs to his Widow, another third Part belongs to his Children unadvanc'd by him in his Life-time, and the other third Part ſuch Freeman by his laſt Will may deviſe as he pleaſeth.

But where a Loſs of a Freeman's Eſtate by the Inſolvency of his Executors doth happen, there is not any Cuſtom of the City of *London*, which directs whether ſuch Loſs ought to be borne out of the Teſtamentary Part of his Eſtate only, or out of his whole perſonal Eſtate as well Cuſtomary as Teſtamentary. Dated the 26th of *April*, 1715.

Gerard Conyers.
Peter Delmé.
George Mertins.
Robert Child.
William Thomſon, Recorder.
Charles Peers.
Francis Forbes.
George Thorold.
William Withers.
William Humphreys, Maior.
William Aſhurſt.
Thomas Abney.
Samuel Garrard.

Gilbert

Gilbert Heathcote.
Richard Hoare.
William Lewen.
John Cafs.

The Report of the Lord Maior and Aldermen being return'd back to the Lord Chancellor *Cowper*, the Matter was again debated by Council on *Trinity Term,* 1715. before his Lordfhip, who was of Opinion, that the Widows and Orphans of a Freeman *Decree* of *London* are in the Nature of Creditors for two Thirds of the Perfonal Eftate he fhall die poffefs'd of; and that if any Lofs happen by the Infolvency of his Executors, fuch Lofs ought to be borne by a Legate of a Freeman, intirely out of his Death's Part, and the fame was decreed accordingly; fo that the Widows and Orphans may have two full Thirds of the Freeman's Eftate, as if no fuch Lofs had been.

Mr. *Readfhaw* was about ten Years in pro- *Note.* fecuting the Suit againft the Executors, which was at laft determined fo much in Favour of the Widow and Orphans.

Sir *Tho. Powis*, } were Counfel for Mr. *Read-*
Mr. *Cowper*, } *fhaw* in Chancery.
Mr. *Sawyer*, }

Mr. *Harris*, Clerk in Court, Mr. *Dixon* of *Lincoln's-Inn*, Sollicitor; Mr. *Major*, &c. were his Counfel before the Court of Aldermen.

Note, It appears by this Cafe, that there is not any Cuftom in the City for afcertaining on which part of a Freeman's Eftate any Lofs by his Executors Infolvency fhould fall: Mr. *Readfhaw* was therefore refolved by the Opinion of the City Counfel to have

Q it

it determined by the Lord Chancellor
in a proper Manner; and (tho' the
View to himſelf as to the Succeſs of the
Cauſe was ſmall) obtained this Decree
whereby it is now ſettled, and become a
Rule in favour of the Widow and Children
of a Freeman, to have a certain Right to
two Thirds of the Perſonal Eſtate, as juſt
Creditors of the Deceaſed.

As to Orphans Portions, the Cuſtom of
the City is, That if any Freeman deviſes
Lands, or Goods, or other Legacies, unto
an Orphan, the Maior and Aldermen are to
take the Profits of the Lands, and to have
the Diſpoſition of the Legacies, till the Legatees attain the Age of 21, or being a
Woman ſhall be marry'd; and if the Diſpoſition of the Profits of the Lands, or of the
perſonal Legacies were declared by the Teſtator in his Will, then the Maior and Aldermen have uſed to convent the Perſons intruſted by the Will before them, and compel him to find Sureties for the true Payment of the Legacies and Performance of the
Will, according to the Law of the Realm,
and the Will of the Teſtator; and if they
refuſe to find Sureties, to impriſon them till
they do ſo.

The

The Practice of the several
Courts belonging to the City
of *London*; with an Account of
their respective Fees, Jurisdiction, &c.

Viz:

The Court of Hustings.
The Lord Maior's Court.
The Sheriffs Court.
The Orphans Court.
The Chamberlain's Court.
The Court of Common Council.
The Court of Aldermen.
The Wardmotes.
The Court of Conservacy for the Ri-
   ver of Thames, *and of Watermen.*
The Court of Requests, or of Con-
   science.

Also the Courts of { *Hallmote.*
                       Coroner.
                       Escheator.
                       Tower.
                       St. Martins le
                          Grand.

Concerning the Court of Huſtings.

THE Court of *Huſtings*, being the ſupreme Court of Judicature within the City of *London* (as that of the Common Council is of its Legiſlature, &c.) is a very antient Court of Record, where all Lands and Tenements, Rents and Services within the City and Liberties of *London* are pleadable, at the *Guild-Hall* of the ſaid City, in two *Huſtings* ; whereof one is called *Huſting of a Plea of Land*; the other, *Huſting of Common Pleas.*

The Judges of this Court are the Lord Maior and Sheriffs for the time being ; and when any Matters of Moment are to be try'd in this Court, the *Recorder* ſits with them, to direct them in Points of Law, and to give Judgment, &c.

This Court is held upon the *Monday* and *Tueſday* of every Week ; upon the *Monday to enter Demands, to award Nonſuits, and allow Eſſoigns* ; and upon *Tueſday, to award Defaults, and to plead*; unleſs it be upon Holy-Days, and other particular Times, when by the Cuſtom of the City, no *Huſtings* is to be kept. 'Tis obſervable, that the *Huſtings of Pleas of Lands*, and the *Huſtings of Common Pleas* muſt be held diſtinctly, notwithſtanding the original Inrolment, &c. that is to ſay, for one Week the Judges ſit upon *Pleas* merely *Real*; and the next Week upon Actions mixt ; the Title of which Court runs thus :

Pl'ita

Pl'ita terre tent. in Huſtingo in Guildhall London die Lunæ prox. &c. Anno Regni, &c.

See 2 *Leon.* 14. That the *Huſtings* are uſually held from three Weeks to three Weeks, but may be every Week if pleaſe.

Of *Pleas* of *Lands* (viz. By *Writ of* Right Patent) *in the Huſtings.*

IN the *Huſting of a Plea of Lands* are pleaded   *Writ.* *Writs of Right Patent,* directed to the Sheriffs of *London,* in which *Writs* there is this Proceſs by Cuſtom of the ſaid City, *viz.* the Tenants, *&c.* ſhall firſt have three Summons at three *Huſtings of a Plea of Land,* next enſuing after the Livery of the *Writ, &c.*

And after the three Summons, as aforeſaid, *Summons.* three *Eſſoigns* at three other *Huſtings of a Plea of Land,* then next enſuing after the third *Eſſoign,* and the Tenants making Default, Proceſs ſhall be made upon them by a *Grand Cape,* or *Petit Cape,* after the manner of an *Appearance,* and other *Proceſs* at Common Law.

And if the Tenants ſhall appear, the De- *Appearance.* mandants ſhall plead againſt them in the Nature of what *Writ* they will, (except certain *Writs* which are pleadable in the *Huſtings of Common-Pleas,* as is afterwards declared) without making Proteſtation to ſue in the Nature of any *Writ.*

And the Tenants ſhall have the View, and *View.* ſhall be eſſoigned after the View, as at Common-Law. And by the Cuſtom of the City

the

the Tenants fhall have an Effoign after every Appearance.

And though fuch *Writ* be abated after the View by Exception of Joint Tenancy, *&c.* and other fuch Writ be revived : The Tenants by the Cuftom of the City fhall have the View in the fecond Writ, notwithftanding the View before had ; and if the Parties *Judgment.* plead to the Judgment, Judgment fhall be pronounced by the *Recorder*'s Mouth. Obferve fix Aldermen at leaft were wont to be prefent at the pronouncing every fuch Judgment.

Jury.   And every *Beadle* of the City, by the Advice of his Alderman, fhall fummon twelve of the beft and moft fubftantial Freeholders in his Ward againft every *Hufting of a Plea of Land,* to come to the *Guild-Hall,* for to pafs in an *Inqueft,* if need require, in Behalf of the reft of the Freeholders of the faid Ward.

Verdict.   And if the Parties plead, and defcend to an *Inqueft,* then fhall the *Inqueft* be taken of the People Inheritory, having at leaft *Franck-Tenements* in the fame Ward, where the faid *Tenements* are; and alfo of other three Wards next to the faid *Tenements* ; fo that forty fufficient Men of the faid Ward, where the faid *Tenements* are, be fworn of the *Inqueft,* if there be fo many.

Damages, &c.   No Damages by the Cuftom of *London* are recoverable in any fuch *Writ of Right Patent,* and the *Inqueft* may pafs the fame Day, by fuch common Summons of the *Beadle,* as aforefaid, provided the Parties be at Iffue, and the *Jurors* come; otherwife *Procefs* fhall be made to caufe the *Inqueft* to come at another *Huftings of Plea of Land,* by a *Precept* from the Maior directed to the Sheriffs; and herein

in the Sheriffs, by the Command of the
Maior, are to be the Officers to ferve the
Writs, and to make Execution thereof, notwithftanding the original *Writ* be directed to
the Maior and Sheriffs jointly. Obferve,
that as well the Tenants, as the Demandants,
may make their *Attornies* in fuch *Pleas.* *Attornies.*

If the Demandants plead againft thofe Tenants in the nature of a *Writ of Right,* and
the Parties defcend to an *Inqueft* upon the *mere* *Inqueft on the*
Right, then fhall the *Inqueft* be taken of Twen- *mere Right.*
ty-four, after the manner of a *Grand Affize,*
according to the Cuftom of the City, provided that Six be of the Ward where the Tenements be, if there be fo many of the
Ward empannelled in the *Inqueft* of Twenty-
four.

The Tenants in all fuch *Writs* may vouch *Vouch to War-*
to *Warranty* within the faid City, and alfo *ranty.*
in a foreign Country, if the Vouchees have
Tenements within the City.

And if the Tenants in fuch a *Writ* do vouch
to *Warranty* in a foreign Country, in which
Cafe *Procefs* may not be made againft the
Vouchees by the Law of the City, then they
fhall be made to bring the Record before the *Removal of*
Juftices of the *Common-Pleas* at the Suit of the *the Record.*
Demandant, and there *Procefs* fhall be made
againft the Vouchee; and when the Voucher
fhall be ended in the faid *Bench,* then fhall all
the *Plea* be fent again to the *Huftings,* there to
proceed in the *Plea,* according to the Cuftom *Procedendo.*
of the City, *&c.*

And likewife if the Tenants in fuch *Writs*
plead in *Bar,* by a Releafe bearing Date in
a foreign County, or plead any other foreign *Foreign Plea.*
Matter, which may not be try'd within the
City, then the Demandant fhall bring the *Pro-*

Q 4 *cefs*

cefs into the *King's-Bench*, to try the matter
as it is alledged; and according as it is found,
the *Plea* fhall be fent back into the *Hufting*,
Procedendo. there to be proceeded as the Cafe requires,
and all the time the *Plea* fhall ceafe in the
Huftings, as it is at this Day.

Error.   If erroneous Judgment be given in the
Huftings before the Maior and Sheriffs, it fhall
be reverfed by Commiffion out of the *Chancery*, directed to certain Perfons to examine
the Record ; or if erroneous Judgment be
given before the Sheriffs in *London*, a *Writ of
Error* may be fued before the Maior and Sheriffs in the *Huftings*. Obferve, that the Summons which are made to the Tenants in fuch
Writs of Right Patent may be made two or
three Days, or the Day next before the faid
Huftings.

Of the Huftings of Common-Pleas.

IN the *Huftings of Common Pleas* are pleadable thefe *Writs* following, *viz. Writs* of
ex gravi Querela, for to have Execution of the
Tenements out of the Teftaments which are
inrolled in the *Huftings: Writs of Dower, unde
nihil habet: Writs of Gavalet of Cuftoms and
Services*, inftead of *Ceffavit: Writs of Error of
Judgment given before the Sheriffs: Writs of Wafte:
Writs de facienda partitione between Copartners :
Writs of Quid Juris clamat, & per quæ Servitia,*
and other *Writs* which are clofed and directed to the Maior and Sheriffs; and alfo all *Replegiaries* of Goods, and *Diftreffes*
wrongfully taken, are pleadable before the
Maior and Sheriffs in the fame *Huftings* of
Pleas, by Plaint without Writ,

Obferve,

Obferve, That the Sheriffs are Minifters to execute the Office, and ferve all the *Writs* and *Replegiaries,* by a Precept from the Maior, directed to the faid Sheriffs ; the *Procefs* in which *Writs* is as followeth.

In a *Writ of Ex gravi querela* Warning fhall be given to the Tenants, two or three Days before the *Hufting,* or in the Morning before, as in a *Plea of Land ;* and fo it fhall be done in all other Summons belonging to the faid *Huftings.* Ex gravi Querela.

If Warning be given, and teftified by the *Sheriff,* or his *Minifter,* the Tenants may be *Effoigned* once ; and if the Tenants make default, and the Warning aforefaid being teftified, then fhall the *Grand Cape* be awarded ; and if they appear, they may be *Effoigned* after the View ; and thereupon all other *Procefs* fhall be made fully as it is faid, as in a *Writ of Right Patent* in the *Huftings of the Pleas of Land.*

In a *Writ of Dower, Unde nihil habet,* the Tenants fhall have at the beginning, *three Summons,* and an *Effoign* after the *three Summons,* and afterwards fhall have the *View,* and after the *View* an *Effoign;* and the Tenants in the fame *Writ of Dower,* fhall have the *View,* notwithftanding they enter by the fame Husband of the *Demandant,* altho' the Husband died feized. *Writ of Dower.*

Alfo the faid Tenants may vouch to *Warranty,* and be *Effoigned* after every Appearance ; and alfo other *Procefs* fhall be made, as in a *Writ of Right in the Hufting of a Plea of Land.*

If the *Demandant* recover *Dower* againft the Tenants by Default, or Judgment in Law, in fuch *Writ of Dower,* and the fame Woman Demandant, fhall alledge in Court of Record, that her Husband died feized, then the *Maior,* Vide ante.

by

by his Precept, fhall give Commandment to the *Sheriffs*, that they fummon an *Inqueft* of Neighbours where the Tenements are, againft the next *Huftings of Common-Pleas*, to enquire whether the Husband died feized, and of the Value of the Tenements, and the *Damages* fhall be enquired of by the fame *Inqueft*.

Writ of Gava-let. In a *Writ* of *Gavalet*, the Tenants fhall have three Summons, and three *Effoigns*, and fhall likewife have the View; they may vouch to *Warranry Denizen* and *Foreigner*, and they fhall be *Effoigned*, and muft enter their Exceptions, and all other Procefs muft be made, as before is declared, in a *Writ* of *Right Patent in the Hufting of-Plea of Land*; faving, that if the Tenant make default, then the Demandant fhall have Judgment to recover, and to hold for a Year and a Day, upon condition that the Tenant may come within the fame Year and a Day next enfuing, and agree for the Arrearages, and find fuch Sureties as the Court fhall award to pay the Rent afterward, and then fhall have again his Tenements: within which Year and Day, the *Tenant* may come and caufe the Demandant to come into Court, by a *Scire Facias*, and have again his Tenements, doing as aforefaid.

Scire Facias. After the End of the Year and the Day, as aforefaid, the Demandant fhall have a *Scire Facias* againft the Tenant, to come and anfwer, if he has any thing to fay, wherefore the faid Demandant ought not to hold the Tenements quietly to himfelf and his Heirs for ever. And if the Tenant do not come, or if he do come, and can fay nothing, &c. then the Judgment fhall be, that the faid Demandant fhall recover the Tenements quietly for ever, according to the Judgments called *Shartford*, by Cuſtom of the City of *London*.

See the Stat. of *Gavalet, poſt,* Tit. *General Statutes* ; and ſee hereafter *pag.* 239, of the Writ of *Partitione Facienda.*

In a *Writ of Waſt,* Proceſs ſhall be made a- *Writ of Waſt.* gainſt the Tenants, by Summons, Attachments, and Diſtreſſes, according to the Statutes thereof made ; and if the Tenant come and plead, then he ſhall have an *Eſſoign,* and ſo after every Appearance ; but if he make default at the Grand Diſtreſs, then there ſhall be a Commandment to the Sheriffs, by a Precept from the Maior, that the Sheriff ſhall come to the Place waſted, and ſhall enquire of the Waſt and Damages according to the Statute, and return the ſame at the next *Huſtings of Common Pleas,* and the Plaintiff ſhall recover the Place waſted, and triple Damage by the Statute.

See after (in this Court) *pag.* 248 to 250, concerning an Action of *Waſt* in *London,* and of a Special Commiſſion of *Errors.*

In a Writ of Error of Judgment, given in *Writ of Error.* Court before the Sheriffs, in Actions Perſonal, *&c.* the Maior ſhall make his Precepts to the Sheriffs, to bring the Proceſs and Record at the next *Huſtings of Common-Pleas,* and warn the Parties to be there to hear the Record.

And after the Record and Proceſs be in the *Huſtings,* altho' the Defendant come not at the Warning, but make default, the Errors ſhall be aſſigned, and there the Judgment ſhall be affirmed, or reverſed, as the Law requireth.

See more of Writs of Error, *&c.* in the *Huſtings, poſt,* 238, 249. (*a* 163, 164)

In

'A Replegiare. 'In a Writ of *Replegiare,* or *Replevin,* the Procefs is thus : If any Man take a Diftrefs within the faid City, he which oweth the Goods, may come to one of the Sheriffs, and fhall have an Officer at the Command of the Court, to go to the Party that took the Goods; and if he may have the View to praife them by two Men, and then a Plaint fhall be made in the Sheriff's Paper Office, to this Effect :

1. H. queritur verfus W. B. de averiis fuis injufte capt' in Dominio fuo vel in libero Tenemento fuo in Parochiâ St. &c.

And the faid Party fhall bring two fufficient Securities to return the Goods, in cafe the fame be awarded.

And the Parties fhall have a Day prefix'd at the next *Huftings of Common-Pleas;* and the Sheriff fhall make a Bill containing the Matter of the Plaint, and fhall bring the faid Bill to the faid *Huftings,* and caufe it to be put upon the File, and the Parties fhall be called for : At which Day, the one or the other, may be effoigned by a Common Effoign.

At what Time foever the Plaintiff makes default, it fhall be awarded, that the Avowant keep the Goods; and fuch Award according to the Cuftom of *London,* fhall be made three times, and after that, it fhall not be reprifable. And if the Avowant makes default, the Goods fhall be awarded to the Plaintiff, *viz.* they fhall remain to him without recovering any damage.

But if it fo happen, that the Sheriff cannot have a view of the Goods, then he fhall certify the fame in the *Huftings,* and there fhall *Withernam.* be awarded a Writ of *Withernam,* and thereupon Procefs made; and if the Parties come, and Avowry be made, they may then plead

to

to *Judgment*, or to an Iffue of *Inqueft*, as the Cafe requires.

The Parties may alfo be Effoigned, after every Appearance; but if the Party claim Property, and certify the fame in the *Hufting*, a Procefs may be made by a Precept to the Sheriff, to try the Property, notwithftanding the Party be *Effoigned* of the King's Service, in a *Replegiare*, and if he make Defaults upon the Effoign Day, he fhall not be charged of the Damage.

The Practice however upon a Replevin, *is briefly faid to be thus,* viz.

He that would replevy Goods in *London*, may go to the Clerk of the Papers belonging to one of the *Compters*, and give in Particulars and Security, to reftore the Goods or the Value, in cafe upon a Trial it fhall appear the fame did not belong to him. And then the Clerk will give a Warrant to one of the Sheriffs Officers, to caufe the Goods to be Appraifed, and to deliver them to the Plaintiff. After the Appraifement is made, and the Goods delivered, the Officer muft make return thereof to the Clerk of the Papers, who will immediately thereupon certify the Record thereof into this Court, where the fame muft be decided: And if Iffue fhall be joined to try in whom the Property of the Goods was when the fame were taken, a Jury muft be fummoned to try the Iffue: And in order thereunto, Precepts muft be iffued to the Beadle of the fix adjacent Wards, to return the Names of the Six fubftantial Freeholders and Inhabitants in each Ward.

When

When the Names are fo returned, a Precept muft be fent to the Sheriffs, to require them to fummon the Jury to appear at the next *Huftings* of Common-Pleas to try the Iffue.

Writ of Error. A Writ of Error may be brought in this Court to reverfe any Judgment given in the Sheriffs Court. The Writ muft be made by the Curfitor for *London*, and directed to the Maior and Sheriffs of *London* ; and when fealed, muft be delivered to Mr. Town-Clerk to allow the fame; and at the fame time, he that fues it, muft enter into Bond with two fufficient Sureties to pay the Debt, or Damages, and Cofts recovered, and which fhall be affeffed, in cafe the Judgment fhould happen to be affirmed; or in cafe the Plaintiff, in the Writ of Error, fhould not profecute the Writ of Error with Effect : And when Security fhall be fo given, Mr. Town-Clerk will make a *Superfedeas* directed to the Sheriffs, to ftay further proceeding upon the Judgment. And it is ufual to move the Court at the next Huftings of Common Pleas, after the allowance of the Writ, that the Proceedings in the Sheriffs Court, may be certified, within fourteen Days then following, into this Court, where Errors may be affigned and argued ; and if Judgment fhall be affirmed, the Plaintiff in the Writ of Error may bring another Writ of Error before the Judges, to examine the former Judgment.

When Judgment fhall be affirmed in this Court, upon a motion, the Court will order the Bond to be delivered up to the Defendant in the Writ of Error, to put the fame in fuit for his Cofts and Damages fuftained, by reafon of the delay of Execution, who fhall not

be

be compelled to cancel or part with the ſame till he ſhall be fully ſatisfied.

If the Plaintiff in the Writ of Error do not certify the Record out of the Sheriffs Court into this Court, according to the time given by the Court, of if he ſhall not aſſign Errors, the Court will give Judgment againſt the Plaintiff, and iſſue out a Warrant, in the nature of a *Procedendo*, to the Sheriffs of *London,* thereby commanding them to proceed to Execution upon the Judgment obtained in that Court.

In a *Writ de Partitione faciend'* to make Partition between Partners of Tenements in *London:* A *Writ* cloſed, ſhall be directed to the Maior and Sheriffs, containing the Matter after the Nature of ſuch Writ, and the Parties ſhall be warned by Precept from the Maior, and the Tenants may be eſſoigned ; or if they come, they may plead ; or if they make Default, the Partition ſhall be awarded by Default. *Writ De Partitione faciend.*

Election of Burgeſſes and other Officers in the Court of Huſtings.

IN this Court, the Burgeſſes to ſerve for the City in Parliament, muſt be Elected by the Livery-men of the reſpective Companies. *Election of Burgeſſes.*

Upon every *Michaelmas* Day, it is the Cuſtom to chuſe a Lord Maior for the Year following; and the uſage is, to put all thoſe Gentlemen in nomination that are Aldermen under the Chair, who have held the Office of Sheriff. The Commons muſt chuſe Two, and return their Names to the Lord Maior and Aldermen, who
elect *Lord Maiors.*

elect which of the Two they think moſt fit to
hold the Place, and ſignify their Choice to the
Commons. And the Perſon ſo elected, muſt
be preſented to the Lord Chancellor, and afterwards muſt be ſworn at *Guild-Hall* on St. *Si-
mon* and *Jude's* Day, and the Day after at
the *Exchequer.*

Sheriffs.   Upon *Midſummer* Day, the Livery-men of
the reſpective Companies do chuſe Sheriffs ;
but 'twas pretended my Lord Maior, by his
Prerogative, may drink to any Citizen, and
nominate him to be one of the Sheriffs ; and
that the uſage hath been for the Commons to
confirm ſuch Perſon, and to elect another to
ſerve with him. *Sed quære.*

Aafter the Sheriffs are elected, the Commons chuſe two Auditors for the Chamber
and Bridge-Houſe Accompts, a Chamberlain,
two Bridge-Maſters, and four Ale-Conners.

Note, That the Sheriffs are Judges of the
Elections, and do declare by Mr. Common-
Serjeant, who are the Perſons elected.

After the Sheriffs are ſo elected, they take
an Oath at *Guild Hall* upon *Michaelmas* Eve,
and the Day after *Michaelmas* Day muſt be
preſented to the Barons of the Exchequer ;
and when they are ſworn, it is not now in
the Power of the Commons to remove them
at their Pleaſure, they being reſtrained by
Stat. 7. *R.* II.

Chamberlain.   The Chamberlain and Bridgmaſters, after
Election, take the uſual Oath before the Lord
Maior and Court of Aldermen.

Attorneys.   *Vide Plus* touching the ſaid Officers, *&c.*
ante Pag. - - -

The Attornies of the Lord Maior's Court,
are Attornies of this Court likewiſe ; and the
Second Attorney is alſo Clerk of the Inrolments

ments, to inroll all Deeds that are brought thither; the Method is thus:

The Perfons that fealed the Deed muft go before the Lord Maior, or the Recorder, and one Alderman, and make Acknowledgment that the fame is their Act and Deed; if a Wife be a Party, fhe is to be examined by them, whether it was done with her full and free Confent, without any kind of Compulfion; in Teftimony of which the Lord Maior, or Recorder and Alderman fet their Hands to it, for which each may demand 4 *d.* and the Attorney's Fee for the Judgment is 2 *s.* Afterwards the Deed muft be deliver'd to the Clerk of the Inrolments, who at the next *Huftings* will caufe Proclamation to be made thereof, according to the Cuftom of the Court.

The Fees for the Inrolment of a Deed are,

	s.	*d.*
To Mr. Recorder — —	06	08
To the Chamberlain — —	01	08
To the Town-Clerk — —	00	10
To the Attorney for every Prefs —	06	00
To his Clerk — —	00	08

Obferve, That a Deed inrolled in the *Huftings,* bars the Wife from claiming her Dower, and is efteemed as good in *London* as a Fine at Common Law.

For proving of Wills in the Huftings, *vide ante pag —*

The Method of paffing *Recoveries* in this Court is, *Firft,* a Writ of *Right Patent* muft be obtain'd from the Curfitor of *London,* which muft be delivered to one of the Attorneys of this Court, who are to prepare the Record, and procure the *Recovery* to pafs.

R *The*

The Charge of paſſing a Recovery, is,

	l.	*s.*	*d.*
For drawing the Writ —	oo	o1	oo
For the Writ of Right —	oo	o5	o6
For Allowance thereof —	oo	o2	oo
For the Attorney's Fee —	oo	o3	o4
For the Warrant of Attorney	oo	oo	o4
For the Precept of Summons	oo	o2	oo
For the Retorn thereof —	oo	o2	o8
For the Declaration —	oo	o2	oo
For the Tenants Plea —	co	o2	oo
For Entring thereof — —	oo	o2	oo
For the Vouchee's Plea —	oo	o2	oo
For Entring thereof — —	oo	.o2	oo
For the Common Vouchee's Plea	oo	o2	oo
For Entring thereof —	oo	o2	oo
For Record for the Pleaders	oo	o2	o6
The Common Cryer —	oo	o1	oo
The Common Voucher —	oo	o1	oo
The Green-Cloth —	oo	o1	oo
The Four Pleaders — —	oo	13	o4
For Entring the Judgment —	oo	o2	oo
The Attorney's Fee thereupon	oo	o3	o4
The Precept for Seizin —	oo	o2	oo
Retorn thereof —	oo	o2	oo
For drawing and ingroſſing the Record — —	oo	13	o4
For exemplifying it —	oo	o6	o8
For the Seal ———	oo	o6	o8
For the Clerk ————	oo	oo	o8
	o4	o7	oo

It is common to have a Deed ſealed to lead the Uſes of the Recovery, and likewiſe to have ſuch Deed inrolled.

It is uſual likewiſe, that if the Vouchees cannot attend the Court in their own Perſons

fons, to fign a Warrant of Attorney, and acknowledge it before the Recorder, and that will be allowed of as well as if they had perfonally attended.

The Form of the faid Warrant, *&c.*

A. B. *& E. uxor ejus, quos* C. D. *vocat ad Warrantizand, &c. po. lo fuis* M. L. *&* J. H. *conjunctim & divifim verfus* W. W. *in placito terre, &c. Viz. de quatuor Meffuagiis & quatuor Gardinis cum pertinentiis fcituat' jacent' & exiftent' in parochia St. Botolphi, &c. in Warda Portfoken, &c. London', ad lucrandum & perdendum, &c. Secundum Confuetud. Civitatis London.*

Primo die, &c. Anno, &c. Capt' & Cognit' coram me.

W. T. *Recordate.*

W. W. H. W.

Note, That in this Court of the *Huftings,* Of Attaints. by Stat. 11. 21 *Hen* VII. an *Attaint* may be fued by Bill upon any falfe Verdict given in any of the Courts of that City; and thereupon the Maior fhall award a Precept to every Alderman to prefent (either by them- *Juries how re-* felves or their Deputies) unto the faid Maior, *turn'd.* at the next *Huftings,* the Names of four indifferent and difcrete Citizens out of each of their Wards, each of them being worth 100 *l.* at leaft; out of which the Maior and fix Aldermen, or more, fhall impannel 48, whom the Maior fhall caufe to be fummoned, together with the Tenants or Defendants in the Attaint, to appear at the next *Huftings*; and

R 2　　　　if

if, upon Default of Appearance, or otherwife, there fhall need a Tales, the Pannel fhall be fupplied out of the reft prefented, or by other fuch Citizens, at the Difcretion of the faid Maior and fix Aldermen.

Attaints.   Alfo that Pleas of Attaints commenced in *London*, fhall be try'd there by *Inquefts* of the faid City, and not elfewhere ; and in an Attaint there no Challenge fhall be for lack of Sufficiency in Eftate.

Judgment.   The Judgment in fuch an Attaint fhall not extend to Lands or Tenements, nor yet to other Punifhment of the Petty Jury, or other Proceffes, than fuch as are limited by this Act.

  Alfo in fuch an Attaint, if the Petty Jury *Attaint of Pet-*be attainted, Judgment fhall be given againft *ty Jury.* the *Defendant*, as at the Common Law, and againft the Petty Jury to forfeit each of them 20 *l.* or more, at the Difcretion of the Court, to be employed as other Penalties forfeited before them, and to fuffer fix Months Imprifonment, or lefs, at the like Difcretion of the Court, and to be for ever after difabled to be a Juror. But if the Verdict be affirm'd, the GrandJury fhall further inquire of the Corruption of the Petty Jurors, and if any of them be found to have taken any Reward or Promifes thereof, he fhall forfeit ten times the Value thereof to the Plaintiff, and fhall further incur Imprifonment and Difability to be a Juror, as aforefaid. The like Forfeiture alfo and Imprifonment fhall be inflicted upon the Tenant or Defendant, that fhall give fuch Reward or Promife, and this laft Forfeiture is to accrue to the City in manner as aforefaid.

Reftitution.   Alfo if a Debt, Cofts, or Damages are recovered in the firft Action (whereupon the Attaint

taint is brought) and that Verdict found
falſe, the Plaintiff in ſuch Attaint may ſue for
Reſtitution of ſuch Debt, Coſts, and Damages, by Writ, Bill, or Plaint, in any of the
King's Courts, wherein no Wager of Law
ſhall be admitted.

And in ſuch Attaint, if the Plaintiff be *Nonſuit, &c.*
Nonſuit, or the firſt Verdict affirm'd, the
Plaintiff ſhall be impriſoned, and make
Fine (to the Uſe of the City) at the Diſcre-
tion of the Court.

Where there are one or more Plaintiffs, if *Grand Jury,*
any of them die, or be Nonſuit, albeit all *&c.*
the Tenants and Defendants, and ſome of the
Petty Jury die, yet ſhall not the Attaint a-
bate, ſo that two of that Jury remain in
Life.

The Grand Jurors that make Default, ſhall
forfeit for the firſt 40 *s.* for the ſecond 5 *l.* and
for every other afterwards 10 *l.*

And ſuch Proceſs ſhall be made againſt
the Jurors and Parties in this Attaint, as
is uſually made in Attaints at the Common
Law, and ſhall be returnable at every
Huſtings.

The Attaint ſhall not remain to be taken
after the firſt Summons for Default of the
Tenant or Defendant, or any of the Petty
Jury ; neither ſhall any Eſſoin be allowed in
the ſame.

When the Trial is to be by *medietatem Lin-* *Trial per Med.*
gua, the Maior and Aldermen ſhall impannel *Linguæ.*
half Strangers worth 100 *l.* apiece.

By Stat. 11 *Hen.* VII. 21. None ſhall be *Jurors how*
empannelled upon a Jury in *London,* except *qualify'd.*
he have Lands and Tenements, or Goods
and Chattels, worth 40 Marks ; and if the
Trial be for Lands or Debts, or Damages a-

R 3   mounting

mounting to 40 Marks or above, his real or Perfonal Eftate fhall be worth 100 Marks, and the Jurors Defect herein is a principal Challenge.

Default.

The Iffues of the Jurors *for Default of appearing fhall be at the firft Summons* 12 d. *at the Second* 2 s. *and double afterwards ; and the Iffues loft in the* Maior's *Court fhall accrue to the* Maior *and* Commonalty, *and thofe loft in the* Sheriffs *Court to the* Sheriffs.

And by Stat. 4. 3 *Hen.* VIII. for the Iffues abovementioned, the Maior and Sheriffs, and their Succeffors may diftrein refpectively, *viz.* the Maior for his, and the Sheriffs for theirs.

Pannel.

And by the faid Statute the Sheriffs of *London* have Power to retorn Pannels of Jurors in Suits depending in any of the Courts at *Weftminfter,* and tryable in *London,* being Citizens, and having Goods of the Value of 100 Marks, who fhall ferve and be fworn in like manner as if they had Lands and Tenements of 40 s. *per Ann.*

Alfo the Sheriffs of *London* fhall return upon the firft Diftrefs upon every Juror 20 d. and upon the fecond Diftrefs 40 d. and upon every other Diftrefs after that, the double, until a full Jury appear and be fworn in pain of 10 l. to be divided between the King and the Profecutor.

And by Stat. 5. 5 *Hen* VIII. the faid Iffues fhall be underftood only of Writs of Diftrefs before Juftices or Juftice of *Nifi prius,* in Suits depending in the Court of *Weftminfter,* and tryable in *London,* and not of other Writs or Proceffes iffuing out of the faid Courts.

And by Stat. 7 *Hen.* VII. 5. *Riens deins le Gard* fhall not be admitted for Challenge in *London.*   3   **And**

And by Stat. 7 & 8 *W.* III. *c.* 32. concerning Juries, no longer time is allow'd for the summoning Juries that are to try Issues joined and tryable in *London*, or County of *Middlesex*, than was by Law required before, nor any longer time for the Return of any Writ, Precept, or Process of *Venire facias*, *Habeas Corpora*, or *Distringas*, than was by Law required before. And the said Act shall not extend to the City of *London*, nor to any other County of any City or Town within this Realm ; nor to any Town Corporate, that hath Power by Charter to hold Sessions of Goal-Delivery, or of the Peace.

By Stat. 27 *H.* VIII. 5. Citizens of *London* being worth 400 Marks in personal Estate, may be impannelled and retorned by the Sheriffs of *London*, upon Attaints there, albeit they have no real Estates, notwithstanding the Stat. of 23 *H.* VIII. 3. And the Justices shall hereafter sit upon Attaints in *London* at *Guild-Hall*, or some other convenient Place in that City, and not elsewhere ; neither shall the Citizens there be compellable to appear upon any such Attaint, in any other Place, notwithstanding the Stat. of 23 *H.* VIII.

Of an Action of Waste in London, *by the Custom ; and of special Commission of Errors.*

Cole in the *Hustings* complains, and counts *Waste in London.* that he was seized of the Reversion in Fee of a Brewhouse which *Green* was possess'd for 51 Years by a Lease, and that *Green fecit vastum, &c. videlicet in prosternendo*

R 4   *unum*

unum Pandoxatorium, &c. pretii mille Librarum.
Defendant pleads no Wafte made, and Iffue,
and a Jury according to the Cuftom of the
City, from the four next adjoining Wards *ef-*
fend' in Cur. ad proxim' Hufting'. The Jury
here made Default, whereupon a *Diftringas*
was awarded againft them, returnable at another Day, *& interim idem Jurat' videant Locum*
vaftatum ; the Jury appear, but it was not returned that they had the View. They found
the Defendant guilty, *viz. ib profternendo unum*
Pandaxatorium, pretii 100 *l.* and other particular Waftes, to the value of 200 *l.* in all ;
(but not any particular Vendition) and affefs 12 *d.* Coft ; and yet here they fay, *quod*
Def. fecit vaftum venditionem, &c. but find not
any Vendition in particular afterward, and
therefore and for that they fhould not have
affefs'd Cofts the Verdict was quafh'd.

     Whereupon, at the Petition of *Green,* ano-
ther Trial was from four Wards (but in the
Record it is not faid, next adjoining) tho' in
truth they were fo, but two were not adjoining by the Record, and thofe Jurors had the
View, and found a general Verdict for the
Defendant, that there was no Wafte done ;
upon which *Cole* the Plaintiff fues a fpecial
Commiffion of Errors in *London,* according
to the Cuftom, directed to feveral Judges,
and *Cole* pray'd Judgment againft himfelf,
which was given ; then the Plaintiff *Cole* proceeds to the Commiffion of Errors, and the
Judges Commiffioners (*Moreton, Turner, Rainf-*
ford, Hales, Vaughan) fent to the Maior and
Sheriffs for the Record at the *Huftings* to be
before them at *Guild-Hall* at a Day affigned ;
the firft Verdict was certified, as parcel of
the Record, and thefe Points were refolved.

                              1. The

A fpecial Com-
miffion of Er-
rors fued in
London.

1. The *Action of Waste* was well maintainable in *London*, for it had Jurisdiction before the Stat. of *Gloc. c.* 5. 2 *Inst.* 299. And 7 *H.* VI. 35. is not Law in this Point.

2. Though the View was not retorned on the first, yet the first Verdict was good, for it is not of Necessity that the other should return it, though they must have the View, and it ought to be examined upon the Trial.
The Jury must have the View, but not necessary to be returned so.

3. The first Verdict was sufficient, and good in Law, upon which the Court of *Hustings* ought to have given Judgment for the Plaintiff, without awarding a new *Venire;* for the Words *vastum venditionem & destructionem,* are but the Title of the Verdict, and not the Substance of it ; and the finding the particular Wastes is the Substance of the Verdict; but if they had not found the particular Wastes, it had been ill.
Finding the particular Waste is the Substance of the Verdict.

4. The last Verdict, and Judgment given on it, was erroneous : *First,* Because it is not said the Precept was to the Beadles of the four next Wards, and so not a Trial according to Custom. *Secondly,* Because the Court quashed the first Verdict, which was sufficient, and so they erred in their Judgment.

5. The Judges Commissioners ought not only to reverse the Judgment in the *Hustings,* given for the Defendant, but ought to give such Judgment upon the Record before them, that the Court of *Hustings* ought to have given, *viz.* That the Plaintiff shall recover the Place wasted, and his Damages *in triplo* upon the first Verdict ; for they are commanded to make *plenam & celerem justitiam,* and if they do it not, the Court
of

of *Huftings* cannot, and fo a Failure of Juftice.

No Cofts of Suit.

6. That Judgment fhall be enter'd for the Plaintiff of the Place wafted, and treble Damages, *nullo habito refpe&u* to the Cofts, for no Cofts of the Suit are recoverable in this Action.

Green the Defendant brought a Writ of Error in Parliament, and affigns Error in Fact, that the four firft Wards, out of which the firft Jury was empannelled, were not the four Wards next adjoining to the Place wafted, and fo the Cuftom not purfued.

Cole pleads, *in nullo eft erratum.*

It was faid, it was an erroneous Act of the Court to award a *Venire* to the Officers of the wrong Ward.

Jeofail.

But it was refolved, that it was a Jeofail, and aided by the Stat 21 *Jac. c.* 13. for two of the Wards appear to be next to the Place wafted, and fo the *Venire* was mifawarded in part.

Q. For the Statute feems to extend only to a Trial at Common Law, and not to a Trial by fpecial Cuftom. 2 *Sanders* 252. & 1 *Mod.* 94. *Green* and *Cole.* But fee this Cafe more at large in 1 *Levins* 309, 310, &c.

Of the Lord Maior's Court.

THE Lord Maior's Court, commonly call' the Maior's Court in *London*, is a Court of Record, and is held in the Chamber of the *Guild-Hall.* The Recorder of the City of *London* for the time being, is Judge of this Court; but the Lord Maior and Aldermen may fit as Judges with him if they
    pleafe

pleafe : This Court is held by Cuftom, and all the Proceedings are faid to be before the Maior and Aldermen. The Sheriffs of *London* may in like manner fit with the Judges of the Sheriffs Court. The Proceedings in that Court being alfo faid to be held before the Sheriffs refpectively, of which more here-after.

And *Note*, This Court is not only a Court of Law, but alfo a Court of Equity, like the Court of Exchequer at *Weftminfter.* See here-after, *p.* —

In this Court all manner of Actions may be enter'd and try'd by a Jury as in other Courts, for any Matters whatfoever arifing within the Liberties of *London*, to any value whatfoever, as for Debt at the Plaintiff's Suit ; Debt at the Chamberlain's Suit ; Debt upon a penal Statute, Trefpafs, Account, Covenant, *&c.* There are only four Attor- *Attornies.* nies belonging to this Court, who upon their Admiffion by the Court of Aldermen, take an Oath for the obferving fuch things as are therein mentioned.

The manner of entering Actions in this *Actions.* Court is different from the Sheriffs Court : For you cannot enter an Action in this Court at either of the Compters, but muft go to one of the four Attornies, and enter your Action with him.

When your Action is enter'd by the At-torney or his Clerk, you muft not employ any of the Sheriffs Officers to arreft the Defen- *Arreft.* dant, but give your Action, or a Note thereof to one of the Serjeants at Mace belonging to the Maior and Aldermen.

There are fix Serjeants belonging to this Court, who are Men of good Eftates, and do

do not belong to either of the Sheriffs. Moſt
of them attend daily at the Attorney's Offices,
and one of them is conſtantly attending at
the Lord Maior's Houſe. If you give any
of them a Note of your Action, he will arreſt the Defendant ; and in caſe ſuch Defendant cannot find Bail, the Officer will carry
Imprisonment. him to one of the Compters, that being the
Priſon as well for this Court as the Sheriffs
Court; which Impriſonment, and the Cauſe
thereof, is conſtantly recorded in a publick
Book, called, the *Niſi prius Book,* by the Attorney that enter'd the Action: But if the
Party arreſted find Bail, the eldeſt of the four
Attornies muſt take the ſame, he being Clerk
of the Bails; and in caſe he ſhall take inſufficient Bail, and the Defendant do abſcond,
the Plaintiff may, after he hath a Judgment
for his Debt or Damages, compel the Clerk
of the Bails to pay the ſame Debt or Damages, by Petition to the Court of Aldermen,
or to Mr. Recorder.

Benefit of ſue- *Note,* 1. That an Action enter'd in this Court
ing in this will remain in force for ever, although no
Court. Proceedings be had thereupon ; whereas an
Action enter'd at either of the Compters
dies, and may be croſſed after ſixteen
Weeks. And the Charge of entering an
Action in this Court, is but four Pence be-
ſides the King's Duty.

2. An Action commenced in this Court may
be brought to a Trial for 30 *s.* Charge,
and in fourteen Days time, whereas in the
Sheriffs Court they require more time, and
much more Money.

3. If there happen to be ſix Weeks time between the putting in Bail to an Action in
this

this Court, and the time of the Defendant's Plea, in such Case the Defendant cannot remove the same Action or Suit into any other Court.

4. That an Action commenced in this Court cannot be removed into the Sheriffs Court; but an Action commenced in the Sheriffs Court, may be removed into this Court, either by the Plaintiff or Defendant, at any time before a Jury is sworn to try the Cause.

Also there is a great Difference in Attachments called foreign Attachments, made in this Court, and those made in the Sheriffs Court. *Vide post.*

Into the Nature of which Attachments in the next Place we shall enquire.

Of Foreign Attachments in the Maiors Court.

BY the Custom of *London* one may attach Money or Goods of the Defendants, either in the Plaintiff's own Hands, or in the Custody of a third Person, and that either in the Maior's Court, or in the Sheriffs Court.

And *Note*, That the Custom of *London* is, That if any Plaint be affirmed in *London* before, *&c.* against any Man, and he is returned *nihil,* if the Plaintiff will surmise any other Man who is within the City, is Debtor to the Defendant, in any Sum, he shall have his Garnishment against him for him to come and answer if he be indebted in the Form which the other hath alledged; and if he comes, and does not
deny

deny it, then this Debt ſhall be attached in his Hands.

Note, The Plaintiff ought to ſurmiſe, that the other Man who is indebted to the Defendant, is within the City, 22 *Ed.* IV. 30. *per Starky* Recorder of *London,* the Cuſtom ſo certify'd.

All *Attachments* are grounded upon Actions of Debt, and the manner of entering *Attachments* is the ſame as is before mentioned for entering Actions: And one of the ſix Officers belonging to this Court muſt be employed to make the ſame.

If *A.* owes *B.* 100 *l.* and *C.* is indebted to *A.* in 100 *l. B.* entereth an Action againſt *A.* of 200 *l.* (in the Sheriffs Court, or the Maior's Court) and by virtue of that Action a Serjeant attacheth 100 *l.* in the Hands of *C.* as the Monies of *A.* to the Uſe of *B.* which is returned upon that Action.

Note, The Return muſt be within certain Hours, for perhaps another Attachment may be made after in the Hands of *C.* ſo that *C.* hath no other way to avoid this other Attachment, but by pleading the former Attachment made as before; then let the Plaintiff fee an Attorney immediately before the next Court holden for the ſame Compter.

The Advantages of making Attachments in this Court rather than in the Sheriffs Court are conſiderable.

1. An *Attachment* made in this Court will continue in force for ever; ſo that the Plaintiff may proceed thereon at his Pleaſure. But an *Attachment* made in the Sheriffs Court is not in force longer than ſixteen Weeks.

For

Secondly, An Attachment for Monies may be made and condemned in this Court in five Days time, if by Confent, or if no Oppofition fhall be made ; and if it be in the Plaintiff's own Hands, may be finifhed for 12 *s*. Charge (befides the King's Duty) the Officers Fees included : And if in a third Perfon's Hands may be condemned for 15 *s*. Charge, the Officers Fees included : Whereas in the Sheriffs Court an Attachment cannot be made and condemned under three Weeks time, or thereabouts, although by Confent ; and the Charge is ufually above a third Part more than is demanded or taken in this Court for condemning an Attachment.

Again, *Thirdly*, If *A.* attaches the Monies or Goods of *M.* in the Hands of *R.* in this Court, and if *R.* have no Monies or Goods in his Hands belonging to *M.* at the time when the Attachment fhall be made ; and it fhall happen that fix Months after *R.* fhall become indebted to *M.* or have Goods in his Hands belonging to *M.* the Plaintiff *A.* by virtue of the Attachment made as aforefaid, fhall recover the Money or Goods he fhall prove came to the Hands of *R.* after the Attachment made. The general Iffue upon all Attachments being, *Whether* R. *who is called the Garnifhee at the time of the Attachment made, or at any time after, had any Monies or Goods of* M. *in his Hands.*

Fourthly, An *Attachment* made in this Court cannot be removed, nor try'd in any other Court ; whereas an *Attachment* made in the Sheriffs Court, may at any time, before Trial, be removed into this Court, by a Warrant figned by the Lord Maior or Recorder ; which

Levetur Que- which Warrant is called a *Levetur Querela,*
rela.   the Charge whereof is 5 s. 10 d.

Note, The *Levetur Querela* muſt be written by
an Attorney of this Court, for which he
receiveth 4 d. and for his Fee 1 s. and 8 d.
and then muſt be delivered to one of the
ſix Officers beforementioned, to procure
my Lord Maior, or the Recorder to ſign
the ſame, for which 4 d. is due to his
Lordſhip. And after the Warrant is ſign'd,
the Officer muſt carry it to the Clerk of
the Papers belonging to the Compter,
where the Action was enter'd, and give
him 2 s. 6 d. to allow the ſame *Levetur,*
and to certify the Action or Attachment,
and the Officer for his Pains hath 1 s.
which makes up the 5 s. 10. d.

Laſtly, An Attachment may be try'd in
this Court for 30 s. although the Concern be
500 l. But by reaſon of Devices of Continu-
ances in the Sheriffs Court, the Charge of a
Trial there comes to much more.

Of the Defen-   *Note,* That in all Attachments, the Perſon
dant and Gar- whoſe Money or Goods is attached, is
niſhee in gene- called the Defendant in the Attachment;
ral.   and the Perſon in whoſe Hands the Attachment is made, is called the Garniſhee, becauſe of his being warn'd not to pay the
Money, but to appear and anſwer the
Plaintiff's Suit; after ſuch Attachment
made, the Garniſhee (if he think fit) may
appear in Court by his Attorney, and wage
Law, or plead, that he has no Money in
his Hands of the Defendants, or other ſpecial Matter, or he may confeſs it.

If the Plaintiff in the Attachment ſhall obtain a Verdict and Judgment for the Money
or Goods attached in the Garniſhees Hands,

           yet

yet the Defendant in the Attachment may at *At what time*
any time before Satisfaction acknowledged *the Defendant*
upon Record, put in Bail to the Plaintiff's *in the Attach-*
ment may put
Action upon which the Attachment is ground- *in Bail, and*
ed, and thereby discharge the Judgment and *discharge the*
Proceedings against the Garnishee; yea, tho' *Attachment.*
the Garnishee be taken in Execution, he shall
be discharged if Bail be put in as aforesaid.

If the Attachment be of Goods only, and *In case of Goods*
the Garnishee pleads he had no Goods in *Judgment for*
an Appraise-
his Hands at the time of the Attachment *ment.*
made, or at any time after, and the Plaintiff
prove the Goods attached, or any part in his
Hands, the Jury in such case must find for
the Plaintiff, and say what Goods they find
in the Defendant's Hands, whereupon Judgment will be enter'd for an Appraisement.

And thereupon a Precept must be made,
and directed to one of the six Officers of this
Court, to appraise the same Goods; and if
the Garnishee shall not produce them, the *Elongavit re-*
Officer must return an *Elongavit*; which is as *turned.*
much as to say, That the Garnishee hath
conveyed the Goods out of the Liberties of
this City.

The next Court Day for Trials after such
Return made, a Jury must be sworn to en- *Jury of En-*
quire of the Value of the Goods found by the *quiry.*
former Jury to be in the Garnishees Hands,
and Judgment must be enter'd for the Value
according to the Verdict of such Jury.

Note, That upon Attachments no Costs are *No Costs.*
allowed to either Party, let the Verdict be
for or against the Plaintiff.

The Day for Trials in this Court, is eve- *Days for Tri-*
ry *Tuesday*, but every Day is a Court for en- *als,* &c.
tering Proceedings, as Appearances, Rules,
Pleas and Judgments, except Holy-Days, the

Week before *Easter*, the firſt three Weeks in *Auguſt*, *i. e.* till the Day after *Bartholomew* Day, from the ſixteenth of *December*, till the *Monday* after *Twelfth-Day*, and during the time of the Seſſions of the *Old Baily*.

After Judgment obtained by the Plaintiff againſt the Garniſhee, on any Attachment, the Plaintiff muſt, before Execution is awarded, find Sureties, who muſt undertake for *Sureties for Re-* the Plaintiff, *If the Defendant in the Attachment* *ſtitution of the* *ſhall within a Year and a Day come into Court,* *Money if the* *and diſprove or avoid the Debt demanded againſt* *Debt be diſ-* *them by the Plaintiff, that then the Plaintiff ſhall* *proved within* *reſtore to the Defendant the Money condemned in* *a Year and a* *the Garniſhees Hands, or ſo much thereof as ſhall* *Day.* *be diſproved, or elſe that they his Sureties will do* *it for him :* And then Execution will be granted againſt the Garniſhee for the Monies. *Vid.* the Pleadings *poſtea.*

Attachment If *A.* attaches Money in the Hands of *B.* as *diſcharged by* the Monies of *C.* and in truth *B.* had no Mo- *the Garniſhee* nies in his Hands belonging to *C.* but expects *for want of a* *Declaration.* to receive it ſhortly, *B.* after four Defaults paſſed (which is uſually in four Court Days) may diſcharge the Attachment by coming into Court perſonally, and giving a Rule to declare upon his Attachment ; and if *A.* do not declare in three Days following, then Judgment will be enter'd againſt *A.* to diſ- *Plea.* charge the Attachment ; but if *A* declare, then *B.* may plead he hath no Monies in his Hands belonging to *C.* at the time of the Attachment, or at any time ſince ; and put the Plaintiff to prove any Money in his Hands ; which if the Plaintiff cannot do, a Verdict will be given for *B.* the Garniſhee ; or elſe *B.* may diſcharge the Attachment by waging of Law in this Form, *viz.* He the ſaid

Garniſhee

Garnishee muſt come into Court, and take *The Manner of* the following Oath : *You ſhall ſwear, That at* *the Garniſhees* *the time of the Attachment made, or at any time* *waging Law.* *ſince, you had not, owed not, nor did detain, nor* *yet have, or owe, or do detain from C. the Defen-* *dant named in the original Bill and Attachment* *aforeſaid, the Sum of* 20 *l. or other Sum, &c. ſo* *as aforeſaid in your Hands attached, nor any Pen-* *ny thereof, in Manner and Form, as the Plaintiff* *by his Bill original and Attachment aforeſaid hath* *ſuppoſed.* So help you God.

The Garniſhees may thus wage Law upon Oath ; but if the Plaintiff hath two Witneſſes that will ſwear that the Garniſhee had Monies in his Hands when the Attachment was made, *What will ſtop* he muſt cauſe their Depoſitions to be taken by *the Garniſhee* the Town-Clerk, and that will ſtop the Garni- *from waging* ſhee from waging his Law, and force him to *his Law.* plead, *&c.*

If the Garniſhee refuſe to wage Law, the Plaintiff may try the Cauſe in four Court Days following, after the *Scire facias* comes into Court.

Note, The Plaintiff at the Trial ſhall not give *Money coming* in Evidence any Monies that came to the *to the Garni-* Garniſhees Hands after the Plea. *Vide* 268. *ſhees Hands af-* *ter the Plea,* Attachment may be made for Goods or *not to be given* Money at the ſame Charge, alſo both upon *in Evidence.* one Attachment, and both in one *Scire facias.*

When Satisfaction is acknowledged, then *After Satisfac-* the Attachment is perfected, ſo that the De- *tion acknow-* *ledged, no Bail* fendant can put in no Bail to diſſolve the *put in can diſ-* Attachment. *ſolve the At-* *tachment.*

The Garniſhee being warned in (after the four Court Days are paſt) to appear to ſhew Cauſe why the Monies and Goods attached in his Hands ſhall not be condemned in Court to the uſe of the Plaintiff, muſt go and fee

S 2 his

If Garnishee will plead, he must put in Bail before the second Court Day after the Scire Fac.

his Attorney, and then if he can wage his Law, he may be difcharged; but if he will plead, he muft put in Bail or Pledges before the fecond Court Day after the *Scire facias* comes in, otherwife for want of Bail put in, he is condemned for the whole Sum, and he is remedilefs as to Trial by Jury; but if he put in Bail and plead, it may be try'd by a Jury.

Attachment dissolved by Garnishee after a Trial.

Note, The Garnifhee after Trial may put in Bail in the Abfence of the Party againft whom the Attachment is made, before the Lord Maior, and fo diffolve the Attachment, and all the Proceedings thereon; but then he and his Security are liable to what Debt the Plaintiff fhall make appear to be due from the Defendant. The Charge of putting in Bail before the Lord Maior is 6 *s.* 8 *d.*

Attachment dissolved by the Defendant.

Alfo the Party againft whom the Attachment is made, may put in Bail in the Compter, or fubmit his Body, which he or the Garnifhee may do before Satisfaction acknowledged by the Plaintiff, and this fhall diffolve the Attachment.

Garnishee for Default of Appearance must pay the Money or go to Prison, Plea when the Day of Payment of a Bond or Specialty is not yet come.

If the Garnifhee fail to appear as he ought, he is taken by Default for want of appearing, and Judgment given againft him for the Goods and Money attached in his Hands, and is remedilefs at Common Law, or in Equity, by reafon of his non-appearance, tho' he hath not one Penny in his Hands; and if taken in Execution, muft pay the Money, or go to Prifon.

If Monies be attached in the Garnifhee's Hand, upon a Bond or other Specialty, and the Money is not become due at the Day therein mentioned, the Garnifhee may by his
Attorney

Attorney put in his Plea, and fet forth, that the Day of Payment is not yet come.

An Attachment in the Sheriffs Court is in force no longer than 16 Weeks. *Vide ante.*

And becaufe this Matter of *Foregn Attachment* is of great Confequence, be the *Attachment* either in the one Court or the other, we will enquire further into the Nature of it, and of the Manner of profecuting and pleading therein.

What things are attachable, or not.

BY the Cuftom of *London* part of a Debt may be attached. *Godb.* 196.

An Attachment may be made for Goods or Money, or both, at the fame Charge, and all upon one Attachment. *Ut ante* 259.

If *B.* attach the Money or Goods of *W.* in *Moneys on Bond before due.* the Hands of *F.* and if *F.* have no Money or Goods in his Hands belonging to *W.* at the time when the Attachment fhall be made ; and it fhall happen that fix Months after (in the Maior's Court) *F.* fhall become indebted to *W.* or have Goods in his Hands belonging to *W. Goods or Money at any time* the Plaintiff by virtue of the Attachment afore- *come to the* faid, fhall recover the Money or Goods he *Garnifhee's* fhall prove came to the Hands of *F.* after the *Hands after* Attachment made, the general Iffue upon all *the Attach-* Attachments, being, whether *F.* (who is called *ment.* the Garnifhee) at the time of the Attachment made, or at any time after, had any Monies or Goods in his Hands of *W.*

A. is indebted to *B.* in 20 *l.* by Bill or Note *When Money* payable at fix Months or more ; in fuch cafe *not due is at-* you cannot enter an Action againft *A.* till the *tached, how to* Money is due ; but if *B.* fhall be indebted to *C. plead.* in any Sum of Money, *C.* may, fo foon as the

S 3 Note

Note is given to *B.* by *A.* caufe an Attachment to be made in the Hands of *A.* as the Monies of *B.* and if *A.* appear, he fhall give Bail within two Days after; and after he hath put in Bail, he muft plead, That it is true he hath fo much Money in his Hands, but that the fame is not due or payable to *B.* the Defendant, till a certain Day to come, *C.* the Plaintiff fhall have Judgment prefently againft *A.* the Garnifhee for the Monies attached, but Execution fhall not be awarded for the Money till it become due according to the time mentioned in the Plea, 1 *Roll's* Abr. 553. *Pierce* and *Calcott* ; but in fuch Cafes it ought to be pleaded, that fuch Debt was attached by the Cuftom before the Debt was due by the Condition of the Obligation fpecially.

The like upon verbal Agreement. If *A.* fhall be indebted to *B.* in a Sum of Money for Goods bought, and a verbal Agreement only, to pay for them at a time to come, and an Attachment fhall be made in the Hands of *A.* for the Money before the time agreed for Payment thereof, fhall be elapfed; in fuch Cafe *A.* the Garnifhee may plead the fame Plea as above, and fhall not be compelled to pay the Money till it become due by the Agreement, but the Plaintiff fhall have Judgment prefently.

Action by Defendant againft the Garnifhee. And if the Defendant in an Attachment after Satisfaction acknowledged upon Record, fhall bring an Action againft the Garnifhee for the Money fo attached, the Garnifhee may in fuch Cafe plead the general Iffue, and give the Attachment in evidence, but muft at the fame time prove the Debt to be a juft Debt for which the Money was condemned, and the Courts above have always allowed it as a good Evidence againft the Plaintiff in the Action.

J. T.

I. T. Citizen of *London*, is indebted 40 *l.* by Specialty unto *A. B.* a Citizen. *A. B.* is indebted to one *Haydon*, another Citizen in 40 *l.* upon a Simple Contract ; *A. B.* dies Inteftate ; *Spinck* adminifters to the faid Inteftate : *I. T.* after the Day of Payment of his 40 *l.* promifeth *Spinck*, in confideration of Forbearance for two Months to pay to *Spinck* the faid 40 *l.* *Spinck* forbears, and the Money is not paid : Afterwards, the Debt due by *I. T.* is attached in his Hands, for the Debt due by the Inteftate to *Haydon* : *Spinck* brings Action on the Cafe againft *J.* for Non-payment of the 40 *l.* according to his Promife ; he pleads that the Debt due by him unto the Inteftate was attached. *Spinck* demurs.

Two Points were debated.

1. Whether for the Debt of the Inteftate, being only a Debt due upon a Simple Contract, a Foreign Attachment may be made ; and it was refolved *per Cur.* a Foreign Attachment may well be fued for it, becaufe by the Cuftom of *London*, the Executor or Adminiftrator be- ing chargeable for a Debt due by the Teftator or Inteftate upon a Simple Contract as well as upon a Specialty, a Foreign Attachment lies for it as well as for a Specialty ; and tho' the Courts of *Weftminfter* are not bound to take notice of this particular Cuftom of *London*, in charging Executors or Adminiftrators on Simple Contract, nor to give Judgment according to the Cuftom ; yet when Judgment hath been given according to that Cuftom, and that Judgment appeareth judicially unto the Judges by the Record, now they ought to allow the Cuftom, and give their Judgment according to that Cuftom : But it was agreed, if there had not been any Debt due by the Inteftate to *Haydon*, though

there

there had been an Attachment made in *London* of the Debt due by *Spinck* to the Inteſtate, and a Judgment given upon it, yet might the Adminiſtrator have relieved himſelf by way of denial, and traverſe, that there had been any Debt due by the Inteſtate to *Haydon*.

A Promiſe to pay upon forbearance, and after the Money is attached in the Aſſurers Hands. 2. Whether the Foreign Attachment for the Debt due unto the Inteſtate, after the Promiſe broken, be ſuch a diſpenſation with the Promiſe, that no Action now lieth for the Adminiſtrator upon the breach of Promiſe.

It was reſolved, that the Promiſe was diſpenſed with, and no Action lay upon the Breach of it : For the Debt due by *J. T.* to the Inteſtate, which was the ground and cauſe of the Promiſe made to *Spinck* the Plaintiff, is taken away by the Judgment had in *London* upon the Foreign Attachment. *Calthorp.* 27. 1 *Roll's* Rep. 105. *Spinck* and *Tenant's.*

The Court ſaid, it was a certain Debt before the Promiſe made ; for the Promiſe is, to pay a Debt due on Bond ; but had the Debt commenced by the Promiſe, it might have been otherwiſe.

Money due upon Account after Promiſe to pay it, and the Day of Payment paſt, may be attached. Agreeable to this Reſolution, was *Bardiſton* and *Humphrey's* Caſe : Where, upon an Account, he that was found in Arrears, upon a conſideration of Forbearance by one Month, promiſeth a Payment of them ; and thoſe Arrearages thus due, being attached in the Hands of the Accomptant, after the Promiſe broken, it was held, that no Action might afterwards be maintained upon the breach of Promiſe. *M.* 37 & 38 *El.* *Rot.* 414.

Where an Account is made upon Debts by Simple Contract, or where Executors give Time for payment of a Bond due to the Teſtator, this ſhall be attached. 1 *Roll's* 551.

Debts

Debts upon Record by Recovery, or otherwife, *Debts on Re-*
as Statute, Recognifance, cannot be attached. *cord.*
Cr. El. 63. 1 *Leon.* 29, 30.

Attachment of the Money after it is in the *Of Money in*
Sheriff's Hands by Execution, is void. 1 *Leon.* *the Sheriffs*
264. *Hands on Exe-*
Debt which is in Suit in the *King's Bench* or *cution and* *Debts that are*
Common Pleas may not be attached. *in Suit in the*

If a Man recover Debt or Damages in *B. R.* *Superior Court.*
this Debt may not be attached in *London,* for an *After Recove-*
Inferiour Court fhall not attach a Debt in a *ry.*
Higher Court. 1 *Roll's* Abr. 552. neither can it
be attached after Iffue joined.

So after an Imparlance to an Action of Debt *After Impar-*
in *B. R.* the Debt may not be attached in *London* *lance.*
for the Caufe aforefaid. 3 *Leon* 232.

If a Writ of Debt retornable in *Banco* be pur- *After a Writ*
chafed before the Attachment, this may not be *purchafed be-*
fore the At-
attached by the Cuftom, *Afton* and *Procter :* aliter *tachment.*
if the Writ be purchafed after the Attachment
by Covin with an *Antedate.* 1 *Roll's* Abr. 552.

Defendant pleads a *Foreign Attachment* in *Lon-* *After Ap-*
don, which was after Appearance, and pending *pearance.*
the Action, it's no good Plea. Cr. El. 157. *Bab-*
ington's Cafe.

The Action was in Debt, upon Condition of
a Bond ; the Defendant demands *Oyer,* which
was to perform an Award, and fets forth, that *On Arbitration*
there were divers Accounts, *&c.* between *J. S.* *between an*
Teftator of the Plaintiff and the Defendant, and *Executor and*
another.
they fubmitted, *&c.* to fuch a one Arbitrator,
who awarded, that the Plaintiff fhould deliver
certain Goods, of which the Teftator died
poffefs'd to the Defendant, and that the Defendant fhould pay to the Plaintiff 320 *l.* and then
fets forth the Cuftom of *Foreign Attachments* in
London, that if a Suit was commenced againft the
Executor of any Perfon, any Debt which was
due

due to the Teſtator *Tempore mortis ſuæ* might be attached; and then ſets forth according to the Common Form, how this 320 *l.* was attached, *&c.* and avers, there were no other Controverſies between the Plaintiff and Defendant, but what concerned the Teſtator of the Plaintiff, and him as Executor only.

The Queſtion was, *Whether this Money was attachable as a Debt due to the Teſtator,* Tempore Mortis ſuæ?

This Money was not attachable.

It was reſolved, That this is not attachable.

For it appears not, that it was any Debt due to the Teſtator at the Time of his Death; and if this Money ſhould be attached, the Executor ſhould be liable to a *Devaſtavit,* and yet ſhould have no Remedy for the Sum awarded.

Executor takes Bond for Debt due to the Teſtator, or ſells Goods not attachable. Damages in Treſpaſs.

Where the Executor takes Bond for a Debt due to the Teſtator, or where he ſells the Goods, the Money for which they were ſold, cannot be attached. 1 *Vent.* 111. *Horſam* and *Turget.*

Executor recovers in Treſpaſs for taking away the Teſtator's Goods, the Damages ſhall be Aſſets, yet they are not attachable; ſo Damages recovered upon Covenants made to the Teſtator.

When a Man dies Inteſtate, and none Adminiſters, againſt whom muſt the Attachment be?

If a Man dies Inteſtate, an Attachment may be made of Monies, or Goods, or both, in a third Perſons Hands; but then the Attachment muſt be enter'd againſt the Lord Biſhop of *London,* reciting his Name: But when there is a Will proved, or Letters of Adminiſtration granted, the Attachment dies, and it muſt again be made againſt ſuch Executor or Adminiſtrator, unleſs it be condemned fully in the Interim.

Cloaths in a Trunk.

Attachment may be made of Boxes or Trunks locked, and it muſt be ſo retorned by the Serjeant upon the Action, and the Court next Day, after the four Court Days paſt, will grant Judgment for the opening it.

If

If Attachment be made of Jewels, either in a *Jewels.*
Man's own Hands, or in a third Parties Hands,
it ought to be retorned fo upon Record.

If Attachment be made of Monies due upon *Penalty at-*
a Bond, the Penalty muft be attached, for the *tached.*
Court will afterward abridge it to the Principal.

No Attachment lieth of Rent. *Rent.*

If *A.* be indebted to *B.* and *J. S.* a Stranger, *Goods in the*
takes the Goods of *A.* as a Trefpaffer, *B.* may *Hands of a*
not attach thefe Goods in the Hands of *J. S. Trefpaffer.*
for the Debt of *A.* for that the Property is out
of *A.* at that Time, and only a Right in him.
Stanmor and *Amone.*

Legacy may not be attached in the Hands of *Legacy.*
an Executor, for that it's uncertain whether the
Executor fhall have Affets to pay Debts. *Page*'s
Cafe, 1 *Roll*'s Abr. 551. 3 *Bulftr.* 244.

If *A.* lend *B.* an 100 *l.* to be repaid by *B.* upon
the Death of the Father of *B.* and this 100 *l.* is
attached by *Foreign Attachment*, and after *A. Foreign At-*
brought Action on the Cafe againft *B.* for the *tachment a*
Money, this *Foreign Attachment* is a good Bar, *good Bar to*
though the Cuftom be to attach Debts, and this *Action on the*
is an Action on the Cafe, in which Damages only *Cafe.*
fhall be given; for it is a Debt, and he may
have Action of Debt for it; and this being once
well attached, he fhall not defeat it by bringing
Action on the Cafe. 1 *Roll's* Abr. 652. *Hales*
and *Walker.*

A. fells Stockings to *B.* on Contract, by which
B. is to give *A.* 10 *l.* and that if he fells the
Stockings before *Auguft* after, then he fhall pay
2 *d.* more for every Pair, the which is attacha- *But aliter if*
ble, but not the 2 *d.* for every Pair, becaufe this *the Suit in*
only refts in Damages to be recovered by Action *Action on the*
on the Cafe, and not Debt, becaufe it's payable *Damages only.*
only upon a poffibility. *Read* and *Hawkins* on
Demurrer.

Where

Where a Foreign Attachment may be given in
Evidence in the Superior Courts. See 1 *Salk.* 280,
291.

What Perſons ſhall be bound by this Cuſtom, or in what other Perſons the Debt may be attached.

Debt may be attached in the Hands of an Attorney of B. R. and he ſhall not be privileged.

HEwes was indebted to *Watkins,* and *Turbill*
having Money of *Hewes* in his Hands, *Watkins* attacheth this Money in the Hands of *Turbill,* by *Foreign Attachment* in *London,* and makes
Mr. *Turbill,* Garniſhee there, according to the
Cuſtom; upon which Mr. *Turbill* being a Clerk
of the Court of *B. R.* prays, That his Privilege
may be allowed: And in *Lodge*'s Caſe, an Attorney of the Court of *Common Pleas,* it was allowed;
but *per* the whole Court, after debate, *Turbill*
was denied Privilege in this Caſe, foraſmuch as
there is no Remedy upon the *Foreign Attachment*
but in *London*; and by ſuch means, if the Defendant will put his Eſtate into his Attorney's
Hands, the Creditor (if ſuch Privilege ſhould be
allowed) ſhall be barred. *Sid.* 362. *Watkins* and
Hewes.

*One may at-
tach a Debt
in his own
Hands.*

A. recovers Debt againſt *B.* in *London, B.* may
attach this Debt in his own Hands for ſo much
due to him. *Lopas* and *Holman.*

*Debt due to
Adminiſtrator
may be at-
tached.*

A Debt due to an Adminiſtrator may be attached within the Cuſtom, for an Adminiſtrator
is within the Cuſtom. *Spinck* and *Tenant*; *vide
ſupra* 263.

Pleadings in Foreign Attachments, and how they ought to be pleaded, as to the Form of the Custom and Matter of Law.

DEbt upon Obligation of 100 *l.* conditioned for the Payment of 50 *l.* before such a Day. The Defendant pleads the Custom of *London* of Foreign Attachments, (*viz.*) That if one (who hath a Debt payable to him by any other in *London*) owes Money to a Third, the Third may attach so much of it as is due to him in the Hands of the Second; and that before the Day of Payment of the Bond, a Creditor of the Plaintiff (such a one) attached the said 50 *l.* in the Defendant's Hands, and gave Security in the Court according to the Custom to repay the Debt, if it be disproved within the Year and Day, *&c.* and that such a Day (which was after the Day in the Original) he paid the 50 *l.* to the said Creditor, upon *Scire Fac.* against him according to the Custom.

Debt on Bond of 100 l. to pay 50 l. and Foreign Attachment of 50 l. pleaded in Bar before the Day of Payment, it is a good Bar for the whole.

Plaintiff demurrs upon this Plea: Because, 1*st*, Its not a good Custom to attach a Debt before its due; but *per Cur.* its a good Custom; for though he cannot attach it as a Debt, yet it may not be levied 'till after the Time of Payment of the Bond, and so the Custom was laid.

2. It was said for the Plaintiff, if it should be a good Bar, yet it is not a Bar but for 50 *l.* which by the Plea, it was not paid till after the Day, and so the Bond forfeited: But *per Cur.* it is a good Bar for the whole, because the *Attachment* which was before the Day of

Pay-

Payment, makes this a Debt to the Creditor, (*viz.*) all that was due, and the Obligee may not take any Advantage of the Obligation afterwards.

If it were for Part, as 20 l. it ſhall be pleaded in Bar for Part.

But if this had been an *Attachment* of 20 *l.* it ſeems the Defendant ſhall plead this Record of the *Attachment* in *London* in Bar, *pro tanto. Sid.* 327. *Robbins* and *Standard.*

Foreign Attachment, in an Inferior Court, was pleaded thus, *That by Cuſtom, Time out of Mind, whoever levied a Plaint*, pro aliquo debito *againſt another upon Surmiſe, that a Stranger was indebted to the Defendant, that Proceſs iſſued forth to attach,* &c.

Pro aliquo debito, and ſaith not, that it did ariſe infra Juriſdictionem.

And the Exception was, that it was not ſaid, *pro aliquo debito*, which did ariſe *infra Juriſdictionem. Per Cur.* it need not be expreſt that the Debt did ariſe *infra Juriſdictionem*, and that if Action be brought in ſuch Caſe, and the Debt be laid to be contracted *infra Juriſdict' Curiæ*, if the Defendant will plead to it, he may, but he ſhall never be admitted to aſſign it for Error, that the Debt did ariſe *extra Juriſdictionem Curiæ*; but if he had tendered ſuch a Plea to the Juriſdiction of the Court upon Oath, then if they had refuſed it, it would have been Error. Wherefore it is enough in this Caſe to ſay, if a Plaint were levied, *pro aliquo debito infra Juriſdictionem Curiæ*, without averring, that the Debt did ariſe *infra Juriſdictionem*: Alſo there cannot be a Cuſtom for a *Foreign Attachment*, before there be ſome default in the Defendant; and for that Cauſe it was held to be ill. 1 *Vent.* 236.

Attachment by Innkeeper for Horſe-meat.

If an *Attachment* be made of an Horſe, or a Mare, in an Inn-keeper's Hands, he appearing by his Attorney, may put in his Plea, ſetting forth, *That there is ſo much Horſemeat due*; and the Court will allow him his Money before the Plaintiff ſhall have Judgment for the Appraiſement of the Horſe or Mare.　　　If

If *A.* be indebted to *B.* who is indebted to *C.* and *C.* sues *B.* in *London,* and by the Custom attaches the Debt of *B.* in the Hands of *A.* and after *B.* brought Action against *C.* for his Debt, and he pleads the Attachment, *B.* may traverse the Cause, *i. e.* That he was not indebted to *C.* for if there were not any just Debt between the Plaintiff, in the first Action, and the Defendant, the Attachment is not any Bar. *Paramour's* Case, cited 1 *Roll's* Rep. 106. 1 *Roll's* Abr. 5 *Vid. infra.* [*The Cause (i. e. that no Debt due) may be traversed.*]

Debt in the *King's Bench* upon *Mutuatus* for 50*l.* The Defendant pleads Attachment in *London,* and that he had found Pledges after four Defaults there of the Plaintiff, to render back the Money *si distrationaretur* within the Year; and it appears that the Pledges were not put in the Day of the last Default, but at a Day after; and *per Cur.* for this the Plea is not good. *Mich.* 40. and 4 *El.* Rot. 604. *Moor* 507. [*Pledges to render back the Money si distrationaretur, &c. not put in the Day of the last Default, it's not good.*]

On a Foreign Attachment (which was used to be pleaded, tho' lately is given in Evidence on the General Issue) if the Custom be not precisely sued, its void. 3 *Keb.* 221. in *Bennet* and *Thorn's* Case. See also 1 *Salk.* 280, 291. [*Foreign Attachment given in Evidence on the General Issue.*]

In Debt on Inland Bill by the Custom of Merchants; the Defendant pleads an Original and Attachment in the Sheriff's Court in *London;* to which the Plaintiff demurs, and *per Cur.* This is but in Abatement, unless it had been pleaded, that a Judgment was thereon: And by *Wild Justice; taliter processum est,* that Judgment was thereon, is not sufficient, but the four Defaults and Judgment must be pleaded specially, as *Cook's* Entry, 3 *Keb.* 627. *Baker* and *Hill.* [*Judgment must be pleaded in Foreign Attachment, and not taliter processum est.*]

Debt for 40 *l.* Defendant pleads that the Plaintiff was indebted to him in 40 *l.* and he therefore sued a Plaint in *London,* and there this Debt in demand was attached in his Hands, and he he pleaded the *Foreign Attachment* in certain, and had Judgment thereupon, *&c.* Plaintiff replies, *He was not indebted to the Defendant in* 40 l. *nor in any other Sum.* Defendant demurs, for that the Debt is not now traversable, because it is recover'd in *London, & non d'frationatur* within the Year and Day, as it might be by the Cuſtom: But *per Cur.* the Replication is good, for whether he were indebted or not, is very well iſſuable; for if he were not indebted, they in *London* could not attach the Plaintiff's Debt by a *Foreign Attachment* for nothing. *Cro. El.* 598. *Paramour* and *Pain:* Though it was held by ſome, that the Debt is not traverſable, for if there were no Debt, he ſhall have Reſtitution upon the Pledges.

Traverſe, that he owed him nothing.

And in *Coke* and *Brainforth*'s Caſe, Debt on Obligation; Defendant pleaded, that the Plaintiff was indebted to him, *& conceſſit ſolvere,* and pleadeth a *Foreign Attachment* in *London*; the Plaintiff *proteſtando quod non habetur tale recordum pro placito dicit;* that he *pro diverſis denariorum ſummis per ipſum præfat R. prius debitis non conceſſit ſolvere,* the ſaid Sum *modo & forma prout:* The Defendant demurs, adjudg'd a good Bar, and the Debt is well traverſable. *Cro. El.* 820.

Action of Debt by *A.* againſt *B.* upon Bond; Defendant pleaded tender of the Money according to the Condition, upon which the Parties were at Iſſue; and after the Defendant pleaded, That after the *Darrain Continuance,* the Debt now in demand was attached in the Defendant's Hands according to the Cuſtom of *London,* for the Debt of *C.* to whom the Plaintiff was indebted; *per Cur.* the Plea is inſufficient, for it is altogether contrary to the firſt Plea; and alſo the Court held, That an Action for the Debt depending here in this Court, the Debt cannot be

the That the Debt was attached after the laſt Continuance is no Plea.

be attached, and the Court would not fuffer a
Demurrer to be joined upon it, but over-ruled
the Cafe without Argument, for it was againft
the Jurifdiction of the Court, and the Privilege
of it. 3 *Leon.* p. 210. *Cor. El.* 101. to the fame
Purpofe is *Pell's* Cafe.

Humphrey's and Barne's Cafe; Debt upon a *Attachment*
Bill obligatory of 13 *l.* 13 *s.* 4 *d.* the Defendant *after the origi-*
pleaded a *Foreign Attachment* in Bar, made in *nal Purchafe.*
London by one *Moulton* (to whom *Humphreys* was
indebted) of 13 *l.* in his Hands after the original Writ purchafed, and before the Return of
the Exigent, or Appearance thereupon, and before he had any Notice of the Suit in the Common Bench; and upon the Demurrer it was adjudged to be no Plea.

1. Becaufe it appeared not that the 13 *l.* attached was part of the faid 13 *l.* 13 *s.* 4 *d.* now
in Demand.

2. Becaufe this Attachment was made while *No Attach-*
the Suit was depending in *C. B.* and the King's *ment to be*
Court being poffeffed of the Caufe, it is infuf- *made while a*
ficient, and cannot be; for the faid Court is *Suit is depend-*
interefted therein, and it is againft the Dignity *ing.*
of the Court to have an inferior Court meddle
therein; alfo while the Suit is depending, it is
quafi in Cuftodia Legis, and cannot be meddled
with by another, as where Goods are diftrained
and impounded, they cannot be attached at
Common Law. *Cro. El.* 691.

Action of *Detinue,* The Plaintiff declared, upon a Bailment of the Cloak of the Value of 10 *l.*
to the Defendant, to be fafely kept, and to be
redelivered to him upon requeft, and fhewed
that he did requeft the Defendant to redeliver
it, and that he doth ftill detain it ad *damnum, &c.*
The Defendant juftified the Detainer by reafon
of a *Foreign Attachment* in *London,* and pleaded,

T   *That*

That London *is an ancient City, and that there is a Cuſtom in* London, *that if any one be indebted to another, that if he will enter his Suit or Plaint in the Compter of the Sheriff of* London, *that a Precept ſhall be awarded to a Serjeant at Mace to Summon the Defendant, and if he return* nihil, *that is to ſay, that he hath nothing in the City by which he can be ſummoned,* & non eſt inventus ; *and if he be ſolemnly called at the next Court, and makes Default, that then if he can ſhew that the Defendant hath Goods in the Hands of one within the Liberty of the City, that the ſaid Goods ſhall be attached, and if the Defendant make Default at four Court Days, being ſolemnly called, that then if the Plaintiff will ſwear his Debt, and put in Bail for the Goods,* viz. *that if the Debt be diſproved within one Year and a Day, or the Judgment be reverſed, that he ſhall have his Judgment for the ſaid Goods:* And he ſhewed, that he enter'd his Plaint againſt the now Plaintiff in the Compter of *Woodſtreet* for the Debt of 20 *l.* and that a Precept was awarded to a Serjeant at Mace to ſummon him, and becauſe he had not any thing by which he could be ſummoned, he ſhewed that the now Plaintiff had Goods in his the Defendant's Hands, which were attached in his Hands, and that he ſwore his Debt, and put in Bail for the Goods, and had Judgment thereupon.   Plaintiff demurs.

The Cauſes.

Exception to Plea of the Cuſtom of Foreign Attachments.

1. He ſets forth, that *J. S.* did levy a Plaint againſt the now Plaintiff, for the Debt of 20 *l.* but ſets not forth expreſly that he did owe him 20 *l.* and he ought to have ſet down how the Debt grew due. *Reſp.* The Action is not brought in that Court to recover a Debt, but he pleaded it in bar to him.

The Cuſtom muſt be ſtrictly purſued in pleading.

2. He pleads a Cuſtom, and doth not purſue it.

The

The Cuſtom is, that if the Serjeant return that he hath nothing within the City, whereby he may be ſummoned, *& non eſt inventus,* and at the next Court Day he be ſolemnly demanded, and make Default, *&c.* and he ſaith, becauſe he hath nothing by which he ſhould be ſummoned, but doth not ſay that the Officer did return, that he had not any thing whereby to be ſummoned, nor doth he plead, or ſay, that at the next Court Day he was ſolemnly demanded; alſo he doth not aver, that he had found Pledges according to the Cuſtom.

3. He ſheweth, that the Goods were attached in the Defendant's Hands, but he doth not ſhew, that it was within the Liberty of the City, and all the Precedents are *infra Juriſdictionem.*

Reſp. We ſay in our Caſe, That the Cuſtom is, that the Goods muſt be in *London. Godb.* 400. *Hern* and *Stubbs's* Caſe, *Latch* 208.

In an Action of Debt for Tobacco in the *Detinet,* a Debt may not be attached within this Cuſtom in Satisfaction; for that it appears not of what value this Tobacco was ; by which it ſhould appear that the Debt is but a Satisfaction to the Value, which cannot be ſupplied by a Plea in Bar in another Action againſt him in whoſe Hands the Debt was attached : But if the Value of the Tobacco had been averred in the Record of the Attachment, the Debt might have been attached in this Action. *Pears* and *Colcott, Tr.* 15. *Car. B. R. Intr. M.* 13. *Car. Rot.* 473.

Debt for Tobacco not to be attached, if the Value does not appear.

If a *Foreign Attachment* be pleaded in Bar of an Action, that the Cuſtom is, [that if any Man brought an Action againſt any other for any Debt, and upon Return made that he *non eſt inventus, & quod nihil unde, &c.* and that

* T 2   upon

upon this, on Surmise that another is indebted to the Defendant in such a Sum, and upon this to pray Process to attach the Sum in his Hands, and to defend, *ita quod,* the Defendant appear to answer to the Plaintiff, and the Serjeant returns, he had attached the Sum in his Hands, and the Defendant appear'd not at four Courts after, &c. That Judgment shall be to recover this in his Hands, &c.] This is not a good Custom, without a Surmise, that the Stranger who is indebted to the Plaintiff is within the Jurisdiction of the Court, and this Return of the Serjeant shall not bind the Party without an actual Surmise of this by the Party himself. Adjudg'd upon Demurrer. Sir *Mich. Hale* and *Walker,* Tr. 1 *Car.* B. R.

The Custom is pleaded, that after the Attachment by Process, if the Defendant make default by four Courts after, that by the Custom at the last of the four Courts the Plaintiff may pray Process against *B.* to come in and shew cause why Judgment should not be against him the next Court after; and when he comes to apply this Custom to his Case, he shews that there were four Defaults, and that at the fourth Default, the Plea was continued for divers Courts, and then Process goes against *B.* and adjudged this doth not warrant the Custom. 1 *Rol.* Abr. 555.

Debt by Administratrix upon a Bond of 26 *l.* made to the Intestate: The Defendant pleaded, That he had commenced an Action of Debt of 30 *l.* against the Plaintiff by the Name of Administratrix to her Husband before the Sheriff of *London,* and upon *nihil* retorned, &c. That Debt was attached in his Hands, and pleaded all the Custom of *Foreign Attachments* in *London,* and
that

that by Judgment this Debt was attached in his
Hands. Adjudg'd no Plea:

1. *Becaufe the Plaintiff fues here as* Administratrix *to her Husband,* & non conftat *by the Bar, that the Debt recover'd in London was the Inteftate's Debt; but only that fhe was fued there by the Name of* Administratrix; *and that might be, although fhe were fued for her proper Debt; as the Books are, that one may be fued by the Name of Heir for his proper Debt, and then the Inteftate's Debt cannot be attached for the proper Debt of the* Administratrix. *Inteftates Debt cannot be attached for the proper Debt of the Adminiftrator.*

2. *It is not fhewed that the Debt recovered in* London *was a Debt by Specialty, otherwife it's not demandable againft an* Administrator. [Q. de hoc; *it's otherwife by the Cuftom of* London, vid. antea.]

3. *It is not fhewed that the Cuftom is, that if the Inteftate was indebted to the Plaintiff there, and the Plaintiff was indebted to the Inteftate, that by an Action brought by the Plaintiff there againft an Administrator, that this Debt might be attached in the Hands of the Plaintiff here; but it is fhewn, that if it be teftified that the Plaintiff was indebted to the fame Perfon whom he fued, that then he might attach. But here the Defendant now, being Plaintiff in* London, *was not indebted to the Plaintiff here, who was there Defendant, but was indebted to the Inteftate. Cuftom not purfued.*

4. *The Judgment in* London *was,* de bonis propriis, *which cannot extend to* bonis Inteftatoris.
Cro El. 843. Hodges *and* Cox.

Debt affigned in Satisfaction of another, is not liable to an Attachment for the Debt of the Affignor; the Cafe of *Lewis* and *Wallis* was remarkable, and a leading Cafe. 3 *Car* II. *B. R.* *Debt affigned in Satisfaction of another Debt is not liable to Attachment for the Debt of the Affignor.*

Wallis was indebted to *Snell* in 500 *l.* and in part of Satisfaction he affigns a Debt of 220 *l.* due by one *Parker. Lewis* after having a Debt of

250 l. juftly due to him by *Wallis*, levies a Plaint in the Sheriffs Court, and after fuggefts that *Parker* was indebted to *Wallis ut fupra*, and by Procefs of *Foreign Attachment*, had the Debt attached in the Hands of *Parker*. *Snell* hearing this, put in Bail for *Wallis* to the Action of *Lewis*, and after brought *Habeas Corpus* to remove this Action into the *King's Bench*, and *Snell* becomes Bail for *Wallis* there, and *Lewis* declares in B. R. upon this. After this, *Wallis*, before Judge *Raymond*, alledged, That he confented not to the Bail upon the *Foreign Attachment*, nor to the *Habeas Corpus*, but that all was done without his Privity, and prays, That a *Procedendo* may be granted to the Action in *London*, which was granted by *Raymond* upon a confident Affertion, That no Bail could be put in, in the Abfence of the Defendant on a *Foreign Attachment*, unlefs in the Prefence of the Lord Maior : Upon this *Procedendo*, *Wallis* confeffeth the Action in *London*, and *Lewis* had Judgment, and *Snell*, as his Bail, was after taken in Execution, and for redemption of his Body, pays the Debt to *Lewis*. The whole Matter being difclos'd, the Court was of Opinion, That after the Affignment by *Wallis* to *Snell* of the Debt of *Parker*, this was in truth, the Right and Property of *Snell*, and *Wallis* had nothing in it but in Truft for *Snell*. Then this Bail by *Snell* on the *Foreign Attachment* was *quafi per Wallis*, and by his Affent ; and when this was done, the *Foreign Attachment*, and all the Proceedings on it were ended, for the *Foreign Attachment* had no other end but to compel the Appearance of the Defendant to the Original Action ; and when the Caufe was removed hither by *Habeas Corpus*, and Bail put in by *Snell*, upon which the *Plaintiff* had declared, this is an Acceptance of the Bail, and

After Habeas Corpus *upon an Action* per Foreign Attachment, and Bail accepted *in* B. R. *the* Foreign Attachment *is difcharged.*

and this Court is poſſeſt of the Cauſe, and no Suggeſtion of the Defendant ſhall ouſt the Court of Juriſdiction, eſpecially as this Caſe is, where it appears, that the Deſign of *Wallis* was to defraud *Snell* of the Satisfaction he had aſſigned to him for part of his Debt. Therefore a *Superſedeas* was awarded to the *Procedendo, Quia improvide emanavit*; by which all the Judgment and Proceedings in *London* were void, *& coram non Judice,* and Reſtitution order'd to be made to *Snell,* and *Lewis* left to proceed in his Action in this Court *per Habeas Corpus,* to which *Snell* was Bail.

Plaintiff declares in *Aſſumpſit* as Adminiſtrator upon *Idebitat.* in 30 *l.* for Wares ſold by the Inteſtate. The Defendant pleads, That after the Death of the Inteſtate, and before Adminiſtration granted, he affirmed a Plaint in the Sheriff's Court againſt the Archbiſhop of *Canterbury,* to whom belonged the Adminiſtration, *ratione Prærogativæ ſuæ.* In treſpaſs on the Caſe *ſur aſſumpſit* of the Inteſtate, and upon Proceſs againſt the Archbiſhop, he was retorned *nihil habet nec eſt Inventus* ; and then ſhews the Cuſtom of *London* of *Foreign Attachments,* and that he himſelf owed to the Inteſtate 30 *l.* and had it in his Hands, and prayed *Attachment* of the ſaid Monies in his Hands, according to the ſaid Cuſtom, and alledgeth their Proceedings and Judgment in good Form as uſual. Demurrer. *(Vide Cumberbach, pag. 330.)*

It was ſhewed to the Court, that the Cuſtom is alledged, that if the Debtor die Inteſtate, and a Plaint be affirmed againſt the Adminiſtrator, and if Proceſs againſt him be retorned, *quod nihil habet nec eſt Inventus,* &c. That this Cuſtom is not purſued in the Plaint affirmed againſt the Archbiſhop, and then the Judgment founded on this Cuſtom will be void. *Quod fuit conceſſum per* *(Cuſtom not purſued in pleading.)*

* T 4 *totam*

totam curiam ; and refolved, that the Plea was infufficient; and that the Judgment upon the *Foreign Attachment* was not any Eftopple to the Plaintiff here, he not being Party. Sir *Tho. Jones* 165. *Smith* and *Rogers*.

By the Cuftom of *Foreign Attachments* in *London*, if *A.* fue *B.* in *London*, &c. and *C.* is indebted to *B.* in the fame Sum, and the faid *C.* is condemned there to *A.* according to the Cuftom, and Judgment given againft him accordingly, yet if no Execution be fued againft *C. A.* may refort to have Judgment and Execution againft *B.* his principal Debtor, and *B.* may fue *C.* for his Debt notwithftanding the Judgment, *per Brook* Recorder of *London : Dyer* 7 *Ed.* VI. 822.

How the Defendant may avoid or difprove a Debt.

The Manner for a Defendant in an Attachment, &c. to difprove or avoid any Debt demanded, is as followeth : The Defendant muft either render his Body to Prifon, or give Security to pay the Debt demanded, and then may bring a *Scire Facias*, which is called a *Scire Facias ad difprobandum debitum* ; and the Plaintiff in the Attachment muft be fummoned to appear, and plead thereunto ; and after the Plaintiff hath pleaded, if the Debt demanded be not a Debt due by Bond, Bill, or Specialty under Hand and Seal, the Defendant may wage his Law, and thereby difcharge himfelf of the Money demanded by the Plaintiff, which muft be done in Court as followeth :

I A. B. do *fwear, That upon the Day of [naming the Day the Action was entered] I did not owe nor detain, nor as yet do owe or detain from* C. D. *the Plaintiff the Sum of* 120 *l. nor any Part or Parcel thereof, in Manner and Form as the Plaintiff by his Bill Original, hath fuppofed.* So help me God.

And

And if the Defendant be a Freeman of *London,* Leg. Gager. he muſt have Six Compurgators, who will Swear, *That they believe in their Conſciences, that what the Defendant ſwears is true :* But if the Defendant be not a Freeman of *London,* then two Compurgators will be ſufficient.

If the Defendant 'ſhall not think fit to wage his Law, but will put the Plaintiff to prove his Debt, he muſt in ſuch Caſe plead that he owes nothing to the Plaintiff, an iſſuable Plea. And in caſe the Plaintiff fail to prove his Debt, a Verdict and Judgment will paſs againſt him for Reſtitution of the Money, or Value of the Goods attached and condemned; and if the Plaintiff in the Attachment ſhall in ſuch caſe be taken in Execution, and ſhall be unable or unwilling to reſtore the Money, his Security or Pledges that he gave when the Money was condemned, will be compelled to pay the Money; for the Sureties cannot Diſcharge themſelves by rendring the Plaintiff's Body to Priſon.

Security to pay the Money if the Plaintiff fail.

But if the Plaintiff prove his Debt, the Verdict will paſs for the Plaintiff in the Attachment, and then Judgment will be entered for the Debt proved to be due; and if ſo much was recovered upon the Attachment or Sequeſtration, the Bail for the Defendant are liable to anſwer, and pay the ſame with Coſts.

Concerning Sequeſtration of a Citizen's Goods, &c.

IF *A. B.* owes Money to *C. D.* and abſconds, and happens to leave Goods in a Houſe or Warehouſe locked up, and no Perſon in the Houſe or Warehouſe; in ſuch Caſe *C. D.* may ſequeſter the Houſe or Warehouſe, and the Goods and Chattels therein contained, and in ſix Days Time, may condemn the Goods. The Man-

Manner of making a Sequeſtration is as follows.
C. D. *muſt enter an Action of Debt againſt* A. B.
*with one of the Four Attorneys of this Court, and
then one of the Officers of this Court muſt go to the
ſame Houſe or Warehouſe, and ſay theſe or the
like Words.*

I Do ſequeſter this Warehouſe, and the Goods
and Chattels therein contained, as the proper
Warehouſe, Goods, and Chattels of *A. B.* to
anſwer *C. D.* in a Plea of Debt, upon a Demand of 120 *l.*

*And then muſt put a Padlock upon the Door of the
Houſe, and ſet a Seal upen the Key-hole of the Padlock. And after four Court Days paſſed, which is
uſual in four Days, the Officer will receive a* Pre-
*cept to open the Warehouſe, and cauſe the Goods
therein to be inventory'd and appraiſ'd by any two
Freemen; and the* Appraiſors *muſt ſet their Names
or Marks to the ſame Inventory, and come to the
next Court, and there take an Oath as followeth :*

The Oath to be taken by the Appraiſors.

Y O U, and either of you, ſhall ſwear, that
the Appraiſement you have made of the
Goods and Chattels in this Schedule or Inventory
ſpecified, whereunto you have ſubſcribed your
Names, is a juſt and true Valuation and Appraiſement of the ſame Goods and Chattels, according to the beſt of your Judgments and Skills.
So help you God.

The ſame Court Day that the Appraiſors are
ſworn, the Plaintiff may have Judgment and Execution for the Goods, bringing two ſufficient
Sureties, who will enter into a Recognizance
to this Effect : *viz. That if the Defendant* A. B.
*ſhall come into Court within a Year and a Day, and
diſprove or avoid the Debt demanded by* C. D. *that
then* C. D. *ſhall reſtore the Goods, or the Value
thereof, to* A. B. *or elſe that they will do it for him.*

Con-

Concerning Guild-Hall, &c.

GUild-Hall has no Jurisdiction to proceed on a Penal Statute-Law, therefore Error of a Judgment given in an in Information at the Court of *Guild-Hall* before the Lord Maior of *London* was brought.

A Question was, *Whether it might be returned here in* B. R. *or whether it ought to be by a special Commission in* London, *according to their Charter ?*

But this being Matter concerning the Crown, a *Certiorari* was awarded to remove the Record; which being done, a Writ of *Error* was brought *Coram vobis residet.*

Certiorari.

The *Error* assigned was, because the Information was brought in *London,* upon the Stat. 5 *El.* for exercising a Trade whereto he was not bound Apprentice, and so demanded 40 *s.* for every Month; and this being a Penal Law, ought not to be sued but in the King's Courts at *Westminster.* 9 Rep. 17. Cro. *Jac.* 538.

Guild-Hall *no Jurisdiction to proceed on a Penal Law.*

The Custom was alledged there were two Officers call'd Bridge-Masters, and that they have certain Fees and Profits belonging to them; and the Citizens assembled in the Common Hall Yearly choose or continue these Bridge-Masters. And another Custom, if there be two Persons upon Election, he that is chosen by the major Number of Votes is elected ; and that if one in such Case, requires the Polls shall be number'd, the Maior ought to allow them the Polls.

Bridgmasters.

Turner brought his Action on the Case against Sir *Samuel Sterling,* Maior, for his refusing to number the Polls, and discharging the Court, so that he lost the Profits.

Verdict was, *pro Quer.*

It was moved in Arrest of Judgment, whether the Action lay ?

Action against Maior for refusing to number the Polls on the Election of a Bridgmaster.

Vaughn

Vaughan, Chief Juftice, was of Opinion, That the Action lies not, for that no Damage appears. If a Maior will not elect a Burgefs, or the Sheriff a Knight, no Action lies, becaufe there is no Election. If twenty had ftood, muft each recover the Value of the Place ? He is to be punifhed by Information or Indictment; and tho' it be averred, he was chofen by the major Part ; yet that cannot be put in Iffue, or tried.

But the others, *Wild*, *Archer*, and *Tirrel*, were for the Action on the Cafe to be good, for tho' *non conftat* whether the Plaintiff fhould have been chofen, yet the Law gives an Action but for the poffibility of Damage. If I have a Beaft-Market, and a Toll for Sale, and one hinders the Beafts from coming thither, *non conftat*, whether they fhould be fold ; yet for the poffibility of that, and of the lofs of the Toll, Action lies. An Action lies as much for injurious preventing him of having the Office, as for hindering him in the executing of the Office. Judgment *pro Quer*.

Cuftom of London *of Foreign Attachment in the Maior's Court, pleaded to a Bond.*

Defendant prays *Oyer* of the Bond, *&c.*

Cuftom of the y fet forth.

——QUibus Lect' & Audit' (actio' non) &c. quia dicit quod Civitas Lond' eft antiqua civitas quodque in ead'·civitate habetur, & à tempore cujus contrarii memoria hominum non exiftit habebatur confuetudo ufitat' & approbat',(viz.) Quod fi aliqua Perfona affirmavit verfus aliquam perfonam aliquam billam Original' debit' in Curia dom' Regis nunc vel predeceflorum fuorum nuper Regum & Reginarum
An-

Angliæ coram Majore & Aldermannis, civitat'
præd' pro tempore exiften' in Camera Guild-Hall
fcituat' in Parochia Sancti Michaelis Bafifhaw in
Warda Bafifhaw Lond' Secundum confuetud' e-
jufdem civitat' tent' feu tenend' & ad Petitionem
Perfone in ead' Bill original' quer' nominat' vel
ejus Attornat' ibid. pro tempore exiften' virtute
bille original' illius per Curiam illam fervien' ad
arma, eorund' Majoris & Aldermannorum infra
eand' civitat' miniftr' ejufdem Curie pro tempore
exiften' precept' fuit ad fummonend' perfonam
in ead' billa nominat' defend' effend' ad eandem
vel prox' curiam dicti dom' Regis nunc vel predeceflorum fuorum prædictorum in dicta Camera
Guild-Hall civitat' prædict' coram Majore & Aldermannis, ejufdem civitat' pro tempore exiften'
tent' feu tenend' ad refpondend'querent' in eadem
Billi Original'de & in placito in eadem Bill. Original' fpecificat.Et fi hujufmodi ferviens ad arma
ac miniftr' Curiæ illius ad eandem vel 'ad hujufmodi prox' curiam virtute præcepti illius coram Majore & Aldermannis civitatis illius pro
tempore exiften' .ore tenus retornavit eidem
Curiæ quod Perfona in billa Original' defendens nominat' nihil habuerit infra Libertat' civitat. præd' per quod aut ubi fum' potuit nec
fuit invent' infra Libertat' civitat' præd' & dicta
perfona in dicta billa Original' defend. nominat'
ab curiam illam ibid. exact. fecerit defaltam. Et
fuper hoc ad eand' curiam teftificat' feu notifi-
cat' fit eidem curiæ per hujufmodi perfonam in
eadem billa original' quer' nominat' in propria
perfona fua vel per Attornat' fuum ibidem pro
tempore exiften' quod aliqua alia perfona fit
indebitat' hujufmodi perfonæ in tali billa original' defend' nominat' in aliqua denariorum fumma ad fummam debi. in eadem billa original'
fpecificat aut ad aliquam parcellam inde & eandem

dem fummam in manibus & cuftod. fuis
habuit & ab hujufmodi defend detineret quod
tunc ad petitionem hujufmodi quer. vel ejus
attornat. ibid. pro tempore exiften. curiæ præd.
fiend. per curiam illam præciperetur ore tenus
hujufmodi Servien. ad arma & minifter. curiæ
illius quod ipfe fecundum confuetud. civitat.
prædict eundem Deft. in eadem billa original.
nominat. per fummam illam fic in manibus &
cuftod. hujufmodi alterius perfonæ exiften. Attach. & quod ipfe fummam illam fic in manibus & cuftod. hujufmodi alterius perfonæ fecundum confuetud. dictæ civitatis Attach. Ita
quod idem defend. effet ad proximam curiam
vel aliquam aliam curiam dict. Dom. Regis nunc
vel prædecefforum fuorum prædictorum coram
Majore & Aldermannis, civitat. præd. pro tempore exiften. in prædicta camera Guild-hall civitat. præd. fecundum confuetud' ejufdem civitat.
tent. feu tenend. ad refpond. eidem quer. de & in
placito in billa original. præd. fpecificat. & fi
idem Servien. ad arma poftea ad hujufmodi
prox. curiam vel ad aliquam hujufmodi aliam curiam ibidem ut præfertur' tent. feu tenend. ore
tenus retornavit, & certificavit eidem curiæ
præd. quod ipfe virtute præcepti illius tal. defend. per fumman illam fic in manibus & cuftod.
hujufmodi alterius perfonæ exiften. fecundum
confuetud. dictæ Civitatis Attach. Ita quod
idem defend. effet tunc ibid. ad eandem curiam
ad refpond. tali quer. de & in placito in billa
original. præd. fpecificat. Et fi hujufmodi defend.
ad curiam illam & ad tres alias Curias ibidem
feperatim prox. & extunc. fecundum confuetud.
civitat. præd. tenend. (vid.) ad quatuor hujufmodi curias feperal. ad peticonem hujufmodi
Quer. vel ejus Attornat. ibid. pro tempore exiften. folempnit. exact. ibid. non venerit fed defalt.

falt. fecerit in eodem placito in billa original.
præd. fpecificat. fecundum confuetud. civitatis
præd. recordat. forent poft prædict. attach. in
forma præd. fact' ipfe quer. in eadem bill. original. nominat. ad quamlibet earund. cur. in propria perfona fua vel per attorn. ibid. pro tempore
exiften. comparen. & feipfum offeren' verfus hujufmodi defend' in præd. placito in Billa original'
præd' fpecificat' fecundum confuet'civitatis præd.
tunc ad ultimam curiam prædictarum quatuor
Curiarum vel ad aliquam aliam curiam poft
præd. quatuor defalt' recordat' ad petitionem
perfonæ in dict' billa original' quer' nominat' vel
per ejus tunc attornat' ibid. pro tempore exiften'
dictæ Curiæ fiend' præciperetur, ore tenus per
eand. Curiam hujufmodi Servien. ad arma quod
ipfe fecundum confuetud. ejufdem curiæ civitat.
præd (quod)præmon. & fcire fac. hujufmodi alteri Perfonæ in cujus manu & cuftod', &c. effend'
ad aliam curiam dict' dom' Regis nunc vel prædecefforum fuorum præd. coram Majore & Aldermannis civitatis præd. pro tempore exiften' in
prædict. camera Guild-Hall ejufdem civitatis fecundum confuetud' dictæ civitatis ex tunc tenend'
oftendend' fi quid pro fe haberet, vel dicere fciat
quare hujufmodi quer. in billa original' præd. nominat. Executionem de præd. fumma fic ut præfertur in manibus fuis attach' & defenf. &c. habere non deberet. Ad quam curiam fi idem
Serviens ad arma retornavit, & teftificavit eid.
curiæ quod ipfe virtute præcepti illius præmon.
& fcire fecit eid. perfonæ in cujus manibus &
cuftod. &c. effend. ibid. in ead. curia ad oftendend' in forma præd. prout ei præcept' fuit & hujufmodi quer. tunc ibidem comparen' in propria
perfona fua vel per Attornat' fuum ad ejus petitionem hujufmodi perfona fic præmonit. tunc &
ibid. fit folempniter exact. & in propria perfona
                                                    fua

sua comparen' & cogn' se tempore hujus Attach.
fact. habuisse debuisse atque detenuisse & ad tunc
se habere & detinere à præd. persona in bill' original. defend. nominat. pecuniæ summan in manibus suis sic Attach. Idemque quer. in propria
persona sua vel per Attor. suum adtunc & ibid.
juravit debitum suum præd. in tali billa original.
petit. tunc talis quer. per consuetud' curiæ illius
haberet, & à toto tempore supradict' habere con-
suevit executionem de hujusmodi summa sic ut
præfertur Attach' in satisfactione debiti in tali
billa original' spec' aut tantàm parcell' inde
quantum ead. summa si attachiat' se extend. per
duos plegios ad minus per ipsum quer' in ead.
curia inveniend' ad hujusmodi summam sic attach. & in executione habit' restituend' hujusmodi defend' si idem defendens infra unum annum & unam diem tunc. prox sequen' secundum
consuetudinem civitat' prædict' ibid. ven' & dis-
rationaverit debitum præd. in præd. billa original
content'. &c. & quod post hujusmodi pleg. invent.
& execution. de hujusmodi summa sic in manibus & custod' hujusmodi alterius personæ attach'
& defens per quer' in ead. billa original' nominat
habit' hujusmodi altera persona in cujus manu &
custod' *&c.* exoneretur versus hujusmodi defend.
de dicta summa ut præfertur attach' & unde executionem sic habit fuit & talis defend' in tali
billa original nominat' exoneretur versus talem
quer. de tanta summa debi' sui in tali original'
per ipsum quer. petit. tam diu quam hujusmodi
judicium & executio' in suis robore permanerent
& effectu per talem defend' minime revocat' vel
disrationat', & si hujusmodi denar' sum' sic attach' & defens. & unde executio sic habetur non
atting' ad integram' summam debit' in præd. billa original per talem quer. versus talem defend'
in curia illa petit. tunc talis quer. per consuetud.

curiæ

curiæ illius haberet, & à totò tempore fupradict.
habere confuevit proceff' verfus talem defend' fecundum confuetud' civitatis præd. pro refiduo fui
debiti præd. per ipfum in tall' billa original' petit.
Et idem H. ulterius dicit quod prædicta confuetudo & omnes aliæ confuetudines civitat' præd. in
ead. civitat' à diu ufitat' authoritate Parliamenti
dom. Rici. quondam Regis Angliæ fecundi poft
conqueftum Anno regni fui feptimo apud Weftm.
in Com. Middlefex tunc Majori & communitati
dictæ civitat' & fucceforibus fuis ratificat. & confirmat' fuere. Et idem defend. ulterius dicit quod
quidam J. J. de London Mercator ante diem
impetrationis brevis originalis præfat' W. L. (fcil.
18 die Martii anno regni dict. dom. Regis nunc
quarto in propria perfona fua ven. in Curia dict'
dom. Regis nunc coram J. B. tunc Majore
præd. civitatis & ejufdem civitatis tunc Aldermannis in prædicta camera *Guildhall* civitat' præd.
fcituat in parochia Sancti Michaelis Bafifhaw in
Warda de Bafifhaw Lond' præd fecundum confuetud' civitatis præd. tent' & adtunc & ibid. in
ead. curia per nomen. J. J. de Lond', mercator'
affirmavit quandam billam original' debi' fuper
demand' duaram mille Librarum Legalis, (&c.)
verfus præd. W. L. civem & haberdafher London'
cujus quidem billæ originalis tenor fequitur in
hæc verba. fcil.

J. J. de Lond' Mercator per J. L. attornat'
fuum petit verfus W. L. civem & Haberdafher
de Lond' duas Mille Libras Legalis, &c. quas ei
debet & injufte detinet. &c. eo quod 26 die Sept.
Anno Dom. 1716. in Paroch. Sancti Sepulchri
Lond' dictus defend. per quoddam fcriptum fuum
obligatorium figillo fuo figillat. & hic in curia
prolat. cujus dat. eft iifdem die & Anno obligavit
fe præfato Querenti in præd. 2000 *l.* folvend. eid.
quer. quo & quando, &c. prout per idem fcrip-

tum

Confirmation of Cuftoms by Stat. 7 R. 2.

Pledges.   tum obligatorium plenius liquet quas prædict.
defend. dicto quer. non dum folvit licet fæpius,
&c. ad damnum dicti Quer. 200 *l.* & inde produc. fectam. Et idem J. J. tunc. & ibid. in ead.
curia fecundum conf. civitatis præd. invenit pleg.
ad billam fuam originalem profequend. videl. J.
Doe & Richardum Roe & tunc & ibid. ponit in
loco fuo J. S. Attornat. fuum verfus præfat.
W. L. in & fuper bill. originalem illam fecundum
confuetud. civitatis præd. &c. Et per eundem
Attornat. fuum adtunc & ibid. idem J. J. petiit

Procefs.   proceffum ei fuperinde fieri verfus præfat. W. L.
fecundum conf. ejufdem civitatis & ei tunc &
ibid. conceff. fuit, &c. fuper quo virtute billæ
originalis præd. ad petitionem præd. J. J. per
tunc attornat. fuum præd. fact. præcept. fuit ore
tenus tunc & ibid. per Cur. illam fecundum confuetud' dictæ civitatis E. A. tunc. Servien' dicto-
rum Majoris & Aldermannorum, ad arma ac miniftro cur. præd. quod ipfe fum. per bonos fum-
monitores præd. W. L. effend. ad eand. cu-

Summons.   riam dicti dom. Regis eod. 18 die Martii Anno
5° fupradict. coram præfato Majore & Aldermannis in præd. camera Guild-Hall civitat. præd;
fecundum coufuetud. civitat' præd. tent' ad refpond' præfato J. de & in placito in præd. billa
fpec. & idem dies dat' fuit adtunc & ibid. per
eand. curiam eid. J. in eod. placito, *&c.* fuper quo
poftea, (fcil.) ad eandem curiam dicti' dom. Regis coram præfat. Majore & Aldermannis in dicta

Retorn.   Camera Guild-Hall 18 die Martii Anno 5° fupradict' fecundum confuetud' civitatis præd. tent.
idem tum Serviens ad arma ac minifter Curiæ
præd. tunc & ibid. ore tenus retornavit & certificavit eid. Curiæ quod præd. W. nihil habuit infra Libertat. civitat' prædict. per quod aut ubi
fum. potuit nec fuit inventus infra eand. Libertat.
civitat præd. Et præd. W. adtunc & ibid. ad e-
andem

andem curiam exactus fuit & non comperuit sed
defaltam fecit, &c. Et super hoc postea ad eand.
curiam præd. J. per tunc Attornat. suum præd.
adtunc & ibid. in ead. curia testificavit & noti-
ficavit eid. curiæ quod præd. defendens per nomen
&c. tunc fuit indebitat' præfato W. in 36 *l.* &
easdem 36 *l.* in manibus & custod. suis tunc habuit & à præfat W. detinuit, & idem J. adtunc &
ibid. per tunc attorn' suum præd. petiit ab eadem curia quod per eandem curiam præciperetur
ore tenus præfato Servienti ad arma & ministro
curiæ præd. quod ipse secundum conf. civitatis
præd. præd. W. per easdem 36 *l.* in manibus &
custod. ipsius defend. ut præfertur tunc existen' secundum confuet' dictæ civitatis attachiar. & quod
ipse summam illam in manibus & custod. ipsius
defend. existen' secundum conf. civitat. præd. defender. ita quod præd. W. esset ad prox' curiam
dicti dom. Regis nunc coram præfato Majore
& Aldermannis. in præd. camera Guild-Hall civitat' præd. secundum confuet' civitatis præd.
tenend' ad respond' præfato J. dé & in placito in
billa sua original' præd. spec. super quo adtunc &
ibid. ad petitionem ejusdem J. per tunc Attornat'
suum. præd. eid. curiæ ut præfertur fact. præcept.
fuit ore tenus per Curiam illam præfato tunc Servien' ad arma ac ministro curiæ illius quod ipse
secundum confuet' civitatis præd. præd. W. per
præd. 36 *l.* in manibus & custodiis ipsius defend'
existen' attach' & ipse easdem 36 *l.* in manibus
& custod. ipsius defend' secundum consuetud' civitat' præd. defender'. Ita quod præd. W. esset
ad proximam curiam dict' dom. Regis nunc in
præd. Camera Guild-Hall civitat' præd. coram
præfat. Majore & Aldermannis 19 die Martii
Anno 5° supradict' secundum confuet' civitat'
præd. tenend' ad respond' præfat' J. de & in placito in billa original' sua prædicta spec'. Et quod

idem

Foreign Attachments

idem tunc Servien' ad arma superius faceret eid.
curiæ tunc & certificaret, &c. Et idem dies dat'
fuit tunc & ib.d. per eandem curiam præfat' J.
in eod. placito. Ad quem diem scil. ad dictam
Curiam dicti dom. Regis coram præfat' tunc
Majore & Aldermannis in prædicta camera
Guild-Hall civitat' præd. prædicto 19° die Martii Anno 5° supradict' secundum consuet' civitatis præd. tent' præd. J. per tunc attornat' suum

Retorn.

præd venit & comparuit, &c. Et præd. Servien'
ad arma tunc & ibid. ore tenus retornavit, & certificavit eid' curiæ quod ipse 19 die Martii Anno
5° supradict' virtute præcepti præd' præd. W. per
præd' 36 l. in manibus & custod. ejusdem H. Def'
tunc existen' secundum consuetud' civitatis præd'
attachiasset & easdem 36 l. sic in manibus & custod' ipsius H. Defend' existen' secundum consuetud' dicte civitat' tunc defendisset. Ita quod
idem W. esset tunc ibidem ad eand' curiam ad
respondend' prafato J. de & in placito in billa
original' sua præd' spec. prout ei superius præcept' fuerat, super quo in ead' curia dicti dom'
Regis coram tunc Majore & Aldermannis in
prædicta Camera Guild-Hall civitat' præd. 19
die Martii Anno 5°. supradict secundum consuet'
civitatis præd. tent. præd. J. per tunc Attorn.
suum optulit se versus præfat' W. de & in placito
in billa original. præd. spec. secundum consuet' civitat' præd. Et præd. W. ad petitionem præd.
J. per tunc Attorn' suum præd. tunc & ibid.
fact' ad eandem curiam solempniter exactus fuit
& non comparuit sed primam tunc & ibid. fecit
defalt. quæ quidem prima defalt. super eund.
W. ad curiam illam in placito in billa original.
præd. spec. secundum consuet' civitatis præd' recordat' fuit &c. Et super hoc tunc & ibid. secundum cons' civitat' præd. dies dat' fuit per eandem curiam eid. W. usque ad prox' curiam dicti

dom'

dom' Regis'coram præfato Majore & Aldermannis, in'præd. camera Guild-Hall civitat' præd'
(ſcil.) 20 die præd. menſis Martii ſupradicto ſecundum conſuetud' civitatis præd' & idem dies
tunc' & ibid' per Curiam illam dat' fuit præfato
J. 'in 'eod. placito &c. ad quam quidem prox
curiam dicti dom' Regis nunc coram præfat' Majore & Aldermannis in prædicta camera Guild-
Hall civitat' præd' præd' 20, die Martii Anno 5°
ſupradict' ſecundum conſuetud' civitatis præd'
tent præd. J. per tunc Attornat' ſuum comparuit
& tunc & ibid' in ead' curia optulit ſe verſus præfat' W. de & in prædicto placito in billa original'
præd' ſpec' ſecundum conſuet' civitatis præd. &
præd. W. ad petitionem præd. J. per tunc Attorn'
ſuum præd. tunc & ibid' fact' tunc & ibid. in ead.
curia ſolempnit' exact' fuit & non compa-
ruit. ſed adtunc & ibidem ſecundam fecit defal- *2d Default.*
tam quæ quidem ſecunda defalta ſuper eand.W.ad
curiam illam in placito in billa original' præd. ſpec'
ſecundum conſuetud' civitatis præd. recordat' fuit,
&c.Et ſuper hoc tunc & ibid ſecundum cons'civitat.
prædict'dies ulterius dat' fuit per eand. curiam præfato W. uſq;prox.curiam dicti dom. Regis nunc coram præfat' Majore & Aldermannis, in præd. Camera Guild-Hall civitat' præd. ſcil. 22 die præd.
menſis Martii Anno 5° ſupradict ſecundum conſuetud' Civit' præd. &c. idem dies tunc & ibid.
dat' fuit per eandem Curiam præfato J. in eod.
placito, &c. ad quam quidem proximam curiam
dicti dom' Regis nunc in camera Guild-Hall civitat' præd. coram præfato tunc Majore & Aldermannis præd. 22 Die Martii Anno 5° ſupradict' ſecundum conſuetud' præd. tent. prædict' J.
per tunc attornat' ſuum prædict' comparuit, &
tunc & ibid. in ead. curia op' ſe verſus præfat' W.
de & in placito prædicto in billa original' prcd'
ſpec. ſecundum cons' civitat' præd. Et præd. W.

ad-

adtunc & ibid. ad petitionem præd. J. tunc attornat. fuum præd. tunc & ibid. fact' in ead' curia
3d Default. folempnitur exact' fuit & non comparuit fed tertiam tunc & ibid. fecit defalt' quæ quidem tertia
defalta fuper eundem W. ad curiam illam in placito in billa original' præd. fpec' fecundum confuetud' civitat' præd. recordatum fuit. Et fuper
4th Default. hoc, (&c. ut fupra ufq; ad quartam defaltam)
quæ quidem quarta defalta fuper eand. W. ad curiam illam, (&c. ut fupra) recordat' fuit. Et idem
W. feipfum per attachiamentum forinfecum præd.
fecundum confuet' civitatis præd. Jufticiar' non
permifit poft quas quidem quatuor defaltas fic
ut præfertur fecundum cons' civitat' præd. in forma præd. fuper præd. W. recordat' (viz.) ad præd.
curiam dict' dom' Regis nunc præd. 24 Die Martii Anno 5° fupradict' coram præfat' tunc Majore
& Aldermannis in præd. camera Guild-Hall civitat' præd. ut prefertur tent' ad petitionem præd.
J. per tunc Attornat' fuum præd. eid' curiæ fact'
præcept' fuit ore tenus per eand' curiam præfat'
tunc Servien' ad arma quod ipfe fecundum confuetud' ejufdem civitat' præmon' & fcire fac. præfato H. defend' effendi ad curiam dicti' dom'
Regis nunc in camera Guild-Hall civitat' præd'
coram præfat' Majore & Aldermannis 26 Die
præd. menfis Martii Anno 5° fupradict. fecundum
confuetudinem civitat' præd' tenend' ad oftendend' & demonftrand' fi quid ipfe haberet, aut dicere fciret quare præd' J. executionem de præd'
36 *l.* in manibus & Cuftod' ipfius H. defend' in
forma præda' attach' & defens', &c. habere non
deberet fecundum confuetud' civitat. præd' &c. &
quid idem tunc Servien' ad arma tunc inde faceret eid' tunc curiæ certificaret, & idem dies tunc
& ibid' dat' fuit per eand' curiam eid' J. effend.
ibid. &c. Ad quam quidem curiam dicti dom'
Regis nunc tent' dicto 26 Die Martii Anno 5° fupradicto

pradicto coram praefato tunc Majore & Aldermannis in praedict. camera Guild-Hall civitat. praed. fecundum confuetud' ejufdem civitat' tent. venit praed. J. per tunc atornatum fuum praed. & idem tunc Servien' ad arma retornavit & certificavit eid. curiae quod ipfe virtute praecepti illius fibi direct. praemon' & fcire fecit praefat' H. defend' effend. ibid. in ead. Curia eod. 26 die Martii prout ei praeceptum fuit fuper quo ad petitionem praed' J. per tunc Attorn' fuum praed. tunc & ibid. fact' praed. H. praemonit', &c. tunc & ibid. folempnit' exact' in ead' Curia in propria perfona fua comparuit & cogn' fe tempore attachiamenti praed. fact' habuiffe atq; detinuiffe adhuc & ibid. habere debere atq; detinere à praefat' W. praed. 36 *l.* in pecuniis numeratis ficut praefertur in manibus praed. H. attach' & defens', &c. Super quo praed' J. per. Attorn' fuum praed' tunc & ibid' in ead' Curia juftum debitum fuum praed' in billa original' praed' petit' fecundum confuetud' praed' Juravit & adtunc & ibid' in ead' Curia petit executionem de praed' 37 *l.* ficut praefertur in manibus & cuftod' praed' H. fic attach' & defens' Secundum confuetud' civitat' praed' fibi adjudicari, &c. Ideo praed' 26 Die Martii Anno 5° fupradicto ad eand' curiam tunc & ibid' tent' fecun- *Judgment.* dum cons' civitat' praed' Confiderat' fuit per eand' curiam quod praed' J. haberet Executionem de praed' 36 *l.* fic ut praefertur fuperius Attach' per duos plegios in ead' curia fecundum confuet' civitatis praed' per ipfum J. inveniend' ad reftituend' praed' W. eafdem 36 *l.* fic attach' fi ipfe idem W. infra unum annum & unum menfem tunc prox' fequen' fecundum cons' civitat' praed' ibid. veniret & difrationaret debitum praed' in billa original' praed. J. content', &c. ac quod idem J. haberet proceffum verfus praed' W. pro refiduo debiti praed' in billa original' praed' fpec'
&c.

&c; Super quo præd' J. ad curiam illam coram
præfat' Majore & Aldermannis, in præd' camerâ
Guild-Hall civitat' præd' præd' 26 Die Martii
Anno 5° fupradict' fecundum cons' civitat' prædict. juxta tenorem judicii præd' inde reddit' &
Secundum cons' præd. inven' fufficien' plegios,
(viz.) F. H. & E. W. mercatores Sciffores cives

Execution. Lond' ad reftituend' præfat' W. præd. 36 *l.* fuperius attach' in forma præd. fi, &c. Et fuper quo
adtunc & ibid. in ead. curia præd. J. per cons' e-
jufdem curiæ habuit executionem de præd. 36 *l.*
fic ut præfertur, &c. fecundum tenorem & demand. judicii inde reddit' & fecundum cons civitat. præd. Et idem J. cognovit tunc & ibid. in
ead. curia fe fatisfact. fuiffe, &c. prout coram
præfat. Majore & Aldermannis in præd. Camera
Guild-Hall civitat. præd. liquet de recordo. Et
idem H. defend. dicit quod præd. 36 *l.* ad fectam

Avertment. præd. J. J: in forma præd. Attach. & defenf. &
in manibus ipfius H. recuperat. & in executionem
habit. fecundum confuetud. ejufdem civitat. &
præd. 36 *l.* in Indorfamento fcripti obligatorii
præd. fpec. funt un. & ead. 36 *l.* & non aliæ neque divers. Et quod præd. H. in billa original.
& in attachiamento præd. præmonit.& nominat. &
præd. H. H. mercator modo hic in brevi & narr.
præd. defend. nominat. eft una & ead. perfona &
non alia neq; diverfa. Et quod præd. W. L. civis
& Haberdafher Lond. in billa original. præd. ad
fectam præd. J. profecut. nominat. defendens. Et
præd. W. L. modo hic in brevi & in narratione
fua nominat. quer. eft un. & ead. perfona, & non
alia neque diverfa : Et quod judicium & executio præd. adhuc in fuo robore perman. & effectu
per præfat. W. minime revocat. five difrationat.
& hoc idem H. paratus eft verificare unde pet.
judicium fi præd. W. L. actionem fuam præd. inde
verfus eum habere feu manutenere debeat, &c

A Foreign Attachment pleaded in an
Action on the Case, on a Promise
made in the hands of an Executrix
in the Sheriffs Court.

ET prædict: W. A. per R. S. Attornatum fuum venit & defendit vim & injuriam quando, *&c.* Et quoad ultimam promiffionem & affumptionem in narratione prædicta fpecificat.
Idem W. dicit quod non affumpfit fuper fe modo & forma prout prædict. A. fuperius narran-
do allegavit & de hoc ponit fe fuper patriam &
prædict. J. fimiliter, *&c.* Et quoad prædictas
quindecim libras in prima promiffione in narratione prædict. fpecificat. Idem W. dicit quod
prædictus J. T. Actionem fuam prædictam verfus
eum habere feu manutenere non debet, quia quoad feptem libras & octodecim folidos parcell.
inde idem W. dicit quod ipfe poft promiffionem
& affumptionem prædict. fact. fcilicet Die &
Anno in narratione prædict. fuperius mentionat'
apud *L.* prædict. in Parochia & Warda prædict.
folvit præfato A. feptem Libras & octodecim
Solidos inde parcel. quos quidem 7*l.*18*s.* prædict.
A. ad tunc & ibidem recepit & habuit, & hoc
paratus eft verificare ; & quoad feptem libr. &
duos Solidos refid. prædicti quindecim libr. in
prædicta prima promiffione mentionat. idem Willielmus dicit quod civitas Lond. eft & à tempore *Cuftom of*
cujus contrarii memoria hominum non exiftit, *Foreign At-*
fuit antiqua civitas, quodque in eadem civitate *tachments*
habetur, & a toto tempore fupradicto habebatur *in London.*
quædam Cur. dicti Domini Regis nunc & prædecefforum fuorum nuper Regum & Reginarum
Angliæ de recordo feperaliter tent. coram fepe-
T   talibus

ralibus Vicecomitibus civitatis prædictæ pro
tempore exiften' de omnibus actionibus debiti
& de omnibus aliis actionibus perfonalibus qui-
bufcunque infra eandem civitatem emergentibus,
quodque etiam in eadem civitate habetur, & à
toto tempore fupradicto habebatur quædam
confuetudo ufitat. & approbat. viz. quod fi aliqua perfona levavit aliquam querelam in placito
debiti fuper demand' alicujus pecuniæ fummæ
in aliqua curia dicti Domini Regis nunc vel
prædeceíforum fuorum tenta infra civitatem
prædictam coram utro Vicecomite ejufdem civitat. fecundum confuetudinem ejufdem civitatis, & dicta perfona in hujufmodi querela nomi-
nata in eadem Cur. fecundum confuetudinem
civitatis prædict. invenit pleg. ad profequend'
eandem querelam fuam ; Et fi ad petitionem
dictæ Perfonæ in eadem querela quer. nominat.
aut Attornati fui præcept. fuit per hujufmodi
Vic. alicui fervien. ad clavam hujufmodi Vic. &
Miniftr. ejufdem Curiæ fecundum confuetud.
civitat. præd. in placito debiti ad fummonend.
perfonam vel perfonas in eadem querela defend.
nominat. effend. in hujufmodi Curia Domini Regis in qua hujufmodi querela levat. vel affirmat.
fuit coram hujufmodi Vic. ejufdem civitatis fecundum confuetudinem civitatis prædict. tenend.
ad refpondendum eidem quer. in eadem querela
nominat. in placito ejufdem querelæ & hujufmodi fervien. ad clavam ac miniftr. Curiæ illius
coram hujufmodi Vic. tent. ad Cur. ill. virtute
præcepti illius retornavit, & certificavit eidem
Curiæ quod perfona defenden. in hujufmodi
querela nominat. nihil habet infra libertatem
civitatis prædict. per quod aut ubi fummonere
potuit nec fuit invent. in eadem civitate & fuper hoc in Curia hujufmodi Vicecomitis coram
hujufmodi Vicecom. tent' pro quærente in eadem
querela

querela nominat' certificat' & teſtificat' fuit quod
aliqua alia perſona ratione quacunq; eſſet indebi-
tat.eidem defend. in eadem querela nominat' ut
executor teſtamenti ejuſdem teſtatoris in aliqua
denariorum ſumma extendend' ad ſummam debiti in eadem querela ſpecificat' aut ad aliquam
parcellam inde & hujuſmodi alia perſona eandem ſummam in manibus & cuſtod. ſuis habet
ut denar' dicti teſtatoris tempore mortis ſuæ
tunc ad petitionem hujuſmodi querentis in eadem querela nominat. vel ejus Attornati per
eandem curiam hujuſmodi Servien. ad clavam
& miniſt. Curiæ illius præciperetur quod hujuſmodi ſerviens ad clavam hujuſmodi defend. in
hujuſmodi querela nominat. per ſummam ill.
ſic in manibus ſive cuſtod. hujuſmodi aliæ perſonæ exiſten. attachiaret & ſummam illam in
manibus ſuis defenderet. Ita quod hujuſmodi
defend. ſit ad primam curiam dicti Domini
Regis coram hujuſmodi Vicecomite ſecundum
conſuetudinem civitatis prædictæ tent. ad reſpondend' hujuſmodi perſonæ in eadem querela
querenti nominat. in placito hujuſmodi querel.
ſuæ & tunc ſi hujuſmodi Serviens ad clavam ad
hujuſmodi primam curiam coram hujuſmodi
Vicecomite tentam retornavit, & certificavit
quod ipſe virtute præcepti præd. præfat. Def.
in eadem querela nominat. per Summam illam
in manibus ſive cuſtod. hujuſmodi aliæ perſonæ
attachiaſſet. Summam illam defendiſſet. Ita quod
in hujuſmodi querela defend. nominat. eſſet
ad eandem curiam ad reſpondendum hujuſmodi querenti in hujuſmodi querela nominat.
in placito hujuſmodi querel. ſuæ & tunc hujuſmodi defend. in eadem querela nominat. ad
curiam illam & ad tres alias ſeperales curias
coram hujuſmodi Vicecomite ſecundum conſuetudinem civitatis prædict. extunc prox.
ſequentes, ad petitionem hujuſmodi perſonæ in

hûjufmodi querela quer. nominat. vel ejus
attornat. folempniter exact. fuit & non venerit
fed defaltam fecit hujufmodi perfona quer. in
hujufmodi querela nominat. ad quamlibet hujufmodi cur. in propria perfona fua vel per
Attornatum fuum comparens ita quod quatuor
defalt. fuper hujufmodi defend. ad quatuor
cur. ill. in placito querel. illius recordat. funt
poft attachiamentum in forma prædicta fact' &
fi tunc ad ultimam eandem cur. alicui Servienti
ad clavam & miniftro ejufdem curiæ præcept.eft
quod fcire faceret hujufmodi aliæ perfonæ in
cujus manibus & cuftod. hujufmodi Summa attachiat' ac defens' fuiffet effend' ad primam
curiam Domini Regis coram hujufmodi Vicecomite ejufdem civitatis fecundum confuetudinem ejufdem civitatis tenend. ad oftenden-
dum fi quid ipfe haberet vel dicere fciret quare
hujufmodi quer. in querela illa nominat' executionem de Summa illa fic in manibus &
cuftod. fuis attachiat' & defens' verfus eum
habere non deberet. Et fi idem Serviens ad
clavam ad primam curiam illam coram hujufmodi Vicecomite tentam retornavit & certificavit, quod ipfe fecundum confuetudinem civitatis prædictæ præmonuiffet & fcire feciffet
hujufmodi al. perfon. ad effend. ibidem ad curiam prout ei præcept' fuiffet & tunc fi hujufmodi alia perfona in eadem cur. folempniter
exact' ad eandem curiam, non comparuit, fed
defalt' fecit, & fi tunc cônfiderat' fuit per eandem curiam coram hujufmodi Vicecomite tent.
fecundum confuetudinem civitatis illius quod
hujufmodi quer' in eadem querela nominat'
habeat executionem de eadem fumma in manibus & cuftod. hujufmodi aliæ perfonæ ut præfertur attachiat. & defens' in plenam folutio-
nem debiti in querela illa fpecificat. aut tant'
partis—— five parcell' inde quant' fumma fic
at-

attachiat' & defens' extenderet, hujufmodi quer' in hujufmodi querela nominat' invenien' & imponen' fufficientes manucapt. five pleg. in eadem curia coram hujufmodi Vic. tenta ad reftituend' hujufmodi Def. in hujufmodi querela nominat. hujufmodi fummam in manibus & cuftod. humoi. aliæ perfonæ fic attachiat' & defens' fi ipfe hujufmodi defend. in hujufmodi querela nominat' infra unum annum & unum diem prox. poft judicium fic ut præfertur reddit' fecundum confuetudinem civitatis prædict' venit in humoi. cur. hujufmodi Vic. & ibidem invenit fufficientes manucaptores ad placitand. cum hujufmodi querente in eadem querela nominat. in placito hujufmodi querel. fuæ & debitum prædictum per hujufmodi querentem per querelam prædictam verfus humoi. defend. petit. & difprobavit & difrationavit, aut fe à debito illo ullo modo exoneravit fecundum confuetudinem civitatis prædict. fic attachiat. & defens' quod tunc poft hujufmodi fecuritatem invent' pro executione fummæ illius in manibus & cuftod' il. alterius perfonæ attachiat. & defens' pro hujufmodi quer. in eadem querela nominat. habit' hujufmodi alia perfona exonerat. fuit verfus defendentem in querela illa nominat. de tanta denariorum fumma debiti fui in eadem querela petit. quant. dict. fumma fic attachiat' & defens. fecundum confuetudinem ejufdem civitatis, & executio inde habita attingeret, tamdiu quam hujufmodi judic. & executio in fuo robore permaneret & effectu. Et ulterius, idem W. dicit quod dict' confuetudo & omnes aliæ confuetudines civitatis prædictæ ufitat. authoritate Parliamenti Dom' Rici. nuper Regis Angliæ fecundi poft conqueftum Angliæ apud Weftm. Anno Regni fui feptimo tent' tunc Majori & communitati civitatis prædict.

dict. & fuccefforibus fuis ratificat' & confirmat fuerunt quodque diu ante impetrationem billæ præd. prædict. A.M. in vita fua indebitat' fuiffet cuidam H. C. in centum libris & fic indebitat' exiften' idem A. M. poftea & ante exhibitionem billæ prædict. prædict. J. apud Lond' prædict. videlt. in parochia Beatæ Mariæ de Arcub. in Warda de Cheap condidit teftamentum & ultimam voluntatem fuam in fcriptis & per eandem conftituit prædictum J. T. Executorem teftamenti fui prædict. & poftea ibidem obiit, & quod poftea fcilicet Die Mercurii quinto decimo die Julii Anno Regni Domini Georgii nunc Regis Magn. Brit. quarto, in curia dicti Domini Regis tenta coram Pet. Delme Milite Aldermanno adtunc uno Vicecomitum civitatis prædict. in computatorio fuo fcituat. in Parochia Sanct. Mildred & Virginis in Pulletra dict. civitatis venit H. T. in propria perfona adtunc & ibid. fecundum confuetudinem ejufdem civitatis, & levavit quandam querelam fuam in placito debi. fupra demand. centum Librarum verfus præfatum J. T. modo quer. per nomen J. T. executoris Teftamenti præfat. A. defunct. cujus quidem querel. tenor fequitur in hæc verba.

ff. J. T. executor Teftamenti A. M. defunct. fum. fuit verfus H. C. in placito debiti fupra demand. centum libr. & fupra hoc adtunc & ibid. in eadem curia fecundum confuetudinem civitatis præd. dictus H. C. invenit. pleg. de profequend' querelam fuam prædictam fic ut præfertur verfus præfatum J. T. Executorem, *&c.* levat. fcilicet. J. D. & J. F. & fuperinde dictus J. C. petiit proceffum fibi fieri in & fuper querelam fuam prædictam verfus J. T. executor. &c. fecundum confuetudinem civi-

civitatis prædiêt. ab omni tempore prædiêto, &c.
super quo adtunc & ibidem secundum confuetudinem diêt. civitatis ad petitionem præfat. H.
C. præcept. fuit per Pet. Delme Militem Al-
dermannum adtunc unum Vicecomitum diêtæ
civitatis cuidam J. S. tunc Servien. ad Clavam
diêti P. D. Militis Alderman. ad tunc unius Vicecomitum diêt. civitatis ac illius cur. miniſtr.
quod ipſe secundum confuetudinem diêt civitatis ſummoniret prædiêtum J. T. Executor. &c.
ad eſſend’ ad Curiam diêti Domini Regis coram
præfato P. D. Milite Aldermanno adtunc uno
Vicecomitum diêt. Civitatis in *Guild-Hall* diêt.
civitatis ſcituat. in Paroch. Sanêti Laurencii
in veteri Judaiſmo ejuſdem Civitat’ die Jovis decimo ſexto die Junii Anno quarto prædiêto ſecundum confuetud. diêt. Civitatis tenend. ad
reſpondend’ præfat. H. C. in placito querel. ſuæ
prædiêt. ſecundum confuetud. Civitatis prædiêt. à toto tempore prædiêto uſitat. Et quod
idem J. S. unus ſervientium ad Clavam diêti P.
D. Militis Aldermanni adtunc Vicecomitis ſu-
perinde faceret ad diêtam Curiam diêti Domini
Regis coram præfato P. D. Milite Alderman. adtunc uno Vicecomitum diêt. civitatis in computatorio prædiêto eodem Die Mercurii decimo
quinto Die Junii Anno quarto prædiêto ſecundum confuetud’ diêt. civitatis, *&c.* tenend’ retornaret & certificaret, *&c.* Cujus quidem præcepti prætextu prædiêtus J. S. unus Servien. ad
Clavam diêti P. D. Militis Alderman. adtunc
unius Vicecomitum diêt. civitat. ac illius Curiæ
Miniſter ad diêtam Curiam diêti Domini Regis
in Computatorio eodem Die Mercurii decimo
quinto Die Junii Anno quarto ſupradiêto coram
præfato P. D. Milite Alderman. ac uno Vicecomitum diêt. Civitat’, *&c.* tunc tent’ retornavit
& certificavit Cur. præd. quod J. T. Executor

nihil

nihil habuit infra Libertat. Civitat. prædict. per
quod aut ubi potuit ipfum præfatum J. fummonere, &c. Supra quo poftea, fcilicet ad eandem
Curiam dicti Dom. Regis coram præfato P. D.
Milit' Aldermanno adtunc uno Vicecomit' dict.
civitat' in Computatorio fuo prædicto eodem Die
Mercurii decimo quinto Die Junii Anno quarto
prædicto fecundum confuetud' dict. civitat. tunc
tentam prædict' H. C. teftificatur & certificat
eidem Cur. dicti dom. Regis coram præfato P.D.
Milite Alderman' adtunc uno Vicecomit' dict.
civitat. in Computatorio fuo prædicto eodem
Die Mercurii Anno quarto fupradicto fecundum
confuetud. dict. civitatis tunc tent. quod quidem
W. A. adtunc debuit præfato J. T. Executor.
&c. quindecim Libr. in manibus alius Perfonæ &
al' pecun' numerat. ut de denariis qui fuer. ipfius
A. M. Teftator. tempore mortis fuæ propr. tunc
habuit in manibus & cuftod. fuis. Et quia prædictus H. C. adtunc & ibidem petiit ab eadem
Curia, quod prædict. J. T. Executor, &c. per
prædict. quindecim Libr. in pecun' numerat. fic
in manu & cuftod. præfati. W. A. exiften. fecun'
confuetud' Civitat' prædict. attachiaretur ad re-
fponden' præfat' H. C. in placito querel. fuæ
prædict' &c. adtunc & ibidem ad petitionem præfat' H. C. in Computatorio prædicto eodem Die
Mercurii decimo quinto Die Jun. Anno quarto
præd. coram præfato P. D. Milit. Aldermanno
adtunc uno Vicecomitum Civitat. præd. præfato
J. S. uno Servien' ad Clavam dict. P. D. Mil.
Alderman. adtunc unius Vicecomitum dict. Civitat. ac illius Cur' Miniftro quod ipfe fecund'
confuetud' Civitat. pred. attachiaret prædictum
J. T. executorem, &c. per prædict' quindecim
Libr. in manibus & cuftod' præfat' W. A. exiften. & eafdem quindecim Libr. in manibus &
cuftod' ejufdem W. A. fecundum confuetud'

civi-

civitatis prædict. defend' ita quod idem J. T.
Executor, *&c.* esset ad dictam curiam dict. Dom.
Regis coram præfato Petro Delme Mil. Aldermanno adtunc uno Vicecomit. civitat. prædict.
in *Guild-Hall* prædict. dicto Die Jovis decimo
sexto Die Junii Anno quarto prædicto secundum
consuetudinem dict. civitat. tenend. ad respon-
dendum præfat. H. C. in placito querel. suæ prædict. secundum consuetudinem civitat. præd. &
quod idem Johan. Stubbs unus Servientium ad
Clavam dict. P. D. Mil. Alderman. adtunc unius
Vicecomitum dict. civitat. ac illius Cur' minister.
interim superinde faceret eidem cur' dict. Dom.
Regis coram præfato Petro Delme Mil. & Aldermanno adtunc uno Vicecomitum dict. civitat.
in Computatorio suo eodem Die Mercurii decimo quinto Die Junii Anno quarto supradicto
secundum consuetudinem dict' civitat' tenend'
retornaret & certificaret, *&c.* super quo idem
Johan. Stubbs unus Servien. ad Clavam dict.
Petri Delme Milit. & Aldermanni adtunc unius
Vicecomitum dict. civitatis ac illius Curiæ mi-
nistr. postea eodem Die Mercurii decimo quinto
Die Junii Anno quarto prædicto retornavit &
certificavit eidem Curiæ dict. Dom. Regis coram
præfato P. D. Mil. & Aldermanno adtunc uno
Vicecomitum dict. Civitatis in Computatorio
suo prædicto eodem Die Mercurii decimo quinto
Die Junii Anno quarto supradicto secundum
Consuetudinem dict. civitat' tunc tent. quod
ipse virtute præcepti prædict. sibi direct. eodem
Die Mercurii decimo quinto Die Junii Anno
quarto prædict. inter horas octavam & nonam
postme ridiem ejusdem diei Junii, secundum con- *Attachment*
suetudinem dict. civitat. attachiasset prædict. *made for Mo-*
J. T. Executorem, *&c.* per prædictas quindecim *ney in ano-*
libr. in pecuniis numeratis ut denar. prædict A. *ther's hand.*
M. Testatoris propr. in manu præfat' W. A. ex-
isten.

iften. & eafdem quindecim libr. in manu & cuftod' ejufdem W. A. fecundum confuetudinem
ejufdem civitatis defendiffet. Ita quod dictus J.
T. executor, &c. effet ad dictam primam curiam
dict. Domini Regis coram præfato P.D. Milite &
Aldermanno adtunc uno Vicecomitum dict. civitatis in Guild-Hall prædict. dicto Die jovis decimo fexto die Junii Anno quarto fupradict' fecundum confuetudinem civitatis præd. tenend'
ad refpond. præfat. H. C. in placito querelæ fuæ
prædict. fecundum confuetudinem civitatis prædict. &c. prout ei fuerat præcept. & idem Dies
dat. eft tunc & ibidem per eandem curiam præfat. H.C. effen. ibidem, &c. fecundum confuetud.
dict. civitatis, &c. ad quam quidem primam curiam dicti Dom. Regis coram præfato Petro
Delme Milite & Aldermanno adtunc uno Vicecomit. dict. civitatis in Guild-Hall præd. dicto
Die jovis decimo fexto Die Junii Anno quarto
prædicto fecundum confuetudinem dict. civitatis
tunc tent. prædictus H. C. in propria perfona fua
Plaintiff comperuit & pofuit loco fuo R. B. attornatum
makes his fuum verfus præfat. J. T. in placito querelæ fuæ
Attorney. prædict. fecundum confuetudinem civitatis prædict. & per eundem R.B. attornatum fuum optulit fe verfus præfat. J. T. executorem, &c. in
placito querelæ fuæ prædict. fecundum confuetudinem civitatis prædict. & fuperinde adtunc &
ibidem ad illam eandem curiam ad petitionem
præfat. H. C. per R.B. attornatum fuum prædictum eidem curiæ inde fact. dict. J. T. executor, &c. folempniter exact' fuit fecundum confuetudinem dict' civitat' & non comperuit, fed
Firft Default. primam tunc & ibidem fecit defaltam, quæ quidem prima defalta tunc & ibid. per eandem cur.
fecundum confued. dict. civitat. fuper præd. J.T.
recordat. fuit ideo Die ; ulterius dat' eft, tunc &
ibidem per eandem cur. præfat. J.T. execut. &c.
ad

ad effend. ad prox. curiam coram præfato P. D.
Milite & Aldermanno adtunc uno Vicecomit.
dict. civitatis in Guild-Hall prædicto Die Sabbati decimo octavo Die Junii Anno quarto præd.
fecundum confuetudinem dict. civitatis tenend.
ad refpondend. præfat. A. C. in placito querelæ
fuæ prædict. fecundum confuetudinem ejufdem
civitatis, &c. & idem dies dat. eft tunc & ibid.
per eandem curiam tunc ibidem præfato H. C.
effend. ibid. &c. fecund. confuet. ejufdem civitat.
ad quam quidem primam curiam dict. Dom. Regis coram præfato P.D. Milite & Aldermanno adtunc uno Vicecomit. civitat. præd. in Guild-Hall
præd. dict. Die Sabbati decimo octavo Die Junii
Anno quarto prædicto fecundum confuetud. dict.
civitatis, &c. tunc tent. præd. H. C. per prædict.
R. B. attornatum fuum comperuit, & optulit fe
verfus præfatum J. T. executorem, &c. in placito querelæ fuæ prædictæ fecundum confuetudinem civitatis prædictæ & tunc ibidem ad illam
eandem curiam ad petitionem præfati H. C. per
eundem R. B. attornatum fuum eidem curiæ inde factam dictus J. T. executor' &c. folempniter
exactus fuit & non comperuit, fed fecundam tunc
ibidem fecit defaltam; quæ quidem fecunda de- *Second De-*
falta tunc & ibidem per eandem curiam fecun- *fault.*
dum confuetudinem civitatis prædict. fupradictum J. T. recordata fuit, &c. Ideo dies datus
eft tunc & ibidem per eandem curiam præfato
J. T. executori, &c. ufque ad primam curiam
dicti Domini Regis coram præfato P. D. Milite
Aldermanno adtunc uno Vicecomitum dict. civitat. in Guild-Hall prædict. die Jovis vicefimo
tertio die Junii Anno quarto prædicto fecundum
confuetud' dict. civitat. &c. tenend. ad refpondend. præfato H. C. in placito querel. fuæ prædict. fecundum confuetud' civitat. præd. &c. &
idem dies datus eft tunc & ibidem per eandem
curiam

curiam præfat. H. C. ad effend. ibidem, &c. fecundum confuetudinem dict. civitatis, &c. ad
quam quidem primam curiam dicti Domini Regis coram præfato P. D. Milite & Aldermanno
adtunc uno Vicecomitum civitatis prædict. in
Guild-Hall prædict. dicto die Jovis vicefimo
tertio die Junii Anno quarto prædict. fecundum
confuetudinem dict. civitatis, &c. tunc tentam
prædict. H. C. per R. B. Attornatum fuum prædictum fecundum confuetudinem civitatis prædict. comperuit & optulit fe verfus præfatum
J. T. executorem, &c. in placito querelæ fuæ
prædict. fecundum confuetudinem civitatis prædict. &c. & tunc & ibidem ad illam eandem curiam ad petitionem præfati H. C. per eundem
R. B. attornatum fuum eidem curiæ inde factam
fecundum confuetudinem dict. civitatis prædict.
J. T. executor, &c. folempniter exact. fuit &
non comperuit, fed tertiam tunc & ibidem fecit

Third De-
fault.

defaltam; quæ quidem tertia defalta tunc &
ibid. per eandem Curiam fecundum confuetudinem civitatis prædict. fupradictum J. T. recordat' fuit, &c. Ideo dies dat' eft tunc & ibid.
per eandem curiam præfato J. T. executori, &c.
ufque ad primam curiam dicti Domini Regis coram præfato P. Delme Milite & Aldermanno adtunc uno Vicecomitum dict. civitatis in Guild-
Hall prædict. Die Sabbati vicefimo quinto Die
Junii Anno quarto prædicto fecundum confuetudinem dictæ civit' &c. tenend' ad refpondendum præfat. H. C. in placito querelæ fuæ prædict. fecundum confuetudinem civitatis præd' &
idem Dies dat' eft tunc & ibid. per eandem Curiam præfato H. C. effend' ibid. &c. fecundum
confuetudinem dict. civitatis, &c. Ad quam quidem primam curiam dicti Domini Regis coram
præfato P. D. Milite & Aldermanno adtunc uno
Vic. dict. civitatis in Guild-Hall prædict. dicto

Die

Die Sabbati vicesimo quinto Die Junii Anno
quarto prædicto secundum consuetudinem civitatis prædict. &c. tent' prædict. H. C. per R. B.
attornatum suum prædictum secundum consuetudinem civitatis prædict. comperuit & optulit
se versus præfat. J. T. executorem, &c. in placito querelæ suæ prædict. secundum consuetud'
civitat' prædict. Et tunc & ibidem ad illam
eandem curiam ad petitionem ejusdem H. C. per
eundem R. B. Attornat. suum eidem Curiæ factam prædictus J. T. Executor, &c. secundum consuetudinem civitat. prædict. solempniter exact'
fuit & non comperuit, sed quartam adtunc &
ibid' defaltam fecit. Quæ quidem quart. defalt. *Fourth De-*
tunc & ibid' per eandem cur. secund. consuetud. *fault.*
civitat. prædict. supradictum T. J. Executorem,
&c. recordat. fuit, postquam quidem quartam
defaltam sic ut præfertur super dictum J. T. ante
recordatam virtute querelæ prædict. scilicet ad
curiam dict. Dom. nostri Georgii nunc Regis
Magnæ Britanniæ, &c. tunc tent. coram præfato
P. D. Milite & Alderman. adtunc uno Vicecomit.
dict. civitat. in Guild-Hall prædict. Die jovis tricesimo Die Junii Anno quarto præd. secund. consuetud. civitat. prædict. præd. H. C. per R. B.
Attornat. suum præd. secund. consuetud. civitat.
præd. comperuit, & per eundem Attornat. petiit
process. sibi fieri in & super querelam suam præd.
secundum consuetudinem civitat. præd. & ei tunc
& ibidem per eandem curiam conceditur, &c.
Et ad istam eandem curiam dict. Domini Regis
Georgii nunc Mag. Brit. &c. tent. in Guild-
Hall civitat. Lond' coram præfato P. D. Milite
& Aldermanno uno Vicecomitum civitat. præd.
Die Jovis præd. tricesimo Die Junii Anno Regni
dict. Dom. Regis nunc Mag. Brit. &c. quarto
præd. (præd. quatuor Defalt. secundum consuetudinem civitat. præd. sic ut præfertur recordat')
præ-

præcept' fuit per eandem curiam præfato J. S.
uno Servien' ad Clavam dict. Vicecom. ac miniftro Curiæ illius quod ipfe fecundum confuetudinem civitat. præd. præmoneret, & Scire fac.
præfat. W. A. ad effend' ad primam curiam dict.

Scire facias
awarded to
the Party in
whofe hands
the Moneys
are.
Dom. Regis coram præfato Vicecomite in Guild-
Hall præd. Die Sabbati fecundo die Julii Anno
fuprad. tenend' ad oftend. & demonftrand' fi
quid pro fe habeat vel dicere fciat quare præd'
A. C. de præd' quindecim libris in pecun. numeratis ut de denariis dicti teftatoris propriis in
manibus & cuftod' præd' W. A. exiftend' prius
attach', & defens' executionem habere non deberet fi fibi viderit expedire.   Ad quam quidem
primam curiam idem Serviens ad clavam retornavit & eidem Cur. certificavit quod ipfe fecundum confuetud. civit. præd' præmonuiffet & Scire feciffet præfat. W. A. ad effend. ad eandem
primam curiam dict. Domini Regis coram præfato Milite & Aldermanno adtunc uno Vicecomitum dict. civitat. in Guild-Hall præd. dicto
Die Sabbati fecundo Die Julii Anno quarto præd.
fecundum confuetud. dict. civitatis præd' tenend'
& tunc & ibid' ad illam eandem Cur' coram
præfat. P. D. Milite & Aldermanno adtunc uno

Scire facias
returned.
Vic' dict' civit' in Guild-Hall prædict' Die Sabbati fecundo die Julii Anno 1716. prædict' fecundum confuetudinem dict' civitat' tunc tent'
dictus H. C. per R. B. attornatum fuum præd.
fecundum confuetud. civit. præd. comperuit &
tunc & ibid' ad ejus petit' per eundem Attornat.
fuum eid' curiæ factam præd' W. A. præmon' in
Attach. folemniter exact. fuit, & tunc & ibid. in
propria perfona comperuit & pofuit loco fuo J.B.
Attornat. fuum verfus præfatum H. C. in placito querelæ fuæ præd. fecundum confuetud. civit.
præd' & Attach' præd' &c. Et tunc & ibid. idem
W. A. per eundem Attornat. fuum petit licentiam
                                                        inter-

interloquendi ufque ad primam curiam dicti
Dom. Regis coram præfat. P. D. Milite & Aldermanno adtunc uno Vicecom. dict. civitat. in
Guild-hall præd. Die Jovis feptimo die Julii Anno
quarto præd. fecundum confuetudinem civitatis
præd. tenend. idem dies dat' eft tunc & ibid. per
eandem curiam partibus præd. ad effend' ibid.
&c. fecundum confuetudinem dict. civitatis. Ad
quam quidem primam curiam dicti Domini Regis
coram præfat. P. D. Milite & Aldermanno adtunc
uno Vicecomitum dict. civitatis in *Guild-hall*
præd. præd. Die Jovis feptimo Die Julii Anno
quarto præd. fecundum confuetud. civitatis
præd. tunc tentam præd. H. C. per R. B. Attornatum fuum comperuit & optulit fe verfus præfat. W. A. præmon. in Attachiamento
præd. in placito querel. præd. & attach. præd.
fecundum confuetud. Civitatis præd. *&c.* &
tunc & ibid. præd. W. A. præmon. in attach.
præd. per J. B. attornat. fuum præd. comperuit,
& in propria perfona fua venit, & cognovit fe
habere in manibus fuis feptem libras & duos folidos cogn. ut denar. dicti teftatoris ideo ad
tunc & ibid. ad illam eandem curiam ad petitionem præfati H. C. per Attornat. fuum præd.
eidem Curiæ inde factam fecundum confuetudinem dict. civitatis confiderat. fuit per eandem
curiam quod præd. H. C. haberet executionem
de præd. fept. libris & duobus folidis per pleg.
fi modo præd. J. T. Exec. per conf. civit. præd.
veniret & inveniret fufficientem fecuritatem five
manucaptor' ad placitandum cum præfat. H. C.
in placito querelæ fuæ præd. vel debitum præd.
difprobaret & difrationaret infra unum annum
& unum diem fecundum confuetud. civit. præd.
&c. Super quo poftea, fcil. ad curiam dicti Dom.
Regis coram præfat. P. D. Milite & Aldermanno
adtunc uno Vicecomitum dict. civitatis in Com-

putatorio

putatorio fuo prædict. Die Sabbati nono Die
Julii Anno quarto præd. fecundum confuetud.
dict. civitat. &c. tunc tent. venit præd. H. C. in
propr. perfon. fua & adtunc & ibid. invenit fufficientes manucaptor. & manucapt. eft per S. B.
de Burchin-Lane Salefman & H. C. de Finch-
Lane Tallowchandler, Cives civitatis præd. ad
reddend. & reftituend. præd. feptem libras &
duos folidos in pecuniis numeratis præfat. J. T.
executor. &c. fi modo ipfe J. T. infra unum annum & unum diem prox. fequend. veniret & inveniret fufficientes manucaptores, vel corpus
prifonæ dicti Dom. Regis redderet parat. ad pli-
tand. cum præfat. H. C. in placito querel. fuæ
præd. fecundum confuetud. dict. civit. & debitum præd. difprobaret & dirationaret aut fe à
debito præd. in querela præd. mentionat. fecundum confuetud. civitat. præd. exoneraret fuper
quo poftea fcil. vicefimo octavo Die Septembris
Anno quarto præd. in *Guildhall* præd. fecundum
confuetud. civitat præd. dictus P. D. Miles &
Alderman. adtunc unus Vicecomitum dict. civit.
fecundum confuetudinem dict. civitatis legitime
amotus fuit, & tunc & ibid. fcil. eod. vicefimo
octavo Die Septembris Anno quarto fupradicto
in *Guild-hall* præd. fecundum confuetud. civitatis
præd. J. B. Aldermannus legitime electus Præ-
fectus admiffus & juratus fuit in officio unius
Vicecom. dict. civitatis in loco præd. P. D. Milit.
Alderman. nuper unius Vicecomit. ejufdem civitatis fecundum confuetud. dict. civitat. pro uno
Anno integro tunc profequend' fecundum confuetud. ejufdem civitatis. Super quo poftea, fcil.ad
Curiam dicti Dom. Regis coram præfat. J. B. Aldermanno modo uno Vicecomitum dict. civitatis
in computatorio fuo fcituat. in parochia prædict.
fcil. Die Veneris vicefimo feptimo Die Januarii
Anno quarto præd. fecundum confuetud. civitat.
præd.

Main-pernors found by the Plaintiff.

The Sheriff removed.

præd. tunc tent. dictus H. C. in propria persona
sua venit in eandem Curiam tunc & ibid tent. &
cognovit se habuisse executionem de præd. septem
libris & duobus solidis in pecuniis numeratis, ut
de denariis præfat. A. in vita sua testatoris propriis in manibus & custod. præfat. W. A. prius
in manibus suis attach' & defens' & de eisdem
septem libris & duobus solidis se fore plene *Satisfaction*
satisfact. & contentat. *&c.* prout per Record. *acknowledg'd*
inde in eadem Curia remanen. plenius liquet &
apparet, *&c.* cum hoc quod idem W. A. verificare vult quod prædictus J. T. in narratione
præd. qui modo quer. sit nominat. & præd. J. T.
in querela & attach. præd. nominat. est una &
eadem persona & non alia neque diversa quodq;
præd. A. in narratione præd. nominat. & præd.
A. M. in querela præd. nominat. est una & eadem
persona & non alia neque diversa quodq; præd.
W. A. in querela & attachiam. præd. nominat. & *Averments*
præd. W. A. qui modo sit Defendens, est una &
eadem persona & non alia neque diversa, quodq;
præd. Summa septem librarum & duorum solidorum superius primo mentionat. parcel' præd.
quindecim librarum in præd. prima promissione
in narratione præd. superius mentionat. & præd.
Summa septem librarum & duorum solidorum
in manibus & custodia ipsius W. A. sic ut præfertur attachiat. & defens. denar. præd. A. M. defunct. est una & eadem Summa & non alia neque
diversa, & quod Executio & Judicium præd. adtunc & adhuc in suis robore & effect. propr.
manet, & præd. debitum in præd. querela speci-
ficat. per eundem J. T. minime distractionatum &
disprobatum existit : Quæ omnia idem W. A. paratus est verificare prout Curia hic, *&c.* unde
petit Judicium si præd. J. actionem suam præd.
inde versus eum habere seu manutenere debeat,
&c.

Farther concerning the Lord Mayor's Court.

Juries return-
ed to try Causes
in the Lord
Mayor's Court.
IT is the Custom of *London*, that every Month there shall be a new Jury to try Causes in this Court and the Sheriffs, and they shall be returned by the several Wards in the City of *London* at their Wardmote-Inquests every *Christmas*; which they constantly do, by an Indenture under their Hands and Seals : in which Indenture they also return the Names of the Common-Council-Men, Constables, and Scavengers. And the particular Wards appointed to serve as Jury-Men for every Month, are divided as followeth :

The Jury-Men returned by

The Wards of *Aldgate*, *Portsoken*, and *Cornhill*, serve for the Month of *January*.

The Ward of *Cheap* for *February*.

The Wards of *Bassishaw*, *Cripplegate within*, and *Cripplegate without*, for *March*.

The Wards of *Vintry*, and *Breadstreet*, for *April*.

The Wards of *Tower*, and *Billingsgate*, for *May*.

The Ward of *Farrindon without* for *June*.

The Ward of *Bridge* for *July*.

The Wards of *Aldersgate*, *Colemanstreet*, and *Broadstreet*, for *August*.

The Wards of *Farrindon within*, and *Castle-baynard*, for *September*.

The Wards of *Queen-hith*, *Dowgate*, and *Walbrooke*, for *October*.

The Wards of *Langhorn*, and *Limestreet*, for *November*.

The

The Wards of *Candlewick, Cordweyner, Bi-ſhopſgate,* for *December.*

When the Names are return'd by the ſeveral Wards, the Town-Clerk writes them into a Book, and gives the Officers of this Court a Copy thereof; and alſo gives a Copy to the Officers of the *Sheriffs Court,* the ſame *Jury* ſerving for both *Courts.*

And the Perſons ſo returned, and no others, muſt ſerve as *Jury-Men* both in this *Court* and the *Sheriffs Court* ; except in ſome ſpecial Caſes, where the *Court,* upon motion, ſhall order a *Jury* of *Merchants,* and in ſuch Caſe the Town-Clerk returns their Names.

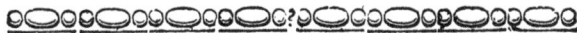

Jury of Merchants.

Of the Lord Mayor's Court of Chancery.

THIS Court is alſo a Court of Equity or Chancery, for any Matters within *London* and the Liberties thereof, and is held before the Lord Mayor and Aldermen ; but the Recorder for the time being, uſually ſits as Judge or Chancellor to determine ſuch Matters : Yet the Lord Mayor and Aldermen may ſit there, if they pleaſe, and determine the Matters depending, as they have formerly done in ſpecial Caſes.

The Manner of exhibiting a Bill in this *Court* is thus : Firſt, it muſt be drawn and ſigned by one of the four City Counſel, whoſe ancient Fee for peruſing and ſigning thereof is 6 *s.* 8 *d.* then it muſt be ingroſſed and entered in Court, and one of the Officers belonging to this Court muſt give the *Defendant* a Summons perſonally within the Liberties of *London* to anſwer ſuch

Summons.

Bill,

Bill, otherwife he is not obliged to appear. The Charge of drawing the Bill is 4 *d.* for every Sheet, and 6 *d.* a Sheet for engroffing thereof, and for the entering it in Court 2 *s.* and for the Attorney's Fees 3 *s.* 4 *d.*

If upon Action depending.　　If an Action at Law fhall be depending in the Mayor's Court, and the Party Defendant cannot be relieved but in Equity ; in fuch Cafe he may exhibit his Bill againft the Plaintiff in the Action, and the entering or fileing the Bill in this Court, is a good Injunction to ftay the *Plaintiff's* Proceedings at Law, without any Motion, until the *Plaintiff* fhall give in a full Anfwer thereto : The Charge whereof will not be near fo much as an Order for an Injunction in the High Court of Chancery.

No Summons.　　And note, That when the Bill is to be relieved againft an Action at Law, the Plaintiff in the Bill fhall not be compell'd to give the Plaintiff at Law any Summons to make anfwer to the Bill ; but if Affidavit fhall be made, *That the Plaintiff at Law was* 100 *Miles from* London *at the time of the exhibiting the Bill,* then upon motion to the *Court,* the *Plaintiff at Law* fhall, and may proceed to Tryal notwithftanding the *Bill ;* but Judgment and Execution muft ftay till the *Plaintiff at Law* anfwer the Bill, or the *Court* fhall make an Order to the contrary.

Action removed out of the Sheriffs Court.　　If an Action at Law fhall be commenced in the Sheriffs Court, the *Defendant* muft caufe the *Action* to be removed into the *Mayor's Court,* before he can ftay the *Plaintiff's* Proceedings at Law, by exhibiting a Bill in this *Court* ; and if the *Plaintiff* at Law anfwer the *Bill,* the *Plaintiff* in Equity may, in eight Days after the *Anfwer* fworn, *Anfwer.*　　put in Exceptions to the *Anfwer* : And after the *Anfwer* filed, if the *Plaintiff* does not give in Exceptions in eight Days, the *Court,* upon

mo-

motion, will order the Bill to be difmift, unlefs
the *Plaintiff* replies in a Week's time; for
which Order the Fee is *6 d.* and if the Bill is
difmift, the Fee for drawing up the Difmiffion
is *6 s. 8 d.* which will be allowed the *Defendant*
in the Cofts. And the next Court-Day after
the Exceptions filed, the *Plaintiff* in Equity muft *Exceptions.*
move for a Day to argue thofe Exceptions, other-
wife they will be over-ruled of courfe; but if
the *Anfwer* fhall be full, and the *Plaintiff* in *Anfwer.*
Equity cannot prove the Matters in his *Bill* fug-
gefted, the *Plaintiff* at Law fhall recover all his
Cofts againft the *Plaintiff* in Equity.

Note; *That where a Bill is exhibited, and no Action* Bill without
at Law depending, the Defendant hath eight Court Action de-
Days given him to anfwer the Bill after his Ap- pending.
pearance, (which ufually happens in ten Days
time;) and if he does not anfwer the Bill in that
time, the Plaintiff in Equity may have an At-
tachment againft him, for which the Fee is 2 s.
6 d. befides the King's Duty, and the Officer's
Fee for ferving thereof is alfo 2 s. 6 d. *which*
Fees the Defendant muft pay when he gives in his
Anfwer.

After Anfwer, the *Plaintiff* may reply generally or fpecially, and may examine Witneffes (in
like manner as is done in the High Court of
Chancery) to prove the Equity of his *Bill*; and *Replication*
within a Month after Replication filed, may *and Examina-*
bring his Caufe to a Hearing. The Town- *tion of Wit-*
Clerk or his Deputy is appointed to examine all *neffes.*
Witneffes on both fides; and his Fee for fwearing and examining every Witnefs is 2 *s.* 4. *d.* and
for the Copies of the *Depofitions* 4 *d.* per Sheet;
but for the Copies, *è contra,* his Fee is 8 *d.* per
Sheet.

If a *Plaintiff* here in Equity fhall be advifed not to examine any Witneffes, he may go to hearing upon the *Bill* and *Anfwer* within fourteen Days after *Anfwer*; and in fuch Cafe, 'tis faid, the whole Charge will not exceed four or five Pounds.

Publication for bearing.

The Town-Clerk's Fees for every Order for publication or hearing of any Caufe, is but 6 *d.* and for an Order at hearing but 1 *s.* But if the Decree be drawn up and inrolled, his Fee is 10 *d. per* Sheet, and for the Copy 4 *d. per* Sheet.

Decree.

After a Decree made, the *Plaintiff* muft ferve the *Defendant* perfonally with a Copy thereof, and make Affidavit of fuch Service before an *Attachment* will be granted againft the *Defendant*

Service of Decree.

for non-performance of the Decree. The *Plaintiff* may ferve the *Defendant* with a Copy of the Decree in any Place whatfoever, although out of the Liberties of *London.*

Bill removed.

A *Bill* may be removed out of this Court into the High Court of *Chancery*, any time before Publication is paffed, after which time the High Court of *Chancery* will not retain the Caufe.

The manner of removing the Bill *into the High Court of* Chancery.

The manner of removing a Bill out of this Court is thus : Firft, The *Defendant* muft file a Bill in the High Court of *Chancery* againft the *Plaintiff* in this *Court*, and then muft at the Regifter's Office give Bond to prove the Suggeftions in his Bill within fourteen Days, and procure Certificate that his Bill is filed, and Security given as aforefaid, and then petition the Lord Chancellor for a *Certiorari* to remove the Bill out of this *Court:* And when the Petition is anfwer'd by his Lordfhip, the Clerk in *Chancery* will make the *Certiorari*, which muft be delivered to the Town-Clerk, and he will allow it, for which his Fee is 2 *s.* and then the Attorney for the *Defendant* in this *Court* will certify the
Bill,

Bill, Anfwer, and Proceedings into the High Court of *Chancery*, for which his Fee is 10 *d.* *per* Sheet.

If the *Defendant* in Equity demur or plead to the *Plaintiff*'s Bill, he muft the next Court after the Demurrer or Plea is entered, move for an Order to argue fuch Demurrer or Plea; other- *Plea or De-* wife the fame will be over-ruled in courfe, and *murrer.* the *Defendant* will be compelled to anfwer, &c.

When a Freeman's Apprentice is legally dif- charged from his Mafter (either by fuing out his Indentures, for want of being inroll'd, &c. or otherwife) his proper way to recover part of *Equity for* the Money which his Mafter received with him *Money to be* as Apprentice, is to exhibit a Bill in this Court *returned to an* againft his Mafter; and if a Decree be, That *Apprentice.* the Mafter fhall return part of the Money, the Apprentice will recover his Cofts, which ufu- ally come to 6 *l.* or more: but if the Appren- tice hath ferved five Years, or near that time, this Court will not relieve him, in ordering any Money to be returned, unlefs there be very ex- traordinary caufe.

Any Perfon may exhibit a Bill in this Court; *By whom* but if fuch Perfon dwell out of the Liberties *Suits may be.* of *London*, this Court, upon a motion, will or- der the *Plaintiff* to give Security by Bond to *Security given* pay the *Defendant*'s Cofts, in cafe the Bill fhall *by an Out-* happen to be difmift, or in default thereof, will *dweller.* difmifs the Bill; and until fuch Security be given, the Court will not compel the *Defendant* to give an Anfwer to the Bill: And the Reafon for fuch Practice, is to prevent vexatious Suits, and becaufe no Attachment for Cofts can be ferved out of the Liberties of *London*.

When a Freeman of *London* dies, leaving Chil- *Freeman's* dren, their readieft and cheapeft way is to ex- *Children.* hibit a Bill in this Court, to have a Difcovery of their Father's Eftate, and for recovering their Part thereof due to them by the Cuftom of *London*.

Freemans Widows may recover cufto-mary Parts.

A Freeman's Widow by a Bill in this Court, may recover her cuftomary Part of her Huf-band's Eftate, againft the Executor of her Huf-band ; but if the Executor live out of the Li-berties of *London*, fhe will be compelled to ex-hibit her Bill in the High Court of *Chancery*.

Suits for Lands in Middlefex *prohibited.*

The Company of Horners in *London* fued in this Court by *Englifh* Bill, concerning a Houfe in *Pettycoat-Lane*, which is in *Middlefex*, ground-ing their Bill upon a Truft, and a Prohibition was awarded ; for tho the Truft was perfonal, yet the Suit arifeth upon the Lands, which are out of their Jurifdiction, as thofe in *Chefter* fhall not meddle with Trufts of Lands here, tho' the Perfons inhabit there, nor *è converfo*.

Depofitions in perpetuam Rei Memori-*am.*

Note ; *By the Cuftom of* London, *the Lord Mayor, Recorder, and Aldermen that are Juftices of Peace, do ufually take Depofitions of Witneffes* in perpetuam Rei Memoriam, *which they pre-ferve upon Record in their Court at* Guild-hall, *and thefe may be given in Evidence to a Jury,* &c. See *Cro. El.* 168, 169.

The Beginning of a Bill in this Court is thus :

To the Right Honourable Sir A. B. *Knight, Lord Mayor of the City of* London, *and to his Right Worſhipful Brethren, the Aldermen of the ſame City.*

" IN all Humility complaining, ſheweth un-
" to your Lordſhip and Worſhips, your
" daily Orator, *C. D. &c.* Or humbly com-
" plaining, ſheweth, *&c.*"

The Concluſion thus :

" May it therefore pleaſe your Lordſhip and
" Worſhips, out of your accuſtomed Goodneſs,
" to cauſe the ſaid *E. F.* to be warned by one
" of your Lordſhip's and Worſhips Serjeants at
" Mace, and Miniſters of this Honourable
" Court, perſonally to be and appear in the
" ſame Court at a Day certain, to be by your
" Lordſhip and Worſhips to him thereunto
" prefixed ; then and there to make anſwer un-
" to all and ſingular the Premiſſes upon his cor-
" poral Oath : And that he may be enjoined to
" ſtand unto, perform, and abide ſuch Order
" and Decree in the Premiſſes, as to your Lord-
" ſhip and Worſhips, upon hearing the Cauſe,
" ſhall ſeem meet."

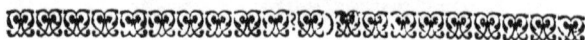

Of the C*o*urt *of* Guild-Hall, *and* Juftice-Hall, *as to* Indi*ct*ments.

IN an A&ctit;ion on the Cafe for falfe Indi&ctit;ment, the Plaintiff faith, one *T.* caufed him to be indi&ctit;ed *Sept.* 12th, at the *Guild-Hall* in *London,* for Perjury, upon the *Stat.* of 5 *El.* and to be arraigned at *Juftice-Hall* in the *Old-Baily Sept.* 18th, and that he was acquitted upon the fame Indi&ctit;ment refident at *Guild-Hall.*

Exc. 1. *He does not fay, he was indi&ctit;ed at the Quarter Seffions as the Statute expreffeth, and the Juftices in* London *hold Seffions every Month.*

R. *It's otherwife here, inafmuch as it is a Special Authority at a certain time.*

In *London* they hold their Seffions of the Peace at *Guild-Hall,* and for Goal-Delivery at the *Juftice-Hall* the next Day after; and their Entries are feveral. In *London* they are Juftices of the Peace by Charter, and not by Commiffion, as in other places, which Cuftom is not to be broken.

The Indi&ctit;ment was at *Guild-Hall,* and the Party is fuppofed to be arraigned at *Juftice-Hall,* and the Ufage is fo, and it is not but an Adjournment from *Guild-Hall* to *Juftice-Hall* to that purpofe; and it is the fame Clerk that removes the Indi&ctit;ment. And when *B. R.* fends for the Indi&ctit;ment, they write to the *Guild-Hall* for

a

a Thing done in *London* ; and to the Clerk of the *Crown* in *Middlesex* for a Thing done in *Middlesex* : And it's reason that Felonies done in *Middlesex*, should be try'd in *London*, according to the Custom and Usage which must not be changed : For *Justice-Hall* is within *London*, and not in *Middlesex*. *Palmer* 45. *Taylor*'s Case.

THE

THE

SHERIFFS COURTS
in *LONDON*.

EACH *Sheriff* holds a Court of Record in *Guild-Hall,* viz. Every *Wednesday* and *Friday,* for *Actions* entered at the *Woodstreet-Compter* ; and every *Thursday* and *Saturday,* for *Actions* entered at the *Poultry-Compter.*

Attorneys.   There are eight Attorneys belonging to these Courts, who of right ought to have three Fees in every Cause that is or shall be brought to Tryal ; viz. A Fee for the Appearance, a Fee at Issue, and a Fee upon Summons for Trial : But if the Cause shall be summoned more than once, he is to have a Fee upon every Summons.

Fees.

Note ; That an *Attorney*'s Fee in this Court is 1 *s.* 8 *d.* and no more.

The *Attorneys* of these Courts are admitted by the Court of Aldermen, and thereupon must take an *Oath.*

Prothonotaries.   There are two Prothonotaries, two Secondaries, two Clerks of the Papers, and eight Clerk-sitters belonging to these Courts.

Secondaries.   The Secondaries allow and return all Writs brought to remove Causes out of these Courts.

The

The Clerks of the Papers file and copy all Clerks of the Papers. *Declarations* upon *Actions* in thefe *Courts.*

The Prothonotaries do draw and ingrofs all fuch *Declarations.*

The Clerk-fitters enter *Actions* and *Attachments,* Clerk-fitters. and take *Bails* and *Verdicts.*

The *Attorneys* have not the Cuftody of any *Record* belonging to thefe Courts; their bufinefs is only to take their Fees due to them in every Caufe, and to give their Clients notice of *Declarations* and *Trials,* and to advife them when and what to plead.

All *Subpœna's* for Witneffes to appear in thefe Courts, are made by the Clerks belonging to the Judges of thefe Courts.

The Fees for a Trial in thefe Courts are faid to be as follows.

	s.	d.
The Action	0	4
The Arreft	1	0
The Attorney's Fee	1	8
The Declaration, if General	1	4
The Court Fees hereon	0	8
The *Deletur*	0	4
The Iffuing and Attorney's Fee	4	0
The Summons of the Jury and Attorney's Fee	4	8
The *Subpœna*	2	0
The Counfel well deferve	5	0
The Juries Verdict	4	6
The Judgment	2	6
The Execution	1	4
If the Declaration be Special, the Prothonotaries Fee for every Sheet drawing and ingroffing is	0	8

The

The Defendant's Fees for a Trial.

	s.	*d.*
The Attorney's Fee for Appearance, and the Court Fees ——— ——— ——	2	6
The Copy of the Declaration 4 *d. per* Sheet.		
The Iffue and Attorney's Fee —— —— —	3	8
Attorney's Fee upon the Summons —— —	1	8

See more of the Fees in thefe Courts hereafter.

Judgment ftayed.　　After a Verdict obtained in either of thefe Courts, and before Judgment entred, the Defendant may ftop Judgment, by marking the Caufe before the Lord-Mayor, for time to pay the Money recovered; which he may do by fpeaking to an Attorney in the *Mayor's-Court*, and giving him 4 *s.* 10 *d.* for that purpofe.

Marked Caufes.　　My Lord-Mayor fits only upon *Saturday* to hear mark'd Caufes; and if upon hearing both Parties, it fhall appear to his Lordfhip that the Plaintiff obtained a Verdict for more than his juft Debt, his Lordfhip may remit the Caufe to Judgment for the juft Debt only, and give fuch time to pay the fame as he fhall think reafonable: But his Lordfhip always orders the Defendant to give good Security to pay the Recovery at fuch times as his Lordfhip directs, and to pay the Cofts in fourteen Days.

The Attorneys in the Mayor's Court always move for time, although the Verdict was in the Sheriffs Court, and his Fee for moving is 1 *s.* 8 *d.*

The Plaintiff muft pay for his Lordfhip's Order, and entering it, 2 *s.* 10 *d.*

Which

Which Charges will be allowed to the Plaintiff upon taxing of Cofts.

In thefe Courts may be tried Actions of Debt, *Actions in Cafe*, Trefpafs, Accompt and Covenants bro-*the Sheriffs* ken ; as alfo Attachments and Sequeftrations, *Court.* as before is obferved.

If either Party fhall have a Witnefs that can-*Witneſſes examined.* not ftay in *London* till the day of Trial, his Teftimony may be taken in Writing ; which will be allowed as good Evidence.

The Method for examining fuch Witnefs is thus : Firft, His Name and Place of Abode muft be delivered in Writing to the adverfe *Attorney ;* and then he muft be examined and fworn by the eldeft *Attorney* in the *Lord-Mayor's Court,* whofe Fee for the Examination and Copy is 3 *s.* 4 *d.*

After the Examination, the adverfe *Attorney* may have a Copy thereof, for which he muft pay 2 *s.*

The two eldeft Clerks in thefe Courts for the Time being, are *Attorneys* of the *Pye-powder Pye-powder Court* held during the firft three Days of *Bartho-Court.* *lomew*-Fair, for the examining and trying all Suits brought for petty Matters and Offences there committed, contrary to the Proclamation *infra.*

Which Proclamation the Lord-Mayor and Aldermen do annually caufe to be made for the better regulating the faid Fair, *viz.*

✿✿✿✿✿✿✿✿✿✿✿✿✿✿✿✿✿✿✿✿✿✿✿

The Tenor of the Proclamation *made on* Bartholomew-Eve *in the Afternoon, at the great Gate going into the* Cloth-Fair, Smithfield.

" THE Right Honourable Sir *A. B.* Knight,
" Lord-Mayor of the City of *London,* and
" his Right Worſhipful Brethren the Aldermen
" of the ſaid City, ſtreightly Charge and Com-
" mand, on the Behalf of our Sovereign Lord
" the King, That all manner of Perſons of
" whatſoever Eſtate, Degree, or Condition they
" be, having recourſe to this Fair, keep the
" Peace of our ſaid Sovereign Lord the King.
    " That no manner of Perſons make any
" Congregation, Conventicles, or Affrays, by
" the which the ſame Peace may be broken or
" diſturbed, upon pain of Impriſonment, and
" Fine, to be made after the Diſcretion of the
" Lord-Mayor and Aldermen.
    " Alſo that all manner of Sellers of Wine,
" Ale, or Beer, ſell by Meaſures enſealed, as
" by Gallon, Pottle, Quart, and Pint, upon
" Pain that will fall thereof.
    " And that no Perſon ſell any Bread, except
" it keep the Aſſize, and that it be good and
" wholeſome for Man's Body, upon Pain that
" will fall thereof.
    " And that no manner of Cook, Pye-baker,
" nor Huckſter, ſell, nor put to ſale, any man-
" ner of Victual, except it be good and whole-
" ſome for Man's Body, upon Pain that will
" fall thereof.

" And

" And that no manner of Perſon buy nor
" ſell, but with true Weights and Meaſures,
" ſealed according to the *Statute* in that behalf
" made, upon Pain that will fall thereof.

" And that no manner of Perſon or Perſons
" take upon him or them within this Fair, to
" make any manner of Arreſt, Attachment,
" Summons, or Execution; except it be done
" by the Officers of this City thereunto aſſign-
" ed, upon Pain that will fall thereof.

" And that no Perſon or Perſons whatſoever,
" within the Limits and Bounds of this Fair,
" preſume to break the Lord's-Day in ſelling,
" ſhewing, or offering to ſale, or in buying, or
" offering to buy, any Commodities whatſoever,
" or in ſitting, tipling, or drinking in any Ta-
" vern, Inn, Ale-houſe, Tipling-houſe, or
" Cook's-houſe, or in doing any other Thing
" that may tend to the Breach thereof, upon
" the Pain and Penalties contained in ſeveral
" *Acts of Parliament*, which will be ſeverely in-
" flicted upon the Breakers thereof. And fi-
" nally, That what Perſons ſoever find them-
" ſelves aggriev'd, injur'd, or wrong'd by any
" manner of Perſon in this Fair, that they come
" with their Plaints before the Stewards in this
" Fair aſſigned to hear and determine Pleas,
" and they will miniſter to all Parties Juſtice
" according to the Laws of this Land, and
" the Cuſtoms of this City.

Con-

Concerning Arrefts, Procefs, Tryal, Judgment, and Execution in London.

Efcape.

AGainft the general Words in an *Act of Parliament*, 2 *Inft.* 20. a Goaler in *London* may permit his Prifoner that is in Execution to go at large with a Battoon in any Place within their Jurifdiction, and it is no Efcape, the Cuftom being fo : *Quo Warranto*, p. 30.

Attachment.

By the Cuftom of *London* after one has arrefted the Goods of his Debtor in his Poffeffion, and without Claim for a Year, they fhall be taken for the Creditors Duty, 35 *H.* VI. 25.

Arrefts without Procefs.

Arreft fans Procefs.

IT is a Cuftom in *London* to arreft a Man without *Procefs* ; or it is a Cuftom there for any Serjeant to arreft after a Plaint entred in any of the Courts of the *Compters*, without other Procefs ; *Co.* 68. *a.* 3 *Cro. Salmon* and *Percival. vide Poft.* 311.

One in Execution in London, *removed by Habeas Corpus in B. R. in Execution there for that Debt; and having difcharged Charges in B. R. remanded.*

Arrefting for better Security, *vide ante.*

One was condemn'd in the *Sheriffs Court* in *London* for Debt, and taken in Execution, and after by an *Habeas Corpus* the Execution with other Caufes were returned ; whereupon he was committed to the *Marfhal* in Execution for that Debt, and other his Executions in *B. R.* and now all the Executions in the *King's-Bench* were difcharged ; and the Judgment in *London* reverfed.

reverfed by a *Writ of Error* in the *Huflings*: The *Queflion* was, *How he fhould be difcharged of this Execution?* For the *King's-Bench* has no Record of the Execution, but by the Return of the *Habeas Corpus*; and of the Reverfal of the Judgment they have no Record, but only what is furmifed. Therefore the Court remitted him to *London* for that Caufe, and there he was difcharged. *Cro. Car.* 128. *Cufack*'s Cafe.

Other Cuftoms of London as to Officers, Courts, Procefs, and Prifons, &c.

NOTE, That both the *Sheriffs* of *London* Both Sheriffs, are in Law but one *Sheriff*, and the one but one Officer. is not of *London*, and the other of *Middlefex*, as is vulgarly fuppofed; *Hob.* p. 70. *Lamb* and *Wifeman.*

And the *Sheriff* of *London* is known·in Law to be two Perfons; therefore if one *Sheriff* of *London* make his Return without his Fellow, this cannot be holpen by *Jeofail*, it being as no Return at all; fo is a Return without the Sheriffs Name fubfcribed: And *London* had no Sheriffs in the 13th of *Ed.* I. 1 *Leon.* 284.

In *London* the Mayor and Commonalty have the Office of Sheriff of *London* and *Middlefex* by Charter, and two Sheriffs are yearly chofen; 3 Rep. *Weftby*'s Cafe.

In the Exchequer *the Cafe was fuch :*

A Man was arraigned and condemned of Fe- *A Felon in* lony, and was imprifon'd in *Newgate*, at the Newgate, Goal Delivery for *Middlefex*; and after a Writ *for a Felony in* Middle-

X 2 of

sex, if
Execution
for Debt a-
gainst him be
delivered to
the Sheriff of
London, it's
ill.

of Execution for Debt issues against him out of the *Exchequer* upon a Recovery there against the Party (the Felon) directed to the Sheriffs of *London,* who serve the Execution upon the Body of the Prisoner in *Newgate,* and after the Felon was pardoned of the Felony, it was now a a *Question,* Whether the Execution were lawful ? and if it were, Then whether the *Pardon* had not discharged it ?

Execution for
Debt against
one condemned
for Felony.

1. *By all the Barons, the Execution served by the Sheriffs* of London, *by force of a Capias directed to the Sheriff of* London, *was not lawful; because the Party was in Prison in the Goal of* Middlesex: *and although* Newgate *was within* London, *yet it is a Prison indifferent for both Counties, and the Prisoner was in the Prison for* Middlesex, *and not for* London; *and the Process ought to have been directed to the Sheriff of* Middlesex.

Attainder
does not ex-
tinct the
Debts as to
other Sub-
jects.

Escape.

2. *The Sheriff may chuse to serve the Execution or not, upon the Body of the Felon for Debt; for that inasmuch as the King, by the Judgment of the Felony, hath Interest in his Person, this Interest is sufficient Privilege against the Action, or Execution of any Subject; yet if the Sheriff will serve the Execution of the Debt, then the Prisoner shall be said to be in Execution for the Debt, and yet subject to the Judgment of the Felony for the King: and if the Felon escape, the Sheriff shall answer to the King, and the Party also : And if the King pardon the Felony, and the Sheriff suffers him to go at large, it's an Escape.*

Newgate a
Prison for both
London and
Middlesex.

Note, *That upon a* Capias ad satisfaciendum *to the Sheriff of* Middlesex, *to take* J. S. *if the Sheriff take him and put him in* Newgate, *which is the Common Prison for* London *and* Middlesex, *and after another* Writ of Execution *comes to the Sheriff*

riff of London ; *although the Sheriffs of* London *are also Sheriffs of* Middlesex, *and* Newgate (*where the Prisoner is*) *is the Prison for both Counties, yet the Prisoner shall not be said to be in Execution upon this new Writ in* London, *nor may the Sheriff of* London *serve it upon him, because he is in another County.*

For when the Commitment is to Newgate *by force of a Writ to the Sheriff of* Middlesex, *he may not be said, in any respect, to be committed in the County of* London; *for the Counties continue several, and the Prison several, in respect of the several Commitments : For there are two several Sides, and a Partition between them.* 1 Rol. Abr. 894. Coas's *Case,* Trin. 16 Jac. B. R.

Commitment for Middlesex, *is not a Commitment for* London, *tho' the Sheriff of* London *and* Middlesex *are one.*

By the Custom of *London* the *Writ of Execution* is directed to the Sheriffs of *London,* and not to the Coroner (who is the Mayor.) 2 *Rol. Abr.* 806.

The Return of the Outlawry out of *London* in *C. B.* is generally made without saying, *Per judicium Coronatorum.*

Custom to remove Pleas and Records out of the Sheriffs Court into the Lord Mayor's.

THE *Custom* is, When a Man is impleaded before the Sheriffs, the *Mayor,* upon Suggestion of the *Defendant,* may send for the Parties, and for the Record, and examine the Parties upon their *Pleas*; and if it be found upon his Examination that the Party *Plaintiff* is satisfied, then he may award that the *Plaintiff* shall be barred. And this is called, *The Court of Conscience*; 4 *Inst. c.* 50. 8 Rep. *City of* London's Case.

Court of Conscience.

X 3   The

The *Plaintiff* in Affault and Battery in his *Replication* faith, *The City of* London *is an ancient City, and hath held Pleas time out of mind,* &c. and *that there was a Plaint in such a Court before* F. M. *by virtue of which Process the Plaintiff was taken.* He fhould have alledged a *Custom* to hold a *Court* before the *Sheriffs*, and that *F. M.* was then *Sheriff :* It is faid, *Coram* F. M. *uno Vicecom.* which is well enough, there being two *Courts,* tho' but one *Sheriff* ; 1 *Keb.* 5 64. *Osborn* and *Parker.*

How to lay the Custom of the Sheriffs Court.

* * *

As to the Difference of Entries in the Mayor's Court and Sheriffs Court.

Computation of Time.

A Clerk of the *Mayor's Court* faid, *That the Figures* 264 (*in their Entries*) *fignify the* 26*th Day of the* 4*th Month,* 26 *the Day, and* 4 *the Month* ; accounting *November* (in which the Mayor is chofen) the firft, and fo the fourth Month is *February.*

But in the *Sheriffs Court* they begin to count their Months in *October.*

And accordingly it was adjudg'd, That *Ashfield* the 26th Day of *February* commenced a *Plaint,* &c. 2 *Rol.* Rep. 380. *Ashfield's* Cafe.

If an Erroneous Judgment be given in any of the *Sheriffs Courts* of the City of *London,* the *Writ of Error* to reverfe this Judgment muft be brought in the *Court* of the *Huftings* before the Lord Mayor ; for that is the *Superior Court.* Pract. Reg. 124. 4 *Inft.* 247.

Writ of Error to be brought in the Huftings.

Direction of Writs.

QUodlibet breve quod tangit liberum tenementum dirigitur Majori & Vicecomitibus, & alia brevia tantum Vicecomitibus.

Of

Of *Proceedings in the Sheriffs Court*.

THE two Sheriffs of *London* do each of *Sheriffs Courts* them keep a Court of Record, where *when kept.* they hold Plea of all perſonal Actions; and the two *Priſons* (called the *Compters*) belong to them.

And they have two Court Days in every Week apiece: For the *Woodſtreet-Compter*, on *Wedneſ-days* and *Fridays*; for the *Poultry-Compter*, on *Thurſdays* and *Saturdays*.

In a *Plaint* of Debt levied before any of the *Sheriffs*, the Cuſtom is, *That the ſaid Sheriffs Ore 'Tenus ſend to the Serjeants of the* Compter, *either to ſummon or attach the Defendant without* Warrant; *and upon* Nihil *returned within the City, Of entring that then the Serjeants, and every of them, by the Actions in Commandment of the Sheriff, have uſed to attach and Compters. arreſt the Defendant, to have his Body at the next Court before the Sheriff at the* Guild-Hall, &c.

In this manner they enter their Records: But the uſual Practice is, to enter an Action in the Office for that purpoſe, at one of the *Comp-ters*; which Action muſt be entered with care: For it is the Original in that Court by which you muſt declare, and from whence there muſt be no variance.

And when an Action is entered, then any one *Arreſts and* of the Serjeants may arreſt the *Defendant*, and *Bail.* bring him into cuſtody until he find Bail to anſwer the Condemnation; which Bail is to be taken by one of the Clerk-ſitters.

X 4 The

Arresting by Serjeants.

The *Defendant* may be arrested by the Custom of *London*, after Entry of the *Plaint* in the *Porters-Book*, before the Entry of it in Court before the *Sheriff*: And after *Plaint* entred, the *Serjeant* may arrest without *Precept*.

Serjeant shewing his Mace.

The Serjeant need not shew his Mace, because he is sworn and known, altho' not to the Party; and a known Bailiff need not shew his Warrant, altho' demanded.

But in *6 Rep.* 52. Countess of *Rutland's* Case, a general Arrest by a Serjeant, by shewing the Mace, and touching his Body with it, and saying, *Sir, I arrest you*, is insufficient; for he ought to shew at whose Suit, out of what Court, for what, and of what Return, &c. that the Party may know, &c.

Escape.

In Escape, the *Defendant* pleads the Custom of *London*; That the Mayor and Sheriffs of *London* have used to enlarge Prisoners that were arrested, in coming and returning from their Courts, having Causes there depending; and sets forth a Plaint in *London* against the Defendant, and that he was arrested, and appeared, and pleaded

Whether the Court can discharge one arrested, who is coming and returning to the Court.

to Issue; and as he was coming to Court, to defend that Action, he was arrested, as is supposed in the Declaration. And *per Cur.* the Court cannot discharge one arrested, except he be arrested in the Face of the Court; 1 *Brownl.* 15. *Wilson* and *the* Sheriffs *of* London.

THE

THE
COURT
OF
ORPHANS.

THE Cuſtom of Orphanage is one of the moſt conſiderable Cuſtoms of *London*, as it reſpects the Children of Freemen who die poſſeſs'd of great perſonal Eſtates; and I ſhall therefore treat,

Firſt, *Of the Cuſtom; and then of the Court.*

By the Cuſtom of *London*, a Freeman's Widow may require a third Part of his Perſonal Eſtate, after Debts and Funeral paid and diſcharged; and his Children may require another third Part thereof; and he may, by Will, give away another third Part of his Eſtate: and if he have no Children, the Widow may require a Moiety of his perſonal Eſtate. But if a Freeman die without a Will, Adminiſtration ſhall be granted to his Wife; and ſhe will claim one third Part by the Cuſtom, and one third Part muſt be divided amongſt the Children, and the other

The Cuſtom of Deviſes in London.

other between the Wife and Children ; and ufually the Woman is allowed two Thirds of the faid third Part.

Cuftom of the Orphanage Court.

It has been refolved, That there hath been a Court of Orphans time out of mind in *London* ; and that there hath been a Cuftom, *If any Freeman, or Freewoman die, leaving Orphans within age unmarried, that the faid Court have had the cuftody of their Body and Goods :* And that the *Executors* and *Adminiftrators* have ufed, and ought to exhibit true Inventories before them ; and if any Debt appear due, to become bound to the Chamberlain to the ufe of the Orphans in a reafonable Sum to make a true Account upon Oath of them, after they have been received : and if they refufe, to commit them till they will become bound ; and this was adjudged to be a reafonable Cuftom.

. *Upon the Return of a* Habeas Corpus, *the Cafe was :*

If Executor or Adminiftrator refufe to give Security for Orphans Portion, Imprifonment lies ; and tho' Security have been given at Common Law, or in the Prerogative Court, yet the Court of Orphans will compel to give them new Security.

One *Jane* (Widow) (Freewoman, and Fifh-monger of *London*) died, leaving divers Orphans, and one *Latch* was *Adminiftrator*, and had exhibited an Inventory of 1000 *l.* Debts unreceived, and was required by this Court to give Bond of 2000 *l.* which he refufed, *per quod, &c.* and this Cuftom in fuch Cafe was adjudged good and reafonable ; and if the Ecclefiaftical Court will compel them to make account there againft this Cuftom, a Prohibition lies. Though it was alledged for the Prifoner in that Cafe, *That he was already bound in the Prerogative Court to make account, and fo he fhould be twice bound ;* Hob. 474. Latch's Cafe.

To

To this purpose is the Case of *Hill*, 13 *Car*. 1. *B. R. Calthrop* 46.

The Custom is, *If any Freeman deviseth Lands or other Legacies of Goods unto an Orphan, that then the Mayor and Aldermen have used to take the Profits of the Land, and to have the disposition of the Legacies, until the Legatees shall attain the Age of 21 Years; or if a Woman, till she be married: And if the disposition of the Profits of the Land, or of the personal Legacies were declared by the Testator in his Will, that then the Mayor and Aldermen have used time out of mind of Man, to convent the Persons trusted by the Will of the Testator before them, and to compel them to find Sureties for the performance of the Legacies; and if they refuse to find Sureties, then it is lawful to imprison them until they do.*

In the Case of *Wilkinson, vers. Boulton, Pasc.* 17. *Cuſtody of Or-* *Car.* 2. *B. R.* 1 *Lev,* 162. 1 *Sid.* 250. *& Raym.* *phans till 21,* 116. it seems agreed, That, by the Cuſtom of *&c.* *London,* the Lord Mayor and Aldermen have the Cuſtody of Male-Orphans till 21, and of Females till 21, or married, and to commit them to the care, *&c.* of Guardians: And if any *Poſt* 317. Perſons take them from ſuch Guardians, *&c.* to bring them in at the next Court, and impriſon them. And alſo, That Peers are not privileged againſt ſuch Cuſtom.

So in the Cafe of the King againſt *Harwood, Marriage Hill.* 23. 24 *Car.* 2. *B. R.* 2 *Lev.* 32. 1 *Mod.* 79. *ſans Aſſent,* 1 *Vent.* 180. it seems agreed, That the Court *Fine and Im-* of Aldermen are, by the Cuſtom of *London, priſonment.* Guardians of all City-Orphans; and if any marry an Orphan under 21, without their Aſſent, they may punish him by Fine and Impriſonment; and this, altho ſhe were married out of the City: For the Orphan is in their cuſtody in all Places within the Kingdom; and every

one

one ought to take Notice (Care) what Perſon he marries.

The Widow of a Freeman of *London* dwelling in *Middleſex*, bequeathed a Legacy of 1000 *l.* to her Daughter, after all Debts and Legacies paid, and upon condition, That *ſhe ſhould not marry without the Conſent of the Executor*; and makes a Freeman her Executor, and dies. The Executor is convented before the Court of the Mayor and Aldermen, and required to put in Sureties to the Chamberlain of *London*, according to the Cuſtom, for the payment of the 1000 *l.* according to the Time limited by the Will, and according to the Will aforeſaid. The Executor denies to find Sureties, whereupon he was committed to Priſon; and an *Habeas Corpus* being awarded out of the *King's Bench*, to have the Body of the Executor, with the Cauſe, all this Matter appeared upon the Return.

And the Court, *Firſt*, reſolved, *That it was a good Cuſtom.*

The Wife of a Freeman is within the Cuſtom.
Secondly, *That the Wife of a Freeman is within this Cuſtom; and the Wife of a Freeman having the liberty and privilege to trade in the City, and ſo able to take benefit by it, ſhe ſhall be bound by the Cuſtoms of it.*

And, Thirdly, *Though ſhe were dwelling out of* London, *at the time of the Will made, ſhe is a Freewoman within the compaſs of the Cuſtom.*

And it was one *Andrew's* Caſe; P. 17 *Jac.* *B. R.* A Freewoman before ſhe contracted Marriage with *J. S.* agrees with him, That ſhe ſhall have power to deviſe a Sum of 200 *l.* to any Perſon; and after her Marriage ſhe, by her Will, gives this to the Children of her firſt Huſband, and dies. The Husband after acknow-
ledgeth

ledgeth a Judgment at Common Law, for the
Security of it; yet by the Cuſtom of the Orphans of *London*, he may be compelled by the
Court of Orphans to give new Security for
this to the Chamberlain of *London*.

Note: *The Security muſt take particular care that* Orphans not
none of the Orphans marry, or be put out Appren- to marry
tices, without leave of the Court of Aldermen ob- without
tained for that purpoſe. leave.

The Court of Aldermen do commit the Cuſtody of Orphans to ſuch Perſon or Perſons as
they ſhall think fit; and if any Perſon do inter- *Marriage*
marry with any Orphan, without the conſent of *without con-*
the ſame Court firſt obtained, ſuch Perſon may be *ſent is finabl:*
fined by them according to the Quality and *and Impriſon-*
Portion of the Orphan; and unleſs ſuch Perſon *ment till paid*
do pay the Fine, or give Security to pay it, the
Court may commit him to *Newgate*, to remain
there till he ſubmit to their Orders. And this
hath been adjudged in the Court of *King's Bench*,
in *Wilkinſon's* Caſe againſt Sir *William Bolton*,
Paſch. 17 *Car.* 2. viz.

An Action of Treſpaſs was brought for Battery and falſe Impriſonment: The Defendant
juſtifies, by the *Cuſtom* of *London* of the *Court* of
Orphans, That a Freeman died and left his Daugh-
ter under 18 *Years of Age;* for ſuch is the Age of *Ante* 315.
a Female and unmarried: *and that the Court com-*
mitted the cuſtody of her to Sir William Bolton; *and*
ſets forth the Cuſtom, That if any ſuch Ward be
taken away, &c. they may commit the Party to Newgate *who does it, to be impriſoned till he produce the*
Infant, or be delivered by due Courſe of Law: And
becauſe the Plaintiff took her away, he was
committed.

The

The Plaintiff *demurs upon the Plea;*

Firſt, *Becauſe the Cuſtom is unreaſonable, for that no time is allowed to the Party to make his Defence.*

Secondly, *Becauſe the Cuſtom is laid generally, to impriſon all ; and ſo a Peer may be impriſoned.*

But, *per Cur.* it's a general Contempt and Offence, and the Cuſtom is reaſonable, but there ſeemed to be a Fault in the *Plea ;* for the Bar was, *That the* Infant *was of ſuch an Age, and unmarried at the time of the Death of the Anceſtor, but does not actually ſay, She was unmarried at the time of the taking :* but it was over-ruled, for that a Bar ſhall be good to *Common Intent.* Vide the Caſes reported in *Raymond,* p. 116. *Hob.* 474.

Bar good to Common Intent.

Note, *The Cuſtom* of London *is ſaid to be, That* if the Father advance any of his Children with any part of his Goods, that that ſhall bar them to demand any further Part, unleſs the Father under his Hand, or by his laſt Will did expreſs and declare, That *it was but in part of Advancement ;* and then that Child ſo partly advanced ſhall put his Part in *Hotchpot* with the Executors and Widow, and have a full third Part of the whole, accounting that which was given to him as a part thereof : *And this is that which the Civilians call* Collatio Bonorum. *Some expound this Cuſtom thus ; As if a Man has two Children, and gives to one of them an* 100 l. *in part of his Advancement, and then dies worth* 900 l. *in this caſe the Wife, the Iſſue not advanced, and the Executors ſhall have but three equal Parts of the* 900 l. *(viz.)* 300 l. *apiece ; and then the Hundred Pounds ſo given ſhall be put in Hotchpot between the Children : which* Sir Edward Coke *conceived cannot be, becauſe*

Hotchpot.

becaufe then there fhould be no Equality among the Iffues, as the Cuftom requireth. 12 Rep. 113.

But in a Book, entitled, *The Privileges of the* Printed 1708. *Lord Mayor and Aldermen of the City,* written by a Perfon very knowing and converfant in the Cuftoms thereof, the faid Cuftom is thus fet down :——' If a Freeman fhall in his Life-time
' give part of his Perfonal Eftate in Marriage
' or otherwife to any of his Children, and fhall
' afterwards make a Will and die, and by fuch
' Will give away all his Perfonal Eftate to his
' other Children ; and it fhall afterwards ap-
' pear by any Writing under the Teftator's
' Hand, or by any thing writ by him, tho it be
' in an Almanack or elfewhere, what Sum he
' gave fuch Child as a Marriage-Portion or
' otherwife; he cannot by any Declaration in
' his Will or other Writing, (importing that he
' *had fully advanced* fuch Child) preclude the fame
' Child from coming in and claiming an equal
' Share with the other Children, of the Perfonal
' Eftate that belong'd to fuch Freeman at the
' time of his Death : Provided fuch Child bring
' the Money fo given him *in full Advancement,* &c.
' into *Hotchpot.* As for inftance,
' If a Freeman has three Children, and to
' one of 'em on his Marriage, *&c.* gives 100 *l.*
' as a Portion *in full Advancement,* &c. and at his
' Death his perfonal Eftate amounts to 350 *l.*
' in this cafe the Child fo married may bring in
' the 100 *l.* fo by him receiv'd, which will make
' the whole to be 450 *l.* which being divided
' into three parts, is 150 *l.* to each Child;
' which Sum the Child fo advanced fhall re-
' ceive, fo as to have an equal Share with the
' two other Children.'

Note,

Note, *It was resolved in* Chancery *in* Beckford's *Case, as to the Hotchpot.*

The unadvan-
ced Children,
by the Custom
of London, *to*
bring in what
they had re-
ceived into
Hotchpot,
with the Or-
phanage
Thirds, after
the Estate is
divided into
Thirds, and
not with the
whole Estate.
R. B. Freeman of *London* had several Children, and by his Will in Writing, after Debts and Funeral paid, appointed one full Third Part of his personal Estate to the Plaintiff *Fr. B.* his Relict, according to the *Custom* of the City of *London*; and declared that *Fr.* and *Eliz.* two of his Daughters had been *fully advanced* in his Lifetime; and that *Mary* and *Jane*, two other Daughters, had not been fully advanced, and directed, *They should bring in their Portions they had received into the third Part of his Personal Estate, belonging unto his unpreferred Children.* The Widow and Relict is Plaintiff in *Chancery*, and the Question between her and the unpreferred Children was,

How the said Estate should be divided by the Custom of London ?

The Plaintiff insisted, *That the Children not fully advanced ought to bring what they had receiv'd into the whole Estate, and that then she ought to have one full Third Part of the whole Personal Estate :* But the Court declared the Custom to be, *That the Testator's two Children,* Mary *and* Jane, *who were not fully advanced, were to bring in what they had received into Hotchpot with the Orphanage Thirds, after the Estate is divided into Thirds, and not with the whole Estate.* 2 Rep. *Ch.* 359. *Beckford's* Case.

What shall be
a good Decla-
ration to let
in the Child to
have a custo-
mary part.
And it was resolved in *Hammond* and *Honnywood's* Case, 32 *Car.* 2. in *Ch.* That by the Custom of *London*, a Declaration made by a Freeman in Writing, tho such Writing was made for his last Will, and revoked, is such a Declaration as will let in the Child to have a customary Part of the Personal Estate.

See

See before, of the Custom of Freemens Wills, and distributing Intestates Estates.

The Portion of an Orphan is of such a nature, that if the Husband of the Orphan die without altering the Property, his Widow, and not his Executors shall have it; which was *Anne Pheasant's* Case, and is reported in 2 *Ventr.* 240. *A. B.* an Orphan of *London* married to *W. Pheasant* before he was 20 Years of Age; he not having taken out the Money dies, but bequeaths this Money to his Wife, provided she should not claim Dower: She brought Dower against *B. P.* Brother of *W. B.* her late Husband; he brings a Bill in *Chancery* against her, to make discovery of the Estate, and to compel her to release Dower, or renounce the Devise: The *Question* was;

If the Money in the Court of Orphans were devisable, or not ?

By *Bridgman Keeper, Twisden,* and *Wild,* this Portion is a Thing in Action, and so not devisable. The Custom of Orphans under Age is, *That they find them Money,* (viz.) *for maintenance, and no more:* Yet when the Orphan comes to Age, or the Female Orphan marry, it is cast up, and the Interest fully paid. Now in this Case it was the Lachess of the Husband, that he did not recover it, for by the Custom it is to be paid at the Marriage, or full Age of the Female Orphan: And the Custom is, upon the Marriage of Orphans, to appoint the *Common Serjeant* to treat and take Security for the Orphans.

But he that marries an Orphan without Licence, must make a Jointure before he receives the Portion. As for Instance,

If the Husband alter not the Property of the Orphan's Portion, and dies, his Widow shall have it.

And the Orphan's Money in the hands of the Chamberlain not devisable by the Husband.

He that marries an Orphan must make a Jointure before he receive the Portion.

Y   The

The Cafe was, a Citizen of *London* dies, and leaves a Daughter; the Portion of the Orphan, according to the Cuftom, is put into the Chamber of *London*, or fecured by the Chamber of *London*: the Orphan marries without Leave or Licence of the *Court of Orphans*. The Husband and Wife bring a *Subpœna* againft the Chamberlain of *London* and the Recognizors for the Portion, and if in the Chamberlain's Hands, then to have the Principal, and account of the Product, or Intereft: Albeit the Husband had a good Eftate which merited the Fortune of the Orphan, yet forafmuch as he had not Licence of the *Court of Orphans*, to marry their *Orphan*; and befides, had not fettled a Jointure upon the Orphan at the Marriage; it was decreed, *That the Husband ſhould firſt make a Jointure for her, before he ſhould receive his Wife's Portion forth of the Chamber of* London. *See hereafter.*

What ſhall be ſaid Part of the Perſonal Eſtate.

Mortgage of an Inheritance.

The Mortgage of an Inheritance to a Citizen of *London*, hath been held to be part of his Perfonal Eftate, and to be divided according to the *Cuſtom: Caſes* in *Ch.* Part 1ſt. 285.

Legacy.

A Citizen of *London* being refiduary Legatee died; the *Queſtion* was, *Whether this being but a Legacy, which till Election veſted,* primâ facie, *in the Legatee, not as Legatee, but as Executor,* (for he was Executor) *and the firſt Teſtator's Eſtate which remains in the Executor, as Executor, ſhall not be ſubject to the Cuſtom, as the Executor's own Eſtate?* In *Civile* and *Rich's* Cafe, the Lord Chancellor decreed the contrary, and faid, I will make Election for him: *Idem.* 310.

A Freeman of *London* purchafeth a Leafe for Years, of fome Houfes in *London* for 700 *l.* and
after-

fterwards for 100 *l.* more buys in the Inheri-
ance, and takes the Conveyance in another's
Name in truſt for him and his Heirs, and dies;
the Queſtion was, *Whether this Leaſe be within
the Cuſtom of* London *to be deviſed as a Chattel?*
For it was agreed by all, that a Leaſe for Years *Leaſes for*
aſſigned over to attend the Inheritance, is not *Years aſſigned*
within it; and the Chancellor's Opinion was, *over to attend
the Inheri-*
That neither can this Leaſe, for 'tis knit to the Inhe- *tance.*
ritance.

If a Father is a Freeman of *London,* he cannot
deviſe the Diſpoſition of the Body of the Infant; *The Body of*
and if he do, yet the Infant ſhall remain in the *an Orphan not
deviſable.*
Cuſtody of the Mayor and Aldermen: And as
well in the *Stat.* of 4 and 5 of *Phil.* and *Mary,* c. 8.
concerning the taking of Infants Female out of
the Poſſeſſion of the Guardian, as in the *Stat.* of
12 *Car.* 2. which impowers Fathers to diſpoſe
of the Cuſtody of their Children, there are Proviſo's, to ſave the Cuſtom of *London; Sid.* 363.
Baſtian's Caſe.

This Cuſtom, to have the cuſtody of the Per- *The Cuſtom to*
ſon and of all the real Eſtate and perſonal, ex- *have the Cuſtody of the*
tends to Lands out of *London.* *Lands, extends
to Lands*
But it has been a Queſtion, *If a Freeman* *out of* Lon-
diſcontinue from the City and his Trade, and dies *don.*
leaving his Children and Eſtate in the Country, whe-
*ther the Court of Orphans ſhall intermeddle with
them?*

And *Hide,* Chief Juſtice, was of Opinion,
They ſhall not intermeddle.

As to the Court of Orphans, *obſerve;*

By an *Act of Parliament, Rot. Pat.* 1 *R.* 2.
N. 130. It was enacted, *That the Mayor and
Chamberlain of* London, *for the time being, ſhall
have the keeping of all the Lands and Goods of ſuch*

Orphans as happen within the City, saving to the King, and other Lords, the Rights of such as hold of them out of the same Liberty.

But notwithstanding the said Stat. it is a Customary Court time out of memory.

Court of Orphans, before whom held. The Court of Orphans is held before the Lord *Mayor* and *Aldermen* of the City of *London,* who are Guardians to Children of all Freemen of *London,* that are or shall be under the Age of 21 Years, at the time of their Father's deceaſe. The common Serjeant of the City is the only Perſon intruſted by the Court of Aldermen, to take all Inventories and Accounts of Freemens Eſtates.

The youngeſt *Attorney* in the Lord Mayor's Court is always Clerk of the *Orphans,* and is appointed to take all Securities for *Orphans* Portions; which Securities are conſtantly taken in the Name of the Chamberlain of *London,* for *Chamberlain a Body Corporate for what purpoſe.* the time being : and to this purpoſe the Chamberlain is a ſole Corporation to him and his Succeſſors for *Orphans*; and in 4 *Rep. Fullwood's* Caſe, a Recognizance or Bond made to him and his Succeſſors, concerning *Orphans,* ſhall, by the Cuſtom of *London,* go to his Succeſſor ; and it is not like the Caſe of a Biſhop, Parſon, Vicar, Maſter of an Hoſpital, *&c.* or ſuch ſole Corporation, for there, no Chattel, either in Action or Poſſeſſion ſhall go in ſucceſſion, becauſe they cannot take Recognizances or Bonds in their politick Capacity, neither have they ſuch a Cuſtom, but the Executors or Adminiſtrators ſhall have them.

In *Spencer's* Caſe, the *Return* was ; If any *Freeman* deviſe any Legacy to an *Orphan,* that the Executor ſhall be conſtrained to find ſufficient Sureties to pay the Legacy according to Law ;

and

and fhews, That a Woman gives a Legacy to
fuch *Orphan*, and returns the Will; by which
it appears fhe was a Widow Inhabitant in *Middlefex*, but Free of *London*, and fhe made *Spencer*
Executor, and devifeth the Legacy to the *Orphan*: and the Legacy was conditional, That
the *Orphan* ought to marry with the Confent of *Imprifonment,*
the Executor; and becaufe he refufed to find &c.
Sureties, he was committed. *Vide antea & poftea.*

It was alledged, The Cuftom was againft
Law; for perhaps he fhall not have Affets beyond Debts to pay it, when the Time of Payment fhall come. *Per Cur.* They ought to have
regard to the Affets, and the Condition. If
they prefs an Obligation upon him that ftands
not with the Rules of Law, we will aid him. Yet
a *Procedendo* was granted.　1 *Rol.* Rep. 316.

Note, *The Committee of an Orphan by the Mayor* Age, Non-
and Aldermen, declaring upon the Cuftom of the age.
City of London, *fhall have the Writ of Ravifh-
ment of Ward, and Age, and Non-age fhall be
limited by them*; Hob. 95. F. N. B. 142.

One affumes, That in confideration that the *Child's Por-*
Plaintiff will marry his Daughter, that he will *tion.*
give to him, at the Time of his Death, a Child's
Portion; If a Citizen of *London* make fuch a Promife, it is good by the Cuftom of *London*, and
the Divifion between the Wife and the Children is certain enough; 2 *Rolle's* Rep. 104.

Note, That when a Freeman of *London* dies,
leaving Children under Age, the Clerks of
the refpective Parifhes within the Bills of
Mortality, ought to give the Name of fuch
Freeman to the Common Cryer of this City,
who is thereupon to fummon the Widow, or

Inventory.

Executor of such Freeman, to appear before the Court of Aldermen, there to be bound to bring in an Inventory of the Teftator's Eftate.

And *Note*, That the Court of Aldermen always allow two Months time for the bringing in and exhibiting fuch Inventories.

If the Party fummoned do not appear, the Lord Mayor may, if he pleafe, fend his Warrant, and force an Appearance : And if any Executor refufe to become bound to bring in an Inventory, the Court of Aldermen may, by *Imprifonment.* their Power, fend fuch Executor to *Newgate*, there to remain till he fubmit ; and the Courts at *Weftminfter* will not releafe fuch Perfon.

After a Bond given, the Executor muft procure four Freemen to appraife the *Teftator's* Goods, and muft caufe them to appear before a *Appraife-* Juftice of the Peace in *London*, and fwear to *ment,* &c. make a juft, true and valuable Appraifement.

The *Common Cryer* muft have Notice when the Appraifement is to be made ; for he is appointed, by the *Court of Aldermen*, to be prefent when all fuch Appraifements are taken, that he may fee the fame be fairly done to the beft Advantage of the *Orphans :* And unlefs the *Common Cryer*, or his *Deputy*, be prefent, and the *Inventory* fhall be figned by the *Common Cryer*, the *Court of Aldmen* will not allow thereof.

The Common Cryer's Fees for figning every Inventory is 10 s. *and for his Attendance, during the Time of the Appraifement, at leaft* 10 s. *per Day.*

When the Appraifement is made, as aforefaid, and figned by the *Common Cryer* and the *Appraifors*, it muft be given to Mr. *Common Serjeant*, or one of his Clerks at his Office in *Guild-Hall-Yard ;*

Yard; and if he approves thereof, he will caufe *Appraifeme^nt* it to be ingroffed, and a Duplicate thereof to be *ingroffed,* &c. made for the Executor, or Adminiftrator: And when the fame is examined by him, and his Hand is fet thereto in Teftimony thereof, the Executor, or Adminiftrator, muft, in the *Court of Aldermen,* fwear the fame Inventory is a true Inventory of the Goods and Chattels of the Party deceafed, according to the beft of his Knowledge.

When the Inventory is fo exhibited, the Executor muft become bound in a confiderable Penalty, either to bring in the Money that fhall appear due to the Orphans, by fuch Inventory, within two Months, or within that time to give good Security to pay the fame into the Chamber of *London,* for the Ufe of the Orphans, when they fhall come to Age, or be married.

But fee hereafter, p. 333. *the late Act, concerning the bringing the Money into the Chamber of* London, *whereby the Cuftom is now altered in this particular.*

When Executors paid the Money into the Chamber of *London,* the Court of Aldermen ufually allow'd 5 *l. per Cent.* Intereft for fuch of the *Teftator's* Eftate as was due to the Orphans by the Cuftom of *London,* fo as the fame exceed not 500 *l.* and for Legacy Money 3 *l.* 6 *s.* 8 *d. per Cent.*

If the Executor fhall not pay the Money into the Chamber, he muft become bound with three Sureties to the Chamberlain of *London* for the Time being, in one or more Recognizances, or elfe by Bond, to pay the Money due to Orphans; and in cafe the Security live within the Liberties of *London,* they muft be bound by Bond.

Y 4   Note,

Note, *That if the Sum be* 900 l. *the Security
must become bound by three Recognizances, each
for the Payment of* 300 l. *the Custom being never
to make any Recognizance touching Orphans of
greater Penalty than* 400 l. *and not for the Payment of above* 300 l.

Note, *The Lord Mayor and Court of Aldermen do
meet at* Guildhall, *and sit in the Orphans Court
there once in every Year, viz. on the* Monday
Morning after Midlent-Sunday, *purposely to hear
the Names of all the Securities that stand bound for
Orphans Portions called over, and therefore that
Day is termed* Call-day ; *upon which Day one
of every of the Sureties ought to appear, to give an
account whether the other Securities are living,
and in good Condition. and whether the Orphans
are living and married.*

If none of the Security appear upon that Day,
they forfeit their Recognizances and Bonds, and
the Clerk of the Orphans in such case must
make out Process against the Security, and force
them to give the Account above required, and
pay the Charges of the Process.

The Security must take particular care that
none of the *Orphans* marry, or be put Apprentice with their Consents, without the Leave of
the Court of Aldermen first obtained for that
Purpose. And as the Orphans come to be of
the Age of one and twenty Years, or shall be
married with the Consent of the Court of Aldermen, they must take care to bring them to
Guildhall, with a Person to prove the Age of
such Orphan ; and then the *Orphan* must acknowledge Satisfaction for the Money due to
him, or her, of the Testator's Estate, which
must be done in the Court of Aldermen ; but
one

one of Mr. Common Serjeant's Clerks muſt
firſt draw up a Note to this, or the like Effect.

" A B. Pariſh Clerk and Regiſter of St. *Mi-*
" A . *chael Baſiſhaw,* London, is come to
" prove unto this Honourable Court, upon his
" Corporal *Oath,* That *C. D.* one of the Sons
" and late *Orphans* of *H. D.* late Citizen and
" Draper of *London,* deceaſed, is of the full Age
" of 21 Years. And the ſaid *C. D.* the Son, is
" come to acknowledge Satisfaction to this Ho-
" nourable Court for 590 *l.* growing due unto
" him for his own Part and Portion of the
" Goods, Chattels, Rights and Credits of the
" ſaid *H. D.* his late Father deceaſed, by the
" Laws and Cuſtoms of the City of *London.*

And Note, *That if a Freeman leaves Lands and*
Tenements to his Children, the Executor muſt be-
come bound with Sureties to account for the Rents
and Profits of ſuch Lands.

Note alſo, *That upon acknowledging Satisfaction, as*
aforeſaid, the Fees to be paid are not to exceed
13 s. 4 d. *for every Thouſand Pound.*

Alſo when any *Orphan* is of full Age,
and ſhall acknowledge Satisfaction in the
Court of Aldermen for all Moneys due to him,
or her, the ſame Court, upon Motion made by
Mr. *Common Serjeant,* doth conſtantly order, That
all Bonds entered into for the Payment of ſuch
Orphans Portion ſhall be delivered up and cancelled; and if the Security became bound by
Recognizances, the Clerk of the *Orphans* will
croſs and diſcharge ſuch Recognizances, for
which his Fee is 2 *s.* upon each Recognizance.
The Widow of every Freeman, if ſhe ſhall
be Executrix or Adminiſtratrix of her Huſband's

band's Eftate, ought, by the Cuftom of *London*, to exhibit a true Inventory of her Husband's Eftate into this Court before fhe contract Marriage; otherwife the *Court of Aldermen* may impofe a reafonable Fine upon fuch Executrix, or Adminiftratrix, to the Ufe of the *Orphans* of fuch Freeman.

Fine.

To prevent Abufes that fometimes happen to Freemens Eftates in Prejudice of *Orphans*, by Executrixes and Adminiftratrixes not giving an Inventory in due time after the *Teftator*'s Deceafe, the *Court of Aldermen* have made an Order, Not to allow any finding Money or Intereft, for any Money that fhall be paid into the Chamber of *London* by any *Executor* or *Adminiftrator* belonging to any Freeman's *Eftate*, until fuch time as the *Executor* or *Adminiftrator* of fuch Freeman do bring in, and exhibit upon *Oath*, a true and perfect Inventory to his Knowledge of all the Goods, Chattels, Plate, Jewels, ready Money, and Debts, which did belong to fuch Freeman at the Time of his Death.

Therefore it is the Intereft and Advantage of all Executors and Adminiftrators of Freemen to exhibit Inventories of the Eftates of fuch Freeman within the Time limited and appointed by the Court of Aldermen for the doing thereof, efpecially fuch as fhall leave no greater Eftate than to pay their Debts : For if upon the bringing any Inventory into the Court of Aldermen, it fhall appear to the Court, that the Teftator did not leave more Eftate than to pay his juft Debts, in fuch cafe the Court will difcharge fuch Executor, or Adminiftrator, of the Recognizance he gave for exhibiting an Inventory without paying any Fee to any Officer whatfoever : Provided fuch Executor, or Adminiftrator, bring in fuch Inventory, when he fhall have

have Notice from Mr. Common Cryer fo to
do.

Note, *The Court of Aldermen do commit the Cuftody
of Orphans to fuch Perfon or Perfons as they fhall
think fit ; and if any Perfon whatfoever do inter-
marry with any Orphan without the Confent of the
fame Court firft obtained, fuch Perfon may be fined* Fine, &c.
*by the faid Court, according to the Quality and
Portion of the Orphan ; and unlefs fuch Perfon do
pay the Fine, or give Bond to pay the fame in fome
reafonable Time, the Court of Aldermen may commit him to* Newgate, *there to remain until he* Imprifonment.
*fubmit to their Order : And although fuch Perfon
fhall have ten times a better Eftate than the Orphan he intermarries with, yet he muft fubmit to pay
fuch Fine as the Court fhall impofe upon him : But
if he fettle an Eftate upon the Orphan as the Court
fhall direct, and make Application to the fame
Court by Petition to have the Fine remitted, they
will in probability fhew Favour to fuch Perfon, as
they have done in the like Cafes.*

This Cuftom, it's faid, hath been adjudged
reafonable, and was argued in the Court of
King's-Bench, in the Cafe of a Merchant that
had a good Eftate, who intermarried with an
Orphan without the Confent of the Court of
Aldermen : The Orphan had but 200 *l.* or
thereabouts in the Chamber of *London*, but her
Portion was 800 *l.* and upon hearing the Matter
in the *Court of Aldermen*, the *Merchant* did feem
to juftify himfelf, becaufe he had the Confent
of the *Orphans* Relations, thereupon the Court
order'd him to pay 40 *l.* as a Fine, which he
refufed, and was committed to *Newgate :* And
after fome confiderable Time he brought a *Habeas Corpus*, which was allowed, and the Caufe
of

of his Imprifonment returned; and upon per-
ufal of the Return, and after long Debate,
had by Counfel on both fides, the *Court of
King's-Bench* remanded the Gentleman back to
Prifon, and directed him to fubmit to the *Court
of Aldermen*; which he did by paying the Fine,
and was thereupon difcharged. But upon his
humble Suit to the Court, a great Part of his
Fine was returned.

When an Inventory is exhibited in this *Court*,
and the Orphans can prove any Goods omitted,
or undervalued, or any Debts charged to be
owing from the Deceafed, which were not real
and juft Debts; in fuch cafe the Clerk, upon
Complaint made, will fummon a Jury to enquire
whether the Inventory fo exhibited, be a true
and perfect Inventory, or not. And if the Jury
find any Omiffions, Undervaluations, or Sur-
charges, then the fame Clerk will fue the Executor upon the Bond he gave for exhibiting an
Inventory, and will thereby compel him to
make good to the Eftate fo much as fhall be
found by the Jury to be omitted, undervalued,
or furcharged; unlefs he can by Proof difcharge
himfelf thereof before the Court of Aldermen,
who, upon Application made by an Executor,
will examine into the Accounts of fuch Executor, and do right to all Parties, without any
Expence to the Executor, or to the Orphans.

When it fhall appear by an Inventory, that
many Debts are ftanding out due to the Deceafed, the *Court* of *Aldermen* do conftantly compel
the Executor to give Bond to render a true Account from time to time, when he fhall be thereunto required.

And it is ufual, once in twelve Months, to
fummon the Executor to give an account; and
if upon the exhibiting thereof, it fhall appear
that

that any Money is due to the Orphans, the Executor muſt either pay the ſame Moneys into the Chamber of *London,* or give good Security to pay the ſame; which if he omit or refuſe, his Bond will be put in ſuit againſt him.

The Method of giving an Account is after this manner.

THE Executor muſt write an Account of *Executors* his Receipts and Payments ſince the In-*Accounts,* ventory exhibited, and give it to Mr. Common Serjeant, who will examine it, and cauſe it to be ingroſſed, and ſet his Hand thereunto, and to a Duplicate thereof for the Executor ; and then the Executor muſt make Oath before the Court of Aldermen that the Account is true.

Note, *That if any Executor cannot give in his Account according to the time mentioned in his Bond, he muſt apply himſelf to the Court of Aldermen for further time, which is uſually granted.*

Note, *That by an Act of Parliament made 5 & 6* Stat. 5, 6 W. *W. & M.* cap. 10. *for the raiſing a perpetual* M. c. 10. *Fund, to pay the yearly Intereſt of* 4 l. *for every* 100 l. *principal Money, and of all the Intereſt thereof due to any Orphan of the City of* London, *or the Executors, Adminiſtrators, or Aſſigns of ſuch Orphan, (in manner as therein is particularly mentioned ;) it is enacted, That no Perſon ſhall be obliged or compelled, by virtue of any Cuſtom within the ſaid City, or by Order or Proceſs of the Court of Orphans, to pay into the Chamber of* London *any Sum of Money, or Perſonal Eſtate, due, or to be due, or belonging to an Orphan of any Freeman, any Law*
or

or Ufage inforcing the fame notwithftanding. But this not to be conftrued to extend to impeach or prevent Procefs upon any Recognizance already given according to the Cuftom.

This Provifion made by the faid Act, for payment of the faid Intereft Money for ever, fhall be in full fatisfaction of the Debts and Intereft thereof due to the faid Orphans and Creditors; and they are to acknowledge Satisfaction of their refpective Debts according to the ufual Cuftom, &c. And the City and their Succeffors (by the faid Act) are acquitted of the fame.

The *Chamberlain* or other Officer, that mifapplies any of the Moneys fo appointed, forfeits treble the Sum to be recovered by any the Orphans or Creditors that will fue for the fame, in any of his Majefty's Courts of Record.

Any Perfon to whom any Money is payable by this Act, may, by writing under his Hand and Seal, transfer his Right and Intereft therein, to be regiftred in a Book to be kept by the Mayor and Court of Aldermen: And fuch Affignee fhall have the Bill, Note, or Writing, and fhall be entituled, and may affign *toties quoties*; and it fhall not be in the power of fuch Perfons who have made fuch Affignments, to releafe or difcharge the fame, or the Moneys thereby affigned.

Note, *There is a Provifion in the faid Act, That on application made to the Mayor and Court of Aldermen, by the Executors or Adminiftrators of the Faeher of fuch Orphan, to pay in, or lodge any Sum of Money of fuch Orphan in the faid Chamber, and to have the Benefit of the faid Provifion*

vifion thereby made ; it fhall be lawful for the faid Mayor and Aldermen to pay off the like Sum to fuch Perfon intitled to the faid yearly Payments, as aforefaid, as they think fit, not being Orphans under the Age of 21 Years, and giving three Months notice to, or for the Perfon fo to be paid off; at the end of which three Months, upon payment or tender of the faid Moneys due for Principal and Intereft to, or for the Perfon to whom fuch Notice fhall be given, according to the Provifion made by the faid Act, at the Office of the faid Chamberlain in Guild-Hall *; That from thenceforth the annual Sum of Money, payable to fuch Perfon, to whom fuch Notice, Payment, or Tender fhall be made, fhall ceafe and determine ; and the fame fhall become due and payable to, or for the ufe of fuch Orphan who fhall have paid in the Moneys for the fame, and fhall be regiftred accordingly, and be affignable as aforefaid : yet the Moneys fo tendered fhall be paid to fuch Perfons upon their demand of the fame, and affigning or giving a difcharge for the fame. And the Provifion made by the faid Act, fhall remain a perpetual Fund for the benefit of the Orphans of the faid City fuccesfively : And the faid Act fhall be reputed a general Act ; and the Judges, upon all Occafions, fhall take notice as if it were a general Act of Parliament relating to the whole Kingdom.*

It is alfo enacted by the faid Act, That all Securities given by the Orphans to any Agents or Sollicitors to obtain Payments of their Debts by Act of Parliament, or otherwife, fhall be null and void : And the *Mayor* and *Court of Aldermen*, out of the Revenue fettled by this *Act*, fhall allow and pay to fuch Agents and Sollicitors, what they judge may be reafonable, and
that

that to be allowed in the Account of the said Revenue : And if they demand or receive more than shall be so adjudg'd due to them, they shall forfeit treble the Sum receiv'd, to be recover'd with Costs of Suit, by such Persons as will sue for the same, in any of his Majesty's Courts of Record at *Westminster.*

Note, *The occasion of making the said Act was this :* K. Ch. II. *to support the Extravagance of his Court,* &c. *being necessitated to use indecent Shifts to procure Money, did about the Years* 1665, 1666, &c. *apply for that purpose to the City of* London; *and by the Treachery or Folly of some Aldermen,* &c. *obtained a Loan on his Privy Seal, or Tallies of Loan, of such Moneys belonging to the said* Orphans, *as were then in the Chamber of the said City, with which for a while he supported his Extravagance, and paid the Interest due thereon till about the Year* 1671. *when finding himself unable to pay the Principal, and scarcely the Interest ; and the Parliament refusing to supply him with Money, he by the Advice of the then Lord* Clifford (*who for that service was made Lord Treasurer of England*) *clos'd the Exchequer, and thereby became not only Bankrupt himself, but occasioned the Chamber of the said City to be so also : whereby many Thousand of City Orphans* (heu Pietas Regum!) *were reduced to Misery and Want, and were not only for ever defrauded of their principal Moneys, but even of Interest for the same, till the said Act* 5, 6 W. M. *which is call'd an Act for their Relief, tho' it utterly deprives them of their Principal, and only allows them* 4 per Cent. *Interest.——Besides the Injury done to the said City in divesting it of its ancient Jurisdiction.*

THE

THE
CHAMBERLAIN's
COURT
OR
OFFICE.

THE Chamberlain of *London* keeps his Office in the Chamber of *Guild-Hall*, and is entrusted not only with *Orphans* Moneys, but also all other the City Cash, (as is before observed :) he is annually elected upon *Mid-summer-Day*, and gives good Security to the Court of Aldermen to pay, and make good whatsoever Cash shall be deliver'd to him, and once every Year gives an account to Auditors appointed and chosen for that purpose. He is also entrusted with the City Leases ; and all Bonds and Securities taken by the Court of Aldermen for *Orphans* Moneys.

He attends at his Office in the Chamber of *Guildhall*, usually every Forenoon, to Inroll and turn over Apprentices, and to make such free as have duly served the full Term of seven Years.

Z   And

And *Note*, That by the Cuſtom of *London*, *Apprentices that are, or ſhall be bound by Indenture above the Age of fourteen Years, and under the Age of twenty one, to Freemen of* London, *for the full Term of ſeven Years, are compellable to ſerve the full Term, and an Action will lie againſt the Apprentice for Breach of any of the Covenants ; as we have before obſerved, and of which we ſhall hereafter ſet down ſome Precedents. But if the Apprentice ſhall be under the Age of fourteen Years at the Time of his binding, or if he be bound for a leſs Term than ſeven Years, his Indenture is not good.*

Maſter neglecting to inroll his Apprentice. And by the ancient and laudable Cuſtom of the City of *London*, every Maſter ought to inroll his Apprentice within the firſt Year of his Term, before the Chamberlain of *London* for the Time being, who uſually attends every Day at his Office in *Guildhall* for that purpoſe, as is aforeſaid. And if the Apprentice be inrolled within the firſt Year of his Term, the Fee is but 2 *s.* 6 *d.* but if he ſhall not be inrolled within the firſt Year, then ſuch Apprentice may be diſcharged from his Maſter's Service.

See before, and ſee after in this Court the Precedents.

By the late *Act* for Orphans, ' An Apprentice muſt pay 2 *s.* 6 *d.* when Bound, and 5 *s.* ' when he is admitted a Freeman, over and ' above the uſual Fees.

Miſdemeanor of Apprentices. If an Apprentice ſhall be unruly or diſorderly in his Maſter's Houſe, or commit any notorious Fault, upon Complaint made thereof, Mr. Chamberlain will ſend one of his *Officers* for ſuch *Apprentice*, and ſend him to *Bridewell*, or

other-

otherwife punifh him, according to the Nature of the *Offence*.

If any *Mafter* fhall mifufe his *Apprentice* by beating him unreafonably, or with unlawful Weapons, or by neglecting to inftruct him, or to find him Neceffaries; upon Complaint thereof made, Mr. Chamberlain will fend a Summons for the Mafter to appear before him: and upon hearing both Parties, will relieve the *Apprentice,* or leave him to take his Remedy againft fuch *Mafter* in the *Lord Mayor's Court.* *Mifufal by Mafters.*

If any Freeman fhall refufe to appear before the *Chamberlain,* being duly fummoned, the *Lord Mayor,* or *Mr. Recorder,* upon Complaint thereof made, will grant a *Warrant* to apprehend fuch Perfon, and compel him to appear; for which *Warrant* the Fee is 1 *s.*

Note, *When an Apprentice is by confent of his Mafter to be turned over to another Mafter of the fame Trade, it cannot be done by any Scrivener; but the Apprentice ought firft to be turned over before the Company where he was bound, and then to be turned over before the Chamberlain: At it is to be obferved, that if an Apprentice be turned over by the Company only, it is no Obligation upon the fecond Mafter to keep fuch Apprentice; nor is the Apprentice compellable thereby to ferve fuch fecond Mafter, but may depart from the Service of fuch fecond Mafter at his pleafure, by fuing out his Indentures againft his firft Mafter, which may be done without the Privity or Knowledge of the fecond Mafter: and therefore it is abfolutely neceffary that all Apprentices fhould be turned over before the Chamberlain, for thereby the firft Mafter is difcharged from him, and the fecond Mafter obliged to keep him; and the Apprentice will be obliged to ferve the fecond Mafter the full Term of his Inden-* Turn-overs before the Company and Chamberlain. Firft Mafter difcharged, and how.

tures;

tures; although the same were made for nine Years or more.

It is thought the Interest and Advantage of every Master and Apprentice, when, any Difference happens between them, to refer the Matter to the *Chamberlain*, who will freely hear both Parties, and decide the Controversy for three Shillings Charge; *viz.* one Shilling to the Officer for the Summons, and two Shillings to the Clerk for the Order. Whereas if they proceed at Law for Relief, it may probably cost each Party six Pounds, if not more, in Charges; and the Conclusion may be less satisfactory than if decided by such Reference, as aforesaid.

Reference to the Chamberlain better than going to Law.

In case any Apprentice shall refuse to be inrolled within the first Year of his Term, the Master may within that Time bring his Indenture to the Chamberlain, or his Clerk, who will record the same; which Record is as good as an Inrollment, and shall bar the Apprentice from discharging himself. There are many Citizens of *London* that neglect to inroll their Apprentices, and the Reason they usually give, is, *That if the Apprentice be inrolled, they are bound to keep him, although he shall be a Thief, or a Gamester; but if he is not inrolled, they can turn him away at their pleasure; but this is a great Mistake: For if an Apprentice shall not be inrolled, and the Master turn him away, the Apprentice may in such case bring his Action upon the Covenants in his Indenture, and recover Damages from time to time against the Master. And if the Apprentice be inrolled and turn'd away, he must take the same Course against his Master. Also if the Apprentice be a Thief, or a Gamester, or absent himself from his Master's Service, or refuse to obey his Master's lawful Commands; in any of these Cases the Master may as lawfully turn him away*

Apprentice refusing to be inrolled.

Supposed Reasons for not inrolling Apprentices.

Answered.

*away when he is inrolled as when he is not inrolled;
for the Inrollment is no Obligation upon the Mafter to
keep the Apprentice more than before when he was not
inrolled.*

*But by the Inrollment the Mafter fuffers no Pre-
judice: For he not only anfwers the Oath he took when
he was made free, but obliges the Apprentice not to go
away at his pleafure, but to ferve out his full Term,
although he were bound for eight Years, or more;
for though he be not inrolled, yet he cannot difcharge
himfelf from his Mafter's Service, unlefs for one of
thofe Caufes hereunder mentioned.*

Alfo every Mafter ought in Confcience to inroll his Note.
*Apprentice, for otherwife he difappoints the Father,
who poffibly paid the Mafter a confiderable Sum with
his Son Apprentice; and if the Apprentice knows he
may leave his Mafter's Service at his pleafure, it
happens very often, (as underftanding Men have obferved) that he neglects his Mafter's Service, and
takes bad Courfes, whereby the Father lofes both his
Money and his Son; which might in all probability
have been prevented, if the Apprentice had been inrolled.*

*Again, Although an Apprentice be inrolled, he
may be difcharged from his Mafter, in cafe the Mafter* Caufes
fhall beat him unreafonably without juft Caufe; or in wherefore
cafe the Mafter refufe to find him fufficient Neceffa- an Appren-
ries; or if the Mafter turn the Apprentice out of his tice may be
Service, or leave off his Trade, or fhall neglect to in- difcharged.
*ftruct his Apprentice, or turn him away: whereas
many Citizens do believe that if an Apprentice be inrolled, he cannot be difcharged from his Mafter for
any Caufe whatfoever.*

Alfo *Note,* By the Cuftom of *London,* an Executor fhall be obliged, on the Teftator's Death,
to place his Apprentice with another Mafter,
&c. *Salk. 66.*

Z 3 The

The *Manner of suing out an Apprentice's Indenture* is thus :

How to sue out the Indentures of an Apprentice.

He muſt bring his Indenture, or a Copy, to an Attorney in the *Lord Mayor's Court*, who will give a Note, or Warrant, to one of the Serjeants before mentioned, to ſignify to the Maſter the Apprentice's Intention of ſuing out his Indenture, and for what Cauſe ; and four Court Days after will leave a Summons in writing at the Maſter's Houſe, for him to appear in the ſaid Court, and ſhew cauſe why his Apprentice ſhall not be diſcharged. And if the Apprentice ſue his Indenture out for not Inrollment, the Maſter may appear, and delay it a ſmall time, but cannot prevent the Apprentice's Diſcharge : But if it be for any other Cauſe, the Maſter may appear by an Attorney of the ſaid Court, and plead, and try the Truth of the Matter complained of by the Apprentice, and the Maſter need not doubt a fair Tryal, the Jurys being all Maſters, and the Court conſtantly ſhews them all juſt and lawful Favour : And if a Verdict paſs for the Apprentice, or the Maſter, no Coſts will be allowed to either Party.

If an Apprentice ſhall be bound for eight, nine, or ten Years, and inrolled, he ſhall be compelled to ſerve the full Term, and cannot *Apprentice bound for 8, 9, or 10 Years.* be diſcharged from his Maſter after ſeven Years Service, unleſs for a very reaſonable Cauſe ; and it often happens that one Year's Service, after ſeven Years ſhall be expired, may be very conſiderable to the Maſter.

Freeman's Widow may take an Apprentice.

A Freeman's Widow may take a Maid Apprentice for ſeven Years, and inroll her in like manner as a Youth, in caſe ſhe be above fourteen Years of Age ; but if the Indenture ſhall be made for leſs than ſeven Years, it is naught, and

and against the Custom of *London*, and will not oblige the Apprentice.

If an Exchange-Woman, or Sempstress, that hath a Husband free of *London*, take a Maid Apprentice, such Apprentice must be bound to the Husband, and not for less than seven Years, and may be Inrolled and made Free at the Expiration of her Term, in case she continue so long unmarried. *Exchange Woman or Sempstress.*

When an Apprentice hath faithfully served the full Term of seven Years, (with a Freeman) and his Master shall refuse to make him Free, Mr. Chamberlain, upon Complaint made, will cause the Master to be summoned to appear before him; and if the Master can not shew good cause for such his Refusal, will make the Apprentice free: and if a Freeman shall refuse to appear before the Chamberlain being duly summoned, my Lord-Mayor, or Mr. Recorder, upon Complaint made, will grant a Warrant to compel him to appear.

If any Master refuse to make his Apprentice free, when the Time mentioned in the Indentures is expired, such Apprentice may (if he have duly served) force his Master to make him free, by summoning him before the *Court of Aldermen*, or before the Chamberlain of *London* for the Time being.

If an Apprentice shall refuse or omit to take his Freedom within convenient time after his Time is expired, Mr. Chamberlain may impose such Fine upon the Apprentice as he shall think fit for such his Neglect.

Every Freeman ought to take particular care not to make an Apprentice free of *London*, by testifying for his Service, unless such Apprentice shall have really served him : For if he shall privately turn his Apprentice over to a Foreigner,

reigner, and let the *Apprentice* ſerve ſuch Foreigner, and teſtify to the Chamberlain that the *Apprentice* ſerved a Freeman; in ſuch caſe the *Maſter* and *Apprentice* may be disfranchiſed, and fined at the pleaſure of Mr. Recorder; and Mr. Chamberlain may, in ſuch caſe, cauſe the Freeman's Shop to be ſhut up.

If a Freeman ſhall make his Apprentice free, by teſtifying he has ſerved him the full Term of ſeven Years, when in truth he has not, both the Maſter and the Apprentice may be disfranchiſed, upon an Information brought againſt them before the Lord Mayor and Aldermen by the Common Serjeant of the City, in whoſe Name all Informations of that nature muſt be brought, and he muſt peruſe and ſign the ſame, for which, in all ordinary Caſes, his Fee is 20 s. but in extraordinary Caſes double or treble that Sum. *See* an Act of Common Council touching this Matter, 18 *H.* VIII. *ante.*

For the Maſter in ſuch caſe ought to be disfranchiſed for teſtifying an Untruth contrary to his Oath of a Freeman; part of which Oath is not to take an Apprentice for a leſs Term than ſeven Year, &c. *Vide poſt.* So that if a Freeman well conſiders his Oath, he will not do any Act contrary thereto, either for Lucre to himſelf, or to pleaſure another.

Note alſo, *A Freeman ought to take care not to make his Apprentice free of* London, *by teſtifying for him, unleſs ſuch Apprentice ſhall have actually ſerved ſome Freeman; for if the Maſter ſhall turn his Apprentice over to a Foreigner, and let the Apprentice ſerve ſuch Foreigner, and yet afterwards teſtify to the Chamberlain that the Apprentice ſerved a Freeman, in ſuch caſe, both the Maſter and the Apprentice may be disfranchiſed*

in

in the Lord-Mayor's Court, and fined at the Plea-
sure of the Court, and 'tis said Mr. Chamberlain
will be directed to shut up both their Shops.

Anno 5 *Car.* I. in the Mayoralty of Sir *Henry*
Garway, one *Tho. Bashfield* testified before the
Chamberlain, that he had served nine Years with
his Master *William Bennet*; for which Term he
was Bound and Inrolled, and thereupon obtained his Freedom: But, in a short Time after,
the Matter being discovered, he was disfranchised because he had not served his Master the
full Term of nine Years.

Anno 10 *Car.* I. Sir *Rob. Parkhurst* Mayor, one
Will. Morrice, a Freeman of *London,* was disfranchised for taking an Apprentice, and contracting that he should serve but five Years, and for
antedating the Indenture and making it for
seven Years, contrary to his Oath taken when
he was made free.

Anno 9 *Jac.* I. Sir *James Pemberton* Mayor,
one *William Whitwell* an Officer, and *Thomas*
Clark, Freemen of *London,* were disfranchised
for fraudulently procuring one *John Lamott,* the
Son of an Alien, to be made a Freeman of *Lon-*
don in the Weavers Company, and they were
fined 20 *l.* a-piece, and their Shop Windows
were ordered to be shut up by the Chamberlain.

The foregoing Precedents of Disfranchise-
ments, *&c.* seem consonant to Law; but I
have seen a Precedent of disfranchising one, for
that he was married within the Term of his
Apprenticeship, which seems not so legal, *viz.*

Anno 18 *Car.* I. Sir *Richard Gurney* Mayor, one
John Wood, who had served seven Years with
John Alte, came before the Chamberlain, and
testified, that he was not married within the
said

faid Term, and thereupon obtained his Free-dom; but was afterwards disfranchifed, becaufe it appeared he was marry'd before the faid Term expired.

But it has been refolved in the Courts at *Weftminfter*, that an Apprentice's marrying within the Term, fhall be no caufe for his Disfran-chifement, or Lofs of Freedom; but he fhall have a *Mandamus*, commanding the Mayor, &c. to make him free notwithftanding his faid *Mar-riage.* See 1 *Levins* 91. 1 *Sid.* 107. 2 *Show.* 154.

Fees due to the City upon the making Free and Inrolling Apprentices.

	s.	d.
An Apprentice made Free, not Inroll-ed, the Mafter pays	13	2
But if Inrolled, the Mafter pays only	4	0
The Apprentice pays, whether Inrolled or not, only	1	0
Befides to the Orphans Fund, as *per Stat.*	5	0
If not turned over before the Chamber-lain, then the Mafter or Miftrefs muft pay extraordinary	2	0
And for Inrolling an Apprentice, with-in the firft Year of his Term	2	0

Fees due to the Clerk of the Chamber.

	s.	d.
For every Copy of a Freedom, if by Service, filing the Indenture, and entring the Name in the Kalendar	2	6
For every Copy of a Freedom, if by Nativity out of *London*, for filing, fealing and entring the Name, &c.	5	0

For

	s.	d.
For every Copy of a Freedom, if by Nativity within *London*, in the same manner	4	0
For the Copy of a Freedom by Redemption, that is, purchased or given, for filing the Order, sealing, &c. and entering the Name	4	0
To the Under-Clerk for each of these Copies	0	6
Note, There is also paid by every Person on his Admission into the Freedom, for *Stamps*, &c.	2	6
For every Second Copy of a Freedom	2	6
To the Under-Clerk	0	6
For every Copy of an Inrollment	2	0
To the Under-Clerk	0	6
For every Indenture that is lost	2	0
For every Search	1	0
For every Inrollment	0	4
For every Turn-over	0	4
For every Order without a Reference	1	0
For every Order upon a Reference	2	0
For every Warrant	1	0
For every Summons within the Liberties	1	0
For evrey Summons without the Liberties	2	0

	s.	d.
Note also, The Clerk of the Chamber formerly took, for engrossing every Lease granted by the City, besides the King's Duty and Parchment	10	0

Upon the Admission of every Person into the Freedom of *London*, Mr. Chamberlain causes them to take an Oath as followeth :

The

The Oath of every Freeman of the City of *London*.

YE *shall swear, That ye shall be good and true to our Sovereign Lord King* George, *and to the Heirs of our said Sovereign Lord the King. Obeysant and obedient ye shall be to the Mayor and Ministers of this City. The Franchises and Customs thereof ye shall maintain, and this City keep harmless in that that in you is. Ye shall be contributary to all manner of Charges within this City, as Summons, Watches, Contributions, Taxes, Tallages, Lot and Scot, and to all other Charges, bearing your part as a Freeman ought to do. Ye shall colour no Foreign Goods under or in your Name, whereby the King or this City might or may lose their Customs or Advantages. Ye shall know no Foreigner to buy or sell any Merchandize with any other Foreigner within this City or Franchise thereof, but ye shall warn the Chamberlain thereof, or some Minister of the Chamber. Ye shall implead or sue no Freeman out of this City, whilst ye may have Right and Law within the same City. Ye shall take no Apprentice, but if he be free-born, that is to say, no Bond-man's Son, nor the Child of any Alien, and for no less Term than for Seven Years, without Fraud or Deceit; and within the first Year ye shall cause him to be Inrolled, or else pay such Fine as shall be reasonably imposed upon you for omitting the same. And after his Term's end, within convenient time (being required). ye shall make him free of this City, if he have well and truly served you. Ye shall also keep the King's Peace in your own Person. Ye shall know no Gatherings, Conventicles, nor Conspiracies made against the King's Peace, but ye shall warn the Mayor thereof, or lett it to your power. All these Points and Articles ye shall well*
and

and truly keep according to the Laws and Customs of this City to your power. So God you help.

If a Freeman well confiders this Oath, he will not do any Act contrary thereunto for lucre, &c. as aforefaid.

When any Freeman's Apprentice is legally difcharged from his Mafter, and it is reafonable that he fhould have part of his Money again, he may have remedy in the Mayor's Court of Equity, as is before obferved.

👑 👑 👑 👑 👑 👑 👑 👑 👑 👑 👑

Here follow certain Precedents of Pleadings between Mafters and Apprentices.

A Declaration by a Mafter againft his Apprentice upon his Indenture, for departing from his Service without leave, wherein the Cuftom of the City of London is fet forth.

London ff. H R. queritur de R. R. in Cuftod. • Marr. &c. de placito convencionis fract' pro eo, *viz.* quod cum Civitas L. eft & à tempore cujus contrar. memoria hominum non exiftit fuit antiqua Civitas, infra quam quidem Civitat. talis habetur & à tempore fupradicto habebatur conf. ufitat' & approbat. quod quilibet civis & liber homo ejufdem Civit. capere poffet & per totum tempus fupradict' capere ufus fuit & confuevit in Apprenticium aliquam perfonam feu aliquas perfonas infra hoc Regnum Angliæ nat. exiften' ultra ætatem quatuordecim Annorum & infra ætat. vigint. & unius Annorum

per

per Indentur. inter hujufmodi Apprentic. ex una
parte & hujufmod. civem & liberum hominem
ex altera parte fiend' ad deferviend. hujufmodi
civi & libero homini civit' præd. pro termin. 7.
Annorum & amplius per hujufmodi Indentur.
obligat. Et præd. talis Apprentic. per conf. civit. præd. à toto tempore cujus contrar. memoria hominum non exiftit ufitat' & approbat' tent'
& obligat. exiftit, & per totum tempus præd. tent'
& obligat' extiterit & teneri confuevit defervire
hujufmodi civi & libero homini Magiftro fuo
per totum tempus Apprenticialitat' fuæ (Anglice
his Apprenticeſhip) in Indentur' illa mencionat' &
content' & bene & fidelit' obfervare, performare
& perimplere omnes & omniod' racionabil. con-
venciones in hujufmodi Indentur. fpec. & content. feu continend. ex parte fua obfervand' tenend' performand' feu perimplend' concernen'
verum juftum & fidel' fervicium dicti Apprenticii erga Magiftrum fuum duran. termin. Ap-
preticialitatis fuæ prædict' fecund' veram intentionem Indentur' præd' acfi hujufmodi Apprenticius tempore confectionis ejufdem Indentur'
fuiffet plene ætatis 21 Annorum & amplius, & fi
talis Apprenticius infringeret aliquam conventionem in eadem Indentur' content' ex parte fua
performand' duran' termin' in eadem content'
quod tunc Magift. talis Apprenticii haberet tale
remedium verfus eundem Apprenticium fuum
qual' haberet fi talis Apprenticius tempore confectionis Indentur. fuæ præd. foret plene ætatis 21
Annorum & amplius : Quæ quidem conf. ac omnes al. confuetud' in eadem Civit' de antiquo

Cuſtoms con-
firmed. ufitat. per Dominum Richardum nuper Regem
Angliæ fecundum in Parliamento ipfius nuper
Regis apud *Weſt.* in Com. *Midd.* Anno regni fui
fexto tent. tunc Majori & Communit' & Civibus
Civit' præd. & fucceſſoribus fuis authoritat' &
con-

cohfenfu Parliament' illius ratificat' & confirmat'
fuer' Cumque per quandam Indentur' factam'.
apud *London,* *viz.* in Paroch. &*c.* (tali die &
Anno)· inter prædictum Richardum adtunc exiften' ætatis 14 Annorum & amplius & infra ætat'
21 Annorum, *viz.* ætatis 15 Annorum, & tunc
ante exiften' natus infra hoc Regnum Magnæ
Britanniæ, *viz.* apud *London'* prædict' in Parochia
& Warda prædict' per nomen R. R. &*c.* Et eundem H. R. tunc exiften' civem & liberum hominem & aurifabrum civitat' prædict' per nomen
H. R. (&*c.*) cujus alteram partem fgillo prædicti R. jam Def. fgnat. prædict' H. hic in cur.
profert cujus dat' eft eifdem Die & Anno prædictus jam Def. pofuiffet feipfum Apprentic. eidem H. civi & aurifabro London' ad difcend'
artem & fuam fecum more Apprent' deferviend'
à fefto Annunciation' Beatæ Mariæ tunc ult.
præterit. ante dat. Indentur' prædict. ufque plenum finem & termin. feptem Annorum extunc
proxime fequen. & plenar. complend. & finiend.
duran. quo termin. idem Apprentic. præfat. Magiftro fuo fideliter deferviret, fecreta fua celaret,
præceptaque fua licita ubique libent. ageret,
dampnu. præfat' Magiftro fuo non faceret aut
ab aliquo fieri videret, quin illum ad poffe fuum
impediret, aut ftatim dictum Magiftrum fuum
inde præmoneret; bona Magiftri fui non devaftaret neque ea illicite alicui perfonæ accommodaret, Fornicationem non committeret, neque Matrimonium contraheret infra prædict. termin.
cartis pictis aleis tabulis luforiis at al. jocis il-
licitis non luderet, quo dictus Magifter fuus ul-
lum detriment' haberet, cum bonis fuis propr.
aut alienis duran. dicto termino abfque licent.
dicti Magiftri fui neque emeret neque venderet,
tabernas non frequentaret, nec feipfum à fervitio
dicti Magiftri fui die vel nocte illicite recederet,

fed

sed in omnibus tanquam fidel. Apprentic. erga
dictum Magistrum suum omnesque suos duran.
dicto termino seipsum gereret. Et præfat. Ma-
gist. Apprentic. suum prædict. in eadem arte qua
tunc utebatur optimo modo quo posset doceret
& erudiret debitâ castigatione, inveniend' dicto
Apprenticio suo sufficien. victum potum losio-
nem lectur. & apparat. omniaque al. necessar. secundum consuetud. dictæ civit. London duran.
dicto termino. Et pro verâ performation' omnium & singulorum convention. & agreament'
præd' prædictus R. prædict. H. per dictam Indentur' firmit. seipsum obligavit prout per eandem Indentur' inter alia plenius apparet. Et
idem H. in facto dicit quod tempore confectionis Indentur' præd. dictus H. fuit civis & liber
homo Civit. prædictæ (*viz.*) artis sive Mysterii de
les aurifabr. (Angliè *Goldsmiths*) infra Civit'
prædict' & eadem arte de les aurifabr. apud
London prædict. in Parochia & Warda prædict.
exercen' idem H. utebatur. Et idem H. ulterius in facto dicit quod idem H. tempore confectionis Indentur. prædict. & ante diem impe-
tration. hujus Billæ scil. prædict. (tali Die &
Anno) supradicto apud London' præd' in Parochia & Warda præd. prædictum R. modo Def.
in Apprenticium suum & servicium suum recepit ad ipsum in arte aurifabr. quam idem H.
tunc utebatur erudiend. secundum formam &
effectum Indentur' præd. qui quidem R. apud
London' præd. in Parochia & Warda prædict.
ab eodem (tali die & anno supradicto) cum eodem
H. ut Apprenticius suus remansit & eidem H.
tanquam Magistro suo deservivit usque (talem
diem & annum) ac licet idem H. bene & fidelit.
performavit perimplevit & custodivit omnes &
singular' conventiones & agreament. in Indentur.
prædicta ex parte sua performand. perimplend.

seu

feu cuſtodiend. ſecundum formam & effectum
Indentur. ill. idem tamen R. modo Def. non
performavit perimplevit, ſeu cuſtodivit aliqua
convention. promiſſion. ſeu agreament. in eadem
Indentur. mentionat. ex parte ſua performand'
perimplend' ſeu cuſtodiend' ſecundum formam
& effectum Indentur. ill. Et idem H. ulterius
in facto dicit quod poſt confectionem Indentur.
prædict. & poſtquam idem H. dictum R. modo
Def. in ſervitium ipſius H. ut præfertur cepiſſet
& duran. tempore quo dictus R. in ſervitio dicti
H. ut Apprenticius ſuus exſtitit & deſervivit &
infra prædict. termin. ſeptem. annorum ſcilicet
(tali Die & Anno) dictus R. modo Def. apud
London' prædict. in Parochia & Warda prædict.
ſine licentia & voluntat. ipſius H. tunc Magiſtri
ſui à ſervitio dicti H. termino Apprenticii ſui
nondum finit. contra formam & effectum Indentur. prædict. deceſſit & receſſit, & adtunc & ibidem bona dicti Henrici ad valent. decem librarum ſine licentia & voluntat. ipſius H. contra
formam & effectum Indentur. prædict. inordinat.
devaſtavit, ſicque prædict. R. licet ſepius requi-
ſit' &c. Conventionem ſuam prædict. de eo quod
idem R. durante termino prædict. in Indentur.
prædict. ſuperius ſpecificat ſeipſum à ſervicio
prædict. H. Magiſtri ſui illicite non recederet, neque bona ipſius H. Magiſtri ſui devaſtaret, neque
ea alicui illicite accommodaret eidem H. non
tenuit ſed infregit. Et ill. huc uſque tenere
contradixit & adhuc contradicit unde idem Henricus dicit quod ipſe deteriorat. eſt. Et dampe-
num habet ad valent. 50 *l*. Et inde producit
Sectam, &c.

*Covenant againft an Apprentice for neg-
lecting his Mafter's Service, and waft-
ing his Money.*

London ſſ.   **T** B. ſummon. fuit ad reſpondendum *W. B.*
. in placito conventionis fracte. Et unde
idem *W.* per *W. R.* attornat. ſuum dicit quod
cum præd. *T. B.* 26. die Feb. anno Regni dom'
reg' nunc tertio apud *C.* in parochia Sancti *A.*
Apoſtoli in Warda de *W.* per ſcriptum ſuum
indentatum, cujus alteram partem Sigillo ipſius
T. B. ſigillat' idem *W. B.* hic in Curiam profert, cujus dat' eſt die & anno ſupradict' per
nomen *T. B.* filii *S. B.* de *L.* in Com' *K. Baker,*
poſuit ſeipſum Apprenticium præfato *W. B.* per
nomen *W. B.* de *L. Grocer,* ad artem ejuſdem
W. B. erudiend' & informand', ac ſecum more
Apprenticii ſui commoratur' & deſervitur' a
feſto St. *M.* Apoſtoli nunc ultimo preterit' ante
dictum viceſimum ſextum diem *F.* uſque finem
termini ſeptem annorum tunc proximo ſequenti-
um & plenarie complend'; prædict' *T.* adtunc
& ibidem per ſcriptum ſuum præd' convenit
cum præfato *W. B.* quod ipſe per tempus præd'
bene & fideliter deſerviret' præfato *W. B.* Magiſtro ſuo, ſecreta ſua celaret, præcepta ſua licita & honeſta libenter ubiq; faceret, fornicationem in domo dicti Magiſtri ſui neq; extra committeret, infra terminum prædictum non recederet, nec diebus nec noctibus ſe elongaret,
damnum ei non faceret, nec fieri videret quod
impedire poſſit, quin illud pro toto poſſe ſuo impediret, aut prædictum Magiſtrum ſuum inde
ſtatim premuniret, bona dicti Magiſtri ſui inordinate

dinate non devaſtaret, nec alteri accommodaret, ſine ejus precepto aut ſpeciali mandato, Tabernas ex conſuetud' non frequentaret, niſi ſit cauſa Mercandiſandi, aut commodum dicti Magiſtri ſui ibidem faciend' Ad Talos neq; ad Scaccarium non luderet, unde idem Magiſter ſuus damnum incurreret, matrimonium neq; contract' cum aliqua muliere infra terminum prædict' non contraheret, nec cum argento ſuo proprio aut alieno non mercandizaret ſine licentia & voluntate dicti Magiſtri ſui, ſed bene & fideliter ſe haberet in omnibus tam in dictis quam in factis, ſicut bonus & fidelis Apprenticius ſe habere deberet, (*&c.*) Prædictuſq; *T. B.* conventionem præd' minime curans, in vigilia Apoſtolorum Petri & Pauli, Anno regni prædicti Domini Regis nunc quarto, apud *L.* in parochia St. *A.* Apoſtoli & in warda de *W.* a ſervitio dicti *W. B.* ſe elongavit, per quod idem *W.* ſervitium ipſius *T.* a prædicta vigilia Apoſtolorum uſq; diem impetrationis hujus loquele *ſcilicet,* (*&c.*) totalit' amiſit, ac ſept' libr' quatuor ſolid' Sterlingorum de denariis ipſius *W.* exiſten' adtunc & ibidem infidelit' & ſubdole ac inordinat' devaſtavit contra exigen' convention' ſue præd' unde idem *W.* dic' quod deteriorat' eſt & damn' het' ad val' 20 *l.* Et inde produc' ſec', *&c.*

A De-

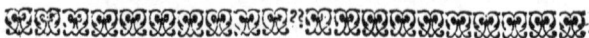

A *Declaration for a Master upon an Indenture of Apprenticeship against his Apprentice, for wasting the Master's Goods.*

Lond. ff. **H**L. queritur de *N. R.* in Custod'
Marr', &c. de placito convenc'
fract', &c. pro eo videlicet quod cum per
quandam Indenturam [factam apud London'
(*viz.*) in paroch'. (&c.) tali die, (&c.) inter
præd. *H. L.* per nomen *H. L.* (&c.) Et præfat'
N. R. per nomen *N. R* (&c.) cujus quidem Indenture alteram partem sigillo ipsius *N.* sigillat'
geren' dat' eisdem die & anno idem *H.* hic in
Cur' profert] Testat existit quod præd. *N.* posuit seipsum Apprenticium præfat' *H. L.* ad artem ejus qua idem *H.* adtunc scilicet præd' tempore confectionis Indentur' **præd'** utebatur erudiend' & secum more Apprenticii sui commoratur' & deservitur' a Festo Annunciacon' beatæ
Mariæ tunc prox. futur' usque ad finem & termin' septem annorum extunc prox' sequen' &
plenar' complend. Et præd. *N. R.* per Indentur'
præd' convenit ad & cum eodem *H. L.* quod
prædict' *N.* duran' termino prædicto præfat. *H.*
tanquam Magistro suo bene & fideliter deserviret, secreta sua celaret, præcept' sua licita &
honesta libenter ubiq; faceret, dampnum eidem
H. Magistro suo non faceret, nec ab aliis fieri
sciret, quin illud pro posse suo impediret, aut
statim dictum *H.* Magistrum suum inde præmoneret ; bona dicti *H.* Magistri sui inordinate non
devastaret, nec ea alicui illicite accommodaret,
Fornicationem non committeret, Matrimonium
non contraheret, ad pictas cartas, talos, seu
aliqua

aliqua al' joca illicita non luderet, Tabernas
non frequentaret, cum bonis fuis propr' aut alienis, durante dicto tempore ; fine licenc' dicti
Magiftri fui non merchandizaret, a fervicio fuo
præd' non recederet, nec fe elongaret, fed in
omnibus tanquam bonus & fidelis Apprentic'
erga dictum *H.* Magiftrum fuum benigne fe gereret & haberet per totum dictum terminum.
Et præd' *H. L.* per Indentur' præd' convenit ad
& cum præfat' *N. R.* quod præd' *H. L.* præd' *N.*
Apprentic' fuum in Arte fua qua idem *H.* adtunc fcilicet prædicto tempore confectionis Indentur' præd' utebatur meliori modo quo fci-
verit aut poterit, doceret, tractaret & informa-
ret, vel doceri & informari faceret, inveniendo
ei victum, veftitum, lineum, laneum, calceos, &
lect' & omnia al' fibi neceffar' per totum dictum
terminum. Et ad conventiones præd' omnes &
fingulas in dict' Indentur' ex parte dicti Apprentic' bene & fideliter tenend' & performand'
in forma ut fupra idem Apprentic' firmit' fe ob-
ligaffet per præd' Indentur' prout per Indentur'
præd' plenius liquet & apparet virtute cujus
quidem Indentur' præfat' *N.* Apprentic' ipfius
H. (tali die, *&c.*) anno decimo præd' ad deferviend' eidem *H.* in forma præd' fecundum formam & effectum Indentur' præd' deven' ac licet
idem *H.* bene & fideliter performavit omnes
conventiones & conceffiones in Indentur' præd'
fpecificat ex parte fua performand' fecundum formam & effectum Indentur' præd' in facto idem *H.*
dic' quod poft confection' Indentur' præd. duran'
termin' præd' videlicet (tali die & anno) præd'
H. L. apud London' præd' in Paroch' & Warda
præd' poffeffionat' fuit de diverfis bonis & merchandiz' ut de bonis & merchandiz' ipfius *H.*
propr' videlicet de, *&c.* (*here name the Goods*) ad
valenc' *&c.* quodque eodem *H* de bonis & ca-

tal. ill. modo quo præfertur posseffionat. existen.
postea duran. termino prædict. (viz. tali die &
anno) præd. *N.* tunc Apprentic. ipsius *H.* modo
quo præfertur existen. apud London. prædict.
viz. in Paroch. & Warda præd. bona & catella
ill. particularit. superius in hac parte recitat.
præfat. *N. R.* per præfat. *H. L.* deliberat. fuer.
ad merchandizand. pro prædict. *H.* Magistro suo,
& ad usum & proficuum ipsius *H.* convertend.
Et idem *H.* ulterius dic. quod præd. *N.* bona &
catalla ill. ad usum & proficuum ipsius *H.* non
convertebat, sed duran. termin. Apprentic. sui
præd. scilicet (tali die & anno) præd. (prefat.
N. tunc Apprentic. ipsius *H.* occasione præd. existen. ac termin. præd. tunc duran.) apud Lond.
præd. in Paroch. & Warda præd. prædicta bona
& catalla, & merchandizas particularit. superius
in hac parte spec. præfat. *N.* ut præmittitur deliberat. subdole ac inordinat. devastabat & ea
in usum & commodum ipsius *N.* propr. adtunc
& ibidem falso & fraudulenter convertit & dif-
posuit. Et sic idem *H.* dic. quod præd. *N.* conventionem præd. in Indentur. præd. spec. de
eo quod præd. *N.* duran. termin. præd. eidem
H. L. tanquam Magistro suo bene & fidelit. non
deservit, eidem *H.* non tenuit, sed infregit, ac
ill. ei hucusque tenere contradixit, & adhuc
contradic. unde dic. quod deteriorat. est &
dampnum habet ad valenc. 100 l. Et inde produc. sectam, &c.

Defendant pleads that his Master delivered him the Goods to sell, and to render his Master an account, and that he accounted, and his Master accepted his account,

Et modo, (&c.) Et præd. *N.* defend. vim. &
injur. quando, &c. Et dic. quod præd. *H. L.* (ac-
con. non, &c.) quia protestando quod bona &
catalla in narr. præd. superius spec. non fuer.
tanti valoris quant. præd. *H.* superius versus eum
narravit pro placito idem *N.* dic. quod bene &
verum est quod præd. *H.* fuit posseffionat. de
bonis & catallis præd. in narr. præd. spec. ut de
bonis

bonis & catallis fuis propr. prout præd. *H.* per
narr. fuam prædict. fuperius fuppon. fed idem
N. ulterius dic. quod præd *H.* fic inde poffeffionat. exiften. prædicto (tali die & anno) fupradicto apud, &c. deliberavit eidem *N.* bona
& catalla præd. ad eadem bona & catalla vendend. & merchandizand. & ad rationabil.
comput. inde eidem *H.* cum inde requifit.
fuiffet reddend. cujus pretextu idem *N.* poftea, fcilicet eifdem die & anno, apud London
præd. in Paroch. & Warda præd. bona & catalla
præd. diverfis perfonis eidem *N.* ignot. ad tam
magnum proficuum quod potuit pro diverfis
pecuniæ fummis attingen. in toto ad 50 l. in
pecuniis numerat. vendidit que eft eadem de-
vaftatio & venditio bonorum & catallorum præd.
unde idem *H.* fuperius fe modo queritur. Et
idem *N.* ulterius dic. quod ipfe poftea & ante
diem exhibitionis bille præd. fcilicet (tali die &
anno) fupradicto apud *L.* præd. in Paroch. &
Warda præd. plene computavit cum præd. *N.*
pro bonis, catallis, & merchandizis præd. fuperius fpec. Et fuperinde idem *N.* 50 l. pro bonis, catallis, & merchandizis prædict. per ipfum
in forma præd. vendit. eidem *H.* ad ufum ipfius
H. propr. adtunc & ibidem folvit & deliberavit
quas quidem 50 l. idem *H.* in plenam conten-
contentacon. & fatisfacon. bonorum, catallorum,
& merchandizarum præd. de eodem *N.* adtunc
& ibidem recepit, acceptavit, & habuit. Et
hoc, &c. unde, &c.

꧁꧂꧁꧂꧁꧂꧁꧂꧁꧂꧁꧂꧁꧂꧁꧂꧁꧂

Action of a Covenant by a Linen-Draper *against his Apprentice, upon an Indenture of Apprenticeship, and Breach alledged for wasting of the Money received by his hands, and the hands of others.*

Lond.ss. G. P. nuper de *G.* in Com. *S.* Linen-Draper alias dictus *G. P. Son of G. P. of (&c.) Yeoman,* Summon' fuit ad respond' *R. J.* de plito' quod teneat conventionem inter eos factam secundum vim formam & effectum quarundam Indenturarum inde inter eos confect', *&c.* & unde idem *R.* per *R. H.* Attornatum suum dic' quod cum per quandam Indenturam factam apud London' in parochia beate Marie de Arcubus in Warda de Cheap, vicesimo die Februarii Anno regni Domini regis nunc Magræ Britanniæ Primo, cujus alteram partem Sigillo prædicti *G. P.* filii signat' idem *R.* hic in Cur' profert cujus dat' est eisdem die & anno testat' existit quod prædictus *G. P.* de *(&c.)* ex suo proprio voluntario, animo, & cum consensu amicorum suorum posuisset & obligasset seipsum apprenticium ad & cum prædicto *R.* per nomen *R. J.* Jun' de *(&c.)* Linen-Draper, secum moratur' scientiam Artem, Anglice *Trade,* sive facultatem suam erudire & ipsum bene & fideliter deservire a die dat' Indent' prædicte quousque prædictus *G.* filius accompleret suam ætatem viginti & quatuor annorum ; duran' quo integro termino prædictus *G. P.* apprenticius prædicti *R. J.* ut magistr' suo bene & fideliter deserviret, secreta sua celaret, precepta sua licita & honesta ubique

ubique faceret, dampnum dicto magistro suo non
faceret nec fieri consentiret si ill' impedire possit,
Tabernas seu domos Cervic', Anglice *Alehouses,*
non frequentaret, ad joca illicita non luderet,
bona dicti Magistri sui inordinate non devastaret
neque expenderet, nec ea alicui persone accommodaret absque licentia dicti Magistri sui, fornicationem non committeret, · matrimonium
durante dicto termino non contraheret, neque
solemnizaret, nec a Servic' dicti Magistri sui
seipsum absentaret, seu prolongaret nocte neque
die absque licentia dicti Magistri sui: Sed in omnibus rebus ut bonus & fidelis Servien' seipsum
gereret, & usus foret erga Magistrum suum &
familiam suam, tam in verbis quam in actis
duran' prædicto termino secundum usum & consuetudinem Civitatis London. Et prædictus *R.J.*
Magister convenisset & concessisset per eandem
Indenturam ad & cum dicto *G. P.* suo Apprenticio docere & instruere, vel doceri & instrui
causare prædictum Apprenticium suum duran'
prædicto termino in tota scientia arte, Anglice
Trade, sive facultate pannarii Linei, Anglice *of a
Linen-Draper,* & in qualibet arte, Anglice *Feat,*
& Mysterio adinde pertinen' in optimo modo
quo ipse potuit sive possit cum debito modo Ca-
stigamen' invenien' sibi duran. prædicto termino
cibum, potum & vestitum, tam linei quam lanei
Calig' Calceos & Lect', Anglice *Bedding,* & omnibus aliis rebus apt' tali Apprenticio tam in æ-
gritudine quam in Salute, & duran' duobus ulte-
riis annis prædicti termini mitteret dict' Apprenticium usque London' ad emend' pro se
Mercimon' ac in fine dicti termini daret & de-
liberaret prædicto Apprenticio suo in recompen-
satione fidelis servicii sui duplicem apparat' &
novum pallium, lati panni, lanei apt' & decen'
pro tali Apprenticio habere & induere, prout per
eandam

eandem indenturam plenius apparet. Et idem *R.*
ulterius dicit quod prædictus *G. P.* filius tempore confectionis Indenture prædicte fuit etatis
fexdecim annorum & non ultra, videlicet apud
London' prædictam in parochia & Warda prædictis; Quodque idem *G. P.* filius per prædictam
Indenturam feipfam pofuit & obligavit Apprenticium ad eidem *R.* deferviend' fecundum formam, tenorem & effect' Statuti de Anno quinto
nuper Regine Elizabeth' in hujufmodi cafu
edit' & provif. & non aliter quodque prædictus
G. filius à tempore confectionis Indenturæ prædictæ ufque ultimam diem Decembris Anno
regni dicti domini regis nunc Anglie feptimo,
& poftea ipfum *R.* ut Apprenticium in prædicta
arte panni linei, Anglice *of a Linen-Draper,* virtute Indenture prædicte apud London' in Parochia & Warda prædict' deferviebat. Idemque *R.*
ulterius dicit quod ipfe a tempore confectionis
Indenture prædicte hucufque performavit, perimplevit & obfervavit omnia & fingula in prædicta Indentur' fpecificat' ex parte fua performand' feu perimplend' fecundum formam &
effectum Indenture illius. In facto idem *R.* dicit
quod prædictus *G. P.* filius poft confectionem
Indenture prædicte, fcilicet inter duodecimum
diem Augufti Anno regni dicti domini regis
nunc Anglie feptimo & vicefimum diem Septembris tunc prox' fequen' apud London in parochia & Warda predict' recepit de denariis
ipfius *R.* per manus fuas proprias ac per manus
diverfarum aliarum perfonar' diverfas feperales
fummas monete in toto fe attingen' ad fummam
mille librarum ; quodque prædictus *G. P.* filius
poft receptionem denariorum prædictorum, fcilicet vicefimo nono die Septembris Anno feptimo fupradicto apud Londinum in Parochia &
Warda prædictis diverfas denariorum fummas in
toto

toto fe attingen' ad fummam ducentarum librarum de prædictis denariis per ipfum ut prefertur recept' fubdole infideliter & inordinate devaftavit contra formam & effectum Indenture
prædicte; ficque prædictus *G.P.* filius licet fæpius
requifit' conventionem prædictam eo quod prædictus *G. P.* Apprenticius ipfum *R. J.* ut fuum
Magiftrum duran' toto prædicto termino bene
& veraciter deferviret, fecreta fua celaret, præcepta fua licita & honefta ubique faceret, dampnum dicto Magiftro fuo non faceret feu fieri
confentiret, fi ipfe eadem impedire poffit; Tabernas feu domus cervic' Anglice *Alehoufes* non
frequentaret, ad Joca illicita non luderet, bona
dicti Magiftri fui inordinate non devaftaret neque expenderet, nec ea alicui perfone accommodaret, abfque licentia dicti Magiftri fui ; fornicationem non committeret, Matrimonium duran'
prædicto termino non contrahereret neque fo-
lemnizaret, nec a Servic' dicti Magiftri fui feipfum abfentaret feu prolongaret nocte neque die
abfque licentia dicti Magiftri fui, fed in omnibus
rebus ut bonus & fidelis Serviens fe gereret &
ufus foret erga dominum fuum & totam familiam
fuam, tam in verbis quam in actis, duran' toto
prædicto termino fecundum ufum & confuetudinem Civitatis London' fecundum formam &
effectum Indenture prædicte eidem *R.* non tenuit fed infregit (* ac ill' ei tenere hucufque
contradixit & adhuc contradicit) unde dicit'
quod deteriorat' eft & dampnum habet ad va-
lentiam ducentarum librarum, & inde producit'
fectam, *&c.*

　Et prædictus *G. P.* filius per *L. E.* Attornatum fuum venit & defend' vim & injur' quando, *&c.* Et dicit' quod prædictus *R. J.* actionem fuam prædictam verfus eum habere non
debet, quia proteftando quod ipfe non recepit
　　　　　　　　　　　　de

*Quere the
ufe of thefe
words.*

Bar by Stat.
of 5 Eliz.
*that none
fhould take
an Apprentice
to fuch a
Trade (but if
he be his Son)*

ex-

except the Father or Mother of the Apprentice hath 40 s. a year in Lands or Tenements which ought to be certified by a Justice of Peace. And the Defendant averred, that he is not the Son of the Plaintiff, and that neither his Father or Mother hath 40 s. per annum, &c.

de denariis prædicti *R.* diverfas feperal' denariorum fummas monete in toto fe attingen' ad fummam mille librarum nec quod ipfe aliquas denariorum fummas ipfius *R.* fubdole infideliter feu inordinate devaftavit, prout prædictus *R.* per narrationem fuam prædictam fuperius fuppon' pro placito idem *G.* dicit quod per quendam Actum in Parliamento apud *W.* in Com' *Middlefex* duodecimo die Januarii Anno domine *Elizabeth*' nuper Regine Anglie quinto tent' edit' (inter alia) provifum & inactitat' fuit authoritate ejufdem Parliamenti, quod non liceat alicui perfone inhabitan' in aliqua civitate five villa corporat' utenti five exercenti aliquo Myfteriorum five artium, Anglice *Crafts*, Mercatoris (negotian') Anglice *Trafficking*, per commercium, Anglice *Traffick*, five artem, Anglice *Trade*, in aliquas partes tranfmarinas Merceri pannarii Aurifabri ferrarii, Anglice *Ironmonger*, fegmentarii, Anglice *Imbroiderer*, five pannularii, Anglice *Clothier*, qui pon' aut ponet pannum ad confectionem & venditionem capere aliquem apprentic' aut fervien' fore inftruct' five doct' in aliquibus artium occupatione artium, Anglice *Crafts*, five Myfteriorum que ipfe feu aliquis eorum utentur five exercentur nifi talis ferviens aut Apprenticius fit filius fuus aut alit' quod pater vel mater talis Apprenticii five fervien' haberet ad tempus captionis talis Apprenticii, five fervien' terras tenementa feu alia hereditamenta clari annui valoris quadraginta folidorum de ftatu hereditario five libero tenemento, ad minus fore certificat' fub manibus & figillis trium Juftic' ad pacem Com' ubi humo' terr' tenementa feu hereditamenta jacent feu jacerent, Majori Ball' aut al' Capitali officiar' talis Civitat. five Vil. corporat. & fore irrotulat. inter recorda ibidem. Et ulterius inactitat. fuit authoritate

thoritate ejufdem Parliamenti quod omnes Indentur. conventiones promiffiones & barganiæ de aut pro habente captione five cuftod. alicujus Apprenticii alit' tunc impofteru. fiend. aut recipiend. quàm per ftatutam prædictum limitatur ordinatur & appunctuatur penitus vacue forent ad omnes intentiones & propofit. prout per eundem actum plenius liquit. Et idem *G.* ulterius dic. quod prædicta villa *G.* in Com. *S.* in narratione prædicta fuperius fpecificat' eft & tempore confectionis Indenture prædicte fuit antiqua Villa corporat' incorporat' per nomen Ballivorum Burgenf. & Comitat' vil (*&c.*) Et quod quidem *E. F.* & *G. H.* tempore confectionis ejufdem Indenture & captionis Apprenticii prædicti fuerunt Ballivi ejufdem Ville, *&c.* Et quod prædictus *R. J.* prædicto tempore confectionis Indenture prædicto ac captionis Apprenticii prædict' inhabitat & adhuc inhabitat infra prædictam villam Gippi' & adtunc & ibidem utebatur & exercebatur & adhuc utitur & exercet' Artem pannarii, Anglice *of a Linen-Draper*, in eadem villa. Et quod ipfe idem *G. P.* modo defendens fuit filius prædicti *G. P.* de, (*&c.*) prædicta in Narratione prædicta fuperius nominar' & Sufanne uxor' ejus & non filius prædicti *R. J.* Quodque non certificat' fuit fub manibus trium Juftic' pacis Ballivis five al' Capitali Officiar' Ville de Gippo prædicta quod pater vel mater prædicti *G. P.* modo defend' habuit terras tenementa feu al' hereditamenta Annui valoris quadraginta folidorum prout per Statut' prædictum limitatur. & ordinatur Sicque Indentur' prædict' hic in Cur' prolat' & in narratione prædicta fuperius fpecificat' Necnon omnes conventiones in eadem Indentur. content. in forma prædicta fact. vigore Statuti prædicti fuerunt, & funt penitus vacue in lege, & hoc

hoc parat. eſt verificare unde pet. Judicium ſi
prædictus *R.* actionem ſuam predictam verſus
eum habere debeat, *&c.*

Repl' ſſ.
That the Fa-
ther of the
Defendant
hath 10 *Acres*
of Land of the
yearly value of
40 s.

Et prædictus *R.* dic' quod ipſe per aliqua
preallegat' ab Actione ſua prædicta habend' pre-
cludi non debet, quia dic' quod prædictus *G. P.*
Pater Apprenticii tempore confectionis Indenture pred' habuit & ſeiſitus fuit in dominico
ſuo ut de feodo de & in decem acris terre tunc
pertin' in, (*&c.*) in Com' prædicto clari Annui
valoris quadragint' Solidorum ultra repriſ. fore
certificat' ſub manibus & ſigillis trium Juſtic'
ad pacem prædict' Com' ubi prædict' terre ut
prefertur jacent & jacebant præfat. tunc Ballivis Ville Gippi' prædicti & fore irrotulat' inter
recorda ibidem ſecundum formam, effectum &
veram intentionem Actus præd. per quod dicta
Indentura & omnes conventiones in eadem content' in ſuo robore, vigore & effectu remanent
& exiſtunt : Et hoc parat' eſt verificare, unde
petit Judicium & dampna ſua occaſione fractionis conventionis præd' ſibi adjudicari, *&c.*

Rejoin. ſſ.
* *That the*
Father of the
Defendant at
the time of the
making of the
ſaid Indenture
was not ſeized
in Fee in the
ſaid 10 *Acres*
of Land, prout,
&c.
† *To which*
the Plaintiff
demurred ſpe-
cially.
|| *Cauſes of the*
Demurrer.

* Et præd' *G. P.* dic' quod prædictus *G. P.*
Pater ipſius tempore confectionis Indenture prædicte non ſeiſitus fuit in dominico ſuo ut de
feodo de & in præd. decem acris terre cum pertin' modo & forma prout præd' *R.* ſuperius re-
plicando allegavit & de hoc pon' ſe ſuper pri-
am' *&c.*

† Et prædictus *R.* dic' quod præd' placitum
prædicti *G. P.* modo & forma præd. ſuperius rejungendo placitat' Ac materia in eodem content' minus ſufficiens in lege exiſtit ad ipſum *R.*
ab Actione ſua præd. verſus præfat' || *G. P.* modo
defend' habend' precludend' tam in hoc quod
præd. *G.* non manutenet materiam in placito ſuo
præd. in barram placitat' Sed ab eadem materia
deceſſit, quam pro deſcu' ſufficien' materie in eo-

dem

dem placito rejungendo placitat content' quodque ipfe ad placitum illud modo & forma præd.
rejungendo placitat' neceffe non habet nec per
legem terre tenetur refpondere, unde pro defectu
fufficien. placiti præd. *G.P.* modo defend' in hac
parte idem *R.* ut prius pet' Judicium & dampna
fua occafione Fractionis conventionis præd' fibi
adjudicari, &c.

Et præd. *G. P.* modo defend' ex quo ipfe fuf- *Joinder in*
ficien? materiam in lege ad præd. *R.* ab actione *Demurrer.*
fua prædicta verfus ipfum *G.* habend' precludend' fuperius rejungendo allegavit, quam ipfe
parat' eft verificare quam quidem materiam
præd. *R.* non dedicit, nec ad eam aliqualit' refpond' fed verificationem illam admittere omnino recufat pet' Judicium & quod præd. *R.* ab
actione fua præd. verfus ipfum habend' preclu-
datur, *&c.* Et quia Juftic' hic fe advifare vo-
lunt de & fuper premiffis priufquam Judicium
inde reddant dies dat' eft partibus præd. hic uf- *Dies datus*
que in Octabis Sancti Michaelis de audiend' in-
de Judicio fuo eo quod ijdem Juftic' hic inde
nondum, *&c.*

---

*A Declaration by an Apprentice againft
his Mafter, for turning him out of his
Service, &c. The Action laid at* Not-
tingham, *where the Indentures are
fuppofed to be made.*

Nott. ff. **G** B. queritur de *J. P.* in Cuftod.
. Marr. *&c.* de placito quod ten'
ei convention' int' ipfum *G.* & præfat. *J.* fact.
fecundum vim formam & effectum quarundam
Indentur. inde inter eos confect. *&c.* Et unde
idem

idem *G.* per *H. S.* & *M. M.* qui admiffi funt per Cur. Dom. Regis hic ad profequend. pro eodem *G.* infra ætat. exiften' ut prox' amici ipfius *G.* dic' quod Civitas *London'* eft & à tempore cujus contrar' memoriam homin. non exiftit, fuit antiqua civitas infra quam quidem civit. talis habetur & à toto tempore fupradicto talis habebatur conf. ufitat. & approbat. in eadem videlicet,(*&c. and fo fets forth the Cuftom of* London *to take Apprentices, as before is obferv'd.*) Et idem *G.* dic' quod præd. *J.* eft & continue per fpacium decem Annorum integrorum jam ult. elapf. & vicefimo fexto die Junii Anno Reg. Dom. Regis nunc tertio fuit civis & liber homo civit. præd. de Societate de les Haberdafhers *London* & per totum fpacium decem Annorum ufus fuit & adhuc utitur & exercet apud *London.* in Paroch. Sti. Martini infra Ludgate in Warda de Farringdon infra artem five myfter. de Haberdafher de Hats & Caps ; quodque idem *G.* præd. vicefimo fexto die Junii Anno tertio fupradicto fuit ætat. quatuordecim Annorum & amplius, & infra ætat. 21 Annorum viz. ætatis fexdecim Annorum ac quod idem *G.* nat. fuit in hoc Regno Angl. viz. apud. *N.* in Com. præd. quodque idem *G.* per nomen *G.* (&c.) per quandam Indentur. factam apud *N.* præd. vicefimo fexto die Junii Anno Regni dicti Dom. Regis nunc tertio fupradicto inter ipfum *G.* ex una parte & præd. *J.* ex altera parte cujus qidem Indentur. alteram partem figillo præd. *J.* figillat. idem *G.* hic in cur. profert cujus dat. eft eifdem die & Anno pofuiffet feipfum Apprentic. præd. *J.* per nomen, (&c.) ad artem ejus erudiend. & fecum more Apprenticii deferviend. à fefto Nativit. Sti. Joh. Bapt. tunc ult. præterit. ufque ad plenum finem & termin. novem Annorum plenar. complend. & finiend. duran. quo termin. dict. Appentic. præfat.

fat. Magiſtro ſuo deſerviret, ſecreta ſua cuſtodiret, præcepta ſua licita libenter ubiq; faceret, damp. eidem Magiſtro ſuo non faceret nec ab aliis fieri videret, ſed pro poſſe ſuo impediret aut ſtatim Magiſtro ſuo inde daret monitionem; bona ejuſdem Magiſtri ſui non devaſtaret nec ea alicui illicite accommodaret, Fornicationem non comitteret, Matrimonium infra eundem termin. non contraheret, ad cartas aleas tales aut aliqua al' joca illicita per quæ dictus Magiſter ſuus aliquod dampnum haberet non luderet, cum bonis ſuis propriis aut alienis duran. dicto tempore ſine licenc. dicti Magiſtri ſui non emet neque venderet, Tabernas non frequentaret, nec ſeipſum à ſervicio dicti Magiſtri ſui die aut nocte illicite abſentaret, ſed in omnibus tanquam fidel. Apprentic. ſeipſum erga dictum Magiſtrum ſuum & omhes alios gereret duran. dicto termino. Et præd. Magiſter eundem Apprentic. ſuum in eadem arte qua utebatur meliori modo quo potuiſſet doceret & inſtrueret cum debit. caſtigatione, inveniend. eidem Apprencic. ſuo eſculent. poculent. veſtit. lect. Anglice *Lodging*, & omnia neceſſar. ſecundum conſuetud. civit. præd. duran. dicto termino, & pro vera performatione omnium & ſingulorum dict. convention. & agreeament. alter partium dictarum ſe obligaſſet alteri per eandem Indentur. prout per eandem Indentur. inter alia plenius appaset & idem *G.* dic. quod licet ipſe bene & fideliter performavit & perimplevit omnes & ſingulas conventiones & conceſſiones in Indentur. præd. ſuperius ſpec. ex parte ſua in Indentur. præd. ſpec. performand. & perimplend. ſecundum formam & effectum Indentur. ill' proteſtandoq; quod præd. *J.* non performavit ſeu perimplevit aliquas convention' ſeu conceſſiones in eadem Indentura ſuperius ſpec' ex parte ſua performand. & perimplend'

fecundum formam & effectum ejufdem Identur.
In facto idem *G.* dic' quod ipfe virtute Indenturæ præd. apud *N.* præd. à Fefto die Nativitat'
Sti. Johannis Baptiftæ Anno quinto fuperdictis
ufq; decimum fextum diem Maii Anno Regni
dicti Domini Regis nunc quinto præfat. *J.* more
Apprenticii fui bene & fideliter confervavit &
defervivit, quodque præd. *J.* poft præd. eund.
diem Maii Anno feptimo fupradicto apud *N.*
prædict. ipfum *G.* à fervicio fuo abfque caufa
rationabili extrapofuit & expulfit, & ad ipfum
G. in fervicio fuo ulterius cuftodiend. duran.
refid' ejufdem Apprentic' & ad artem præd.
qua idem *J.* tunc utebatur ulterius docend. &
informand. adtunc & ibidem penitus recufavit &
non inveniebat eidem *G.* Apprentic. fuo præd.
efculent. poculent. veftit. lect. Anglice *Lodging,*
& omnia al' neceffar. duran. termino Apprenticialitat. fuæ præd. fecundum formam & effectum
conventionis fuæ præd. in ea parte in Indentur.
præd. mentionat' ficque præd. *J.* licet fæpius requifit' convention' præd. de eo quod præd. *J.*
eundem Apprenticium fuum in eadem arte qua
utebatur meliori modo quo potuiffet doceret &
inftrueret, & inveniret eidem Apprentic' fuo
efculent' poculent' veftit' lect' Anglice *Lodging,*
& omnia al' neceffar' fecundum conf. Civit. London' per totum dictum tempus Apprenticialitat'
præd. *G.* præd. in forma præd. eidem *G.* non
tenuit fed infregit & ill' ei hucufque tenere contradixit & adhuc contradic' unde dic' quod deteriorat' eft & dampnum habet ad valenc' 60 l.
& inde produc' fectam, &c.

Plea that the
Plaintiff left
his Service
without his
Licence; and
that he there-
upon

Et prædictus *J.* per *T. A.* (&c) Action. non
(&c.) quia dic' quod ipfe diu ante præd. tempus
quo fupponitur ipfum *G.* pofuiffe fe Apprentic'
præfat' *J.* necnon eodem tempore quo, &c. necnon continue extunc hucufq; fuit liber homo &
civis

civis Civit' London' præd. viz. artis five myfterii
de les Haberdafhers London' & arte five myfte-
rio de les Haberdafhers infra eandem Civit' &
non alibi per totum tempus præd. ufus fuit oc-
cupavit & exercuit quodque idem *J.* artem
five myfterium de les Haberdafhers Londo' prædicto tempore præd. pofitionis ipfius *G.* Apprenticii præfat' *J.* apud *L.* viz. in Paroch' (&c.)
uten' occupan' & exercen' idem *G.* præd. tempore quo, &c. tunc & ibidem pofuit fe Appren'
eidem *J.* ad artem ejus difcend' & erudiend' &
fecum more Apprentic' deferviend' pro præd.
termino *9* Annorum prout præd. *G.* fuperius
allegavit & idem *J.* ulterius dic' quod prædict.
G. à præd. tempore confectionis Indentur' præd.
ufque decimum quintum diem Maii Anno Reg.
Dom. Regis nunc quinto fupradicto apud Lond'
in Paroch' & Warda præd. eidem *J.* ut Apprentic' ipfius *J.* cum eodem *J.* commoravit &
habitavit quo quidem decimo quinto die Maii
Anno quinto fupradicto idem *G.* illicite & abfque licenc' & notic' ipfius *J.* apud London' in
Paroch' & Warda præd. deceffit & fe elongavit
& fe à fervicio ipfius *J.* à prædict. 25 die Maii
Anno quinto fupradicto ufque quintum diem
Julii tunc prox' fequen' abfque licenc' ipfius *J.*
abfentavit, quo quidem quinto die Julii Anno
quinto fupradicto idem *G.* apud London' præd.
in Paroch. & Warda præd. optulit fe eidem *J.*
ad eum extunc deferviend. ufque finem dicti
termini *9* Annorum, quodque ipfe idem *J.* ipfum
G. in fervitium fuum recipere recufavit prout
ei bene licuit abfque hoc quod ipfe idem *J.*
præd. decimo fexto die Maii Anno quinto fupradicto apud *N.* prædict. ipfum *G.* è fervicio
fuo extrapofuit feu expulfit prout præd. *G.* fuperius narrand' allegavit & hoc, &c. unde, &c.

Quer'

Quer' moratur in leg' & causa moration' in lege fuit pro eo quod præd. *J.* in barr' sua prædict. per traversiam suam deduc. diem & locum extrapositionis & expulsionis præd. *G.* à servicio suo in exitu ubi dies & locus per præd. *G.* allegat' non sunt traversibil.

See *T.* 7 *Jac.* 1. *rot.* 503. *Brownlow's Office.* Covenant brought by *J.* Apprentice against *V.* his Master, and Breach that he did not find his Apprentice Meat and Drink, *&c.*——— Barr, that he did find sufficient Meat, *&c.* to his Apprentice, until such time that he departed from his Service.

H. 14. *Jac.* 1. *rot.* 63. *Br.* Covenant brought by an Apprentice against his Master, and Breach that he did not instruct and inform him in his Art.

T. 19. *Jac.* 1. *rot.* 2862. *Br.* Covenant brought by an Apprentice against his Master. ——— Barr, that the Apprentice did depart his Service before the Term ended.

For receiving and detaining the Plain-
tiff's Apprentice, having left his Ma-
ster's Service.

Lond. ss. **A**B. queritur de *C. D.* in custodia Marr' &c. pro eo videl' quod cum præd. *C.* (tali die & Anno) apud London' &c. quendam *E. F.* adtunc & adhuc Apprentic' ipsius *A.* (tunc & ibidem existen' scien' eundem *E.* fore Apprentic' ipsius *A.*) à servicio ipsius *A.* illicite recepit & eundem *E.* extra & à servicio ipsius *A.* à præd'——— die ——— Anno
super-

fuperdicto ufque——— diem——— tunc prox'
fequen' cuftodivit & retinuit & adhuc cuftodit
& retinit contra voluntat' ipfius *A.* idemque *C.*
D. fcien' præfat' *E.* fore Apprentic' prædict' *A.*
eundem *E.* præfat' *A.* nondum deliberavit licet
ad hoc idem *C.*——— die——— Anno———
fuperdicto apud London' præd. in Paroch' &
Warda præd. per præd. *A.* requifit' fuiffet fed
præfat' *E.* eidem *A.* hucufque deliberare omnino
contradixit & adhuc contradic' per quod idem
A. non folum fervicium prædicti *E.* Apprenticii
fui per totum tempus præd. predidit verum etiam diverfa grandia Lucra commoda & proficua
quæ ipfe fervicium ipfius *E.* per idem tempus
habuiffe percepiffe & obtinuiffe potuiffet, fi præd.
C. D. præfat' *E.* à dicto fervicio præd. *A.* non
recepiffet, cuftodiviffet & retinuiffet, totaliter a-
mifit unde dic' quod deteriorat' eft & dampn-
num habet ad valenc' 50 l. & inde produc' Sectam, &c.

Aliter *for procuring the Plaintiff's Ap-*
prentice to leave his Service, and for
that the Defendant receiv'd and de-
tain'd him in his Service.

Lond. ff.   A B. queritur de *C. D.* in cuftodia
Marr' &c. pro eo videlicet quod
cum quidem *R. M.* (tali die & Anno) apud London' (&c.) exiftebat fervien' ejufdem *A.* & in
fervicio dicti *A.* tunc exercen' artem de les *Cloth-*
workers infra Civitat' London. præd. eidem *A.*
tanquam Apprentic' pro termino feptem Annorum extunc prox' fequen' in arte ill' deferviend'
fecundum conf. Civit' London. prædict. retent'
Bb 3   fuit

fuit idemque *R. M.* eo prætextu in servicio ill'
per spacium trium Annorum diligent' occupat'
& usitat' fuit per quod idem *A.* nonnullos la-
bores & expensas ad eundem *R. M.* in arte ill.
erudiend' diversimodo habuisset & expendidisset
prædictus tamen *C. D.* præmissorum non ignar'
machinan' præd. *A.* de servicio servien' sui præd.
ac de eo proficuo commodo & advantag' quæ
ipse idem *A.* ratione servicii servient' sui præd.
habere & percipere potuisset callide & subdole
decipere & defraudare (tali die & Anno) apud
London' præd. in Paroch' & Warda præd. prædict. *R. M.* adtunc servien' ejusdem *A.* a servicio præd. prædicti *A.* existen' recedere procuravit cujus prætextu postea scilicet (tali die &
Anno) apud *L.* præd. in Paroch' & Warda præd.
præd. *R. M.* à servicio ejusdem *A.* absque licenc'
& bona voluntat' ipsius *A.* Magistri sui recessit
idemq; *C. D.* (licet bene sciebat quod præd. *R.*
M. existebat servien' ejusdem *A.* per diversos
Annos adtunc ventur' deservitur' retent' scilicet
quod præd. *R. M.* adtunc à servicio ipsius *A.*
Magistri sui absque licentia & bona voluntat'
ipsius *A.* recessisset) nihilominus postea scilicet
(tali die & Anno) præd. apud London' præd. in
Paroch' & Warda præd. præfat' *R. M.* in servicium suum contra voluntat' præd. *A.* ad eidem
C. D. in servicio suo deserviend. procuravit &
retinuit per quod idem *A.* totum proficuum
commodum & easiament' quæ ipse ratione servicii servientis sui præd. per totum tempus præd.
perdidit & amisit unde dicit quod deteriorat.
est & dampnum habet ad valenc' 40 l. & inde
produc' Sectam, &c.

Hambleton verf. Veere, Trin' 21. *Car.* 2.
Rot. 1750.

'ACtion' *fur le Cafe le Plant. declare* q' *lou*
'un Henry Veere vicefimo nono Sept.
'Anno Regni Regis decimo fexto apud, &c. in
'Servicio (*del Plant'*) tanquam Apprenticius
'pro termino novem Annorum extunc prox.
'fequen. deferviend. in arte Laterarii, Anglice
'*a Bricklayer*, retent. fuit idemq; Henricus Veere
'eo pretextu in fervicio prædicto per fpatium
'quinq; Annor' diligenter occupat. & ufitat.
'fuit (*le dit Defend.*) præmiffor. non ignarus
'fed Machinan. *le Plant.* de fervicio fervientis
'præd. ac omni proficuo & commodo quæ ipfe
'ratione fervicii illius habere callide & fubdole
'decipere & defraudare ultimo die Octob. An-
'no Regni Regis nunc vicefimo primo apud,
'(&c.) prædictum Henricum Veere adtunc fer-
'vientem præd. Clementis (*le Plant'*) à præd.
'fervicio ipfius (*le Plant'*) recedere procuravit
'& abduxit prætextu cujus procurationis & ab-
'ductionis poftea fc. primo die Novembris, An-
'no, (&c.) apud, (&c.) præd. Henricus à fer-
'vicio præd. Clementis (*ff. le Plant.*) abfque
'licentia & contra voluntatem ipfius Clementis
'receffit per quod idem (*le Plant.*) totum pro-
'ficuum commodum & eafiamentum quæ rati-
'one fervitii fervientis præd. per totum refi-
'duum termini præd. ventur' recipere potuiffet
'totaliter perdidit & amifit *ad damnum del*
'*Plant.* 100 *l.* For which he brought this Action : And upon the general Iffue of Not Guilty
pleaded, a Verdict was found for the Plaintiff

at the Affizes in *Effex,* and Damages affefs'd generally with Coft of Suit. And now it was moved in Arreft of Judgment for the Defendant, that the Plaintiff had declared, and had a Ver- dict for more Damages than by his own fhew- ing he ought to recover, &c. 2 *Saund.* 170.

And Judgment was ftayed for the Uncertain- ty of the Damages.

See alfo the feveral Statutes of 7 H. 4. cap. 7. 11 H. 7. cap. 9. *or* 11. 19 H. 7. cap. 17. 7 H. 8. cap. 6. 5 Eliz. cap. 4. *concerning Apprentices in Cities, Burroughs, and* Towns *Corporate, where- in a fpecial Regard is had to the Cuftoms of the City of* London.

T H E

THE
COURT
OF
COMMON-COUNCIL.

HIS being the fupreme and legiflative Court of the City, is held in the Chamber of *Guild-Hall*, before the Lord-Mayor, Aldermen, and Common-Council-Men of the City of *London*, at fuch times as the Lord-Mayor fhall appoint and direct, it being in his Lordfhip's power to call and difmifs this Court at his Pleafure. It's faid to have Refemblance to the High-Court of *Parliament*, becaufe it confifts of two Houfes. And fee 3 *Leon.* 264. *per Fleetwood.* This Court confifts of the Mayor and Aldermen, and four Perfons chofen out of each Ward by the Commonalty : Thefe may make Ordinances, which they call *Acts of Common-Council*, which fhall bind every Citizen and Freeman. In this Court are made Laws for Advance of Trade, and for the better Government of the City.

Several Committees are annually appointed and elected by this Court for the better and more fpeedy Difpatch of the City Affairs, who
make

make Report to this Court of their Doings and Proceedings, as Occasion requires, *viz.*

1. A Committee of six Aldermen and twelve Commoners, for letting and demising the City's Lands and Tenements, who usually meet every *Wednesday* in the Afternoon at *Guild-Hall*, for that Purpose.

2. A Committee of four Aldermen and eight Commoners to let and dispose of the Lands and Tenements given by Sir *Thomas Gresham*, who usually meet at *Mercer's-Hall*, at such times as the Lord-Mayor for the time being directs and appoints : It being the Custom to elect the Lord-Mayor one of this Committee.

3. This Court doth also annually elect Commissioners for the Sewers and Pavements.

4. This Court doth also annually elect a Governour, Deputy-Governour and Assistants, for Management of the City's Lands in *Ulster* in *Ireland*, pursuant to the King's Charter, which it's said is as followeth, *viz.*

'WE will also, and by these Presents for
' Us, our Heirs and Successors, do
' Grant, Constitute, and Ordain, That the a-
' foresaid Society of the Governour and Assist-
' ants of *London*, of the New Plantation in *Ulster*,
' within the Realm of *Ireland*, for ever hereaf-
' ter shall be Yearly elected and appointed by
' the Mayor, Aldermen, and Commonalty of
' the said City of *London*, at the first Common-
' Council to be holden in the same City of
' *London*, next after the Feast of the Purifica-
' tion of the blessed Virgin *Mary* ; at which
' time the Deputy of the Governour, and twelve
' of the same Persons which have been Assist-
' ants for the Year precedent, shall be removed
' from their Office, and one other Deputy and
' twelve

' twelve other Affiftants fhall be of new named,
' fupplied, and appointed into the Places of the
' fame Deputy and Affiftants, fo as aforefaid to
' be removed, for the Help of the Governour
' and Affiftants not removed, for One Year next
' following : And that at the End of that Year
' then next following, fuch former Affiftants which
' continued in the fame Office in that Year
' then preceding, fhall be then likewife remo-
' ved, and others fhall be likewife of new na-
' med, fupplied, elected, and appointed into
' their Places ; and fo by an interchangeable
' Courfe, fo that twelve of the fame Affiftants
' fhall be, and continue in their Places, during
' the Term of two Years.

' And further, We Will, Ordain, and Con-
' ftitute for Us, our Heirs, and Succeffors, That
' at a Common-Council in the aforefaid City of
' *London*, next after the Feaft of the Purification
' of the bleffed Virgin *Mary*, next after the
' Date of thefe Prefents, the Nomination and
' Election of the aforefaid Governour, Deputy,
' and Affiftants be, and fhall be made in Form
' aforefaid, and fo from thenceforth Yearly from
' time to time for ever.

Note, A Stranger born may be made Free of
this City by Order of this Court, and not o-
therwife.

The feveral Places of Common-Serjeant,
Town-Clerk, and Common-Crier, are in the
Gift of this Court.

The Judges of the Sheriffs Courts have fometimes been elected by this Court, and fome
times by the Court of Aldermen.

Note, After the Death of *J. White*, late Clerk
of the Court of Requefts, commonly called the
Court of Confcience in *London*, this Court did elect and
chufe

chufe Maj. *Gunftone* in his ftead ; but Mr. *White*
was elected by the Court of Aldermen : And
always before and fince Maj. *Gunftone*'s Election,
the Court of Aldermen have elected the refpective Clerks of that Court. And it hath been
declared by Council Learned in the Law, That
the Right of electing the Clerk of the Court of
Requefts is not in this Court. *Quære.*

The Court of Aldermen.

THis feems to be divided into two Courts,
viz. the Inner and Outer : The former is
a Court of Record, and held in the Inner Chamber of *Guild-hall* every *Tuefday* and *Thurfday*, except Holy-Days, and in the Time of Seffions of
Goal-Delivery.

All Matters touching Lights, Water-courfes,
and Party-walls may be determined in this
Court. *See the Cafe of* Arnot *and* Brown
infra.

The Affize of Bread is conftantly appointed
by this Court.

All Bonds and Leafes that pafs under the
City Seal, muft be fealed in this Court.

Several Places are in the Gift of the Lord-
Mayor and this Court, *viz.*

The Recorder.
Sword-Bearer.
Four City-Council.
City-Remembrancer.
Common-Hunt.
Water-Bailiff.
City-Solicitor.

Compt-

Comptroller of the Chamber.
Two Secondaries.
Four Attorneys of the Lord-Mayor's Court.
Clerk of the Chamber.
Hall-Keeper.
Three Serjeant-Carvers.
Three Serjeants of the Chamber.
Serjeant of the Channel.
Yeomen of the Chamber.
Four Yeomen of the Water-fide. ?
Yeomen of the Channel.
Under Water-Bailiff.
Meal-weighers.
Clerk of the City's Works.
Six Young-men.
Two Clerks of the Papers.
Eight Attorneys in the Sheriffs Court.
Eight Clerk-Sitters.
Two Prothonotaries.
Clerk of the Bridge-Houfe.
Clerk of the Court of Requefts.
Beadle of the Court of Requefts.
Thirty fix Serjeants at Mace.
Thirty fix Yeomen.
The Gauger.
The Sealers and Searchers of Leather.
Keeper of the Green-yard.
Two Keepers of the Compters.
Keeper of *Newgate.*
Keeper of *Ludgate.*
Meafurer.
Steward of *Southwark.*
Bailiff of *Southwark.*
Bailiff of the Hundred of *Offulfton.*
City Carpenter, and other Artificers.
The Rent-Gatherer hath been put in by Mr.
    Chamberlain.

The Cafe of Arnot *and* Brown, *Mich.* 7 Will. *in* B.
R. *was thus.* *They were Owners of two conti-*
guous Houfes in London, *and* Brown *having*
Lights in his Houfe towards Arnot's *Yard,* Ar-
not *made up Blinds with Boards,* &c. *The*
Court of Aldermen, upon the Stat. 19 Car. 2
c. 3. *ordered, they fhould be pull'd down. But a*
Prohibition was granted in B. R. *For whatever*
Note. *they may do in their Inner-Court by* Quod Permit-
tat, *where* they have Power *to determine real*
Aétions, yet 'tis plain the Court of Aldermen have
no Power in this fummary Way, unlefs by 19 Car.
2. c. 3. *And that gave 'em only a temporary*
Power, viz. *during the rebuilding of the City.*
Alfo, while the City was rebuilding, they had
Power to affign Lights, but being once affign'd, the
Party gain'd a legalTitle to'em,and may maintain
an Aétion for the Obftruétion, and the faid Court
of Aldermen have no further Power.

Ward-

Wardmote Courts.

Wardmote is as much as *Folkſmote* among the *Saxons*, or *Plebiſcitum* among the *Romans*, and is defined to be an Aſſembly of the whole People (*i. e.* Free Citizens) of one Ward duly ſummoned by the Lord Mayor, (the Alderman of the Ward, as Head of the Aſſembly, or his Deputy being preſent) in order to correct Defects and Diſorders, remove Annoyances, and promote the common Intereſt and Commodity of the ſaid Ward.

Theſe Wardmote Courts are like the Leet Courts in the County ; for as thoſe were derived out of the County Court, ſo theſe were derived out of the Lord Mayor's Court, which is a Court of Record, and erected for the better Government of the City; and the Aldermen of every Ward had an antient right to hold Leets there.

Note, The *Lord Mayor* doth annually iſſue out his Precept to the Aldermen of every Ward, to hold his Wardmote for the Election of Common-Council-Men, and other Officers. The Tenor of which Precept is to the effect following.

To

To Sir R. C. *Knt. Alderman of the*
    Ward of, &c.

Wardmote. ‘ WE charge and command you, that up-
‘   on St. *Thomas's* Day, the Apoſtle, next
‘ coming, you do hold your Wardmote, and
‘ that you have afore us at our General Court
‘ of Aldermen to be holden the *Tueſday* next
‘ coming, all the Defaults that ſhall be pre-
‘ ſented afore you by Inqueſt in the ſaid Ward-
Inqueſt for ‘ mote ; and the ſaid Inqueſt ſhall have full
the Year. ‘ Power and Authority by one whole Year, to
‘ enquire and preſent all ſuch Defaults as ſhall
‘ be found within your ſaid Ward, as often-
‘ times as ſhall be thought to you expedient
‘ and needful, which we will ſhall be once eve-
‘ ry Month at the leaſt.’

Inqueſt dying.   2. ‘ And if it happen any of your ſaid In-
‘ queſt to die, or depart out of your ſaid Ward
‘ within the ſaid Year, that then, in place of
‘ him, or them ſo dying or departing out of
‘ your ſaid Ward, you cauſe to be choſen one
‘ able Perſon in his ſtead, to enquire and pre-
‘ ſent with the others in manner and form
‘ abovefaid.’

Non-appear-   3. ‘ And that, at the ſaid general Court,
ance. ‘ you give afore us the Names and Sirnames of
‘ all them of your ſaid Ward that come not
‘ to your ſaid Wardmote, if they be duly
‘ warned, ſo that due Redreſs and Puniſhment
‘ of them may be had, as the Caſe ſhall require,
‘ according to the Law.’

Watch, Light,   4. ‘ And that you do provide, that at all
Vizard. ‘ times convenient, a ſufficient Watch be kept :
‘ And that Lanthorns with Lights, *&c.* by night,
‘ in old manner accuſtomed, be hanged forth :
Quære. ‘ And that no Man go by night without
    ‘ Light,

' Light, nor with Vizard, on the Peril that be-
' longeth thereto.'

5. ' And alfo that you do caufe to be chofen *Common-*
' .... Men, of the moft fufficient, honeft, and *Council*
' difcreet Men of your faid Ward, to be for
' your faid Ward of the Common-Council of this
' City for the Year enfuing, according to the
' Cuftom in that Behalf yearly ufed. And al-
' fo, that you do caufe the faid Men fo to be
' chofen to be of the Common-Council, to be
' fworn before you, and in your prefence, ac-
' cording to the Oaths and Declarations by
' them for this purpofe ufed and accuftomed.'

6. ' And that alfo in the faid Wardmote, *Conftables,*
' you caufe to be chofen certain other honeft *Scavengers,*
' Perfons to be Conftables and Scavengers, and *Beadle, Rakers*
' a common Beadle, and a Raker to make clean
' the Streets and Lanes of all your faid Ward,
' according to the Cuftom yearly ufed in that
' behalf: Which Conftables have, and fhall
' have full Power and Authority to diftrain
' for the Salary and Quarterage of the faid
' Beadle and Raker, as oftentimes as it fhall be
' behind or unpaid.'

7. ' Alfo that you keep a Roll of the Names, *Roll of Names*
' Sirnames, Dwelling-places, Profeffions, and
' Trades of all Perfons dwelling within your
' Ward, and within what Conftable's Precinct
' they dwell ; wherein the Place is to be fpeci-
' ally noted by Street, Lane, Alley, or Sign.

8. ' Alfo that you caufe every Conftable from *Conftables*
' time to time, to certify unto you the Name,
' Sirname, Dwelling-place, Profeffion and Trade
' of every Perfon who fhall newly come to
' dwell within his Precinct, whereby you may
' make and keep your Roll perfect : And that *Roll*
' you caufe every Conftable for his Precinct, to

C c   ' that

' that purpose, to make and keep a perfect Roll
' in like manner.'

Innholder.
Lodger.
Sojourner.

9. ' Also that you give special Charge, that
' every Inn-holder, and other Person within
' your Ward, who shall receive any Person to
' lodge or sojourn in his House above twoDays,
' shall, before the third Day after his coming
' thither, give knowledge to the Constable of
' the Precinct, where he shall be so received,
' of the Name, Sirname, Dwelling-place, Pro-
' fession and Trade of Life, or Place of Ser-
' vice of such Person, and for what cause he
' shall come to reside there : And that the said
' Constable give present notice thereof to you.

Suspected Per-
sons.

' And that the said Inn-holder lodge no sus-
' pected Person, or Men or Women of evil
' Name.'

Constables
Search.

10. ' Also that you cause every Constable
' within his Precinct, once every Month at the
' furthest, and oftner, if need require, to make
' diligent search and inquiry, what Persons be
' newly come into his Precinct to dwell, sojourn
' or lodge : And that you give special charge,
' that no Inn-holder or Person shall resist or
' deny any Constable in making such Search or
' Inquiry, but shall do his best Endeavour to
' aid and assist him therein.'

11. ' And for that of late, there is more re-
' sort to the City of Persons evil-affected in
' Religion and otherwise, than in former times
' hath been ; you shall diligently inquire if any
' Man be received to dwell or abide within

Frank-pledge.

' your Ward, that is not put under Frank-
' pledge, as he ought to be by the Custom of
' the City : And whether any Person hath con-
' tinued in the said Ward by the space of one
' Year, being above the Age of twelve Years,
' and not sworn to be faithful and loyal to the

King's

' King's Majesty, in such sort as by the Law
' and Custom of this City he ought to be.'

12. ' To all these Purposes the Beadle of *Beadle.*
' every Ward shall employ his Diligence, and
' give his best Furtherance.'

13. ' Also you are to take order, that there *Stocks, &c.*
' be provided and set up a Pair of Stocks and a
' Whipping-Post in some convenient Place in
' every Parish within your Ward, for the pu-
' nishing of Vagrants and other Offenders.'

14. ' Also that you have special regard that *Fire.*
' from time to time there be convenient Provi-
' sion for Hooks, Ladders, Buckets, Spouts,
' and Engines, in meet Places within the several
' Parishes of your Ward, for avoiding the Peril
' of Fire.'

15. ' Also that the Streets and Lanes of this *Streets.*
' City be from time to time kept clean before
' every Church, House, Shop, Ware-house,
' Door, Dead-wall, and in all other common
' Passages and Streets of the said Ward.'

16. ' And where by divers Acts of Com-
' mon-Council, aforetime made and established
' for the Common-weal of this City, among
' other things, it is ordained and enacted, as
' hereafter ensueth :

' Also it is ordained and enacted, That from *Hucksters of*
' henceforth no Huckster of Ale or Beer be *Ale and Beer.*
' within any Ward of the City of *London*, but
' honest Persons, and of good Name and Fame,
' and so taken and admitted by the Alderman
' of the Ward for the time being ; and that the
' same Hucksters do find sufficient Surety afore
' the Mayor and Aldermen for the time being,
' to be of good guiding and rule : And that
' the same Hucksters shall keep no Bawdry,
' nor suffer no Lechery, Dice-playing, Carding,
' or any other unlawful Games to be done,

' ex-

' exercifed or ufed within their Houfes: And
' to fhut in their Doors' at nine of the clock
' in the Night, from *Michaelmas* to *Eafter*, and
' from *Eafter* to *Michaelmas*, at ten of the clock
' in the Night, and after that Hour fell no Ale
' or Beer. And if any Huckfter of Beer or
' Ale, after this Act publifhed and proclaimed,
' fell any Ale or Beer within any Ward of the
' City of *London*, and be not admitted by the
' Alderman of the fame Ward fo to do, or find
' not fufficient Surety, as it is above rehearfed,
' the fame Huckfter to have Imprifonment, and
' make Fine and Ranfom for his Contempt,
' after the Difcretion of the Lord Mayor and
' Aldermen: And alfo that the faid Huckfters
' fuffer no manner of common Eating and
' Drinking within their Cellars or Vaults, con-
' trary to the Ordinance thereof ordained and
' provided, as in the faid Act more plainly ap-
' peareth at large. We charge you that you
' put the fame in due execution accordingly.'

Meafures
fealed.

   17. ' And alfo that you fee all Tiplers, and
' other Sellers of Ale or Beer, as well privy
' Ofteries, as Brewers and Inn-holders, within
' your Ward, not felling by lawful Meafures
' fealed and marked with the City Arms or
' Dagger, be prefented, and their Names in your
' faid Indentures be expreffed, with their De-
' faults, fo that the Chamberlain may be law-
' fully anfwered of their Amercements.

Strangers
born.

   18. ' And alfo that you fuffer no Alien, or
' Son of any born an Alien, to be of the Com-
' mon-Council, nor to exercife or ufe any other
' Office within this City, nor receive or ac-
' cept any Perfon into your Watch, privy or
' open, but *Englifhmen* born: And if any Stran-
' ger born out of this Realm, made Denizen
' by Letters Patents, or any other after his
                        ' Courfe

‘ Courfe or Lot be appointed to any Watch,
‘ that then ye command and compel him or
‘ them to find in his Stead and Place, an *Eng-*
‘ *lifhman* to fupply the fame.

19. ‘ And alfo that you caufe an Abftract of
‘ the Affize appointed by Act of Parliament for
‘ Billets and other Fire-wood, to be fair writ-
‘ ten in Parchment, and to be fixed or hanged
‘ up in a Table, in fome fit and convenient
‘ Place in the Parifh within your Ward, where
‘ the common People may beft fee the fame.

20. ‘ And furthermore, we charge and com- *Streets.*
‘ mand you, that you caufe fuch Provifion to *Pain* 40 s.
‘ be had in your faid Ward, that all the Streets
‘ and Lanes within the faid Ward, be from
‘ time to time cleanfed and clearly voided of
‘ Ordure, Dung, Mire, Rubbifh, and other
‘ filthy Things whatfoever be to the Annoy-
‘ ance of the King’s Majefty’s Subjects.

21. ‘ And alfo, that at all times as you fhall *Vagrants.*
‘ think neceffary, you do caufe Search to be
‘ made within your faid Ward for all Vagrant
‘ Beggars, fufpicious and idle People, and fuch
‘ as cannot fhew how to live, and fuch as fhall
‘ be found within your faid Ward, that you caufe
‘ to be punifhed, and dealt with according to
‘ the Laws and Statutes in fuch Cafe ordained
‘ and provided.

22. ‘ And alfo we Will and Charge you the *Jurymen.*
‘ faid Aldermen, that your felf certify and pre-
‘ fent before us at the faid general Court, to be
‘ holden the aforefaid *Munday* next after the
‘ Feaft of the *Epiphany*, all the Names and Sir-
‘ names truly written of fuch Perfons within
‘ your faid Ward, as be able to pafs in a Grand
‘ Jury by themfelves: And alfo all the Names and
‘ Sir-names truly written of fuch Perfons being
‘ and dwelling within your faid Ward, as be

‘ able

'able to pafs in-a Petty Jury by themfelves:
'That is to fay, Every Grand Juryman to be
'worth in Goods an hundred Marks, and every
'Petty-Juryman forty Marks, according to an
'Act in that Cafe ordained and provided: And
'the fame you fhall indorfe on the Backfide of
'your Indenture.

Harlots.

23. 'Item, For divers reafonable and urgent
'Confiderations us efpecially moving, we
'ftraitly charge and command you on the
'King our Sovereign Lord's Behalf, That you
'diligently provide and forefee, that no man-
'ner of Perfon or Perfons within your faid
'Ward, what Condition or Degree foever he
'or they be of, keeping any Tavern or Ale-
'houfe, Ale-cellar, or any other Victualling-
'houfe, or Place of common Refort to eat or
'drink in within the fame Ward, permit or
'fuffer at any time hereafter any common Wo-
'men of their Bodies, or Harlots, to refort and
'come into their faid Houfe, or other the Pla-
'ces aforefaid, to eat or drink, or otherwife
'to be converfant or abide, or thither to haunt
'or frequent, upon pain of Imprifonment, as
'well of the Tenant and Keeper of every fuch
'Houfe or Houfes, and all other the Places a-
'fore remembred, as of the common Women
'or Harlots.

Articles.

24. 'Alfo that you do give in Charge to the
'Wardmote Inqueft of your Ward, all the Ar-
'ticles delivered to you herewith, and that
'you have a fpecial Care of keeping the Peace
'and good Order during your Wardmote; and
'if any offend herein, you fine or punifh him
'or them according to Law.

25. 'And whereas the Moneys received for
'the Fines of Perfons refufing to hold Ward-
'Offices within your Ward, ought to be employed

ployed in the Service, and for the publick Be-
‘ nefit of the whole Ward, and not of any par-
‘ ticular Precinct or Parish within the Ward :
‘ Thefe are therefore to require you to take
‘ Care, that all fuch Fines be from time to time
‘ difpofed of accordingly for the Benefit of the
‘ whole Ward, as you with the Deputy and
‘ Common-Council-Men of your Ward fhall
‘ think moft fitting and convenient ; and that
‘ no fuch Fines be received or employed in any
‘ particular Precinct or Parifh : not failing here-
‘ of, as ye tender the common Weal of this
‘ City, and Advancement of good Juftice, and
‘ as you will anfwer the contrary at your ut-
‘ termoft Peril. Dated at ... *&c.* under the
‘ Seal-Office of Mayoralty of the faid City,
‘ the .... Day of .... *&c.*

In a Cafe between the King and *Sellars, Sellars* was indicted at the Seffions in *London,* for
not attending at the Wardmote Inqueft, being
chofen of the Jury for fuch a Year.

To this Indictment he pleaded the King’s
Grant to the Company of Cooks, of which he
was a Member ; by which Grant that Company
is exempted from being put or fummoned upon
a Jury or Inqueft, before the Mayor or Sheriffs,
or Coroner of *London ;* and upon Demand, it
was a Queftion, Whether the Cooks are difcharged by that Grant, from their Attendance
at the faid Wardmote Inqueft ? It was argued,
that they are not difcharged, for the Words of
this Grant do not extend to that Cafe ; for the
Cooks are thereby difcharged only before the
Mayor, Sheriffs or Coroners, *&c.* but the Court
of Wardmote is held before neither, for it is
held before the Alderman of the Ward, and the
Words of the Grant ought to be taken ftrictly,

Cc 4   *viz.*

viz. that Cooks fhall be exempted, if there be other fufficient Men to ferve in the Ward befides ; and if this does not appear, the Grant is void : but this is not alledged.

To the firft Exception it was faid, that the Wardmote Inqueft was held before the Mayor ; for the Jury there are not to try any Matter, but only to make Prefentments, which are carried before the Mayor.

Exceptions were taken againft the Indictment, which was for not ferving at a Wardmote Inqueft for fuch a Year.

1. Becaufe it's a thing not known at the Common Law, that a Man fhould be of a Jury for a whole Year.

2. The Indictment faith, the Defendant was Inhabitant of fuch a Place, and elected a Juryman.

But faith not, that he ought to hold the Office to which he was elected. It was quafh'd, 3 *Mod. Rep.* 167. 168.

THE

THE
COURT
OF
Confervacy for the River THAMES.

THIS Court is held before the Lord Mayor, at fuch times as he fhall appoint and direct, within the refpective Counties near adjacent to the Cities of *London* and *Weftminfter*, and adjoining to the River *Thames*.

The Water-Bayliff is the Lord Mayor's Deputy, and ought to give notice to his Lordfhip of all Offences committed by any Perfons contrary to the Orders made for Prefervation of the Brood and Fry of Fifh in the faid River.

The Title of the Lord Mayor of the City of London, *to and for the Confervacy of the River of* Thames, *may be collected from what follows.*

INprimis, The Mayor of the faid City for the time being, and all other his Predeceffors, Governours of the fame City, time out of Mind have had and exercifed the Rule of the Confervacy of the River of *Thames*, and the Corre-

&ion and Punishment of all manner of Fisher-
men, and all other Persons offending within the
said River.

Item, King *Edward* the Third by his Charter
hath granted, That the Citizens of *London* shall
remove and take away all Kidels in the Water of
the Rivers of *Thames* and *Medway*, and shall
have the Punishment to the King belonging
thereof coming.

Item, By the Statute made in the Seventeenth
Year of the Reign of King *Richard* the Second,
it is ordained, That the Mayor of *London* for
the time being, shall have the Conservacy of
the *Thames*, and put in Execution the Statute
of 13 *Edw.* 1. and 13 *Rich.* 2. from the Bridge
of *Stanes* to *London*, and from thence over the
same Water, and in the Water of *Medway*.

Item, By a Statute made 4 *H.* 7. 15. The
Mayor of *London*, and his Successors, shall have
the like Conservation and Authority in all the
Issues, Breaches, and Ground overflown, as far
as the Water Ebbeth and Floweth, grown out
of the River of *Thames*, (as touching the Punishment for using unlawful Nets and Engines),
as he hath within the same River.

Item, King *James* by his Charter to the City,
dated the 20th of *August*, in the third Year of
his Reign, takes notice of the Lord Mayor's
Right to the Office of Bailiff, and Conservation of the River of *Thames*, in these Words, or
to this Effect :

Charta

Charta Jacobi *Regis conceſſa Civibus*
Londini *de Conſervatione Rivi* Tha-
meſis, *inter alia geren' Dat' vice-*
ſimo die Auguſti, *Anno Regni ſui*
Tertio.

‘ J *A M E S,* by the Grace of God, of *Eng-*
‘ *land, Scotland, France,* and *Ireland,* King,
‘ Defender of the Faith, *&c.* To all to whom
‘ our preſent LettersPatents ſhall come, Greeting.
‘ Whereas our Beloved in Chriſtian part, the
‘ Mayor and Commonalty, and Citizens of our
‘ City of *London,* time out of Memory of Man,
‘ have had, exerciſed, and ought and have ac-
‘ cuſtomed to have, and exerciſe the Office of
‘ Bailiff and Conſervation of the Water of
‘ *Thames,* to be exerciſed and occupied by the
‘ Mayor of the ſame City for the time being,
‘ during the time of his Mayoralty, or by his
‘ ſufficient Deputies, in and upon and about
‘ the Water of *Thames :* That is to ſay, from
‘ the Bridge of the Town of *Stanes* in the
‘ County of *Middleſex,* and towards the Weſt
‘ unto *London-Bridge,* and from thence to a cer-
‘ tain Place called *Yendal,* otherwiſe *Yenland,*
‘ otherwiſe *Yenleet,* towards the Sea, and Eaſt
‘ in *Medway,* and in the part of the City of
‘ *London* aforeſaid ; and upon whatſoever Bank,
‘ and upon every Shoar, and every Wharf of
‘ the ſame Water of *Thames* within the Li-
‘ mits and Bounds aforeſaid : And in, upon,
‘ and about all and every of them. And alſo
‘ for the time aforeſaid, have had and taken,
‘ and ought and have accuſtomed to have and
‘ take to their own proper Uſe, by the Mayor
‘ of the aforeſaid City for the time being, du-
‘ ring

' ring the time of his Mayoralty, or his suffi-
' cient Deputies, all Wages, Regards, Fees and
' Profits appertaining and belonging to the same
' Office of a Bailiff : We therefore, to
' the intent that the said Mayor and Com-
' monalty and Citizens may more securely,
' freely, and quietly use, have, exercise, and en-
' joy the Office aforesaid, and the Fees, Wages,
' Regards, and Profits thereunto belonging,
' to them and their Successors for ever, of our
' special Grace, and certain Knowledge, and
' meer Motion, have granted, and by these
' Presents for Us, our Heirs and Successors, do
' grant to the foresaid Mayor and Commonalty
' and Citizens, and their Successors, That
' they the aforesaid Mayor and Commonalty
' and Citizens, and their Successors, may exer-
' cise and execute the aforesaid Office of Bailiff
' and Conservation of the Water of *Thames* by
' the Mayor of the said City for the time be-
' ing, during the Time of his Mayoralty, or
' his sufficient Deputies, from time to time for
' ever, in, upon, or about the same Water of
' *Thames* : That is to say, from the aforesaid
' Bridge of *Staines*, in the County of *Middlesex*
' towards the West, to the Bridge of *London*,
' and from thence to a certain Place called
' *Yendal*, otherwise *Yenland*, otherwise *Yenleet*,
' towards the Sea and East and in *Medway*, and
' in the Port of the City of *London* aforesaid,
' and upon whatsoever Bank, and whatsoever
' Shear, and whatsoever Wharf of the same
' Water of *Thames*, within the Limits and
' Bounds aforesaid, in, upon, and about every
' one of the same, and to have, receive, collect,
' and enjoy all and singular Wages, Regards,
' Fees, and Profits to the same Office of Bailiff
' pertaining and belonging, to the proper Use of
' the

' the fame Mayor and Commonalty and Citi-
' zens, by the Mayor of the City aforefaid for
' the time being, during the time of his Mayor-
' alty, or by his fufficient Deputies, without
' the Hindrance of Us, our Heirs or Succef-
' fors, or any of our Officers, Bailiffs, or Mi-
' nifters, or of our Heirs or Succeffors, or our
' Admiral of *England,* or of our Succeffors, or
' any others of our Subjects, or of our Heirs
' or Succeffors whatfoever, or of any Grant by
' Us, our Heirs or Succeffors to be made to
' the contrary; To have, hold, and enjoy the
' aforefaid Office, and all and fingular the Pre-
' miffes, with all and fingular Wages, Regards,
' Fees, Profits, and Appurtenances what-
' foever, to the faid Office belonging or apper-
' taining, to the aforefaid Mayor and Common-
' alty and Citizens, and their Succeffors for ever,
' by the Mayor of the aforefaid City for the
' time being, during the time of his Mayoralty,
' or by his fufficient Deputies to be exercifed
' and executed without any Accompt, or any
' thing to be rendred or made thereof to Us,
' our Heirs, or Succeffors, fo as no other Bai-
' liff or Confervator of the aforefaid Water,
' fhall be, or fhall in any wife intermeddle in
' the Premiffes.'

Note, That by *Stat.* 27 *H.* 8. 18. If any Perfon do, or procure any thing to be done to the
annoying of the *Thames,* making of Shelves
there by Mining, Digging, cafting of Dung,
Rubbifh, or other thing therein, or otherwife
howfoever, or convey away any Boards, Stakes,
Timber-work, Pillars, or other things, from
Banks or Walls thereof, except it be to repair
them; or undermine any Banks, or Wall there,
to the Damage of the faid River; he fhall for-
' feit

feit for every fuch Offence 5 *l.* to the King, and
the Mayor and Commonalty of *London,* to be
recovered by the faid Mayor and Commonalty.

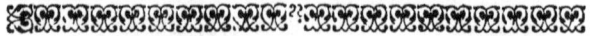

Anno 1630.

*Here follow feveral Orders devifed and
agreed upon by the Right Honourable
Sir* Robert Ducie, *Knight and Baro-
net, Lord Mayor of the City of* London,
and Confervator of the River Thames,
and Waters of Medway, *for the Prefervation of the Brood and Fry of Fifh
within the Weft Part of the faid
River.*

'Irft, That no Man, upon Penalty and
'   Forfeiture of his Net and Ten Pounds,
' with Imprifonment at the Difcretion of the
' Lord Mayor, fhall prefume to fhoot any
' Draw-net or Coulter-net, at any Time of the
' Year, before Sun-rifing, nor after Sun-fetting;
' (for that in the Night-time unlawful Nets
' be ufed, and other Abufes offered, to the
' great Hurt and Annoyance of the faid River
' of *Thames*) and to fhoot in their feveral
' Rooms well known.
'   2. *Item,* ' That no Fifherman or other fhall
' ftill, lie, or bend over any Net during the
' time of the Flood, whereby both Salmons and
' other kinds of Fifh may be hindred, and kept
' back from fwimming upwards, to the Benefit
' and Profit of fuch Fifher-men as dwell in the
' Weft part of the faid River, upon the like
' Pain and Penalty.
'   3. *Item,* ' That no Fifher-man or other fhall
' fhoot any Draw-net, Cod-net, or other Net
                                              or

' or Engine, whereby any Salmon-fish shall be
' taken after *Holyrood* Day is past, being the
' Fourteenth Day of *September* ; because at that
' time they are out of Season, and remain here
' upon the River only to Spawn and Breed, up-
' on the like Payment.

4. *Item,* ' That no Fisher-man or other shall
' fish with any Net, or lay or hale any Weel, or
' use any other Net or Engine whatsoever, from
' Sun-setting on Saturday at Night, until Sun-
' rising upon Monday Morning, no, not during
' all the time of *Lent,* as being a thing not only
' very hurtful to the said River, but also a great
' Abuse and Profaning of the Lord's Sabbath ;
' upon the like Payment.

5. *Item,* ' That no Fisher-man or other shall
' at any time hereafter ship their Draw-nets
' (called Shipping a-stern) into their Boats, be-
' fore such time as they have laid forth all their
' whole Net, as they do when they land to-
' wards a low Water, nor that they ship some
' part of their said Net, and land the rest ; but
' that from henceforth they shall fulfil and ob-
' serve that ancient Order of landing their
' Nets (as they have heretofore usually done)
' at low Water ; upon the like Payment.

6. ' *Item,* That no Fisher-man or other Per-
' son whatsoever shall use any Spear, called an
' Eel-spear, at any Time of the Year, for that
' they are likewise very great Destroyers of Bar-
' bels, and other kinds of Fish ; nor shall work
' with any Bley-net, Rugge-net, or Smelt-net,
' upon the said Water westward, farther than
' *Isleworth* Church, from the tenth Day of *March*
' yearly, until *Holyrood* Day be past, being the
' fourteenth Day of *September* ; upon the like
' Payment.'

7. *Item,*

7. *Item,* 'That no Fisher-man or other shall
' at any time of the Year use or exercise any
' Flue, Trammel, Doublewalled-Net or Hoop-
' ed-Net whatsoever; for that they are not
' only the utter Destruction of all breeding Bar-
' bels, but also a great Spoil and Hurt to other
' forts of the young Brood and Fry of Fish, be-
' ing with those kind of Nets infinitely de-
' ftroy'd, to the general Ruin of the River a-
' forefaid; upon the like Payment.'

8. *Item,* ' That no Fisher-man or other shall
' lay any Weels called Kills in any place of the
' River, from the tenth of *March,* till the tenth
' of *May* yearly, for that all Roaches do then
' fhed their Spawn; nor that no Man what-
' foever cut any Bull-Rushes, or other Flags
' or Sedges growing upon the River, from
' *Richmond* unto the *Markftone* above *Stanef-*
' *Bridge,* for that they are a great Succour and
' Safeguard unto the Fish; upon the like Pay-
' ment.'

9. *Item,* ' That no Fisher-man or other shall
' ufe within the faid River of *Thames,* any Weel
' called a Lomb or a Mill-pot, or any other
' Engine with the Head thereof againft the
' Stream, upon Pain of forfeiture of ten Pounds,
' and Imprifonment at the difcretion of the
' Lord Mayor: Nor that no Man whatfoever
' fhall occupy upon the faid River of *Thames,*
' any Nets called Purfe-Nets, otherwife Cafting-
' Nets, upon the like Payment.'

10. *Item,* ' That no Fisher-man or others
' fhall be fuffered to rug for Flounders, either
' by Ebb or by Flood, at any time of the Year,
' between *London-Bridge* and *Stran-gate* on the
' South-fide, and *Weftminfter-Bridge* on the
' North-fide; but only two Cafts at low Water,
' and two Cafts at full Sea or high Water, for
' the

' the Safeguard of the Fry and Brood of Fifh ;
' and no Flounder fhall be taken under the af-
' fize of fix Inches : Nor that no Fifher-man or
' other fhall fleet with any Bley-net upon the
' Benches from *Whitehall* to the *Temple-ftairs*
' upon high Waters, from *Whitfontide* to *Bar-*
' *tholomewtide,* upon like Payment.

11. *Item,* ' That no Fifher-man or other Per-
' fon whatfoever fhall caft, bring, or caufe to
' be brought, any Carrion, Soil, Gravel, Rub-
' bifh, Sods of Earth, or any other Filth or An-
' noyance, whereby Banks or Shelves are raifed,
' and the common Paffage hindred, to the great
' danger of Fares, Boats, and Barges paffing to
' and fro upon the faid River : Nor that no
' Fifher-man or other fhall drive, or caufe to
' be driven any Piles, Stumps, or Stakes with-
' in the faid River of *Thames,* upon which the
' like Mifchief and Dangers may arife, until
' fuch time as they be lawfully licenfed fo to
' do ; upon the like Pain and Penalty as afore-
' faid.'

12. *Item,* ' That no Fifher-man or other fhall
' prefume to take up any Rack or Drifth upon
' the Water of *Thames,* without notice given
' thereof to the Water-Bailiff, or his Subftitute,
' within convenient time, he fatisfying him for
' his Pains, as fhall be reafonable and thought
' fitting ; nor fhall conceal and keep fecret the
' faid Rack or Drifth from the faid Water-
' Bailiff, to the end that fuch order and care
' may be taken therein, as hath been accuftomed,
' according to the Laws and Ordinances or-
' dained for the Prefervation of the faid River ;
' upon like Payment and Penalty.'

13. *Item,* ' That no Fifherman or other fhall
' fifh with any kind of Net, or ufe any Angle-
' Rod with more than two Hooks upon a Line,

' or faw or fcratch for Barbel within the Limits
' of *London-bridge*, or fhall ufe any other Engine
' nearer unto the *Bridge* than St. *Botolphs Wharf*,
' and the *Bridge-Houfe Wharf* on the Eaft fide,
' nor nearer on the Weft fide than St. *Mary*
' *Overies* Stairs and the *Old Swan*; upon pain of
' Imprifonment at the difcretion of the Lord
' Mayor, and fix Shillings eight Pence to the
' Chamber of *London*.'

14. *Item*, ' That no Peter-man fhall at any
' time hereafter fifh or work with any manner
' of Net upon the faid Water weftward, farther
' than *Richmond Crane*; unto which Place, or
' near thereabouts, the Water ebbeth and flow-
' eth, for that the Fifhing beyond that Place,
' hath caufed a great deftruction of Fifh; upon
' pain of forfeiture of twenty Shillings for
' every time they fhall fo offend, and farther
' Punifhment according to the Quality of his
' Offence.'

15. *Item*, ' It is ordered that no Peter-man
' fhall hereafter at any time of the Year take
' the Tides above *Richmond*, nor go in company
' together, it being found very prejudicial and
' hurtful both to the River and Fifher-men,
' and nothing available for the furnifhing of
' any Markets; nor fhall go to fifh more than
' five together in one Company between *Rich-*
' *mond* and *London Bridge*, upon pain of forfeit-
' ing for every time ten Shillings, and Imprifon-
' ment during pleafure.'

16. *Item*, ' That no Peter-man, or any other
' take any Flounders, or any other fhort Fifh,
' which they have ufually called Kettle-Fifh,
' not being fix Inches of affize, being found to
' be to the great deftruction of the Fifh; upon
' the like Penalty and Pain.'

17. *Item*,

17. *Item,* 'That whereas many Inconveni-
' encies have heretofore rifen to the River of
' *Thames,* by divers Fifher-mens keeping of
' Boys, who had neither fufficiency to take the
' charge of Fifhing, nor bound Apprentice to
' the fame : Therefore from henceforth it fhall
' not be lawful for any Fifher-man to keep two
' Boys in one Boat, unlefs the one of them be
' at Man's Eftate, or thought fufficient by the
' Water-Bailiff to take the charge, or elfe that
' one of them be an Owner : Nor that no
' Fifher-man from henceforth do take any Ap-
' prentice to the faid Trade of Fifhing, unlefs
' he firft enter his Name into the Regifter-
' Book of the Water-Bailiff of this City, kept
' for that purpofe, nor under the Term of feven
' Years ; and that, after the Expiration of
' his faid Term, he likewife come again be-
' fore the faid Water-Bailiff, to be by him
' admitted a lawful Fifher-man, (as of ancient
' time hath been accuftomed) upon like Pay-
' ment.'

. 18. *Laftly,* ' That every Fifher-man upon the
' River of *Thames,* from *London-Bridge* unto
' *Stanes-Bridge,* fhall once every Year (*viz.* upon
' St. *Paul's* Day, being the five-and-twentieth
' Day of *January*) appear before the Water-
' Bailiff of this City, at the Chapel of the *Guild-*
' *Hall,* by ten of the clock in the Forenoon of
' the fame Day, there to enter their feveral
' Names into his Regifter-Book kept for that
' purpofe : And farther, to hear the Orders
' and Inftitutions ordained for the prefervation
' of the faid River, to be openly and publickly
' read, to the intent that they and every of
' them may the better perform the fame ; upon
' pain of fix Shillings eight Pence for every
' Default fo made. And if any Man whatfo-

' ever,

‘ ever, Fifherman or other, fhall contemptu-
‘ oufly or ftubbornly refift the Water-Bailiff,
‘ being Sub-Confervator under the Lord Mayor,
‘ in the due Performance and Execution of his
‘ faid Office, he fhall make fuch Fine, or be
‘ imprifoned at the difcretion of the Lord Mayor
‘ for the time being, as unto his Lordfhip fhall
‘ feem moft fitting.’

*Articles to be inquired upon by the Jury
for the River of* Thames *Eaftward.*

‘ I *Mprimis,* You fhall faithfully and truly pre-
‘ fent (without any refpeƈt) all fuch Per-
‘ fons, Fifher-men and others, as do prophane
‘ the Lord’s Sabbaths in their unlawful Fifh-
‘ ings, and going forth that Day to their La-
‘ bour, being to the high Difpleafure of Al-
‘ mighty God, and availeth not to the furnifh-
‘ ing of any Market. And if any fuch Fifher-
‘ men have gone forth to fifh, having been at
‘ Home before *Sunday* at Night Sun-down, you
‘ fhall faithfully and truly prefent them.’

Trinker-men. 2. *Item,* ‘ That no Trinke fhall ftand for
‘ Smelts till the one and twentieth Day of *October*
‘ yearly, and fo to continue until *Good-friday*
‘ following. And to ufe no manner of Net for
‘ Smelts than full two Inches in the forepart,
‘ Inch and a half in the fecond part ; and in
‘ the third part, which is the Hofe or Cod,
‘ an Inch and quarter wet and dry. And the
‘ Hofe not to exceed eleven Foot in length,
‘ and in compafs fixty Meifhes, and not above.
‘ And five Hoops placed a Foot and a half
‘ afunder in the faid Cod ; the laft Hoop to be
‘ placed

' placed within two Foot of the end of the Cod,
' and each·Hoop to be a Foot and a half over
' every way, upright within the Hoop, and not
' otherwise.'

   3. *Item,* ' That no Trinke fhall ftand to fifh
' above nine Tides in the Week, *viz.* Three
' Tides againft *Wednefday,* three Tides againft
' *Friday,* and three Tides againft *Saturday* Mar-
' ket, and fo likewife three Tides againft Saints
' Eves and other Fafting-Days; and then to
' wafh, hale up, and .go home with their faid
' Nets and Boats every *Saturday* Morning to
' their own Houfes. And in *Lent* time they
' may ftand every Day, the Sabbath-day ex-
' cepted.'

   4. *Item,* ' That no Trinke fhall ftand in any
' Byrth more than is allowed him to ftand, but
' fhall ftand ,in all fuch feveral places, and in
' fuch manner as hereafter followeth, and in no
' other place; that is to fay, he fhall keep his
' Cooplement.'

At *Blackwall-Ferry* two, one Breaft or Front, and no more.

At *Ley-fhelp* two, and no more.

At *Woolwich-fhelp* two, and no more.

At *Woolwich Town* five, and·no more.

At *Gallions-naffe* three, and no more.

At *Buzards-bufh* five, and no more.

At the Eaft and Weft End of *Barkin-fhelp,* two at each Place, and no more.

At *Dagnam-fhelp* fix, and no more.

At the *Carrick* four, and no more.

At *Julian-tre-job* three, and no more.

At *Dartford-job* three, and no more.

At the *Bight* at *Erith-naffe* three, and no more.

At *Stokefleet-naffe,* alias *Stakes-end,* five, and no more.

At *Avely-hole* five, and no more.
At *Purfleet* five, and no more.
At *Grayes Thorough* fix, and no more.
At the *Two Thoroughs* three, and no more.
And every Trinke to keep his true Coople-
ment, and to ftand no more in a Byrth.

5. ' *Item*, That no Trinke fhall ftand to
' fifh for Whitings till the Ember-Week before
' *Michaelmas* Yearly, and to come no higher
' than *Purfleet*, and to have the Hofe or Cod of
' his Net full Inch and a half. And upon *Sa-*
' *turday* Sun-up to wafh off his Net, hale up,
' and go home, and not to return to his La-
' bour again till *Monday* Morning Day-light.
' And fo likewife fhall every Fifherman do
' from *London-Bridge* Weftward, to *Graves-End-*
' *Bridge.* in the Eaft, and not otherwife.
6. *Item*, ' That no Trinkerman, or other
' Fifherman, fhall buy any Trinke, or take to
' receive any Copy under the Seal of the Office
' of Mayoralty, until he be allowed and thought
' fit by the Lord Mayor of *London*, or by his
' Subftitute, the Water-Bailiff for the time be-
' ing, with the general Liking and Confents of
' the faid Company of Trinkermen, and fe-
' venteen Trinkes allowed, and no more.
7. *Item*, ' That no Trinke fhall ftand to
' fifh before any Breach-mouth at the rifing or
' finking of any Mother-fifhes, or in the time
' of Spawn or Brood of Fifh ; and that every
' Trinke fhall at all Times and Seafons take up
' and carry away his Anchor at the time of his
' leaving off from Fifhing, and not leave his
' faid Anchor behind him to keep his Byrth,
' contrary to the ancient Order and Cuftom.
8. *Item*, ' That each Trinke fhall every
' dark and foggy Night hang forth out of his
' faid

'said Trinke-Boat one Lanthorn with sufficient
'Candle-light, for the better and safer Passage
'of Ships, Boats, and Vessels passing to and
'fro upon the said River: And that every
'Trinke-Cable be no more than twenty Fa-
'thom long at the most; or any Henbilt above
'twenty two Fathom. And likewise to have
'a Warp of forty Fathom to sheer off and
'give way, if any Ship, Crayer, or any other
'Vessel shall chance to drive upon them.

9. *Item,* 'That every Trinker-man shall
'one Week before his going forth to fish,
'come up to the Chapel of *Guildhall, London,*
'and there appear before the Water-Bailiff, as
'well to receive Leave and Licence for their
'going forth, as also to hear the Orders and
'Institutions ordained for the Preservation of
'the said River, to be there openly and pub-
'lickly read, to the end that they may the bet-
'ter observe and keep the said Orders, and eve-
'ry thing therein contained.

10. *Item,* That no Hebberman shall fish for Hebberman.
'Smelts before the twenty fourth Day of *Au-*
'*gust* yearly, and so to continue till *Good-Fri-*
'*day:* And that no Hebberman shall fish in
'any Haven, Creek, Breach, or Issue, with
'any Net of less Assize than three Inches for
'Flounders, from the Feast of *Easter,* until the
'said twenty fourth Day of *August* yearly.
'And shall likewise appear before the Water-
'Bailiff of *London* at the Chapel of *Guild-hall,*
'there to receive Leave and Licence for their
'said going forth. And that the Meish of their
'said Smelt-Nets be full Inch wet and dry,
'and not otherwise.

11. *Item,* 'That every Hebberman shall fish
'by the Shore, and pitch their Pole at half
'Ebb, and shall have but forty Fathom Rope

'allowed

' allowed from the Pitch of their Pole into the
' River, and not to lie a floating or flatting
' for Smelts between two Anchors in the midst
" of the Stream, nor shall have any kind of
' Weight of Lead, Iron, Stone, Barrel, Firkin,
' Kilderkin, Cask, or with any Wherry, or
' other Device. Nor shall fish from *Good-Friday*
' till *Bartholomew-tide* yearly, betwixt *London-*
' *Bridge* and *Graves-end*, with any Net under
' two Inches, except with a Wade-net for Bait
' only.

    12. *Item*, ' That no Hebberman shall work
' any higher for Whitings than *Dartford-Creek*,
' and to work with no manner of Net for
' Whitings of less Assize than full Inch and half
' wet and dry : Nor shall go forth to take any
' of the said Whitings yearly, until they be
' lawfully licensed by the Water-Bailiff of *Lon-*
' *don*, before whom they are severally to appear
' at the said Chapel of *Guildhall, London*, one
' Week before *Gang-tide* yearly.

Trawlerman.   13. *Item*, ' You shall present the Names and
' Surnames of every Trawler unto the Lord-
' Mayor of *London*, or his Substitute the Wa-
' ter-Bailiff for the time being. And that no
' Trawler shall fish above *Holl* Haven on the
' North-side, and *Porsing* on the South-side, till
' a Fortnight after *Michaelmas* yearly ; and all
' the Summer to use no Net for Soals under two
' Inches and a half in the Cod, being two
' Yards long, and the rest of the Net to be
' three Inches. And no Trawler to work in
' *Tilbury-hope* after *Michaelmas*, with any man-
' ner of Net under four Inches for Plaice all
' the Net over. And no Trawler to come
' upon any Trawl with any other Net at any
' time of the Year.

                 14. *Item*,

14. *Item,* ' To prefent all fuch as have pitch-
' ed, fet, or erected any Riff-hedge, or Half-
' Nets upon Stakes or otherwife within the full
' Sea and low Water, being an Engine utterly
' to kill fmall Fifh, and what Land-men they
' be upon *Kentifh-Shore,* or in any other Place
' within the Waters of *Thames* and *Medway,*
'-that do or have ufed the fame.

15. *Item,* ' That no Trawler do ftay abroad
' to fifh after *Whitfontide* againft *Wednefday*-Mar-
' ket till *Bartholomew-tide* yearly, nor that no
' Trawler do fifh in *Tilbury-hope* upon the *Sa-*
' *turday* after Sun-rifing; but to wafh off, hale
' up, and go home, as all other Fifhermen ought
' to do, and according to the old and ancient
' Cuftom of the River of *Thames* and Waters
' of *Medway.*

16. *Item,* ' That every Trawler upon the
' River Eaftwards, do yearly appear before the
' Water-Bailiff of *London,* at the Chapel of
' *Guild-hall,* one Week before their true times
' and Seafons of going forth to fifh, then and
' there to receive Leave and Licence for their
' faid going forth, and to hear the Orders and
' Inftitutions ordained for the Prefervation and
' Government of the River of *Thames,* to be there
' openly and publickly read, to the end that
' they may the better obferve and perform the
' fame.

17. *Item,* ' That no Trawler that hath or
' doth ufe to Trawl to take Soals, Chate, Plaice,
' or Thornback, fhall take or bring any fuch
' Fifh to any Maket, or to any Country-Town
' to fell, except they contain the Affize as fol-
' loweth ; that is to fay, every fuch Soal,
' Chate, Plaice, and Thornback to contain in
' Length feven Inches with the Head and Tail,
' and not under.

18. *Item,*

Dragger-man. 18. *Item*, ' That no Dragger-man that hath
' or doth ufe to drag for Shrimps, fhall go forth
' to fifh till the firft Day of *November* yearly,
' and to continue till *Good-Friday* : Nor fhall ufe
' any fuch Drag at any time of the Year above
' *Maggot-Naffe* on the Southfide, and *Stake-Brake*
' Creek on the Northfide, and not otherwife.
' And that every Dragger-man fhall upon the
' firft Day of *November* yearly, appear before
' the Water-Bailiff of *London*, to receive Leave
' and Licence for going forth.

Shadders. 19. *Item*, ' That all manner of Fifhermen
' whatfoever, that ufe to take Shads in Shad-
' ding-time, fhall obferve and keep their true
' Order of fhooting a Drove's Length off from
' one another; and to prefent what Diforder is
' kept amongft them, both in going forth upon
' *Sundays*, or otherwife. And that none of the
' faid Shadders fhall go forth to fifh until they
' have received Leave and Licence of the Lord
' Mayor of *London*, or his Subftitute the Water-
' Bailiff for the time being ; their true time of
' going forth to be the Week before *Eafter* year-
' ly, and not before.

Peter-men. 20. *Item*, ' That no Peter-man whatfoever,
' from *London-Bridge* in the Weft, as far as the
' River of *Medway* in the Eaft, fhall fleet for
' Flounders with any Rugge-Net in the Night-
' time, from Sun going down until Day-light
' the next Morning betwixt *Michaelmas* and
' *Chriftmas* ; becaufe in the Night-time they
' make great Deftruction of fmall Flounders,
' and carry them away both unfeen and un-
' known. Nor that no Peter-man do fifh with
' any Hagan or Smelt-Net below *London-Bridge*
' at any time of the Year.

21. *Item*, ' That no Peter-man, or other Per-
' fon whatfoever, fhall fifh betwixt *London-Bridge*
                                 ' and

'and *Lime-houfe-Naffe*, with any manner of Net
'to fleet, beat, or rugge at any time of the
'Year, except for Shads only: Nor that no
'Peter-man do rugge from *London-Bridge* to
'*Blackwall*, and fo Eaftward, from *Michaelmas*
'yearly till *Whitfontide*, but only three Cafts at
'High-water, and three Cafts at Low-water
'in and out; and every Rugge-Net is to con-
'tain two Inches three quarters in the Meifh
'wet and dry, and every Bley-Net two Inches
'and a half throughout wet and dry.

22. *Item,* 'That no Fifher-man or other *Smelt-leaps.*
'Perfon whatfoever, fhall lay down in the Ri-
'ver of *Thames* Eaftward, any Smelt-leaps be-
'fore St. *Paul's*-Day yearly, and fo continue
'till *Good-Friday* next following, and no longer.
'Nor that no Fifherman or other Perfon fhall
'lay in the faid River any more than only one
'Wand of eighteen and no more, and not to
'lay them down until they be lawfully licenfed
'thereunto by the Lord Mayor, or Water-Bai-
'liff, and none to ufe them but Fifhermen and
'Houfholders.

23. *Item,* 'That no Fifherman, or other Per- *Eel-leaps.*
'fon, fhall lay in the faid River of *Thames* any
'Eel-leaps, till fourteen Days after *Eafter* year-
'ly, and fo to continue until *Michaelmas* next
'following: Nor fhall lay any more or greater
'quantity than only two dozen, and no more:
'Nor fhall lay any of the faid Eel-leaps until
'they be lawfully licenfed thereunto as afore-
'faid, and not otherwife.

24. *Item,* 'That no Fifher-man, or other *Eel-fpear.*
'Perfon whatfoever, fhall ufe upon the River
'of *Thames*, at any time of the Year, any
'Spear called an Eel-fpear, or any other kind
'of Spear whatfoever, for that they are great
'Deftroyers of young Brood, and other kind of
'Fifh

' Fifh in great abundance, and therefore alto-
' gether unlawful; no Man to ufe them upon
' pain of Imprifonment, and further Fine at
' the Difcretion of the Lord Mayor.

Forftalling.   25. *Item,* ' You fhall further inquire, and true
' Prefentment make, of all fuch Perfons as do
' ufe to go down the River to buy up either
' Fifh, or Victuals, other Commodities, before
' the fame cometh to *Billingfgate* and other
' Keys, being known and appointed Places of
' Sale, Vent, and Difcharge thereof : if you
' know any fuch, you fhall prefent who they
' be, and how often they have fo done.

Fifh out of Seafon.   26. ' *Item,* That no Fifher-man or other Perfon
' whatfoever, fhall work with any manner of
' Net or Engine whatfoever, to take or kill
' any Dace or Roach from the Tenth of *March*
' till the Tenth of *May* yearly, for that they
' do then fhed their Spawn : Nor that they
' take or kill any of the faid Dace, Roch, or
' other kind of Fifh, out of their due kind or
' feafon, nor except they contain in Length ac-
' cording to the true Scantling and Affize, and
' not otherwife.

Soil and Rubbifh.   27. *Item,* You fhall further inquire, and true
' Prefentment make, whether any Butcher,
' Brewer, Inn-keeper, or any other Perfon or
' Perfons, as well within the City of *London,*
' as in any other Country Town or Village (as
' far as the Liberty of the Lord-Mayor ex-
' tendeth) have caft or put into the faid River,
' any Paunches, Grains, Horfe-dung, or any
' other Rubbifh, Soil, or Filth whatfoever, to
' the very great Annoyance and Hurt of the
' faid River, on pain of Imprifonment, and
' further Fine, at the Difcretion of the Lord-
' Mayor of *London* : If you know any fuch,
' you fhall prefent them.

28. *Item,*

28. *Item,* ' You fhall further inquire what *Royal-Fifh.*
' Royal-Fifhes have been taken within the Ju-
' rifdiction and Royalty of the Lord Mayor
' of *London*; as namely, Whales, Sturgeons,
' Porpuffes, and fuch like, and to prefent the
' Name and Names of all fuch Perfons as fhall
' take them to the Lord-Mayor of *London* for
' the time being.

29. *Item,* ' That no Fifher-man, or other *Lampern-*
' Perfon whatfoever, fhall lay in the faid River *Rods.*
' of *Thames* any Lampern-Leaps to take Lam-
' perns, before *Bartholomew-tide* yearly, and fo
' to continue till *Good-Friday*; nor fhall lay any
' more or greater quantity than only one Rod
' of forty Fathom, containing feven dozen of
' Leaps, and not above : Nor fhall lay any of
' the faid Rods until they fhall be lawfully
' licenfed by the Lord Mayor of *London,* or by
' his Subftitute, the Water-Bailiff for the time
' being.

30. *Laftly,* ' Becaufe the number of Fifher-
' men do daily increafe, and not only Fifher-
' men, but alfo a great number of Cable-hang-
' ers and Tradefmen, fuch as were never bound
' Apprentice to the Craft and Science of Fifh-
' ing, to the great Hurt of the River, and Hin-
' drance of Fifhermen, the faid River being
' not able to relieve and fuccour, the Multipli-
' city of them being fo great : It is now or-
' dained, That every Fifher-man dwelling near
' unto the faid River, that doth take and receive
' into his or their Cuftody, any Apprentice to
' the faid Trade of Fifhing, fhall within one
' Month next after, repair unto the Water-
' Bailiff of *London,* to have his Indenture writ-
' ten and ingroffed, to the end that after he
' may prefent him to the Chamberlain of *Lon-*
' *don,* to be Enrolled, according to ancient
' Cuftom.

' Cuſtom. And not to receive any Apprentice
' under the Term of Seven Years. And at the
' end and expiration of the ſaid Term, that the
' Maſter of the ſaid Apprentice do again preſent
' him to the ſaid Water-Bailiff, to be by him
' admitted and allowed a Fiſherman. And
' finally, You ſhall inquire, and true Preſentment
' make, by the Oaths that you, and every of
' you have taken, whether any Fiſherman, or
' other Perſon whatſoever they be, have with
' any manner of Net or Engine offended or
' miſuſed himſelf in fiſhing within the ſaid
' River ; or whether they have any manner of
' ways made deſtruction of the Brood and Fry
' of any kind of Fiſh therein contained, con-
' trary to the good and ancient Laws, Ordi-
' nances, and Conſtitutions of the ſaid River
' of *Thames*. And to make a true, perfect, and
' faithful Preſentment of all other kind of Enor-
' mities, Hurts, Offences, and Annoyances,
' touching as well Fiſhermen, as any other
' Perſon or Perſons within the ſaid Juriſdiction,
' being any manner of ways hurtful or offenſive
' to the ſame.

At a Court of Aldermen the Tenth of July, 1673.
an Order was made as followeth, viz.

' THis Court conſidering the great Decay of
' the Fiſhing-Trade in the River of *Thames*,
' and conceiving, The drawing the Shores
' (of late ſo frequently practiſed) is the chief
' Ground thereof, as tending to the great Pre-
' judice and utter Deſtruction of the Brood and
' Fry of all ſorts of Fiſh, did thereupon this
' Day ſtrictly order and enjoin, That no Per-
' ſon do hereafter preſume to draw the Shores
' in the River of *Thames* upon any Pretence
' whatſoever,

' whatfoever, at any Time or Seafon of the
' Year, either with lawful or unlawful Nets,
· fave only for Salmons in Rooms appointed
' and fet out for that purpofe by this Court :
' And that none do fiſh for Salmons in fuch
' Rooms, but only fuch as fhall be impowered
' thereunto under the Seal of the Mayoralty of
' this City: And alfo that none fiſh with a
' Net under fix Inches in the Meiſh, upon pain
' that every Offender fhall forfeit for every
' fuch Offence, his Nets, and pay as a Fine,
' the Sum of Twenty Pounds, and fuffer Im-
' prifonment during the Pleafure of this Court.
' And to the end more diligent and ſtrict Search
' may for the future be made upon the faid Ri-
' ver than heretofore hath been, or poffibly can
' be by one fingle Perfon, for fuch as fiſh with
' unlawful Nets, at unlawful times, and in un-
' lawful manner ; the Water-Bailiff for the
' time being, is by this Court ordered and im-
' powered, from time to time, to authorize
' two or more houeſt Fiſhermen, in fuch Town
' and Places as he fhall think convenient, as
' well below as above the Bridge, to be affiftant
' to him in the Execution of his Duty ; and
' when they fhall think fit, to go out and fearch
' for any fuch Offenders, and to take away
' their Nets, and give their Names to Mr. Wa-
' ter-Bailiff, that he may take effectual Care,
' that they be feverely proceeded againſt
' according to Law.

Wagſtaffe.

Con-

Concerning the Company of Watermen for the River of Thames.

BY a *Stat.* 2 & 3 *P.* and *M.* it was enacted, That at the first Court of Aldermen in *London*, next after the first of *March*, out of the Watermen betwixt *Gravesend* and *Windsor*, eight Overseers are to to be chosen to keep order among the rest.

That two Watermen shall not carry any, but where one of them hath exercised that Profession two Years before that time, and hath been allowed by the greater part of the said Overseers, under the known Seal; on pain to be committed to one of the Compters, by the said Overseers, for a Month, or for less time, as the Offence shall deserve.

That no single Man, that is no Housholder, nor retained as an Apprentice, or as a Servant, for one Year at least, shall exercise that Profession, betwixt the Places aforesaid, on pain of like Punishment.

The Lord Mayor and Aldermen of *London*, and the Justices of Peace within the Counties adjoining to the River of *Thames*, upon Complaint of any two of the Overseers, or of any Waterman's Master, have Power not only to hear and determine any Offences committed against this Act, and to enlarge any Waterman unjustly punished by the said Overseers, but likewise to punish the Overseers themselves, in case they unjustly punish any Person by colour of this Act.

Also

Alfo a *Wherry* that is not twelve Foot and a half long, and four Foot and a half broad in the Midfhip, and fufficient to carry two Perfons on one fide right, fhall be forfeit, and the King fhall have one Moiety, and the Informer the other.

Again, That Waterman that withdraws himfelf in time of Preffing, (it being proved by two Witneffes before the faid Mayor, Aldermen, or Juftice, and two of the faid Overfeers) fhall fuffer a Fortnight's Imprifonment, and fhall be prohibited to row any more upon the *Thames* for a Year and a Day after.

Alfo, The Overfeers fhall not only call the Watermen before them, and direct them, and regifter their Names, but likewife examine their Boats before they be launched, whether they have due Proportion and Goodnefs, according to this Act: And if the Overfeers refufe or neglect their Office, they fhall forfeit 5 *l.* between the King and Informer.

Alfo, The Court of Aldermen fhall affefs the Fares of Watermen, which being fubfcribed by two of the Privy-Council (at leaft) fhall be fet up in *Guild-Hall, Weftminfter-Hall,* &c. and the Waterman that takes more than according to the Fare fo affeffed, fhall for every fuch Offence *See after.* fuffer half a Year's Imprifonment, and forfeit 40 *s.* to be divided as before.

And by the 1 *Jac.* 1. 16. No Waterman fhall *Stat.* 1 *Jac.* 1. retain any Servant or Apprentice, unlefs he *c.* 16. himfelf hath been an Apprentice to a Waterman by the fpace of five Years before; and not an Apprentice under the Age of eighteen Years, or for lefs time than feven Years, in pain to forfeit for every fuch Offence 10 *l.* to be divided betwixt the King and the Profecutor.

E e

But

But this Act shall not restrain Watermens Sons, of convenient Growth and Strength, and formerly trained up in rowing, but that they be allowed to serve as Apprentices, and to carry Passengers from place to place, at the Age of sixteen Years.

Also, That eight Overseers shall yearly, upon the first Day of *March*, and the first Day of *September*, cause openly to be read in the Common-Hall, all their Orders made, or to be made, in pain that every of them, for every such Default, shall forfeit twenty Nobles to be divided betwixt the King and the Prosecutor.

See the Rates following.

Rates signed and agreed upon by the Privy-Council, and the Lord Mayor and Court of Aldermen, to be taken by Watermen.

From London to	Limehouse, Newcrane, Shadwell-Dock, Bell-Wharf, Ratcliff-Cross,	Oars. 1 s.	Sculler. 6 d.

From

From Lon-
don to
{
Wapping-Dock,
Wapping New-
stairs,
Wapping Old-
stairs,
The Hermitage,
Rotherhith-
Church-Stairs,
Rotherhith-
Stairs,
}
Oars. Skuller.
6 d.   3 d.

From St. O-
lave's to
{
Rotherhith-
Church-Stairs,
and
Rotherhith-Stairs.
}
Oars. Skuller.
6 d.   3 d.

From *Billingsgate* to St. *Saviour's-Mill*, Oars 6 d.
Skuller 3 d.
From St. *Olave's* to St. *Saviour's-Mill*, Oars 6 d.
Skuller 3 d.
All the Stairs between *London-Bridge* and *West-minster*, Oars 6 d. Skuller 3 d.

From either side
above *London-*
Bridge to
{
Lambeth,
Fox-hall,
}
Oars. Skuller.
1 s.   6 d.

From *White-*
Hall to
{
Lambeth,
Fox-hall,
}
Oars. Skuller.
6 d.   3 d.

From
{
Temple,
Dorset-stairs,
Black-Frier-
stairs,
Paul's-Wharf,
}
to *Lambeth.* Oars. Skull.
8 d.   4 d.

E e 2   Over

Over the Water directly in the next Skuller,
between *London-Bridge* and *Lime-house*, or
London-Bridge and *Fox-hall*, 2 d.

From *London* to *Gravesend*, whole Fare 4 s. 6 d.
with Company, 9 d.

From *London* to *Grayes*, or *Greenhive*, whole Fare
4 s. with Company 8 d.

From *London* to *Purfleet* or *Eriff*, whole Fare 3 s.
with Company 6 d.

From *London* to *Woolwich*, whole Fare 2 s. 6 d.
with Company 4 d.

From *London* to *Blackwall*, whole Fare 2 s. with
Company 4 d.

From *London* to *Greenwich*, whole Fare 1 s. 6 d.
with Company 3 d.

From *London* to *Deptford*, whole Fare 1 s. 6 d.
with Company 3 d.

From *London* to { *Chelsey*, *Battersey*, *Wandsworth*, } whole Fare 1 s.
6 d. with Company 3 d.

From *London* to { *Putney*, *Fulham*, *Barn-Elms*, } whole Fare 2 s.
with Company 4 d.

From *London* to { *Hammersmith*, *Chiswick*, *Mortlack*, } whole Fare 2 s.
6 d. with Company 6 d.

From *London* to { *Brentford*, *Isleworth*, *Richmond*, } whole Fare 3 s.
6 d. with Company 6 d.

From *London* to *Twickenham*, whole Fare 4 s.
with Company 6 d.

From *London* to *Kingston*, whole Fare 5 s. with
Company 9 d.

From

From *London* to *Hampton-Court,* whole Fare 6 *s.* with Company 1 *s.*

From *London* to { *Hampton-Town,* *Sunbury,* *Walton,* } whole Fare 7*s.* with Company 1 *s.*

From *London* to { *Walton,* *Weybridge,* *Chertsey,* } whole Fare 10 *s.* with Company 1*s.*

From *London* to *Stanes,* whole Fare 12 *s.* with Company 1 *s.*

From *London* to *Windsor,* whole Fare 14 *s.* with Company 2 *s.*

Rates for carrying Goods in the Tilt-Boat between London and Gravesend.

For a half Firkin — 1 *d.*
For a whole Firkin — 2 *d.*
For a Hogshead — 2 *s.*
For a hundred Weight of Cheese, Iron, or any heavy Goods — 4 *d.*
For a Sack of Salt or Corn — 6 *d.*
For an ordinary Chest or Trunk 6 *d.*
For an ordinary Hamper — 6 *d.*
For every single Person in the ordinary Passage — 6 *d.*
For the Hire of the whole Tilt-Boat 1 *l.* 2 *s.* 6 *d.*

The Lord Mayor for the time being may cause any Person inhabiting within *London,* or

E e 3　　　　the

the Liberties to be fummoned to appear before his Lordfhip upon the Complaint of any
Citizen ; and for non-appearance, may grant
his Warrant to bring fuch Perfon before him,
and hath Power to hear and determine Differences between Party and Party.

If any Apprentice or other Perfon fhall be
carried on Ship-board, or there detained againft
his Will, the Lord Mayor may fend his Warrant
by his Water-Bailiff, and compel the Captain
or Commander of the Veffel to releafe fuch
Perfon.

Wherrymen, Watermen and Lighter-men made a Company. By a late Statute made, *An.* 11 & 12 *W.* 3.
cap. 21. For the better ordering and governing
the Watermen, Wherrymen and Lightermen on
the River of *Thames*, between *Gravefend* and
Windfor, it is enacted, That all Laws in Force
touching Watermen and Wherrymen, not thereby altered or repealed, fhall be duly put in Execution under the Penalties therein contained :
And that every Lighterman, or Owner, Keeper,
or Worker of any Lighter, or other large Craft
on the *Thames*, between *Gravefend* and *Windfor*,
fhall be taken to be of the Society or Company
of Wherrymen and Watermen ; which Wherrymen, Watermen and Lightermen, are by the faid
Act made a Society or Company.

That all fuch Lightermen on the River of
Thames (except Trinity-men, Fifhermen, Ballaft-
men, Weftern Barges and Mill-boats, Chalk-
hoys, Faggot and Wood Lighters, and other
Craft carrying the fame) fhall be regiftred in a
Book kept by the Company of Watermen and
Lightermen, and be liable to the Rules of the
faid Company.

That the Lord Mayor and Court of Aldermen fhall yearly elect eight of the beft Watermen, and three of the beft Lightermen, at the
firft

firſt Court of Aldermen next after the firſt Day
of *June*, to be Overſeers and Rulers of the ſaid *Overſeers.*
Wherrymen, *&c.* who are to maintain good
Orders amongſt them, and to cauſe the Names
of the Lightermen to be regiſtred at their
Hall, after the 29th Day of *June* 1700, then
coming.

That the ſaid Rulers and Aſſiſtants were on
the firſt Court-day after the firſt day of *June*
then next, and ſo yearly to appoint Watermen
of the principal Towns and Stairs, between
Graveſend and *Windſor*, to chuſe their Aſſiſtants, *Aſſiſtants.*
not exceeding ſixty, nor leſs than forty Water-
men. And the Lightermen on the firſt of *June*
then next, and ſo yearly, are to chuſe nine
Lightermen, who with the Watermen ſhall be
the Aſſiſtants of the ſaid Company for pre-
ſerving good Government amongſt them ; who
on the firſt Day of *July* yearly, ſhall preſent
to the Court of Aldermen five Watermen, and
two Lightermen to be Auditors of the ſaid
Company, for auditing the Accounts of the
Rulers, *&c.* And Perſons elected Rulers, Aſſiſtants, or Auditors, refuſing or not well exerciſing
their Places, ſhall forfeit five Pounds.

The ſaid Rulers, Auditors and Aſſiſtants,
may make Rules with Penalties, for the good
Government of their Society; which, firſt appro-
ved by the Court of Aldermen, and after by the
Lord Chief Juſtice of either Bench ſhall be
binding.

That the Lord Mayor and Aldermen of
London, and the Juſtices of Peace in the Shires
next adjoining to the *Thames*, between *Graveſend* and *Windſor* in their ſeveral Juriſdictions,
upon Complaint of the Overſeers and Rulers,
ſhall hear and determine Offences contrary to
this Act, and levy the Penalties by Diſtreſs.

That Perfons owning or working any Lighter, or flat Boat for unlading Goods and Merchandizes from Ships, &c. and Regiftring themfelves and Servants in the faid Company's Books by the 29th Day of *Sept.* 1700. were thereby declared Lightermen ; and none but fuch Regiftred Perfons (befides free Watermen then after to be Regiftred as Lightermen, and fuch as had ferv'd their Time to Lightermen) fhall keep or work any Lighters, under penalty of five Pounds *per* Week.

That none (except *Trinity-men*) fhall row or ply on the faid River, &c. in Boats, &c. for carrying Paffengers for Profit, but fuch as have ferved their Time, or are Servants or Apprentices to Watermen; and all the Penalties of this Act fhall be paid to the faid Rulers and Overfeers, for the ufe of the Poor and Decay'd of the faid Society.

Poor.

Owners of Keys, &c.
That the Owners, &c. of any Keys betwixt *Hermitage-Bridge* and *London-Bridge*, may ufe their own Lighters, as heretofore, imploying therein qualified Watermen or Lightermen : And Woodmongers may keep and work Lighters by themfelves, and Servants for carrying their own Goods only.

Layftals, &c.
That Perfons keeping Layftals, may carry the Soyl thence as heretofore : And Gard'ners may bring to the Markets of *London*, &c. their Fruit, Herbs, Roots, &c. and carry Soyl in their Boats by their own Servants, as heretofore.

And that Offences againft this Act fhall be profecuted within 30 days. And that Perfons profecuted for any thing done in purfuance thereof, may plead the general Iffue, or vouch this Act in Juftification ; and if a Verdict pafs for the Defendant, &c. he fhall have double Cofts. And that

Offenders

Offenders punished by this Act, shall not incur the penalty of any other for the same Offence.

That after the first Day of *June* then next, the said Rulers and Overseers, Auditors and Assistants on their Court-Days, might appoint forty Watermen to ply on every Lord's Day, *Lord's Day.* between *Vauxhall* and *Limehouse*, for carrying Passengers cross the River at a Penny each : Which Watermen shall account next Day for the Money to the said Rulers, *&c.* who are to pay them for their Labour, and apply the Overplus to the poor decay'd Watermen and Ligh- *Poor.* termen of the Company, and their Widows.

And the Watermen neglecting every *Monday* to pay the whole, so earn'd and receiv'd, shall forfeit 40 *s.*

But this Act is not to impeach the Right of *Charles* late Duke of *Richmond* and *Lenox*, Lord of the Manor of *Gravesend*, his Heirs, Executors, *&c.* for holding there the Court of the Watercourse for the better Government of Barges, Boats, *&c.* ferrying from *Gravesend* to *London*, and of the Persons owning or working of the same ; nor prejudice any Liberties, *&c.* of the Mayor, Jurats, *&c.* of *Gravesend* and *Milton* in *Kent*, touching the said Passage or Ferry thence to *London*, or the Government thereof.

Nor to hinder the Watermen of St. *Margaret's Westminster*, from plying cross the *St. Margarets Westminster.* *Thames* from *Westminster-Bridge* to *Stand-Gate*, and from the *Horse-Ferry* to *Lambeth-Bridge* on the Lord's Day, by turns, as of late ; the Moneys earned thereby, being applied to the poor decay'd Watermen and their Widows of the said Parish of St. *Margaret.* And any two Justices of the Peace of the said Parish, may call the

Watermen

Watermen fo working, to Account, and
caufe the Moneys by them earned, to be
applied as aforefaid : Which Watermen of
St. *Margaret's*, fhall chufe two Stewards
and a Clerk on the 23*d* Day of *April*
yearly ; and fhall, at a Meeting of their
Society, appoint the Watermen fo to
work in their turns on the Lord's Day.

An Order made by the Court of Rulers,
Auditors, *and* Affiftants *of the Company of* Watermen *and* Lightermen,
of the River of Thames.

WHereas feveral Watermen and Lightermen, and the Apprentices of fuch, whilft
they are rowing or working upon the River of
Thames, and at their feveral refpective Places of
Refort, or plying Places, between *Gravefend* and
Windfor, do often ufe fuch immodeft, obfcene
and leud Expreffions towards Paffengers, and
to each other, as they are offenfive to all fober
Perfons, and tend extreamly to the Corrupting
and Debauchery of Youth : For Prevention
therefore of fuch ill Practices for the future, it
is hereby declared and ordained by the Court
aforefaid, That if any Waterman or Lighterman, after the 16*th* Day of *October* 1701. fhall
upon the faid River, or at any Place of their
Refort, as aforefaid, be guilty of ufing any fuch
leud Expreffions, and be thereof duly convicted,
by one or more Witnefs or Witneffes, or by the
Confeffion of the Offender, before the Rulers of
this Company, he fhall forfeit and pay for every
fuch Offence, the Sum of two Shillings and Six
Pence. And if any Waterman or Lighterman's
Apprentice

Apprentice fhall herein offend, the Mafter or Miſtreſs of every fuch Offender, (the Offender being duly convicted as aforefaid) fhall forfeit and pay the like Sum of two Shillings and fix Pence ; and in cafe of Refufal, the Offender fhall fuffer Correction, as the Rulers of this Company fhall in their Difcretion think fit and neceffary. Which faid Forfeitures (when paid) fhall be applied to the ufe of the poor, aged, decayed, and maimed Members of this Company, their Widows and Children. Dated at the Hall of the faid Company, this 8*th* Day of *October,* 1701.

E. Knight, Clerk.

THE

THE
Court of REQUESTS,

Commonly called the

Court of Conscience.

HE first beginning of this Court (by as much as appears from any Record) was in the ninth Year of King *Henry* the Eighth, by Act of Common Council then made; whereby it was ordained, That the Mayor and Aldermen of the City of *London*, should Monthly assign and appoint two Aldermen and four Commons to be Commissioners, to sit in the same Court in *Guildhall*, upon *Wednesday* and *Saturday* in every Week, there to hear, examine, and determine all Matters brought before them, between Party and Party, Citizens of *London*, where the Debt did not exceed forty Shillings, which Act was to continue two Years, and no longer. But being found beneficial for the Relief of such poor Debtors, as could not make present Payment of their Debts, and also to be a great Ease and Help to such poor Persons as had small Debts owing to them, and were not able to prosecute a Suit in Law for the same: The said Act hath since been continued by divers other Acts of Common Council; and besides the two Aldermen monthly assigned, the number

of

of Commiffioners was encreafed from four to twelve, and by that Authority the fame Court continued till the firft Year of the Reign of King *James* : And then divers malicious People flighting the Authority of the fame Court, and not regarding the Expence, how great foever, if they might ruin their poor Debtors ; and being often animated thereunto by divers covetous Attorneys, Petty-Foggers and Solicitors, did frequently commence Suits for petty Debts and Caufes againft poor Men (Citizens of *London*) in the High Courts at *Weftminfter*, or elfewhere, out of the faid Court of Requefts, to avoid the Jurifdiction thereof, and to bar the faid Commiffioners from ftaying fuch Suits, and examining the faid Caufes ; and thereby caufed fuch poor Men many times to pay ten times as much Charges as the principal Debt did amount unto, to the undoing fuch poor Men, their Wives, and Children, and alfo to the filling of the Prifons with the poor fo fued. For Remedy whereof, and for the ftrengthning and eftablifhing the faid Court, an Act of Parliament was made, *Anno primo Jacobi*, That every Citizen and Freeman of *London*, that had or fhould have any Debts owing unto him, not amounting to 40 *s.*, by any Debtors (Citizens and Freemen of *London*) inhabiting in *London*, or the Liberties thereof, fhould or might caufe fuch Debtors to be warn'd to appear before the Commiffioners of the faid Court : And that the faid Commiffioners, or the greater number of them, fhould from time to time fet down fuch Orders between fuch Parties, Plaintiff and Defendant, Creditor and Debtor, touching fuch Debts not exceeding 40 *s.* as they fhould find to ftand with Equity and good Confcience.

But

But after the making the ſaid Act, divers Evil-minded Perſons took hold of ſome doubtful and ambiguous Words therein, and wreſted the ſame to a wrong Senſe, that they might avoid the Juriſdiction of the ſaid Court, contrary to the true Meaning of the ſaid Act.

For remedy whereof, and for the farther ſtrengthening and eſtabliſhing the ſaid Court; an Act of Parliament was made in the third Year of the ſaid King *James*, intitled, *An Act for the recovering of ſmall Debts, and for the relieving of poor Debtors in* London. The Tenor whereof is as followeth.

Stat. 3. Jac. cap. 15. *See* Cro. Car. 413. *and* Chart. 1. Car. 1.

'WHereas by virtue of divers Acts of Common Council made within the City of *London*, the Lord Mayor and Aldermen of the ſame City, for the Relief of poor Debtors dwelling within the ſaid City, have accuſtomed monthly to aſſign two Aldermen, and twelve diſcreet Commoners to be Commiſſioners, and ſit in the Court of Requeſts, commonly called the Court of Conſcience, in the *Guildhall* of the ſame City, there to hear and determine all Matters of Debt not amounting to the Sum of 40 s. to be brought before them : And whereas at the Seſſions of Parliament holden at *Weſtminſter*, the Nineteenth Day of *March*, in the firſt Year of the Reign of our Sovereign Lord the King's Majeſty that now is, for the further Relief of ſuch poor Debtors, and more perfect eſtabliſhing of the ſaid Court, there was made and provided an Act, entitled, *An Act for recovery of ſmall Debts, and relieving of poor Debtors in* London : And whereas ſince the making of the ſaid Act, divers Perſons intending to ſubvert the good and charitable Intent
'tent

' tent of the fame, and taking hold of fome
' doubtful and ambiguous Words therein, do
' wreft the fame for their own Lucre and Gain,
' to the avoiding the Jurifdiction of the faid
' Court, contrary to the godly Meaning of the
' faid Act.

' For the Remedy whereof, and to the in-
' tent that fome more full and ample Provifion
' may be made for the Relief of fuch poor
' Debtors; Be it enacted by Authority of this
' prefent Parliament, that every Citizen and
' Freeman of the City of *London*, and every
' other Perfon and Perfons inhabiting, or that
' fhall inhabit within the faid City, or the Li-
' berties thereof, being a Tradefman, Victual-
' ler, or a Labouring Man, which now have,
' or hereafter fhall have any Debt or Debts ow-
' ing unto him or them, not amounting to
' forty Shillings, by any Citizen, or by any o-
' ther Perfon or Perfons being a Victualler,
' Tradefman, or Labouring Man, inhabiting,
' or that fhall inhabit within the faid City,
' or the Liberties thereof, fhall or may caufe
' fuch Debtor or Debtors to be warned or fum-
' moned by the Beadle or Officer of the faid
' Court of Requefts for the time being, by
' writing to be left at the Dwelling-houfe of
' fuch Debtor or Debtors, or by any other reafo-
' nable warning or notice to be given to the faid
' Debtor or Debtors to appear before the Com-
' miffioners of the faid Court of Requefts, hol-
' den in the *Guildhall* of the faid City : And
' that the faid Commiffioners, or any three of
' them or more, fhall have Power and Autho-
' rity by virtue of this Act, from time to time,
' to fet down fuch Order and Orders between
' fuch Party and Parties Plaintiffs, and his or
' their fuch Debtor and Debtors Defendants,
' touching

' touching fuch Debts not amounting to the
' value of forty Shillings, in queftion before
' them, as they fhall find to ftand with Equity
' and good Confcience : All their Order or
' Orders to be regiftred in a Book, as they
' have been accuftomed, and as well the Party
' Plaintiff, as the Debtor or Defendant, to ob-
' ferve, perform, and keep the fame in all
' Points. And for the more due proceeding
' herein, it fhall be lawful for the fame Com-
' miffioners, or any three or more of them, to
' minifter an Oath to the Plaintiff or Defen-
' dant, and alfo to fuch Witneffes as fhall be
' produced on each Party, if the fame Com-
' miffioners, or any three of them or more fhall
' fo think it meet.

  ' And be it further enacted by the Authori-
' ty aforefaid, That if in any Action of Debt, or
' Action upon the Cafe upon any *Affumpfit* for
' the Recovery of any Debt, to be fued or pro-
' fecuted againft any the Perfon or Perfons a-
' forefaid, in any of the King's Courts at *Weft-*
' *minfter*, or elfewhere out of the faid Courts
' of Requefts, it fhall appear to the Judge or
' Judges of the Court where fuch Action fhall
' be fued or profecuted, that the Debt to be
' recovered by the Plaintiff in fuch Action doth
' not amount to the Sum of forty Shillings, and
' the Defendant in fuch Action fhall duly prove
' either by fufficient Teftimony, or by his own
' Oath, to be allowed by any the Judge or
' Judges of the faid Court where fuch Action
' fhall depend, that at the time of the com-
' mencing of fuch Action, fuch Defendant
' was inhabiting and refident in the City of
' *London*, or the Liberties thereof, as above,
' That in fuch cafe the faid Judge or Judges
: fhall not allow to the faid Plaintiff any Cofts
: of

' of Suit, but fhall award that the fame Plain-
' tiff fhall pay fo much ordinary Cofts to the
' Party Defendant, as fuch Defendant fhall
' juftly prove before the faid Judge or Judges,
' it hath truly coft him in Defence of the faid
' Suit.

' And be it further enacted, That if any
' Plaintiff or Creditor, Defendant or Debtor,
' after warning given to him or them, in man-
' ner and form before in this Act mentioned,
' by the faid Officer of the faid Court of Re-
' quefts, fhall without fome juft or reafonable
' Caufe of Excufe refufe to appear in the faid
' Court before the faid Commiffioners, or fhall
' not perform fuch order as the faid Commiffi-
' oners, or any three or more of them, fhall
' fet down, of or concerning fuch Debts as a-
' forefaid; That then it fhall be lawful for the
' Officers of the faid Court, or any other of
' the Serjeants at Mace of the faid City, by
' Order of the faid Commiffioners, or any three
' or more of them, to commit fuch Party or
' Parties to Prifon, into one of the Counters
' of the faid City, there to remain until he or
' they fhall perform the Order of the faid Com-
' miffioners in that behalf.

' Provided always, That this Act, or any
' thing therein contained, fhall not extend to
' any Debt for any Rent upon any Leafe of
' Lands or Tenements, or any other real Con-
' tracts, nor to any other Debt that fhall arife
' by reafon of any Caufe concerning a Tefta-
' ment or Matrimony, or any thing concern-
' ing or properly belonging to the Ecclefiaftical
' Court, albeit the fame fhall be under forty
' Shillings : Any thing before contained to the
' contrary in any wife notwithftanding.

And thus by this laſt repeated Act, this Court is eſtabliſhed and continued to this Day. The Courſe and Practice thereof is by Summons; to which if the Party ſummoned appear not, the Commiſſioners may make an Order to commit him: and if he appear, they proceed ſummarily to Judgment, examining both Parties and Witneſſes upon Oath, and as they ſee cauſe give Judgment without more ado.

And *Note*, That the Lord Mayor and Court of Aldermen do monthly aſſign ſuch Aldermen and Commons to ſit as Commiſſioners in the ſaid Court, as they think fit: And the ſame Perſons, or any three of them, make a Court, and do ſit in *Guildhall* every *Wedneſday* and *Saturday* in the Forenoon, to hear and determine ſuch Cauſes as come before them.

A Cauſe may be brought and determined in this Court for 10 *d.* Charge, in caſe the Defendant appear the firſt or ſecond Court Day after the Summons left, *viz.* Six-Pence for the Plaint and the Summons, and 4 *d.* for the Order: But if the Defendant do not appear the ſecond Court-Day after Summons, an Attachment will be awarded againſt him, which will compel him to appear, and encreaſe the Charge: And on his refuſing or neglecting then to appear, they will commit him to Priſon.

If any Citizen ſhall be arreſted for a Debt under 40 *s.* this Court will grant a Summons for the Plaintiff in the Action; and if he appear not the firſt Court-Day after the Summons left at his Houſe, will grant an Attachment againſt him, and force him to take his Debt, and pay the Defendant his Coſts. And if any Attorney in *London* ſhall preſume to go on in any ſuch Suit, after notice to the contrary, or ſhall refuſe to obey the Order of this Court,

upon

upon Complaint thereof made to the Court of
Aldermen, they will fufpend fuch Perfon : As
foon after the making the laft recited Act, hap-
pened to one *Hutton*, one of the Attorneys of
the Sheriffs Court, for a Contempt againft the
faid Court.

In the Mayoralty of Sir *William Craven*, *Anno* 1610. this *Hutton* was fent for by the Commiffioners fitting in this Court ; and he refufing
to come before them, they made Complaint to
the Court of Aldermen, who thereupon made
an Order to difmifs him from his Office of an
Attorney ; which Order followeth in thefe
Words.

Craven, Mayor.

Jovis 24 *die* Januarii, *Anno Domini*
1610. *Annoque Regis* Jacobi *Angl.
&c. octavo.*

'THis Day Sir *John Jolls*, Knight and Al-
' derman of this City, did declare unto
' this Court, That he and three difcreet Com-
' moners of this City (amongft others) affign-
' ed by this Court to be Commiffioners for this
' Inftant Month of *January* for the Court of
' Requefts, commonly called the Court of Con-
' fcience, according to an Act of Parliament
' made in the Third Year of the Reign of the
' King's Majefty that now is : And that they
' fitting in the faid Court of Confcience in the
' *Guildhall* of this City, yefterday laft, being
' *Wednefday* the three and twentieth of this In-
' ftant *January*, to hear and determine Matters
' for the Recovering of fmall Debts, and relie-

' ving of poor Debtors in this City, according
' as by the said Act of Parliament they are au-
' thorized, and only out of a conscionable
' Care to be certainly informed of the true
' State of a Case brought before them, and
' which was depending in the Sheriffs Court,
' where they were informed that *Thomas Hutton,*
' one of the Attorneys in the Sheriffs Court,
' was retained for the Plaintiff in the said Court :
' And the said *Hutton* being in the *Guildhall,* in
' the View of the said Sir *John Jolls,* and other
' the Commissioners ; the said Commissioners
' commanded the Beadle of the said Court to
' go to the said *Hutton,* and require him pre-
' sently to come to the said Sir *John Jolls,* and
' the other Commissioners. And albeit the
' Beadle went two several times to him, yet
' the said *Hutton* peremptorily and contemptu-
' ously made answer, *That he neither could nor*
' *would come to them.* The which being here
' examined in full and open Court, and the said
' *Hutton* called to answer thereto, the same was
' in part confessed by the said *Hutton,* and also
' proved by the Oath of the Clerk and Beadle
' of the said Court of Requests. And to ag-
' gravate the said Offence and Contempt, the
' said *Hutton* here in open Court, did affirm,
' *That he knew not what Authority that Court had*
' *to send for him.* The which Indignities and
' Contempts offered to Commissioners chosen
' by this Court, and established by Act of Par-
' liament, and to an Alderman of the City of
' *London,* by a subordinate Officer of this City ;
' this Court do generally hold the same in-
' tolerable, and the said *Hutton* worthy of se-
' vere and condign Punishment : And therefore
' do order and decree that the said *Thomas Hut-*
' *ton* shall be presently and absolutely dismissed ;
' and

' and this Court doth abfolutely difmifs him of
' and from his faid Place and Office of one of
' the Attorneys of the faid Sheriffs Court afore-
' faid. And Mr. *Dale*, one of the Judges of
' the faid Court, was fent for, and being here
' prefent, was required to take notice thereof,
' and to publifh the fame in the Sheriffs-Court,
' and to take   Order that the faid *Thomas*
' *Hutton* be not admitted hereafter to practife
' any more in the faid Court.'

It is before obferv'd, pag.   That the
Clerk of this Court has been fometimes elected
by the Court of Common-Council ; but it properly belongs to the Court of Aldermen, *i. e.*
the Lord Mayor and Aldermen. *Quære*.

And note, the Beadlefhip of this Court is
faid to be in the Gift of the Lord Mayor.

The Clerks Fees of this Court.

FOr every Plaint — — 2 *d.*
    For every Appearance — — 2 *d.*
For every Order — — 4 *d.*
For every Precept or Warrant to commit to
    Prifon — — 6 *d.*
For every Search — — 2 *d.*
For every Satisfaction acknowledged upon an
    Order — — — 6 *d.*

Beadles Fees.

FOr warning every Perfon within the Liber-
    ties — — — 4 *d.*
For warning every Perfon without the Liber-
    ties — — 6 *d.*
For ferving every Precept or Warrant — 4 *d.*

There

Here are several other Courts kept within the City of *London*; as,

1. The Halmote.
2. The Court of the Coroner.
3. The Court of the Escheator.
4. The Court of the *Tower*.
5. *St. Martins-le-Grand.*

The Halmote.

1. The Halmote, or Court of the Hall, is that Court which every Company in *London* keep in their Halls, which was anciently call'd the Halmote or Folkmote.

The Court of the Coroner.

2. The Mayor is Coroner within the City, and this Court is held before him or his Deputy. *See the Office of Coroner in* London, ante.

Escheators Court.

3. And the Lord Mayor is also Escheator within the said City; and this Court of Escheator is also held before him or his Deputy.

The Court of the Tower.

4. This Court is held within the Verge of the Tower of *London*, before the Steward there, by Prescription, for Debt, Trespass, and other Actions of any Sum greater or lesser.

St. Mar-

St. Martins le Grand.

There is alfo a Court held at St. *Martins le Grand*, but is diftinct from the Government of the City of *London*, and is fubject to the Liberty of the Deanery of *Weftminfter*. It is a Liberty wherein a Court of Record is kept Weekly every *Wednefday*, for the Tryal of all perfonal Actions, of what nature foever ; and there is a Court-Houfe and a Prifon. The leading Procefs is a *Capias* againft the Body, or an Attachment againft the Goods ; fo that a Man's Goods may be arrefted in his own Houfe upon the firft Procefs, if he be not taken : which is according to the Practice of all ancient Liberties or Franchifes.

Prerogative Court, &c.

There is alfo the Prerogative Court, and Court of Admiralty, held at *Doctors-Commons*, within the City of *London* ; of which we fhall add no more in this Place, they being elfewhere treated of at large.

Here

Here follow several Certificates of Fees, accustomed to be taken by the several Prothonotaries, Secondaries, Attorneys, and Sitting Clerks, belonging to the Sheriffs of the City of London. *And also of the several and particular Fees taken of Prisoners committed to either of the Compters in* Wood-street *or the* Poultry, London. *With Notes of the ancient Fees, Duties and Claims of the Keeper of* Ludgate, *for all Persons committed to that Prison.*

✿✿✿✿✿✿✿✿✿✿✿✿✿✿✿✿✿✿✿✿✿✿

Fees of the Prothonotaries of the Sheriffs Court.

In Obedience to the Command of this Honourable Court, I Roger Goodday, *one of the two Prothonotaries of the Sheriffs Courts held in the* Guildhall, London, *do humbly certify, That the Fees taken by me for any Business by me done, appertaining to the same Courts, by virtue of my said Office (which is only for Declarations of the same Courts made by me) are as followeth, viz.*

FOr these general Declarations intituled as followeth, to wit, *Assumpsit, Insult' fecit, Domu' fregit, Ejection' Firme, Verbis Scandalosis, Trover pro Bonis, Trover pro Pecuniis, Concessit solvere, Billa Penalis, Billa simplex, & Scriptum obligatorium,* Twelve-pence a-piece is taken, and no more.

Item,

Item, For thefe other general Declarations, intituled as followeth, to wit, *Aſſumpſit ad ſeɛt.Aminiſtratricis maritat' Aſſumpſit ad ſeɛt' Adminiſtrator.vel Adminiſtratric' ſol. Aſſumpſit verſus Adminiſtrator.vel.Adminiſtratric' ſol.vel verſus Adminiſtratric' maritat. Aſſumpſit ad ſeɛt' Executor. vel Executric' ſol. vel ad ſeɛt' Executric' maritat' Aſſumpſit verſus Executor' vel verſus Executric' ſol. vel verſus Executric' maritat' Aſſumpſit ad ſeɛt' viri & uxoris dum ſol. vel verſus virum & uxorem dum ſol.Aſſumpſit pro ſupeovivent. Conceſſit ſolvere pro Executor' vel pro Executric' ſol. vel pro Executric' maritat', vel verſus Executor, vel verſus Executric' ſolam,vel verſus Executric' maritat' Conceſſ. ſolvere pro Adminiſtrator' vel pro Adminiſtratric' ſol. vel pro Adminiſtratric' maritat', vel verſus Adminiſtrator. vel verſus Adminiſtratric' ſolam, vel verſus Adminiſtratric' maritat; Scriptum vel Billa ſimplex pro Executor', vel pro Executric' ſol. vel pro Executric' maritat' vel verſus Executor. vel verſus Executric' ſol. vel verſus Executric' maritat' & Billa ſimplex vel Scriptum. pro Adminiſtrator' vel pro Adminiſtratric' vel pro Adminiſtratric' maritat. vel verſus Adminiſtrator. vel verſus Adminiſtratricem ſolam, vel verſus Adminiſtraticem maritat' Duo ſcripta, due Bille ſimplices, un' Script. cum un' Billa ſimplice,Scriptum cumCon' ſol. Billa ſimplex cumCon' ſol. Scriptum unde ſatisfecit, Billa ſimplex unde ſatisfecit, Scriptum pro ſupervivent. Billa ſimplex pro ſupervivent. Scriptum ad ſeɛt' viri & uxor. dum ſol. vel verſus virum & uxor. dum ſol. Billa ſimplex pro viro & uxor. dum ſol.vel verſus virum & uxor. dum ſol' & Conceſſit ſolvere verſus uxorem ſol. mercandizan' abſq; viro.* Sixteen Pence a piece is taken, and no more.

Item, For thefe other general Declarations, intituled as followeth, *viz. Quantum meruit pro eſculent' & poculen' allocat.Defend. ſol. & Aſſumpſit, &*

& *Quantum meruit* general *pro bonis* (*fi Schedula fit brevis*) & *Affumpfit* ; Twenty Pence a piece only is taken, and no more.

Item, For a Declaration upon an Apprentice's Indenture, if for Abfence only, or for imbezeling Goods only, but two Shillings fix Pence is taken, and no more ; but if there be more Breaches than one, it is to be drawn by Council, and then it is reckoned for a fpecial Declaration.

Item, All other Declarations (together alfo with *Trover pro bonis* & *Quantum meruit pro bonis*, if the Goods be many, and cannot be contained within the fpace left in the general Blank) are to be drawn firft, and afterwards to be fairly ingroffed, and are therefore called Special Declarations ; for which there is taken four Pence *per* Sheet for every Sheet drawn, and four Pence *per* Sheet for every Sheet ingroffed, and no more. And thefe, as I am informed, are the ancient and accuftomed Fees.

But it is to be underftood, that I have to my felf but the Moiety of thefe Fees for Declarations, as they happen ; and *William Newbold*, the other Prothonotary, hath the other Moiety thereof. And fo in the like manner for Declarations of the fame Court, done by the faid *William Newbold*, he hath the one Moiety of the Fees thereof to himfelf, and I the other. Moiety thereof.

17 *March*
1663.
                                        R. *Goodday*.

The Fees due to and usually taken 'by William Newbold, *the Younger*, *by Vertue of his Office of one of the two Prothonotaries of the Courts held before both and either of the Sheriffs of the City of* London, *(pro tempore) in the Guild-hall of the same City, for any Declaration whatsoever, upon any Plaint or Action levied before both or either of the said Sheriffs, are as followeth,* viz.

FOr every General Declaration upon, 1. An *Assumpsit.* 2. Upon an Assault. 3. Upon a *Domum fregit.* 4. Upon an Ejectment. 5. Upon a Trover for *English* Moneys. 6. Upon a *Concessit solvere.* 7. Upon a single Bond. 8. Upon a single Bill. 9. Upon a single Bill Penal. 10. Upon general scandalous Words, as Thief, Whore, and the like : When it is only written and ingrossed by me into Parchment, and not drawn into Paper, Twelve Pence. But when such a Declaration is drawn by me into Paper, for the Client to go to Council with, or otherwise to use at his pleasure, for every Sheet thereof, drawing four Pence ; and for every Sheet thereof, ingrossing, four Pence.

For every General Declaration upon a Trover for Goods, if it be ordinary, that is to say, if the Goods contained in the Schedule be but of few Parcels, and may be contained in the two Lines Space usually left in the Ingrossment of a Blank Trover for Goods, Twelve Pence. But if it be extraordinary, that is to say, the Goods contained in the Schedule be many and

divers

divers for kind, and cannot be contained in the two Lines ufually left in the Blank, as before; then for every Sheet thereof drawing, four Pence; and for every Sheet thereof ingroffing, four Pence.

. For every General Declaration upon, 1. An *Affumpfit* at the Suit of an Adminiftrator. 2. Upon a *Conceffit Solvere* at the Suit of the fame. 3. Upon a fingle Bill or a fingle Bond at the Suit of the fame. 4. Upon an *Affumpfit* againft an Adminiftrator. 5. Upon an *Affumpfit* againft an Executor. 6. Upon an *Affumpfit* againft an Executrix married or unmarried. 7. Upon an *Affumpfit* againft an Adminiftratrix married or unmarried. 8. Upon a *Conceffit Solvere* againft the fame. 9. Upon a fingle Bill or a fingle Bond againft the fame. 10. Upon a *Conceffit Solvere* againft an Adminiftrator. 11. Upon a *Conceffit Solvere* at the Suit of an Executor. 12. Upon a *Conceffit Solvere* at the Suit of an Executrix, married or unmarried. 13. Upon a *Conceffit Solvere* againft an Executor. 14. Upon a *Conceffit Solvere* againft an Executrix, married or unmarried. 15. Upon a fingle Bill or fingle Bond againft an Adminiftrator. 16. Upon the like at the Suit of an Executor. 17. Upon the like at the Suit of an Executrix, married or unmarried. 18. Upon a fingle Bill or fingle Bond againft an Executor. 19. Upon a fingle Bill or fingle Bond againft an Executrix, married or unmarried. 20. Upon an *Affumpfit* at the Suit of an Executor. 21. Upon an *Affumpfit* at the Suit of an Executrix, married or unmarried. 22. Upon an *Affumpfit* at the Suit of an Adminiftratrix, married or unmarried. 23. Upon a *Conceffit Solvere* at the Suit of the fame. 24. Upon a fingle Bill or fingle Bond at the Suit of the fame. 25. Upon two fingle Bonds, or two
fingle

single Bills. 26. Upon a single Bond and a *Concessit Solvere*. 27. Upon a single Bill, and *Concessit Solvere*. 28. Upon a Bond *Unde satisfecit*. 29. Upon a single Bill *Unde satisfecit*. 30. Upon a Bond or Bill at the Suit of a Survivor. 31. Upon an *Assumpsit* at the Suit of the same. 32. Upon a Bond or single Bill made to the Wife when unmarried. 33. Upon a Bond or single Bill made by the Wife when unmarried. 34. Upon an *Assumpsit* made to the Wife when unmarried. 35. Upon an *Assumpsit* made by the Wife when unmarried. 36. Upon a *Concessit Solvere* against a Wife trading without her Husband : When it is only written and ingrossed by me into Parchment, and not drawn into Paper, Twelve Pence. But when it is drawn by me into Paper, as is before expressed ; then for every Sheet thereof drawing, four Pence ; and for every Sheet thereof ingrossing, four Pence.

For every general Declaration upon a *Quantum meruit* for Meat, Drink, and Lodging, allowed to the Defendant in the Plaint only, when only ingrossed as before, twenty Pence ; but if drawn as before, for drawing fourPence a Sheet ; and for ingrossing, four Pence a Sheet.

For every General Declaration upon a *Quantum meruit*, for Goods sold and delivered, if the Goods in the Schedule be few, and may be contained in two Lines (according as it is before expressed, for a Declaration upon a Trover for Goods) Twenty Pence ; but if not, then for drawing four Pence a Sheet, and for ingrossing four Pence a Sheet.

For every General Declaration upon an Indenture of Apprenticehood, if for Absence only, or for purloining his Master's Moneys and Goods, it being ingross'd, only two Shillings and fix Pence. But if it be for more Breaches than one, then for every Sheet thereof drawing four Pence ; and for every Sheet thereof ingroffing, four Pence.

For every other Declaration, which is not a general one, as before, but a fpecial one, for every Sheet thereof drawing, four Pence ; and for every Sheet thereof ingroffing, four Pence.

Tuefday 22d Day of *March,*
Anno Dom. 1663. *Annoq;*
Regni Regis, Caroli Se-
cundi,Angliæ, &c. 16.

William Newbold, Jun'
Prothonotary.

A Particular of Fees taken and due to the Secondaries in London, *for Return and Execution of Procefs returnable in the Courts at* Weftminfter, *and elfewhere.*

1. FOr returning a Nichil upon an Original Writ in Trefpafs —— 4 *d.*
2. For Return of a Summons upon any fuch Writ —— —— 2 *s.*
3. For Return of Iffues upon any Diftringas fued out upon any Original —— 2 *s.*
4. For a Warrant upon a *Lat.* or any Procefs before Judgment —— 4 *d.*
5. For charging a Prifoner with any Writ 2*s.* 4*d.*

6. For

6. For Return of *Non est Inventus,* upon any Writ ——— ——— — 4 *d.*

7. For Return of a *Cep' Cor'* upon any Writ 4 *d.*

8. For Return of a *Ha. Cor.* upon a *Cep' Cor'* or *distr* nuper vic'* ——— : 4 *d.*

9. For a Return of a special *Cep' Cor'* where the Defendant is Prisoner, or in any other special Case. ——— ——— 2 *s.*

10. For Allowance of a *Supersed'* upon a Writ of Error, or upon any other Writ for every Name ——— ——— 2 *s.* 4 *d.*

11. For a Bail for a Bond for Appearance 2 *s.* 4 *d.*

12. For a Release upon any Writ before Judgment ——— ——— 2 *s.* 4 *d.*

13. For a Warrant upon a Writ of the Peace, and good Behaviour out of the *Crown-Office* ——— ——— ——— — 2 *s.* 4 *d.*

14. For a Warrant upon a Writ of *Haber' fac' Possess'* ——— 2 *s.* 4 *d.*

15. For a Return of the same Writ, and Entry thereof ——— ——— 6 *s.* 8 *d.*

16. For executing a Writ of Inquiry of *Dam'* 10 *s.*

17. For executing a Writ of Inquiry for a *Devastavit* ——— ——— 13 *s.* 4 *d.*

18. For executing a Writ of *Eleg.* or *Fi. Fa* whereby any Lands or Goods are seized, or of a *Ca. Sa'* the Statute allows Poundage, though we take under the Allowance, respecting what Benefit the Plaintiff makes, and what Trouble we are at, the Officer and Appraisers being paid.

For Return of a *Devastavit* upon a *Fi. Fa.* where Assets are found upon fully Admin' and Entry ——— ——— 6 *s.* 8 *d.*

For a Return of a *Fier' Fec'* upon a *Fi. Fa.* 2 *s.*

For Return of a *Null' bon'* upon a *Fi. Fa.* 4 *d.*

For Return of a *Ven.Fa.* for an ordinary Jury 4 *d.*

For

For Return of a *Ven. Fa.* to a Party Jury   2 s.

For Return of an ordinary *Diſtr' Jur'* 2 s.   4 d.

For Return of a Party or Special *Diſtr' Jur'* 4 s. 8 d.

For a *Tales* upon an ordinar' *Jur'* ——— 2 s.

For a *Tales* upon a ſpecial *Jur'* ———— 4 s.

For a *Nichil* or a *Mortuus* upon a *Sc' Fa'*   12 d.

For a *Sc' Fec.* or a Summons upon a *Sc' Fa'*   2 s.

For a Warrant upon a *Sci' Fa'* ——— 12 d.

Upon a Writ of *Ha. Cor. cum cauſa,* to remove any Action unto any Court at *Weſtminſter.*

For the Allowance to the firſt Action —2 s. 4 d.

For every other Action ———— 4 d.

For Return of the firſt Action ——— 2 s. 6 d.

For every other Action ——— 1 s.

For Return of every Writ, if not judicial, 2 s. 4 d.

For Return of every judicial Writ — 3 s. 4 d.

For a Bill to certify the Cauſe from one Compter to another ——— ——— 4 d.

For Allowance of a *Certiorari* to remove an Attachment —— —— 2 s. 8 d.

For Return of the ſame if no Proceedings —— —— —— 6 s. 8 d.

If proceeded upon, or more Attachments than one returned, according to the Length and and Difficulty thereof.

For Return of an *Exigent* allowed for every Name outlawed or waived ——— 4 d.

For a *Reddidit ſe,* or *Retraxit* for every Name —— —— —— 12 d.

For Allowance of a *Superſed'* to an *Exigent,* for every Name before the Return —— 12 d.

For every Name after the Return —— 2 s.

For the Clerk for filing of it —— 4 d.

For Allowance and Return of a *Certiorari* upon an *exegi Fa'* —— —— 4 s. 10 d.

For Return of a Proclamation upon an *Exigent* or other Writ —— —— 12 d.

For

For the Copy of an ordinary *Exigent,* or other
  Writ ——— ——— 4 *d.*
For the Copy of an extraordinary long Writ, ac-
  cording to the Length of it.
For the Copy of a Pannel for a Jury ——— 4 *d.*
For Executing and Return of any Precept in
  Dower or Partition, according to the Length
  and Trouble.

{ *Edw. Trotman.*
{ *Edw. Leigh.*

---

*The several Fees accustomed to be ta-
ken as of Right belonging to the Attorneys of the Worshipful the Sheriffs
Courts in* London.

UPon every Retainer by Plaintiff or Defen-
dant ——— ——— 1 *s.* 8 *d.*
After Appearance and Declaration upon every
  further Imparlance or Issue ——— 1 *s.* 8 *d.*
Upon the Summons of a Jury ——— 1 *s.* 8 *d.*
Upon any Proviso craved by the Defendant's
  Attorney ——— ——— 1 *s.* 8 *d.*
Upon any Motion whereupon the Court puts
  off a Tryal ——— ——— 1 *s.* 8 *d.*
Upon Argument upon a Demurrer joined,
  special Verdict or Motion in Arrest of Judg-
  ment ——— ——— 3 *s.* 4 *d.*
Upon Imparlance to special Pleadings 1 *s.* 8 *d.*
For drawing special Pleadings *per* Sheet 4 *d.*
For ingrossing thereof ——— 4 *d.*
Upon a Wager of Law perfected or tendred
                                          1 *s.* 8 *d.*
Upon any Judgment obtained by Default upon
  Attachment, or otherwise ——— 1 *s.* 8 *d.*

G g   Upon

Upon Revival of a Judgment by *Scir' fac'* 1 *s.* 8 *d.*
Upon Satisfaction entred upon a Judgment by
Warrant — — 1 *s.* 8 *d.*

> *Nath. Barker.* } { *Longworth Croſſe.*
> *Richard Bincks.* } { *Jo. Ayres.*
> *Jo. Baynes.* } { *Ja. Jobſon.*

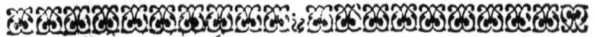

'*A Table of the Fees due, and uſually
taken by the Clerkſitters belonging
to the Sheriffs Courts in both Compters,* London, *as followeth.*

IMprimis, For Entry of every Action   4 *d.*
  Item, For the Copy of the Bail   4 *d.*
Item, If the Defendant be a Freeman, and re-
quire Defaults for entring the ſame   4 *d.*
Item, If the Defendant yield himſelf to an
Action without an Arreſt, or for Diſcharge
of his Sureties after Arreſt, or to an Action
in Diſſolution of an Attachment for entring
the ſame   4 *d.*
Item, If the Defendant undertakes to ſave his
Bail harmleſs, for recording the ſame   4 *d.*
Item, If the Bail reprieve the Defendant, the
Bail payeth for entring the ſame, and for
his Diſcharge   4 *d.*
Item, For the Return of every Attachment or
Sequeſtration   4 *d.*
Item, For the Copy of every Action, and of
every Attachment   4 *d.*
Item, For every brief Copy to make the Plain-
tiff's Declaration, and for his Warrant of
Attorney   4 *d.*
                Item,

Item, For every Warrant of Attorney for the Defendant 2 *d.*

Item, For entring of a Nonfuit for want of a Declaration 2 *d.*

Item, For the Amendment of an Action in the Name or Sum 2 *d.*

Item, For altering the Nature of an Action, from one kind to another 4 *d.*

Item, for Entry of a *Si procedatur* for the Garnifhee's Attorney 4 *d.*

Item, For perfecting an Action according to a Speciality, for every perfection 2 *d.*

Item, For every Warrant of Attorney for the Plaintiff, upon an Attachment or Sequeftration 4 *d.*

Item, For Bail in Diffolution of an Attachment 1 *s.* 4 *d.*
And for entring fuch Diffolution 1 *s.*

Item, For a Note teftifying fuch Diffolution 6 *d.*

Item, For every *Scire fac'*, Bill of Appraifement or Sequeftration for Goods, unlefs they confift of very many Parcels, in which cafe they ever took according to the length 2 *s.*

Item, For every Precept to appraife Goods upon an Attachment 2 *s.* 4 *d.*

Item, For Return of every *Elongavit* upon every fuch Precept 1 *s.*

Item, For every Bail in the Office 1 *s.* 4 *d.*

Item, For every Bail taken out of the Office 2 *s.* 8 *d.*

Item, For a Bail upon an Attachment, to reftore the Money or Goods condemned, in cafe the Defendant fhall difprove the Plaintiff's Debt within a year and a day 1 *s.* 4 *d.*

Item, For awarding every *Venire fac'* for Tryal of an Iffue, and the Return thereof, 8 *d.*
Whereof we allow to the Clerk of the Papers in Cafe he makes the *Venire fac'* 2 *d.*

Item,

Item, For every Verdict Juror withdrawn, and drawing up thereof, or Non-fuit upon Tryal   1 *s.* 6 *d.*

Item, For drawing every Special Verdict, for every Sheet   8 *d.*

Item, For the Copy of every fpecial Verdict, for every Sheet   4 *d.*

Item, For Ingroffing of every fpecial Verdict, for every Sheet   4 *d.*

Item, For marking a Caufe before the Lord Mayor   2 *d.*

Item, When a Caufe is by the Lord Mayor generally remitted to Judgment, for entring thereof   2 *d.*

Item, When the Caufe is remitted by the Lord Mayor, with an Order for time of Payment, for entring that Order   4 *d.*

Item, Upon a *Hab. Corpus* brought to remove a Prifoner, when a *Mittatis Caufas* is brought from one Compter to th'other, or from the Lord Mayor's Court for fearching and figning, if no Caufe be,   4 *d.*

If there be Caufes, for certifying every Action   4 *d.*

Item, For certifying every Writ   1 *s.*

Item, For a Bill of Charge or Difcharge of Actions, from one Compter to the other 4 *d.*

Item, For every Search   4 *d.*

And for the Difcharge of every Prifoner by the Clerkfitter's fetting his Hand, for that purpofe, to the Keeper's Book   1 *s.*

Thefe belong to the Sheriffs, and are accompted and paid accordingly.

Item, For withdrawing every Action of Debt above forty Shillings, Actions of Accompt, or Breach of Covenant   1 *s.*

Item, For every Action of Debt under forty Shillings   4 *d.*

Item, For withdrawing every Action of Trefpafs, or Action upon the Cafe   6 *d.*

Item,

Item, For every Protection   2 *s.* 6 *d.*

Item, For a Bail taken before the Lord Mayor in the Defendant's abfence   2 *s.* 8 *d.*

Item, For the Diffolution of an Attachment thereupon, and Entry thereof   2 *s.* 8 *d.*

Item, For a Note, if required, teftifying fuch Diffolution   1 *s.*

Item, For every *Decem Tales*   8 *d.*

Item, For charging a Prifoner with an Action out of the Lord Mayor's Court   4 *d.*

Item, For Difcharge thereof   4 *d.*

Item, For Charging a Prifoner with a Caufe out of the Court of Requefts, *London,*   4 *d.*

Item, For Difcharge thereof   4 *d.*

Item, for continuance of every Caufe ready for Tryal   8 *d.*

Item, For a Copy of the Juries Names (if required)   4 *d.*

H. Cotton.	*Fran. Mitchell.*
Ed. Sayer.	*Henry Hearne.*
Geo. Gaell.	*Edw. Maynard.*
Matthew Petley.	*Will. Gardner.*

A Certificate of the feveral Fees taken in the Compter of Woodftreet.

Prifoners charged by Writs, Actions or Warrants, if lodged in the Mafterfide Ward,

Pay to the Keeper ——— ——	6 *s.* 8 *d.*
To the Book-keeper ——— —	2 *s.*
To the Turnkey ——— ——	1 *s.*
To the Chamberlains — ——	2 *s.* 6 *d.*
	12 *s.* 2 *d.*

If

If lodged in the Knight's Ward,

To the Keeper	3 s. 6 d.
To the Book-keeper	1 s.
To the Turnkey	6 d.
To the Chamberlains	1 s. 6 d.
	6 s. 6 d.

If lodged in the Two-penny Ward,

To the Keeper	2 s. 6 d.
To the Book-keeper	1 s.
To the Turnkey	6 d.
To the Chamberlains	1 s.
	5 s.

If lodged in the Common Ward, or discharged the same,

To the Keeper	2 s.
To the Book-keeper	1 s.
To the Turnkey	6 d.
	3 s. 6 d.

If any Prisoner be charged in Execution, he is to pay for his Fine of Irons for all Sums under 30 l. Two Pence a pound; and all Sums above, Penny half penny.

The Command Prisoners if discharged the same day, or lodge in the Common Ward,

Pay to the Keeper	1 s. 10 d.
To the Book-keeper	8 d.
To the Turnkey	6 d.
To the Beadle of the Ward	6 d.
	3 s. 6 d.

If the Command Prisoner have a Bed, he payeth to the Keeper

	2 s. 6 d.
To the Book-keeper	1 s.
To the Turnkey	8 d.
To the Chamberlains	1 s.
To the Beadle	6 d.
	5 s. 8 d.

I

If on the Lord Mayor's Command, to the
Carver — — — — 12 *d.*
If committed by the Marſhal, his Fee is 12 *d.*

Rich. Hackett.

The 22d of *November*, 1663.
A Particular of the Fees and Rates for Priſoners committed to the Poultry *Counter,* London.

FOr each Priſoner to the Maſter-Keeper,
his Turnkeys, Book-keepers, *&c.*
In the Maſter-ſide or Houſe   9 *s.* 8 *d.*
In the Knights Ward ſide   5 *s.*
In the Twopenny Ward ſide   4 *s.*
In the Two-hole Wards   3 *s.* 6 *d.*
In the Book-houſe on the Maſter ſide   6 *s.*
For a mark'd Priſoner removed by *Habeas Cor-*
pus, &c.   2 *s.* 6 *d.*

To the Serjeant, Warden and his Yeoman, for
Dogget Bill of each Priſoner Arreſted and
Committed   4 *d.*
To the Lord Mayor's Carvers for each Priſoner
committed by the Lord Mayor's particular
Warrant or ſpecial Command,   1 *s.*
To the City Marſhals, for each Priſoner com-
mitted by them upon any ſpecial Warrant or
Command,   1 *s.*
To the Stock of the poor Priſoners of the Hole
Wards, towards common Fire, Candles, and
other Proviſions for each Arreſted Perſon in
their Wards, and for Command,   1 *s.*

For each Prifoner in the feveral Wards, to the Mafter-Keeper for Chamber-Rent, Beds, Sheets, &c.

In the Mafters fide *per* Night.   6 *d.*

In the Knights Ward *per* Night   3 *d.*

In the Twopenny Ward *per* Night   2 *d.*

To the Mafter Keeper for Sheets at entrance and change, in the Mafter-fide 1 *s.* the other Lodging Wards   8 *d.*

To the Chamberlains and Turnkeys of each Ward, in the Mafters fide 1 *s.* the other Lodging Wards   8 *d.*

For each Prifoner in the Hole Wards due 1 *d.* *per* Night Rent and Accommodations, but take nothing.

For each Prifoner lying upon Statute, Condemnation or Execution, not giving in Security for their being a true Prifoner for 30 *l.* and under 2 *d. per* pound, and for all Sums above 30 *l.* 1½. *per* pound Money.

For each Prifoner's Chamber-rent, Dyet, Beer, Fire, Candles, Attendance, and other Accommodations in the Mafters Houfe, according to the Ability and Quality of the Perfon, but generally is 30 *s. per* Week.

For a Prifoner going abroad with one or more Under-keepers in cafe of Neceffity, or fome extraordinary occafion, is at an uncertain Rate, differing according to the number and value of the Actions, and the quality and the condition of the Prifoner, and according to the more or lefs Time, Places, and other material Circumftances.

Humphry Gyffard.

A

A Note of all the Fees, Duties, and Claims of the Keeper of Ludgate, *for all Persons committed to that Prison.*

AT the coming in of every Prisoner, to the Turnkey   1 *s.*   *Time out of Mind.*

To the Officer that brings him   2 *d.*

When the Prisoner is discharged, to the Turnkey   1 *s.*

To the Chamberlain   2 *d.*

To the Keeper his Fee for every Prisoner when discharged   2 *s.*

To the Chamberlain once every Month for washing of Sheets   8 *d.*

Prisoners lying in the best Lodgings, are to pay by the Night   3 *d.*

In the Second   2 *d.*   *By Act of*

In the meanest Lodging   1 *d.*   *Common*

* Prisoners in Execution for all matters under *Council the* 30 *l.* are to pay by the pound   2 *d.*   *25th of Septemb.* 1621.

And if above 30 *l.* to pay *per* pound   1 *d. ob.*   * *By Act of*

I take not this Fee of Poundage, but on Fee *Common* of a Writ, which is but   2 *s.* 6 *d.*   *Council the*

† The Prisoner charged with Actions, for every *1st of August, the 1* Action I know of   1 *s.*   *Ed.* 6.

For a Writ   2 *s.* 6 *d.*   † *Ordered the*

The Prisoner that goeth abroad with a Keeper, *14th of June* is to pay *per diem*   1 *s.* 4 *d.*   1598.

The Keeper that goeth with him to have his Dinner, or in Money   4 *d.*

Robert Nicols Keeper.
Bl. B.

Fees

※※※※※※※※※※※※※※※-※※※※※※※※※※※

Fees incident to the Sheriffs Court, &c. *of* London.

WE have before occasionally seen some Fees in several Courts, but being short in the Sheriffs-Court, we will now inquire further after them.

First, It is to be observed, that the Plaintiff in the Sherriffs-Court hath four Court-Days to declare against the Defendant (unless the Defendant be a Prisoner,) if he fee his Attorney; otherwise he may be nonsuited the first.

Bail.   Also the Defendant upon an Action of **Debt** hath liberty (if a Freeman) upon his putting in Bail, to mark his four Defaults, which will cost 4 *d.* more than the Fees of the Bail; and hereupon he may chuse to appear by Attorney, till the fourth Court-Day after his putting in Bail.

And unless the Defendant mark his four Defaults, the Plaintiff ought to appear the first Court-Day after Bail to the Action, by his Attorney, or he may be non-suited; and if the Defendant be a Prisoner, no Attorney appearing, a Non-suit may be had; and the Charges of the Defendant, upon a Non-suit, are,

For Appearance	2 *s.* 6 *d.*
Non-Suit	1 *s.* 4 *d.*
Judgment	2 *s.* 6 *d.*
Execution	4 *d.*

If he appear not then, Judgment passeth against him by Default, and Execution may be had in the Afternoon.

And

And if the Defendant be a Foreigner and bail'd, if he appear not the firſt Court-Day by his Attorney, Judgment will paſs alſo againſt him and his Bail. *See after for Waggoners and Carriers. Pag.* 461.

The Plaintiff's Charge thereupon is

To his Attorney, and for the Declaration and
  Count. 3 *s.* 10 *d.*
Judgment by Default. 4 *s.* 4 *d.*
And *Note,* The Plaintiff always pays 4 *d.* for not Filing his Bond in Court.

Note, When a Defendant puts in Bail to an Aƈtion, he pays 16 *d.* but if it be againſt him and his Wife, he pays 2 *s.* 8 *d.* And if there be a ſaving harmleſs on Record, he pays more 4 *d.*

The withdrawing an Aƈtion of Treſpaſs, or *Aƈtion withdrawn* Treſpaſs on the Caſe, or Treſpaſs upon Eject- ment, 6 *d.* If Debt, Account, or Breach of Covenant 12 *d.* The withdrawing a Declaration, 16 *d.* And ſo if at Iſſue or after Summons of the Jury upon the Pannel, 16 *d.* If withdrawn by conſent, always 4 *d.* more, *ex aſſenſu partium,* and then the Defendant cannot have Judgment for Charges, otherwiſe he may.

After Judgment given in Court upon a Try- *Execution after Judgment upon Tryal.* al, you may have Execution preſently againſt the Body or Goods of the Defendant, and the next Day againſt the Bail, which will coſt 4 *d.* But if you take the Defendant in Execution, you cannot afterwards have a *Fieri Facias* againſt the Defendant's Goods.

And if you take out a *Fieri Facias* againſt the Goods of the Defendant, it will coſt 2 *s.* 4 *d.*

You

You muft agree with the Serjeant and Clerk of the Papers for the executing your *Fi. Fa.* And if the Goods feized and inventory'd do not amount to the Sum in the Judgment, you may afterwards have execution againft the Defendant's Body or againft the Bail for the remainder.

Bail dif-charg'd. If the Bail be taken in Execution, the Defendant may render his Body and difcharge them; or the Bail may carry the Defendant to Prifon without an Officer, and difcharge themfelves, by paying the Clerk 4 *d.* for marking the Reprieve to the Action.

The Fees of the Plaintiff, upon a Tryal in the Sheriffs-Court, are fet down before, *Page*

As alfo the Defendant's Fees in part. But it is to be obferv'd, that if the Defendant plead fpecially he muft pay 4 *d. per* Sheet for his fpecial Plea, and 4 *d. per* Sheet Ingroffing; alfo 4 *d.* more for his Imparlance (and the Plaintiff the like) and 12 *d.* more upon the Iffue: and if Council thereon, 3 *s.* 4 *d.* all which are allowed. A Fee upon a Summons 1 *s.* 8 *d.* if *Special Decla-*Council 3 *s.* 4 *d.* Alfo for every Declaration *rations, &c.* that is fpecial you pay 4 *d. per* Sheet for Drawing, and 4 *d. per* Sheet Ingroffing, befides 8 *d.* the Court Fees; and if Council, 3 *s.* 4 *d.* which is allowed by the Court.

Every Council extraordinary, though the Plaintiff pay 10 *s.* or 20 *s.* he fhall be allowed by the Court but 3 *s.* 4 *d.* to each.

All other Charge is loft, as what you pay to the Quarterman for fwearing the Witneffes, which is of Courtefy, not due, who is to attend the Court: Alfo what you pay above One Shilling for the Arreft is not allowed; and alfo what you pay for taking the Defendant in Execution, or for ferving the *Fi. Fa.* againft the

Goods

Goods of the Defendant, and all Charges issuing thereon.

The Plaintiff pays for Continuance of his Cause, after Summons before the Court sits, but 8 *d.* If afterward his Witnesses come not, and he moves the Court for a Continuance, then 4 *s.* 4 *d.* So likewise if the Defendant moves to put off the Tryal, 4 *s.* 4 *d.* which is lost on both sides.

Note, That every Carrier and Waggoner hath of course his Return-day given him, if desired by his Attorney, Charge 4 *d.* <small>*Carrier and Waggoner.*</small>

If the Plaintiff, after the Defendant hath removed his Cause, bring down the Cause again by a *Procedendo,* for want of putting in Bail, his Charge thereof he is allowed, and also 2 *s.* 8 *d.* for Attendance, and what other Charge he is at more, in relation to a Trial, to his Attorney. An Action is usually tried in four Court Days. <small>*Procedendo.*</small>

Note, The Defendant hath two ways of Removal; the one by a *Levata Querela* into the Mayor's Court, the other by *Habeas Corpus.* <small>*Removing Causes out of the Sheriffs-Court.*</small>

The Charge of the *Levata Querela* is 5 *s.* 10 *d.* and for carrying up the Record, as you agree with the Clerk of the Papers.

The Defendant, after the Plaint is certified up, may prefer his Bill there in the Mayor's Court, if he hath Equity, or afterwards remove it from thence by *Habeas Corpus;* but if the Defendant carry not up his Plaint in time, the Plaintiff will have a *Remandetur,* and so try it in the Sheriffs Court. <small>*Equity.*</small> <small>*Remandetur,*</small>

If the Defendant bring his *Habeas Corpus* to remove it, the Charge is,

The Writ,	13 *s.* 7 *d.*
The Allowance,	2 *s.* 4 *d.*
The Return,	2 *s.* 6 *d.*

If

If any other Actions, 4 d. a piece for the Allowance, and 6 d. a piece for the Return.

Note, That in all Actions under 4 l. 19 s. unless it be where Trial of Title of Land is concerned, though the Writ be allowed and the Plaint returned, the Plaintiffs Attorney may proceed to Tryal against the Defendant, notwithstanding the Removal and Return, and shall recover his Debt against the Defendant, but his Bail are freed. But it is otherwise if the Defendant turns himself over to the *King's-Bench* or *Fleet.*

Also observe, That if there be six Weeks between the Bail and Issue joyning, the Defendant shall not remove his Plaint by Writ, but shall stand Tryal below.

The Defendant, after Recovery against him by a Jury, may before a Judgment mark his Cause before the Lord Mayor, as before observ'd, Charge 5 s. 10 d. Then he or some other Person enters into a Recognizance double the Recovery to the Chamber of *London,* to stand to such Order as the Lord-Mayor shall make therein.

After such Order made by the Lord Mayor, the Defendant pays the Plaintiff's Costs into the Court within fourteen Days, and gives Security in the *Compter* by Bond to pay the Recovery, according to such Order, to the Plaintiff; the Plaintiff pays for the bringing down such Order, 4 s. 6 d. which Charge is allowed.

The Plaintiff may sometimes get a *Procedendo ad judicium* out of the Chancery, and so prevent the Lord-Mayor's Order; but it must be done before the Lord-Mayor make his Orders.

The Defendant cannot mark his Cause before the Lord Mayor, if it be once removed by *Habeas Corpus.*

Note,

Note, That if a Recovery be obtained on *Thurſday,* the Defendant muſt be ſure to mark the Cauſe before the next Court, elſe Judgment will be entred *ſedente Curia.*

Note, If the Verdict be found for the Defendant, the Court always abateth out of the Defendants Coſts 3 *s.* 4 *d.* out of favour to the Plaintiff.

If there be a Rule or Stay of Execution entred upon Record, you always pay 4 *d.*

If a Freeman be arreſted for a Debt under *Court of Con-* 40 *s.* though he put in Bail after the Arreſt, *ſcience.* yet if he warn the Plaintiff to the Court of Conſcience, though on Bond, that Court will order it, and compel the Plaintiff to loſe his Charge, and ſtand to their Order; which is alſo before-mentioned, in the Practice of the Lord Mayor's Court.

If the Defendant be a Priſoner, the Plaintiff may enter his Action againſt him, fee his Attorney, ſend for him to Court by a *Duc. Fac.* and proceed to Tryal : The Charge of the *Duc. Fac.* is 12 *d.* if in Execution, 2 *s.* 6 *d.* And ſo if in *Ludgate,* which is a Priſon of Eaſe for Freemen in reſpect of Charge, but thoſe Coſts are all one, and the Proceedings as from either *Compter* alike.

A Priſoner's Charge in going from the *Removal from* *Compter* to *Ludgate,* which is called his *Houſe,* *the Compter* is 16 *d.* *to Ludgate.*

Miniſters, commonly called Clerks, have the like Privilege.

A *Scire fac. poſt annum,* for reviving a Judgment after a Year and a Day, will coſt uſually 12 or 13 *s.*

To the Attorney more, 2 *s.* 6 *d.* And Judgment thereon, 2 *s.* 8 *d.*

If

Proceedings
against a Ser-
jeant at Mace
for his ne-
gleat, &c.

If an Action be entred againſt a Man, and the Plaintiff employs a Serjeant, gives him his Fee, and afterwards arreſts the Party and takes his Word, the Plaintiff having feed his Attorney, may give a Warning to the Quarterman, Charge thereof, 4 *d.* viz. *Warn in* A. B. *Serjeant at Mace, to appear at the next Court, to ſhew Cauſe why he arreſted* C. D. *and let him go without Bail to the Plaintiff's Action.* If the Officer do not appear on the Warning, the Plaintiff may have an Attachment againſt him, which is deliver'd to the Quaterman, who by virtue thereof compels him to come in the next Court. And he pays for the Attachment 1 *s.* to the Officer 1 *s.* The Officer appearing, the Court orders him to pay the Fees of the Attachment and Officer, the Plaintiff proving the Arreſt; then if the Officer deſires farther Day to bring in the Defendant, with the Conſent of the Plaintiff, it will be granted : Or the Plaintiff may bring a ſpecial Action of the Caſe againſt the Officer, but it muſt be entred againſt him as Serjeant at Mace: then he muſt declare ſpecially, ſetting forth the Debt, the former Action and the Arreſt; which three being proved, they may and do commonly find the Plaintiff's Debt and Damages.

Defendants
Proceeding by
Proviſo.

If a Defendant will, he may go on by *Proviſo*; and if no Iſſue, tender an Iſſue after Declaration; and upon the Plaintiff's neglect of Summons of one Court-day after Iſſue joyned, the Defendant may crave his *Proviſo* (Charge 2 *s.*) and ſo proceed to Tryal, and his Coſts ſhall be allowed as before, all but 3 *s.* 4 *d.* only the Court will allow but 12 *d.* for putting in Bail.

If a Man under Arreſt give any Money to an Officer, it is of Courteſy, and not of Right; and not a Penny thereof allowed.

Note,

Note, That if a Caufe be removed by *Habeas Corpus,* and Pledges given for the Defendant before a Judge, the Bail are liable to all other Declarations given to the Defendant's Attorney the next Term after Bail ; and the Defendant's Attorney will be compell'd to receive the Declarations.

The Garnifhee's Charge upon an Attachment, if he wage Law only, is,

FOR the Appearance —— 2 s. 6 d.
The Wager of Law —— 4 s. 8 d.

Fees upon Attachments in the Sheriffs-Court.

But if the Garnifhee refufe to wage Law, the Plaintiff may try the Caufe in four Court-Days following after the *Scire Facias* comes into Court. If the Garnifhee will plead that he hath no Money in the Hands of *A.* the Charge then of the Plaintiff, and before, is

The Action and Return ——	8 d.
The Officer —— ——	1 s.
But if the Garnifhee be not prefent he will have —— ——	2 s.
The Warning in the Garnifhee ——	1 s.
The Appearance by an Attorney——	2 s. 6 d.
The *Scire Facias* ufually —	2 s.
The Iffue ——	4 s.
The Summons of the Jury —	4 s. 8 d.
If a *Subpœna* —— ——	2 s.
The Council ——	3 s. 4 d.
The Verdict of the Jury ——	4 s. 6 d.
The Judgment ——	2 s. 8 d.

H h

Then

Then the Plaintiff, as is before obferv'd, muft put in Bail or Pledge, that if the Defendant fhall come within the Year and the Day next enfuing into the Court, and that he can difcharge himfelf of the faid Moneys fo condemned in Court, and that he owed nothing unto the Plaintiff at the time in the Plaint mentioned, the faid Money fhall be forth coming, *&c.*

The Plaintiff's Bail ——— 1 *s.* 4 *d.*
Satisfaction upon Record — 1 *s.* 4 *d.*
If Warrants of Attorney be given, for two
　Warrants ——— 8 *d.*
Attorney's Fee ——— 1 *s.* 8 *d.*
If the Plaintiff gives Warrant to acknow-
　ledge Satisfaction upon Record, upon an
　Action, he pays ——— 2 *s.* 4 *d.*
If the Sum attach'd be under forty Mark,
　then he pays but ——— 3 *s.* 8 *d.*
For the Summons, and to the Jury 3 *s.* 6 *d.*
The Charge of the Plaintiff's Affidavits to
　hinder the Garnifhee from waging Law,
　——— ——— 6 *s.* 8 *d.*
The Plea of *Eftopel* to which they are an-
　nex'd — — 7 *s.*
Plaintiff pays for bringing the Rolls into Court
　1 *s.* 4 *d.* and 2 *s.* 6 *d.* his Attorney.

The *Garnifhee's* Charge to a Tryal, when he pleads.

THE Appearance by an Attorney 2 *s.* 6 *d.*
　The Bail ——— — 1 *s.* 4 *d.*
Copy of the *Scire Facias* ——— 1 *s.*
The Iffue ——— 4 *s.* 8 *d.*
　　　　　　　　　　　　　　　The

The Attorney's Fee at Tryal — 1 *s.* 8 *d.*
The Council (if any) —— 3 *s.* 4 *d.*

The Garnifhee after Trial may put in Bail in the Abfence of the Party againft whom the Attachment is made before the Lord Mayor, and fo diffolve the Attachment.

After Satisfaction upon Record, and when the Money is fully condemned by the Plaintiff, the Party againft whom the Action is, and whofe Goods are attached, may come and put in Bail *ad difprobandum Debitum* ; the Charge whereof is for the Bail 2 *s.* 8 *d.* The Appearance, 2 *s.* 6 *d.*

Then he muft put into the Court his *Scire Facias*, 13 *s.* But it muft be within the Year and Day next enfuing after Satisfaction.

Bail being put in, the Defendant may give a Rule, by his Attorney, for the Plaintiff to declare ; and if he declare not, he fhall be Nonfuited, and the Moneys given again to the Defendant. The Defendant alfo fhall have Reftitution, if he can difcharge himfelf of the Debt ; and fo for a parcel thereof.

All Charges upon an Attachment are loft on the Garnifhee's and Plaintiff's part.

It was obferv'd before, that an Attachment may be made for Goods and Moneys at the fame Charge (but the Sum muft be certain) all upon one Attachment, and both in one *Scire Facias*: If for Goods, then a Judgment for an Appraifement (if no Appearance by the Garnifhee) the Charge 2 *s.* Then the Plaintiff proceeds to a Bill of Appraifement, and to Charge for fummoning of the Jury ; then he muft prove the Value of the Goods, and Judgment then paffeth ; this cofts 2 *s.* 8 *d.* then Bail and Satisfaction.

H h 2   Upon

Upon an Attachment made in the Plaintiff's own Hands, either of Moneys, or Goods, or both :

If of Money, then the Charge is as followeth :

The Action and Return ———	8 *d.*
The Appearance by an Attorney —	2 *s.* 6 *d.*
The *Scire Facias* ———	2 *s.*
The *Fiat Executio* ———	2 *s.* 8 *d.*
The Plaintiff 's Bail ——	1 *s.* 4 *d.*
The Satisfaction — —	1 *s.* 4 *d.*

Then the Attachment is perfected, so that the Defendant can put in no Bail to diffolve the Attachment.

If the Attachment be made of Goods in the Plaintiff's Hands, then the Charge is as followeth :

The Action and Return —— ——	8 *d.*
The Officer ———	1 *s.*
The Appearance by Attorney —	2 *s.* 6 *d.*
The *Scire Facias* —— —	2 *s.*
The Judgment for Appraifement —	2 *s.*
The Bill of Appraifement ——	2 *s.*
The *Fiat Executio,* or Judgment —	2 *s.* 8 *d.*
The Bail ——— ——	1 *s.* 4 *d.*
The Satisfaction ———	1 *s.* 4 *d.*

Note, The Plaintiff muft obferve, that after Judgment is given by the Court for the Appraifement of the Goods, he muft bring two Freemen of *London* into the Court, the next Court-Day following, there to be fworn, *That they have made an Appraifement of the Goods to the beft of their Skill and Knowledge* ; who put their Hands to the Appraifement.

An Attachment is never throughly perfected till there be Bail and Satisfaction upon Record ; becaufe otherwife Bail may be put in by the Defendant to diffolve the Attachment, as aforefaid, ſaid, and then all the Plaintiff's Charge is loſt, and himſelf never the nearer. The Charge of a Judgment for opening of Trunks is 2 *s.*

The Charge of a Sequeſtration for the Plaintiff.

THE Action and Return —— 8 *d.*
The Officer for making the Sequeſtration —— —— 2 *s.*
The Padlock
The Appearance —— — 2 *s.* 6 *d.*
The *Scire Facias* —— 2 *s.*
The Judgment for opening, and the Appraiſement —— —— 2 *s.* 4 *d.*
The Officer for going to break open the Door —— —— 2 *s.*
The Bill of Appraiſement, 2 *s.* 6 *d.* ſometimes more.
The Officer's Hand —— 1 *s.*
The *Fiat Executio*, or Judgment — 2 *s.* 8 *d.*
The Bail —— —— 1 *s.* 4 *d.*
The Satisfaction. —— 1 *s.* 4 *d.*

Note, That upon a Bill of Appraiſement for a Sequeſtration, the Court granteth Judgment, as upon an Attachment.

The Defendant upon the Action may put in Bail before Satisfaction, as upon an Attachment, and ſo diſſolve the Sequeſtration, or after Satisfaction put in Bail *ad diſprobandum Debitum.*

The Proceedings after Bail alike as upon Attachment.

✦✦✦✦✦✦✦✦✦✦✦✦✦✦✦✦✦✦✦✦✦✦

The Charge in confeſſing a Judgment, by an Adminiſtratrix, &c. to one Creditor, when ſhe intends to plead it in barr of other Debtors.

THE Action and Bail   —   2 *s.*
    The Declaration, Attorney, and Court
   —   —   —   4 *s.* 4 *d.*
The Judgment   —   —   4 *s.* 4 *d.*
TheAttorney to confeſs theJudgment 2 *s.*
The Warrant   —   —   4 *d.*

If a Judgment be pleaded in *Guildhall*, ſhe ſhall recover her Charge againſt the Plaintiff, if the Judgment be confeſſed in that Court. And as to Priorities of Judgments, there is no ſuch thing ; for firſt come, firſt paid : for he that hath the laſt Judgment, if he levy the Goods in Execution firſt, he ſhall be paid, and the reſt laid aſide, unleſs there be an Overplus of the Goods, amonnting to more than the Sum contained in the Judgment.

✦✦✦✦✦✦✦✦✦✦✦✦ ✦✦✦ ✦✦✦✦✦✦✦✦✦✦✦✦

Fees ſaid due to be paid upon giving Security for Orphans Money.

IF the Sum to be ſecured amount to 100 *l.* and do not exceed 300 *l.*
To the Common Serjeant   —   6 *s.* 8 *d.*
To the Common Cryer   —   6 *s.* 8 *d.*
To the Town Clerk   ——   2 *s.*
To the Clerk of the Orphans   —   1 *s.* 4 *d.*

The like Fees muſt be paid for every 300 *l.*
that is ſecured ; and if the Sum ſecured be
1000 *l.* then the Security muſt enter into four
Recognizances, the laſt of which muſt be for
100 *l.* only. And the Fees in ſuch caſe will
amount to — — 3 *l.* 6 *s.* 8 *d.*

If the Sum ſecured is but 20 *l.* then the
Fees are as followeth :

		s.	*d.*
To the Common Serjeant	—	3	4
To the Common Cryer	—	3	4
To the Town Clerk	—	2	0
To the Clerk of the Orphans	—	1	4
		10	0

If the Sum of any Recognizance ſhall be
under 20 *l.* then the Common Serjeant's Fees
and Common Cryer's Fees are but one Penny
in every Pound : But the Town Clerk and
the Clerk of the Orphans have the ſame Fees
as above is mentioned.

✿✿✿✿✿✿✿✿✿✿✿✿✿✿✿✿✿✿✿✿✿

*Fees to be paid for acknowledging
Satisfaction upon four Recognizances
for* 1000 l.

	s.	*d.*
TO the Common Serjeant upon every Recogniznnce	6	8
To the Common Cryer	5	6
To the Town Clerk	2	0
To the Clerk of the Orphans	1	4

The Fees in ſuch caſe will in the whole a-
mount to three Pounds.

If

If Satisfaction is to be acknowledged upon
a Recognizance but for 20 *l.* then the Fees are
as followeth :

	s.	*d.*
To the Common Serjeant	3	4
To the Common Cryer	2	6
To the Town Clerk	2	0
To the Clerk of the Orphans	1	4
	9	2

But if the Moneys due to the Orphans shall
be paid into the Chamber of *London,* then there
are no Fees due to any Person.

General

General Statutes relating to the City of LONDON.

E fhall now give the Reader an Account of fuch Statutes, or Acts of Parliament, as refpect the City of *London, viz.* 1*ft*, Of fuch as relate to the faid City in general ; and, 2*dly*, Of fuch as may be reduced under particular Alphabetical Titles.

And firft of fome Statutes that concern the faid City in general.

By *Magna Charta, cap. 9.* 'tis provided, That the City of *London* fhall have all their antient Liberties and Cuftoms which they have ufed to have. *See* 2 Inft. 20.

The Stat. 10 *Ed.* 2. of *Gavelet*, fays, That the Lords of Rents in *London*, may recover the faidRents by a Writ of *Gavelet* in their Huftings, or in Default thereof the Lands themfelves.

1. By Stat. 28 *E.* 3. *c.* 10. The Mayors, Sheriffs and Aldermen of *London*, fhall caufe Errors, Defaults and Mifprifions there, to be redrefs'd on pain to forfeit for the firft Default 1000 Marks, for the fecond 2000 Marks, and for the third the Franchife and Liberty of the City to be feized.

2. That the faid Defaults fhall be inquired of by Inquefts of *Kent, Effex, Suffex, Hertford, Buckingham* and *Berks,* as well at the King's Suit, as of others that will complain.

3. That the Mayor, Sheriffs and Aldermen being indicted, fhall be caufed by due Procefs

to

to come before the King's Juſtices aſſigned thereto out of the City, and ſhall there be made to anſwer as well to the King, as to the Party grieved.

4. That their Tryal ſhall be by foreign Inqueſts as aforeſaid ; whereupon, if they are attainted, the ſaid Penalties ſhall be levied upon them, and the Plaintiffs ſhall alſo recover treble Damages.

5. In the Proſecution of ſuch Suits, the Conſtable of the *Tower*, or his Lieutenant, ſhall execute all Proceſſes in the City ; which Proceſſes ſhall be by Attachment, Diſtreſs and Exigent.

6. And in the King's Caſe, the *Exigent* ſhall be awarded on Return of the firſt *Capias* ; but at the Suit of the Party, after the Return of the third *Capias*.

7. If they have Lands out of the City, Proceſs ſhall iſſue againſt them into the Country where ſuch Lands lie, by Attachment and Diſtreſs.

8. Every of them that appear ſhall anſwer particularly for himſelf, as well at the Peril of him that is abſent as of himſelf.

This *Ordinance* ſhall extend to all other Cities and Burroughs throughout the Realm ; but by Stat. 1 *H.* 4. *c.* 15. 'tis ſaid, The Penalties of 1000 and 2000 Marks impoſed by the Stat. 28 *E.* 3. ſhall not be limited to a Certainty, but be left to the Diſcretion (*i. e.* the Moderation) of the Juſtices thereto aſſigned, in like manner as it is for other Cities and Burroughs.

I confeſs my ſelf at firſt ſurprized to find ſuch an Act as that of 28 *E.* 3. *ſupra* (ſo highly injurious not only to the City of *London*, but to the Nation in general) to have been paſs'd in an *Engliſh* Parliament. But afterwards obſerving

from

from a Manufcript of Mr. *Rymer's*, now in my Cuftody, how eafily and often Parliaments were at that Time abufed, by having Acts impofed upon them by the King's Council which the Commons never affented to, I could not forbear concluding the faid Act to be one of that kind ; and the rather fo, for that in the laft Claufe, 'tis only called an Ordinance, as if it were only at firft an Ordinance of the Lords, and afterwards impofed on the Commons without their Confent, by ingroffing it on the Parliament Roll, after the Parliament was up, as the manner then was.

But however this Statute was obtained, 'tis evident it continued not long in Force : For in the firft Year of *R.* 2. all the Liberties of the City of *London* are confirmed in Parliament, notwithftanding any Statute to the contrary ; *Cotton* 165. And *6 R.* 2. 'tis enacted, at the Requeft of the Commons, That the City of *London* fhall enjoy all fuch Liberties, as they had, *Temp. E.* 3. or fince; *Cotton*. 281. Alfo 7 *R.* 2. 'tis enacted, That the Citizens of *London* fhall enjoy all their whole Liberties whatfoever, with this Claufe, *Licet non ufi vel abufi fuerunt*, and notwithftanding any Statute to the contrary, *&c.* Which implicitly repeals the faid Stat. 28 *E.* 3. *See* Cotton. 294.

But further, 'tis certain that the faid Stat. 28 *E.* 3. was exprefly repealed by a Stat. made 17 *R.* 2. which enacts, That it is not the King's Meaning or Intent, nor the Meaning of the Stat. made 28 *E.* 3. That the Mayors, Sheriffs and Aldermen of *London*, that now are, heretofore have been, or hereafter fhall be, fhould incur or bear the Pains contain'd in the faid Stat. of *E.* 3. for any erroneous Judgment given or to be given in the faid City. *See* Cotton 354.

And

And as to the Stat. 1 *H.* 4. I find, that 9 *H.* 4. on the Petitions of the Citizens of *London*, the King grants in Parliament, That they fhall enjoy all their Liberties, notwithftanding the Act made in the late Parliament, *i. e.* 1 *H.* 4. So that both the faid Acts of 28 *E.* 3. and 1 *H.* 4. feem now to to ftand repealed.

See alfo divers otherStatutes for faving or confirming the Liberties of *London*, *viz.* 8 *H.* 6. *c.* 4. 31 *H.* 6. *Pulton* Office 8. 1 *E.* 4. *c.* 1. 13 *E.* 4. *c.* 3. 17 *E.* 4. *c.* 5. 1 *R.* 3. *c.* 8. 3 *H.* 7. *c.* 7. 4 *H.* 7. *c.* 3. & 15. 6 *H.* 7. *c.* 18. 19 *H.* 7. *c.* 8. & 21. 1 *H.* 8. *c.* 5. *of* Prifage. 3 *H.* 8. *c.* 14. *of* Oils, &c. 6 *H.* 8. *c.* 7. *of* Watermen. 13 *H.* 8. *c.* 8. *of* Orphans. 27 *H.* 8. *c.* 21. *of* Tythes. & 24. *of* Franchifes. 32 *H.* 8. *c.* 14. *of* Freight. & 20. *of* Franchifes. 33 *H.* 8. *c.* 39. *of* Courts. 37 *H.* 8. *c.* 12. *of* Tythes. & 35 *H.* 8. *of* Conduits. See alfo 1 *Mary*, *c.* 9. *of* Phyficians. 1, 2 M. *c.* 13. *of* Bail. 2, 3 P. M. *c.* 36. *of* Watermen. 4, 5 P. M. *c.* 18. *of* Drapery.

Stat. 19 *Car.* 2. *cap.* 2. For erecting a Judicature for determining of Differences touching Houfes burnt or demolifhed by reafon of the Fire of *London*. 4, 5 W. M. *c.* 12. and a *Stat.* 7 *Ann.* *c.* 9. explanatory of the former.

Stat. 19 *Car.* 2. *cap.* 3. For the fpeedy rebuilding of the faid City, and the Uniformity of the new Buildings, and for preventing of outrageous Fires there.

Stat. 22 *Car.* 2. *cap.* 11. Another Act concerning rebuilding of the faid City, *viz.* For fetting forth Market-places, &c. repairing of Wharfs and Docks, Number of Parifhes fetled, and 51 Parifh Churches to be rebuilt ; their Names, Dimenfions, and Method of Building, with their Unions, Rates, Charges, &c.

Stat. 22,23 *Car.2.c.* 14. For determining of Differences touching Houfes burnt or demolifhed within four Years fince the late dreadful Fire.

Stat. 22,23 *Car.* 2. *cap.* 15. Touching Tythes in *Lond. vid. ante.*

Stat. 22, 23 *Car.* 2. *cap.* 17. Alfo concerning the rebuilding of the faid City, *viz.* of affigning Places for Common-Sewers, Dreins and Vaults, and pitching and paving the Streets. *See alfo the Stat.* 2 W. M. *Seff.* 1. *c.* 8. & *Seff.* 2. *cap.* 8. 9 W. 3. *c.* 37. & *poft tit.* Paving.

Stat. 1 *Jac. cap.* 15. For finifhing the Cathedral Church of St. *Paul. See that and the other fubfequent Statutes for that purpofe, viz.* 8, 9 W. 3.

Alfo the Stat. 9 *Ann. c.* 22. & 10 *Ann. c.* 11. For building 50 new Churches in or near *London.*

See the Statutes touching Markets in London, poft, *under the Titles* Billingfgate *and* Blackwellhall.

And for other Statutes touching the faid City, fee the refpective Alphabetical Titles following.

✠✠✠✠✠✠✠✠✠✠✠✠✠✠✠✠✠✠✠✠✠✠✠✠✠✠✠✠✠✠✠✠✠✠✠

Particular Statutes relating to the faid City, alphabetically digefted.

THE Cuftoms of the City of *London* are faved by the Act for committing the Adminiftration of Inteftates Eftates, 22 & 23 *Car.* 2. *cap.* 10.

Adminiftration.

By the Act 14 *H.* 8. 2. All Aliens in or about *London,* fhall be within the Governance of the Corporation of the Myftery or Craft whereof they are, and taxable to their Myftery. Here Strangers dwelling in St. *Martins-le-Grand, London,* are excepted.

Aliens.

And a Decree made in the *Star-Chamber,* 20 *H.* 8. was by *Stat.* 21 *H.* 8. 16. confirm'd, and thereby enacted, that fuch Strangers fhould pay Scot and Lot, Tax and Tallage, &c. as

the

the Mafters, Wardens, and Companies do, and that they fhall make Oaths and other things; here alfo Strangers dwelling in St. *Martins le Grand* are excepted. And by *Stat.* 22 *H.* 8. *c.* 8. there is an Exception for the Merchants of the *Stillyard*, that they fhall not pay any other Cuftoms than they ufed by their Franchifes. By *Act* 32 *H.* 8. 16. No Alien, Artificer, Denizen, or not Denizen, in St. *Martins le Grand*, fhall keep above two Strangers Servants at one time, on pain to incur the penalty of 14 *H.* 8. 2.

Apothecaries. By *Stat.* 6 *W.* 3. *cap.* 3. Apothecaries of the City of *London* are exempted from the Offices of Conftable, Scavenger, Overfeers of the Poor, and other Parifh, Ward and Leet Offices, and of and from ferving upon any Juries or Inquefts.

Attaints. We have obferv'd before, how far the Citizens of *London* are concern'd as Jurymen, &c. by the Statutes relating to Attaints. See in the Court of *Huftings, ante.*

Bowyers. By the *Stat.* 8 *Eliz.* 10. A Bowyer dwelling in *London* or the *Suburbs*, fhall have always ready 50 Bows of *Elm*, &c. upon penalty of 10 *s.* for every Bow failing of that number.

Brafs and Pewter. By *Stat.* 19 *H.* 7. 6. None fhall caft Brafs or Pewter, but according to the goodnefs of the Metal wrought in *London*, in pain to forfeit one Moiety thereof to the King, and the other to the Finder.

Alfo hollow Ware of Pewter, called Laymetal, fhall be wrought after the Affize of Laymetal in *London*, and fhall be mark'd, in pain to forfeit the faid Wares, or (being fold) the price thereof, which fhall be divided as aforefaid.

By

By *Stat.* 1 *Jac.* 21. The Sale of Goods _{*Brokers.*}
wrongfully gotten to any Brokers in *London*,
Weftminfter, *Southwark*, or within two Miles
of *London*, fhall not alter the property thereof :
And if a Broker having receiv'd fuch Goods,
fhall not upon the requeft of the true Owner
truly difcover them, how and when he came
by them, and to whom they are convey'd, he
fhall forfeit double the value thereof to the faid
Owner.

This Act fhall not prejudice the ancient
Trade of Brokers in *London*, being Settled and
Sworn for that purpofe, it being only intended
againft Frippers, and Pawn-takers, who for
the moft part keep open Shop.

By *Stat.* 8 *&* 9 *W.* 3. *cap.* 32. a Broker for
making or concluding Bargains between Merchant and Merchant, or others in *London*, fhall
be Admitted and Licenfed by the Lord Mayor
and Court of Aldermen of *Londou*, and is to
take Oaths, *&c.* and upon his Admittance,
give Bond to the Lord Mayor, Citizens and
Commonalty of *London* in the penalty of 500 *l.*
with Condition, That if he do, and fhall well
and truly ufe, execute, and perform the Office
and Imployment of a Broker, between Party
and Party, without Fraud, Covin, or any
Corrupt or Crafty Devices, according to the
purport, true intent and meaning of the Statute in that cafe lately made and provided,
then the Obligation to be void.

The number of fuch Brokers fhall not at
one time exceed 100. and the Fees of Admittance into the faid Employment, fhall not exceed 40 *s.* their Names and Places of Habitation are to be publickly affixed on the *Royal Exchange*, in *Guildhall*, and in fuch other publick
Places

Butchers.

Places in *London*, as the Lord Mayor and Court of Aldermen shall think fit.

By *Stat.* 4 *H.* 7. 3. No Butcher shall kill any Flesh within his Scalding-house, or within the Walls of *London*; in pain to forfeit for every Ox so killed 12 *d.* and for every other Beast 8 *d.* to be divided between the King and the Prosecutor.

By *Stat.* 22, & 23 *Car.* 2. *cap.* 19. If any Butcher in *London* or *Westminster*, or within ten Miles thereof, buy fat Cattel, and sell them again alive or dead, to another Butcher, the Seller shall forfeit the value of such Cattle.

Drovers.

Also no Drover shall be licensed by the Justices of Peace within *London* and *Westminster*, or 80 Miles of the same. And those that exercise the Trade of Grasiers or Butchers, shall not have Licence to be Drovers.

Butter and Cheese.

Though by the *Stat.* 3, & 4 *Ed.* 6. 21. None (Except Innholders or Victuallers in their Houses) shall buy any Butter or Cheese to sell again, save only by Retail, in open Shop, Fair, or Market; and so not above a Wey of Cheese, or Barrel of Butter at one time, without fraud, in pain to forfeit the double value, to be divided betwixt the King and the Prosecutor; yet by *Stat.* 21 *Jac.* 1. 22. the foresaid Statute, as also so much of the Statue 5 & 6 *E.* 6. 14. which concerns the Buying and Retailing of Butter and Cheese, shall not extend to the Retailers of Cheese in *London*, *Westminster*, or *Southwark*; having served Seven Years in that Trade: nor uttering above four Wey of Cheese, or four Barrels of Butter at one time, without fraud.

And by the *Stat.* 4, & 5 *W.* & *M. c.* 7. there is a Charge and Penalty upon Warehouse-keepers, Weighers and Searchers, or Shippers of Butter and Cheese, neglecting their Duties concerning the Butter and Cheese that shall be

brought

brought to them, for any Cheefemonger free of the City of *London,* &c. And alfo a Penalty upon Mafters of Veffels, refufing to take on board any fuch Butter and Cheefe : Yet this Act fhall not exclude Cheefemongers free of the City of *London,* from fending their own Veffels, or fuch as they fhall hire for their own Goods.

By *Stat.* 10, & 11 *W.* 3. c. 24. it is Enacted, *Billingfgate* that *Billingfgate Market* within the City of *Lon- Market.* *don,* fhall be every day (except *Sundays*) a Free Market for all forts of Fifh ; and that any Per- fons may Buy or Sell any fort of Fifh in the faid Market.

And all Perfons buying any Fifh in the faid Market, may fell the fame again in any other Market or Place within *London,* or elfewhere, by Retail; being found and wholefom Fifh : only none but Fifhmongers fhall fell in publick or fixed Shops or Houfes.

Alfo no Perfons fhall employ, or be employed by any other Perfon in buying at *Billingfgate* any quantity of Fifh to be divided by Lots or in Shares amongft any Fifhmongers or others, to be afterwards fold by Retail or otherwife : nor fhall any Fifhmonger ingrofs or buy in the faid Market any quantity of Fifh, but what fhall be for his own Sale or Ufe, and not for any other Fifhmonger to fell again, under penalty of 20 *l.* for each Offence, one moiety to the Poor of the Parifh, the other to the Profecutor. See the *Stat.*

By *Stat.* 8 & 9 *W.* 3. *cap.* 9. it is Enacted, *a* *well-* That the publick Market of *Blackwell-Hall, Hall Market.* fhall be held every *Thurfday, Friday,* and *Satur-* vid. *poft,*Dra- *day,* from eight till twelve in the Forenoon, and pery. from two till five in the Afternoon, except days of Humiliation or Thankfgiving ; and the Kee- pers are not to admit any buying or felling of any Woollen Cloth at the said Hall, upon any other Days or Hours than aforesaid; upon the penalty of 100 *l.* And no Factor, or any Person whatsoever, other than the Owner of the Cloth, shall sell or expose to sale, out of the said Market of *Blackwell-Hall*, any Cloth directed to be brought to the said Market, or any Factor there; upon penalty of 5 *l.* for every Cloth so sold. With several other Penalties upon the Hall-Keepers, Clerks, and Master-Porters neglecting their Duties; and upon Factors, for not giving true Accounts to the Clothiers.

Smithfield-Market

By *Stat.* 22 & 23 *Car.* 2. *cap.* 19. If any fat Cattel bought in *Smithfield* Market shall be brought again into the said Market to be sold alive, they shall be seized by the Bailiff, Toll-Keeper, or other Officer, having oversight of the Market; to the use of the Mayor and Aldermen, &c. For discovery whereof, all Cattel sold shall be mark'd, by cutting off two Inches of the further Horn. And by this Act, Foreigners, as well as Freemen, may buy and sell any Cattel in the Market of *Smithfield,* the Custom of Foreign bought and Foreign sold, or other Usage notwithstanding. By *Stat.* 11 & 12 *W.* 3. *c.* 13. the Act made 22 & 23 *Car.* 2. for preventing Frauds in the buying and selling of Cattel in *Smithfield* and elsewhere, revived by 1 *Jac.* 2. with a *Proviso,* not to extend to Salesmen and Factors, employed by Farmers or Feeders, and continued with the said *Proviso* for 7 years, from 23 of *Febr.* 1692. and thence to the end of the next Session ; is with the said *Proviso* continued for 7 years, from the 29th of *Sept.* 1700. and from thence to the end of the next Session of Parliament.

See the Act 22 Car. 2. cap. 11. *For setting forth Market-places,* &c. ante.

Also

Alſo, See before the Orders for Regulating publick Markets within the City of London, *from pag.* 122, *to* 137. *and ſee after* Tit. Victual *and* Victuallers, pag. 495, 496.

There is a Privilege granted to the City of *Captains* London, upon the Act 43 *Eliz.* 3. made for Re- *and Soldiers.* lief of Maimed Soldiers, that the ſaid Act ſhall not prohibit the City of *London* to make a Tax (if need require) differing from that limited in the ſaid Act : So that no Pariſh pay above 3 *s.* weekly, nor above or under 12 *d.* weekly, one Pariſh with another. *See after* Tit. Soldiers.

By 8 *& 9. W.* 3. *c.* 14. An Impoſition is put *Churches.* upon Coals, for compleating the Cathedral of St. *Paul, London*; and repairing the Cathedral of St. *Peter's Weſtminſter.*

An Act was made 5 *& 6. W. &. M. cap.* 22. *Coaches and* for Regulating and Licenſing the Hackney *Chairs.* Coaches within the Cities of *London* and *Weſt-minſter. See* pag. 118, 120, *&c.*

A Statute made 16, 17 *Car.* 2. for the ſelling *Coals.* of Sea-Coals (brought into the River of *Thames*) by the Chaldron to contain 36 Buſhels heap'd, and according to the Buſhel ſealed for that purpoſe at *Guildhall, London*; and Coals ſold by Weight, are to be after 112 pound to the hun-dred, upon forfeiture of all the Coals, and double value thereof, to be recovered in any Court of Record; or upon complaint to the Lord Mayor and Juſtices of Peace within the City and Liberties: one half to the Perſon complaining, the other to the Poor, or Re-pairing the Highways within the Pariſh, *&c.* Alſo the Lord Mayor and Court of Aldermen of *London*, may ſet Rates and Prices upon Coals to be ſold by Retail, allowing competent clear

I i 2   Profit

Profit to the Retailer. This *Stat.* by 7 & 8 *W.* 3. *cap.* 36. is made perpetual.

Conduits. A *Stat.* 35 *H.* 8. *cap.* 10. For repairing, making and mending the Conduits in *London.*

Cordwainers, Curriers and Tanners, &c. There are several Statutes made for Regulating the *Cordwainers, Curriers,* and *Tanners* within the City of *London, &c.* 1 *M. Parl.* 3. 8. 1 *Jac.* 1. 22. 13, 14 *Car.* 2. *cap.* 7. See after *Tit.* Leather.

Coopers. Also a Statute made 23 *H.* 8. 4. to give power to the Wardens of the Mystery of *Coopers* within the City of *London,* to search for, and gauge all Vessels made for Ale, Beer, and Soap, to be put to Sale within *London* and the *Suburbs,* and within two Miles compass without the *Suburbs,* (as well within the Liberties as without) and to examine their Contents and Weight; and being found right, to mark them with St. *Anthony's* Cross, &c. See after *Tit.* Gauging.

Customs. Acts made to regulate the Customs within the Ports of *London, &c.* and the Commissioners and Officers belonging to the same. 12 *Car.* 2. *cap.* 4. 13, 14 *Car.* 2. *cap.* 11. 4 & 5 *W.* & *M. cap.* 15. 8 & 9 *W.* 3. *cap.* 24. 9 & 10 *W.* 3. *cap.* 23. 11, & 12 *W.* 3. *cap.* 3.

Damages. There is a Statute which gives Damages to Disseisees in *London,* by Recognizance of the same Assize, whereby they recover their Lands. *Glouc.* 14. 6 *Ed.* 2.

Debt of 40 s. or under. The 3 of *Jac.* 1. 15. concerning Debts of 40 *s.* due to or by Citizens of *London, &c.* See before in the *Court of Conscience.*

Drapery. By *Stat.* 17 *E.* 4. 5. there is an Exception as to *London* and *Bristol,* concerning sealing with Wax at both ends, Woollen Cloths, half Cloths, Streats and Kerseys, being perfect in making and measure; but those in *London* and *Bristol,* are to be sealed with Lead.

Also

Alfo by *Stat.* 39 *Eliz.* 20. The Owner of *Northern* Cloths brought up to be fold in *London*, fhall caufe them to be brought to *Blackwell Hall* to be fearch'd dry, without wetting ; in pain of 40 *s.* between the Queen and Informer.

The *Stat.* 22 & 23 *Car.* 2. *cap.* 22. concern- *Fines.* ing the Eftreating all Fines, Poftfines, Iffues, Amerciaments, &*c.* into the *Exchequer*, fhall not prejudice the Privileges of the City of *London.*

A Forfeiture is impofed, by 31 *E.* 3. *Stat. Fish and* 2. upon any Piker of *London*, that at the *Fishmongers.* Fair of Great *Yarmouth* for Herrings, fhall enter into the *Haven* there to abate the Fair ; the Forfeiture is of the Veffel, and all the Goods thereof. Alfo by 1 *Geo. c.* 18. no Salmon is to be brought to *London* under 6 Pound Weight.

And for preferving the Fry of Fifh, the Mayor or Warden of *London*, hath power to hear and determine Offences, &*c.* in *Thames*, from *Stanes* to *London* ; and in *Medway*, as far as the Citizens Grant extends. 17 *R.* 2. 9.

By 43 *Eliz.* 9. No Ordinance made by the Fifhmongers in *London*, or any other Corporation, reftraining any Coaftman, Fifherman, or other, from taking, bringing in, putting to Sale, or buying of Salt-fifh or Herrings (being wholefom) fhall be put in execution in pain of 100 *l.*

There is an Exemption of the Franchifes and *Franchifes.* Liberties of *London*, notwithftanding the powers given to Purvcyors to take Provifion within the Liberties. See *Stat.* 27 *H.* 8. 24. Neither fhall the *Stat.* 32 *H.* 8. 20. (concerning the Franchifes of the late Religious Houfes) be prejudicial to the City of *London.*

The Affize of Fuel ordained by 7 *E.* 6. 7. is *Fuel.* by *Stat.* 43 *Eliz.* 14. continued and enjoyed to be obferved in *London* and *Weftminfter*, and all other Corporations, where Tall-wood, Billet and Faggots are ufed to be fold.

I i 3   There

Fletchers.　There is an Act extant, made 33 *H.* 8. concerning Fletchers and Artificers in Archery, in and about the City of *London.*

Fuſtians, &c.　The *Stat.* 11 *H.* 7. 27. provides, that the Maſter and Wardens of Sheermen in *London,* ſhall have power to ſearch the Workmanſhip of ſuch as uſe the broad Sheer, as well for Fuſtian as Cloth, and that as well againſt Denizens as Strangers. And by the *Act* 39 *Eliz.* 13. the Mayor of *London* or his Deputy, and the Maſter and Wardens of the Myſtery of Clothworkers there, or ſuch diſcreet Perſons as they ſhall appoint, may make the like ſearch, as the ſaid Maſter and Wardens of Sheermen.

Gauging.　By *Stat.* 31 *Eliz.* 8. No Brewers ſhall ſell or put to Sale in *London,* the *Suburbs,* or within two Miles compaſs of the *Suburbs,* any Beer or Ale in Buts, Pipes, Punchions, Hogſheads, Teirſes, or ſuch other Veſſel brought from beyond Sea, and never lawfully gauged within this Realm, before the ſame be lawfully gauged, &c. by the Maſter and Wardens of the Coopers of the City of *London,* or their Deputies ; who, upon Requeſt, are obliged to go and mark ſuch Veſſels, under a Penalty.

Gavelet.　The *Stat.* 10 *E.* 2. concerning the Writ of *Gavelet,* ſays, That the Lords of Rents in *London* may recover them by a Writ of *Gavelet* in their *Huſtings,* and in Default thereof the Lands themſelves in *Demeſn.*

Goldſmiths.　There are ſeveral Acts made to regulate Goldſmiths of the City of *London,* &c. As *Artic. ſuper Chart. cap.* 20. 28 *E.* 1. 27 *E.* 3. 14. 2 *H.* 6. 14. 4 *H.* 7. 2. 18 *Eliz.* 15. And a late Act made 6 & 7 *W.* 3.

Gunpowder.　See alſo a late *Stat.* 5 *Geo.* c. 26. againſt keeping large Quantities of *Gunpowder* in *Lon.* or *Weſtminſter.*

Hats and Haberdaſhers.　By *Stat.* 8. *Eliz.* 11. The Maſter and Wardens of *Haberdaſhers* in *London,* calling to them one

one of the Company of *Cappers*, and another of the *Hatmakers*, have power to fearch in *London*, and within three Miles round, all Cappers and Hatters, and to punifh the Offenders, *&c.*

Concerning the Haven of the River of *Thames*, &c. we have treated before in the Court for the *Confervacy* thereof.   See alfo *Stat.* 27 *H.* 8. 18. & 7 *Ann. c.* 9. *Haven of the River of Thames, &c.*

By *Stat.* 22 *Car.* 2. *cap.* 12. The Occupiers, and where there are none, the Owners of Lands, Houfes, *&c.* adjoining to the High-ways, Streets, *&c.* in the Suburbs and Liber-ties of *London*, *Southwark*, and *Weftminfter*, which are or fhall be paved, fhall be liable to the Scavengers Rates, as by 14 *Car.* 2. *cap.* 2. *Highways.*

Touching Juries in the City of *London*, and the Iffues by them loft, *&c.* we have treated before in the Court of *Huftings* for the City of *London*. *Juries.*

The *Stat.* 5 *Eliz.* 4. concerning Labourers, *&c.* fhall not reftrain the Cities of *London* and *Norwich*, from taking Apprentices as in times paft. *Labourers.*

By *Stat.* 1 *W.* & *M. Seff.* 1. *cap.* 33. Leather fhaved, liquor'd, and curried, is made fubject to the View, Search and Seizure of the Mafter of the feveral Myfteries of the *Cordwainers*, *Curriers*, *Girdlers*, and *Sadlers* of the City of *London*, according to *Stat.* 1 *Jac.* 1. *Leather.*

But nothing in this Act fhall give Power to the Mafter and Wardens of the Company of *Curriers*, to fearch or feize any Leather, Hide, or Skin, but fuch as fhall be curried in *London*, or within three Miles thereof, by fome Mem-bers of their own Company, nor in any other place, but the open Market-place, or in the Shops, Houfes, or Warehoufes of fuch *Curriers*.

Touching *Billingfgate*, *Blackwellhall*, and *Smith-field* Markets within the City of *London*, fee fe-veral Statutes touching *Billingfgate*, &c. before in this Alphabet. And fee after *Victual* and *Victuallers*. *Markets.*

488   *Particular Statutes*

Mainprizal.

The Act against Mainprizal, 1 & 2 *P. M.* 13. That none shall be let to Bail, which are forbidden to be bailed by 3 *Ed.* 1. 15. does not extend to restrain Justices within *London* and *Middlesex*, to set to Bail Prisoners, as thentofore they have used, &c.

Malt.

The Mayor of *London* has Power (by *Stat.* 17 *R.* II. 4.) to search and see that Malt made in the Counties of *Huntingdon, Cambridge, Northampton,* and *Bedford,* and brought to *London* for the Provision of the Court and City, be well cleansed from Dust and other Filth.

Merchants.

By *Stat.* 6 *E.* IV. 4. the Clause of the *Statute* 5. *H.* IV. 9. enjoining Merchant Strangers to sell their Commodities within a Quarter of a Year next after their Arrival is repealed, saving the Liberties of *London.*

By the *Stat.* 12 *H.* VII. 6. the Fellowship of Merchants in *London* shall not exact or levy upon every *Englishman* (being the King's true Liege-Man trading at the Marts in *Flanders, Holland, Zealand, Brabant,* and other the Arch-Duke of *Burgoin*'s Countries) more than ten Marks, in pain of 20 *l.* to the King, and ten times so much as they shall overtake, to be recovered by Action of Debt.

Merchandizes.

A Statute was made 1 *Eliz.* 11. That none should lade or unlade into, or out of any Ship or other Vessel, any Goods, Wares, or Merchandizes whatsoever, (Fish taken by *Englishmen* only excepted) and unless it be upon a Leak or Wreck, to be imported or exported but only in the Day-time, *viz.* from the first of *March* until the last of *September,* betwixt Sun-rising and Sun-set; and from the last of *September* to the first of *March,* between the Hours of Seven and Four, (and that in such Places as should e appointed by Commission)

in

in pain to forfeit the Wares, Goods, and Merchandizes, otherwife laden or unladen, or the
value thereof.

Amongft the Places fo to be affign'd, *London*
is firft named, and all other Places (*Hull* only
excepted) where there is a Cuftomer, Con-
troller, and Searcher.

By *Stat.* 43 *Eliz.* 12. the Lord Chancellor *Policies of*
or Keeper fhall award a ftanding Commiffion *Affurance.*
(to be renew'd Yearly, or as often as to him
fhall feem meet) for the hearing and determining of all fuch Caufes arifing, and Policies
of Affurance, as fhall be entred in the Office
of Affurance, *London* ; and this Commiffion is
to be directed to the Judge of the Admiralty,
the Recorder of *London*, two Doctors of the
Civil Law, two Common Lawyers, and eight
grave and difcreet Merchants, or to any five
of them : Which Commiffioners, or the major part of them, fhall have Power to hear and
examine, order and decree all fuch Caufes in
a brief and fummary Courfe, as to their Difcretion fhall feem meet, without formality of
Pleadings or Proceedings.

And by the *Stat.* 13 & 14 *Car.* II. *cap.* 23.
the faid Commiffioners, or three of them,
whereof a Doctor of the Civil Law, or Bar-
rifter of the Law of five Years ftanding to be
one, may proceed as five might have done ;
and in cafe of wilful delay of Witneffes, upon
the firft Summons, and Tender of the Charges ;
and of Parties upon the fecond Summons, may
punifh the Offenders by Imprifonment or Cofts :
And every fuch Commiffioner may proceed, having taken an Oath, before the Lord Mayor of
London only, to proceed uprightly. Alfo Commiffions fhall iffue out of the Admiralty returnable before the faid Commiffioners, to examine

Witneffes

Witneſſes beyond Sea, or in any remote Parts of the King's Dominions: The Commiſſioners, or three of them, may paſs Sentence and Execution againſt the Body and Goods, and againſt the Executors, &c. or the Party evicted, and aſſeſs Coſts of Suit. And any one Commiſſioner may adminiſter an Oath to a Witneſs, notice being given to the adverſe Party, and ſet up in the Office, that ſuch Witneſs may be croſs examined: But the Commiſſioners ſhall not proceed againſt Body and Goods for the ſame Debt.

Militia.

By Statute 13 & 14 *Car.* 2. *cap.* 3. the Lieutenants of the Militia of *London* have power to continue to liſt and levy the Train-Bands and Auxiliaries there, in ſuch manner as was uſed in forming the then preſent Forces raiſed by the King's Commiſſion, and may levy Yearly ſo much Moneys as they ſhall judge needful, as was the preſent Aſſeſſment then levied; not exceeding in one Year one Month's Tax which the City then paid towards the Tax of 70000 *l.* per *Menſem. See* Soldiers, *and ſeveral late Statutes for raiſing the ſaid* Militia.

Monopolies.

The Statute againſt Monopolies made 21 *Jac. c.* 3. ſhall not be prejudicial to *London,* or any other Corporation, for any Grant made then concerning their Cuſtoms, nor any Corporation, Company or Fellowſhip of any Art, Trade or Myſtery, nor to any Company or Society of Merchants.

Orphans.

Concerning the Statute for Orphans of the City of *London,* we have ſpoken heretofore. *See before in the Court of Orphans.*

Oil and Oil-men.

By *Statute* 3 *H.* 8. 14. the Mayor of *London,* together with the Maſter and Wardens of the Myſtery of Tallow-Chandlers there, have Power to ſearch all Oils brought to *London* to be ſold; and to overſee that the ſame be not mixed

mixed or altered from their right kinds; and what they fhall find deceitfully mixed, they are to caft away, and punifh the Offender by Imprifonment, or otherwife at their Difcretions, according to the Laws and Cuftoms of the faid City.

There is a Statute which was made 1 *Jac.* 1. *Painters and* cap. 20. for the Benefit of the Painters of Lon-*Plaifterers.* don, that no Plaifterer fhall ufe or exercife the Art of Painter in *London*, or the *Suburbs* thereof, or lay any manner of Colour or Painting whatfoever, unlefs he be a Servant or Apprentice to a Painter, or have ferved feven Years Apprentice to that Art; under penalty of 5 *l.* a time, to be divided betwixt the King and the Profecutor.

Provided the Plaifterers may ufe Whiting, Blacking, Red-Lead, Red-Oker, and Ruffet, mingled with Size only, and not with Oil.

And provided alfo, that no Painter fhall take above 16 *d.* the Day for laying any flat Colour whatfoever, mingled or mixt with Oyl or Size, upon any Timber, Stone or Lead.

Concerning paving the Streets between *Ald-Paving* gate and *White-Chapel, Shoe-Lane, Fetter-Lane,* &c. *Streets,* &c. there is a Statute extant, made 32 *H.* 8. 17. whereby the Mayor, Aldermen and Juftices of Peace in *Middlefex,* have power within their refpective Jurifdictions, to inquire, hear and *vid. Conduits.* determine in Seffions, the Defaults of paving and repairing of Streets; and in cafe the faid Juftices fhall be found remifs therein, they fhall refpectively forfeit 5 *l.*

Alfo any three Juftices in *London,* whereof the Mayor is to be one, have power to fet Fines upon fuch as do not pave and repair any Street or Lane in *London,* or the Liberties thereof, to be levied by Diftrefs, Plaint or Action,

by

by the Chamberlain, to the ufe of the Mayor and Commonalty of the faid City.

A like Statute made 34 and 35 *H.* 8. 12. for paving and repairing of *White-crofs-ftreet, Chifwell-ftreet, Long-lane,* St. *John's-ftreet,* &c.

Another like Act, made 13 *Eliz.* 23. for paving and keeping in Repair the Way without *Aldgate,* called the Bars without *Aldgate,* &c.

Alfo another additional Act, made 23 *Eliz.* 12. for paving of the *Minories. See the Acts, and* vide pag. 112, *&c.*

Petitions. By *Stat.* 13 *Car.* 2. *Stat.* 1. *cap.* 5. none fhall labour or procure Hands or Confent of above 20 Perfons to any Petition, Remonftrance, *&c.* to the King, or both, or either Houfes of Parliament for Alteration in Church or State, unlefs by Confent (if arifing in *London*) of the Mayor, Aldermen and Commons in the Common Council; and not above ten Perfons are to repair to deliver fuch Petition, upon penalty not exceeding above 100 *l.* and three Months Imprifonment.

Phyficians, &c. There are feveral Statutes extant concerning the Phyficians and Chirurgeons in and about the City of *London:* The Jurifdiction and Authority of the Prefident, Cenfors and Commonalty of the College of Phyficians in *London,* extends alfo to others within feven Miles compafs of *London. Note,* That of this College of Phyficians, and of their Jurifdiction and Authority, much may be read in the eighth Report of *Coke,* in Dr. *Bonham's* Cafe.

Policies of Affurance. See before, Title, *Merchants* and *Merchandizes.*

Poor People. There are feveral Statutes relating to the poor People in and about the City of *London,* &c. as 43 *Eliz.* 2. 13, 14 *Car.* 2. *cap.* 12, &c.

Note,

Note, The *Stat.* 3 *Jac.* 1. *cap.* 15 . *ante*, under ^{Poor Debtors.} the Title *Court of Conscience*, pag. 430.

By an Act made, 22 and 23 *Car.* 2. *cap.* 20. *Poor Prisoners*. Authority is given to find out all Gifts and Bequests for the Benefit of poor Prisoners for Debt in *London*, &c.

See the Statute for reversing the Judgment in *Quo Warranto*. the *Quo Warranto* against the City of *London*, *ante.* pag. 47, & 48.

Power given to the Mayor of *London*, &c. *Recognizances*. to take Recognizance of Statutes Merchant, and of the Staple, by 13 *Ed.* 1. *Acton Burnell*, also 13 *Ed.* 1. *de Mercatoribus*, and 23 *H.* 8. 6. for the *Staple*.

An Act made 13 & 14 *Car.* 2. *cap.* 15. con-*Silk-throwers*. cerning the Silk-throwers Trade.

Also by *Stat.* 20. *Car.* 2. *cap.* a By-Law of the Silk-throwers in *London*, stinting the Freemen of the said Company, not to work with above 160 Spindles at one time, and the Affistants with above 240, is made void, and the Company disabled from making any By-Law, which shall limit the number of Utensils about the said Mystery.

Also no By-Law made, or to be made by the said Company, shall confine any Freeman to take a less number than three Apprentices at any time.

The Justices in *London* are to be present at the *Soldiers*. Musters of the Militia, according to Act 6 & 7 *W.* 8. *cap.* 8. and upon this Act upon the Quartering any Troops of Horse in the Liberties of *London*, every Officer and Soldier is to pay 8 *d.* *per* Night for Hay. But by 4 *Geo.c.* 4. & 5.*Geo.c.* 5. no Justice is obliged to be present at such Musters.

The Lord Mayor of *London*, Recorder and *Southwark* every Aldermon that hath been Mayor, are *Buildings*. with several others constituted by 29 *Car.*2. *cap.* 4. to determine Differences concerning the building-

ing

ing or not building the Houses burnt down by the Fire happening in *Southwark*, on the 26th of *May* then laft ; the Judgments, Orders and Decrees, to be delivered to the Town-Clerk of *London*, to be kept among the Records of the City. Alfo the Lord Mayor has power to give an Oath to the other Commiffioners for executing their Authorities, other, than the Juftices of either Bench and Barons of the *Exchequer*. And five of fuch Perfons after they have taken it, may adminifter it to the Lord Mayor.

Taxes. By *Stat.* 19 *H.* 7. 8. Scavage Money to be taken of Denizens, is faved to the Mayor and Commonalty of *London*.

Tunnage. By *Stat.* 5, 6 *W. & M. cap.* 21. being an Act upon Tunnage, for eftablifhing the Bank of *England*, there is a Tax of 10 *s. per* Tun for Blubber, &c. to be paid by the Merchants of *London* trading to *Greenland*, and 10 *s. per* Tun for Oil, and other Merchandize, to *Newfound-Land*.

Salt. By *Stat.* 7, & 8*W.* 8. *cap.*31. The Lord Mayor and Court of Aldermen of *London*, &c. have Authority to fet Prices for Salt to be fold in *London*, and the Perfon forfeits 5 *l.* which may be levied by the Lord Mayor's Warrant ; the one Moiety to the King, the other to the Informer and Profecutor for the fame, before the faid Lord Mayor.

By *Stat.* 9, & 10 *W.*3. *cap.* 44. The like Power for Salt is given them to be fetled by *July* 98. and after, upon the like Forfeiture upon Offenders.

Aid-Tax. By the *Stat.* 11, 12 *W.* 3. *cap.* 2. for granting an Aid to his Majefty, and for Maintenance of his Navy and Guards, &c. the Inhabitants of *London*, &c. are to be taxed in the Wards where they dwell.

Thames. The River *Thames*, vide *Haven*, ante.

Trade and Commerce. By *Stat.* 1 *Jac.* 2. 19. (concerning what time foreign Corn is imported, and the Prices of middling

dling *English* Corn then to be determined) what is thereby required to be done by the Juftices at their Quarter Seffions, fhall be done in *London* in *October* and *April*, by the Mayor and Aldermen, and Juftices of the Peace there.

An Act made 1 *W.* & *M. Seff.* 1. *cap.* 34. concerning the Incorporation of the Company of Merchants of *London* trading to *Greenland*.

Stat. made 9 & 10 *W.* 3. *cap.* 17. concerning *Trading and* Bills of *Exchange* drawn or dated, at and from *Inland Bills.* any Place in this Kingdom of 5 *l.* Sterling or upwards, upon any Perfon in *London*, or other *Vid. another* trading City, to be protefted in *London* by a No- *Act made 3* tary -Publick, and in default of fuch Notary-& 4.*An.Reg.* publick by any fubftantial Perfon of the Place before two Witneffes after Acceptance in Writing, and Expiration of three Days after the fame fhall be due, (refufal or neglect being firft made of due Payment) the Proteft is to be notified within fourteen Days after to the Party from whom the Bills were received ; who upon producing fuch Proteft, is to repay the faid Bill with Intereft andCharges from theTime of protefting, for whichProteft there isnot to bepaid above 6*d.* In default of fuch Proteft and due notice, the Perfon failing fhall be liable to all Cofts, Damages and Intereft thereupon. And if fuch Inland Bills be loft or mifcarry, within the time limited for Payment of the fame, the Drawer fhall give others of the fame Tenour ; Security being given to indemnify him, in cafe the loft Bills be found again. . See the Act.

Tryals, fee feveral Statutes touching Tryals *Tryals.* in *London*, ante, *Tit.* Court of *Huftings*, 250, &c.

Tythes, fee the *Stat.* relating to Tythes within *Tythes.* *London*, ante, 87.

By *Stat.* 31 *E.* 3. 10. Every Man that bring- *Victual and* eth Victual to *London*, may freely fell the fame, *Victuallers.*
without

without the Interruption or Impeachment of any. And the Mayor and Aldermen of *London* may rule and regulate the Defaults of *Fishmongers*, *Butchers* and *Poulterers*, as they do of such as sell Beer, Ale or Wine.

By *Stat. 6 R. 2. Stat. 1. 9.* No Victualler in *London*, or any other City, Borough, or Port of the Sea, shall exercise any judicial Office there; and in case any be chosen into such Office, he shall forbear to use Victualling during his Office, in pain to forfeit the Victuals sold.

And by *Stat. 7 R. 2. 11.* All Vintners and Victuallers, as well Fishmongers as others, coming with their Victuals to *London*, shall be under the Governance of the Mayor and Aldermen of that City, as hath been heretofore used.

The *Stat. 3 H. 8. 8.* says, when a Victualler in a City or Corporation is chosen to bear an Office, by reason whereof he ought to have the Assizing of Victuals, two others (being no Victuallers) shall be joyn'd and sworn with him, truly to Assess and Assize, &c. but here the Officers in *London*, *York* and *Coventry* are excepted.

Voucher. See *Stat.* of *Glouc. 12. 6 E. 1.* concerning one being impleaded for a Tenement in *London*, and vouching a Foreigner to Warrantry, with the manner of the Process relating thereto.

Wager of Law. By *Stat. 38 E. 3. 5.* Any Man may wage his Law, by sufficient People of his Condition against *Londoners* Papers, and the Creditor shall take Surety otherwise, (if he please); but shall not put the Party to plead to the Inquest, unless he will do so of his own accord.

Watermen. Of them it is treated before in the Court of Conservacy of the River of *Thames*.

Weights and Measures. By *Stat. 11 H. 6. 8.* The Mayor of *London*, and all other Mayors and Bailiffs on their Oaths, shall be charged to keep and execute the

Statutes

Statutes for obferving due Weights and Meafures.

By *Stat.* of *Gloucefter*, 15, 16 *E.* 1. the Mayor and Bayliffs (now Sheriffs) of *London*, are to inquire of Wine fold againft the Affize.

By *Stat.* 28 *H.* 8. 14. The Lord Chancellor, *Wines.* Treafurer, Prefident of the Council, Privy Seal, or the two Chief Juftices, or five, four or three of them have power at their Difcretions, to fet the Prices of all kind of Wines, *viz.* of the Butt, Tun, Pipe, Hogfliead, Puncheon, Tierce, Barrel 'or Rundlet, when they fhall be fold in grofs. The Prices then are to be written and proclaimed in *Chancery* in the Term-time, or elfe in the City, Borough or Town where any fuch Wines are fold in grofs , 40 *l.* forfeiture for every Veffel otherwife fold, betwixt the King and Head Rulers in a Corporation ; but out of a Corporation, betwixt the King and the Profecutor.

And by *Stat.* 37 *H.* 8. 23. None that fell Wines either in Grofs or by Retail, fhall fell them above the Prices fet by the Great Officers, upon the Penalty aforefaid.

And if any refufe to fell their Wines accordingly in *London*, the Mayor, Recorder, and two antient Aldermen being no Vintners, in other Places the chief Officers, *&c.* may enter the Houfes of fuch Perfons, and fell their Wines at the Prices fo affeffed.

The *Stat.* 7 *E.* 6. 5. provides for Licences for fuch as fell Wine by Retail in *London*, &c. and only forty Licences are allowed in *London* by this Act.

Alfo the *Stat.* 12 *Car.* 2. *cap.* 25. is made for licenfing Retailers of Wine, and the King may iffue out Commiffions for the Commiffioners to licenfe whom they think fit, for 21 Years, or under, and for fuch Rent as they can agree ; and here the Privileges of the Univerfities,

K k and

and of the Company of Vintners in *London,* and other Cities, *&c.* are faved.

The laſt mentioned Aɛt ſays, That all Perſons that ſell Wines in groſs, mingled or abuſed, ſhall forfeit 100 *l.* for every Offence, and all ſelling ſuch Wines by Retail 40 *l.* one half to the King, the other to the Informer. That no *Spaniſh* or ſweet Wines ſhall be ſold for above 18 *d. per* Quart by Retail. No *French* Wines above 8 *d.* No *Rheniſh* above 12 *d.* and ſo proportionably; on pain of 5 *l.* for every quantity ſo ſold, one Moiety to the King, the other to him that will ſue.

But the Chancellor, and other great Officers, may ſet the Prices at higher or lower Rates than as aforeſaid ; Proclamation to be made thereof as aforeſaid ; and in default of ſuch ſetting, the Prices ſet by this Aɛt ſhall be obſerv'd, Confirm'd, 13 *Car.* 2. *cap.* 7.

Note, the *Stat.* 15 *Car.* 2. *cap.* 14. gives the powers of granting Licences as aforeſaid, and the Moiety of the Forfeitures to *James* Duke of *York,* and the Heirs Males of his Body. Here alſo the Privileges of the Company of Vintners, *London,* &c. are ſaved.

And by *Stat.* 22, & 23 *Car.* 2. *cap.* 6. the Powers and Revenues are again veſted in the King, and in Satisfaɛtion thereof, the King's Letters Patents whereby there ſhould be granted to the Duke and his Heirs Males 24000 *l.* of the Revenues of the Exciſe of Beer and Ale, *&c.* ſhall be good in Law.

Exciſe.

And by *Stat.* 1 *Jac.* 2. *cap.* 12. it is enaɛted, That the King from thenceforth ſtand and be ſeized of, and in the ſaid yearly Rent or Sum of 24000 *l.* of one entire and indefeazable Eſtate in Fee Simple ; the aforeſaid laſt Aɛt of Parliament notwithſtanding. *See alſo the Stat.* 4, 5 W. M. *c.* 15.

F I N I S.

THE
TABLE

A.

The TABLE.

Ap-

The TABLE.

Kk 3

The TABLE.

The TABLE.

Kk 4   Charters

The TABLE.

The TABLE.

Courts

The TABLE.

Cuftom

The TABLE.

The TABLE.

Decla-

The TABLE.

The TABLE.

The TABLE.

The TABLE.

The TABLE.

The TABLE.

The TABLE.

L l 2 O.

The TABLE.

O.

The TABLE.

The TABLE.

The TABLE.

W.

A

A TABLE

OF THE

Statute Law relating to the City of
LONDON.

The End of the Table.

www.ingramcontent.com/pod-product-compliance
Lightning Source LLC
Chambersburg PA
CBHW020752300326
41914CB00050B/173